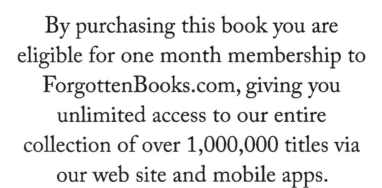

ISBN 978-1-5279-8750-0
PIBN 10157108

This book is a reproduction of an important historical work. Forgotten Books uses
state-of-the-art technology to digitally reconstruct the work, preserving the original format
whilst repairing imperfections present in the aged copy. In rare cases, an imperfection in
the original, such as a blemish or missing page, may be replicated in our edition. We do,
however, repair the vast majority of imperfections successfully; any imperfections that
remain are intentionally left to preserve the state of such historical works.

For true title-pages of vol. see after p. clx.,
contents & index

ACTS

OF THE

PARLIAMENT OF THE UNITED KINGDOM

OF

GREAT BRITAIN AND IRELAND

PASSED IN THE SESSIONS HELD IN THE

37TH–38TH & 38TH–39TH YEARS OF THE REIGN OF HER MAJESTY,

QUEEN VICTORIA,

BEING THE FIRST AND SECOND SESSIONS OF THE TWENTY-FIRST PARLIAMENT
OF THE UNITED KINGDOM.

OTTAWA :

37-38 VICTORIA.

CHAP. 41.

An Act to amend "The Colonial Attorneys' Relief Act." A. D. 1874.

[*30th July*, 1874.]

WHEREAS by the Colonial Attorneys' Relief Act certain 20 & 21 Vict., provisions are made for regulating the admission of c. 39. attornies and solicitors of Colonial Courts in Her Majesty's Superior Courts of Law and Equity in England in certain cases, and it is considered just and equitable to amend the said Act:

Be it therefore enacted by the Queen's most Excellent Majesty, by and with the advice and consent of the Lords' Spiritual and Temporal, and Commons, in this present Parliament assembled, and by the authority of the same, as follows :—

1. So much of the Colonial Attorneys' Relief Act as enacts that no person shall be deemed qualified to be admitted as attorney or solicitor under the provisions of the said Act unless he shall pass an examination to test his fitness and capacity, and shall further make affidavit that he has ceased for the space of twelve calendar months at the least to practice as attorney or solicitor in any colonial court of law, and also so much of the said Act and of any orders and regulations made thereunder as relate to such examination, shall not apply to nor shall compliance therewith respectively be required of any person seeking to be admitted as attorney or solicitor under the provisions of the said Act who shall have been in actual practice for the period of seven years at the least as attorney and solicitor in any colony or dependency as to which an Order in Council has been or may be made as mentioned in the said Act, and who shall have served under articles and passed an examination previously to his admission as attorney and solicitor in any such colony or dependency.

Examination and ceasing to practice dispensed with where Colonial Attorney and Solicitor has actually practiced for seven years and passed examination previous to admission.

2. The expression "The Colonial Attorneys' Relief Act" shall henceforth be deemed to include this Act.

Short title.

38-39 VICTORIA.

CHAP. 38.

A.D. 1875   An Act to remove certain doubts with respect to the powers of the Parliament of Canada under section eighteen of the British North America Act, 1867.

[*19th July*, 1875.]

30 & 31 Vict.
c. 3.

WHEREAS by section eighteen of the British North America Act, 1867, it is provided as follows: "The privileges, immunities, and powers to be held, enjoyed, and exercised by the Senate and by the House of Commons, and by the Members thereof respectively shall be such as are, from time to time, defined by Act of the Parliament of Canada, but so that the same shall never exceed those at the passing of this Act held, enjoyed, and exercised by the Commons House of Parliament of the United Kingdom of Great Britain and Ireland, and by the Members thereof;"

And whereas doubts have arisen with regard to the power of defining by an Act of the Parliament of Canada, in pursuance of the said section, the said privileges, powers, or immunities; and it is expedient to remove such doubts:

Be it therefore enacted by the Queen's Most Excellent Majesty, by and with the advice and consent of the Lords, Spiritual and Temporal, and Commons in this present Parliament assembled and by the authority of the same, as follows:—

Substitution of new section for section 18 of 30 & 31 Vict., c. 3.   **1.** Section eighteen of the British North America Act, 1867, is hereby repealed, without prejudice to anything done under that section, and the following section shall be substituted for the section so repealed:—

The privileges, immunities, and powers to be held, enjoyed and exercised by the Senate and by the House of Commons, and by the Members thereof respectively, shall be such as are from time to time defined by Act of the Parliament of Canada, but

Parliament of Canada.

but so that any Act of the Parliament of Canada defining such privileges, immunities and powers shall not confer any privileges, immunities or powers exceeding those at the passing of such Act, held, enjoyed and exercised by the Commons House of Parliament of the United Kingdom of Great Britain and Ireland, and by the Members thereof.

2. The Act of the Parliament of Canada passed in the thirty-first year of the reign of Her present Majesty, chapter twenty-four, intituled "An Act to provide for oaths to witnesses being administered in certain cases for the purposes of either House of Parliament" shall be deemed to be valid, and to have been valid as from the date at which the Royal Assent was given thereto by the Governor General of the Dominion of Canada. _{Confirmation of Act of Parliament of Canada 31 & 32 Vict., c. 24.}

3. This Act may be cited as "The Parliament of Canada Act, 1875." _{Short title}

38-39 VICTORIA.

CHAP. 53.

A. D. 1875. An Act to give effect to an Act of the Parliament of the Dominion of Canada respecting Copyright.

[*2nd August*, 1875.]

WHEREAS by an Order of Her Majesty in Council, dated the 7th day of July, 1868, it was ordered that all prohibitions contained in Acts of the Imperial Parliament against the importing into the Province of Canada, or against the selling, letting out to hire, exposing for sale or hire. or possessing therein foreign reprints of books first composed, written, printed or published in the United Kingdom, and entitled to copyright therein, should be suspended so far as regarded Canada :

And whereas the Senate and House of Commons of Canada did in the second session of the third Parliament of the Dominion of Canada, held in the thirty-eighth year of Her Majesty's Reign, pass a Bill intituled : " An Act respect- " ing Copyrights," which Bill has been reserved by the Governor General for the signification of Her Majesty's pleasure thereon :

And whereas by the said reserved Bill provision is made, subject to such conditions as in the said Bill are mentioned. for securing in Canada the rights of authors in respect of matters of copyright, and for prohibiting the importation into Canada of any work for which copyright under the said reserved Bill has been secured ; and whereas doubts have arisen whether the said reserved Bill may not be repugnant to the said Order in Council, and it is expedient to remove such doubts and to confirm the said Bill :

Be it enacted by the Queen's Most Excellent Majesty, by and with the advice and consent of the Lords Spiritual and Temporal, and Commons, in this present Parliament assembled, and by the authority of the same, as follows :—

1.

Canada Copyright Act.

1. This Act may be cited for all purposes as " The Canada Short title of Copyright Act, 1875."

2. In the construction of this Act the words " book " and Definition of " copyright " shall have respectively the same meaning as terms. in the Act of the fifth and sixth years of Her Majesty's reign, chapter forty-five, intituled " An Act to amend the Law of Copyright."

3. It shall be lawful for Her Majesty in Council to assent Her Majesty to the said reserved Bill, as contained in the schedule to this may assent to Act annexed,* and if Her Majesty shall be pleased to signify schedule. Her assent thereto, the said Bill shall come into operation at such time and in such manner as Her Majesty may by Order in Council direct ; anything in the Act of the twenty-eighth and twenty-ninth years of the reign of Her Majesty, chapter ninety-three, or in any other Act to the contrary notwithstanding.

4. Where any book in which, at the time when the said Colonial re-reserved Bill comes into operation, there is copyright in the prints not to United Kingdom, or any book in which thereafter there into United shall be such copyright, becomes entitled to copyright in Kingdom. Canada in pursuance of the provisions of the said reserved Bill, it shall be unlawful for any person, not being the owner, in the United Kingdom, of the copyright in such book, or some person authorized by him, to import into the United Kingdom any copies of such book reprinted or republished in Canada ; and for the purposes of such importation the seventeenth section of the said Act of the fifth and sixth years of the reign of Her Majesty, chapter forty-five, shall apply to all such books in the same manner as if they had been reprinted out of the British dominions.

5. The said Order in Council, dated the seventh day of Order in July one thousand eight hundred and sixty-eight, shall con- Council of 7th tinue in force so far as relates to books which are not entitled continue in to copyright for the time being, in pursuance of the said force subject reserved Bill. to this Act.

* For Schedule see reserved Act elsewhere.

38-39 VICTORIA.

CHAP. 88.

A. D. 1875 An Act to make provision for giving further powers to the Board of Trade for stopping Unseaworthy Ships.

[*13th August*, 1875.]

BE it enacted by the Queen's Most Excellent Majesty, by and with the advice and consent of the Lords, Spiritual and Temporal, and Commons in this present Parliament assembled, and by the authority of the same as follows :—

Appointment and powers of officers having authority to detain unseaworthy ships. **1.** The Board of Trade may forthwith and from time to time by special order appoint a sufficient number of fit and proper persons, from their own staff or otherwise, to be officers having authority to detain unseaworthy ships, and may, from time to time, revoke any such appointment.

If any officer so appointed has reason to believe, upon inspection or otherwise, that any British ship is, by reason of the defective condition of her hull, equipments, or machinery, or by reason of overloading or improper loading, unfit to proceed to sea without serious danger to human life, he may order that the ship be detained for the purpose of being surveyed.

Any such order shall have the same effect as if it were an order of the Board of Trade under section twelve of the Merchants' Shipping Act, 1873.

For the purpose of ascertaining whether a British ship is fit to proceed to sea, any officer so appointed may go on board the ship and inspect the same, or any part thereof, or any of the machinery, boats, equipments, or other articles on board thereof, not unnecessarily detaining or delaying her from proceeding on her voyage ; and any person who wilfully impedes him in the execution of his duty shall be liable to the same penalties, and may be dealt with in the same manner as if the officer were an Inspector appointed by the Board of Trade under the Merchants' Shipping Act, 1854.

When

Unseaworthy Ships.

When any officer so appointed orders a ship to be detained, he shall forthwith report his proceedings to the Board of Trade.

An officer so appointed shall receive such remuneration for his services under this Act as the Treasury from time to time direct, and such remuneration shall be paid out of moneys to be provided by Parliament.

2. Whenever a complaint is made to the Board of Trade or to any officer so appointed by one-fourth of the seamen belonging to any British ship, that the ship is, by reason of the defective condition of her hull, equipments, or machinery or by reason of overloading or improper loading, unfit to proceed to sea without serious danger to human life, it shall be the duty of the Board or officer, as the case may be, if the complaint is made within time sufficient for that purpose before the sailing of the ship, without requiring any security for the payment of costs and expenses, to take proper steps for ascertaining whether the ship ought to be detained for the purpose of being surveyed under the Merchant Shipping Act, 1873. *Ship to be detained on complaint of crew.*

3. From and after the first day of October, one thousand eight hundred and seventy-five, no cargo of which more than one-third consists of any kind of grain, corn, rice, paddy, pulse, seeds, nuts or nut kernels, shall be carried on board any British ship, unless such grain, corn, rice, paddy, pulse, seeds, nuts or nut kernels be contained in bags, sacks or barrels, or secured from shifting by boards, bulkheads or otherwise. *Cargo of grain, &c*

This section shall not apply to any grain shipped previous to the first October, one thousand eight hundred and seventy-five.

The master of any British ship who shall knowingly allow any cargo or part of a cargo to be shipped therein for carriage, contrary to the provisions of this section, shall, for every such offence, incur a penalty not exceeding two hundred pounds.

4. Section eleven of "The Merchants' Shipping Act, 1871," shall be repealed, and in lieu thereof it shall be enacted,— *Penalties on sending unseaworthy ships to sea.*

1. Every person who sends a ship to sea in such unseaworthy state that the life of any person would be likely to be thereby endangered, and the managing owner of any
British

Unseaworthy Ships.

British ship so sent to sea from any port in the United Kingdom, shall be guilty of a misdemeanor, unless he prove that he used all reasonable means to ensure her being sent to sea in a seaworthy state, or prove that her going to sea in such unseaworthy state, was, under the circumstances, reasonable and justifiable; and for the purpose of giving such proofs, such person may give evidence in the same manner as any other witness:

2. Every person who attempts, or is party to any attempt to send to sea any ship in such unseaworthy state that the life of any person would be likely to be thereby endangered, shall be guilty of a misdemeanor, unless he give such proof as aforesaid; and for the purpose of giving such proof such person may give evidence as aforesaid:

3. Every master of a British ship who knowingly takes the same to sea in such unseaworthy state that the life of any person would be likely to be thereby endangered, shall be guilty of a misdemeanor, unless he prove that her going to sea in such unseaworthy state, was, under the circumstances, reasonable and justifiable; and for the purpose of giving such proof, such person may give evidence as aforesaid:

4. The owner of every British ship shall from time to time register at the Custom House of the port in the United Kingdom at which such ship is registered, the name of the managing owner of such ship, and if there be no managing owner, then of the person to whom the management of the ship is entrusted, by and on behalf of the owner; and in case the owner fail or neglect to register the name of such managing owner or manager as aforesaid, he shall be liable, or if there be more owners than one, each owner shall be liable in proportion to his interest in the ship, to a penalty not exceeding in the whole five hundred pounds each time that the said ship leaves any port in the United Kingdom after the first day of November, one thousand eight hundred and seventy-five, without the name being duly registered as aforesaid:

5. The term "managing owner" in sub-section one shall include every person so registered as managing owner or as having the management of the ship for and on behalf of the owner:

6. No prosecution under this section shall be instituted except by or with the consent of the Board of Trade:

Unseaworthy Ships.

---

7. No misdemeanor under this section shall be punishable upon summary conviction; Provided that the repeal enacted by this section shall not affect any punishment incurred or to be incurred in respect of any offence against the enactment hereby repealed, or any legal proceeding in respect of any such punishment; and any such legal proceeding may be carried on as if this Act had not passed.

5. Every British ship not registered on or after the first Marking of day of November, one thousand eight hundred and seventy- deck lines. five, shall before registry, and every British ship registered before that day shall on or before that day, be permanently and conspicuously marked with lines of not less than twelve inches in length and one inch in breadth, painted longitudinally on each side amidships, or as near thereto as is practicable, and indicating the position of each deck which is above water :

The upper edge of each of these lines shall be level with the upper side of the deck plank next the waterway at the place of marking. The lines shall be white or yellow on a dark ground or black on a light ground :
Provided that—

(1) This section shall not apply to ships employed in the coasting trade or in fishing, nor to pleasure yachts ; and—

(2) If a registered British ship is not within a British port of registry at any time before the first day of November one thousand eight hundred and seventy-five, she shall be marked as by this section required within one month after her next return to a British port of registry subsequent to that date.

6. With respect to the marking of a load-line on British Statement of ships, the following provisions shall have effect :— load-line.

(1) From and after the first day of November one thousand eight hundred and seventy-five the owner of every British ship shall, before entering his ship outwards from any port in the United Kingdom upon any voyage for which he is required so to enter her, or if that is not practicable, as soon after as may be, mark upon each of her sides amidships, or as near thereto as is practicable, in white or yellow on a dark ground, or in black on a light ground, a circular disc twelve inches in diameter, with a horizontal line eighteen inches in length, drawn through its centre ;

(2)

Unseaworthy Ships.

(2) The centre of this disc shall indicate the maximum load-line in salt water to which the owner intends to load the ship for that voyage ;

(3) He shall also, upon so entering her, insert in the form of entry delivered to the Collector or other principal officer of Customs, a statement in writing of the distance in feet and inches between the centre of this disc and the upper edge of each of the lines indicating the position of the ship's decks which is above that centre ;

(4) If default is made in delivering this statement in the case of any ship, any officer of Customs may refuse to enter the ship outwards ;

(5) The master of the ship shall enter a copy of this statement in the agreement with the crew before it is signed by any member of the crew, and no superintendent of any mercantile marine office shall proceed with the engagement of the crew until this entry is made ;

(6) The master of the ship shall also enter a copy of this statement in the official log book ;

(7) When a ship has been marked as by this section required, she shall be kept so marked until her next return to a port of discharge in the United Kingdom.

Penalty for offences in relation to marks on ships.

7. Any owner or master of a British ship who neglects to cause his ship to be marked as by this Act required, or to keep her so marked, and any person who conceals, removes, alters, defaces, or obliterates, or suffers any person under his control to conceal, remove, alter, deface, or obliterate any of the said marks, except in the event of the particulars thereby denoted being lawfully altered, or except for the purpose of escaping capture by an enemy, shall, for each offence, incur a penalty not exceeding one hundred pounds.

If any of the marks required by this Act is in any respect inaccurate so as to be likely to mislead, the owner of the ship shall incur a penalty not exceeding one hundred pounds.

Proceedings may be taken against the Board of

8. Where a claim of compensation under the Merchant Shipping Act, 1873, is made against the Board of Trade, and liability to pay compensation, or the amount thereof is in dispute,

Unseaworthy Ships.

dispute, proceedings may be taken against the Board of Trade by action against the principal Secretary thereof as nominal defendant. Trade by action against the principal secretary.

9. In every contract, of service, express or implied between the owner of a ship and the master or any seaman thereof, and in every instrument of apprenticeship whereby any person is bound to serve as an apprentice on board any ship, there shall be implied, notwithstanding any agreement to the contrary, an obligation on the part of the owner of the ship to the master, seaman, or apprentice, that the owner of the ship, his agents and servants, shall use all reasonable efforts to ensure the seaworthiness of the ship for the voyage at the commencement thereof, and to keep her in a seaworthy condition during the voyage. Liability of ship owner to crew.

Provided that nothing in this section shall make the owner of a ship, liable for the death of or any injury to a master, seaman, or apprentice belonging to any ship when caused by the wrongful act, neglect, or default of a seaman or apprentice belonging to the same ship, in any case where he would not otherwise be so liable.

10. This Act may be cited as the Merchant Shipping Act, 1875, and shall be construed as one with the Merchants Shipping Act, 1854, and the Acts amending the same, and the said Acts and this Act may be cited collectively as "The Merchant Shipping Acts, 1854 to 1875." Short title.

11. This Act shall continue in force until the first day of October one thousand eight hundred and seventy-six. Duration of Act.

ACT

OF THE

PARLIAMENT

OF THE

DOMINION OF CANADA,

PASSED IN THE

THIRTY-EIGHTH YEAR OF THE REIGN OF HER MAJESTY

QUEEN VICTORIA,

AND IN THE

SEDOND SESSION OF THE THIRD PARLIAMENT,

Begun and holden at Ottawa, on the fourth day of February, and closed by Prorogation on the eighth day of April, 1875.

RESERVED.

HIS EXCELLENCY

THE RIGHT HONORABLE, SIR FREDERICK TEMPLE, EARL OF DUFFERIN,

GOVERNOR GENERAL.

OTTAWA:

PRINTED BY BROWN CHAMBERLIN,
LAW PRINTER TO THE QUEEN'S MOST EXCELLENT MAJESTY.
ANNO DOMINI, 1876.

38 VICTORIA.

CHAP. 88.

An Act respecting Copyrights.

[Reserved for the signification of Her Majesty's pleasure, 8th April, 1875; Royal assent given 26th October, 1875, and proclaimed 3rd December, 1875, to take effect from 11th December, 1875.]

HER Majesty, by and with the advice and consent of the Senate and House of Commons of Canada, enacts as follows:— *Preamble.*

1. The Minister of Agriculture shall cause to be kept in his office books to be called the "Registers of Copyrights," in which proprietors of literary, scientific and artistic works or compositions, may have the same registered in accordance with the provisions of this Act. *Minister of Agriculture to keep registers of copyrights.*

2. The Minister of Agriculture may, from time to time, subject to the approval of the Governor in Council, make such rules and regulations, and prescribe such forms as may appear to him necessary and expedient for the purposes of this Act: such regulations and forms being circulated in print for the use of the public shall be deemed to be correct for the purposes of this Act; and all documents, executed and accepted by the said Minister of Agriculture, shall be held valid so far as relates to all official proceedings under this Act. *Minister to make rules, forms, &c.* *Their effect.*

3. If any person prints, or publishes, or causes to be printed or published, any manuscript whatever, (the said manuscript having not yet been printed in Canada or elsewhere), without the consent of the author or legal proprietor first obtained, such person shall be liable to the author or proprietor for all damages occasioned by such publication, to be recovered in any court of competent jurisdiction. *Liability of persons printing MSS. without owner's consent.*

4. Any person domiciled in Canada or in any part of the British Possessions, or being a citizen of any country having an international copyright treaty with the United Kingdom, *Who may obtain copyrights.*

2   dom,

dom, who is the author of any book, map, chart, or musical composition, or of any original painting, drawing, statue, sculpture or photograph, or who invents, designs, etches, engraves or causes to be engraved, etched or made from his own design, any print or engraving, and the legal representatives of such person shall have the sole right and liberty of printing, reprinting, publishing, reproducing and vending such literary, scientific or artistic works or com-

Translations. positions, in whole or in part, and of allowing translations to be printed or reprinted and sold, of such literary works

Term of copy-right. from one language into other languages, for the term of twenty-eight years, from the time of recording the copyright thereof in the manner hereinafter directed.

Condition for obtaining copyright. 2. The condition for obtaining such copyright shall be that the said literary, scientific or artistic works be printed and published or reprinted and republished in Canada, or in the case of works of art that it be produced or reproduced in Canada, whether they be so published or produced for the first time, or contemporaneously with or subsequently to

Proviso. publication or production elsewhere: Provided that in no case the exclusive privilege in Canada shall continue to exist after it has expired anywhere else.

Exception as to immoral works, &c. 3. No immoral, or licentious, or irreligious, or treasonable, or seditious literary, scientific or artistic work shall be the legitimate subject of such registration or copyright.

Renewal of copyright, for what term and on what conditions. 5. If at the expiration of the aforesaid term of twenty-eight years, such author, or any of the authors (when the work has been originally composed and made by more than one person) be still living, or being dead, have left a widow or a child, or children living, the same exclusive right shall be continued to such author, or if dead, then to such widow and child or children, (as the case may be) for the further term of fourteen years: but in such case within one year after the expiration of the first term, the title of the work secured shall be a second time recorded, and all other regulations herein required to be observed in regard to original copyrights shall be complied with in respect to such renewed copyright.

Record of re-newal to be published. 6. In all cases of renewal of copyright under this Act, the author or proprietor shall, within two months from the date of such renewal, cause a copy of the record thereof to be published once in the *Canada Gazette.*

Deposit of copies &c., in the Minister of Agriculture's office 7. No person shall be entitled to the benefit of this Act, unless he has deposited in the office of the Minister of Agriculture two copies of such book, map, chart, musical composition, photograph, print, cut or engraving, and in case of paintings, drawings, statuary and sculpture, unless

he

he has furnished a written description of such works of art; and the Minister of Agriculture shall cause the copy-right of the same to be recorded forthwith in a book to be kept for that purpose, in the manner adopted by the Minister of Agriculture, or prescribed by the rules and forms which may be made, from time to time, as herein-before provided. Record of copyright.

8. The Minister of Agriculture shall cause one of the two copies of such book, map, chart, musical composition, photo-graph, print, cut or engraving aforesaid, to be deposited in the Library of the Parliament of Canada. Copies to be sent to the Library of Parliament.

9. No person shall be entitled to the benefit of this Act, unless he gives information of the Copyright being secured, by causing to be inserted in the several copies of every edition published during the term secured, on the title-page, or the page immediately following, if it be a book, or if a map, chart, musical composition, print, cut, engraving or photograph, by causing to be impressed on the face thereof, or if a volume of maps, charts, music, engravings or photographs, upon the title-page or frontispiece thereof, the following words, that is to say : " Entered according to Act of Parliament of " Canadà, in the year   by A. B., in the Office " of the Minister of Agriculture." But as regards paintings, drawings, statuary and sculptures, the signature of the artist shall be deemed a sufficient notice of such proprietorship. Notice of copyright to appear on the work.
Form.
Exception.

10. Pending the publication or republication in Canada of a literary, scientific or artistic work, the author or his legal representatives or assigns, may obtain an interim copyright by depositing in the office of the Minister of Agriculture a copy of the title, or a designation of such work intended for publica-tion or republication in Canada,—the said title or designation to be registered in an interim copyright register in the said office,—to secure to the author aforesaid, or his legal repre-sentatives or assigns the exclusive rights recognized by this Act, previous to publication or republication in Canada,—the said interim registration, however, not to endure for more than one month from the date of the original publication elsewhere, within which period the work shall be printed or reprinted and published in Canada. Interim copyright, how obtain-able, and its effect.

And duration.

2. In all cases of interim registration under this Act, the author or proprietor shall cause notice of such registration to be inserted once in the *Canada Gazette.* Notice to be given.

3. A literary work, intended to be published in pamphlet or book form, but which is first published in separate articles in a newspaper or periodical, may be the subject of registra-tion within the meaning of this Act, while it is so preliminarily published, provided that the title of the man- Registration of work first published in separate articles in a periodical.—conditions.

2½   uscript

uscript and a short analysis of the work are deposited in the Office of the Minister of Agriculture, and that every separate article so published is preceded by the words "Registered in accordance with the Copyright Act of 1875;" but the work when published in book or pamphlet form, shall be subject, besides, to the other requirements of this Act.

As to newspapers &c., containing portions of British copyright works.

4. The importation of newspapers and magazines published in foreign countries, and containing, together with foreign original matter, portions of British copyright works republished with the consent of the author or his assigns or under the law of the country where such copyright exists shall not be prohibited.

Penalty for the infringement of copyright of a book.

11. If any other person, after the interim registration of the title of any book according to this Act, within the term herein limited, or after the copyright is secured and for the term or terms of its duration, prints, publishes, or reprints, or republishes, or imports, or causes to be so printed, published or imported, any copy or any translation of such book without the consent of the person legally entitled to the copyright thereof, first had and obtained by assignment, or, knowing the same to be so printed or imported, publishes, sells or exposes for sale or causes to be published, sold or exposed for sale any copy of such book without such consent, such offender shall forfeit every copy of such book to the person then legally entitled to the copyright thereof; and shall forfeit and pay for every such copy which may be found in his possession, either printed or printing, published, imported or exposed for sale, contrary to the intent of this Act such sum, not being less than ten cents nor more than one dollar, as the *Recovery and application.* court shall determine; of which penalty one moiety shall be to the use of Her Majesty, and the other to the legal owner of such copyright, and such penalty may be recovered in any court of competent jurisdiction

Penalty for the infringement of copyright of a painting, &c.

12. If any person, after the recording of any painting, drawing, statue or other work of art, within the term or terms limited by this Act, reproduces in any manner or causes to be reproduced, made or sold, in whole or in part, copies of the said works of art, without the consent of the proprietor or proprietors, such offender or offenders shall forfeit the plate or plates on which such reproduction has been made, and also every sheet thereof so copied, printed or photographed to the proprietor or proprietors of the copyright thereof, and shall further forfeit for every sheet of the same reproduction so published or exposed for sale contrary to the true intent and meaning of this Act such sum, not being less than ten cents *Recovery and application.* nor more than one dollar, as the court shall determine; and one moiety of such forfeiture shall go to the proprietor or proprietors and the other moiety to the use of Her Majesty; and such forfeiture may be recovered in any court of competent jurisdiction.

13.

13. If any person after the recording of any print, cut or engraving, map, chart, musical composition or photograph, according to the provisions of this Act, within the term or terms limited by this Act, engraves, etches or works, sells or copies, or causes to be engraved, etched or copied, made or sold, either in the whole or by varying, adding to or diminishing the main design, with intent to evade the law, or prints, or reprints or imports for sale, or causes to be so printed or imported for sale, any such map, chart, musical composition, print, cut or engraving, or any part thereof, without the consent of the proprietor or proprietors of the copyright thereof, first obtained as aforesaid, or, knowing the same to be so printed or imported without such consent, publishes, sells or. exposes for sale, or in any manner disposes of any such map, chart, musical composition engraving, cut, photograph or print, without such consent as aforesaid, such offender or offenders shall forfeit the plate or plates on which such map, chart, musical composition, engraving, cut, photograph or print has been copied, and also every sheet thereof, so copied or printed as aforesaid, to the proprietor or proprietors of the copyright thereof, and shall further forfeit for every sheet of such map, musical composition, print, cut or engraving which may be found in his or their possession, printed or published or exposed for sale, contrary to the true intent and meaning of this Act, such sum, not being less than ten cents nor more than one dollar, as the court shall determine; and one moiety of such forfeiture shall go to the proprietor or proprietors, and the other moiety to the use of Her Majesty; and such forfeiture may be recovered in any court of competent jurisdiction. *Penalty for the infringement of copyright of a print, chart, music, photograph, &c.* *Recovery and application*

14. Nothing herein contained, shall prejudice the right of any person to represent any scene or object, notwithstanding that there may be copyright in some other representation of such scene or object. *Proviso as to scenery &c.*

15. Works of which the copyright has been granted and is subsisting in the United Kingdom, and copyright of which is not secured or subsisting in Canada, under any Canadian or Provincial Act, shall, upon being printed and published, or reprinted and republished in Canada, be entitled to copyright under this Act; but nothing in this Act shall be held to prohibit the importation from the United Kingdom of copies of such works legally printed there. *Copyright in Canada of British copyright works— on what conditions obtainable. Proviso.*

2. In the case of the reprinting of any such copyright work subsequent to its publication in the United Kingdom any person who may have, previous to the date of entry of such work upon the registers of copyright, imported any foreign reprints shall have the privilege of disposing of such reprints by sale or otherwise; the burden of proof, however, in such a case will lie with such person to establish the extent and regularity of the transaction. *As to foreign reprints imported before copyright is obtained in Canada.*

16.

16. Whenever the author of a literary, scientific or artistic work or composition which may be the subject ot copyright, has executed the same for another person or has sold the same to another person for due consideration, such author shall not be entitled to obtain or to retain the proprietorship of such copyright, which is, by the said transaction, virtually transferred to the purchaser, who may avail himself Proviso. of such privilege, unless a reserve of the said privilege is specially made by the author or artist in a deed duly executed.

17. If any person not having legally acquired the copyright of a literary, scientific or artistic work, inserts in any copy thereof printed, produced,reproduced or imported, or impresses on any such copy, that the same hath been entered according to this Act, or words purporting to assert the existence of a Canadian copyright in relation thereto, every person so offending, shall incur a penalty not exceeding three hundred Recovery and dollars (one moiety whereof shall be paid to the person who application. sues for the same, and the other moiety to the use of Her Majesty,) to be recovered in any court of competent jurisdiction.

2. If any person causes any work to be inserted in the register of interim copyright and fails to print and publish, or reprint and republish the same within the time prescribed he shall incur a penalty not exceeding one hundred dollars (one moiety whereof shall be paid to the person who sueth for the same, and the other moiety to the use of Her Majesty), to be recovered in any court of competent jurisdiction.

18. The right of an author of a literary, scientific or artistic work, to obtain a copyright, and the copyright when obtained shall be assignable in law, either as to the whole interest or any part thereof, by an instrument in writing made in duplicate and to be recorded in the office of the Minister of Agriculture, on production of both duplicates Condition. and payment of the fee hereinafter provided. One of the duplicates shall be retained in the office of the Minister of Agriculture, and the other returned, with certificate of registration, to the party depositing it.

Cases of con-
flicting claims
in respect of
copyright
to be settled
before a
competent
court.

19. In case of any person making application to register as his own, the copyright of a literary, scientific or artistic work already registered in another person's name, or in case of simultaneous conflicting applications, or of an application made, by any person other than the person entered as proprietor of a registered copyright, to cancel the said copyright, the party so applying shall be notified that the question is to be settled before a court of competent jurisdiction, and no further proceedings shall be had concerning the subject before a judgment is produced maintaining, cancelling or otherwise settling the matter ; and this registration or cancellation

cellation or adjustment of the said right shall then be made by the Minister of Agriculture in accordance with such decision. Action on decision.

20. Clerical errors happening in the framing or copying of any instrument drawn in the office of the Minister of Agriculture, shall not be construed as invalidating the same, but when discovered they may be corrected under the authority of the Minister of Agriculture. Clerical errors how corrected.

21. All copies or extracts certified, from the office of the Minister of Agriculture shall be received in evidence, without further proof and without production of the originals. Certified copies or extracts,— their effect.

22. Should a work copyrighted in Canada become out of print, a complaint may be lodged by any person with the Minister of Agriculture, who, on the fact being ascertained to his satisfaction, shall notify the copyright owner of the complaint and of the fact ; and if, within a reasonable time, no remedy is applied by such owner, the Minister of Agriculture may grant a license to any person to publish a new edition or to import the work, specifying the number of copies and the royalty to be paid on each to the copyright owner. Provision for the case of a copyrighted work being out of print.
Licence to print it, &c.

23. The application for the registration of an interim copyright, of a temporary copyright and of a copyright, may be made in the name of the author or of his legal representative, by any person purporting to be the agent of the said author ; and any fraudulent assumption of such authority shall be a misdemeanor and shall be punished by fine and imprisonment accordingly ; and any damage caused by a fraudulent or an erroneous assumption of such authority shall be recoverable before any court of competent jurisdiction. Application for registration may be made through an agent.
Punishment of pretended agents.

24. If any person shall wilfully make or cause to be made any false entry in the registry books of the Minister of Agriculture, or shall wilfully produce or cause to be tendered in evidence any paper falsely purporting to be a copy of an entry in the said books, he shall be guilty of a misdemeanor, and shall be punished accordingly. Making false entries &c., to be a misdemeanor.

25. If a book be published anonymously, it shall be sufficient to enter it in the name of the first publisher thereof either on behalf of the un-named author or on behalf of such first publisher, as the case may be. Anonymous books may be entered in the name of first publisher.

26. It shall not be requisite to deliver any printed copy of the second or of any subsequent edition of any book or books, unless the same shall contain very important alterations or additions. As to second and subsequent editions.

Limitation of actions.

27. No action or prosecution for the recovery of any penalty under this Act, shall be commenced more than two years after the cause of action arose.

Fees payable under this Act.

28. The following fees shall be payable to the Minister of Agriculture before an application for any of the purposes. hereinafter mentioned shall be entertained, that is to say :

On registering a Copyright $1 00
On registering an Interim Copyright 0 50
On registering a Temporary Copyright ... 0 50
On recording an assignment 1 00
On Certified copy of Registration........... 0 50
On registering any decision of a Court
   of Justice, for every folio.................... 0 50

On office copies.

On office copies of documents not above mentioned, the following charges shall be made :

For every single or first folio certified copy $0 50
For every subsequent hundred words
(fractions from and under fifty being not
  counted and over fifty being counted
  for one hundred)............................... 0 25

Proviso.

2. The said fees shall be in full of all services performed under this Act by the Minister of Agriculture or by any person employed by him in pursuance of this Act.

To be part of Con. Rev. Fund.

3. All fees received under this Act shall be paid over to the Receiver-General and form part of the Consolidated Revenue Fund of Canada. No fees shall be made the subject

Proviso.

of exemption in favour of any person ; and no fee, exacted by this Act, once paid, shall be returned to the person who paid it.

Repeal of inconsistent Acts.

29. "The Copyright Act of 1868," being the Act Thirty first Victoria, Chapter Fifty-four, and all other Acts or parts. of Acts, inconsistent with the provisions of this Act, are hereby repealed, subject to the provisions of the next following section.

Unexpired copyrights to continue unimpaired.

30. All copyrights heretofore acquired under the Acts or parts of Acts repealed shall, in respect of the unexpired terms thereof, continue unimpaired, and shall have the same force and effect as regards the Province or Provinces to which they now extend and shall be assignable and renewable, and all penalties and forfeitures incurred and to be incurred under the same may be sued for and enforced, and all prosecutions commenced before the passing of this Act for any such penalties or forfeitures already incurred may be continued and completed, as if such Acts were not repealed.

Short title.

31. In citing this Act it shall be sufficient to call it " The Copyright Act of 1875."

TREATIES AND CONVENTIONS

OF

HER MAJESTY, THE QUEEN

AND THE

GOVERNMENT OF CANADA

WITH

FOREIGN POWERS

AND THEIR REPRESENTATIVES.

OTTAWA:

PRINTED BY BROWN CHAMBERLIN,

LAW PRINTER FOR CANADA, TO THE QUEEN'S MOST EXCELLENT MAJESTY.

1876.

TREATIES AND CONVENTIONS.

TREATY

Concerning the formation of a General Postal Union, concluded between Germany, Austro-Hungary, Belgium, Denmark, Egypt, Spain, the United States of America, France, Great Britain, Greece, Italy Luxemburg, Norway, the Netherlands, Portugal, Roumania, Russia, Servia, Sweden, Switzerland, and Turkey.

The undersigned, Plenipotentiaries of the Governments of the countries above enumerated, have, by common consent and subject to ratification, agreed upon the following Convention :

ARTICLE I.

The countries between which the present Treaty is concluded shall form, under the title of " General Postal Union," a single postal territory for the reciprocal exchange of correspondence between their Post Offices.

ARTICLE II.

The stipulations of this Treaty shall extend to letters, post-cards, books, newspapers and other printed papers, patterns of merchandise, and legal and commercial documents originating in one of the countries of the Union and intended for another of those countries. They shall also apply to the exchange by post of the articles above mentioned between the countries of the Union and countries foreign to the Union whenever such exchange takes place over the territory of two at least of the contracting parties.

ARTICE III.

The general Union rate of postage is fixed at 25 centimes for the single prepaid letter.

Nevertheless, as a measure of conversion, the option is reserved to each country, in order to suit its monetary or other requirements, of levying a rate higher or lower than this charge, provided that it does not exceed 32 centimes or go below 20 centimes.

Every letter which does not exceed 15 grammes in weight shall be considered a single letter. The charge upon letters exceeding that weight shall be a single rate for every 15 grammes or fraction of 15 grammes.*

---

*By Article 24 of the Detailed Regulations for carrying this Treaty into effect, any country which has not adopted the decimal metrical system of weight may substitute half an ounce for 15 grammes

The charge on unpaid letters shall be double the rate levied in the country of destination on prepaid letters.

The prepayment of post cards is compulsory. The postage to be charged on them is fixed at one-half of that on paid letters, with power to round off the fractions.

For all conveyance by sea of more than 300 nautical miles within the district of the Union, there may be joined to the ordinary postage an additional charge, which shall not exceed the half of the general Union rate fixed for a paid letter.

ARTICLE IV.

The general Union rate for legal and commercial documents, patterns of merchandise, newspapers, stitched or bound books, pamphlets, music, visiting cards, catalogues, prospectuses, announcements and notices of various kinds, whether printed, engraved or lithographed, as well as for photographs, is fixed at 7 centimes for each single packet.

Nevertheless, as a measure of conversion, the option is reserved to each country, in order to suit its monetary or other requirements, of levying a rate higher or lower than this charge, provided that it does not exceed 11 centimes or go below 5 centimes.

Every packet which does not exceeed 50 grammes in weight shall be considered a single packet. The charge upon packets exceeding that weight shall be a single rate for every 50 grammes or fractions of 50 grammes.*

For all conveyance by sea of more than three hundred nautical miles within the district of the Union, there may be joined to the ordinary postage an additional charge which shall not exceed the half of the general Union rate fixed for articles of this class.

The maximum weight of the articles mentioned above is fixed at 250 grammes for patterns of merchandise, and at 1,000 grammes for all the others.

There is reserved to the Government of each country of the Union the right to refuse to convey over its territory or to deliver articles specified in the present Article with regard to which the laws, orders and decrees which regulate the conditions of their publication and circulation have not been observed.

ARTICLE V.

The articles specified in Article II., may be registered.

Every registered packet must be prepaid.

The postage payable on registered articles is the same as that on articles not registered.

The charge to be made for registration and for acknowledgments of receipt must not exceed that made in the inland service of the country of origin.

---

* By Article 24 of the Detailed Regulations for carrying this Treaty into effect, any country which has not adopted the decimal metrical system of weight may substitute two ounces for 50 grammes, and may raise to four ounces the weight to be allowed for a single newspaper.

In case of the loss of a registered article, and except in case of *force majeure*, there shall be paid an indemnity of 50 francs to the sender, or at his request, to the addressee, by the office of the country in the territory or in the maritime service of which the loss has occurred—that is to say, where the trace of the article has been lost,—unless, according to the legislation of such country, the office is not responsible for the loss of registered articles sent through its inland post.

The payment of this indemnity shall be effected with the least possible delay, and, at the latest, within a year dating from the date of application.

All claim for an indemnity is excluded if it be not made within one year, counting from the date on which the registered article was posted.

ARTICLE VI

Prepayment of postage on every description of article can be effected only by means of postage stamps or stamped envelopes valid in the country of origin.

Newspaper and other printed papers unpaid or insufficiently paid shall not be forwarded. Other articles when unpaid or insufficiently paid shall be charged as unpaid letters, after deducting the value of the stamped envelopes or postage stamps, if any, employed.

ARTICLE VII.

No additional postage shall be charged for the re-transmission of postal articles within the interior of the union.

But in case an article which has only passed through the inland service of one of the countries of the Union should, by being re-directed, enter into the inland service of another country of the Union, the Post Office of the country of destination shall add its inland rate.

ARTICLE VIII.

Official correspondence relative to the Postal Service is exempt from postage ; with this exception, no franking or reduction of postage is allowed.

ARTICLE IX.

Each office shall keep the whole of the sums which it collects by virtue of of the foregoing Articles, 3, 4, 5, 6 and 7. Consequently there will be no necessity on this head for any accounts between the several offices of the Union.

Neither the senders nor the addressees of letters and other postal packets shall be called upon to pay, either in the country of origin, or in that of destination, any tax or duty other than those contemplated by the articles above mentioned.

ARTICLE X.

The right of transit is guaranteed throughout the entire territory of the Union.

General Postal Union.

Consequently, there shall be full and entire liberty of exchange, the several Post Offices of the Union being able to send, reciprocally, in transit through intermediate countries, closed mails as well as correspondence in open mails, according to the wants of the traffic, and the exigencies of the Postal Service.

Closed mails and correspondence sent in open mails must always be forwarded by the most rapid routes at the command of the Post Offices concerned.

When several routes offer the same advantages of speed, the despatching office shall have the right of choosing the route to be adopted.

It is obligatory to make up closed mails whenever the number of letters and other postal packets is of a nature to hinder the operations of the transit office, according to the declaration of the office interested.

The despatching office shall pay to the office of the territory providing the transit, the sum of two francs per kilogramme for letters and 25 centimes per kilogramme for the several articles specified in Article IV, net weight, whether the transit takes place in closed mails or in open mails.

This payment may be increased to 4 francs for letters and to 50 centimes for the articles specified in Article IV, when a transit is provided of more than 750 kilometres in length over the territory of one office.

It is understood, however, that in any case in which the transit is already actually gratuitous or subject to lower rates, those conditions shall be maintained.

Whenever a transit shall take place by sea over a distance exceeding 300 nautical miles within the district of the Union, the Office by or at the expense of which this sea service is performed, shall have the right to a payment of the expenses attending this transport.

The members of the Union engage to reduce those expenses as much as possible. The payment which the office providing the sea conveyance may claim on this account from the despatching office, shall not exceed 6 francs 50 centimes per kilogramme for letters and 50 centimes per kilogramme for the articles specified in Article IV., net weight.

In no case shall these expenses be higher than those now paid; consequently, no payment shall be made upon the sea routes on which nothing is paid at the present time.

In order to ascertain the weight of the correspondence forwarded in transit, whether in closed mails or in open mails, there shall be taken, at periods which shall be determined upon by common consent, an account of such correspondence during two weeks. Until revised, the result of that account shall serve as the basis of the accounts of the Post Offices between themselves.

Each office may demand a revision,—

1. In case of any important modification in the direction of the correspondence;

2. At the expiration of a year after the date of the last account.

The provisions of the present article are not applicable to the Indian Mail, nor to the mails conveyed across the territory of the United States of America by the railways between New York and San Francisco. Those services shall continue to form the object of special arrangements between the Post Offices concerned.

ARTICLE XI.

The relations of the countries of the Union with the countries foreign to the Union shall be regulated by the separate conventions which now exist, or which may be concluded between them.

The rates of postage chargeable for the conveyance beyond the limits of the Union shall be determined by those conventions ; they shall be added, in such case, to the Union rate.

In conformity with the stipulations of Article IX, the Union rate shall be appropriated in the following manner :—

1. The despatching office of the Union shall keep the whole of the Union rate for the prepaid correspondence addressed to foreign countries.
2. The receiving office of the Union shall keep the whole of the Union rate for the unpaid correspondence originating in foreign countries.
3. The office of the Union which exchanges closed mails with foreign countries shall keep the whole of the Union rate for the paid correspondence originating in foreign countries and for the unpaid correspondence addressed to foreign countries.

In the cases mentioned under the numbers 1, 2 and 3, the office which exchanges the mails is not entitled to any payment for transit. In all the other cases the transit rates shall be paid according to the stipulations of Article X.

ARTICLE XII.

The exchange of letters with value declared and of Post Office money orders, shall form the subject of ulterior arrangements between the various countries or groups of countries composing the Union.

ARTICLE XIII

The Post Offices of the various countries composing the Union are competent to draw up, by common consent, in the form of detailed regulations, all the measures of Order and detail necessary with a view to the execution of the present Treaty. It is understood that the stipulations of these detailed regulations may always be modified by the common consent of the offices of the Union.

The several offices may make amongst themselves the necessary arrangement on the subject of questions which do not concern the Union generally ; such as the regulations of exchange at the frontier, the determination of radii in adjacent countries within which a lower rate of postage may be taken, the conditions of the exchange of Post Office money orders, and of letters with declared value, &c., &c.

General Postal Union.

ARTICLE XIV.

The stipulations of the present Treaty do not involve any alteration in the inland postal legislation of any country, nor any restriction on the right of the contracting parties to maintain and to conclude treaties, as well as to maintain and to establish more restricted unions with a view to a progressive improvement of postal relations.

ARTICLE XV.

There shall be organized, under the name of the International Office of the General Postal Union, a central office, which shall be conducted under the surveillance of a Postal Administration to be chosen by the Congress, and the expenses of which shall be borne by all the offices of the contracting States.

This office shall be charged with the duty of collecting, publishing and distributing information of every kind which concerns the International Postal Service; of giving, at the request of the parties concerned, an opinion upon questions in dispute; of making known proposals for modifying the detailed regulations; of notifying alterations adopted; of facilitating operations relating to the international accounts, especially in the cases referred to in Article X. foregoing; and in general of considering and working out all questions in the interest of the Postal Union.

ARTICLE XVI.

In case of disagreement between two or more members of the Union as to the interpretation of the present Treaty, the question in dispute shall be decided by arbitration. To that end, each of the offices concerned shall choose another member of the Union not interested in the affair.

The decision of the arbitrators shall be given by an absolute majority of votes.

In case of an equality of votes the arbitrators shall choose, with the view of settling the difference, another Administration equally uninterested in the question in dispute.

ARTICLE XVII.

The entry into the Union of countries beyond sea not yet forming part of it, shall be effected on the following conditions:

1. They shall make their application to the Administration charged with the management of the International Office of the Union.
2. They shall submit to the stipulations of the Treaty of the Union, subject to an ulterior understanding on the subject of the cost of sea conveyance.
3. Their adhesion to the Union must be preceded by an understanding between the Administration having postal conventions or direct relations with them.

General Postal Union.

4. In order to bring about this understanding, the Administration charged with the management of the International Office of the Union shall convene, if there be occasion, a meeting of the Administrations interested, and of the Administration desiring admission.

5. When the understanding has been arrived at, the Administration charged with the management of the International Office of the Union shall give notice of the same to all the members of the General Postal Union.

6. If in a period of six weeks, counting from the date of that communication, no objections are presented, the adhesion shall be considered as accomplished, and notice thereof shall be given by the managing Administration to the Administration joining the Union. The definitive adhesion shall be completed by a diplomatic act between the Government of the managing Administration and the Government of the Administration admitted into the Union.

ARTICLE XVIII.

Every three years at least a Congress of plenipotentiaries of the countries participating in the Treaty shall be held with a view of perfecting the system of the Union, of introducing into it improvements found necessary, and of discussing common affairs.

Each country has one vote.

Each country may be represented either by one or several delegates, or by the delegation of another country.

Nevertheless, it is understood that the delegate or delegates of one country can be charged with the representation of two countries only; including the one they represent.

The next meeting shall take place at Paris in 1877.

Nevertheless, the period of this meeting may be advanced, if a demand to that effect be made by one-third at least of the members of the Union.

ARTICLE XIX.

The present Treaty shall come into force on the 1st July, 1875.

It is concluded for three years from that date. When that term is passed, it shall be considered as indefinitely prolonged, but each contracting party will have the right to withdraw from the Union on giving notice one year in advance.

ARTICLE XX.

After the date on which the present Treaty comes into effect, all the stipulations of the special treaties concluded between the various countries and Administrations, in so far as they may be at variance with the terms of the present Treaty, and without prejudice to the stipulations of Article XIV., are abrogated.

8

General Postal Union.

The present Treaty shall be ratified as soon as possible, and, at the latest, three months previous to the date on which it is to come into force. The acts of ratification shall be exchanged at Berne.

In faith of which the plenipotentiaries of the Governments of the countries above enumerated have signed it at Berne, the 9th October, 1874.

WM. JAS. PAGE, for Great Britain.
STEPHAN, } for Germany.
GUNTHER, }
LE BARON DE KOLBENSTEINER, } for Austria.
PILHA', }
M. GERVAY, } for Hungary.
P. HEIM, }
FASSIAUX,)
VINCHENT, } for Belgium.
J. GIFE,)
FENGER, for Denmark.
MUZZI BEY, for Egypt.
ANGEL MANSI, } for Spain.
EMILIO C. DE NAVASCUES, }
JOSEPH H. BLACKFAN, for United States of America.
B. D'HARCOURT, for France, (3rd May, 1875.)
A. MANSOLAS, } Greece.
ALB. BETANT, }
TANTESIO, for Italy.
VON ROEBE, for Luxembourg.
C. OPPEN, for Norway.
HOFSTEDE, } for Holland.
B. SWEERTS DE LANDAS WYBORGH, }
EDUARDO LESSA, for Portugal.
GEORGE F. LAHOVARI, for Roumania.
BARON VELHO, } for Russia.
GEORGE POGGENPOHL, }
MLADEN Z. RADOJKOVITSCH, for Servia.
W. ROOS, for Sweden.
EUGÈNE BOREL,)
NAEFF, } for Switzerland.
DR. J. HEER,)
YANCO MACRIDI, for Turkey.

POSTAL ARRANGEMENT BETWEEN THE DOMINION OF CANADA AND THE UNITED STATES.

The Post Office Department of the United States of America and the Post Office Department of the Dominion of Canada being desirous of effecting, by means of a new arrangement, the unification of the postal systems of the United States and Canada, in respect to correspondence exchanged between them ; the undersigned duly authorized for that purpose by their respective Governments, have agreed upon the following articles :—

ARTICLE I.

Correspondence of every kind, written and printed, embracing letters, postal cards, newspapers, pamphlets, magazines, books, maps, plans, engravings, drawings, photographs, lithographs, sheets of music, &c., and patterns and samples of merchandise, including grains and seeds, mailed in the United States and addressed to Canada, or, *vice versâ*, mailed in Canada and addressed to the United States, shall be fully prepaid at the domestic postage rates of the country of origin, and the country of destination will receive, forward and deliver the same free of charge.

ARTICLE II.

Each country will transport the domestic mails of the other by its ordinary mail routes in closed pouches through its territory, free of charge.

ARTICLE III.

Patterns and samples of merchandise not exceeding the weight of eight ounces may be exchanged in the mails between the two countries under such regulations in regard to the forwarding and delivery of the same as either of the Post Office Departments shall prescribe to prevent violations of the revenue laws.

They must never be closed against inspection, but must always be so wrapped or enclosed that they may be readily and thoroughly examined by Postmasters. The postage on each pattern or sample shall be ten cents, —prepayment obligatory.

ARTICLE IV.

No accounts shall be kept between the Post Office Departments of the two countries in regard to international correspondence of any kind exchanged between them, but each Department will retain to its exclusive use all the postage it collects on mail matters of every kind sent to the other for delivery.

ARTICLE V.

The Post Office Department of the United States and Canada shall each return to the other all dead letters, unopened and without charge, monthly or oftener, as may best suit the regulations of each Department.

Postal arrangement between Canada and United States.

ARTICLE VI.

The expense of transporting the mails between the frontier exchange offices where the conveyance is by water, shall be borne equally by the two Departments ; but when the transportation is by land, the expense shall be borne by each in proportion to the distance travelled over the territory of each country. All contracts for such transportation shall, before they go into operation, be approved by the Post Office Department of each country.

ARTICLE VII.

All offices now exchanging mails shall continue to act as offices of exchange under this convention.

The two Departments may, at any time, by mutual agreement, discontinue any of said offices of exchange, or establish others.

ARTICLE VIII.

The existing arrangement for the exchange of registered letters between the two countries shall continue in full force ; but the registration fee on registered letters sent from the United States to Canada, shall be the same as the registration fee charged in the United States for domestic registered letters.

ARTICLE IX.

This arrangement, except so far as it relates to letter postage, shall take effect from the 1st of January, 1875. The reduced letter rate will come into operation on the 1st of February, 1875. It shall continue in force until terminated by mutual agreement ; and it may be annulled at the desire of either Department upon six months previous notice given to the other.

Done in duplicate and signed at Ottawa the 27th day of January, 1875.

(Signed,)   D. A. MACDONALD,

Postmaster-General, Canada.

MARSHALL JEWELL,

Postmaster-General, United States.

I hereby approve the aforegoing postal arrangement, and in testimony thereof, I have caused the seal of the United States to be affixed.

U. S. GRANT,

By the President

(L.S.)

HAMILTON FISH,

Secretary of State.

WASHINGTON, February 1st, 1875.

MONEY ORDER SYSTEM BETWEEN CANADA AND THE UNITED STATES

CONVENTION

Between the Postal Department of the United States of America and the Postal Department of the Dominion of Canada.

The Postal Department of the United States of America and the Postal Department of the Dominion of Canada being desirous of establishing an exchange of money-orders between the two countries, the undersigned, duly authorised for that purpose, have agreed upon the following articles :—

ARTICLE I.

There shall be a regular exchange of money-orders between the two countries for sums received from remitters in one country for payment to beneficiaries in the other.

The maximum of each order is fixed at forty dollars, gold value, when issued in the Dominion of Canada, and when issued in the United States at fifty dollars in the national paper currency of that country; but no money-order shall include the fractional part of a cent.

ARTICLE II.

The Postal Department of the Dominion of Canada shall have the power to fix the rates of commission on all money-orders issued in the Dominion of Canada, and the Postal Department of the United States shall have the same power in regard to all money-orders issued in the United States. Each Postal Department shall communicate to the other its tariff of charges or rates of commission; and these rates shall, in all cases, be paid in advance by the remitter, who shall not be entitled to repayment thereof. It is understood, moreover, that each Department is authorized to suspend temporarily, after having given sixty days' notice of such intention to the other, the exchange of money-orders, in case the course of exchange, or any other circumstances, should give rise to abuses, or cause detriment to the postal revenue.

ARTICLE III.

Each country shall keep the commission charged on all money-orders issued within it, but shall pay to the other country one half of one per cent on the total amount of such orders.

ARTICLE IV

The service of the postal money-order system between the two countries shall be performed exclusively through the agency of offices of exchange which shall be established in the United States by the Postmaster General of that country.

Money Order Convention between Canada and United States.

Eight such offices are hereby designated, viz : Bangor, Me., Boston, Mass., New York, Ogdensburgh and Buffalo, N.Y., Detroit, Mich., Saint Paul, Minn., and Portland, Oreg., and the number and location of these offices may be changed from time to time by said Postmaster General as the interest of the service may require.

ARTICLE V.

Any person in the United States desiring to remit to the Dominion of Canada a sum of money, within the limits prescribed by Article I hereof, may pay it into any post office in the United States, designated; from time to time by the Postmaster General of that country for the transaction of Canadian money-order business. Such person shall, at the same time, give the name and address of the person to whom the amount is to be paid in said Dominion, and also his own name and address.

Any person in the Dominion of Canada desiring to remit to the United States a sum of money, within the same limits, may pay it into any money-order office of said Dominion, designated by the Postmaster General thereof for the said purpose, giving at the same time the name and address of the person to whom the amount is to be paid in the United States, and also his own name and address.

The receiving postmaster in either country shall, in accordance with the rules established by its Postal Department, forward a coupon, an advice and a money order to the Exchange Office in the United States, most convenient to the residence of the beneficiary for whom the money is intended; the postmaster of which Exchange Office shall immediately after the receipt thereof certify upon the coupon, the advice, and the order the value of the same in currency of the country in which payment is to be made, and he shall likewise enter therein the name of the inland office at which the same is to be paid, and shall at once forward the advice to said office, and the order to the beneficiary for whom the money is intended, retaining the coupon on file in his office as a voucher for his own protection and information.

ARTICLE VI.

The money-orders, advices and coupons issued in each country shall have, printed thereon, consecutive local or inland numbers, the number upon each advice and coupon being the same as upon its corresponding order, and in addition thereto all such orders, advices and coupons shall be numbered consecutively at the Exchange Office at which they are certified, which numbers shall be in the order of their receipt and certification, and shall be designated as "International numbers."

The discovery, by an inland postmaster, of any error in a money-order or advice shall be by him promptly reported to the Exchange Office through which the same was certified, and any error coming to the notice of an Exchange Office shall at once be reported to the Money Order Office at Washington, D.C., in order that an explanation or correction may be given or asked for, as the case may be,—which explanation or correction shall be afforded with the least possible delay.

Money Order Convention between Canada and United States.

ARTICLE VII.

Lists of all orders issued during each week by postmasters in either country, for payment in the other, shall at the close of the week, or as soon thereafter as practicable, be transmitted by the Postal Department of the issuing to that of the paying country, and at the close of each fiscal quarter two copies of an account shall be prepared and transmitted to the Postal Department of the United States by the Postal Department of the Dominion of Canada, exhibiting the balance found due on the exchanges of money-orders during the quarter, one copy of which, after proper verification and acknowledgment, shall be returned to the Postal Department of the Dominion of Canada. If this verified account shows a balance in favor of the Postal Department of the Dominion of Canada, that of the United States will transmit, with such verified copy of the quarterly account, a bill of exchange on Montreal, Canada, for the amount of said balance, payable to the Postal Department of the Dominion of Canada. The latter will then send an acknowledgment of receipt to the Postal Department of the United States. If, on the other hand, said account, after verification and acknowledgment as aforesaid, shows a balance in favor of the Postal Department of the United States then the Postal Department of the Dominion of Canada will, upon receipt of the certified copy of the same transmit to that of the United States a bill of exchange for the amount thereof on New York. The United States Postal Department will then send in return an acknowledgment of receipt.

If, pending the settlement of an account, one of the two Postal Departments shall ascertain that it owes the other a balance not exceeding five thousand dollars, the indebted administration shall promptly remit the approximate amount of such balance to the credit of the other. The expenses attending the remittance of bills of exchange shall invariably be borne by the Postal Department having to make the payment.

This account and the letters which accompany such intermediate remittances shall be in accordance with the forms A, B and C hereto annexed.

ARTICLE VIII.

Until the two Postal Departments shall consent to an alteration, it is agreed that, in all matters relative to money-orders which shall result from the execution of the present convention, the Canadian dollar shall be considered equivalent to one dollar of the gold coin of the United States, and the Exchange Offices in the United States shall certify all orders upon the basis of gold.

ARTICLE IX.

The value, in gold coin, of deposits made in the United States, in paper money, for payment to beneficiaries in the Dominion of Canada, and the value in United States paper money, of deposits made in the Dominion of Canada, in gold coin or currency of par value, for payment in the United States, shall be determined according to the rate of premium on gold in New York, N. Y., in the following manner, viz : The postmaster at New

York shall, at three o'clock p. m., of each day, except Sunday, telegraph to each of the above named Exchange Offices in the United States, the rate of premium on gold at that hour, which rate shall, when received by such Exchange Office, be taken as the basis of conversion of money values. for the next, and for all subsequent orders and advices dispatched and received, until the receipt of the next telegram from the postmaster at New York.

ARTICLE X.

A duplicate order shall only be issued by the Postal Department of the country on which the original order was drawn, and in conformity with the regulations established, or to be established in that country.

ARTICLE XI.

A money order returned on application by a dispatching Exchange Office to the inland issuing postmaster, as "not certified for payment," may be repaid, by said postmaster, to the remitter, in the same manner as a domestic order.

ARTICLE XII.

An order which shall not have been paid within twelve calendar months after the month of its issue shall become void, and the sum received therefor shall accrue to and remain at the disposal of the country of origin; and the advice shall be returned by the inland postmaster holding the same to his Postal Department, to be by it returned to the Postal Department of the country in which it originated. The Postal Department of the Dominion of Canada shall therefore enter to the credit of the United States, in the quarterly account, all sums certified from the latter country, which remain unpaid at the end of the period specified. On the other hand, the United States Postal Department shall, at the close of each month, transmit to the Postal Department of the Dominion of Canada, for entry in the quarterly account, a detailed statement of all orders dispatched from said Dominion which under this article become void.

ARTICLE XIII.

Repayment of an order, not void, to a remitter shall not be made until an authorization therefor shall first have been obtained by the Postal Department of the country of issue from the Postal Department of the country where such order was made payable: and the amount of the repaid order shall be duly credited to the former country in the quarterly account. It is the province of each Postal Department to determine the manner in which repayment to the remitter is to be made.

ARTICLE XIV.

The orders drawn by each country upon the other shall be subject, as regards payment, to the regulations which govern the payment of domestic orders in the country on which they are drawn.

Money Order Convention between Canada and United States.

ARTICLE XV.

The Postal Department of each country shall be authorized to adopt any additional rules, not repugnant to the foregoing, for greater security against fraud, or for the better working of the system generally. All such additional rules, however, must be promptly communicated to the Postal Department of the other country.

ARTICLE XVI.

The present Convention shall take effect on Monday, the second day of August, 1875, and shall continue in force until twelve months after the date at which one of the contracting parties shall have notified to the other its intention to terminate it.

Done in duplicate and signed at Washington, on the eighth day of June in the year of Our Lord one thousand eight hundred and seventy-five, and at Ottawa, Canada, on the twenty-third day of June in the year of Our Lord one thousand eight hundred and seventy-five.

(L.S.)
    (Signed,)   MARSHALL JEWELL,
Postmaster General of the United States.

(L.S.)
    (Signed,)   T. FOURNIER,
Postmaster General of Canada.

I hereby approve the foregoing Convention, and in testimony thereof, I have caused the seal of the United States to be hereto affixed.

(L.S.)
    (Signed,)   U. S. GRANT,
By the President.

    (Signed,)   JOHN L. CADWALADER,
Acting Secretary of State

7th July, 1875.

GENERAL CONVENTION BETWEEN THE GOVERNMENTS OF GREAT BRITAIN AND OF TUNIS.

Signed in the English and Arabic Languages, July 19, 1875.

The Government of Her Majesty the Queen of the United Kingdom of Great Britain and Ireland, and His Most Serene Highness Mohammed Essaddock Bey, Lord of the Regency of Tunis, being desirous to maintain and improve the relations of friendship and commerce which have long subsisted between them, and between British and Tunisian subjects, have resolved to proceed to a revision and improvement of the Treaties subsisting between the respective countries ; in consequence of which the following stipulations have been entered into and concluded between His Most Serene Highness the Bey, and Richard Wood, Esquire, Companion of the Most Honourable Order of the Bath, Her Majesty's Agent and Consul General, duly authorized to that effect.

ARTICLE I.

Her Majesty the Queen of the United Kingdom of Great Britain and Ireland may appoint, besides her Political Agent, such Consuls, Vice-Consuls, and Consular Agents in the Regency of Tunis, as she may deem necessary ; and such Consuls, Vice-Consuls and Consular Agents shall be at liberty to reside in any of the seaports or cities of His Highness the Bey, which they or the British Government may choose and find most convenient for the affairs and service of Her Majesty, and for the assistance of her subjects.

ARTICLE II.

Every mark of honour and respect shall, at all times, be paid, and every privilege and immunity allowed to Her Majesty's Agent and Consul-General, accredited to His Highness the Bey, which is paid or allowed to the Representative of any other nation whatsoever ; and respect and honour shall be shown to the British Consuls, Vice-Consuls and Consular Agents, who shall reside in the Regency of Tunis. Their houses and families shall be safe and protected. No one shall interfere with them, or commit any act of oppression or disrespect towards them, either by word or deed ; and if any one should do so, the Tunisian authorities shall take immediate measures for the punishment of the offender. The British Consuls, Vice-Consuls and Consular Agents, shall, moreover, continue to enjoy, in the most ample sense, all the privileges and immunities which are now, or may be hereafter accorded to the Consuls, Vice-Consuls, and Consular Agents of the most favoured nation.

ARTICLE III.

The British Agent and Consul-General shall be at liberty to choose his own interpreters, brokers, guards and servants, either from among the natives or others. His interpreters, brokers, guards and servants shall be exempt from the conscription, and from the payment of any poll tax, forced contribution or other similar or corresponding charge.   In like manner, the Consuls, Vice-Consuls and Consular Agents, residing at the Tunisian ports, under the orders of the said Agent and Consul-General, shall be at liberty to choose, that is to say, the Consuls, each one interpreter, one broker, two guards and three servants; the Vice-Consuls and Consular Agents, each one interpreter, one broker, one guard, and two servants, not being in the military service, who shall likewise be exempt from the conscription, from the payment of any poll tax, forced contribution, or other similar or corresponding charge.   No prohibition nor tax shall be put upon the provisions, furniture, or any other articles which may come to the said Agent and Consul-General, Consuls or Vice Consuls, for their own use, and for the use of their families, upon their delivering to the Officer of the Customs a note under their hand, specifying the number of articles which they shall require to be passed on that ground ; but this privilege shall only be accorded to Consular Officers who are not engaged in trade.   If the service of their Sovereign should require their attendance in their own country, no impediment shall be offered to their departure, and no hindrance shall be offered either to themselves or their servants, or in regard to their property, but they shall be at liberty to go and come respected and honoured.   If they should depute another person to act for them in their absence, they shall not be prevented in any way from so doing; nor shall the deputy be prevented from acting in that capacity.

ARTICLE IV.

There shall be reciprocal freedom of commerce between the Dominions of Her Majesty the Queen and the Regency of Tunis.   British merchants or their agents and brokers shall be permitted to purchase at all places within the Regency, whether for the purposes of internal trade or of exportation, all articles, without any exception whatsoever, being the produce or manufacture of the said Regency : and the purchaser shall be free to remove his goods, when purchased, from one place to another, without any attempt being made on the part of the Local Governors to interfere with them.

ARTICLE V.

In accordance with the friendship which has, at all times, existed between the two Governments, His Highness the Bey engages to protect British subjects who may come to this country either for the purposes of trade or for travelling.   They shall be free to travel or to reside in any part of the Regency without hindrance or molestation ; and they shall be treated with respect, love and honour.   They shall be exempt from forced military service, whether by land or by sea; from forced loans, and from every extraordinary contribution.   Their dwellings and warehouses destined for purposes of residence and commerce, as well as their property, both real and personal, of every kind, shall be respected ; and, in particular, all the stipulations of the Convention concluded between Her Majesty's Government and His Highness the Bey on the 10th of October, 1863, relative to the permission granted to British subjects to hold real property in the Regency, of Tunis, are hereby confirmed. And British subjects, vessels, commerce, and navigation shall enjoy, without any restriction or diminution, all the privileges, favours and immunities which are now or may hereafter be granted to the subjects, vessels, commerce and navigation of any other nation whatever.

Her Britannic Majesty, on her part, engages to insure to Tunisian subjects, vessels, commerce and navigation within her Dominions, the enjoyment of the same protection and privileges which are or may be enjoyed by the subjects, vessels, commerce and navigation of the most favoured nation.

ARTICLE VI.

The perfect security which His Highness the Bey accords to the British merchants and subjects who may reside in the Regency extends likewise to the exercise of the free rites of their religion. They shall be free to erect churches, upon the application of the British Agent and Consul-General to His Highness the Bey, who will grant the necessary permission. The British Cemetery of Saint George, and other burial places, now or hereafter to be established, shall be protected and respected as heretofore.

ARTICLE VII.

His Highness the Bey engages that he will not prohibit the importation into the Regency of any article the product and manufacture of the dominions and possessions of Her Britannic Majesty, from whatever place arriving, and that the duties to be levied upon such articles of produce or manufacture so imported shall in no case exceed one fixed rate of eight per cent., *ad valorem*, to be calculated upon the value of such merchandise at the place of landing, or a specific duty fixed by common consent, equivalent thereto.

Such articles, after paying eight per cent. import duty, shall not be subject to any other internal charge or impost whatsoever, whether the buyer be a Tunisian or a foreigner. And if such articles should not be sold for consumption in the Regency, but should be re-exported within the space of one year, the Administration of the Customs shall be bound, provided the bales or packages have not been opened, to restore, at the time of their re-exportation, the duty levied, to the merchant, who shall be required first to furnish proofs that the goods so exported have paid the said import duty.

After the expiration of one year the merchant shall be free to re-export his foreign goods without claiming the drawback, and the Custom House shall not levy upon them any duty whatsoever on re-exportation.

Should a British merchant or his agent desire to convey, by sea or by land, from one port or place to another port or place in the Regency of Tunis, goods upon which the *ad valorem* duty above mentioned has already been paid, such goods shall be subject to no further duty, either on their embarkation or disembarkation, provided they be accompanied by a certificate from the Tunisian Administrator of Customs that the duty has been paid.

General Convention between Great Britain and Tunis.

And it is moreover agreed that no other or higher duties shall be imposed on the importation of any article the produce or manufacture of one of the Contracting Parties into the country of the other, which shall not equally extend to the like articles being the produce or manufacture of any other country.

ARTICLE VIII.

Vessels navigating under the British flag and vessels navigating under the Tunisian flag shall be free to carry on the coasting trade in the States and Dominions of the Contracting Parties. They shall enjoy the same rights and immunities as are enjoyed by national vessels, and they shall be free either to land a portion of their cargoes, or to embark goods, foreign or native, to complete their cargoes in each other's ports, without being obliged in each case to procure any special license from the local authorities, or to pay any charges and dues that are not paid by national vessels.

The stipulations of this Article shall, however, as regards the Colonial coasting trade, be deemed to extend only to the coasting trade of such of the Colonial possessions of Her Britannic Majesty as, under the provisions of the Act relating thereto, may have opened their coasting trade to foreign vessels.

ARTICLE IX.

His Highness the Bey formally engages to abolish all monopolies of agricultural produce or any other article whatsoever, save and except tobacco and salt, and save and except the fisheries, and the tannery of hides of oxen, camels and horses.

British subjects, however, or their agents, buying or selling salt and tobacco in virtue of licenses or permits for consumption in the Regency of Tunis, shall be subject to the same regulations as the most favored Tunisian subjects trading in the two articles aforesaid; and, furthermore, they shall be free to compete for, obtain, and exercise the right of fishery, subject to the local laws and regulations.

ARTICLE X.

If British merchants or their agents in the Regency of Tunis should purchase any article of Tunisian produce or manufacture for internal consumption, the said merchants or their agents shall not pay, on the purchase and sale of such articles, any higher duties or charges than are paid, under similar circumstances, by the most favoured class of Tunisians or foreigners engaged in the internal trade of the Regency of Tunis. In like manner, Tunisian merchants or their agents in the British dominions shall not pay on the purchase and sale of British produce or manufactures, for internal consumption in the said dominions, higher duties or charges than are paid by British subjects or the most favoured foreigners engaged in the internal trade of the said dominions, upon similar articles of produce or manufacture.

ARTICLE XI.

If a British merchant or his agent shall purchase for exportation any article of Tunisian produce or manufacture, either at the place where such article is produced or in its transit from that place to another, upon which article of produce or manufacture the internal taxes known by the names of "Ushr," "Kanoon," and "Mahsoulat," and others, have been already levied, such article of produce or manufacture shall be subject at the port of shipment to the payment of the export duty only, and the notarial fees and charges for measurement established by law.

ARTICLE XII.

In case of any dispute arising between the Custom House and a merchant regarding the value to be put upon any merchandise or goods imported by him into the Regency of Tunis, the merchant shall be free to pay the duty in kind, in the most equitable manner.

Should, however, the merchant be unwilling to make use of the above faculty, the Custom House shall have the right to purchase such merchandise or goods at the price at which the merchant has valued them, with an augmentation of 5 per cent.

But should the foregoing two modes fail to solve the difficulty His Highness the Bey and Her Majesty's Agent and Consul-General shall each name an arbitrator, being a merchant, and, in case of a divergence of opinion, the two arbitrators shall name an umpire, also a merchant, whose decision shall be final.

ARTICLE XIII.

With a view to the encouragement of agriculture, His Highness the Bey furthermore engages to permit the importation, free of import duty and of every other internal charge, of agricultural implements and machinery, as well as of cattle and animals for the improvement of the native breeds, whenever such agricultural implements, machinery, cattle, and animals are proved to be for private use and not for purposes of trade,—in which latter case they shall be subject to the payment of an import duty not exceeding 8 per cent.

ARTICLE XIV.

In case the importation of foreign wheat, barley and Indian corn should be rendered necessary in consequence of the failure of the crops, in consequence of famine or other causes, which God forbid, such foreign wheat, barley and Indian corn shall be as heretofore exempt from the payment of any import duty, and shall be subject only to the payment of 20 karoobs (7½d.) per kaffis.

With the exception of the above three articles, all other foreign provisions, such as rice, lentils, beans, and other pulse know by the appellation of "Hashahesh" (dried vegetables) shall pay an import duty not exceeding eight per cent., but the importer or his agent shall be free to sell such provisions in retail or in any other manner without the payment of any other charge whatsoever.

ARTICLE XV.

It is understood between the Contracting Parties, that the Tunisian Government reserves to itself the faculty and right of issuing a general prohibition against the importation into the Regency of gunpowder, unless Her Majesty's Agent and Consul-General shall think fit to apply for a special license, which license shall, in that case, be granted, provided no valid objection thereto can be alleged.

Gunpowder, when allowed to be imported, shall be subject to a duty not exceeding eight per cent., and shall be liable to the following regulations :—

1. It shall not be sold by subjects of Her Britannic Majesty in quantities exceeding the quantities prescribed by the local regulations.

2. When a cargo, or a large quantity of gunpowder arrives in a Tunisian port on board a British vessel, such vessel shall be anchored at a particular spot, to be designated by the local authorities, and the gunpowder shall then be conveyed, under the inspection of such authorities, to depôts or fitting places designated by the Government, to which the parties interested shall have access under due regulations.

Gunpowder imported in contravention of the prohibition, or in the absence of the license aforementioned, shall be liable to confiscation, save and except small quantities of gunpowder for sporting reserved for private use, which shall not be subject to the regulations of the present Article.

Cannon, arms of war, or military stores, as well as anchors, masts, and chains cables, shall be imported free of duty, provided they are landed at the opened and recognised ports ; provided, also, that previous to the landing of cannon the permission of the Government is obtained.

ARTICLE XVI.

The people of the Contracting Parties shall have the right to establish in each other's country, commercial, industrial, and banking companies, co-operative, or mutual or shareholding associations, or any other association, whether between and amongst themselves, or between them and Tunisian subjects or subjects of any other Power : provided the object of such companies and associations be lawful, and subject always to the laws of the country in which they shall be established.

It is, however, understood, that no joint stock companies limited, whose capital is made up of nominal shares to bearer, and no anonymous association shall be established in their respective territories without the authorization of the Local Government.

ARTICLE XVII.

British subjects and Tunisian subjects shall be free to exercise in each other's country any art, profession, or industry; to establish manufactories and factories, and to introduce steam machinery, or machinery moved by any other power, without being subjected to any other formality or to the payment of higher or other taxes and imposts than those prescribed by the laws or municipal regulations, or which are paid by natives.

It is understood that the manufactories and their appurtenances, being immovable property, shall be subject to the provisions of the Convention of the 10th October, 1863, relative to the permission granted to British subjects to hold real property in the Regency of Tunis.

ARTICLE XVIII.

No harbour, pilotage, light-house or quarantine dues, or other local dues, shall be levied upon British vessels, which are not imposed upon Tunisian vessels or upon the vessels of the most favored nation.   .

If a British vessel shall enter a Tunisian port from stress of weather and depart, it shall not be subject to the payment of the aforesaid dues, but shall pay only the fee to the pilot, should a pilot be required. Should such vessel, however, visit a Tunisian port for the purpose of procuring water and of purchasing provisions, it shall pay only a portion, not exceeding half, of the harbour, pilotage, light-house and quarantine or other local dues payable at the said port.

In like manner Tunisian vessels which shall visit any of the ports of Her Majesty's dominions shall pay only the harbour, quarantine and other dues which are levied upon British vessels.

ARTICLE XIX.

The captains of merchant vessels having goods on board destined for the Regency of Tunis shall, on their arrival at the port where such goods are to be landed, deposit in the Custom-house of such port a true copy of their manifest.

ARTICLE XX.

If a British subject be detected in smuggling into the Regency any description of goods, or should be detected in embarking any goods, the produce of Tunis, for which he can exhibit no Custom-house permit, such goods shall be confiscated by the Tunisian Treasury; but the report or *procès-verbal* of the alleged contraband must, as soon as the said goods are seized by the authorities, be drawn up and communicated to the British consular authorities, and no goods can be confiscated as contraband unless the fraud with regard to them shall be duly and legally proved.

It is stipulated that vessels navigating under the British flag shall submit to the regulations of the port ; that such vessels, speronaras, boats, and the like craft shall not serve as depots for merchandize ; and that whenever their detention in the Tunisian ports shall exceed eight calendar months, they shall, when required to do so, give satisfactory explanations to the British Consular authority and to the local authorities in regard to the motive of their detention in such ports. Should such explanations be deemed unsatisfactory, the Custom-house may, with the consent of Her Majesty's Agent and Consul-General, place a guard on board for the prevention of fraud, the expenses for such guard being at the charge of the vessel.

General Convention between Great Britain and Tunis.

ARTICLE XXI.

Should British subjects desire to embark in, or discharge goods from, any vessel, they can employ the Tunisian Custom-house boats, paying the usual charges for the use of such boats. They are free, however, to discharge their merchandise without using the Custom-house boats, in which case they will apprise the Administration of the Customs of it in writing, taking care to mention, on the arrival of each steamer or vessel having goods on board to their consignment, that they will be present themselves, or be represented by their agents, to assist at the discharge of said goods. In case of their absence, however, the Custom-house will proceed to discharge their goods, rendering itself responsible as heretofore, unless in a case of *force majeure.* No sort of claim can be preferred by the consignee against the Custom-house on the plea that it had not the right to discharge his goods, seeing that the discharge is made with the sanction of the master of the vessel, and not with that of the Custom-house.

Every consignee who discharges his goods after making the demand in writing, will provide himself with a Custom-house officer, who will accompany him to the vessel and return with him to the Custom-house. The fee to the Custom-house officer shall be paid by the merchant.

ARTICLE XXII

Whenever the Tunisian Government shall temporarily prohibit the exportation of wheat, barley, cattle, or any other article of native produce, such prohibition shall not come into operation until three months after official notification shall have been given, and shall apply only to the specific article or articles mentioned in the Decree enacting the prohibition.

ARTICLE XXIII.

No British subject, nor any person under British protection, shall, in the Regency of Tunis, be made liable to pay a debt due from another person of his nation, unless he shall have made himself responsible or guarantee for the debtor by a valid document. Neither shall any British subject be compelled to sell anything to, or to buy anything from, a Tunisian without his own free will. The seller shall be obliged to deliver up to the purchaser only that portion of the goods which he voluntarily sold to him, and the purchaser shall have no claim or right upon the remaining portion of such goods or merchandise.

In like manner, no Tunisian subject in the Dominions of the Queen of Great Britain shall be made liable to pay a debt due from another person of his nation to a British subject, unless he shall have made himself responsible or guarantee for the debtor by a valid document.

ARTICLE XXIV.

In all criminal cases and complaints where the prosecutor and prisoner are British subjects, and in all civil differences, disputes or litigation which may occur between British subjects exclusively, the Agent and Consul-

4

General, Consul or other British authority, shall be sole judge or arbiter. No one shall interfere, but they shall be amenable to the British Consular Courts only.

All civil differences, disputes or litigations between British subjects and the subjects of any foreign country other than Great Britain, shall be decided solely in the Tribunals of the foreign Consuls, according to the usages heretofore established, or which may hereafter be arranged between such Consuls, without the interference of the Tunisian Courts or Government.

ARTICLE XXV.

Disputes and differences arising between a British and a Tunisian subject, whether the British subject is plaintiff or defendant, of a commercial and civil nature (criminal and correctional excepted), shall be settled by His Highness the Bey, or his delegate, in the presence and with the concurrence of the British Consul-General or Consul.

It is likewise agreed that, should any new procedure, differing from the above, be adopted and applied at present, or in future, in the treatment of any other nation, the British subjects, without exception, shall be entitled to the enjoyment thereof, whenever Her Majesty's Government shall request it.

It is, however, understood that if Mixed Courts should be at any time established in Tunis with the assent and approval of Her Majesty's Government, in that case all civil and commercial suits and disputes arising between British and Tunisian subjects shall be heard and determined by such Mixed Courts and Tribunals, according to the rules and procedure that may be agreed upon between the Contracting Parties.

ARTICLE XXVI

The cognizance of crimes committed by British subjects in the Tunisian territory, as well as all contraventions of the police and other regulations, shall devolve upon the Consul-General or Consul; and the punishment thereof shall be applied by the said Consul-General or Consul, in concurrence with His Highness the Bey. In case the criminal or offender should escape from the Consular or other prison, the Consul-General or Consul shall not be held responsible in any matter whatsoever.

ARTICLE XXVII.

No quittance or receipt presented by a British subject to a Court, purporting to be a discharge of a debt which he has contracted towards a Tunisian subject, shall be held as a legal and a valid discharge, unless he can show that such quittance or receipt is under the handwriting, seal, or signature of the Tunisian subject, or duly executed by native notaries, and attested by the Cadi or the Governor of the place. And in like manner, no quittance or receipt presented by a Tunisian subject, purporting to be a discharge of a debt which he has contracted towards a British subject, shall be held as a legal and valid discharge of his debt, unless he can show that such quittance or discharge is under the handwriting, signature or mark of the British subject, duly attested by the Consul, or unless the discharge is drawn up by two notaries and attested by the British Consul.

ARTICLE XXVIII.

Should any Tunisian subject be found guilty before the Tunisian Courts of procuring false evidence to the injury or prejudice of a British subject, he shall be severely punished by the Tunisian Government. In like manner, the competent British Consular authorities shall severely punish, according to English law, any British subject who may be convicted of the same offence against a Tunisian subject.

ARTICLE XXIX.

If, at any time, Her Majesty's Agent and Consul-General, Consul, Vice-Consul or Consular Agent, should require the assistance of soldiers, guards, armed boats or other aid for the purpose of arresting or transporting any British subject, the Tunisian authorities shall immediately comply with the demand, on payment of the usual fees given on such occasions by Tunisian subjects.

ARTICLE XXX.

If a ship belonging to the Queen of Great Britain, or to any of Her subjects, should be wrecked or stranded on any part of the coast of the Regency of Tunis, the Tunisian authorities within whose jurisdiction the accident may occur shall, in accordance with the rules of friendship, respect her and assist her in all her wants. They shall allow and enable the master to take such steps as he may think necessary or desirable, and shall take immediate steps for the protection of her crew and of her cargo, and of any goods, papers or other articles which may be saved from her at the time of the wreck or afterwards; and, moreover, they shall lose no time in informing the nearest British authority of the accident. They shall deliver over to him, without exception or loss, all the cargo, goods, papers and articles which have been saved and preserved from the wreck, and they shall likewise furnish the master and the crew of the wrecked ship with such victuals and provisions as they may require, for which they shall receive payment. For their friendly aid and services in protecting, saving, preserving and restoring to the British Consular authorities the goods and contents saved through their exertions from the wrecked vessel, or any portion thereof, they shall be entitled to such an amount of salvage as Her Majesty's Agent and Consul-General and the Chief Tusinian authority on the spot shall judge a fair compensation for their services. The master and crew shall be at liberty to proceed to any place they please, and at any time they may think proper, without any hindrance.

In like manner, the ships of His Highness the Bey, or of Tunisian subjects, shall be assisted and protected in the dominions of the Queen of Great Britain as though they were British ships, and shall be subject only to the same lawful charges of salvage to which British ships under similar circumstances are liable.

4½

ARTICLE XXXI.

Should, however (which God forbid), the crew or any portion of the crew of a wrecked or stranded British vessel be murdered by the natives. or its cargo, or any part of its cargo or contents, be stolen by them, the Tunisian Government binds itself to take the most prompt and energetic measures for seizing the marauders or robbers, in order to proceed to their severe punishment. It, moreover, engages to make the most diligent search for the recovery and restitution of the stolen property ; and whatever compensation for the damage done to individuals or to their effects, under similar circumstances, is granted, or may hereafter be granted to the subjects of the most favored nation, or the equivalent of it, shall be also accorded to the subjects of the Queen of Great Britain.

ARTICLE XXXII.

It is agreed and covenanted that if any of the crew of Her Majesty's ships of war, or of British merchant vessels, of whatever nationality they may be, borne on the papers of the said ships, shall desert within any port in the Regency of Tunis, the authorities of such port or territory shall be bound to give every assistance in their power for the apprehension of such deserters, on the application of the British authority. In like manner, if any of the crew of the ships of His Highness the Bey, or of Tunisian merchant vessels, not being slaves, shall desert in any of the ports or harbours within the dominions of Her Majesty the Queen of Great Britain, the authorities of such ports or harbours shall give every assistance in their power for the apprehenson of such deserters on the application of the Commanding Officer, Captain. or other Tunisian authority ; and no person whatsoever shall protect or harbour such deserters.

ARTICLE XXXIII.

The ships of war belonging to Her Majesty the Queen, and the ships belonging to His Highness the Bey, shall have free liberty to use the ports of each country for washing, cleansing and repairing any of their defects. and to buy for their use any sort of provisions, alive or dead, or any other necessaries, at the market price, without paying custom to any officer.

And it is moreover agreed that, whenever any of Her Majesty's ships of war shall arrive in the Bay of Tunis, and shall fire a salute of twenty-one guns, the Castle of the Goletta, or the Tunisian ships of war, shall return the same number of guns as the Royal salute to Her Majesty's colours, according to ancient usage.

ARTICLE XXXIV.

The Government of the Queen of the United Kingdom of Great Britain and Ireland, in consideration of the sincere friendship that has at all times existed between Her Majesty and His Highness the Bey, agrees that Tunisian ships and cargoes shall be received at the ports and harbours of the British dominions upon the same footing as British vessels and cargoes.

General Convention between Great Britain and Tunis.

ARTICLE XXXV.

British vessels arriving in any of the Tunisian ports for the purpose of trade, or by reason of stress of weather, or to repair damages, shall not be compelled to discharge their cargoes or any portion of their cargoes, and they shall not be made to change their destination or to receive any passengers on board unless it be with their own free will, but they shall be respected, and they shall be allowed to depart without any hindrance. Should they be compelled to land their cargoes, or a portion thereof, in order to effect repairs, they shall also be permitted to re-embark such goods free of any duty or charge whatsoever.

Tunisian vessels shall receive the like friendly treatment in ports and harbours of the British Dominions.

ARTICLE XXXVI.

If any British subject should die in any place or territory appertaining to His Highness the Bey, no Governor, or other Tunisian officer shall, on any pretence whatsoever, take possession or dispose of, or interfere with the goods and property of the deceased; but such goods and property, of whatever description, may be taken possession of by his heirs, or by the British Consular authority, without any hindrance or impediment whatsoever on the part of such Governor or Tunisian officer.

If, however, a British subject should die at a place where there is no British Consul, or whilst travelling, in such case the Tunisian authorities of the place where he died shall be bound to preserve and protect his goods and effects; they shall make, with the assistance of notaries, a faithful inventory of them, which inventory they shall lose no time in sending to the nearest Governor of a place where an English Consul resides.

Should the deceased British subject leave behind him debts due from him to a native, the Consul-General or his deputy shall assist the creditor in the recovery of his claim upon the estate of the deceased; and likewise, if the deceased should leave behind debts due to him from Tunisians, the Governor, or those who have such power, shall compel the debtors to pay what is due by them to the Consul-General or his deputy, for the benefit of the estate of the deceased.

ARTICLE XXXVII.

The British Government and His Highness the Bey, ·moved by sentiments of humanity and having regard to the free institutions which, under Providence, their respective countries happily enjoy, mutually engage to do all in their power for the suppression of slavery. Whilst, on the one part, the British Government engage not to relax their efforts with friendly powers for the prevention of the barbarous traffic in human beings, and for the emancipation of slaves, His Highness the Bey especially engages, on the other to cause the Declaration of Moharem, 1262 (23rd January, 1846) abolishing for ever slavery in the Regency, to be obeyed and respected, and to use his utmost efforts to discover and punish all persons within his Regency who contravene or act contrary thereto.

ARTICLE XXXVIII.

The British Government and His Highness the Bey engage to do all in their power for the suppression of piracy; and His Highness especially engages to use his utmost efforts to discover and punish all persons on his coasts or within his territory who may be guilty of that crime, and to aid the British Government in so doing.

ARTICLE XXXIX.

Privateering is now and forever abolished : His Highness the Bey being desirous to maintain inviolable, the neutrality of the Regency of Tunis, it has been established and agreed that, in case of war or hostilities, he shall not permit the enemies of Her Majesty the Queen of Great Britain to fit out privateers in the ports of the Regency, or to sail from them to prey upon the ships and commerce of Her subjects ; and it is moreover established that His Highness shall not permit or tolerate in the Regency of Tunis the sale of any prize whatsoever which shall have belonged, or may belong to the belligerents.

The Queen of Great Britain will cause to be observed the same rules of neutrality towards Tunisian ships and subjects in all the seaports of Her Majesty's dominions.

ARTICLE XL.

In order that the two Contracting Parties may have the opportunity of hereafter treating and agreeing upon such other arrangements as may tend still further to the improvement of their mutual intercourse, and to the advancement of the interests of their respective people, it is agreed that at any time after the expiration of seven years from the date of the present Convention of Commerce and Navigation, either of the High Contracting parties shall have the right to call upon the other to enter upon a revision of the same ; but until such revision shall have been accomplished by common consent, and a new Convention shall have been concluded and put into operation, the present Convention shall continue and remain in full force and effect.

ARTICLE XLI.

If any doubt shall arise with regard to the interpretation or the application of any of the stipulations of the present Convention, it is agreed that in Tunis the interpretation the most favourable to British subjects shall be given, and in Her Majesty's Dominions that most favorable to Tunisians. It is not pretended by any of the foregoing Articles to stipulate for more than the plain and fair construction of the terms employed, nor to preclude in any manner the Tunisian Government from the exercise of its rights of internal Administration where the exercise of those rights does not evidently infringe upon the privileges accorded by the present Convention to British subjects or British Commerce.

ARTICLE XLII.

The stipulations of the present Convention shall come into immediate operation and shall be substituted for the stipulations of all preceding Treaties between Great Britain and Tunis, with the exception of the Convention of the 10th of October, 1863, already referred to in Article XVII preceding, which is renewed and confirmed.

This Convention has been written in triplicate, consisting in forty-two Articles besides the introduction, and contained in the preceding forty-three pages, to be signed by both parties, and to be executed in the manner explained and clearly set forth in its several provisions, having for their object the duration, confirmation, and maintenance of amity between them.

Dated Monday, the sixteenth day of Gumad-el-Thany, 1292 of the Hegira, corresponding to the nineteenth day of July, 1875.

[L.S.]　　RICHARD WOOD.
[L.S.]　　MUHAMMAD AS-SADIG, PASHA,
Bey.

AT THE COURT AT OSBORNE HOUSE, ISLE OF WIGHT, THE 5TH DAY OF FEBRUARY, 1876.

Present :

THE QUEEN'S MOST EXCELLENT MAJESTY IN COUNCIL.

WHEREAS by an Act of Parliament made and passed in the Session of Parliament holden in the thirty-third and thirty-fourth years of the reign of Her present Majesty, intituled : " An Act for amending the law relat- "ing to the Extradition of Criminals," and also by an Act of Parliament made and passed in the Session of Parliament holden in the thirty-sixth and thirty-seventh years of the reign of Her present Majesty, intituled : "An " Act to amend the Extradition Act, 1870," it was amongst other things enacted, that where an arrangement has been made with any foreign State with respect to the surrender to such State, of any fugitive criminals, Her Majesty may, by Order in Council, direct that the said Acts shall apply in the case of such foreign State ; and that Her Majesty may, by the same or any subsequent Order, limit the operation of the Order and restrict the same to fugitive criminals who are in or suspected of being in the part of Her Majesty's dominions specified in the Order, and render the operation thereof subject to such conditions, exceptions, and qualifications as may be deemed expedient.

Extradition Treaty with Hayti.

And whereas a Treaty was concluded on the seventh day of December, one thousand eight hundred and seventy-four, between Her Majesty and the President of the Republic of Hayti, for the mutual extradition of fugitive criminals, which Treaty is in the terms following ;—

Her Majesty the Queen of the United Kingdom of Great Britain and Ireland, and His Excellency the President of the Republic of Hayti, having judged it expedient with a view to a better administration of justice, and to the prevention of crime within the two countries and their jurisdictions, that persons charged with or convicted of the crimes hereinafter enumerated, and being fugitives from justice, should, under certain circumstances, be reciprocally delivered up ;

Her Britannic Majesty and the President of Hayti have named as their Plenipotentaries to conclude a Treaty for this purpose, that is to say :

Her Majesty the Queen of the United Kingdom of Great Britain and Ireland, Spencer St. John, Esq., Minister-Resident and Consul-General of Her Britannic Majesty in the Republic of Hayti and Her Chargé d'Affaires in the Dominican Republic ;

And His Excellency the President of the Republic of Hayti, M. Surville Toussaint, ex-Senator.

Who, after having communicated to each other their respective full powers, found in good and due form, have agreed upon and concluded the following Articles :--

ARTICLE I.

The High Contracting Parties engage to deliver up to each other those persons who, being accused or convicted of a crime committed in the territory of the one party, shall be found within the territory of the other party under the circumstances and conditions stated in the present Treaty,

ARTICLE II.

The crimes for which the extradition is to be granted, are the following :—
1. Murder, or attempt to murder ;
2. Manslaughter ;
3. Counterfeiting or altering money, uttering or bringing into circulation counterfeit or altered money ;
4. Forgery, or counterfeiting, or altering or uttering what is forged or counterfeit or altered ;
5. Embezzlement or larceny ;
6. Obtaining money or goods by false pretences ;
7. Malicious injury to property, if the offence be indictable ;
8. Crimes against bankruptcy law ;
9. Fraud by a bailee, banker, agent, factor, trustee, or director, or member or public officer of any company, made criminal by any law for the time being in force ;
10. Perjury or subornation of perjury ;
11. Rape ;
12. Abduction ;

13. Child-stealing ;
14. False imprisonment ;
15. Burglary or house-breaking ;
16. Arson ;
17. Robbery with violence ;
18. Threats, by letter or otherwise, with intent to extort ;
19. Piracy by law of nations ;
20. Sinking or destroying a vessel at sea, or attempting or conspiring to do so ;
21. Assaults on board a ship on the high seas, with intent to destroy life or to do grievous bodily harm ;
22. Revolt, or conspiracy to revolt, by two or more persons on board a ship on the high seas, against the authority of the master.

The extradition is also to take place for participation in any of the aforesaid crimes, provided such participation be punishable by the laws of both the Contracting Parties.

ARTICLE III.

No Haytian shall be delivered up by the Government of Hayti to the United Kingdom, and no subject of the United Kingdom shall be delivered up by the Government thereof to the Government of Hayti.

ARTICLE IV.

The extradition shall not take place if the person claimed on the part of the Government of the United Kingdom, or the person claimed on the part of the Government of the Republic of Hayti, has already been tried and discharged, or punished, or is still under trial in Hayti or in the United Kingdom respectively, for the crime for which his extradition is demanded.

If the person claimed on the part of the Government of the United Kingdom, or if the person claimed on the part of the Government of the Republic of Hayti should be under examination for any other crime in Hayti or in the United Kingdom respectively, his extradition shall be deferred until the conclusion of the trial, and the full execution of any punishment awarded to him.

ARTICLE V.

The extradition shall not take place if, subsequently to the commission of the crime, or the institution of the penal prosecution, or the conviction thereon, exemption from prosecution or punishment has been acquired by lapse of time, according to the laws of the State applied to.

ARTICLE VI.

A fugitive criminal shall not be surrendered if the offence in respect, of which his surrender is demanded, is one of a political character, or if he prove that the requisition for his surrender has, in fact, been made with a view to try or punish him for an offence of a political character.

ARTICLE VII.

A person surrendered can in no case be kept in prison, or be brought to trial in the State in which the surrender has been made, for any other crime or on account of any other matters than those for which the extradition shall have taken place.

This stipulation does not apply to crimes committed after the extradition.

ARTICLE VIII.

The requisition for extradition shall be made through the Diplomatic Agents of the High Contracting Parties respectively.

The requisition for the extradition of an accused person must be accompanied by a warrant of arrest, issued by the competent authority of the State requiring the extradition, and by such evidence as, according to the laws of the place where the accused is found, would justify his arrest if the crime had been committed there.

If the requisition relates to a person already convicted, it must be accompanied by the sentence of condemnation passed against the convicted person by the competent court of the State that makes the requisition for extradition.

A requisition for extradition cannot be founded on sentences passed *in contumaciam.*

ARTICLE IX.

If the requisition for extradition be in accordance with the foregoing stipulations, the competent authorities of the State applied to shall proceed to the arrest of the fugitive.

The prisoner is then to be brought before a competent magistrate, who is to examine him, and to conduct the preliminary investigation of the case, just as if the apprehension had taken place for a crime committed in the same country.

ARTICLE X.

The extradition shall not take place before the expiration of fifteen days from the apprehension, and then only if the evidence be found sufficient, according to the laws of the State applied to, either to justify the committal of the prisoner for trial, in case the crime had been committed in the territory of the said State, or to prove that the prisoner is the identical person convicted by the Courts of the State which makes the requisition.

ARTICLE XI.

In the examinations which they have to make, in accordance with the foregoing stipulations, the authorities of the State applied to shall admit as entirely valid evidence the sworn depositions or statements of witnesses taken in the other State, or copies thereof, and likewise the warrants and sentences issued therein, provided such documents are signed or certified by a judge, magistrate or officer of such State, and are authenticated by the oath of some witnesses, or by being sealed with the official seal of the Minister of Justice or some other Minister of State.

ARTICLE XII.

If sufficient evidence for the extradition be not produced within two months from the date of the apprehension of the fugitive, he shall be set at liberty.

ARTICLE XIII.

All articles seized, which were in the possession of the person to be surrendered at the time of his apprehension, shall, if the competent authority of the State applied to for the extradition has ordered the delivery thereof, be given up when the extradition takes place, and the said delivery shall extend not merely to the stolen articles, but to everything that may serve as a proof of the crime.

ARTICLE XIV.

The High Contracting Parties renounce any claim for the reimbursement of the expenses incurred by them in the arrest and maintenance of the person to be surrendered, and his conveyance till placed on board ship: they reciprocally agree to bear such expenses themselves.

ARTICLE XV.

The stipulations of the present Treaty shall be applicable to the Colonies and foreign possessions of Her Britannic Majesty.

The requisition for the surrender of a fugitive criminal who has taken refuge in any of such Colonies or foreign possessions shall be made to the Governor or chief authority of such Colony or possession, by the Chief Consular officer of Hayti in such Colony or possession.

Such requisitions may be disposed of, subject always, as nearly as may be, to the provisions of this Treaty, by the said Government or chief authority, who, however, shall be at liberty either to grant the surrender, or to refer the matter to his Government.

Her Britannic Majesty shall, however, be at liberty to make special arrangements in the British Colonies and foreign possessions for the surrender of Haytian criminals who may take refuge within such Colonies and foreign possessions, on the basis, as nearly as may be, of the provisions of the present Treaty.

The requisition for the surrender of a fugitive criminal from any Colony or foreign possession of Her Britannic Majesty shall be governed by the rules laid down in the preceding Articles of the present Treaty.

ARTICLE XVI.

The present Treaty shall come into force ten days after its publication, in conformity with the forms prescribed by the laws of the High Contracting Parties. It may be terminated by either of the High Contracting Parties, but shall remain in force for six months after notice has been given for its termination.

The President of the Republic of Hayti engages to apply to the Senate for the necessary authorization to give effect to the present Treaty, immediately after its meeting.

The present Treaty shall be ratified, and the ratifications shall be exchanged as soon as possible.

In witness whereof, the respective Plenipotentiaries have signed the same, and have affixed thereto the seals of their arms.

Done at Port au Prince the seventh day of December, in the year of Our Lord One thousand eight hundred and seventy-four.

(L.S.)   SPENSER ST. JOHN.

(L.S.)   SURVILLE TOUSSAINT.

And whereas the ratifications of the said Treaty were exchanged at Port au Prince on the second day of September last :

Now, therefore, Her Majesty, by and with the advice of Her Privy Council, and in virtue of the authority committed to Her by the said recited Acts, doth order, and it is hereby ordered, that from and after the twenty-first day of February, One thousand eight hundred and seventy-six, the said Acts shall apply in the case of the said Treaty with the President of the Republic of Hayti.

(Signed),   C. L. PEEL.

AT THE COURT AT OSBORNE HOUSE, ISLE OF WIGHT, THE 5TH DAY OF FEBRUARY, 1876.

Present:

THE QUEEN'S MOST EXCELLENT MAJESTY IN COUNCIL.

WHEREAS by an Act of Parliament made and passed in the Session of Parliament holden in the Thirty-third and Thirty-fourth years of the Reign of Her present Majesty, intituled: "An Act for amending the Law "relating to the Extradition of Criminals," and also by an Act of Parliament made and passed in the Session of Parliament holden in the Thirty-sixth and Thirty-seventh years of the Reign of Her present Majesty, intituled: "An Act to amend the Extradition Act, 1870," it was amongst other things enacted, that where an arrangement has been made with any foreign State with respect to the surrender to such State of any fugitive criminals, Her Majesty may, by Order in Council, direct that the said Acts shall apply in the case of such foreign State; and that Her Majesty may, by the same or any subsequent Order, limit the operation of the Order, and restrict the same to fugitive criminals who are in or suspected of being in the part of Her Majesty's dominions specified in the Order, and render the operation thereof subject to such conditions, exceptions, and qualifications as may be deemed expedient:

And whereas a Treaty was concluded on the sixth day of January, 1874, between Her Majesty and the President of the Republic of Honduras, for the mutual extradition of fugitive criminals, which Treaty is in the terms following:—

Her Majesty the Queen of the United Kingdom of Great Britain and Ireland, and His Excellency the President of the Republic of Honduras, having judged it expedient, with a view to the better administration of justice and to the prevention of crime within the two countries and their jurisdictions, that persons charged with or convicted of the crimes hereinafter enumerated, and being fugitives from justice, should, under certain circumstances, be reciprocally delivered up, have named as their Plenipotentiaries to conclude a Treaty for this purpose, that is to say:—

Her Majesty the Queen of the United Kingdom of Great Britain and Ireland, Edwin Corbett, Esq., Her Majesty's Chargé d'Affaires and Consul-General to said Republic of Honduras, &c.:

And His Excellency the President of the Republic of Honduras, the Senor Don Augustin Gomez Carrillo, Deputy to the present Legislature of Guatemala, &c.

Who, after having communicated to each other their respective full powers, found in good and due form, have agreed upon and concluded the following articles:—

ARTICLE I.

The High Contracting Parties engage to deliver up to each other those persons who, being accused or convicted of a crime committed in the territory of the one Party, shall be found within the territory of the other Party, under the circumstances and conditions stated in the present Treaty.

ARTICLE II.

It is agreed that Her Britannic Majesty and His Excellency the President of Honduras shall, on requisition made in their name by their respective Diplomatic Agents, deliver up to each other reciprocally any persons, except native subjects or citizens of the Party upon whom the requisition may be made who, being accused or convicted, whether as a principal or an accessory, either before or after the fact, of any of the crimes hereinafter specified, committed within the jurisdiction of the requiring Party, shall be found within the territories of the other Party:—

1. Murder, or attempt or conspiracy to murder;
2. Manslaughter;
3. Counterfeiting or altering money, or uttering counterfeit or altered money;

4. Forgery, counterfeiting or altering, or uttering what is forged or counterfeited or altered ;

5. Embezzlement or larceny ;

6. Obtaining money or goods by false pretences ;

7. Malicious injury to property, if the offence be indictable ;

8. Crimes against bankruptcy law ;

9. Fraud by a bailee, banker, agent, factor, trustee or director or member or public officer of any Company made criminal by any law for the time being in force ;

10. Perjury or subornation of perjury ;

11. Rape ;

12. Abduction ;

13. Child-stealing ;

14. False imprisonment ;

15. Burglary or house-breaking ;

16. Arson ;

17. Robbery with violence ;

18. Threats by letter or otherwise with intent to extort ;

19. Piracy by law of nations ;

20. Sinking or destroying a vessel at sea, or attempting or conspiring to do so ;

21. Assaults on board a ship on the high seas with intent to destroy life or to do grievous bodily harm ;

22. Revolt, or conspiracy to revolt, by two or more persons on board a ship on the high seas against the authority of the master :

Provided that the surrender shall be made only when, in the case of a person accused, the commission of the crime shall be so established as that the laws of the country where the fugitive or person so accused shall be found would justify his apprehension and commitment for trial if the crime had been there committed ; and, in the case of a person alleged to have been convicted on such evidence as according to the laws of the country where he is found, would prove that he had been convicted.

ARTICLE III.

No Honduran, as above stated, shall be delivered up by the Government of Honduras to the Government of the United Kingdom, and no subject of the United Kingdom shall be delivered up by the Government thereof to the Government of Honduras.

ARTICLE IV.

The extradition shall not take place if the person claimed on the part of the Government of the United Kingdom, or the person claimed on the part of the Government of Honduras, has already been tried and discharged or punished, or is still under trial, in the territory of the United Kingdom or of Honduras respectively for the crime for which his extradition is demanded.

If the person claimed on the part of the Government of the United

Extradition Treaty with Honduras.

Kingdom, or if the person claimed on the part of the Government of Honduras, should be under examination for any other crime in the territory of the United Kingdom or in the Republic of Honduras respectively, his extradition shall be deferred until the conclusion of the trial and the full execution of any punishment awarded to him.

ARTICLE V.

The extradition shall not take place if, subsequently to the commission of the crime or the institution of the penal prosecution or the conviction thereon, exemption from prosecution or punishment has been acquired by lapse of time, according to the laws of the State applied to.

ARTICLE VI.

A fugitive criminal shall not be surrendered if the offence, in respect of which his surrender is demanded is one of a political character, or if he prove that the requisition for his surrender has, in fact, been made with a view to try or punish him for an offence of a political character.

ARTICLE VII.

A person surrendered can in no case be kept in prison, or be brought to trial in the State to which the surrender has been made, for any other crime, or on account of any other matters, than those for which the extradition shall have taken place. This stipulation does not apply to crimes committed after the extradition.

ARTICLE VIII.

The requisition for extradition shall be made through the Diplomatic Agents of the High Contracting Parties respectively.

The requisition for the extradition of an accused person must be accompanied by a warrant of arrest issued by the competent authority of the State requiring the extradition, and by such evidence as, according to the laws of the place where the accused is found, would justify his arrest if the crime had been committed there.

If the requisition relates to a person already convicted, it must be accompanied by the sentence of condemnation passed against the convicted person by the competent Court of the State that makes the requisition for extradition.

A requisition for extradition cannot be founded on sentences passed *in contumaciam.*

ARTICLE IX

If the requisition for extradition be in accordance with the foregoing stipulations, the competent authorities of the State applied to shall proceed to the arrest of the fugitive.

The prisoner is then to be brought before a competent Magistrate, who is to examine him and conduct the preliminary investigation of the case, just as if the apprehension had taken place for a crime committed in the same country.

ARTICLE X.

The extradition shall not take place before the expiration of fifteen days from the apprehension, and then only if the evidence be found sufficient, according to the laws of the State applied to, either to justify the committal of the prisoner for trial, in case the crime had been committed in the territory of the said State, or to prove that the prisoner is the identical person convicted by the Courts of the State which makes the requisition.

ARTICLE XI.

In the examination which they have to make, in accordance with the foregoing stipulations, the authorities of the State applied to shall admit as entirely valid evidence the sworn depositions or statements of witnesses taken in the other State, or copies thereof, and likewise the warrants and sentences issued therein, provided such documents are signed or certified by a Judge, Magistrate, or officer of such State, and are authenticated by the oath of some witness, or by being sealed with the official seal of the Minister of Justice or some other Minister of State.

ARTICLE XII.

If sufficient evidence for extradition be not produced within two months from the date of the apprehension of the fugitive, he shall be set at liberty.

ARTICLE XIII.

All articles seized, which were in the possession of the person to be surrendered at the time of his apprehension, shall, if the competent authority of the State applied to for the extradition has ordered the delivery thereof, be given up when the extradition takes place; and the said delivery shall extend, not merely to the stolen articles, but to everything that may serve as a proof of the crime.

ARTICLE XIV.

The High Contracting Parties renounce any claim for the reimbursement of the expenses incurred by them in the arrest and maintenance of the person to be surrendered and his conveyance till placed on board ship; they reciprocally agree to bear such expenses themselves.

ARTICLE XV

The stipulations of the present Treaty shall be applicable to the Colonies and foreign possessions of Her Britannic Majesty.

The requisition for the surrender of a fugitive criminal who has taken refuge in any of such Colonies or foreign possessions shall be made to the Governor or chief authority of such Colony or possession by the Chief Consular Officer of the Republic of Honduras, in such Colony or possession.

Such requisition may be disposed of (subject always, as near as may be, to the provisions of this Treaty) by the said Governor or chief authority, who, however, shall be at liberty either to grant the surrender, or to refer the matter to his Government.

Her Britannic Majesty shall, however, be at liberty to make special arrangements in the British Colonies and foreign possessions, for the surrender of Honduran criminals who may take refuge within such Colonies and foreign possessions, on the basis, as nearly as may be, of the provisions of the present Treaty.

The requisition for the surrender of a fugitive criminal from any Colony or foreign possession of Her Britannic Majesty shall be governed by the rules laid down in the preceding Articles of the present Treaty.

ARTICLE XVI.

The present Treaty shall come into force ten days after its publication, in conformity with the forms prescribed by the laws of the High Contracting Parties. It may be terminated by either of the High Contracting Parties, but shall remain in force for six months after notice has been given for its termination.

The Treaty shall be ratified, and the ratifications shall be exchanged at Guatemala, in twelve months, counted from this day.

In witness whereof, the respective Plenipotentiaries have signed the same, and have affixed thereto the seal of their arms.

Done at Gautemala, the sixth day of the month of January, in the year of Our Lord One thousand eight hundred and seventy-four.

[L.S.]   EDWIN CORBETT.
[L.S.]   AUGN. GOMEZ CARRILLO.

And whereas the ratifications of the Treaty were exchanged at Guatemala on the 12th day of October last:

Now, therefore, Her Majesty, by and with the advice of Her Privy Council, and in virtue of the authority committed to Her by the said recited Acts, doth order, and it is hereby ordered, that from and after the twenty-first day of February, One thousand eight hundred and seventy-six, the said Acts shall apply in the case of the said Treaty with the President of the Republic of Honduras.

(Signed),   C. L PEEL.

5

ORDERS IN COUNCIL

PROCLAMATIONS AND REGULATIONS

HAVING FORCE OF LAW

IN THE

DOMINION OF CANADA,

ISSUED DURING THE YEARS 1874, 1875 AND 1876.

HIS EXCELLENCY

THE RIGHT HONORABLE, SIR FREDERICK TEMPLE, EARL OF DUFFERIN,

GOVERNOR GENERAL.

OTTAWA:

PRINTED BY BROWN CHAMBERLIN,
LAW PRINTER TO THE QUEEN'S MOST EXCELLENT MAJESTY.
ANNO DOMINI, 1876.

ORDERS IN COUNCIL

PROCLAMATIONS AND REGULATIONS

DOMINION OF CANADA

IMPERIAL ORDERS IN COUNCIL.

INTERNATIONAL TONNAGE

THE following copy of an Order issued by Her Majesty in Council extends to ships of Spain, the measurement whereof has been ascertained and denoted in the registers and other national papers, after the 2nd day of December, 1874, the advantages held out by the 60th Section of "The "Merchant Shipping Act, 1862," and exempts them from re-measurement in any port or place in Her Majesty's Dominions according to the rules relating to the measurement of tonnage of merchant ships now in force under the Merchant Shipping Act 1854, and directs that such ships shall be deemed to be of the tonnage denoted on their Spanish certificates of nationality and registry or certificates of measurement. The Order also provides that in case the Owner or Master of any Spanish steam-ship desires the deduction for engine-room in his ship to be estimated under the rules for engine-room measurement and deduction applicable to British ships instead of under the Spanish rule, the engine-room shall be measured and the deduction calculated according to the British rules.

The foreign countries which had previously adopted the British system of measurement, and whose ships were admitted to the advantages held out by the 60th Section of the "Merchant Shipping Act 1862," are Austro-Hungary, Denmark, France, Germany, Italy, United States of America, Sweden, to which are now added those of Spain. *

WM. SMITH,
Deputy Minister of Marine and Fisheries.

DEPARTMENT OF MARINE AND FISHERIES,
OTTAWA, 20th October, 1875.

---

* By Order in Council of the 26th October, 1875, this privilege is also extended to Dutch vessels.

AT THE COURT AT WINDSOR, THE 17TH DAY OF MARCH, 1875.

Present :

THE QUEEN'S MOST EXCELLENT MAJESTY IN COUNCIL.

WHEREAS, by the "Merchant Shipping Act Amendment Act, 1862," it is enacted that whenever it is made to appear to Her Majesty that the rules concerning the measurement of tonnage of merchant ships for the time being in force under the principal Act have been adopted by the Government of any foreign country, and are in force in that country, it shall be lawful for Her Majesty, by Order in Council, to direct that the ships of such foreign country shall be deemed to be of the tonnage denoted in their certificate of registry or other national papers, and thereupon it shall no longer be necessary for such ships to be remeasured in any port or place in Her Majesty's Dominions ; but such ships shall be deemed to be of the tonnage denoted in their certificates of registry or other papers in the same manner, to the same extent, and for the same purposes, in, to and for which the tonnage denoted in the certificate of registry of British ships is to be deemed the tonnage of such ships :

And whereas it has been made to appear to Her Majesty that the rules concerning the measurement of tonnage of merchant ships now in force under "The Merchant Shipping Act, 1854," have been adopted by the Government of His Majesty the King of Spain, with the exception of a difference in the mode, in certain steamers, of estimating the allowance for engine room, and such rules are now in force in that country, having come into operation on the 2nd day of December, 1874, Her Majesty is hereby pleased, by and with the advice of Her Privy Council, to direct as follows :—

1. As regards sailing ships, that merchant sailing ships of the said kingdom of Spain, the measurement whereof after the said 2nd day of December, 1874, has been ascertained and denoted in the registers and other national papers of such sailing ships, testified by the date thereof, shall be deemed to be of the tonnage denoted in such registers and other national papers, in the same manner and to the same extent, and for the same purpose, in, to and for which the tonnage denoted in the certificate of registry of British sailing ships is deemed to be the tonnage of such ships.

2. As regards steamships, that merchant ships belonging to the said kingdom of Spain which are propelled by steam or any other power requiring engine room, the measurement whereof shall, after the said 2nd day of December, 1874, have been ascertained and denoted in the registers and other national papers of such steam ships, testified by the dates thereof, shall be deemed to be of the tonnage denoted in such registers or other national papers, in the same manner and to the same extent, and for the same purpose, in, to and for which the tonnage denoted in the certificate of registry of British ships is deemed to be the tonnage of such ships : Provided, nevertheless, that if the owner or master of any such Spanish steam ship desires the deduction for engine room in his ships to be estimated under the rules for engine room measurement and deduction applicable to British ships instead of under the Spanish rule, the engine room shall be measured and the deduction calculated according to the British rules.

Imperial—Foreign Deserters.

AT THE COURT AT WINDSOR, THE 12TH DAY OF FEBRUARY, 1876.

Present :

THE QUEEN'S MOST EXCELLENT MAJESTY IN COUNCIL.

WHEREAS by the "Foreign Deserters Act, 1852," it is provided that whenever it is made to appear to Her Majesty that due facilities are or will be given for recovering or apprehending seamen who desert from British merchant ships in the Territories of any foreign power. Her Majesty may, by Order in Council, stating that such facilities are or will be given, declare that seamen not being slaves who desert from Merchant ships belonging to such power, when within Her Majesty's Dominions, shall be liable to be apprehended and carried on board their respective ships, and may limit the operation of such Order, and may render the operation thereof subject to such conditions and qualifications, if any, as may be deemed expedient :

And whereas it has been made to appear to Her Majesty that due facilities are given for recovering and apprehending Seamen who desert from British merchant ships in the Territories of His Majesty the King of the Hellenes : Now, therefore, Her Majesty, by virtue of the powers vested in Her by the said "Foreign Deserters Act, 1852," and by and with the advice of Her Privy Council, is pleased to order and declare, and it is hereby ordered and declared, that from and after the publication hereof in the *London Gazette*, Seamen, not being slaves, and not being British subjects, who, within Her Majesty's Dominions, desert from Merchant ships belonging to the Kingdom of Greece, shall be apprehended and carried on board their respective ships : Provided always, that if any such deserter has committed any crime in Her Majesty's Dominions he may be detained until he has been tried by a competent Court, and until his sentence if any, has been fully carried into effect.

And the Secretaries of State for India in Council, the Home Department and the Colonies, are to give the necessary directions herein accordingly.

(Signed),   C. L. PEEL.

Note.—By Order in Council of the 17th May, 1876, this law is extended to deserters from Brazilian ships.

ORDERS IN COUNCIL, &c.

By Orders in Council of 7th Sept., 1874, His Excellency disallowed two Acts of the Manitoba Legislature, entitled respectively "An Act to define " the privileges, immunities and powers of the Legislative Council and Leg- " islative Assembly of Manitoba, and to give summary protection to persons " employed in the publication of Sessional Papers," and "An Act to incor- porate the Winnipeg Board of Trade."
Vide Canada Gazette, Vol. 8, p. 262.

(*Circular Despatch.*)

DOWNING STREET,
10th September, 1874.

SIR,—In consequence of an application made to this Office by a gentle- man naturalized in 1873 in this country, to be allowed the rights and privi- leges of a British subject in Gibraltar, the opinion of the Law Officers of the Crown has been taken as to whether Certificates of Naturalization granted in the United Kingdom extend to the Colonies.

2. The Act 7 and 8 Vict. (1844), c. 66, sec. 6, provided that upon obtaining the Certificate, and taking the Oath therein mentioned, every alien then residing in, or who shall thereafter come to reside in, any part of Great Britain or Ireland, should enjoy all the rights of a British subject. The Act 10 and 11 Vict., c. 83, sec. 3, expressly enacted that the above Act of 1844 should not extend to the Colonies. The Act 33 Vict. (1870), c. 14, sec. 7, enacted that an alien to whom a Certificate of Naturalization should be granted, should, in the United Kingdom, be entitled to all political and other rights, &c., of a British subject.

3. Her Majesty's Government are advised that the operation of the above enactments is clearly confined to the United Kingdom, and that a Certificate of Naturalization, granted under either of the Acts of 1844 or 1870, confers upon an alien no rights or privileges in a British Colony.

4. As this subject is one of general interest, and with a view to remove any doubts which may exist in the Colony under your Government upon the point, I have thought it desirable that the state of the Law should be made known in a Circular Despatch to all the Colonies.

I have the honor to be, Sir,
Your most obedient humble servant,
CARNARVON.

The Officer Administering
the Government of Canada.

Governor General.

(*Circular Despatch.*)

APPEALS TO PRIVY COUNCIL.

DOWNING STREET,
28th November, 1874.

SIR,—The Administrator of a Colonial Government has recently forwarded to me a Petition to the Queen in Council from one of the parties in a private suit, for leave to appeal to Her Majesty in Council from a judgment of the Supreme Court of the Colony.

2. I take this opportunity to inform you that it is no part of the duty of the Governor of a Colony to forward such Petitions, but that they should be brought before the Lords of the Judicial Committee of the Privy Council by a professional agent of the Petitioner in the usual manner.

3. I have further to inform you that it is not the practice of the Judicial Committee to return any answer to such Petitions until an appearance has been entered on behalf of the Petitioner.

4. If, therefore, application should be made to you by a party in a private suit to transmit a Petition of this nature to the Secretary of State, you will decline to do so; and you will inform the Petitioner what are the proper steps to be taken in the matter.

I have honor to be, Sir,
Your most obedient humble servant,
CARNARVON.

The Officer Administering
the Government of Canada.

———

By Order in Council of the 12th day of December, 1874, His Excellency declared his assent to "An Act to facilitate arrangements between Railway Companies and their creditors," passed by the Legislature of Nova Scotia.
Vide Canada Gazette, Vol. 8, p. 659.

———

By Order in Council of the 12th day of December, 1874, His Excellency the Governor General declared his disallowance of the Act passed by the Legislature of Nova Scotia, entitled viz. : "An Act to incorporate the Anglo-French Steamship Company."
Vide Canada Gazette, Vol. 8, p. 660.

———

By Order in Council of the 12th day of December, 1874, His Excellency the Governor General declared his disallowance of the Act passed by the Legislature of Nova Scotia, entitled: "An Act to incorporate 'The Halifax Company, Limited."
Vide Canada Gazette, Vol. 8, p. 660.

By Order in Council of the 16th March, 1875, His Excellency disallowed the Act of the Legislature of British Columbia, passed in the Session of 1874, intituled: "An Act to amend and consolidate the laws affecting Crown Lands in British Columbia."
Vide Canada Gazette, Vol. 8, p. 1134.

By another Order in Council of the same date, His Excellency disallowed an Act of the same Legislature, passed in the same Session, intituled: "An Act to make provision for the better administration of Justice."
Vide Canada Gazette, Vol. 8, p. 1134.

By an Order in Council of the 31st day of March, 1875, His Excellency disallowed an Act passed by the Legislature of Nova Scotia, in the Session of 1874, intituled: "An Act to incorporate the Eastern Steamship Company."
Vide Canada Gazette, Vol. 8, p. 1189.

By an Order in Council of the 1st day of April, 1875, His Excellency disallowed an Act passed by the Legislature of Ontario, at its Session held in 1874, intituled: "An Act to amend the Law respecting Escheats and Forfeitures."
Vide Canada Gazette, Vol. 8, p. 1189.

By an Order in Council of the 15th June, 1875, His Excellency assented to an Act of the Legislature of Prince Edward Island, intituled: "The Land Purchase Act, 1875," reserved by the Lieutenant Governor of that Province.
Vide Canada Gazette Vol. 8, p. 1712

By a Proclamation of the 6th August, 1875, His Excellency the Administrator, under Her Majesty's name, announced Her Majesty's sanction to "An Act for the relief of Henry William Peterson."
Vide Canada Gazette, Vol. 9, p. 166.

By a Proclamation of 17th September, 1875, His Excellency, in Her Majesty's name, proclaimed, ordered and directed that the Act made and passed in the thirty-eighth year of Our Reign, intituled: "An Act to establish a Supreme Court and a Court of Exchequer for the Dominion of

Governor General, &c.

Canada," should come into force as respects the appointment of Judges, Registrar, Clerks and Servants of the said Courts, the organization thereof and the making of general rules and orders under the seventy-ninth section of the said Act, on the Eighteenth day of September, in the year one thousand eight hundred and seventy-five.

Vide Canada Gazette, Vol. 9, p. 374.

By a Proclamation of the 10th January, 1876, His Excellency, in Her Majesty's name, proclaimed, ordered and directed that the Eleventh day of January, in the year of Our Lord one thousand eight hundred and seventy-six, had been and was appointed as the day and time at and after which the judicial functions of the said Courts respectively, and the provisions of the said Act, other than those proclaimed as in force on the Eighteenth day of September then last past, should take effect and be exercised.

Vide Canada Gazette Vol. 9. p. 905.

By Proclamation bearing date 15th July, 1875, His Excellency, in Her Majesty's name, published the following regulations made under authority of the Act, 35th Vict., chap. 27, intituled : "An Act relating to Quarantine" :—

1. All boats, ships and vessels coming into the Harbour of Charlottetown, in the Province of Prince Edward Island, which shall have at the time of their said arrival, or shall have had during their passage from the places where they respectively cleared, any person on board laboring under Asiatic Cholera, Fever, Small Pox, Scarlatina or Measles, or other infectious and dangerous disease, or on board of which any person shall have died during such passage, or which, being of less tonnage than seven hundred tons measurement, shall have on board thirteen or more steerage passengers, or which being of greater tonnage than seven hundred tons measurement shall have on board fifty or more steerage passengers, or which shall have come from some infected port, shall make their quarantine in the said harbor on board such vessels or at such place on shore, and in such manner as shall be directed by the Inspecting Physicians of the said harbour, and there remain and continue until such ships or vessels shall be discharged from such Quarantine, by such license or passport and discharge, given without fee or emolument of any kind, as shall be directed or permitted by such order or orders as shall be made by the Governor, with the advice of the Privy Council ; and until the said ships and vessels shall respectively have performed such quarantine, and shall be discharged therefrom by such license or passport and discharge as aforesaid, persons, goods or merchandise, which shall be on board such boats, ships or vessels, shall not come or be brought on shore, or go or be put on board of any other ship or vessel in Canada, except at such place indicated as aforesaid when duly required by competent authority.

Agriculture, &c.

2. All boats, ships and vessels of the class and description mentioned in the preceding regulation as liable to make their quarantine in the said Harbour of Charlottetown, shall anchor as near as may be safe to the Quarantine Station, there to be inspected by the Inspecting Physician, and ordered, according to circumstances, as aforesaid.

3. The Inspecting Physician of the Port of Charlottetown, shall visit, on his arrival, such boats, ships and vessels, and shall direct them as best calculated for the Public Health, and in accordance with the intent and meaning of the present regulations, and of any Orders in Council, which may be communicated to him from time to time.

4. The Inspecting Physician appointed for the Port of Charlottetown, shall have the power to go on board, examine and inspect boats, ships and vessels entering the said harbour and to direct such boats, ships and vessels to go to such place or places within the shelter of the said harbour to perform quarantine as it may be necessary to send them to, and shall grant to such boats, ships and vessels permission to dispense with further quarantine whenever he is satisfied that no further dangers are threatened by the admission of the same to *pratique.* The said Inspecting Physician shall have the medical attendance over the sick and healthy on board of such boats. ships and vessels, or on shore, if allowed to perform their quarantine on shore, and shall be the judge of the preventive and precautionary measures to be taken, either in the treatment of persons or in the washing, cleansing and purifying of luggage and other articles, and shall have power to order such preventive and precautionary measures to be taken as aforesaid.

5. Every Master and every Pilot having charge of a boat, ship or vessel of the class and description hereinbefore mentioned as liable to make their quarantine at the said Port of Charlottetown, shall bring such boat, ship or vessel to anchor within the limits of the anchorage grounds hereinbefore defined for the said port, and shall keep a Union Jack flying at the peak of such boat, ship or vessel until boarded by the Inspecting Physician as aforesaid.

6. These regulations shall not apply to any vessel of war, or to transports or vessels having Queen's Troops on board accompanied by a medical officer, and in a healthy state, or to any steamer unless sickness or death may have occurred during the passage.

7. No boat, ship or vessel shall be entered and cleared at the Port of Charlottetown aforesaid, until all the requirements of the foregoing regulations in reference to such boat, ship or vessel shall have been fully complied with.

8. Any person who shall contravene, either by omission or commission, any of the foregoing regulations, shall, for every such offence, incur and pay a fine not exceeding one hundred dollars, to be recovered in the manner prescribed by the said Act; and every person who, upon conviction of any such offence, shall fail to pay the amount of fine which he shall have been condemned to pay, shall be imprisoned until such fine be paid.

Vide Canada Gazette, Vol. 9, p. 89:

COPYRIGHT.

PRIVY COUNCIL CHAMBERS,
OTTAWA, 7th December, 1875.

I hereby certify that the following Rules, Regulations and Forms of the Department of Agriculture framed under the provisions of "The Copyright Act of 1875," were on this day submitted to and approved by His Excellency the Governor General in Council, as provided by the 2nd section of the said Act.

W. A. HIMSWORTH,
Clerk, Privy Council.

RULES, REGULATIONS AND FORMS OF THE DEPARTMENT OF AGRICULTURE, RESPECTING "THE COPYRIGHT ACT OF 1875."

GENERAL RULES.

1. There is no necessity for any personal appearance at the Department of Agriculture, unless specially called for by order of the Minister or the Deputy, every transaction being carried on by writing.

2. In every case the applicant or depositor of any paper is responsible for the merits of his allegations and of the validity of the instruments furnished by him or his agent.

3. The correspondence is carried on with the applicant, or with the agent who has remitted or transmitted the papers to the office, but with one person only.

4. All papers are to be clearly and neatly written on foolscap paper, and every word of them is to be distinctly legible, in order that no difficulty should be met with in the taking cognizance of, and in registering and copying them.

5. All copies of books deposited in accordance with section 7 of "The Copyright Act of 1875" must be furnished with board covers or full bound, and all copies of maps deposited must be mounted.

6. All communications to be addressed in the following words : *To the Minister of Agriculture, (Copyright Branch), Ottawa.*

7. In preparing an assignment in duplicate pursuant to section 18 of "The Copyright Act of 1875," care should be taken to allow on the back of the document a sufficient space for the insertion of the certificate.

8. As regards proceedings not specially provided for in the following forms, any form being conformable to the letter and spirit of the law will be accepted, and if not conformable will be returned for correction.

9. A copy of the Act and the Rules with a particular section marked, sent to any person making an inquiry is intended as a respectful answer by the office.

Agriculture, &c.

COPYRIGHTS.

10. An application for the registration of a Copyright, *if made by the proprietor himself*, shall be made after the following form :—

To the Minister of Agriculture,
     (*Copyright Branch*), *Ottawa.*

I, (*name of person*) domiciled in (*Canada, state the place and Province, or in any other part of the British Possessions. state the place, or being a citizen of any country, state the Country, having an International Copyright treaty with the United Kingdom, as the case may be*) hereby declare that I am the proprietor of the (*book, map, chart, &c., &c., as the case may be*), called (*title or name as the case may be*) and that the said (*book, map, &c., as the case may be*) has been published in Canada by (*name of the publisher thereof*) in the (*name of the locality where the publication has taken place*) in the Province of (*Quebec, Nova Scotia, New Brunswick, &c., as the case may be*) and hereby request the Registration of the same, and for that purpose I herewith forward the fee required by the Copyright Act of 1875, together with two copies of the (*book, map, chart, &c., as the case may be ; if the object is a painting, a sculpture or any other work of art, a written description of such work of art.*)

In testimony thereof, I have signed in the presence of the two undersigned witnesses at the place and date hereinafter mentioned.

(*Place and date.*)

                                         (Signature of the Proprietor.)

Signature of the two witnesses }

11. An application for the registration of a Copyright, *if made by the Agent of the Proprietor*, shall be made after the following form :—

To the Minister of Agriculture,
     (*Copyright Branch,*) *Ottawa.*

The undersigned, resident in the (*designation and name of the locality and Province where the Agent resides,*) being the Agent authorized by (*name of the Proprietor, stating where domiciled in Canada or in any other part of the British Possessions, or being a Citizen of any Country, stating the Country, having an International Copyright treaty with the United Kingdom, as the case may be*) hereby declare that (*name of the Proprietor*) is the Proprietor of the (*book, map, chart, &c., &c., as the case may be*) called (*title or name, as the case may be*), and that the said (*book, map, chart, &c., as the case may be*) has been published in Canada by (*name of the publisher thereof*) in the (*designation and name of the locality where the publication has taken place*) in the Province of (*Ontario, Quebec, Nova Scotia, New Brunswick, &c., as the case may be*) and hereby request the registration of the same, and for that purpose I herewith forward the fee required by "The Copyright Act of 1875," together with two copies of the (*book, map, chart, &c., &c., as the case may be ; if the object is a painting, a sculpture, or any other work of art, a written description of such work of art*).

Agriculture, &c.

In testimony thereof, I have signed this application in the presence of the two undersigned witnesses at the place and date hereunder mentioned.

(*Place and date.*)

(Signature of the Agent of the Proprietor.)

Signature of the two witnesses }

INTERIM COPYRIGHT.

12. An application for the registration of an Interim Copyright, *if made by the proprietor himself*, shall be made after the following form :—

To the Minister of Agriculture,
(Copyright Branch), Ottawa.

I, (*name of person*) domiciled in (*Canada,—state the place and Province, or in any other part of the British Possessions, state the place, or being a citizen of any country, state the country, having an International Copyright treaty with the United Kingdom, as the case may be*) hereby declare that I am the proprietor of a (*book, map, chart, &c., as the case may be*) called (*title or name, as the case may be*) for which I hereby request the privilege of an Interim Copyright, in the terms of the Act, and for that purpose I herewith forward the fee required by "The Copyright Act of 1875," together with a copy of the title of the said (*book, map, chart, &c., as the case may be*).

In testimony thereof, I have signed in the presence of the two undersigned witnesses, at the place and date herewith mentioned.

(*Place and date.*)

(Signature of the Proprietor.)

Signature of the two witnesses. }

13. An application for the registration of an Interim Copyright, (*if made by the Agent of the proprietor*), shall be made after the following form :—

To the Minister of Agriculture,
(Copyright Branch), Ottawa.

The undersigned, resident in the (*designation and name of the locality and Province where the Agent resides*) being the Agent authorized by (*name of the proprietor, stating where domiciled, in Canada or in any other part of the British Possessions, or being a citizen of any country, stating the country, having an International Copyright treaty with the United Kingdom, as the case may be*) hereby declare that (*name of the proprietor*) is the proprietor of the (*book, map, chart, &c., &c., as the case may be*) called (*title or name, as the case may be*) for which I hereby request the privilege of an Interim Copyright, in the terms of the Act, and for that purpose I herewith forward the fee required by "The Copyright Act of 1875," together with a copy of the title of the said (*book, map, chart, &c., &c., as the case may be.*)

Agriculture, &c.

In testimony thereof, I have signed in the presence of the two under-signed witnesses, at the place and date hereunder mentioned.

(*Place and date.*)

(Signature of the Agent of the Proprietor.)

Signatures of the two witnesses. }

TEMPORARY COPYRIGHTS.

14. An application for the registration of a Temporary Copyright, *if made by the proprietor himself*, shall be made after the following form :—

To the Minister of Agriculture,
   (*Copyright Branch*), *Ottawa.*

I (*name of person*) domiciled in (*Canada, state the place and Province, or in any other part of the British Possessions, state the place, or being a citizen of any country, state the country, having an International Copyright treaty with the United Kingdom, as the case may be*) hereby declare that I am the proprietor of the (*book, story, novel, &c, &c., as the case may be*) called (*title or name*) which is now being preliminarily published in separate articles, in the (*state the name, place and Province of the newspaper or periodical in which the work is being published*) for which I hereby request the privilege of a temporary copyright in the terms of the Act, and for that purpose I here-with forward the fee required by "The Copyright Act of 1875," together with a short analysis of the said work.

In testimony thereof, I have signed in the presence of the two under-signed witnesses, at the place and date hereunder mentioned.

(*Place and date.*)

(Signature of the Proprietor.)

˙gnature of the two witnesses. }

15. An application for the registration of a temporary copyright, *if made by the Agent of the proprietor*, shall be made after the following form :—

To the Minister of Agriculture,
   (*Copyright Branch*), *Ottawa.*

The undersigned, resident in the (*designation and name of the locality and Province where the Agent resides*) being the Agent authorized by (*name of the proprietor, stating where domiciled in Canada, or in any other part o the British Possessions, or being a citizen of any country, stating the country, having an International Copyright Treaty with the United Kingdom, as the case may be*) hereby declare that (*name of the proprietor*) is the proprietor of the (*book, story, novel, &c., &c., as the case may be*) called (*title or name*) which is now being preliminarily published in separate articles in the (*state the name, place, and Province of the newspaper or periodical in which the work is being published*) for which I hereby request the privilege of a

Agriculture.

temporary copyright in the terms of the Act, and for that purpose I herewith forward the fee required by "The Copyright Act of 1875," together with a short analysis of the said work.

In testimony thereof, I have signed in the presence of the two undersigned witnesses, at the place and date hereunder mentioned.

(*Place and date.*)

(Signature of the Agent of the Proprietor.)

Signatures of the two witnesses. }

NOTICE.—The correspondence with this Department is carried, through the Canadian mail, free of postage.

The forwarding of any paper should always be accompanied by a letter, and a separate letter should be written in relation to each distinct subject.

It is particularly recommended that reference should be made to the law, before writing on any subject to the Department, in order to avoid unnecessary explanations and useless loss of time and labor.

A sufficient margin should be left on every paper, and specially on specifications and assignments for the insertion of references or certificates, and for the affixing of the seal thereto.

It must be remembered that the better papers are executed, the sooner the work is dispatched at the office, and the surer the regularity of the proceedings is guaranteed.

GOVERNMENT HOUSE, OTTAWA.

Thursday, 20th day of April, 1876]

Present:

HIS EXCELLENCY THE GOVERNOR GENERAL IN COUNCIL.

WHEREAS a contagious disease affecting cattle and other animals prevails in many parts of Europe, and it is expedient, in order to prevent the introduction of the same into Canada, that the importation of cattle and certain other animals be subjected to restriction and regulations,—

His Excellency, on the recommendation of the Hon. the Minister of Agriculture, and under the provisions of the Act passed in the 32nd and 33rd years of Her Majesty's reign, and intituled: "An Act respecting "contagious diseases affecting Animals," has been pleased to make the following regulations, that is to say:—

1. From and after the 25th day of April instant, the importation into the Provinces of Nova Scotia, New Brunswick and Quebec, of live cattle, sheep and swine, coming from Europe, shall be prohibited, except at the Ports of Halifax, St. John, N.B., and Quebec.

2. All cattle, sheep and swine arriving in Canada through either of the said Ports of Halifax, St. John, or Quebec, shall be subject to inspection by officers who may, from time to time, be appointed for that purpose ; and such cattle, sheep and swine may, in the discretion of any such officer,

6

Agriculture. &c.

either be permitted to enter or be detained in quarantine, at such place and in such manner as shall be directed by the Quarantine Officer, until duly discharged therefrom.

3. The Inspecting Officers shall visit the boats, ships, vessels, cars or vans, and the cattle, sheep and swine coming into the said ports, and superintend the landing of such animals, and order them, according to the requirements of the case, to be allowed free entry, or to be conveyed to the grounds assigned for quarantine, and shall also superintend the landing and disposal of fodder, litter, blankets, troughs and other objects having been used by or for the said animals.

4. The animals thus subjected to quarantine shall be treated and dealt with under the direction of the Inspecting Officer, and the articles used in connection with the said animals shall be in like manner employed in their care and maintenance, under the same direction and supervision.

5. Should it be found necessary to destroy any of the said animals, or all or any portion of the articles used in the care of the said animals, such destruction shall take place under the orders and supervision of the Superintending Officer, and in the manner prescribed by him, but not unless permission to that effect has been previously given by the Minister of Agriculture.

6. The Officers appointed to carry out the Law and the foregoing Regulations, shall have free access to any boat, ship, vessel, car, van, or to any place where cattle, sheep or swine imported from Europe may be found, in order to inspect the same, and under instructions from the Minister of Agriculture, deal with infected animals and the articles employed in their service, in the manner contemplated by the Act, under the penalties prescribed thereby against any person contravening any of the provisions thereof, or of any Regulation made thereunder.

The said Inspectors or Officers may, if it be deemed necessary, order the cleansing and purifying of any infected place, vehicle or other article so inspected, and direct such precautionary measures to be taken as may by him or them be considered advisable, pending the decision of the Minister of Agriculture as to their ultimate disposal.

7. The expense of feeding, attending to, and of providing for any cattle, sheep or swine detained in quarantine, shall be borne by the owner thereof, with the exception of that for the use of grounds and shelter; and such cost, if incurred by the Inspector of Quarantine shall, in the event of the owner failing to comply with the said Inspector's requisition, be paid before the animals are permitted to leave the quarantine, and in case of refusal or neglect to pay the same, the Inspector shall, on being so ordered by the Minister of Agriculture, cause the said animals to be sold to meet the said cost; the balance, if any, to be handed over to the owner.

8. The quarantine shall be under the care and subject to the orders of the Officers appointed for that purpose, who shall have the general superintendence of the servants or other persons, and of all other matters connected therewith.

W. A. HIMSWORTH,
Clerk, Privy Council.

Customs.

By Order of Council of 6th April 1875, "Ground Gypsum for agricultural purposes," is admitted free of duty.
Vide Canada Gazette, Vol. 8, p. 1222.

GOVERNMENT HOUSE, OTTAWA,

Friday, 7th day of May, 1875.

Present:

HIS EXCELLENCY THE GOVERNOR GENERAL IN COUNCIL.

WHEREAS it is provided by the 58th Section of the Act 31 Victoria, Chapter 6, intituled : "An Act respecting the Customs," that the importer of any cattle or swine may slaughter and cure and pack the same in bond, under such Regulations and restrictions as the Governor in Council may from time to time make for this purpose ;

And whereas it has been found expedient to give effect to the said Section 58, in so far as regards the importation of swine, and to alter the terms of the Regulations for this purpose, adopted by Order in Council of 22nd day of May, 1868,—

His Excellency, on the recommendation of the Honorable the Minister of Customs and under the provisions of the said Act has been pleased to order, and it is hereby ordered, that the said Order in Council of the 22nd day of May, 1868, and the Regulations thereby established be and the same are hereby repealed, and that the following Regulations be and are hereby adopted and established in lieu thereof—that is to say :

1. Upon the importation of swine for the purpose of slaughter, the Importer shall enter the same for Warehouse, upon the usual form of such entries, stating upon its face, the number and value of the herd, and also the quantity of pork, bacon, hams and lard, which the number stated will produce when slaughtered and dressed at 113 pounds weight for each live hog so imported, and the amount of duty to which such produce is or may be liable under the rate prescribed by the tariff in force at the time being as the proper duty on meat of that kind. Such Importer shall then execute a bond to the Queen, in double the amount of such duty, the conditions of which bond shall be, that upon the due exportation within one year of the said products of the swine so imported and converted into pork, bacon, hams and lard, or payment of the duty secured by the said bond, then the said bond shall be and become null and void, otherwise shall remain in full force and virtue.

2. Upon the reception into the Bonding Warehouse, the swine shall be regarded only as meat, and it shall not be lawful to remove any of them from such Warehouse alive ; nor shall any part of the produce of such swine be removed therefrom, for any purpose, without a permit from the Collector, or proper Officer of Customs, as in the case of all other bonded goods.

3. Swine imported in the carcass to be cured and packed in bond, may

6½

Customs.

be entered in the usual way for Warehouse, and be placed in the premises established as a Warehouse of this class for the special purpose of curing and packing. The weight of such carcasses to be duly ascertained by the proper Officer of Customs, and the Importer shall give bonds to the Queen in double the amount of duties accruing thereupon under the tariff then in force, conditioned for the due exportation of the same, or payment of duty within two years from the date of first entry.

4. The killing pen, curing and packing houses and all cellars, stores or other apartments included in such Warehouse, shall be accessible at all times between sunrise and sunset to the inspection and survey of the Collector or Inspector of Customs, or of any Officer of Customs to whom the duty of such inspection may be assigned by them or either of them.

5. The produce of swine imported alive and warehoused for slaughter, at the said rate of 113 pounds for each hog, and the meat of the swine imported in carcass for curing and packing, at the actual ascertained weight on first entry, shall be subject while in bond to all changes in the tariff rates of duty, and when entered out of bond for home consumption, shall pay the rate of duty in force at the date of such entry.

W. A. HIMSWORTH,
Clerk, Privy Council.

———

By Order in Council of 10th May, 1875, "Sheet German Silver" and "Box Wood" are also admitted free.
Vide Canada Gazette, Vol 8, p. 1514.

———

By Order in Council of 14th June, 1875, Galt was constituted a Port of Entry and Warehousing Port from 1st July, 1875.
Vide Canada Gazette, Vol. 8, p. 1710.

———

By Order in Council of same date, Liscomb, N.S., was made an Outport under the Survey of Guysboro', from 1st July.
Vide Canada Gazette, Vol. 8, p. 1710.

———

By Order in Council of same date, Port Credit and Wellington Square Outports were placed under the Survey of the Port of Oakville.
Vide Canada Gazette, Vol. 8, p 1710.

———

By Order in Council of the same date, Pembroke, Ont., was made a Port of Entry and Warehousing Port.
Vide Canada Gazette, Vol. 8, p. 1710.

———

By Order in Council of same date, St. Hyacinthe was made a Port of Entry and Warehousing Port.
Vide Canada Gazette, Vol. 8, p. 1711.

Customs.

GOVERNMENT HOUSE, OTTAWA,

Monday, 14th day of June, 1875.

Present:

HIS EXCELLENCY THE ADMINISTRATOR IN COUNCIL.

ON the recommendation of the Honorable the Minister of Customs, and under the provisions of the 123rd section of the Act passed in the Session of the Parliament of Canada, held in the 31st year of Her Majesty's reign, chaptered 6, and intituled: "An Act respecting the Customs," His Excellency, by and with the advice of the Queen's Privy Council for Canada, has been pleased to order, and it is hereby ordered, that the following Regulations respecting the Bonding Warehouses in the Dominion be and the same are hereby adopted and established, that is to say :—

REGULATIONS.

ARTICLE I.—Warehouses for the storage of imported goods shall be known and designated as follows:—

Class 1.—Stores occupied by the Government of Canada.

Class 2.—Warehouses occupied by importers exclusively for the storage of goods imported by, or consigned to them, or purchased by them in bond.

Class 3.—Warehouses occupied for the general storage of imported goods.

Class 4.—Yards, sheds and other buildings used for the storing and slaughtering of animals in bond.

Class 5.—Warehouses exclusively for the manufacture or refining of sugar.

Class 6.—Sufferance Warehouses.

Applications for establishment of Bonded Warehouses.

ARTICLE II.—For a Warehouse of the second or third class, the owner shall make application in writing to the Collector of the Port, describing the premises, the location and capacity of the same, and stating the purpose for which the building is to be used, whether for the storage of merchandise imported by, or consigned to himself exclusively or for the general storage of merchandise in bond.

The Collector will thereupon examine or direct the Surveyor or other proper officer of Customs, in whom he can repose confidence, to examine and inspect the premises and to report to him in writing the particulars of the location, construction and dimensions of the building, its capabilities for the safe keeping of merchandise, and all other facts bearing upon the subject.

When the examination has been made, the Collector will transmit the report, together with the proprietor's application, with his own report as to the necessity of granting the application to the Commissioner of Customs.

ARTICLE III.—If on examination of the foregoing documents the Minister of Customs is satisfied that the public interest will be subserved thereby, the application will be granted, whereupon the owner or occupant will be notified by the Collector, and on fulfilment of the conditions hereinafter provided, the Collector will assign a number for the Warehouse and add the same to his register, placing a Warehouse Locker in charge thereof.

Warehouses of Class 1.

ARTICLE IV.—At all ports where there are Government stores, they shall be used for the examination and appraisement of imported goods, and for the storage of unclaimed and seized goods, and where there are no such stores, the Collector may, under the direction of the Minister of Customs, make temporary arrangements for suitable premises for those purposes, or may deposit such unclaimed or seized goods in any Warehouse of Class 3.

Warehouses of Class 2.

ARTICLE V.—A Warehouse of Class 2 shall consist of an entire building, or not less than one whole floor of such building, and in the latter case must be so arranged as that the Customs locks will prevent all access to the floor set apart and established as a Bonded Warehouse, and no partitions of slats shall in any case be allowed, but all divisions between the part of a building occupied as a Warehouse, whether door or partition shall be of the most solid and secure description possible in each case.

Warehouses of Class 3.

ARTICLE VI.—A Warehouse of Class 3 shall in every case consist of an entire building and shall be used solely for the storage of bonded merchandise, or of unclaimed and seized goods ordered thereto by the Collector of Customs.

The rates of storage and compensation for labour in the handling of bonded goods in Warehouses of this class shall be subject to agreement between the owner or importer of the goods and the proprietor of the Warehouse, who will collect all amounts due for storage and labour, the duty of the Collector or proper officer of Customs being to look after the safe custody of the goods for the security of the revenue only.

Should the Collector of Customs require to deposit in any such Warehouse unclaimed and seized goods, the charges for storage and labour thereupon shall not exceed the regular rates, and the proprietor shall be liable as in other cases for their safe keeping.

ARTICLE VII.—All Warehouses of either Class 2 or Class 3 shall be secured by Customs locks, provided by the Department of Customs; but this will not prevent the proprietors or occupants of the building from having their own locks on the same doors in addition thereto.

ARTICLE VIII.—No free or duty paid goods shall be stored in any Bonded Warehouse; and all bonded goods, when entered for consumption, removal or exportation, shall immediately be removed therefrom, unless permission to the contrary be first obtained from the Collector upon an application made to him in writing, specifying the goods and the time for which it is desired they should remain, and in such case the goods shall be legibly and conspicuously marked and set apart from those remaining in bond; but no such privilege shall be granted in any case except for good and urgent reasons.

Applications for Warehouses of Class 4.

ARTICLE IX.—Application for the establishment of a Warehouse of this class shall be made in the same manner as for Classes 2 and 3, and shall be subject to the regulations adopted by Order in Council of 7th May, 1875.

Class 5.—Warehouses for refining Sugar in Bond.

ARTICLE X.—Applications for the establishment of Warehouses of Class 5 shall be made in accordance with the terms of the Order in Council, regulating the refining of sugar in Bond, dated 31st January, 1855, except that the application and description shall be submitted for approval of the Minister of Customs before acceptance, as in the case of Warehouses of Classes 2 and 3.

Class 6.—Sufferance Warehouses.

ARTICLE XI.—Warehouses of this class for the accommodation of steamers and other vessels may be established in accordance with the Order in Council relating thereto of 23rd October, 1868.

Sufferance Warehouses at Railway Stations and Depots shall be established in accordance with Section 1 of Order in Council bearing date 4th December, 1856, and shall be subject to all the rules for safe keeping of merchandise stored therein, provided in the case of Warehouses of any other class.

ARTICLE XII.—The proprietor of every Warehouse of Class 2 and Class 4 shall pay, for the privileges granted him in the use of such Warehouse, the sum of forty dollars per annum, in half-yearly payments, in advance to the Collector of Customs.

The proprietor of every Warehouse of Class 3 and Class 5 shall pay in like manner not less than forty dollars, nor more than one hundred dollars per annum, according to the capacity of the building and the nature and amount of business—the exact sum to be determined by the Minister of Customs at the time of accepting the proprietor's application.

All the foregoing payments shall in future date from the establishment of each Warehouse, and in the case of Warehouses already established in the ports named in the Order in Council of 25th June, 1869, from the expiration of the time for which the proprietors have already paid, and in all other ports, in the case of Warehouses already established but not heretofore subjected to any payment, from the first day of July, 1875; and no Warehouse of either of the classes named in this Article shall be recognized by the Collector of Customs as an established Warehouse until or unless the said quarterly payments are made within not over ten days after the proper date.

Customs.

General Provisions.

ARTICLE XIII.—No alteration can be made in any Bonded Warehouse without permission of the Collector of Customs; and if any material change in the premises is contemplated it must be submitted for approval of the Minister of Customs.

The Collector of Customs shall advise the Commissioner of Customs of any changes in the surroundings of bonded premises likely to affect their general security, and if burned or plundered immediate notice must be given to the Commissioner, with full particulars of all facts connected therewith.

Proprietors of Bonded Warehouses may relinquish the business at any time, on giving timely notice to the owners of merchandise deposited therein, but no part of any quarterly payment made by them shall be refunded for any portion of a term unexpired.

The Minister of Customs may, at any time, for reasonable cause, order the discontinuance of the right to store bonded goods in any premises established as a Bonded Warehouse; and when thus discontinued such Warehouse can only be re-established after renewed application as at first.

All moneys received from proprietors of Warehouses, as provided in Art. 12, shall be paid over by the Collector of Customs to the Receiver General, and shall form part of the Consolidated Revenue Fund of Canada.

ARTICLE XIV.—The Collector of Customs will cause the proprietor or occupant to place over the gate or door leading into, or on some conspicuous place on every Customs Warehouse, a board or sign with the following painted thereon:

" V. R.

No. ————.

Customs Warehouse."

ARTICLE XV.—Sections 12, 13, 14 and 15 of Regulations dated 30th March, 1850, and the Order in Council dated 25th June, 1869, relating to payments for the privilege of using stores as Bonding Warehouses in certain ports, are hereby repealed.

W. A. HIMSWORTH,

Clerk, Privy Council.

By Order in Council of 11th August, 1875, Ingersoll is made an Outport, under the survey of Woodstock, Ontario.
Vide Canada Gazette, Vol. 9, p. 265.

By Order in Council of the 8th day of October, 1875, Kincardine, late Penetangore, was constituted a Port of Entry and a Warehousing Port
Vide Canada Gazette, Vol. 9, p. 504.

Customs.

By Order in Council of the 30th October, 1875, the Outport of La Have was thereafter to be known as the Outport of Bridgewater and the Outport of Getson's Cove, to be known as the Outport of La Have.
Vide Canada Gazette, Vol. 9, p. 588,

By Order in Council of the 15th November, 1875, the Town of Berlin, Ontario, was made an Outport under the survey of Guelph.
Vide Canada Gazette, Vol. 9, p. 638.

By Order in Council of the 21st day of February, 1876, Brockville was constituted a port at which Raw or Leaf Tobacco Tobacco may be imported into Canada, under the 31 Vict., chap., 51.
Vide Canada Gazette, Vol. 9, p. 1130.

Inland Revenue.

PRIVY COUNCIL CHAMBER,
OTTAWA, 1st April, 1875.

NOTICE is hereby given that on the recommendation of the Honorable the Minister of Inland Revenue and under the provisions of the 1st Section of "The General Inspection Act," "His Excellency the Governor General in Council has, by Order in Council of this day's date, been pleased to constitute the Counties of Temiscouata and Kamouraska, in the Province of Quebec, an Inspection Division for all the purposes of the said Act.

W. A. HIMSWORTH,
Clerk, Privy Council.

By Order in Council of the 26th day of April, 1875, the Inspection Division of Toronto, in the Province of Ontario, was declared to be composed of the City of Toronto and the Counties of York and Peel in the said Province.
Vide Canada Gazette, Vol. 8, p. 1860.

By Order in Council of the 9th July, 1875, Prince County, in the Province of Prince Edward Island, was constituted an Inland Revenue Division to be known and designated as the "Inland Revenue Division of Summerside."
Vide Canada Gazette, Vol, 9, p. 67.

By Order in Council of the 22nd July, 1875, the town of Chatham, in the Province of Ontario, be, and it is hereby constituted a Port from which goods subject to Duties of Excise may be exported in Bond.
Vide Canada Gazette, Vol. 9, p. 93.

By Order in Council of the 22nd day of July, 1875, the Town of Chatham, in the Province of Ontario, was constituted a Port from which goods subject to Duties of Excise may be exported in Bond.
Vide Canada Gazette, Vol. 9, p. 178.

By Order in Council of the 22nd day of July, 1875, the boundaries of the Inspection District of Algoma, in the Province of Ontario, were made the same as the boundaries of the Electoral District of Algoma, in the said Province.
Vide Canada Gazette, Vol. 9, p. 178.

Inland Revenue.

GOVERNMENT HOUSE, OTTAWA,
Monday, 26th day of July, 1875.

Present :

HIS EXCELLENCY THE ADMINISTRATOR OF THE GOVERNMENT IN COUNCIL.

ON the recommendation of the Honorable the Minister of Inland Revenue, and under the provisions of the Act passed in the Session of the Parliament of Canada, held in the 36th year of Her Majesty's reign, chaptered 47 and intituled: "An Act respecting Weights and Measures," His Excellency, by and with the advice of the Queen's Privy Council for Canada, has been pleased to order, and it is hereby ordered, that the accompanying Regulations as to the descriptions of Weighing Machines, Weights and Measures that will be admitted to verification and as to fees to be charged for such service, be and they are hereby approved.

REGULATIONS AS TO THE DESCRIPTIONS OF BALANCES AND WEIGHING MACHINES THAT WILL BE ADMITTED TO VERIFICATION.

The following balances are to be admitted to verification :—

A. BALANCES HAVING EQUAL ARMS.

B. BALANCES COMMONLY KNOWN AS STEELYARDS, OR ROMAN BALANCES, HAVING UNEQUAL ARMS.

C. WEIGH BRIDGES.

A. Balances with equal arms are only to be admitted to verification when—

1. The beam shows no perceptible difference as regards the form of the two arms ;

2. It is provided with a tongue pointing upwards or downwards from its centre, at right angles with a line joining the extreme bearings ;

3. It is in equilibrium when a line joining the extreme bearings is perfectly horizontal and returns to that position after being put into vibration ;

4. Its arms are equal within the specified limit of error ;

5. The balance is sufficiently sensitive to be turned decidedly and promptly by the addition or withdrawal of so much of the load as represents the error tolerated by regulations ;

6. No balance balls or other detached parts other than the pans are used for adjusting the balance ;

7. The balance, as a whole, is of sufficient strength, and on a sufficiently stable base to secure it against change of form or position under the maximum load it is to carry ;

8. The beam will carry its maximum load without deflection ;

Inland Revenue.

9. The maximum load for which it is to be used, is distinctly engraved or marked on the beam;

10. The knife edges are permanently fixed to the beam.

B. Balances commonly known as *steelyards* or Roman balances having unequal arms, are only to be admitted to verification when—

1. There is sufficient room for oscillation, and the knife edges on which the beam oscillates, are sufficiently fine to permit it to move freely;

2. The beam is sufficiently strong to carry its load without deflection;

3. The bottom of the notches by which the divisions of the long arm of the lever are indicated and from which the weight is suspended, are in a right line drawn through the knife edges forming the points of suspension, and when such straight line passes near to and a little above the centre of gravity of the whole apparatus;

4. The divisions on the long arm of the lever are equal among themselves;

5. The weight used with the lever is some multiple or sub-multiple of the pound avoirdupois, and has distinctly marked on it its true weight;

6. The maximum weight intended to be weighed on it is distinctly marked on the beam;

7. The position of equilibrium is indicated by a tongue or pointer exactily vertical when the line defined in section 3 is horizontal.

C. Weigh Bridges, Hay Scales, and Platform Scales, will only be admitted to verification when—

1. The foundation or supporting base is sufficiently firm and capable of carrying without change of level or of form, or other disturbance, the maximum load for which it is to be used;

2. If movable from place to place, some satisfactory arrangement, such as a level or plummet is provided and permanently attached, for indicating whether the machine is perfectly level;

3. The platform is so arranged that any obstruction to its free movement can be easily detected;

4. All the beams, levers, and other parts are of sufficient strength to carry the maximum load to which they will be respectively subjected without deflection;

5. The knife edges are firmly and permanently fixed in the levers, have sufficient room to permit free oscillation, and are sufficiently firm;

6. The oscillations are sufficiently evident;

7. The weights used with the instrument are multiples or authorized sub-multiples of the avoirdupois pound, plainly marked with their actual weight, and with the weight they are intended to indicate on the scale;

8. The weights used as above are a decimal sub-multiple, as $\frac{1}{10}$, $\frac{1}{100}$, $\frac{1}{1000}$ of the load indicated by them;

9. There are no movable balls or detached parts for the adjustment of the balance accessible or so placed that they can be changed without breaking a seal, or without the change coming to the knowledge of the Deputy Inspector;

Inland Revenue.

10. The apparatus indicates the same weight, whether the load is placed in the centre of the platform, on one side of it or at either corner.

11. The maximum load which the apparatus is intended to weigh, is conspicuously marked on some essential part of it.

———

No balances other than such as will come within the conditions under one or other of the heads A, B or C., are to be verified or stamped.

———

SCHEDULE A.

WEIGHTS to be admitted to Verification.

Dominion Weights				Weights to be tolerated till 1st July, 1878.		
Avoirdupois Weights.			Troy or Bul.ion Weights.	Avoirdupois Weights.		
In Bronze.	In Iron.	In Soft Metal Cased.	In Bronze only.	In Bronze.	In Iron.	In Soft Metal Cased.
50 lbs.	50 lbs.	50 lbs.	500 ozs.	56 lbs.	56 lbs.	56 lbs.
30 "	30 "	30 "	300 "	28 "	28 "	28 "
20 "	20 "	20 "	200 "	.14 "	14 "	14 "
10 "	10 "	10 "	100 "	7 "	7 "	7 "
5 "	5 "	5 "	50 "	4 "	4 "	4 "
3 "	3 "	3 "	30 "	2 "	2 "	2 "
2 "	2 "	2 "	20 "	1 "	1 "	1 "
1 "	1 "	1 "	10 "			
8 ozs.			5 "			
4 "			3 "			
2 "			2 "			
1 "			1 "			
8 drs.			·5 "			
4 "			·3 "			
2 "			·2 "			
1 "			·1 "			
½ "			·03 "			
1000 grs.			·03 "			
600 "			·02 "			
300 "			.01 "			
200 "			·005 "			
100 "			·003 "			
60 "			·002 "			
30 "			·001 "			
20 "						
10 "						
6 "						
3 "						
2 "						
1 "						
·6 "						
·3 "						
·2 "						
·1 "						
·06 "						
·03 "						
·02 "						
·01 "						

Inland Revenue.

SCHEDULE B.

FORMS of Weights that will be admitted to Verification.

FORMS OF DOMINION WEIGHTS.

Avoirdupois Weights

From 50 lbs. down to one pound, cylindrical, with knob.
The same with ring.
Rectangular block, with ring or handle, cast solid.
Truncated square pyramid.
From 3 lbs. down to one-half dram. Any of the above forms ; also flat discs in nests.

Grain Weights.

From 1,000 grains down to ten grains. Cylindrical, with a small rising stem and knob.

Six grains and under. Bent platinum or aluminum wire so bent as to represent the number of grains, or decimal parts of a grain.

In every case the denomination of the weight, when of sufficient size, must be cast, engraved or stamped on them in bold legible numerals, of a size duly proportioned to the size of the weight.

Troy Weights.

From 500 ounces down to one ounce. Truncated cone with knob.

From ·5 ounces down to ·001 ounce, flat square plates.

The denomination to be engraved on the top of the knob of each weight, in as large numerals as the size of the weight will admit ; and also on the face of the smaller weights.

FORMS OF WEIGHTS TOLERATED TILL JULY 1ST, 1878.

Avoirdupois Weights.

The ordinary bell shape.
Flat discs for 4 lbs. and under.
Rectangular blocks with rings or with handles cast solid.
Truncated square pyramids with rings.

In every case the denomination of the weight must be cast, engraved or stamped on them in bold legible numerals, proportioned to the size of the weight.

Inland Revenue.

SCHEDULE C.

FEES to be collected for Verification of Weights, under the Order in Council of 26th July, 1875.

	Dominion Weights.					Weights to be tolerated till 1st July, '78			
Avoirdupois Weight.				Troy Weight.		Avoirdupois Weight.			
Denominati'n	Verification Fees.			Denominat'n	Verification Fees.	Denominat'n	Verification Fees.		
	Bronze.	Iron.	Cased.		Bronze only.		Bronze.	Iron.	Cased.
	cts.	cts.	cts.		cts.		cts.	cts.	cts.
50 lbs.	25	25	30	500 oz.	50	56 oz.	30	30	35
30 "	20	20	25	300 "	40	28 "	25	25	30
20 "	20	20	25	200 "	35	14 "	20	20	25
10 "	15	15	20	100 "	30	7 "	15	15	20
5 "	10	10	15	50 "	20	4 "	10	10	15
3 "	5	10	15	30 "	20	2 "	5	10	15
2 "	5	10	15	20 "	20	1 "	5	10	15
1 "	5	10	15	10 "	20				
8 oz.	5 ⎫			5 "	15				
4 "	5			3 "	10				
2 "	5			2 "	10				
1 "	5	Not admitted.	Not admitted.	1 "	10				
8 drams	5			·5	10				
4 "	5			·3	10				
2 "	5			·2	10				
1 "	5			·1	10				
½ "	5 ⎭			.05	10				
				·03	10				
				·02	10				
Set as above from 50 lb. down to 1 lb	$1.00	$1.10	$1.50	·01	10				
				·005	10				
				·003	10				
do from 8 oz to ½ dram	$0.40			·002	10				
				·001	10				
Set of grain weights from 1,000 grains down to ·01 of a grain, in authorized series	$1.00			Set as above from 500 oz. to 1 oz........	$2.50				
				do from ·5 oz down to ·001	$1.00				

Inland Revenue.

SCHEDULE D.

DOMINION MEASURES of Capacity that may be admitted to Verification.

Denominations.	Materials.
A.—Bushel. Half Bushel. Peck.	May be made of— 1. Bronze or Brass, cast. 2. Hammered Sheet Brass or Copper, strengthened by rims of similar metal, and upright straps. 3. Sheet Iron, strengthened by iron rim top and bottom, and by upright straps. 4. Wood, Oak, Elm, or Ash, with iron rim.
B.—Gallon. Half Gallon. Quart. Pint. Half Pint. Gill. Half Gill.	May be made of— 1. Bronze or Brass, cast. 2. Hammered Sheet, Brass or Copper, with suitable rim of similar metal. 3. Hard Pewter.

1. NOTE.—Every measure must have cast, engraved, stamped or branded on it its denomination or capacity, in bold, legible characters, duly proportioned to the size of the measure.
2. No measure of capacity, of which the sides or bottom are indented, battered or knocked out of the regular form will be admitted to verification.

SCHEDULE E.

MEASURES of capacity that will be tolerated until the 23rd May, 1880, under the Act 36 Vict., chap. 47, sect. 5, sub-secs. 2 and 3.

The Winchester Bushel and the Wine Gallon, with their submultiples, when made of any of the materials specified for the Dominion Standards of corresponding names, may be verified, and certificates of such verification granted, when it becomes necessary for the determination of quantities in any special cases that may arise under the provisions of the Act above cited.

In all such cases the standards to be used for such verification are to be specially applied for to the District Inspector, and must be returned to him as soon as the purpose for which they were obtained is accomplished.

SCHEDULE F.

FORMS of Measures of capacity that may be admitted to Verification.

DOMINION MEASURES.

Cylindrical.

For the Bushel, Half Bushel, and Peck, the depth must not be less than four-ninths of the diameter.

For the Gallon and smaller measures, the depth shall not be less than the diameter.

MEASURES TOLERATED UNDER SECT. 5 OF 36 VICT., CHAP. 47.

Cylindrical or Conical.

In no case to be verified if the sides or bottoms are battered, indented, or otherwise put out of their original and regular shape.

Inland Revenue.

SCHEDULE G.

Fees to be collected for the verification of Measures of Capacity under the Order in Council of July 26, 1875.

Denomination.	Bronze Cast.	Sheet Brass or Copper.	Sheet Iron.	Hard Pewter.	Wood.	Denomination.	Any Material.
	cts.	cts.	cts.	cts.	cts.		cts.
Bushel	50	50	50	....	25	Bushel	50
½ bushel	40	40	40	....	20	½ bushel	40
Peck	30	30	30	....	15	Peck	30
Gallon	25	15	....	15	....	Gallon	25
½ gallon	15	10	....	10	....	½ gallon	15
Quart	10	10	....	10	....	Quart	10
Pint	5	5	....	5	....	Pint	5
½ pint	5	5	....	5	....	½ pint	5
Gill	5	5	....	5	....	Gill	5
½ gill	5	5	....	5	....	½ gill	5
Set from bushel to Peck	1.00	1.00	....	....	50		
Set from gallon to ½ gill	50	50	....	50	....		

Dominion Measures — Material. Tolerated Measures till 1880.

SCHEDULE H.

Fees to be charged for Verification of Weigh-Bridges, Platform Scales, Weighing Machines, Balances and Steelyards.

Balances with equal arms :

　　To weigh 5 lbs. and under in each pan...................... $0 50
　　To weigh from 5 lbs. up to 50, each pan..................... 1 00
　　To weigh from 50 lbs. up to 100, each pan................. 1 50
　　To weigh from 100 lbs upwards............................. 2 00

Steel-yards with divided arm :

　　To weigh 500 lbs. and under........... $0 50
　　To weigh 500 to 1,000 lbs............... 0 75
　　To weigh 1,000 to 2,000 lbs............. 1 00
　　To weigh 2,000 and upwards........... 1 50

To be verified at the Inspector's Office. If verified elsewhere cost of cartage of weights used for verification to be charged extra.

Balances with unequal arms, not divided :

　　To weigh 1,000 lbs. and under......... $0 75
　　To weigh 1,000 lbs. up to 2,000 lbs... 1 00
　　To weigh 2,000 lbs. and up to 4,000 lbs 1 50

Same as above as to cartage.

7

Inland Revenue.

Weigh-bridges or Platform Scales :
   To weigh 2,000 lbs. and under......... $1 00
   To weigh 2,000 to 4,000 lbs............. 1 50
   To weigh 4,000 to 6,000 lbs............. 2 00
And for each additional ton................ 0 50

And in addition to these rates the cost of cartage the weights used for verification.

SCHEDULE I.

LINEAL MEASURES that may be admitted to Verification.

DENOMINATION.	MATERIAL.
10 feet measures.	
6 " "	These measures may be made of any suitable hard metal, or of straight grained wood. When of wood the ends must be protected by metal tips, well secured.
5 " "	
3 " " or yard	
½ yard	
2 feet "	
1 foot "	
½ " "	
Chain in Riban, 100 feet.	The chains of iron or steel with solid joints. The Ribands may be of steel or of metal wire woven with other fibre.
" " 50 "	
" Divided into "	
" in Riband, 66 "	
" 33 "	
" Divided into links.	

SCHEDULE K.

FEES to be charged for verification of Lineal Measures.

	Of Metal.	Of Wood.
10 feet..	30 cts.	20 cts
6 "	25	20
5 "	25	20
3 " or yard....................................	20	10
½ yard..	10	5
2 feet...	5	5
1 foot	5	5
½ "	5	5
Chain or Riband, 100 feet....................	$1 00	
" " 50 "	0 75	
" " 66 "	1 00	
33 "	0 75	

W. A. HIMSWORTH,
Clerk, Privy Council.

Inland Revenue.

NOTICE.

DEPARTMENT OF INLAND REVENUE,
OTTAWA, 2nd August, 1875

NOTICE is hereby given that by an Order of His Excellency the Governor General in Council, bearing date the 19th May, 1875, the Tariff of Tolls on Dominion Canals was amended and modified as follows, viz :—

1. Bricks, clay, sand, cement and water lime to be added to Class 3 instead of Class 4.

2. Under head of Standard for estimating weights, all reference to the bushel to be omitted in respect of grains.

2000 lbs avoirdupois (or 20 centals) to constitute the ton weight.

EDWD. MIALL, jr.,
Acting Commissioner, I. R.

Inland Revenue.

PRIVY COUNCIL CHAMBER,
OTTAWA, 2nd September, 1875.

NOTICE is hereby given, that on the recommendation of the Honorable the Minister of Inland Revenue, and under the provisions of the Act 38 Victoria, Chapter 34, intituled: "An Act to amend the Act Chapter forty-six of the Consolidated Statutes of Canada, intituled: 'An Act respecting Culling and measuring of Timber,'" His Excellency the Administrator of the Government, by Order in Council of the 27th day of August, ultimo, has been pleased to approve of the following amended Tariff of Cullers' Fees for measuring off or counting Hemlock Lumber and Timber, that is to say:—

Tariff.	Total Fees in cents & tenths of a cent.	Office Fees in cents & tenths of a cent.	Cullers Fees in cents & tenths of a cent.
For measuring off or counting Hemlock per ton	4	$1\frac{7}{10}$	$2\frac{3}{10}$
Deals, counted off, 100 Standard..................	,8	3	5
Plank, 2 inches thick and under, 100 pieces.....	25	5	20
For culling and measuring in a Merchantable state or measuring in "Shipping order," or counting off when not otherwise herein provided:			
Waney, string measurement, per ton	10	3	7
Square and waney, per ton......................	$7\frac{4}{10}$	$2\frac{3}{10}$	$5\frac{1}{10}$
Deals---per 100 standard.......................	45	8	37
Plank, 2 inches thick and under, 100 pieces......	35	10	25
Boards, 100 pieces.............................	28	5	23
Flatted and round timber, Spruce or Hemlock, per 1,000 lineal feet.	56	20	36

W. A. HIMSWORTH,
Clerk, Privy Council.

Inland Revenue.

GOVERNMENT HOUSE, OTTAWA,
Thursday, 30th day of September, 1875.

Present :

HIS EXCELLENCY THE ADMINISTRATOR OF THE GOVERNMENT IN COUNCIL.

ON the recommendation of the Honorable the Minister of Inland Revenue, His Excellency, by and with the advice of the Queen's Privy Council for Canada, has been pleased to Order, and it is hereby Ordered, that the Order in Council, bearing date the 17th day of May A.D. 1875, establishing Inspection Districts under the provisions of the 16th section of the Act passed in the thirty-sixth year of Her Majesty's reign, chaptered 47, and intituled : " An Act respecting Weights and Measures," be, and the same is hereby cancelled, and that under the provisions of the same section the following Districts be, and they are hereby set apart and established as Districts for the Inspection of Weights and Measures, viz. :—

1. Windsor.	4. Kingston.	7. Nova Scotia.
2. London.	5. Montreal.	8. New Brunswick.
3. Toronto.	6. Quebec.	9. Manitoba.
	10. British Columbia.	

And it is further ordered that under the provisions of the 20th section of the said Act the said Districts be, and they are hereby respectively subdivided into Inspection Divisions in accordance with the following Schedule. Each such Division to comprise the Territory set opposite thereto, that is to say :—

SCHEDULE.

Province.	District.	Division.	Territory Comprising the Division.
ONTARIO.	Windsor............	Essex...................	County of Essex.
		Kent.....................	do Kent.
		Lambton...............	do Lambton.
		Bruce...................	do Bruce.
		Huron	do Huron.
		Stratford	do Perth.
	London...............	London....	City of London and that portion of the county, comprising the Electoral District of East Middlesex.
		Middlesex.............	That portion of the county, comprising the Electoral Districts of North and West Middlesex.
		Elgin....................	County of Elgin.
		Wellington............	do Wellington.
		Waterloo...............	do Waterloo.
		Brant...................	do Brant.
		Norfolk.................	do Norfolk.
		Oxford..................	do Oxford.
		Hamilton...............	City of Hamilton and County of Wentworth.
		Halton	Counties of Halton and Peel.
		Niagara.................	Town of Niagara and County of Lincoln.
		Welland	Counties of Haldimand and Welland.

Inland Revenue.

SCHEDULE.—*Continued.*

Province.	District.	Division.	Territory Comprising the Division.
ONTARIO.	Toronto.............	Toronto................	City of Toronto.
		York......................	County of York.
		Ontario.................	do Ontario.
		Algoma	From Thunder Bay East.*
		Grey	County of Grey.
		Simcoe	do Simcoe.
		Muskoka...............	Muskoka, Nipissing, Parry Sound and Manitoulin. *
		Durham............. ..	County of Durham.
		Northumberland....	do Northumberland.
		Peterborough........	do Peterborough.
		Victoria	do Victoria.
		Hastings..	do Hastings.
		Prince Edward......	do Prince Edward.
	Kingston............	Kingston.....	City of Kingston and County Frontenac.
		Lennox.................	County of Lennox and Addington.
		Lanark.................	do Lanark.
		Renfrew................	do Renfrew.
		Ottawa.................	City of Ottawa and County of Carleton.
		Dundas................	Counties of Russell and Dundas.
		Brockville............	do Grenville and Leeds, Town of Brockville and the Township of Elizabethtown.
		Glengarry	Counties of Prescott, Glengarry, Stormont and the Town and Township of Cornwall.
QUEBEC.	Montreal........	Hull...................	Counties of Ottawa and Pontiac.
		Montreal	City of Montreal and County of Hochelaga.
		Laval ..:...............	Counties of Jacques-Cartier, Laval, Vaudreuil and Soulanges.
		Chambly...............	Counties of Laprairie, Chambly and Verchères.
		Joliette.................	do Montcalm, Joliette, and L'Assomption.
		Terrebonne...........	do Terrebonne, Argenteuil and Two M'tains.
		Richelieu..............	do Richelieu and Yamaska.
		Berthier...............	do Berthier and Maskinongé.
		St. Hyacinthe.......	City and County of St. Hyacinthe and the Counties of Rouville and Bagot.
		Missisquoi	Counties of Shefford, Brome and Missisquoi.
		Iberville...............	do Napierville, St. Johns and Iberville.
		Beauharnois..........	do Beauharnois, Chateauguay and Huntingdon.
		Sherbrooke..	Counties of Wolfe, Richmond, Compton and Stanstead and Town of Sherbrooke.
		Three Rivers.........	County of St. Maurice and City of Three Rivers.
		Drummond...........	Counties of Drummond and Arthabaska.
		Champlain...	do Champlain and Nicolet.
	Quebec..............	Lotbinière.............	Counties of Lotbinière and Portneuf.
		Quebec.................	City of Quebec.
		Montmorency........	Counties of Quebec and Montmorency.
		Lévis	County of Lévis.
		Beauce.................	Counties of Beauce and Megantic.
		Bellechasse...........	do Dorchester and Bellechasse.
		Saguenay..............	do Charlevoix, Saguenay and Chicoutimi.
		Montmagny...........	do Montmagny and L'Islet.
		Kamouraska..........	do Kamouraska and Temiscouata.
		Rimouski..............	County of Rimouski.
		Gaspé..................	Counties of Gaspé and Bonaventure.
		Labrador..............	Labrador and Magdalen Islands.

* See next page.

Inland Revenue.

SCHEDULE.—*Continued.*

Province.	District.	Division.	Territory Comprising the Division.
NOVA SCOTIA.	Nova Scotia......	Halifax..............	City of Halifax and Town of Dartmouth, and that part of the County of Halifax, known as the Electoral District of West Halifax.
		Guysborough.........	Counties of Guysborough and that portion of the County of Halifax known as the Electoral District of East Halifax.
		Lunenburg............	Counties of Lunenburg and Queens.
		Pictou...............	do Antigonish and Pictou.
		Colchester...........	do Colchester and Cumberland.
		Hants	do Hants and Kings.
		Annapolis............	do Annapolis and Digby.
		Yarmouth.............	do Yarmouth and Shelburne.
		Cape Breton..........	do Victoria and Cape Breton.
		Inverness	do Inverness and Richmond.
NEW BRUNSWICK.	New Brunswick..	Restigouche	Counties of Restigouche and Gloucester.
		Northumberland...	do Northumberland and Kent.
		St. John.............	City of St. John and County of St. John.
		Fredericton.........	Counties of York and Sunbury.
		Moncton	do Westmoreland and Albert.
		Woodstock............	do Victoria, Carleton and Charlotte.
		Kings	do Kings and Queens.
MANITOBA			The whole Province.
BRITISH COLUMBIA			The whole Province.

W. A. HIMSWORTH,
Clerk, Privy Council.

* By Order in Council of the 15th November, 1875, the Division of Algoma is made the same as the Electoral District, and that of Muskoka is to contain Muskoka, Nipissing and Parry Sound.

Vide Canada Gazette, Vol. 9, p. 638.

Inland Revenue.

REGULATIONS

Respecting the Verification and Testing of Gas and Gas Meters, under the Acts 36 Vict., chap. 48, and 88 Vict., chap 37.

1st. Copies of all models deposited in the Department of Inland Revenue and legalized by the Order in Council of 18th December, 1874, having been verified under the direction of the Minister of Inland Revenue, such copies shall hereafter be known as "*Local Gas Standards*" and a sufficient set thereof shall be placed in such places as may be necessary for carrying out the provisions of the Acts above cited, in suitable offices provided for that purpose.

2nd. The "Local Gas Standards" shall be placed in the custody of duly appointed Inspectors or Deputy Inspectors, who shall be responsible for their safety and shall have sole possession of them; and it shall not be lawful for any person—except such as are duly authorized thereto—to have access to or use any of the said "*Local Gas Standards.*"

3rd. Whenever there is reason for supposing that any of the said Standards have become inaccurate—as to which the Inspector of Gas or some superior officer of the Inland Revenue Department shall be the sole judge— such Standards shall be tested by such portable instruments as may be determined by Departmental Regulations, or the Standards supposed to be defective may, if deemed necessary by the Department of Inland Revenue, be removed to Ottawa and verified by the original models.

4th. When Gas Meters have been verified and found to be correct within the limit of error tolerated by the Statute, the Inspector or Deputy Inspector shall affix a seal thereto, which seal shall be of wax bearing such device as may be directed by departmental regulations.

5th. Under the authority of the Act 38 Vic., chap. 37, sec. 37, it is hereby declared that sulphur in gas shall be considered as in excess, when found in greater quantity than twenty grains in one hundred cubic feet of gas, and that ammonia shall be considered as being in excess, when the quantity found is greater than two grains in one hundred cubic feet of gas.

6th. The forms in Schedule A shall be used for granting certificates respecting the verification of Meters and the testing of Gas, and no certificate shall be valid unless it is given on the form hereby authorized, nor unless stamps representing the authorized fees payable for such a certificate are attached thereto and cancelled in accordance with' the Departmental Regulations then in force.

7th. Schedule B attached hereto is a Schedule of fees which shall be paid for the verification of Meters and for testing Gas, and the fees made payable simply for testing or verifying Meters shall be payable whether such Meters are stamped or rejected.

Inland Revenue.

SCHEDULE A 1.

GAS INSPECTOR'S OFFICE,

18

I hereby certify that   I have tested the Illuminating
Power of the Gas furnished by   in accordance with the
provisions of the Act to provide for the inspection of Gas and Gas Meters,
and that the Illuminating Power of the said Gas was
equal to that of

[*Attach stamps here.*]   Standard Candles. The fees amounting to $ have
been paid and the stamps Nos.   representing
said fees, are hereto attached.

Inspector.

See particulars of experiments hereto attached.

SCHEDULE A 2.

GAS INSPECTOR'S OFFICE,

18

I hereby certify that   I have tested the purity
of the Gas furnished by the   and after testing such Gas in
accordance with the provisions of the Act to provide
for the inspection of Gas and Gas Meters, I find the
quantity of sulphur contained therein

[*Stamps to be attached*   and the quantity of ammonia contained therein
here.]   The fees amounting to $ have been
paid, and the stamps Nos.   representing
said fees are attached hereto.

Inspector

See particulars of experiments hereto attached.

SCHEDULE A 3.

GAS INSPECTOR'S OFFICE,

18

I hereby certify that   I have this day inspected
the   Light Meter No.
manufactured by   and found the same

[*Attach stamps here.*]   The fees amounting to $ have
been paid and the stamps Nos.   representing
said fees are attached hereto.

Inspector

Inland Revenue.

SCHEDULE B..

Verification and testing of Gas and Gas Meters.

Fee to be charged for the verification of gas meters and the testing of gas under the Act 36 Vict., Chap. 48 :—

1st. *Verification of Meters.*

			$.	c.
5 lights and under			0	50
10	"	"	0	75
20	"	"	1	00
30	"	"	1	50
50	"	"	2	00
60	"	"	2	50
80	"	"	3	50
100	"	"	4	50

and for every addition of twenty lights or under a charge of 80 cents.

2nd. *Inspection as to Illuminating Power.*

For every Certificate as to illuminating power, $3 00

For a Certificate as to average illuminating power during one week.................................... 6 00

For a Certificate of illuminating power by inspection made at the request of, and in the presence of a Consumer after due notification. 4 00

For a Certificate as to the presence or absence of Sulphurated Hydrogen............................. 1 50

For a Certificate of an Analysis for quantity of Sulphur... 4 00

For a Certificate of an Analysis for quantity of Ammonia... 3 00

For a Certificate of Analysis, for average quantity of Sulphur and Ammonia during one month 10 00

3rd. For each requisition for Meter or Gas inspection with notice to opposite party........ 0 25

PRIVY COUNCIL CHAMBER,
OTTAWA, 11th February, 1876.

I hereby certify that the foregoing Regulations respecting the verification and testing of Gas and Gas Meters with the Schedule thereto annexed were submitted to and approved by His Excellency the Governor General in Council on the 10th day of February instant.

W. A. HIMSWORTH,
Clerk, Privy Council.

Inland Revenue.

By Order in Council of the 6th March, 1876, Brockville is declared to be a port from which goods subject to duties of Excise, may be exported in bond.

Vide Canada Gazette, Vol. 9, p. 1,211.

GOVERNMENT HOUSE, OTTAWA,
Wednesday, 8th day of March, 1876.

Present:

HIS EXCELLENCY THE GOVERNOR GENERAL IN COUNCIL.

ON the recommendation of the Honorable the Minister of Inland Revenue, and under the provisions of the 26th section of the Act passed in the Session of the Parliament of Canada, held in the thirty-seventh year of Her Majesty's reign, chaptered 8, and intituled : "An Act to prevent the Adulteration of Food," His Excellency, by and with the advice of the Queen's Privy Council for Canada, has been pleased to make the following Regulations for carrying into effect the provisions of the said Act, that is to say :

1st. That Analysts be appointed only at the Cities of Montreal, Quebec, Halifax, St. John and Toronto.

2nd. (*Has reference only to the remuneration of the Analysts.*)

3rd. That the following tariff of fees be authorized :—

For Gas Analysis for Sulphur, Ammonia and Sulphuretted Hydrogen....................................	$10 00
For Analysis of Milk, Bread, Butter and Sweets...	5 00
For Analysis of Malt Liquors, Cider, Light Wines, Drugs, Alcoholic Liquors, Liqueurs and Condiments	8 00
For Analysis of Tea, Tobacco, Cocoa and Chocolate	10 00
For Analysis of Unenumerated Articles.............	5 00

4th. That all fees collected under the above tariff shall, when collected, be paid to the credit of the Consolidated Revenue Fund.

5th. That the Analysts appointed shall be governed by the following regulations :—

(*a*) On receipt of sample from the Revenue Officer authorized as provided in the Act above cited, to take such samples, the Analyst shall open sample, and, in the presence of that officer, shall carefully mix equally and divide the sample into two parcels—one of which he shall keep for analysis, the other he shall seal up with his own seal, and deposit with the Inland Revenue Officer.

(*b*) The Analyst shall reserve a portion of his own sample for future examination. But if the substance be of such a nature as to undergo alteration by keeping a short time (such as milk), the first analysis shall be final, and in such case no analysis shall be held valid unless report be sent in within twelve hours of the taking of the sample, and in such case duplicate samples shall be unnecessary.

Inland Revenue.

(c) That the Analyst shall impartially perform the duties of his office, and shall not give the result of his analysis or the names or addresses of parties whose samples may be submitted to him, to any one except when called upon to do so in his report to the Department, or before a Court of Law, in conformity with his duties under this Act.

(d) The Form of Certificate given in each case shall be as in Schedule A.

SCHEDULE A.

M. I 187

I, Public Analyst for Inland Revenue Division of appointed under Inland Revenue Act of 1875, hereby certify that I received from(1) , Inland Revenue Officer for District of on the day of 187 , a sample sealed according to Act, Seals unbroken, bearing (2) marks. That I opened such package in presence of (3) , an officer designated by the Department, and the sample then (4) I then carefully mixed such sample equally, and divided into two parcels, one of which I handed to said Inland Revenue Officer, the other I have submitted to analysis, and find (5)

I have further reserved a portion of the sample myself.
    As witness my hand.

        (Signed)

                  A. B.,
                  Analyst

Instructions as to filling in blanks, &c.

1. Here insert the name of the person submitting the sample for analysis.

2. Here insert a description of the Seals, Marks, Numbers, or other devices used for securing the vessel or package in which the article is contained.

3. Here insert the name of some officer designated by the Department of Inland Revenue, in whose presence the package was opened.

4. Here insert the weight or measure of the sample, or, when the article cannot be conveniently weighed or measured, this passage may be erased or the blank left unfilled.

5. Here the Analyst will insert the result of his analysis and, at his discretion, his opinion as to whether the mixture (if any) was for the purpose of reducing the article potable or palatable, or of preserving it, or of improving its appearance, or was unavoidable; and may state whether it is

in excess of what is ordinary or otherwise, and whether the ingredients or materials mixed are or are not injurious to health. In case of a certificate regarding Milk, Butter, or any article liable to decomposition, the Analyst shall specially report whether any change had taken place in the constitution of the article that would interfere with the analysis.

W A. HIMSWORTH,

Clerk, Privy Council.

GOVERNMENT HOUSE, OTTAWA.

Monday, 13th day of March, 1876.

Present :

HIS EXCELLENCY THE GOVERNOR GENERAL IN COUNCIL.

ON the recommendation of the Honorable the Minister of Inland Revenue and under the provisions of the 11th section of the Act passed in the Session of the Parliament of Canada, held in the thirty-first year of Her Majesty's reign, chaptered 50, and intituled: "An Act to increase the "Excise Duty on Spirits; to impose an Excise Duty on Refined Petroleum, "and to provide for the Inspection thereof:"

His Excellency, by and with the advice of the Queen's Privy Council for Canada, has been pleased to Order, and it is hereby Ordered, that the Order in Council of the 15th of June, 1869, passed under the provisions of the said Act, be amended by adding thereto the following Regulations:

Licenses to use the light products of petroleum for illuminating purposes, which will not stand a fire test of 105 degrees, may be granted upon the following conditions :—

(a) The parties so licensed shall conform, as to the storage and use of Petroleum and its products, to all Municipal Regulations of the Municipality in which they propose to use them.

(b) Such light products of Petroleum shall not be used for illuminating purposes in any place occupied as a dwelling-house, workshop, manufactory or other place, otherwise than in the form of vapour or gas flowing through pipes.

(c) The supply or store of such light products of Petroleum shall be stored in suitable metal reservoirs sunk below the surface of the ground, and safely covered with earth, at a distance of not less than fifty feet from any dwelling-house, workshop, manufactory or other place in which it is proposed to use it.

(d) If any pumps or apparatus used for forcing air or vapour into the reservoir be placed within any dwelling-house or work-shop they shall be so arranged that there can be no back-flow of the Petroleum or its light products, or of any vapour or gas arising therefrom into the building.

(e) The pipes for conveying the gas or vapour to the jets or burners within the dwelling-house, work-shop, manufactory, or other place where it is proposed to use it, shall be so arranged as to have a descent or decline from the burners to the reservoir, or to some other receptacle placed outside such building, and sunk below the surface of the earth at a distance of not less than fifty feet; all such pipes being so arranged as to carry away any condensed vapour that may be formed therein.

(*f*) Pendents from ceilings to which burners are attached, and from which the condensed vapour cannot be taken off, as provided in paragraph 5, shall be connected from the top of the supply pipe in such a way as to prevent the condensed vapour that may accumulate in the supply pipes flowing into the pendents.

(*g*) All apertures, pipes or inlets to the reservoirs shall be covered by fine wire gauze.

(*h*) All apertures in tanks and reservoirs used for storing the light products of Petroleum shall be fitted with self-acting stoppers or valves, which will close automatically.

W. A. HIMSWORTH,
Clerk, Privy Council.

By Order in Council, dated 18th March, 1876, it was declared that that portion of the City and County of St. John lying to the East of the River shall constitute the Inspection Division of St. John, and that portion of the County of St. John including the Town of Carleton, lying to the westward of the River, shall constitute the Inspection Division of Carleton, in so far as relates to the Inspection of Pickled Fish and Fish Oils.

Vide Canada Gazette, Vol. 9, p. 1276.

By Order in Council of the 20th April, 1876, the Inspection District of Shelburne was subdivided into two Districts under the respective names of Shelburne and Barrington, embracing the Townships of those names.

Vide Canada Gazette, Vol. 9, p. 1391.

By Order in Council of the 20th day of April, 1876, the Port of Victoria in Province of British Columbia, was made a Port, from which goods subject to duties of Excise shall be exported in Bond.

Vide Canada Gazette, Vol. 9, p. 1391.

Interior.

Copy of a Report of a Committee of the Honorable the Privy Council, approved by His Excellency the Governor General in Council on the 26th March, 1874.

On a Memorandum dated 20th March, 1874, from the Surveyor-General of Dominion Lands, referring to the letter of Mr. Codd, Acting Agent of Dominion Lands, dated the 7th March instant, requesting authority to deal with trespassers on the timber of the Dominion Lands, in addition to that given by the Order in Council of the 13th January, 1873, establishing Timber Regulations in Manitoba, and the 60th section of the Dominion Lands Act;—

The Surveyor-General alludes to the case of firewood or timber seized because cut without authority and being in too small quantities to justify the expense of placing men in charge of the several seizures, and which would consequently, as experience shows, be gradually carried away by the parties trespassing, before the expiration of the time fixed by the said section of the Act for the sale thereof for the benefit of the Crown; and with a view to shorten this time he recommends that under the provisions of the 105th section of the Dominion Lands Act, the Agent of the Dominion Lands in Manitoba be authorized to order the sale of the timber cut without authority on which the claimant refuses or neglects, within fifteen days from the date of seizure, to pay three times the amount of the dues authorized under the regulations before mentioned to be collected.

On the recommendation of the Honorable the Minister of the Interior, the Committee advise that the authority requested be granted.

Certified.

W. A. HIMSWORTH,
Clerk, Privy Council.

BY Proclamation bearing date 27th August, 1874, His Excellency, in Her Majesty's name, declares and makes subject to the provisions of the eighteenth, nineteenth, twentieth, twenty-first and twenty-second sections of the Act of the Parliament of Canada, made and passed in the thirty-first year of Our Reign, and intituled : " An Act providing for the organization of the Department of the Secretary of State of Canada, and for the management of Indian and Ordnance Lands,"—

Firstly,—All and singular the following Indian Lands situate in the Province of Ontario, being land belonging to or occupied by the Tribe of the Mississagua Indians of Alnwick, that is to say : all and every the lots and other lands in the first and second concessions respectively of the Township of Alnwick, in the County of Northumberland and the Province of Ontario, and also all those the unsold islands belonging to them in the Bay of Quinté, Lake Ontario, Weller's Bay and the River St. Lawrence ; and secondly,—all and singular the following Indian Land situate in the said Province of Ontario belonging to or occupied by the Tribe of Mississagua at the Rice, Mud and Scugog Lakes, that is to say: all those reserves

Interior.

occupied and owned by them on the shores of the Rice, Mud and Scugog Lakes respectively, and also all those, the unsold islands belonging to them in Rice Lake and all rivers and waters situated between the Counties of Peterborough, Victoria, Northumberland and Durham in the Province of Ontario.

Vide Canada Gazette, Vol. 8, p. 234.

GOVERNMENT HOUSE, OTTAWA,
Saturday, 10th day of October, 1874
Present :

HIS EXCELLENCY THE GOVERNOR GENERAL IN COUNCIL.

ON the recommendation of the Honorable the Minister of Justice, and under the provisions of the 33rd section of the Act passed in the Session of the Parliament of Canada, held in the 33rd year of Her Majesty's reign, intituled : " An Act to amend and continue the Act 32 and 33 Victoria, " chapter 3, and to establish and provide for the Government of the Pro- " vince of Manitoba," as amended by the third section of the Act passed in the 37th year of Her Majesty's reign, intituled : " An Act respecting the " appropriation of certain Dominion Lands in Manitoba," His Excellency, by and with the advice of the Queen's Privy Council for Canada, has been pleased to settle and approve the form of Letters Patent hereunto appended as the mode and form by which Lands applied for under the sub-section 3 of Section 32 of the Act first above mentioned shall be granted to Appli cants complying with the requirements of the Law :—

CANADA.

VICTORIA, by the Grace of God of the United Kingdom of Great Britain and Ireland, Queen, Defender of the Faith, &c., &c., &c.

To all to whom these Presents shall come—GREETING :

WHEREAS the Lands hereinafter described are part and parcel of the lands surrendered to Her Majesty by the Governor and Company of Adventurers, trading into Hudson's Bay, commonly called the Hudson's Bay Company :

And whereas, by the 3rd sub-section of the 32nd section of an Act of the Parliament of Canada, passed in the thirty-third year of Our Reign, intituled : " An Act to amend and continue the Act 32nd and 33rd Vic- " toria, chapter 3, and to establish and provide for the Government of the Province of Manitoba," it is, amongst other things in effect, enacted (for the quieting of titles, and securing to the settlers in the Province of Manitoba the peaceable possession of the lands held by them,) that "all titles by occupancy, with the sanction and under the license and authority of the Hudson's Bay Company, up to the 8th day of March, 1869, of land in that Province, in which the Indian title has been extinguished, shall, if required by the owner, be converted into an estate in freehold, by grant from the Crown :"

And whereas, by the 3rd Section of another Act of the said Parliament of Canada, passed in the thirty-seventh year of Our Reign, intituled: "An Act respecting the appropriation of certain Dominion Lands in Manitoba," after reciting that it is expedient to afford facilities to parties claiming lands under the 3rd and 4th sub-sections of the 82nd section of the Act 33rd Victoria, chapter 3 to obtain Letters Patent for the same; it is enacted, "That persons satisfactorily establishing undisturbed occupancy of any lands within the Province prior to, and being by themselves, or their servants, tenants or agents, or those through whom they claim, in actual and peaceable possession thereof, on the eighth day of March, one thousand eight hundred and sixty-nine, shall be entitled to receive letters patent therefor, granting the same absolutely to them respectively in fee simple:"

And whereas it has been represented and satisfactorily established to Us that previous to and on the eighth day of March, 1869,

was in undisturbed occupancy and in actual and peaceable possession of the lands hereinafter described, being land in that part of the said Province of Manitoba, in which the Indian Title had on the last mentioned date been extinguished:

And whereas, the claims of the said

to the said lands hereinafter named, have by assignment (or intermediate assignments) since the said eighth day of March, 1869, become vested in

who, pursuant to the Act firstly above-mentioned, has required the said title by occupancy to be converted into an estate in freehold by grant from us:

Now KNOW YE, that in consideration of the premises, and in pursuance of the powers vested in us by the said hereinbefore in part recited Acts, We by these presents do grant unto the said

and assigns forever; all th   parcel   or tract   of land, situate, lying, and being in the
in the said Province of Manitoba, in Our Dominion of Canada, described and known as, and being composed of

containing by admeasurement
Acre   more or less.
To have and to hold the said parcel   or tract   of land, hereby granted, unto the said

and Assigns for ever; saving, excepting and reserving, nevertheless, unto us, Our Heirs and Successors, all mines of gold and silver, and the free uses, passages and enjoyment of, in, over and upon all navigable waters
8

Interior.

---

that shall or may be hereafter found on or under, or be flowing through or upon any part of the said parcel or tract of land hereby granted as aforesaid.

Given under the Great Seal of Canada :—WITNESS, &c., &c.

At Ottawa, this   day of   in the year of Our Lord one thousand eight hundred and seventy-   and in the thirty-   year of Our Reign.

His Excellency has been pleased to order that the Order in Council of the 28th day of February last, be and the same is hereby rescinded.

W. A. HIMSWORTH,

Clerk, Privy Council.

By Proclamation bearing date 26th November, 1874, His Excellency, in Her Majesty's name, declares and makes subject to the provisions of the eighteenth, nineteenth, twentieth, twenty-first and twenty-second sections of the Act of the Parliament of Canada, made and passed in the thirty-first year of H. M. Reign, and intituled : " An Act providing for the Organization of the Department of the Secretary of State of Canada, and for the Management of Indian and Ordnance Lands,"—

"All and singular the following lands situate in the Province of Quebec, being land belonging to or occupied by the Tribe of Montagnais Indians at Point Bleu, that is to say :

" The Reserve belonging to the Tribe of Montagnais Indians of Point Bleu, which is situated on Lake St. Jean, in the County of Chicoutimi, and Province of Quebec, together with all roads, or allowances for roads, running through the said lands."

Vide Canada Gazette, Vol. 8, p. 592.

By Proclamation bearing date 13th February, 1875, His Excellency, in Her Majesty's name, declares and makes subject to the provisions of the eighteenth, nineteenth, twentieth, twenty-first and twenty-second sections of the Act of the Parliament of Canada, made and passed in the thirty-first year of H. M. Reign, and intituled : " An Act providing for the organization of the Department of the Secretary of State of Canada, and for the management of Indian and Ordnance Lands,"—

" All and singular the following Indian Lands situate in the Province of Ontario, being the Reserve Lands belonging to or occupied by the Tribe of the Six Nation Indians, in the Township of Tuscarora, and in the Township of Onondaga, in the County of Brant and in the Township of Oneida, in the County of Haldimand, and also all and singular the Reserve Lands occupied by the Mississagua Indians, in the aforesaid Township of Tuscarora ; and also all and singular the following Indian Lands, in the Province of Quebec, namely : the Reserve Lands occupied by the Tribes respectively of Algonquins, Têtes de Boule, and Nipissingues Indians, in

Interior.

the Township of Maniwaki, in the County of Ottawa, and occupied by the Tribe of Iroquois Indians, in the Village of St. Regis, in the County of Huntingdon ; and also all and singular the islands in the River St. Lawrence owned by the last named Indians, together with all roads or allowances for roads running through the said Lands."
Vide Canada Gazette, Vol. 8, p. 1053.

———

By a Proclamation of the 16th July, 1875, His Excellency in Her Majesty's name, declares and makes, subject to the provisions of the eighteenth, nineteenth, twentieth, twenty-first and twenty-second sections of the Act of the Parliament of Canada, made and passed in the thirty-first year of H.M. Reign, and intituled " An Act providing for the organization of " the Department of the Secretary of State of Canada, and for the manage-" ment of Indian and Ordnance Lands,"—

" All and singular the following Indian Lands situate in the Province of Quebec, being the Reserve Lands belonging to or occupied by the Abenaki Tribe or Band of Indians of St. Francis and situated on the north-east side of the River St. Francis, in the County of Yamaska, in the Province of Quebec, and commonly known as the Indian Reserve, which includes the Indian Village ; and also the Islands in the River St. Francis claimed by the said Indians, together with the lands situated near the village of Beçan-cour, in the County of Nicolet, in the said Province of Quebec, known as the Indian Reserve, which lands belong to the Abenaki Indians residing therein who are commonly called the Abenakis of Beçancour."
Vide Canada Gazette, Vol. 9, p. 91.

———

PRIVY COUNCIL CHAMBER,
OTTAWA, 17th January, 1876

NOTICE is hereby given that on the recommendation of the Honorable the Minister of the Interior, and under the provisions of the " *Dominion Lands Act,*" and Acts amending the same, His Excellency the Governor General in Council has this day been pleased to authorize the Minister of the Interior to issue special temporary Permits or Licenses for the cutting of timber in certain cases upon Dominion Lands in the Province of Manitoba, subject to the following conditions, that is to say :

1. The term to be one year.

2. The dues to be paid by way of stumpage, such stumpage to be one cent and a half per inch across the stump, for trees seven inches and under in diameter, and for trees over that size three cents per inch across the stump : such dues to be paid, in all cases, according to the quantity of mber cut under such Permits, from time to time, on the report and return f the Timber Inspector.

3. No tree less than three inches in diameter to be cut under such ermit.

Interior.

With a view to guard against fires—should damage to growing timber or to private property, other than that of the holder of the Permit, be caused by a fire which may have originated on the ground covered by the Permit, the latter to be subject to immediate forfeiture.

4. Such Permit to be liable also to forfeiture for non-compliance with any of the other conditions above set forth.

W. A HIMSWORTH,
Clerk. Privy Council

Justice.

IN PURSUANCE of the provisions contained in the 79th section of the 38th Victoria, Chapter 11, intituled : " An Act to establish a Supreme Court and a Court of Exchequer for the Dominion of Canada," it is Ordered that the following Rules, in respect of the matters hereafter mentioned, shall be in force in the Supreme Court of Canada.

SUPREME COURT.

Appeals.

1. The first proceeding in appeal in this Court shall be the filing in the office of the Registrar of a case, pursuant to section 29 of the Act, certified under the seal of the Court appealed from.

2. The case, in addition to the proceedings mentioned in the said section 29, shall invariably contain a transcript of all the opinions or reasons for their judgment delivered by the Judges of the Court or Courts below, or an affidavit that such reasons cannot be procured, with a statement of the efforts made to procure the same.

3. The case shall also contain a copy of any order which may have been made by the Court below or any Judge thereof enlarging the time for appealing.

4. The Court or Judge thereof may order the case to be remitted to the Court below, in order that it may be made more complete by the addition thereto of further matter.

5. If the appellant does not file his case in appeal with the Registrar within *one month* after the security required by the Act shall be allowed, he shall be considered as not duly prosecuting his appeal, and the respondent may move to dismiss the appeal pursuant to sect. 41 of the Act.

6. The case shall be accompanied by a certificate under the seal of the Court below, stating that the appellant has given proper security to the satisfaction of the Court whose judgment is appealed from, or of a Judge thereof, and setting forth the nature of the security, to the amount of $500, as required by the 31st section of the said Act ; and a copy of any bond or other instrument by which security may have been given shall be annexed to the certificate.

7. The case shall be printed by the party appellant, and twenty-five printed copies thereof shall be deposited with the Registrar for the use of the Judges and officers of the Court.

8. The case shall be in demy quarto form. It shall be printed on paper of good quality, and on one side of the paper only, and the type shall be small pica, leaded, and the size of the case shall be *eleven inches* by *eight and one half inches* and every tenth line shall be numbered in the margin. An index to the pleadings, depositions and other principal matters shall be added.

9. The Registrar shall not file the case without the leave of the Court or a Judge, if the foregoing order has not been complied with, nor if it shall appear that the press has not been properly corrected, and no costs shall be taxed for any case not prepared in accordance with this order.

10. Together with the case, certified copies of all original documents and exhibits used in evidence in the Court of first instance, are to be de-

posited with the Registrar, unless their production shall be dispensed with by order of a Judge of this Court; but the Court or a Judge may order that all or any of the originals shall be transmitted by the officer having the custody thereof to the Registrar of this Court in which case the apellant shall pay the postage for such transmission.

11. Immediately after the filing of the case, a notice of the hearing of the appeal shall be given by the appellant for the next following session of the Court as fixed by the Act, or as specially convened for hearing appeals according to the provisions thereof, if sufficient time shall intervene for that purpose; and if between the filing of the case and the first day of the next ensuing session there shall not be sufficient time to enable the appellant to serve the notice as hereinafter prescribed, then such notice of hearing shall be given for the session following the then next ensuing session.

12. The notice convening the Court under section 14 of the Act for the purpose of hearing election or criminal appeals or appeals in matters of *habeas corpus* or for other purposes shall, pursuant to the directions of the Chief Justice or Senior Puisné Judge, as the case may be, be published by the Registrar in the *Canada Gazette* and shall be inserted therein for such time before the day appointed for such special session as the said Chief Justice or Senior Puisné Judge may direct, and may be in the form given in Schedule A to these Rules appended.

13. The notice of hearing may be in the form given in Schedule B to these Rules appended.

14. The notice of hearing shall be served at least *one month* before the first day of the session at which the appeal is to be heard.

15. Such notice shall be served on the Attorney or Solicitor who shall have represented the respondent in the Court below, at his usual place of business, or on the booked agent or at the elected domicile of such Attorney or Solicitor at the City of Ottawa; and if such Attorney or Solicitor shall have no booked agent or elected domicile at the City of Ottawa, the notice may be served by affixing the same in some conspicuous place in the office of the Registrar, and mailing a copy thereof prepaid to the address of such Attorney or Solicitor in sufficient time to reach him in due course of mail before the time required for service.

16. There shall be kept in the office of the Registrar of this Court a book to be called the "Agents' Book," in which all Advocates, Solicitors, Attorneys and Proctors practising in the said Supreme Court may enter the name of an Agent (such Agent being himself a person entitled to practise in the said Court) at the said City of Ottawa, or elect a domicile at the said city.

17. In case any respondent who may have been represented by Attorney or Solicitor in the Court below, shall desire to appear in person in the appeal he shall, immediately after the allowance by the Court appealed from or a Judge thereof of the security required by the Act, file with the Registrar a suggestion in the form following:—

"A. *vs.* B."

" I, A. B., intend to appear in person in this appeal."

(Signed) "A. B."

Justice.

18. If no such suggestion shall be filed, and until an order shall have been obtained as hereinafter provided for a change of solicitor or attorney, the solicitor or attorney who appeared for any party respondent in the Court below shall be deemed to be his solicitor or attorney in the appeal to this Court.

19. When a respondent has appeared in person in the Court below he may elect to appear by attorney or solicitor in the appeal, in which case the attorney or solicitor shall file a suggestion to that effect in the office of the Registrar, and thereafter the notice of hearing and all other papers are to be served on such attorney or solicitor as hereinbefore provided.

20. A respondent who appears in person may, by a suggestion filed in the Registrar's office, elect some domicile or place at the City of Ottawa, at which all notices and papers may be served upon him, in which case service at such place of the notice of hearing and all other notices and papers shall be deemed good service on the respondent.

21. In case the respondent, who shall have appeared in person in the Court appealed from, or shall have filed a suggestion pursuant to Rule 17, shall not, before service, have elected a domicile at the City of Ottawa, the notice of hearing may be served by affixing the same in some conspicuous place in the office of the Registrar.

22. Any party to an appeal may, on an *ex parte* application to a Judge, obtain an order to change his attorney or solicitor, and, after service of such order on the opposite party, all services of notices and other papers are to be made on the new attorney or solicitor.

23 At least *one month* before the first day of the session at which the appeal is to be heard, the parties appellant and respondent shall each deposit with the Registrar, for the use of the Court and its officers, *twenty-five* copies of his factum or points for argument in appeal.

24. The factum or points for argument in appeal shall contain a concise statement of the facts, and of the points of law intended to be relied on, and of the arguments and authorities to be urged and cited at the hearing, arranged under the appropriate heads.

25. The factum or points for argument in appeal shall be printed in the same form and manner as hereinbefore provided for with regard to the case in appeal, and shall not be received by the Registrar unless the requirements hereinbefore contained, as regards the case, are all complied with.

26. If the appellant does not deposit his factum or points for argument in appeal within the time limited by order 23, the respondent shall be at liberty to move to dismiss the appeal on the ground of undue delay, as provided for by section 41 of the Act.

27. If the respondent fails to deposit his factum or points for argument in appeal within the said prescribed period, the appellant may set down or inscribe the cause for hearing *ex parte.*

28. Such setting down or inscription *ex parte* may be set aside or discharged upon an application to a judge in chambers sufficiently supported by affidavits

29. The factum or points for argument in appeal first deposited with the Registrar shall be kept by him under seal, and shall in no case be com-

municated to the opposite party until the latter shall himself bring in and deposit his own factum or points.

30. So soon as both parties shall have deposited their said factum or points in argument in appeal, each party shall, at the request of the other, deliver to him *three* copies of his said factum or points.

31. Appeals shall be set down or inscribed for hearing in a book to be kept for that purpose by the Registrar at least *one month* before the first day of the session of the Court fixed for the hearing of the 'appeal.

Hearing.

32. No more than two Counsel on each side shall be heard on any appeal, and but one Counsel shall be heard in reply.

33. The Court may in its discretion postpone the hearing until any future day during the same session, or at any following session.

34. Appeals shall be heard in the order in which they have been set down, and if either party neglect to appear at the proper day to support or resist the appeal the Court may hear the other party and may give judgment without the intervention of the party so neglecting to appear, or may postpone the hearing upon such terms as to payment of costs or otherwise as the Court shall direct.

35. All orders of this Court in cases of appeal shall bear date on the day of the judgment or decision being pronounced, and shall be signed by the Registrar.

Adding Parties to the Appeal.

36. In any case not already provided for by the Act, in which it becomes essential to make an additional party to the appeal, either as apellant or respondent, and whether such proceeding becomes necessary in consequence of the death or insolvency of any original party, or from any other cause, such additional party may be added to the appeal by filing a suggestion as nearly as may be in the form provided for by section 43 of the Act.

37. The suggestion referred to in the next preceding rule may be set aside, on motion, by the Court or a Judge thereof.

38. Upon any such motion the Court or a Judge thereof may, in their or his discretion, direct evidence to be taken before a proper officer for that purpose, or may direct that the parties shall proceed in the proper Court for that purpose, to have any question tried and determined ; and in such case all proceedings in appeal may be stayed until after the trial and determination of the said question.

Motions.

39. All interlocutory applications in appeals shall be made by motion, supported by affidavit, to be filed in the office of the Registrar before the notice of motion is served. The notice of motion shall be served at least *four clear days* before the time of hearing.

Justice.

40. Such notice of motion may be served upon the solicitor or attorney of the opposite party by delivering a copy thereof to the booked agent or at the elected domicile of such solicitor or attorney to whom it is addressed at the City of Ottawa. If the solicitor or attorney has no booked agent, or has elected no domicile at the City of Ottawa, or, if a party to be served with the notice of motion has not elected a domicile at the City of Ottawa, such notice may be served by affixing a copy thereof in some conspicuous place in the office of the Registrar of this Court.

41. Service of a notice of motion shall be accompanied with copies of affidavits filed in support of the motion.

42. Upon application supported by affidavit, and after notice to the opposite party, the Court or a Judge thereof may give further reasonable time for filing the printed case, depositing the printed factum or points of either party, and setting down or inscribing the appeal for hearing, as required by the foregoing rules.

43. Motions to be made before the Court are to be set down in a list or paper, and are to be called on each morning of the Session before the hearing of appeals is proceeded with.

Appeals to be deemed out of Court for delay.

44. Unless the appeal is brought on for hearing by the appellant within *one year* next after the security shall have been allowed, it shall be held to have been abandoned without any order to ·dismiss being required, unless the Court or a Judge thereof shall otherwise order.

45. The foregoing Rules shall be applicable to appeals from the Exchequer Court of Canada, except in so far as the Act has otherwise provided.

Criminal Appeals.

46. The foregoing rules shall not, except as hereinbefore provided, apply to criminal appeals, nor to appeals in matters of Habeas Corpus.

47. In the cases mentioned in the next preceding rule no printed case shall be required, and no factum or points for argument in appeal need be deposited with the Registrar, but such appeals may be heard on a written case, certified under the seal of the Court appealed from, and which case shall contain all judgments and opinions pronounced in the Court below.

48. In criminal appeals and in appeals in cases of Habeas Corpus, and unless the Court or a Judge shall otherwise order, the case must be filed as follows :—

1. In appeals from any of the Provinces other than British Columbia, at least *one month* before the first day of the Session at which it is set down to be heard.

2. In appeals from British Columbia, at least *two months* before the said day.

49. In cases of criminal appeals and appeals in matters of Habeas Corpus, notice of hearing shall be served the respective times hereinafter fixed before the first day of the general or special session at which the same is appointed to be heard ; that is to say :—

1. In appeals from Ontario and Quebec, *two weeks.*

Justice.

2. In appeals from Nova Scotia, New Brunswick, and Prince Edward's Islands, *three weeks*

3. In appeals from Manitoba, *one month*.

4. In appeals from British Columbia, *six weeks*.

Election Appeals.

50. The foregoing rules are not to apply to appeals in Controverted Election cases.

51 In such election appeals the party appellant shall deposit with the Registrar such sum as shall be required for printing the record or so much thereof as a Judge may direct to be printed at the rate of thirty cents per folio of one hundred words.

52. The Registrar shall cause *twenty-five* copies of the said record to be printed in the same form as hereinbefore provided for the case in ordinary appeals for the use of the Court and its officers, and also *twenty* additional copies, *ten* of which are, upon his request, to be delivered to the appellant free of charge, and *ten* to the respondent upon payment of thirty cents for each folio of one hundred words in the record so printed.

53. The factum or points for argument in appeal in Controverted Election appeals shall be printed as hereinbefore provided in the case of ordinary appeals.

54. The points for argument in appeal or factum in Controverted Election cases shall be deposited with the Registrar at least *three days* before the first day of the session fixed for the hearing of the appeal, and are to be interchanged by the parties in manner hereinbefore provided with regard to the factum or points in ordinary appeals.

55. In Election appeals a judge in chambers may, upon the application of the appellant, make an order dispensing with the printing of the whole or any part of the record, and may also dispense with the delivery of any factum or points for argument in appeal. Such order may be obtained *ex parte*, and the party obtaining it shall forthwith cause it to be served upon the adverse party

Fees.

56. The fees mentioned in Schedule C to these orders shall be paid to the Registrar by stamps to be prepared for that purpose,

Costs.

57. Costs in appeal between party and party shall be taxed pursuant to the tariff of fees contained in Schedule D to these orders.

58. The Court or a Judge may direct a fixed sum for costs to be paid in lieu of directing the payment of costs to be taxed.

59. The payment of costs, if so ordered, may be enforced by process of execution in the same manner and by means of the same writ and according to the same practice as may be in use from time to time in the Exchequer Court of Canada.

Justice.

60. Contempts incurred by reason of non-compliance with any order of the Court other than order for payment of money may be punished in the same manner and by means of the same process and writs and according to the same practice as may be in use from time to time in the Exchequer Court of Canada.

Cross Appeals.

61. It shall not, under any circumstances, be necessary for a respondent to give notice of motion by way of cross appeal, but if a respondent intends, upon the hearing of an appeal, to contend that the decision of the Court below should be varied, he shall, within the time specified in the next Rule, or such time as may be prescribed by the special order of a Judge, give notice of such intention to any parties who may be affected by such contention. The omission to give such notice shall not in any way interfere with the power of the Court on the hearing of an appeal to treat the whole case as open, but may, in the discretion of the Court, be ground for an adjournment of the appeal, or for a special order as to costs.

62. Subject to any special order which may be made, notice by a respondent under the last preceding Rule shall be *one month's* notice.

63. A respondent who gives a notice pursuant to the two last preceding Rules shall, before or within *two days* after he has served such notice, deposit a printed factum or points for argument in appeal with the Registrar as hereinbefore provided as regards the principal appeal, and the parties upon whom such notice has been served shall, within *two weeks* after service thereof upon them, deposit their printed factum or points with the Registrar, and such factum or points shall be interchanged between the parties as hereinbefore provided as to the principal appeal.

Translations.

64. Any Judge may require that the factum or points for argument in appeal of any party shall be translated into the language with which such judge is most familiar; and in that case the Judge shall direct the Registrar to cause the same to be translated, and shall fix the number of copies of the translation to be printed, and the time within which the same shall be deposited with the Registrar; and the party depositing such factum shall thereupon cause the same forthwith to be printed at his own expense, and such party shall not be deemed to have deposited his factum until the required number of the printed copies of the translation shall have been deposited with the Registrar.

65. Any Judge may also require the Registrar to cause the judgments and opinions of the Judges in the Court below to be translated, and in that case the Judge shall fix the number of copies of the translation to be printed and the term within which they shall be deposited with the Registrar, and such translation shall thereupon be printed at the expense of the appellant.

Payment of Money into Court.

66. Any party directed by any order of the Court or a Judge to pay money into Court must apply at the office of the Registrar for a direction

Justice.

so to do, which direction must be taken to the Ottawa Branch or Agency of the Bank of Montreal and the money there paid to the credit of the cause or matter ; and after payment the receipt obtained from the Bank must be filed at the Registrar's office.

Payment of Money out of Court.

67. If money is to be paid out of Court, an order of the Court or a Judge must be obtained for that purpose, upon notice to the opposite party.

68. Money ordered to be paid out of Court is to be so paid upon the cheque of the Registrar, countersigned by a Judge.

Formal objections not to prevail.

69. No proceeding in the said Court shall be defeated by any formal objection.

Extending or abridging time.

70. In any appeal or other proceeding the Court or a Judge may enlarge or abridge the time for doing any act, or taking any proceeding, upon such (if any) terms as the justice of the case may require.

71. The Registrar is to keep in his office all appropriate books for recording the proceedings in all suits and matters in the said Supreme Court.

Computation of Time.

72. In all cases in which any particular number of days not expressed to be clear days, is prescribed by the foregoing rules, the same shall be reckoned exclusively of the first day and inclusively of the last day, unless such last day shall happen to fall on a Sunday, or a day appointed by the Governor General for a public fast or thanksgiving, or any other legal holiday or non-juridical day, as provided by the Statutes of the Dominion of Canada.

73. If it happens at any time that the number of Judges necessary to constitute a quorum for the transaction of the business to be brought before the Court is not present, the Judge or Judges then present may adjourn the sittings of the Court to the next or some other day and so on from day to day until a quorum shall be present.

Vacations.

74. There shall be a vacation at Christmas, commencing on the 15th of December and ending on the 10th of January.

75. The long vacation shall comprise the months of July and August.

Interpretation.

76. In the preceding rules the term " A Judge " means any Judge of the said Supreme Court, transacting business out of Court.

Justice.

77. In the preceding rules the following words have the several meanings hereby assigned to them over and above their several ordinary meanings, unless there be something in the subject or context repugnant to such construction, that is to say :—

(1) Words importing the singular number include the plural number, and words importing the plural number include the singular number.

(2) Words importing the masculine gender include females.

(3) The word " party " or " parties " includes a body politic or corporate and also Her Majesty the Queen and Her Majesty's Attorney-General.

(4) The word " Affidavit " includes affirmation.

(5) The words " The Act " mean " The Supreme and Exchequer Court Act."

Dated this seventh day of February A.D. 1876.

Certified.

ROBERT CASSELS,
Registrar, S.C.C.

SCHEDULE A.

Dominion of }
  Canada. }

The Supreme Court will hold a special session at the City of Ottawa on   the   day of   187 for the purpose of hearing causes and disposing of such other business as may be brought before the Court (*or* for the purpose of hearing Election appeals, criminal appeals, *or* appeals in cases of *habeas corpus, or* for the purpose of giving judgments only *as the case may be.*)

By order of the Chief Justice,
or
By order of Mr. Justice,
(Signed)

R. C.
Registrar.

Dated this   day of   187

Justice.

SCHEDULE B.

FORM OF NOTICE OF HEARING APPEAL.

In the Supreme Court }
    of Canada. }

A. B., Appellant and C. D., Respondent.

Take notice that this appeal will be heard at the next session of the Court to be held at the City of Ottawa, on   the day of   187

To

Appellant's Solicitor or Attorney,
or
Appellant in person.

Dated this   day of }
      187 }

SCHEDULE C,

TARIFF OF FEES TO BE PAID TO THE REGISTRAR OF THE SUPREME COURT OF CANADA.

On entering every appeal.................................\$10 00
On entering every judgment, decree or order in the
      nature of a final judgment........................ 10 00
On entering every other judgment, decree or order   2 00

In other matters the fees shall be regulated by the Tariff in force in the Exchequer Court of Canada in actions of the first class, and in every case not thereby provided for, the fees to be paid shall be in the discretion of the Registrar, subject to revision by the Court or a Judge.

Marine.

By Order in Council of 23rd July, 1874, Port Maitland, N.S., is made a Port for Registration of Shipping,
Vide Canada Gazette, Vol. 8, p. 82.

By Order in Council of 10th October, 1874, a By-Law of the Quebec Harbour Commissioners, to prevent injury to the Commissioners' Wharves by rapid travel over them, was approved.
Vide Canada Gazette, Vol. 8, p. 402.

By Order in Council, of 8th March, 1875, His Excellency declares the Ports of Victoria and Esquimalt, in the Province of British Columbia, Ports at and for which Port Wardens may be appointed for all the purposes of the "Act to provide for the appointment of Port Wardens at certain Ports of the Dominion."
Vide Canada Gazette, Vol. 8, p. 1190.

By Order in Council, of the 29th March, 1875, His Excellency declares the Port of Halifax, in the Province of Nova Scotia, to be a Port at and for which a Port Warden may be appointed for all the purposes of the "Act to provide for the appointment of Port Wardens at certain Ports of the Dominion."
Vide Canada Gazette. Vol. 8. p. 1190

By Order in Council of the 3rd April, 1875, certain rules and regulations for the government of the Port of Lunenburg, in the Province of Nova Scotia, under the Acts 36 Vict., chap 9, 38 Vict., chap. 80, and for the government of the office of Harbour Master for the said Ports, were sanctioned.
Vide Canada Gazette, Vol 9, page 135.

By Order in Council of 3rd April, 1875, His Excellency, on the recommendation of the Honorable the Minister of Marine and Fisheries, and under the provisions of the Act passed in the 36th year of Her Majesty's Reign, and intituled : "An Act respecting Pilotage," by and with the advice of the Queen's Privy Council for Canada, was pleased to order that a Pilotage District be and the same was thereby formed for the County of Richmond, in the Province of Nova Scotia, "the limits of which district extend from the entrance of Arichat Harbor to Cape Canso, and from Cape Canso to Fourchu, in the County referred to ;" and His Excellency, under the

Marine.

authority aforesaid, was further pleased to make the payment of Pilotage Dues compulsory within the limits of the said District.
Vide Canada Gazette, Vol. 8, p. 1221.

———

By Order in Council of the 4th day of April, 1875, certain By-Laws of the Trinity House of Quebec, relating to the mooring of steamships, &c., passed on the 4th March, 1875, were approved and sanctioned.
Vide Canada Gazette, Vol. 8, p. 1810.

———

By Order in Council of the 7th day of April, 1875, on the recommendation of the Honorable the Minister of Marine and Fisheries, and under the provisions of the 4th section of the Act passed in the Session of Parliament of Canada, held in the 36th year of Her Majesty's Reign, chaptered 55, and intituled : "An Act respecting Wreck and Salvage," His Excellency, by and with the advice of the Queen's Privy Council for Canada, was pleased to constitute and establish the County of Yarmouth, in the Province of Nova Scotia, a District for all the purposes of the said Act.
Vide Canada Gazette, Vol. 8, p. 1221.

———

By a Proclamation of the 10th April, 1875, His Excellency, in Her Majesty's name, declared the Act intituled "An Act to provide for " the appointment of Harbour Masters for certain Ports in the Provinces of " Quebec, Ontario, British Columbia and Prince Edward Island," to be in force at, and with respect to, the Port of Nanaimo, in the Province of British Columbia.
Vide Canada Gazette, Vol. 8, p. 1247.

———

By a Proclamation of the 10th April, 1875, His Excellency, in Her Majesty's name, declared the Act intituled "An Act to provide for " the appointment of Harbour Masters for certain Ports in the Provinces " of Nova Scotia and New Brunswick," to be in force at, and with respect to, the Port of Harvey, in the County of Albert, in the Province of New Brunswick.
Vide Canada Gazette, Vol. 8, p. 1248.

———

By a Proclamation of the 8th March, 1876, His Excellency, in Her Majesty's name, declared the Act intituled : "An Act to provide for the " appointment of Harbour Masters for certain Ports in the Provinces of Nova " Scotia and New Brunswick" to be in force at, and with respect to the Port of Mulgrave, in the County of Guysboro', in the Province of Nova Scotia one of the Provinces of Our Dominion of Canada.
Vide Canada Gazette, Vol. 9, p. 1201.

Marine.

By a Proclamation of the 10th April, 1875, His Excellency, in Her Majesty's name, declared the Act intituled "An Act to provide for "the appointment of Harbour Masters for certain Ports in the Provinces of "Quebec, Ontario, British Columbia and Prince Edward Island," to be in force at, and with respect to, the Ports of Grand River, Rollo Bay, Bay Fortune, Souris and St. Peter's Bay, in the County of Kings, in the Province of Prince Edward Island.
Vide Canada Gazette, Vol. 8, p. 1248.

———

By Order in Council of the 12th day of April, 1875, certain By-Laws of a general nature, of the Harbour Commissioners of Montreal, passed on the 26th day of January, 1875, were approved and sanctioned.
Vide Canada Gazette, Vol. 8, p. 1259.

———

GOVERNMENT HOUSE, OTTAWA,
Wednesday, 5th day of May, 1875.

Present :

HIS EXCELLENCY THE GOVERNOR GENERAL IN COUNCIL.

ON the recommendation of the Honorable the Minister of Marine and Fisheries, and under the provisions of the Act passed in the 36th year of Her Majesty's Reign, and intituled : "An Act respecting Pilotage ;" His Excellency the Governor General, by and with the advice of the Queen's Privy Council for Canada, has been pleased to order, and it is hereby ordered, that a Pilotage District be, and the same is hereby formed for the Province of British Columbia, the limits of which district shall extend from the shores of Washington Territory to the Northern Boundary of the Province, and include the entire Coast of British Columbia with its Rivers and Harbors.

And His Excellency, under the authority aforesaid, has been further pleased to make the payment of Pilotage Dues compulsory within the limits of the said District.

W. A. HIMSWORTH,
Clerk, Privy Council.

———

RULES AND REGULATIONS

Made by the Board of Steamboat Inspection for the guidance of Engineers of Steamboats under the provisions of the Act 31 Vict., chap. 65, intituled : "An Act respecting the Inspection of Steamboats and for the greater safety "of passengers by them," as amended by the 1st section of the Act 36 Vict., chap. 53 intituled : "An Act to amend the Acts respecting the Inspection of "Steamboats."

9

Marine.

RULE I.

Engineers are required in all cases, upon the stopping of the engine to open the safety-valve, so as to keep the steam in the boiler below the limit allowed by the Inspector's Certificate, as prescribed by law, to open the furnace doors or close the dampers ; and when from accident or other cause the water in the boiler has fallen below the point of safety, to put out the fires immediately.

RULE II.

Engineers shall keep the fire-pumps and hose and their connections in perfect condition ready for immediate use, and when found unfit for use from age or other cause, shall report their condition to the Inspector by whom the steamer was last inspected.

RULE III.

Engineers when laying up a steamer in the Fall, or when finally leaving her, are required to report to the owner, and also to the Inspector of the nearest District, any defects of or injury to the Boilers or Machinery by which the safety of the same may be endangered. They shall also report to the Inspector of the District at which the steamer next arrives any accident happening to the boilers or machinery during the trip, and in case of omission to make such report, the license of the Engineer so omitting shall be revoked.

RULE IV.

The Chief Engineer of a steamer is held accountable by the Board for the proper care and management of the boilers and machinery under his charge. He is therefore in no case to absent himself from the vessel while on her regular trips unless a competent substitute be provided to fill his place during such absence.

RULE V.

Engineers on first taking charge of a steamer, and at least once a year thereafter, shall satisfy themselves by close examination that the braces, stays and pins of the boiler are in good order, and sufficient for the strain to which they may be subjected ; they shall also satisfy themselves that the safety-valves are in good working order and sufficient for the requirements named in Rule I. hereof.

RULE VI.

Engineers holding temporary certificates requiring a further license must go before the Board as soon as possible after the expiration of the time for which the temporary certificate has been granted, for the purpose of obtaining an annual certificate. No re-issue of a temporary certificate will be made unless the applicant shews good and sufficient reason for not appearing before the Board as required.

Marine.

RULE VII.

Engineers are to exhibit their certificates in the engine room along with a copy of these Rules.

Inspectors of steamboats are hereby directed to see that the foregoing Rules and Regulations are strictly enforced.

PRIVY COUNCIL CHAMBERS,
OTTAWA, 14th May, 1875.

I hereby certify that the foregoing Rules and Regulations made by the Board of Steamboat Inspectors were submitted to and approved by His Excellency the Governor General in Council, on the 5th day of May instant.

W. A. HIMSWORTH,
Clerk, Privy Council.

By Proclamation of the 17th day of May, 1875, His Excellency, in Her Majesty's name, declared the "Act to provide for the appointment of Harbour Masters for certain ports in Nova Scotia and New Brunswick" to be in force at, and with respect to, Great Shemogue, New Brunswick.
Vide Canada Gazette, Vol. 8, p. 1545.

By a Proclamation dated 17th May, 1875, His Excellency, in Her Majesty's name, declared that the Act intituled: "An Act to provide for the appointment of Harbour Masters for certain Ports in the Provinces of Nova Scotia and New Brunswick," was in force at, and with respect to, the Port of Shediac, in the County of Westmoreland, in the Province of New Brunswick.
Vide Canada Gazette, Vol. 8, p 1546.

By a Proclamation of the 17th May, 1875, His Excellency, in Her Majesty's name, declared the Act intituled: "An Act to provide for the "appointment of Harbour Masters for certain Ports in the Provinces of "Quebec, Ontario, British Columbia and Prince Edward Island" to be in force at, and with respect to, the Port of Tracadie, West River and Rustico, in the Province of Prince Edward Island.
Vide Canada Gazette, Vol. 8, p. 1545.

Marine.

By Order in Council of the 14th June, 1875, His Excellency established in the County of Inverness, in the Province of Nova Scotia, a Wreck and Salvage District to be called the Southern District of that County, and to extend from the County line of Inverness, on the said Strait of Canso to Mabou Harbor, and also in said County, a District to be called the Northern District, and to extend from Mabou Harbour to the County line of Inverness aforesaid, at Cape North.
Vide Canada Gazette, Vol. 8, p. 1711.

———

By Order in Council of 14th June, 1875, a Shipping Office for the shipping of seamen, &c., was constituted at Port Hawkesbury, N. S.
Vide Canada Gazette, Vol. 8, p. 1711.

———

By Order in Council of the same date, the payment of pilotage dues was made compulsory in the Pilotage District of King's and Hants, N. S.
Vide Canada Gazette, Vol. 8, p. 1711.

———

By an Order in Council of the 21st day of June, 1875, a tariff of fees to be paid to the Port Warden of Halifax, Nova Scotia, made by the Chamber of Commerce of that city, was approved.
Vide Canada Gazette, Vol. 8, p. 1712.

———

By Order in Council of 22nd June, 1875, Rules and Regulations for the Port of Shediac and the Harbour Master there were approved.
Vide Canada Gazette, Vol. 8, p. 1713.

———

By Order in Council of 22nd June, 1875, Pilotage Rules for the Sydney (N.S.) District were approved.
Vide Canada Gazette, vol. 8, p. 1715.

———

By Order in Council of 25th June, 1875, Pilotage Rules for the Port of Halifax were approved.
Vide Canada Gazette, Vol. 8, p. 1712.

———

By Order in Council of 25th June, 1875, additional rules for the Pilotage District of Pictou, N.S., were approved.
Vide Canada Gazette, vol. 8, p. 1716.

Marine.

By Order in Council of the 9th day of July, 1875, the Port of Truro, in the County of Colchester, in the Province of Nova Scotia, was constituted a Port for the registration of Shipping; Collector of Customs at the said Port to be Registrar of Shipping, and to superintend the Survey and Measurement of Ships thereat under the provisions of the 3rd section of the Imperial Colonial Shipping Act, 1868, the 11th section of the Act 36 Vict., chap. 128, and the 77th section of the Act 36 Vict., chap. 129, respecting the Shipping of Seamen. Londonderry to cease to be a Port for the registration of Shipping.
Vide Canada Gazette, Vol. 9, p. 67.

By Order in Council of the same date, the Port of Winnipeg, in the Province of Manitoba, was also constituted a Port for the registration of Shipping; Collector of Customs at that Port to be Registrar of Shipping, and to superintend the Survey and Measurement of Ships thereat, under the provisions of the 3rd section of the Imperial Colonial Shipping Act of 1868, the 11th section of the Act 36 Vict., chap. 128, and the 77th section of the Act 36 Vic., chap. 129, respecting the Shipping of Seamen.
Vide Canada Gazette, Vol. 9, p. 67.

By Orders in Council of the 9th and 14th July, 1875, certain Rules and Regulations of the Pilotage Authority for the District of St. John, N.B., were sanctioned.
Vide Canada Gazette, Vol. 9, p. 68.

By Order in Council of 14th July, 1875, certain Rules and Regulations for the Pilotage District of Richibucto, N.B., were sanctioned.
Vide Canada Gazette, Vol. 9, p. 69.

By a Proclamation of 16th July 1876, His Excellency, in Her Majesty's name, declares that the Act intituled : "An Act to provide for the appointment of Harbour Masters for certain Ports in the Provinces of Nova Scotia "and New Brunswick" shall henceforth be in force at, and with respect to, the Port of Tracadie, in the County of Gloucester, in the Province of New Brunswick.
Vide Canada Gazette, Vol. 9, p. 91.

By a Proclamation of the 16th July, 1875, His Excellency, in Her Majesty's name, declares that the Act intituled : "An Act to provide for the "appointment of Harbour Masters for certain Ports in the Province of Nova "Scotia and New Brunswick," shall henceforth be in force at, and with respect to the Ports of port Hood and Port Hawkesbury, in the County of Inverness, in the Province of Nova Scotia.
Vide Canada Gazette, Vol. 9, p. 92.

Marine.

By a Proclamation of 16th July, 1875, His Excellency in Her Majesty's name, declares that the Act intituled : "An Act to provide for the appoint- "ment of Harbour Masters for certain Ports in the Provinces of Nova Scotia "and New Brunswick," shall henceforth be in force at, and with respect to, the Port at Margaret's Bay, in the County of Halifax, in the Province of Nova Scotia.
Vide Canada Gazette, Vol. 9. p. 92.

By Order in Council of the 22nd day of July, 1875, Port Mulgrave, in the County of Guysborough and Province of Nova Scotia, was constituted a Port at and for which a Port Warden may be appointed.
Vide Canada Gazette, Vol. 9, p. 188.

By Order in Council of the 22nd July, 1875, a Shipping Office is established at the Port of Charlottetown, in the Province of Prince Edward Island.
Vide Canada Gazette, Vol. 9, p. 94.

By Order in Council of the 27th July, 1875, certain Rules and Regula- tions for the Government of the Port of Getson's Cove, in the Province of Nova Scotia, and of the office of Harbour Master of the said Port, were sanctioned.
Vide Canada Gazette, Vol. 9, p. 181.

By Order in Council of the 28th July, 1875, His Excellency the Administrator of the Government declared and determined that Port Hawkesbury, in the County of Inverness, in the Province of Nova Scotia, be a Port at and for which a Port Warden may be appointed.
Vide Canada Gazette, Vol. 9, p. 281.

GOVERNMENT HOUSE, OTTAWA,
Monday, 13th day of September, 1875.

Present :

HIS EXCELLENCY THE ADMINISTRATOR OF THE GOVERNMENT IN COUNCIL

ON the recommendation of the Honorable the Minister of Marine and Fisheries, and under the provisions of the 16th section of the Act passed in the Session of the Parliament of Canada, held in the Thirty-first year of Her Majesty's Reign, chaptered 65, and intituled "An Act respecting "the Inspection of Steamboats and for the greater safety of passengers by "them," as amended by the 2nd section of the Act 32 and 33 Victoria, chap. 89, and the 2nd, 5th and 7th sections of the Act 37 Victoria, chap. 30, His Excellency, by and with the advice of the Queen's Privy Council for Canada, has been pleased to order, and it is hereby ordered, that the follow- ing Rules and Regulations respecting Life-Boats, Yawl Boats and Fire Extinguishers on Steamers, passed by the Board of Steamboat Inspection at Ottawa on the 19th day of November, 1874, be and the same are hereby approved and adopted, that is to say :—

Marine.

Rule I.—The Life-Boat required by Section 16, 31 Victoria, chap. 65, may be considered of sufficient capacity, if made of the following dimensions :—

	Ft.	in.
Length of Keel	22	0
Breadth of Beam from metal to metal	5	6
Depth from top of Keel to top of Gunwale	2	9

Rule II.—The Life-Boat required by Section 5 of the amended Act 37 Victoria, chap. 30, may be considered of sufficient capacity, if made of the following dimensions :—

	Ft.	in.
Length of Keel	18	0
Breadth between metal and metal	5	2
Depth from top of Keel to top of Gunwale	2	2

Rule III.—The carrying capacity in number of persons of Yawl Boats shall be determined as follows, viz. :—

By multiplying the length of the Keel by the breadth and by the depth from top of Keel to Gunwale in feet, and then dividing the product by ten, the quotient will be the number of persons allowable to each boat.

Rule IV.—It is hereby required that the following number of Chemical Fire Extinguishers shall be carried on board Steamboats of the undermentioned sizes and classes, viz. :—

On every Freight and Tug Steamboat of more than one hundred tons gross measurement, one such Extinguisher.

On every Freight and Tug Steamboat of more than five hundred tons, two such Extinguishers.

On every Steamboat of the gross tonnage of one hundred tons and upwards, but less than three hundred tons, carrying passengers, two such Extinguishers.

On every Steamboat of the gross tonnage of three hundred tons and upwards, carrying passengers, three such Extinguishers.

On every Steamboat employed chiefly in the carriage of Freight, when not carrying more than fifty passengers, two such Extinguishers.

W. A. HIMSWORTH,
Clerk, Privy Council.

———

By a Proclamation of the 23rd September, 1875, His Excellency, in Her Majesty's name, declared the Act intituled : "An Act to provide for the "appointment of Harbour Masters for certain Ports in the Provinces of Nova "Scotia and New Brunswick," to be in force at, and with respect to, the Port of Baddeck, in the County of Victoria, in the Province of Nova Scotia.
Vide Canada Gazette, Vol. 9, p. 406.

———

Marine.

By a Proclamation of the 23rd day of September, 1875, His Excellency, in Her Majesty's name, declared the Act intituled: "An Act to provide " for the appointment of Harbour Masters for certain Ports in the Provinces of "Quebec, Ontario, British Columbia and Prince Edward Island," to be in force at, and with respect to, the Port of Southampton, in the Province of Ontario.
Vide Canada Gazette, Vol. 9, p. 406.

———

By a Proclamation of the 29th October, 1875, His Excellency, in Her Majesty's name, declared the Act intituled: "An Act to provide for " the appointment of Harbour Masters for certain Ports in the Provinces of " Nova Scotia and New Brunswick," to be in force at, and with respect to, the Port of Whycocomah, in the County of Inverness, in the Province of Nova Scotia.
Vide Canada Gazette, Vol. 9, p. 560.

———

By Order in Council of the 23rd day of November, 1875, His Excellency has constituted and established a District for the purposes of the Act respecting Wreck and Salvage, to extend from Fox Point, in the County of Gaspé, and Province of Quebec, to the boundary line between the Counties of Gaspé and Rimouski, in said Province.
Vide Canada Gazette, Vol. 9, p. 665.

———

By Proclamation of the 20th April, 1876, His Excellency, in Her Majesty's name, declared the Act intituled " An Act to provide for appointment " of Harbour Masters for certain Ports in the Provinces of Nova Scotia and " New Brunswick " to be in force at, and with respect to the Port of Cheti-camp, in the County of Inverness, in the Province of Nova Scotia.
Vide Canada Gazette, Vol. 9, p. 1385.

———

NOTE—See also pp. clix and clx.

Fisheries.

GOVERNMENT HOUSE, OTTAWA,
Saturday, 3rd day of April, 1875.

Present :

HIS EXCELLENCY THE GOVERNOR GENERAL IN COUNCIL.

ON the recommendation of the Honorable the Minister of Marine and Fisheries, and under the provisions of the 19th section of " The Fisheries Act," His Excellency, by and with the advice of the Queen's Privy Council for Canada, has been pleased to make the following Special Fishery Regulation :

" No person shall carry on Cod-fishing with seines at a less distance " than one-half mile from any fishing grounds where fishing boats are " anchored and fishermen actually engaged fishing for Cod-fish with hooks " and lines."

W. A. HIMSWORTH,
Clerk, Privy Council.

By Order in Council of the 3rd day of April, 1875, the following Regulations were approved :

GENERAL FISHERY REGULATIONS FOR THE PROVINCE OF ONTARIO.

*Close-time for Whitefish.

" No person shall fish for, catch, kill, buy, sell, or have in possession, any Whitefish, between the 10th day of November and the 1st day of December in each year, in the Province of Ontario."

*Close-time for Salmon-Trout and Lake-Trout.

" No person shall fish for, catch, kill, buy, sell, or have in possession, any Salmon-Trout or Lake-Trout, between the 15th day of October and the 1st day of December in each year, in the Province of Ontario."

Close-time for Speckled-Trout, Brook or River-Trout.

" No person shall fish for, catch, kill, buy, sell, or have in possession, any Speckled-Trout, Brook or River-Trout, between the 15th day of September and the 1st day of January in each year, in the Province of Ontario."

*Close-time for Fresh-Water Herrings.

" No person shall fish for, catch, kill, buy, sell, or have in possession, any Fresh-Water Herrings, between the 15th day of October and the 1st day of December in each year, in the Province of Ontario."

* But see O. in C. of 30th September, 1875.—p. cxli.

Fisheries.

Close-time for Bass.

" No person shall fish for, catch, kill, buy, sell, or have in possession, any Bass, between the 15th day of May and the 15th day of June in each year, in the Province of Ontario."

Close-time for Pickerel (Dorée) and Maskinongé.

" No person shall fish for, catch, kill, buy, sell, or have in possession, any Pickerel (*Dorée*), or Maskinongé, between the 15th day of April and the 15th day of May in each year, in the Province of Ontario."

Fishery Leases and Licenses in the Province of Ontario.

" Fishing by means of nets or other apparatus without leases or licenses from the Department of Marine and Fisheries, is prohibited in all waters situated within the Province of Ontario."

GENERAL FISHERY REGULATIONS FOR THE PROVINCE OF QUEBEC.

Close-time for Whitefish.

" No person shall fish for, catch, kill, buy, sell, or have in possession, any Whitefish, between the 10th day of November and the 1st day of December in each year, in the Province of Quebec."

Close-time for Salmon-Trout, Lake-Trout or "Lunge" and "Winnoniche."

" No person shall fish for, catch, kill, buy, sell, or have in possession, any Salmon-Trout, Lake-Trout or "Lunge," between the 15th day of October and the 1st day of December in each year, in the Province of Quebec."

Close-time for Speckled-Trout, Brook or River-Trout.

" No person shall fish for, catch, kill, buy, sell, or have in possession, any Speckled-Trout, Brook or River-Trout, between the 15th day of September and the 1st day of January in each year, in the Province of Quebec."

Close-time for Bass.

" No person shall fish for, catch, kill, buy, sell, or have in possession, any Bass, between the 15th day of May and the 15th day of June in each year, in the Province of Quebec."

Close-time for Pickerel (Dorée), and Maskinongé.

" No person shall fish for, catch, kill, buy, sell, or have in possession, any Pickerel (*Dorée*), or Maskinongé, between the 15th day of April and the 15th day of May in each year, in the Province of Quebec."

Fisheries.

Close-time for Lobsters.

" In the Province of Quebec, no person shall, during the months of July and August, fish for, catch, kill, buy, sell, or have in possession, any soft shelled Lobsters or female Lobsters, with eggs attached, nor shall Lobsters of a less size than nine inches in length, measuring from head to tail, exclusive of claws or feelers, be at any time fished for, caught, killed, bought, sold or had in possession; but when caught by accident in nets or other fishing apparatus lawfully used for other fish, Lobsters with eggs attached, soft shelled and young Lobsters of a less size than nine inches, shall be liberated alive, at the risk and cost of the owner of the net or apparatus, or by the occupier of the fishery, on whom, in every case, shall devolve the proof of such actual liberation."

Fishery Leases and Licenses in the Province of Quebec.

" Fishing by means of nets or other apparatus without leases or licenses from the Department of Marine and Fisheries, is prohibited in all waters situated within the Province of Quebec."
Vide Canada Gazette, Vol. 8, p. 1219.

RECAPITULATION OF CLOSE SEASONS FOR FISH IN THE PROVINCES OF ONTARIO AND QUEBEC.

ONTARIO.

Speckled-Trout, Brook or River-Trout.—From 15th September to 1st January.
Bass.—From 15th May to 15th June.
Pickerel (Dorée).—From 15th April to 15th May.
Maskinongé.—From 15th April to 15th May.

QUEBEC.

Whitefish.—From 10th November to 1st December.
Salmon-Trout, Lake-Trout, or "Lunge."—From 15th October to 1st December.
Speckled-Trout, Brook or River Trout—From 15th September to 1st January.
Bass.—From 15th May to 15th June.
Pickerel (Dorée).—From 15th April to 15th May.
Maskinonge.—From 15th April to 15th May.
Lobsters—From 1st July to 31st August.

---

* But see O. in C., 20th April.—p. cxliv.

Fisheries.

By Order in Council of the 28th day of April, 1875, Fishery Regulations for the following Counties in the Provinces of Nova Scotia and New Brunswick respectively were established, viz.:

NOVA SCOTIA.

For the County of Halifax; for the District of Chester, Lunenburg County; for the Western District of Lunenburg; for the County of Queens; for the County of Shelburne; for the County of Yarmouth; Argyle River, Yarmouth County; for the County of Digby; for the County of Kings; for the County of Hants; for the County of Cumberland; for the County of Colchester; for the County of Pictou; for the County of Guysborough; for the County of Inverness; for the County of Victoria; for the County of Richmond; for the County of Cape Breton.

NEW BRUNSWICK.

For the County of Restigouche; for the County of Colchester; for the County of Northumberland; for the County of Kent; for the Counties of Westmoreland and Albert; for the Counties of St. John, Kings, Queens, Sunbury, York, Carleton and Victoria; for the County of Charlotte.
Vide Canada Gazette, Vol. 8, p. 1360 *et seq.*

By Order in Council of the 7th day of May, 1875, the special Fishery Regulations established by the Orders in Council hereinafter mentioned, were repealed, such Regulations having been superseded by the General Fishing Regulations established by the Order in Council of the third day of April, 1875, that is to say:—
The Orders in Council of the 18th day of May, 1868; the 10th day of September, 1868; the 9th day of April, 1869; the 9th day of June, 1869; the 30th day of June, 1869; the 14th day of February, 1870; the 22nd day of March, 1870; the 1st day of April, 1870; the 9th day of June, 1870; and the 17th day of August, 1870.
Vide Canada Gazette, Vol. 8, p. 1490.

GOVERNMENT HOUSE, OTTAWA.
Monday, 14th day of June, 1875.

PRESENT:

HIS EXCELLENCY THE ADMINISTRATOR IN COUNCIL.

ON the recommendation of the Honorable the Minister of Marine and Fisheries, and under the provisions of the "Fisheries Act," His Excellency, by and with the advice of the Queen's Privy Council for Canada, has been pleased to make the following Fishery Regulation for the County of Yarmouth, Province of Nova Scotia, in addition to the General Fishery Regulations adopted on the 28th April, 1875:

Fisheries.

" No Salmon or Alewives shall be taken in any manner on any stream
" in the County of Yarmouth from one hour after sunrise on Friday morning
" till an hour after sunrise on Monday morning."

W. A. HIMSWORTH,
Clerk, Privy Council.

GOVERNMENT HOUSE, OTTAWA.
Thursday, 22nd day of July, 1875.
Present :

HIS EXCELLENCY THE ADMINISTRATOR IN COUNCIL.

ON the recommendation of the Honorable the Minister of Marine and
Fisheries, and under the provisions of the " Fisheries Act," His Excellency, by and with the advice of the Queen's Privy Council for Canada,
has been pleased to make the following amendments in each of the Fishery
Regulations for the respective Counties in the Province of New Brunswick,
adopted by Order in Council of 28th April last.

" SALMON FISHING.

" The annual tax payable on every 200 lbs. weight of Salmon caught
" by nets shall be rated at forty cents."

" BASS FISHING.

" The annual tax payable on every 200 lbs. weight of Bass caught by
" nets shall be rated at twenty cents."

W. A. HIMSWORTH,
Clerk, Privy Council.

GOVERNMENT HOUSE, OTTAWA,
Thursday, 30th day of September, 1875.
Present :

HIS EXCELLENCY THE ADMINISTRATOR OF THE GOVERNMENT IN COUNCIL.

ON the recommendation of the Honorable the Minister of Marine and
Fisheries, and under the provisions of the 19th section of the Act
passed in the Session of the Parliament of Canada, held in the thirty-first
year of Her Majesty's Reign, chaptered 60, and known as " The Fisheries
Act," His Excellency, by and with the advice of the Queen's Privy Council
for Canada, has been pleased to Order, and it is hereby Ordered, that the
Regulations for the Province of Ontario relating to Whitefish, Salmon Trout
or Lake Trout and Herrings, adopted by the Governor General in Council
on the 3rd of April last, under the said Act, be, and the same are hereby
rescinded, and the following regulation be, and the same is hereby adopted
in lieu thereof:

Fisheries.

REGULATION.

Close Time for Whitefish, Salmon Trout or Lake Trout.

" No person shall fish for, catch, kill, buy, sell or possess any Whitefish, " Salmon Trout, or take Trout between the twelfth day of November and " the first day of December, in each year, in the Province of Ontario."

W. A. HIMSWORTH,
Clerk, Privy Council.

By a Proclamation of the 7th October, 1875, His Excellency, in Her Majesty's name, declared that the Act of the Parliament of Canada passed in the 31st year of Her Majesty's Reign and intituled " An Act for " the Regulation of Fishing and Protection of Fisheries," shall, upon, from and after this present seventh day of October instant, come into operation and be enforced in the Province of Prince Edward Island, and that the said seventh day of October was appointed for the coming in operation and being enforced in the Province of Prince Edward Island of said Act. *Vide Canada Gazette*, Vol. 9, p. 504.

GOVERNMENT HOUSE, OTTAWA.
Friday, 8th day of October, 1875.

Present :

HIS EXCELLENCY THE ADMINISTRATOR OF THE GOVERNMENT IN COUNCIL.

ON the recommendation of the Honorable the Minister of Marine and Fisheries, and under the provisions of the 19th section of the Act passed in the Session of the Parliament of Canada, held in the thirty-first year of Her Majesty's Reign, chaptered 60, and known as " The Fisheries Act," His Excellency, by and with the advice of the Queen's Privy Council for Canada, has been pleased to Order, and it is hereby Ordered, that the following Special Fishery Regulations for the Province of Prince Edward Island be, and they are hereby adopted :

REGULATIONS.

Salmon Fishery.

1. No person shall fish for, catch, kill, buy, sell or have in possession any Salmon between the first day of September and the thirty-first day of December, in each year, in the Province of Prince Edward Island ; nor shall any person fish for, catch, kill, buy, sell or possess at any time foul or spent Salmon, or Salmon fry in the said Province.

2. The Midgell, Morell, Dunk and Winter Rivers, in the aforesaid Province, are set apart for the natural and artificial propagation of fish.

Fisheries.

Trout Fishery.

3. No person shall fish for, catch, kill, buy, sell or possess any Trout between the first day of October and the first day of December, in each year, in the Province of Prince Edward Island; and Trout shall not at any time be fished for or taken by spears, sweep-nets or seines, in any river, stream or pond within the said Island.

W. A. HIMSWORTH,
Clerk, Privy Council.

GOVERNMENT HOUSE, OTTAWA,
Monday, 6th day of March, 1876.

Present :

HIS EXCELLENCY THE GOVERNOR GENERAL IN COUNCIL.

ON the recommendation of the Honorable the Minister of Marine and Fisheries, and under the provisions of " The Fisheries Act," His Excellency, by and with the advice of the Queen's Privy Council for Canada, has been pleased to Order, that so much of the Fishery Regulations for the Province of New Brunswick as relate to the size of the meshes of nets used for Bass fishing, passed on the 18th December, 1874, be, and the same is hereby rescinded, and that the following Regulation be, and the same is hereby adopted in its stead :

" In the Province of New Brunswick Bass shall not be fished for, " caught or killed by means of any kind of net having meshes of a less size " than five inches, extension measure."

W. A. HIMSWORTH,
Clerk, Privy Council.

GOVERNMENT HOUSE, OTTAWA,
Monday, 6th day of March, 1876.

Present :

HIS EXCELLENCY THE GOVERNOR GENERAL IN COUNCIL.

ON the recommendation of the Honorable the Minister of Marine and Fisheries, and under the provisions of " The Fisheries Act," His Excellency, by and with the advice of the Queen's Privy Council for Canada, has been pleased to make the following amendment to that part of the Revised Fishery Regulations having reference to the Close Season for Bass in the County of Northumberland, New Brunswick, adopted in Council on 28th April, 1875, viz. :

Fisheries.

"Fishing for bass in the Napan and Black Rivers, in the County of
"Northumberland, and along the shores of the main River Miramichi,
"between the mouths of Napan and Black Rivers, in the aforesaid County,
"in the Province of New Brunswick shall be permitted from the opening
"of navigation in the spring time until the 25th day of May, in each year."

W. A. HIMSWORTH,
Clerk, Privy Council.

GOVERNMENT HOUSE, OTTAWA,
Thursday, 20th day of April, 1876.

Present:

HIS EXCELLENCY THE GOVERNOR GENERAL IN COUNCIL.

ON the recommendation of the Honorable the Minister of Marine and
Fisheries, and under the provisions of the Act passed in the Session of
the Parliament of Canada, held in the 31st year of Her Majesty's Reign,
chaptered 60, and known as "The Fisheries Act," His Excellency, by and
with the advice of the Queen's Privy Council for Canada, has been pleased
to make the following Fishery Regulations:—
    "No person shall fish for, catch, kill, buy, sell, or possess any lobsters
"between the 10th day of July and the 20th day of August in each year:—
    "Female lobsters in spawn, or with eggs attached, soft shelled and
"young lobsters of less size than nine inches in length, measuring from
"head to tail, exclusive of claws or feelers, shall not be at any time fished
"for, caught, killed, bought, sold or possessed; but when caught by accident
"in nets or other fishing apparatus, lawfully used for other fish, lobsters
"in spawn, or with eggs attached, soft shelled and young lobsters of a less
"size than nine inches, shall be liberated alive, at the risk and cost of the
"owner of the net or apparatus, or by the occupier of the fishery, on whom,
"in every case, shall devolve the proof of such actual liberation."
    His Excellency has also been pleased to Order that the regulation
passed on the *24th of April, 1874, respecting "Lobster Fishing" be and the
same is hereby repealed.

W. A. HIMSWORTH,
Clerk, Privy Council.

GOVERNMENT HOUSE, OTTAWA,
Thursday, 20th day of April, 1876.

Present:

HIS EXCELLENCY THE GOVERNOR GENERAL IN COUNCIL.

ON the recommendation of the Honorable the Minister of Marine and
Fisheries, and under the provisions of the Act passed in the Session
of the Parliament of Canada held in the 31st year of Her Majesty's Reign,

---

* Qy.—3rd April (?) *ante.*

Fisheries.

chaptered 60, and known as "The Fisheries Act ; " His Excellency, by and with the advice of the Queen's Privy Council for Canada, has been pleased to make the following Fishery Regulation :

"Nets used for catching Shad in the Counties of Albert and Westmore-"land, in the Province of New Brunswick, shall not exceed two hundred "and fifty fathoms in length, each, and every boat engaged in fishing for "Shad shall be entered with the local Fishery Officer who will number the "same on the bow or stern thereof, and the owner shall also mark such "number on the sail, in legible characters."

W. A. HIMSWORTH,
Clerk, Privy Council.

GOVERNMENT HOUSE, OTTAWA,
Thursday, 20th day of April; 1876.

Present :

HIS EXCELLENCY THE GOVERNOR GENERAL IN COUNCIL.

ON the recommendation of the Honorable the Minister of Marine and Fisheries, and under the provisions of the Act passed in the Session of the Parliament of Canada, held in the 31st year of Her Majesty's Reign, chaptered 60, and known as "The Fisheries Act," His Excellency, by and with the advice of the Queen's Privy Council for Canada, has been pleased to make the following Fishery Regulation :—

"The use of explosive materials to catch or kill fish is forbidden in the Dominion of Canada."

W. A. HIMSWORTH,
Clerk, Privy Council.

Militia.

GENERAL REGULATIONS FOR THE GOVERNMENT OF THE MILITARY COLLEGE AT KINGSTON.

OBJECTS OF THE COLLEGE.

1. The Military College is established for the purpose of imparti ng a complete education in all branches of military tactics, fortification, engineering, and general scientific knowledge in subjects connected with, and necessary to. a thorough knowledge of the military profession, and for qualifying officers for command and for staff appointments.

(*a*) The length of the course of instruction will be four years.

REGULATIONS FOR ADMISSION.

2. Admission to the College as Cadets will be granted to the successful candidates at an open competitive examination.

3. The examinations will be conducted by Examiners appointed annually by the Governor in Council, as provided by law.

4. Notice will be given from time to time of the day and place of the examinations, and the vacancies to be competed for at each examination.

5. Boards will be appointed by the Governor in Council in each Military District to supervise the examination of candidates.

(*c*) These Boards will assemble for the first examinations at the office of the Deputy Adjutant General, at the Head Quarters in the several Military Districts, viz:—At Victoria, B. C., Winnipeg, Man., London, Toronto, Kingston, Brockville, Montreal, Quebec, Fredericton, Halifax and Charlottetown, at ten o'clock, a.m., on the fourth day of January, 1876.

6. No person will be accepted as a Cadet who is not considered eligible as to stature and physical power. The limits of age will for the present be from 15 to 20, the candidates being required to be within those limits on the first day of the month following the examination.

(*a*) The number of Cadets with which the College may be opened shall not exceed 22; the selections will be made by the Governor in Council from the lists of names forwarded by the Boards of Examiners, having reference to the order of merit in which the candidates pass their examinations.

7. Each Candidate for admission must send to the Adjutant General of Militia, not less than one month before the examination is held. an application accompanied by the following papers in duplicate.

(*a*) A certified abstract from the register of his birth, or, in default, a declaration by one of his parents or guardians before a magistrate, giving his exact age.

(*b*) A certificate of good moral character. signed by a clergyman of the locality in which he has recently resided, or by the head of the school or college at which he has received his education for at least the two preceding years.

8. When a candidate who has once been examined applies to be examined again. he will only be required to forward a certificate of his moral character for the interval between the two examinations.

Militia.

9. The number of trials allowed will not exceed three.

10. All candidates will be examined by a medical officer to be appointed by the Minister of Militia, and no candidate will be allowed to proceed to examination unless certified by this officer to be free from all bodily defects or ailments, and in all respects, as to height and physical qualities, fit for the military service.

(a) Each Cadet will be examined annually by a medical officer, and if from any cause he is found to be unlikely to become physically qualified for the military service, he will be required to resign.

11. Only persons who are British subjects and who have resided, or whose parents have resided in Canada for five years immediately preceding the date of examination, shall be eligible as candidates for admission as Cadets, and all such persons shall be eligible. Short periods of absence in Europe for purposes of education to be considered as residence.

12. Each Cadet before being examined will be required to sign a certificate that he is not married, and no Cadet will be permitted to marry during the period he remains in the college.

13. The candidates will be required to satisfy the Examiners appointed under paragraph 8 in the subjects subjoined.

14. The examination will be divided into two parts, viz.: "preliminary" or qualifying, and "further examination"; the former is obligatory, the latter optional.

15. The subjects of "preliminary" examination will be as follows:

	Marks.
(1) Mathematics:	
(a) Arithmetic, including vulgar and decimal fractions, simple and compound proportion, partnership, profit and loss	500
(b) Algebra, including simple equations	500
(c) Geometry, first book of Euclid	500
(2) (a) Grammar and writing English correctly, and in a good legible hand from dictation	500
(b) Composition, as tested by the power of writing an essay, precis or letter.	500
(3) Geography, general and descriptive	500
(4) History, British and Canadian, general	500
(5) French; grammar and translation from the language	500
(6) German; grammar and translation from the language	500
(7) Latin; grammar and simple translation from the language	500
(8) Elements of freehand drawing, viz: simple copies from the flat	300

(16) French and German to be considered under clause 13 as alternative subjects, in either but in only one of which the candidate need be qualified.

(17) No candidate will be considered qualified for a cadetship or be allowed to count marks in the further examination unless he obtain a minimum of half the total number of marks in each of the subjects. Paragraph 15—one,(a. b. c. together); two,(a. and b. together) three, four and eight, and a minimum of one-third in each of the subjects, five, six and seven.

Militia.

(18) The subjects of " further" examination will be as follows :—

	Marks.
(1) Mathematics :	
(*a*) Algebra, up to and including simple and quadratic equations...	1000
(*b*) Geometry up to and including third book of Euclid....	1000
(*c*) Theory and use of common logarithms, plain trigonometry, mensuration..	1000
(2) English literature, limited to specified authors, the names of the authors being given beforehand..........	1000
(*a*) The examination in January, 1876, to include the first seven chapters of Spalding's English literature.	
(3) Geography, physical, particularly of the Dominion of Canada and United States..................................	1000
(*a*) For the examinations in January, 1876, Page's Introductory Book, and Colton's Outline of Physical Geography.	
(4) History, British and Canadian, limited to certain fixed periods, the names of the authors and periods being specified beforehand..	1000
(*a*) For the examinations in January, 1876, Collier's History of the British Empire, embracing the Tudor and Stuart periods, and the first ten chapters of Hodgins' History of Canada.	
(5) French ; translation from English into French................	1200
(6) German ; translation from English into German..............	1200
(7) Latin ; Including the fifth book of Cæsar's Commentaries, to end of 23rd chap., and 2nd book of Virgil's Ænead	1500
(8) Drawing ; Copy from flat, shaded, and simple object drawing..	1000

(19). No optional subject, except mathematics and drawing, shall gain a Cadet any marks, unless he obtain a minimum of one-third of the marks assigned to that subject.

(20) The marks gained in the obligatory subjects, as laid down in paragraph 17, will be added to those gained in the optional subjects, as laid down in par. 19, to make a second total.

The resulting total will determine the candidate's place in the competitive list,—the successful candidates being those who stand first on the list up to the number of vacancies competed for, if otherwise qualified.

(21) Blank forms of certificates, and the necessary printed questions for use at the examinations, will be forwarded to the several Boards from Head Quarters, Ottawa, and a list of successful candidates, together with the total number of marks gained by each, and the date when the Cadets are required to report themselves at the College, will be published in the *Canada Gazette.*

Every Cadet entering upon a course of instruction in the College, will be required to sign a roll of entry, and be thenceforward for the term of his pupilage subject to the Queen's Rules and Regulations, the Mutiny Act, the

Militia.

Rules and Articles of War, and to such other rules and regulations as Her Majesty's troops are subjected to.

REWARDS.

(22) A sword will be given at each final examination as a special reward for excellence of conduct.

(23) The commissions in the militia service of not less than three Cadets who are recommended by the Commandant on their finally leaving the College as having specially distinguished themselves, and who at the end of twelve months are reported by the officer commanding the Militia as having performed their duty in a satisfactory manner for that period, shall be ante-dated twelve months.

PAYMENTS AND ALLOWANCES.

(24) Each Cadet will be required to provide himself with and keep in repair at his own expense, such articles of uniform, boots, and personal clothing as may be determined.

(25) Each Cadet will be required to provide himself with such books, instruments and apparatus as may be determined.

(26) Articles required under pars. 24 and 25 must be obtained by the Cadet from the Government stores, and will be issued to him at cost price.

(27) Each Cadet will be provided free of expense with barrack furniture, board, washing and attendance.

(28) Each Cadet will be required to pay in advance, previous to joining, a contribution of $200 to cover the value of articles under pars. 24 and 25, and in every future year a sum of $150 in advance, for the same purpose.

(29) These sums will be accounted for annually to the Cadet; any surplus will be carried to his credit towards his next annual contribution, and any deficit must be paid by the Cadet in addition to his next annual contribution.

(30) On finally leaving the College each Cadet will be allowed to take with him all articles obtained under pars. 24 and 25.

(31) In the case of a Cadet who is absent a whole term on account of sickness or *rusticating*, a payment of $50 shall be required of him for the privilege of his name being kept on the rolls of the College, and for a vacancy being guaranteed at the commencement of the next term.

(32) An allowance for travelling expenses at the rate of four cents a mile, for the number of miles beyond 500 necessarily travelled between the Head Quarters of the Military District in which he resides and the College, will be paid to each Cadet at the time he is first admitted, and a similar allowance for travelling expenses to Head Quarters of the same Military District will be paid to each such Cadet who has satisfactorily passed final examination at the College.

(a) No allowance for travelling expenses will be granted to those who reside within 500 miles from the College.

Militia.

PRIVY COUNCIL CHAMBERS,
OTTAWA, 29th October, 1875.

I hereby certify that the foregoing General Regulations for the government of the Military College at Kingston, were submitted to, and approved by His Excellency the Governor General in Council on the 26th day of October instant.

W. A. HIMSWORTH,
Clerk, Privy Council.

REGULATIONS RESPECTING THE MILITARY COLLEGE AT
KINGSTON.

GOVERNMENT AND ORGANIZATION.

1. The General Officer commanding the Militia will be *ex-officio* President of the Military College.

2. An independent inspection by a Board of Visitors appointed by the Governor in Council, and reporting to the Minister of Militia, will be made once a year. Such Board will not be a permanent body, but will consist of five members, of whom three shall be members of the Militia Staff, not less than two to retire annually. The first report will be made as soon after the expiration of twelve months from the opening of the College as may be determined.

3. The Commandant shall have power to suspend any Professor, Instructor or other officer or employee, pending the result of a report to the Governor in Council through the General Officer commanding.

4. The organization to be on a military basis.

5. The Commandant to be solely responsible for discipline and for the general superintendence of the studies.

6. The Commandant to have power to issue such standing orders as he may deem necessary,—provided that they are not opposed to anything contained in the Act for the establishment of the College or to the Regulations approved by the Governor in Council,—subject to the approval of the President.

7. The Commandant will be assisted in the arrangement of the studies by an Academy Board, composed of the Professors or senior Instructors of the different branches. The head of each branch will have the general power of supervision and inspection of the studies in his department, with the duty of reporting on them to the Commandant.

8. The Commandant will, from time to time, assemble and confer with all the Professors and Instructors of each separate branch on matters relating to it.

9. The Military Officers and Military and Civil Instructors will have the power of placing any Cadet in arrest pending the decision of the Commandant, to whom a report in writing, or personally in presence of the

Militia.

Cadet, of the cause of the arrest will be made. The Commandant may, at his discretion, permit Military Instructors and Officers to award extra drill to a Cadet for a period not exceeding two days; all such punishments to be reported to the Commandant.

10. The Professors and Instructors will perform such duties connected with the Cadet company as may be assigned to them by the Commandant.

11. The Officers, Professors and Instructors, both military and civil, will at all times be liable to be required to afford assistance in other branches of instruction than their own.

12. The Commandant will be assisted by a Captain of Cadets, and by a Staff Officer who will have charge of the records, correspondence, stores and accounts of the establishment, and make all local payments connected therewith.

13. The Commandant will have the absolute power of rustication or removal, and also of sentencing a Cadet to lose places in the list of successful candidates for employment. When expulsion is necessary the case will be referred to the Governor General in Council, through the general officer commanding the Militia.

14. The Commandant will cause records to be kept of all serious punishments awarded and of the offences which have caused them, which records must be confidential and open only to the General commanding and the Visitors.

15. The Commandant will inspect accounts of every description connected with the College, and certify those which require it.

16. The name of any Cadet expelled for misconduct will be gazetted, and recorded in the offices of the various public Departments, in order to prevent his being admitted to any branch of the public service.

17. No person belonging to the Military College is to receive a present from any Cadet, or from the relations or friends of any Cadet.

18. No Professor or Instructor will be permitted to give private instruction to a Cadet, either during the vacations or at any other time ; or be allowed to prepare Candidates for admission to the College.

COURSE OF INSTRUCTION.

1. The length of the course will be four years. If any Cadet fail to come up to the required standard at any two periodical examinations, or be found unable to qualify in his studies, or to acquire sufficient proficiency in military exercises, he will be removed. No extension of the above period on account of absence from any cause, except illness, will be granted. Cases of protracted absence on account of illness will be specially referred to the General Officer commanding.

2. The following subjects will form the course of obligatory studies:—

    (1) Mathematics, including plane trigonometry, practical mechanics with application of mathematics to machinery.
    (2) Fortification, field and permanent. Geometrical drawing.
    (3) Artillery.
    (4) Military drawing, reconnaissance, surveying.
    (5) Military history, administration, law, strategy and tactics.

Militia.

  (6) French or German at the student's choice.
  (7) Elementary chemistry, geology, &c.
  (8) Drawing, free hand figure and landscape.

  (9) Drills and Exercises.
{
  Infantry.
  Artillery.
  Engineer.
  Riding, sword exercise, &c.
  Gymnastics.
  Swimming.
}

  (10) Discipline.

  3. In addition to the obligatory course, every Cadet will be allowed at his option to take up certain voluntary subjects, viz. :—
    (1) Higher mathematics.
    (2) Higher fortification.
    (8) Higher chemistry, physics.
    (4) French or German (other than language taken up in obligatory examination).
    (5) Architecture, construction, estimating, &c.
    (6) Hydraulic engineering, &c., &c.

  4. No obligatory subject shall obtain a Cadet any marks unless he obtain a minimum of one-half marks in it.

  5. No Cadet will be considered qualified unless he obtain at least one-half marks in the obligatory course in Mathematics, Fortification, Artillery, Military History, Administration, &c., &c., and one-half the total aggregate of the marks allotted to all the obligatory subjects.

  6. No voluntary subject shall gain a Cadet any marks unless he obtain a minimum of at least one-third of the marks assigned to that portion of it in which he is examined. The marks gained in the voluntary subjects will be added to those obtained in the obligatory subjects and to those gained during the College course, the whole to make a second total, according to which the Cadets shall be finally placed.

  7. The final examination will be conducted by examiners independent of the College.

———

PRIVY COUNCIL CHAMBERS,
    17th December, 1875.

  I certify that the foregoing Regulations were on this day submitted to and approved by His Excellency the Governor General in Council

      W. A. HIMSWORTH
        Clerk. Privy Council.

Public Works.

GOVERNMENT HOUSE,
Friday, 14th day of May,   875.

Present :

HIS EXCELLENCY THE GOVERNOR GENERAL IN COUNCIL.

ON the recommendation of the Honorable the Minister of Public Works, and under the provisions of the 65th and 66th sections of the Act passed in the Session of the Parliament of Canada held in the 31st year of Her Majesty's Reign, chaptered 12 and intituled : "An Act respecting the Public Works of Canada ; " His Excellency, by and with the advice of the Queen's Privy Council for Canada, has been pleased to order, and it is hereby ordered, that the following regulations for the management, proper use and protection of the wharves around the Rideau Canal Basin and the approaches thereto in the City of Ottawa be and the same are hereby adopted and established, and that such Regulations shall apply to that portion of the Canal from and including the first lock to the Bridge known as the Maria Street Bridge

REGULATIONS.

ARTICLE I.

The Wharfinger shall, according to his discretion, assign to each vessel, steamer or barge the berth it shall occupy, giving precedence when practicable, to a vessel or barge with cargo over a vessel or barge taking in cargo, and shall have power to change such berth from time to time as he may see fit; and such assignment of a berth may be made by verbal notice to the master or person in charge of such vessel or barge, either on each trip or for the whole business season, and no vessel or barge shall take up or occupy any berth in the said Basin or the approaches, unless such berth shall have been assigned to her by the Wharfinger ; provided always, that the Wharfinger assigns a berth within twelve hours after her arrival; but if the wharves are full, such vessel shall lie where indicated until a berth has been assigned by the Wharfinger

ARTICLE II.

All vessels or barges in the said Canal Basin and its approaches shall be under the control of the Wharfinger, so far as regards their position, mooring fastening, removal and extent of accommodation, the Masters or persons in charge thereof may require from each other; and no person on board or in charge of any vessel or barge in said Basin shall disregard or disobey the orders of the Wharfinger in such respect ; and in the event of such refusal or disregard of the orders of the Wharfinger, it shall be lawful for such Wharfinger to cast off or cut away the hawsers or other fastenings of such vessels or barges, or cut away any ring or post to which such hawsers or other fastenings may be attached ; and in such event, in addition to the penalty hereinafter provided for, the master or person in

---

---

charge of such vessel shall be bound to pay to the Department of Public Works of Canada the damage (if any) caused to the wharf by the cutting away of such ring or post ; and the Wharfinger shall have power to hold any vessel disobeying his orders and causing damage, until such damages be paid.

ARTICLE III.

In the event of the resistance of any person or persons on board of any vessel to the orders of the Wharfinger to remove the same under the powers conferred upon him by the last preceding section, whether such resistance be active or passive, it shall be lawful for the Wharfinger to take possession of such vessel or barge, and to remove the same, and he shall have the power of employing a sufficient number of men for that purpose, at the expense of the master, owner or person in charge of such vessel, to aid him in forcing such removal, and have the right to move anchor, or make fast such vessel at such place as he shall see fit.

ARTICLE IV.

No raft, crib, floats or floating timber shall be or remain attached or secured to any wharf in said Basin or its approaches, without the express permission of the Wharfinger, and irrespective of the penalty hereafter provided for, and the Wharfinger shall have the power, without any notice to any person whomsoever, to cut adrift any raft, crib or timber, or hire tugs to remove, or may otherwise remove the same, which shall be so attached or secured without his permission; and such raft, crib or timber, so cut adrift or towed out, shall thereafter continue to be and remain at the proper risk of the owner thereof, respectively, and the owner shall be liable for all costs connected with towing or cutting adrift or otherwise removing such raft, crib, or timber ; and no raft shall enter the Deep Cut without the permission of the Wharfinger being first had ; no vessel or barge shall lay within the limits of said Basin or its approaches in such a place or position as to prevent a free and unobstructed passage for all other vessels or barges in the said Basin to any wharf in the said Basin.

ARTICLE V.

Lessees of lots facing the Basin shall have the first privilege of unloading or loading vessels or barges opposite their respective lots, but the Wharfinger may, if he sees fit, allow any vessel or barge to discharge on the wharves, although fronting on private lots.

ARTICLE VI.

Rafts or cribs, floats, barges or vessels loaded with cordwood, boards, lumber, ties, brick, cedar posts, stone, or other freight, shall not be permitted to remain in the berths assigned to them, unless the unloading of the cargo thereof be commenced immediately and diligently, and continually proceeded with, and when unloading firewood alongside any wharf at the rate of not less than twenty-five cords a day ; and all cordwood, lumber, ties, posts, brick, stone, or other freight, must be carted clear of the canal lands, unless special permission to deposit the same on the canal lands be given beforehand by the Wharfinger.

Public Works.

ARTICLE VII.

Vessels or barges arriving in the Canal Basin or its approaches, shall be allowed for unloading, as follows :—Two working days for 50 tons of cargo, or less than 50 tons. Three working days for over 50 tons, and not exceeding 100 tons ; and one working day for every 50 tons of cargo exceeding 100 tons. Cordwood, not less than 25 cords a day.

For Loading.—One working day for 50 tons and under, and two working days for 50 tons and under 100 tons ; one working day additional for every 50 tons of cargo exceeding 100 tons ; provided always that vessels or barges that shall be discharged or loaded in a shorter time, or that shall have ceased discharging or loading from any cause, shall not be entitled to retain their berths, should the Wharfinger see fit to order them to remove ; and provided also that on application to that effect the Wharfinger shall have the power, if he sees fit, to extend such time for a further period. And every such working day shall consist of ten hours.

ARTICLE VIII.

No goods, coal, firewood or cargo of any kind landed from any vessel, barge or raft and placed upon any wharf or the canal lands shall remain for a longer period than twenty-four hours, Sundays excepted, after being landed or placed there before the owners, master or person in charge shall commence removing the same off the wharves or canal lands at the rate specified by Article Seven, and a like penalty to that hereinafter provided shall be incurred for every twenty-four hours of working days during which such goods shall remain upon such wharf or canal lands without being removed.

ARTICLE IX.

No goods placed on the wharves or the canal lands for shipment on any vessel or barge shall be allowed to remain on the wharves or canal lands for a longer period than twenty-four hours, unless under special permission from the Wharfinger, and a like penalty to that hereinafter provided shall be incurred for every twenty-four hours of working days during which such goods shall remain upon such wharf or canal lands until shipped.

ARTICLE X.

No goods shall be placed on the wharves in said basin or the canal lands, so as to obstruct the thoroughfare therein, under the penalty provided for the breach of any by-law; and if so placed, shall be removed forthwith by the owner or person in charge thereof, upon the orders of the Wharfinger to that effect under a further like penalty.

ARTICLE XI.

In the event of the breach of either of the last three foregoing by-laws, or any part of them, it shall be lawful for the Wharfinger to remove

Public Works.

or cause to be removed any goods, coal, wood, lumber or other thing which shall remain on the wharf or canal lands longer than it or they are permitted to do by the last three foregoing by-laws, or by any of them, and such removal shall be made at the cost and charges of the owner or consignee of such effects, or of the master or person in charge of said vessel or barge from which they are landed or shipped, at the option of the Minister of Public Works, and such costs and charges, and any further or other reasonable costs and charges in respect thereof, and of the custody and safe keeping of the same, and all penalties incurred in respect thereof shall be a lien upon such effects which shall not be delivered up to any person whomsoever until all such costs, charges and penalties be paid; and, notwithstanding such removal, such effects shall continue to be at the risk of the owners thereof, and if the costs and charges thereon, and all penalties due in respect thereof be not paid, and such effects taken away by the owners thereof, or their representative, within thirty days after such removal, such effects may be sold by public auction for the benefit of whom it may concern, and the Minister of Public Works shall only be accountable in respect of such effects for the nett proceeds of such sale, less all such costs, charges and penalties.

ARTICLE XII.

No person shall make or dress any timbers, or do any repairs on any of the wharves or canal lands, except with the express permission of the Wharfinger previously obtained, and at such places as he shall have designated.

ARTICLE XIII.

No rubbish or thing whatsoever shall be thrown from any vessel, barge, raft, or from the wharves into the water of the Canal Basin; and no person shall place, pile or deposit any dirt, rubbish, snow, ice or other thing upon said wharves.

ARTICLE XIV.

The Wharfinger shall have power, under the direction of the Superintendent, to allot, let or lease any space or vacant ground adjoining the Canal Basin for piling thereon cordwood, lumber, &c., subject to such rate of charges, and for such time and times as from time to time may be fixed by the Minister of Public Works.

Fines and Penalties and their Collection.

ARTICLE XV.

Every person, in whatsoever capacity he may be acting, who shall violate or infringe any of the by-laws hereinbefore contained and passed this day, shall be subject to a fine of five dollars currency.

ARTICLE XVI.

Every person, in whatsoever capacity he may be acting, who shall fail or neglect to obey any one of the aforesaid by-laws, or any portion of one of them, shall be subject to a penalty of five dollars currency.

Public Works.

ARTICLE XVII.

The master or person in charge of any vessel or barge which shall violate or infringe, or fail or neglect to obey any one of the aforesaid by-laws, or any part or portion of them, or any one of them, and the master or person in charge of any vessel or barge, in the conduct and management of which any one of the said by-laws, or any portion of one of them shall be violated, infringed or destroyed, shall be subject to a penalty of five dollars currency.

ARTICLE XVIII.

The owner of any cargo, lumber or effects, or of any matters or things whatsoever landed from any barge in respect of which cargo, lumber or effects, matters or things, there shall be any violation or infringement of, or disobedience to any one of the aforesaid by-laws, or of any part of them, shall be subject to a penalty of five dollars currency.

ARTICLE XIX.

The owner or person in charge of any goods, lumber or other effects deposited for shipment on any wharf or elsewhere on the said basin, or its approaches, in respect of which goods, lumber or effects there shall be any violation or infringement of, or disobedience to, any one of the aforesaid by-laws, or of or to any part of any one of them, shall be subject to a penalty of five dollars.

INTERPRETATION.

The word " vessel," when made use of in the foregoing Regulations, is to be understood as comprehending and including vessels, boats and barges, whether propelled by steam or otherwise, scows, pontoons or other floating conveyance of freight, or for the purposes of transport. The word " rafts," when made use of in the foregoing Regulations, is to be taken as including rafts or cribs of timber of every description, whether manufactured or unmanufactured, lumber, logs, floating timber, rafting materials, ties and wood, or of material used for conveyance of freight, or purposes of transport. The words " working days " are to be understood as comprehending and meaning days on which work can be legally performed. The word " owner " shall comprehend or mean a part-owner or owners. The word " wharfinger " shall comprehend the person appointed to act by the Minister of Public Works of Canada. The word " goods " shall be understood as comprehending coal, ore and other mineral products, lumber, firewood, cordwood, ties, staves, laths, brick, stone, sand or earth, or any goods, wares or merchandise of any description or nature whatsoever ; when more persons than one are hereinbefore made subject to a penalty, the Minister of Public Works shall have the option of proceeding for such penalty against such one of such persons as he may see fit.

His Excellency has been further pleased to order that all previous Order in Council or Regulations inconsistent with the Regulations hereby adopted be, and the same are hereby cancelled.

W. A. HIMSWORTH,
Clerk Privy Council.

Public Works.

By a Proclamation dated 5th November, 1874, His Excellency, in Her Majesty's name, declared that upon and after the Seventh day of November instant, the Public Works, formerly known as the Public Toll Bridge, situate in the Town of Brantford, in the County of Wentworth, as it stood on the Eleventh day of April, in the year of Our Lord One thousand eight hundred and fifty-one, known as the "Brantford Bridge," and the macadamized, planked and gravelled Toll Road, situate in the said County. commencing at the City of Hamilton, and thence running westerly to the westerly boundary line of the said County of Wentworth, being composed of all those parts of the Public Toll Roads known as the Hamilton and Brantford Road and the Brantford and London Road, lying between the western limits of the City of Hamilton and the western limits of the County of Wentworth (excepting such parts thereof as lie within the limits of the said Town of Brantford), and now known and described as the Public Toll Bridge situate in the Town of Brantford, in the County of Brant, known as the "Brantford Bridge," and the macadamized, planked and gravelled Toll Road running through the Township of Brantford, in the County of Brant aforesaid, and the Township of Ancaster and Barton, in the County of Wentworth, commencing at the western boundary line of the County of Wentworth, as it stood on the Eleventh day of April, in the year of Our Lord One thousand eight hundred and fifty-one, thence easterly through the Town and Township of Brantford, and the Townships of Ancaster and Barton aforesaid, to the City of Hamilton, in the said County of Wentworth, being composed of all those parts of the Public Roads formerly known as the Hamilton and Brantford Road and the Brantford and London Road, lying between the said western boundary line of the County of Wentworth, as it stood on the said Eleventh day of April, in the year of Our Lord One thousand eight hundred and fifty-one, and the western limits of the said City of Hamilton (excepting such parts of the said road as lie within the limits of the said Town of Brantford), together with all the bridges thereon and all toll-gates, toll-bars and toll-houses on the said road now under the management and control of the Minister of Public Works, shall be no longer under his control.
Vide Canada Gazette, Vol. 8, p. 468.

By Order in Council of the 5th November, 1874, the Harbour of Oakville, Ont., was declared no longer a public work, but vested in the Corporation of that town, and certain regulations respecting its management. and the tolls, were approved.
Vide Canada Gazette, Vol. 8, p. 472.

By a Proclamation dated the 30th day of July, 1875 His Excellency, in Her Majesty's name, declared that, upon and after that day, the Public Bridge situate in the Village of Portage du Fort, in the County of Pontiac, in the Province of Quebec, and known as the "Portage du Fort Bridge," then under the management and control of Our Minister of Public Works, should be no longer under his control.
Vide Canada Gazette, Vol. 9, p. 166.

By Order in Council of the 3rd day of 'April, 1875, Tonnage Dues at the rate of ten cents per ton of the registered measurement thereof are imposed and authorized to be levied on each and every Vessel entering the Harbor of Cow Bay, N. S.
Vide Canada Gazette. Vol. 8, p. 1221.

———

By Order in Council of the 10th day of April, 1875, the following rates of toll were imposed and authorized to be levied and collected on Merchandise landed on the Pier at Cow Bay, that is to say : Three cents per barrel and a proportionate rate on all other goods or packages ; and that such tolls be cellected by the Collector of Customs at Cow Bay.
Vide Canada Gazette, Vol. 8, p. 1256.

———

By Order in Council of the 13th day of April, 1875, the ferry steamer "St. Jean Baptiste," plying between Prescott, in the County of Grenville, and Province of Ontario, and Ogdensburg, in the State of New York, U.S., was exempted from the requirements of the second section of the Act 37 Vict., chap. 30, relating to Steamboat Inspection, in so far as the same pre- scribes the carrying of a metallic life-boat, on condition that a suitable wooden boat be carried by the said steamer in place of a metallic life-boat, such wooden boat to be fitted with air-tight compartments under the direc- tions of the Inspector of Steamboats for the District to which the said steamer belongs.
Vide Canada Gazette Vol. 8, 1256.

———

By Order in Council of the 21st day of April, 1875, His Excellency was pleased, on the recommendation of the Honorable Minister of Marine and Fisheries, and under the provisions of the Act passed in the 36th year of Her Majesty's Reign, and intituled : " An Act respecting Pilotage," by and with the advice of the Queen's Privy Council for Canada, to order that a Pilotage District be formed for the Port of Richibucto, in the County of Kent and Province of New Brunswick, the limits of which District shall extend from Point Escuminac, on the north, to Cassey Cape, on the south, and as far as North Point, Prince Edward Island on the east ; and His Excellency was further pleased to make the payment of Pilotage Dues compulsory within the limits of the said District.
Vide Can da Gazette, Vol. 8, p. 1307.

———

By Order in Council of the 21st day of April, 1875, a Pilotage District was formed for the Counties of Kings and Hants, in the Province of Nova Scotia, the limits of which District shall embrace Cobequid Bay, the Basin of Minas, Minas Channel, and extend down the Bay of Fundy until they strike a line drawn from Cape Chignecto, in the County of Cumberland, to a point in the County of Kings, where the division line between the Counties of Kings and Annapolis strikes the Bay of Fundy ; such limits also to include the several rivers and creeks in the Counties of Kings and Hants, which fall into the Bay of Fundy, Basin of Minas, Minas Channel and Cobequid Bay ; and the payment of Pilotage Dues was made non-compulsory within the limits of the said District.

Vide Canada Gazette, Vol. 8, p. 1307.

By Order in Council of the 8th day of September, 1875, the Lower Ottawa Boom Company were authorized to collect the following rates of toll for the use of their works at Duck and Kettle Islands, that is to say :

Saw logs, flat and round timber or cedars.. 30 cents per piece.
Square timber.. 40   do   do

Vide Canada Gazette, Vol 9, p. 348.

By Order in Council of the 15th day of April, 1876, the Upper Ottawa Improvement Company were authorized to levy and collect the following rates of toll, viz. :—

Through Des Joachim Boom, Saw-Logs not over 16 feet,—per piece. 3 cents.

Through Fort William and Lepasse Booms or either of them, Saw-Logs not over 16 feet long,—per piece, 1¼ cents.

Through Allumette Boom, Saw-Logs not over 16 feet long,—per piece. 2 cents.

Through Melons Chenail Boom, Saw-Logs not over 16 feet long,—per piece, ¾ cents.

Through improvements in Mississippi Chenail, Chat Rapids and Quio Boom, or any of them, Saw-Logs not over 16 feet long,—per piece, 2¼ cents.

Through improvements in Thompson's Bay, Saw-Logs not over 16 feet long,—per piece, 1 cent.

Vide Canada Gazette, Vol. 9. p. 1392

TABLE OF CONTENTS

A

INDEX

ACTS OF IMPERIAL PARLIAMENT, RESERVED ACT, TREATIES, AND ORDERS IN COUNCIL, &c.,

PREFIXED.

ACTS OF IMPERIAL PARLIAMENT.

INDEX.

·ACTS

PARLIAMENT

OF THE

DOMINION OF CANADA,

PASSED IN THE

THIRTY-NINTH YEAR OF THE REIGN OF HER MAJESTY

QUEEN VICTORIA,

AND IN THE

THIRD SESSION OF THE THIRD PARLIAMENT,

Begun and holden at Ottawa, on the tenth day of February, and closed by Prorogation on the twelfth day of April, 1876.

HIS EXCELLENCY

THE RIGHT HONORABLE, SIR FREDERICK TEMPLE, EARL OF DUFFERIN,
GOVERNOR GENERAL.

VOL. I.
PUBLIC GENERAL ACTS.

OTTAWA:
PRINTED BY BROWN CHAMBERLIN,
LAW PRINTER TO THE QUEEN'S MOST EXCELLENT MAJESTY.
ANNO DOMINI, 1876.

39 VICTORIA.

CHAP. I.

An Act for granting to Her Majesty certain sums of money required for defraying certain expenses of the public service, for . the financial years ending respectively the 30th June, 1876, and the 30th June, 1877, and for other purposes relating to the public service.

[Assented to 12th April, 1876.]

MOST GRACIOUS SOVEREIGN,

WHEREAS it appears by messages from His Excellency the Right Honorable Sir Frederick Temple, Earl of Dufferin, Governor General of the Dominion of Canada, and the estimates accompanying the same, that the sums hereinafter mentioned are required to defray certain expenses of the public service of the Dominion not otherwise provided for, for the financial years ending respectively the thirtieth day of June, one thousand eight hundred and seventy-six, and the thirtieth day of June, one thousand eight hundred and seventy-seven, and for other purposes connected with the public service : May it therefore please Your Majesty that it may be enacted, and be it enacted by the Queen's Most Excellent Majesty, by and with the advice and consent of the Senate and House of Commons of Canada, that— Preamble.

1. From and out of the Consolidated Revenue Fund of Canada, there shall and may be paid and applied a sum not exceeding in the whole one million one hundred and thirty-nine thousand three hundred and thirty-eight dollars and twenty-eight cents, towards defraying the several charges and expenses of the public service of the Dominion, from the first day of July, in the year of Our Lord one thousand eight hundred and seventy-five, to the thirtieth day of June, in the year of Our Lord one thousand eight hundred and seventy-six not otherwise provided for, and set forth in Schedule A. to this Act, and also for the other purposes in the said schedule mentioned. Sum granted
for 1875-76.
$1,139,338.28.

2.

Sum granted
for 1876-77.

\$19,486,616.02

2. From and out of the Consolidated Revenue Fund of Canada; there shall and may be paid and applied a sum not exceeding in the whole nineteen million four hundred and eighty-six thousand six hundred and sixteen dollars and two cents, towards defraying the several charges and expenses of the Dominion, from the first day of July, in the year of Our Lord one thousand eight hundred and seventy-six to the thirtieth day of June, in the year of Our Lord one thousand eight hundred and seventy-seven, not otherwise provided for, and set forth in the Schedule B. to this Act, and for other purposes in the said schedule mentioned.

Account to be rendered.

3. A detailed account of the sums expended under the authority of this Act, shall be laid before the House of Commons of Canada during the first fifteen days of the then next session of Parliament.

Recital as to amounts of authorized loans remaining unborrowed.

4. And whereas there remained on the thirty-first day of December last unborrowed and negotiable of the loans authorized by Parliament for the several works hereinafter mentioned, and for general purposes the sums opposite to each respectively, viz :—

	\$	cts.
For Intercolonial Railway............................	2,433,333	33
For opening communication and administration of the Government in the North-West Territories...	1,460,000	00
For improvement of the River St. Lawrence	1,500,000	00
For the improvement of Quebec Harbour......	1,200,000	00
For the Pacific Railway and Canals..............	12,166,666	66

For general purposes, balance,   \$ cts.
30th June, 1875.............. 18,242,279 70
Redeemed to 31st December....   865,866 27

              19,108,145 97
Issued............. .... 4,866,666 67

           14,241,479 30

        \$33,001,479 29

Such sums may be raised under 35 V., c. 6, and 38 V., c. 4.

Therefore it is declared and enacted, that the Governor in Council may authorize the raising of the several sums above mentioned, as they may be required for the purposes aforesaid, respectively, under the provisions of the Act passed in the thirty-fifth year of Her Majesty's reign, intituled : " *An Act respecting the Public Debt, and the raising of Loans authorized by Parliament,*" as amended by the Act passed in the thirty-eighth year of Her Majesty's reign, intituled : " *An Act to amend the Act respecting the Public Debt and the raising of loans authorized by Parliament,*" and the sums so raised shall form part of the Consolidated Revenue Fund of Canada, out of which like sums shall be applicable to the several purposes aforesaid, under the Acts and provisions thereunto relating respectively

                      SCHEDULE A.

SCHEDULE A.

SUMS granted to Her Majesty by this Act, for the financial year ending 30th June, 1876, and the purpose for which they are granted.

SERVICE.	Amount.	Total.
	$ cts.	$ cts
CHARGES OF MANAGEMENT.		
To provide for further expenses in connection with the Seigniorial Commission...		1,500 00
ADMINISTRATION OF JUSTICE.		
Miscellaneous Justice........	10,000 00	
SUPREME COURT OF CANADA AND EXCHEQUER COURT OF CANADA.		
Salaries of Precis Writer, Clerk and Messenger.................... $1,170 00		
Printing, stationery and contingencies 1,000 00		
	2,170 00	
NORTH-WEST TERRITORIES.		
Travelling expenses of two Stipendiary Magistrates........................	1,500 00	
		13,670 00
POLICE.		
NORTH-WEST MOUNTED POLICE.		
To provide for further expenses for current fiscal year ($50,000 advanced under special warrant of His Excellency the Governor General)......	119,435 32	
To meet arrears of fiscal years 1873-74 and 1874-75........	41,184 47	
		160,619 79
LEGISLATION.		
To provide for increased cost of parliamentary printing........................	20,000 00	
To provide for law books for Supreme Court.........................	6,000 00	
To provide for cost of increased staff, &c., for Parliamentary Library, in accordance with the report of the Committee.....................	4,000 00	
		30,000 00
IMMIGRATION AND QUARANTINE.		
Part of unexpended balance of 1874-75................................		25,000 00
MILITIA.		
Drill pay and all other incidental expenses connected with the drill and training of the Militia...		20,000 00
PUBLIC WORKS AND BUILDINGS.		
CHARGEABLE TO CAPITAL.		
Workshops, Public Buildings, Ottawa, from 1874-75..............................		3,000 00
Carried forward........		253,789 79

SCHEDULE A.

SCHEDULE A.—*Continued.*

SERVICE.	Amount.	Total.
	$ cts.	$ cts.
Brought forward..	....	253,789 79
PUBLIC WORKS AND BUILDINGS.		
CHARGEABLE TO INCOME.		
To provide for the cost of lock boxes for the new Post Office Building, Montreal	4,100 00	
To provide for additional cost, new Custom House, Pictou, N.S., $1,750, and $4,800 from 1874-75.....	6,550 00	
To provide for Barracks, Battle River, North-West Territories...............	8,000 00	
To pay cost of buildings, Fort Pelly	33,966 94	
Toronto Custom House, from 1874-75...	7,000 00	
Toronto Examining Warehouse, from 1874-75	8,000 00	
Ottawa Post Office and Custom House, from 1874-75........................	7,000 00	
Grosse Isle Quarantine Station, from 1874-75.................................	4,000 00	
Montreal Examining Warehouse, from 1874-75	49,796 59	
Sydney Quarantine Station, from 1874-75	2,000 00	
Sydney Marine Hospital, from 1874-75...	5,000 00	135,413 53
OCEAN AND RIVER STEAM SERVICE.		
To provide for additional cost for maintenance of Dominion steamers ...	18,000 00	
To provide for the cost of building and equipping a steam boat to maintain communication between Prince Edward Island and the mainland during winter months, in accordance with the terms of Union..	30,000 00	48,000 00
FISHERIES.		
To provide for the following additional expenditure :—		
· Ontario—fishery overseers' salaries and disbursements.. $1,900 00		
Quebec do do do ... 3,500 00		
	5,400 00	
Maintenance of steamer for protection of Fisheries ......:	2,500 00	
Fish-breeding, &c.........	11,500 00	19,400 00
INDIANS.		
To bring up the annuities payable under the Robinson Treaty to the Chippewas of Lakes Huron and Superior, from 96 cents to $4 per head	11,000 00	
To purchase presents for the Indians in the neighbourhood of Fort Carleton, on the River Saskatchewan	5,000 00	
To complete the payment of annuities under Treaty No. 4, and the purchase of provisions for Indians assembled to receive those annuities for which a Special Warrant from His Excellency the Governor General has been issued.....................................	34,000 00	
To aid in the publication of a Grammar and Dictionary in Saulteau or Chippewa and English	500 00	50,500 00
MISCELLANEOUS.		
To provide for expenditure under the Fishery Commission	3,200 00	
Carried forward	3,200 00	507,103 32

SCHEDULE A.

SCHEDULE A.—*Continued.*

SERVICE.	Amount.	Total.
	$ cts.	$ cts.
Brought forward	3,200 00	507,103 32
MISCELLANEOUS.—*Continued.*		
Miscellaneous printing	4,200 00	
To provide for the relief of settlers in Manitoba, rendered destitute by grasshopper ravages, for which a special warrant has been issued by His Excellency the Governor General	60,000 00	
To defray appropriation for the relief of distressed settlers in the Province of Manitoba	25,000 00	
To meet probable claims of the Hon. Ambrose Shea	11,866 30	104,266 30
BOUNDARY SURVEYS.		
Unexpended balance of 1874–75 for survey of boundary between Canada and United States	147,457 14	
Unexpended balance of 1874–75 for survey of boundary between Ontario and the North-West	21,692 40	169,149 54
PUBLIC WORKS AND BUILDINGS.		
RAILWAYS.		
To provide for additional rolling stock, &c., Prince Edward Island Railway	44,000 00	
To pay for balance of cost of change of gauge, railway lines of Nova Scotia and New Brunswick ($38,758.12, from 1874–75)	168,758 12	212,758 12
CHARGES ON REVENUE.		
WEIGHTS AND MEASURES.		
To meet the salaries of Inspectors of Weights and Measures, Gas and Gas Metres	....	21,284 00
UNPROVIDED ITEMS OF 1874-75.		
Vide Public Accounts 1874–75, part 2, page 398	....	124,777 00
Total........	....	1,139,338 28

SCHEDULE B.

SUMs granted to Her Majesty by this Act, for the financial year ending 30th June, 1877, and the purposes for which they are granted.

SERVICE.	Amount.	Total.
	$ cts.	$ cts.
CHARGES OF MANAGEMENT.		
Financial Inspector	2,600 00	
Office of Assistant Receiver-General, Toronto	8,000 00	
do Montreal	5,500 00	
Auditor and do Halifax, N.S	10,000 00	
do do St. John, N.B	11,000 00	
do do Fort Garry	6,500 00	
do do Victoria, B.C.	7,000 00	
do do Charlottetown, P.E.I.	4,000 00	
Country Savings Banks, New Brunswick, Nova Scotia and British Columbia	12,000 00	
Seigniorial Tenure and Commission	2,500 00	
		69,100 00
CIVIL GOVERNMENT.		
The Governor General's Secretary's Office	8,180 00	
The Department of the Queen's Privy Council for Canada	14,540 00	
do Justice	16,200 00	
do Militia and Defence	35,150 00	
do the Secretary of State	30,140 00	
do the Minister of the Interior	39,680 00	
do the Receiver-General	20,720 00	
do Finance	48,250 00	
do Customs	27,500 00	
do Inland Revenue	24,982 50	
do Public Works	48,934 00	
The Post Office Department	84,990 00	
The Department of Agriculture	28,240 00	
do Marine and Fisheries	23,815 00	
Treasury Board Office	3,300 00	
Office of Inspector of Penitentiaries	3,150 00	
Departmental Contingencies	175,000 00	
Stationery Office for Stationery	20,000 00	
Readjustment of Salaries (including promotions)	35,000 00	
To provide for the salaries of two clerks in the Indian Branch, Department of the Interior, inadvertently omitted in first estimate	1,250 00	
		689,021 50
ADMINISTRATION OF JUSTICE.		
Miscellaneous	10,000 00	
do North-West Territories	10,000 00	
Circuit Allowances, British Columbia	15,000 00	
do Manitoba	3,000 00	
Travelling expenses of Stipendiary Magistrates in North-West Territories	3,000 00	
Precis Writer of the Supreme Court of Canada and Exchequer Court	1,800 00	
Clerk of Supreme Court of Canada and Exchequer Court	300 00	
Messenger of Supreme Court of Canada and Exchequer Court	300 00	
Contingencies and Disbursements, including salaries of officers to be appointed in the Supreme Court of Canada and Exchequer Court	10,000 00	
Law Books for Supreme Court	1,000 00	
Carried forward	54,400 00	758,121 50

SCHEDULE B.—*Continued.*

Service.	Amount.	Total.
	$ cts.	$ cts.
Brought forward	54,400 00	758,121 50
ADMINISTRATION OF JUSTICE.—*Continued.*		
Province of British Columbia. For the salary of one Stipendiary Magistrate, or County Court Judge, to provide, if necessary, for the vacancy created by the death of the late A. T. Bushby, Esq...	2,425 00	
North-West Territories. Travelling expenses of one Stipendiary Magistrate.........................	1,500 00	58,325 00
POLICE.		
Dominion Police...	....	15,000 00
PENITENTIARIES.		
Kingston Penitentiary, Ontario...	97,841 75	
Rockwood Asylum, Ontario..	61,977 50	
Halifax Penitentiary, N.S..	27,532 13	
St. John do N.B...	38,944 25	
St. Vincent de Paul Penitentiary, Quebec...........................	52,230 06	
Manitoba Penitentiary...	17,650 00	
Maintenance of Convicts, British Columbia.........................	10,000 00	306,175 69
LEGISLATION.		
SENATE.		
Salaries and Contingent Expenses of the Senate.....................	50,718 00	
HOUSE OF COMMONS.		
Salaries, per Clerk's estimate...	60,850 00	
Expenses of Committees, Extra Sessional Clerks, &c...............	13,000 00	
Contingencies...	20,140 00	
Publishing Debates...	15,000 00	
Salaries and Contingencies, per Sergeant at Arms' Estimate.....	35,450 00	
MISCELLANEOUS.		
Grant to Parliamentary Library, including provision for Law Books......	12,000 00	
For readjustment of salaries of Librarian and Assistant...........	400 00	
Printing, Binding and Distributing the Laws.........................	12,500 00	
To meet the estimated expenses in connection with Consolidation of the Laws..	8,000 00	
Printing, Printing Paper and Bookbinding.............................	70,000 00	
Contingencies of the Clerk of the Crown in Chancery...............	1,200 00	
Miscellaneous Printing...	2,000 00	
Carried forward..	301,258 00	1,137,622 19

SCHEDULE B.

SCHEDULE B.—*Continued.*

SERVICE.	Amount.	Total.
	$ cts.	$ cts.
Brought forward..	301,258 00	1,137,622 19
LEGISLATION.—*Continued.*		
MISCELLANEOUS.—*Continued.*		
To provide for salaries of Draughtsmen, and other expenses in connection with the preparation of Maps for Railway Committee, to be expended under the supervision of the Clerk of the House of Commons	2,900 00	
		304,158 00
ARTS, AGRICULTURE AND STATISTICS.		
To meet expenses in connection with the care of the Archives	3,000 00	
To meet expenses in connection with the organization of the Patent Record...	6,500 00	
To meet expenses in connection with the preparation of Criminal Statistics..	5,000 00	
Salaries and contingent expenses of Statistical Office, Halifax	4,100 00	
Salaries of 316 Deputy Registrars, Province of Nova Scotia, and allowances for getting marriage returns..	1,880 00	
		20,480 00
IMMIGRATION AND QUARANTINE.		
Salaries of Immigration Agents and Employés	26,950 00	
Salaries of Immigration Travelling Agents.	12,000 00	
Medical Inspection of the Port of Quebec......................................	2,600 00	
Quarantine, Grosse Isle	12,000 00	
do St. John, N.B...	3,000 00	
do Miramichi, N.B.; Pictou, N.S	1,000 00	
do Halifax, N.S...	3,600 00	
do Charlottetown, P.E.I.......	1,000 00	
To meet expenses of further precautionary measures for the Public Health and for the prevention of disease among animals...............	20,000 00	
Contingencies of Canadian and other regular Agencies........	24,000 00	
Travelling Expenses of Travelling Agents......................................	14,000 00	
Towards assisting Immigration and meeting Immigration expenses, including estimated expense of transport of Mennonites...................	170,000 00	
		290,150 00
PENSIONS.		
Samuel Waller, late Clerk, House of Assembly............................	400 00	
L. Gagné, Messenger, do	72 00	
John Bright, do do	80 00	
Mrs. Antrobus..	800 00	
New Militia Pensions.		
Mrs. Caroline McEachern and four children...... .... 265 00		
Jane Lakey.. 146 00		
Rhoda Smith....... ,................ .... 110 00		
Janet Anderson.. 110 00		
Margaret Mackenzie.................................... 80 00		
Mary Ann Richey and two children...... .... 336 00		
Mary Morrison....................................... .. 80 00		
Louise Prud'homme and two children............ 110 00		
Virginia Charron and four children............ 150 00		
Paul M. Robins.................................... 146 40		
Charles T. Bell..................................... 73 20		
Alex. Oliphant.................... .... 109 80		
Charles Lugsden.................................. 91 50		
Carried forward 1,807 90	1,852 00	1,752,410 19

SCHEDULE B.—*Continued.*

SERVICE.	.	Amount.	Total.
		$ cts.	$ cts.
Brought forward	$1,807 90	1,352 00	1,752,410 19
PENSIONS.—*Continued.*			
Thomas Charters	91 50		
Charles T. Robertson	110 00		
Percy G. Routh	400 00		
Richard S. King	400 00		
George A. Mackenzie	73 20		
Edward Hilder	146 40		
Fergus Schofield	73 20		
John Bradley	109 80		
Richard Penticost	91 50		
James Bryan	109 80		
Jacob Stubbs	73 20		
Mary Connor	110 00		
Mary Hodgins and three children	191 00		
John Martin	110 00		
A. W. Stevenson	110 00		
Mrs. J. Thorburn	150 00		
Mrs. P. T. Worthington and children	378 00		
Mrs. J. H. Elliot and children	130 00		
Ellen Kirkpatrick and three children.	266 00		
Mrs. George Prentice and children	400 00		
Mary Hannah Temple and child	298 00		
To provide for a pension to Ensign Fahey, in accordance with a report of the Medical Board	200 00		
		5,829 50	
To meet the probable amount required for Pensions to Veterans of the War of 1812		50,000 00	
Compensation to Pensioners in lieu of land		8,000 00	
			65,181 50
MILITIA.			
ORDINARY.			
Salaries of Military Branch and District Staff		29,400 00	
Salaries of Brigade Majors		28,500 00	
Allowances for Drill Instruction		40,000 00	
Ammunition		40,000 00	
Clothing		40,000 00	
Military Stores		40,000 00	
Public Armouries and care of arms, including the pay of Storekeepers and Caretakers, Storemen, and the rents, fuel and light of Public Armouries		52,000 00	
Drill pay and other incidental expenses connected with the Drill and Training of the Militia		125,000 00	
Contingencies and general service not otherwise provided for, including assistance to Rifle Associations and Bands of Efficient Corps		50,000 00	
Targets (Revote)		2,000 00	
Drill Sheds and Rifle Ranges		10,000 00	
EXTRAORDINARY.			
Care and Maintenance of Properties transferred from the Ordnance and the Imperial Governments, including Rents		7,000 00	
Ordnance and Equipment of Garrison Artillery		10,000 00	
Carried forward		473,900 00	1,817,591 69

SCHEDULE B.

SCHEDULE B.—*Continued.*

SERVICE.	Amount.	Total.
	$ cts.	$ cts.
Brought forward..	473,900 00	1,817,591 69
MILITIA.—*Continued.*		
SPECIAL.		
Pay, Maintenance and Equipment of "A" and "B" Batteries Garrison Artillery and School of Gunnery, Kingston and Quebec..................	110,000 00	
Military College..	26,000 00	
Military Schools, Nova Scotia and New Brunswick...........................	10,000 00	
Pay and Maintenance of Dominion Force in Manitoba........................	30,000 00	
Mounted Police, North-West Territories...........	292,651 50	
do do do forage and contingencies..........	10,000 00	
		952,551 50
PUBLIC WORKS AND BUILDINGS.		
(*Chargeable to Capital.*)		
RAILWAYS.		
Intercolonial Railway completion.....................................	500,000 00	
do extension into Halifax..	175,000 00	
do to deep water at St. John, N.B...............................	200,000 00	
Prince Edward Island Railway..	200,000 00	
Pacific Railway, this grant being made with the view that the arrangements for the construction of the Canadian Pacific Railway should be such as the resources of the country will permit, without increasing the existing rates of taxation............	2,810,000 00	
Pacific Railway Survey and Engineering..........	500,000 00	
CANALS.		
For Works of Construction, viz. :—		
Lachine Canal.. ...	·1,200,000 00	
St. Lawrence Canals..	60,000 00	
Cornwall Canal..	200,000 00	
Welland Canal..	2,000,000 00	
St. Anne's Lock..	160,000 00	
Carillon and Chute à Blondeau..	330,000 00	
Grenville Canal..	200,000 00	
Rideau Canal..	6,000 00	
Culbute Canal..	35,000 00	
Chambly Canal..	10,000 00	
St. Peter's Canal..	50,000 00	
Miscellaneous work on Canals..	10,000 00	
PUBLIC BUILDINGS, OTTAWA.		
Tower.. 9,000 00		
Grounds.. 18,900 00		
Retaining walls, gates, footpaths, painting, &c............. 8,000 00		
Extension, West Block......... .... 296,000 00		
	331,900 00	
Total chargeable to Capital........................	....	8,977,900 00
Carried forward	....	11,748,043 19

SCHEDULE B.—*Continued.*

SERVICE.	Amount.	Total.
	$ cts.	$ cts
Brought forward..	....	11,748,043 19
PUBLIC WORKS AND BUILDINGS.		
(Chargeable to Income.)		
IMPROVEMENT OF NAVIGABLE RIVERS.		
Improvements of Navigable Rivers...	10,000 00	
St. Lawrence, removal of chains and anchors............	15,000 00	
Neebish Rapids.............. ,...	10,000 00	
		35,000 00
ROADS AND BRIDGES.		
Lake Superior and Red River route............		25,000 00
PUBLIC BUILDING .		
Ontario.		
Examining Warehouse, Toronto.	39,000 00	
Guelph Custom House, Excise and Post Office....................	25,000 00	
Kingston Military School and Repairing Fortifications.........	40,000 00	
Quebec.		
Repairing Fortifications..........	5,000 00	
Examining Warehouse, Montreal..	60,000 00	
Montreal Examining Warehouse............................	50,000 00	
Nova Scotia.		
Sydney Marine Hospital..................................	3,000 00	
Prince Edward Island.		
Souris Marine Hospital..	500 00	
North-West Territories.		
Public Buildings, &c...	25,000 00	
Mounted Police Buildings and River Crossings............	30,000 00	
Public Buildings generally	5,000 00	
		282,500 00
PENITENTIARIES.		
General Penitentiary for the Maritime Provinces	30,000 00	
St. Vincent de Paul........	20,000 00	
Carried forward	50,000 00	342,500 00	11,748,043 19

SCHEDULE B.— *Continued.*

SERVICE.	Amount.	Total.
	$ cts.	$ cts.
Brought forward... 50,000 00	342,500 00	11,748,043 19
PUBLIC WORKS AND BUILDINGS.—*Continued.*		
(Chargeable to Income.)		
PENITENTIARIES.—*Continued.*		
Manitoba Penitentiary......... .... 52,400 00		
do Furniture 2,000 00		
British Columbia Penitentiary 66,000 00		
Penitentiaries generally additions and repairs 5,000 00	175,400 00	
RENTS, REPAIRS, &c.		
Rents, repairs, furniture and heating, &c...................... 182,000 00		
Heating Public Buildings.... .... 40,000 00		
Removal of snow, Public Buildings, Ottawa.................. 2,500 00		
Gas, Public Buildings, Ottawa......... .... 12,000 00		
Allowance for Fuel and Light, Rideau Hall...................... 5,000 00		
Repairs and Miscellaneous Expenses, Rideau Hall....... .... 10,000 00	251,500 00	
HARBOURS AND BREAKWATERS.		
Ontario.		
Cobourg Harbour, Lake Ontario.......... .... 15,000 00		
Bayfield do Lake Huron 5,600 00		
Kincardine do do 3,100 00		
Goderich do do 32,500 00		
Thunder Bay.. 6,000 00		
Quebec.		
Breakwaters, Lower St. Lawrence................................... 5,000 00		
New Brunswick.		
Richibucto Harbour... 10,000 00		
Shippegan Breakwater 11,000 00		
St. John Harbour 65,000 00		
Nova Scotia.		
Musquodoboit, Halifax County.. 1,000 00		
Cow Bay, C.B... .... 10,000 00		
Ingonish South, C.B.............................. .... 15,000 00		
Breakwater between Michaud and Mark Points, Richmond Co 5,000 00		
Chipman's Brook, Kings County........................ .... 2,750 00		
Lingan Beach, C.B................................... .... 2,000 00		
Tracadie, Antigonish County....................................... 750 00		
Carried forward............. .... 189,700 00	769,400 00	11,748,043 19

SCHEDULE B.—*Continued.*

SERVICE.	Amount	Total.
	$ cts.	$ cts.
Brought forward..$189,700 00	769,400 00	11,748,043 19
PUBLIC WORKS AND BUILDINGS.—*Continued.*		
(*Chargeable to Income.*)		
HARBOURS AND BREAKWATERS.—*Continued.*		
Prince Edward Island.		
Tignish.. 4,750 00		
Colville Bay (Souris).. 20,000 00	214,450 00	
SLIDES AND BOOMS..	10,000 00	
MISCELLANEOUS.		
Dredge Vessels...	11,000 00	
Dredging	102,000 00	
Miscellaneous Works not otherwise provided for........................	10,000 00	
Surveys and Inspections..	45,000 00	
Arbitrations and Awards..	15,000 00	
Total chargeable to Income...............................	....	1,176,850 00
OCEAN AND RIVER SERVICE.		
DOMINION STEAMERS.		
Maintenance and repairs of steamers *Napoleon III, Newfield, Druid, Lady Head* and *Sir James Douglas*..............................	80,000 00	
MAIL SUBSIDIES.		
Moiety payable to Allan Line between Halifax and Cork..... 39,541 67		
Steam Communication between Halifax and St. John, *viâ* Yarmouth... 10,000 00		
Steam Communication on Lakes Huron and Superior.......... 12,500 00		
Steam Service between San Francisco and Victoria, British Columbia 54,000 00		
Steam Communication with the Magdalen Islands.............. 4,200 00		
Winter Service by Steamer between Prince Edward Island and the Mainland 15,000 00		
Steam Communication between Nova Scotia and Newfoundland... 5,000 00		
Steam Communication between Grand Manan Island, N.B., and the Mainland.................................... 1,500 00		
To provide for the cost of building and equipping a steamboat to maintain communication between Prince Edward Island and the Mainland during winter months, in accordance with the Terms of Union................. 25,000 00	166,741 67	
To provide for the examination of Masters and Mates........................	4,250 00	
For purchase of Life Boats, Life Preservers and Rewards for Saving Life	7,000 00	
Carried forward	257,991 67	12,924,893 19

SCHEDULE B.

SCHEDULE B.--*Continued.*

SERVICE.	Amount.	Total.
	$ cts.	$ cts.
Brought forward..	257,991 67	12,924,893 19
OCEAN AND RIVER SERVICE.---*Continued.*		
To provide for investigation into Wrecks and Casualties, and Collection of information relating to disasters to Shipping	1,000 00	
Expenses in connection with Canadian Register and Classification of Shipping	6,000 00	
Montreal Water Police	14,090 00	
River Police, Quebec	21,700 00	
Removal of obstructions in navigable rivers......................................	500 00	
		301,281 67
LIGHTHOUSE AND COAST SERVICE.		
Salaries and Allowance of Lighthouse Keepers......................................	142,917 50	
Maintenance and Repairs........... :	213,000 00	
For construction of Lighthouses, and completion of Lighthouses in course of construction................................ ....|	30,000 00	
Salary of Keeper, Time Ball, Halifax (15 months)............................	125 00	
		386,042 50
FISHERIES.		
Salaries and Disbursements of Fishery Overseers and Wardens :—		
Ontario.............	8,860 00	
Quebec	10,000 00	
Nova Scotia, including Inspector and Clerk............................	14,375 00	
New Brunswick, do do	10,085 00	
Prince Edward Island and Manitoba...............	1,500 00	
British Columbia......	1,000 00	
Maintenance and repairs of steamer for protection of fisheries.................	17,000 00	
Fish-breeding, Fishways and Oyster Beds..	16,000 00	
		78,820 00
GEOLOGICAL SURVEY AND OBSERVATORIES.		
Observatory, Quebec	2,400 00	
do Toronto	4,800 00	
do Kingston	500 00	
do Montreal	500 00	
do New Brunswick......	850 00	
Grant for Meteorological Observations, including Instruments and cost of Telegraphing Weather Warnings...	37,000 00	
Additional for Geological Survey..	5,000 00	
		51,050 00
MARINE HOSPITALS AND SICK AND DISTRESSED SEAMEN.		
MARINE HOSPITALS.		
Marine and Emigrant Hospital, Quebec...........	20,000 00	
Montreal General Hospital...... .... 3,000 00		
Other ports in Quebec............. .... 2,000 00		
	5,000 00	
Carried forward...	25,000 00	13,742,087 36

SCHEDULE B.

SCHEDULE B.—*Continued.*

SERVICE.	Amount.	Total.
	$ cts.	$ cts.
Brought forward...	25,000 00	13,742,087 36
MARINE HOSPITALS, &c.—*Continued.*		
MARINE HOSPITALS.—*Continued.*		
St. Catharines Hospital, Ontario......................................	500 00	
Kingston Hospital...	500 00	
	1,000 00	
Halifax General Hospital...	‹3,500 00	
Other ports in Nova Scotia	10,000 00	
	13,500 00	
Hospital of St. John..	4,000 00	
Other ports in New Brunswick......................................	8,000 00	
	12,800 00	
Ports in British Columbia	3,000 00	
Ports in Prince Edward Island	2,000 00	
EXPENSE OF SHIPWRECKED AND DISABLED SEAMEN.		
Province of Quebec..	1,000 00	
do Nova Scotia	2,000 00	
do New Brunswick	1,000 00	
do British Columbia	1,000 00	
do Prince Edward Island....................................	500 00	
To reimburse Board of Trade, London, for expenses incurred in connection with shipwrecked and distressed seamen of the Dominion.........	3,000 00	
		65,000 00
STEAMBOAT INSPECTION.		
SALARIES.		
Chairman...	1,800 00	
Deputy Chairman	1,400 00	
Inspector, Toronto District	1,200 00	
do Three Rivers District...................................	1,000 00	
do Quebec District	1,000 00	
do East Ontario District...................................	1,000 00	
do Montreal	1,200 00	
do British Columbia.......................................	750 00	
Travelling expenses of Chairman, and expenses in connection with Steamboat Inspection..	1,100 00	
Clerk to Board of Inspection.......................................	300 00	
Travelling and incidental expenses of Inspector of New Brunswick and Nova Scotia, and contingencies of Office.......................	865 00	
Travelling expenses of Inspector of Toronto District, and contingencies of Office..	600 00	
Travelling expenses of Inspector, Three Rivers	200 00	
do do Quebec	250 00	
do do East Ontario.........................	330 00	
do do Montreal............................	405 00	
To provide for expenses, inspecting Prince Edward Island steamers.......	500 00	
For purchase of instruments and steam guages......................	550 00	
To provide travelling expenses of Inspector, British Columbia...........	200 00	
		14,650 00
INSPECTION OF INSURANCE COMPANIES.		
To meet expenses in connection with the Inspection of Insurance Companies..	....	6,000 00
Carried forward...	....	13,827,737 36

SCHEDULE B.--*Continued.*

SERVICE.	Amount.	Total.
	$ cts.	$ cts.
Brought forward	....	13,827,737 35
INDIANS.		
For Indians, Quebec..	2,200 00	
Purchase of blankets for aged and infirm Indians of Ontario and Quebec	1,600 00	
Indians of Nova Scotia, relief, &c	4,500 00	
Indians of New Brunswick, relief, &c	4,500 00	
Indians of Prince Edward Island, relief, &c..........................	2,000 00	
Indians of British Columbia :—		
Victoria Superintendency. 15,000 00		
Fraser do 10,000 00		
	25,000 00	
Manitoba Superintendency.		
Annuities under Treaties Nos. 1 and 2..................................	22,926 00	
do do 3..	17,440 00	
do do 5......................................	14,660 00	
Agricultural implements, ammunition, twine, farming stock and tools to be furnished under the above-mentioned Treaties Nos. 1 & 2.	4,000 00	
do do do 3......	8,000 00	
do do do 5......	3,000 00	
Provisions for Indians assembled to receive annuities under the above-mentioned Treaties...	10,000 00	
Salaries and Office Expenses..	18,660 00	
North West Superintendency.		
For annuities under Treaty No. 4	27,610 00	
Agricultural Implements, &c., under Treaty No. 4	8,000 00	
Provisions for Indians assembled to receive annuities	12,000 00	
Ammunition and twine under this Treaty	1,500 00	
Salaries and Office Expenses...	19,000 00	
Probable expense in connection with New Treaties	80,000 00	
Miscellaneous.		
To aid Indians' Schools where most required..	2,000 00	
To meet anticipated expenses in connection with the Sioux..........	2,000 00	
To bring up the annuities payable under the Robinson Treaty to the Chippewas of Lakes Huron and Superior, from 96 cents to $4 per head	11,000 00	
		301,596 00
MISCELLANEOUS.		
Canada *Gazette*..	4,000 00	
Miscellaneous Printing	8,000 00	
Unforeseen expenses : Expenditure thereof under Order in Council, and a detailed statement to be laid before Parliament during the first fifteen days of the next Session	50,000 00	
Commutation in lieu of remission of duties on articles imported for the use of the Army and Navy..	12,000 00	
For the organization of Government in the North-West Territories	12,000 00	
		86,000 00
Carried forward..	....	14,215,333 35

SCHEDULE B.

SCHEDULE B.--*Continued.*

SERVICE.	Amount.	Total.
	$ cts.	$ cts.
Brought forward......	....	14,215,333 36
COLLECTION OF REVENUES.		
CUSTOMS		
Salaries and contingent expenses of the several ports :—		
In Province of Ontario	$219,054 00	
do Quebec..	199,510 00	
do New Brunswick...........	92,329 00	
do Nova Scotia	103,250 00	
do Manitoba and North-West Territories	10,250 00	
do British Columbia	20,208 00	
do Prince Edward Island	21,990 00	
Salaries and travelling expenses of Inspectors of Ports, and travelling expenses of other Officers on Inspection.	16,000 00	
Contingencies of Head Office, covering printing, stationery, advertising, telegraphing, &c., for the several Ports of Entry............	15,000 000	
		697,591 00
EXCISE.		
Salaries of Officers and Inspectors of Excise	177,800 00	
Travelling expenses, rent, fuel, stationery, &c....................	45,000 00	
Preventive Service..........	3,000 00	
To provide for payment of additional salary to special class of Excisemen.......................	3,000 00	
To provide for additions to outside service	5,000 00	
To pay Collectors of Customs allowance on duties collected by them	2,000 00	
		235,800 00
CULLING TIMBER.		
Quebec Office.		
Supervisor..	2,000 00	
Deputy Supervisor and Book-keeper....	1,600 00	
Cashier...	1,200 00	
Specification Clerks	1,900 00	
Messenger	400 00	
Specification Clerks, viz : 4 at $600, 2 at $700, 1 at $500, 2 at $1,000 (8 months)	6,300 00	
Pay of Cullers	57,000 00	
Contingencies	5,000 00	
Montreal and Sorel Offices.		
Deputy Supervisor	800 00	
Book-keeper and Specification Clerks..........	1,000 00	
Pay of Cullers	4,000 00	
Contingencies	300 00	
		81,500 00
WEIGHTS AND MEASURES.		
Equipment.		
For Standards ordered in England, but not yet delivered ...	20,000 00	
Carried forward........	20,000 00	1,014,891 00	14,215,333 36

2½   SCHEDULE B.

SCHEDULE B.—*Continued.*

SERVICE.	Amount.	Total.
	$ cts.	$ cts.
Brought forward.. 20,000 00	1,014,891 00	14,215,333 38
COLLECTION OF REVENUES.—*Continued.*		
WEIGHTS AND MEASURES.—*Continued.*		
Inspection.		
Salaries and expenses of 93 Inspectors of Weights and Measures. (Will be recouped by fees) 72,000 00		
Salaries and expenses of 32 Gas Inspectors.. .... 18,600 00	110,600 00	
INSPECTION OF STAPLES.		
For the purchase and distribution of Standards of Flour, &c., and for other Expenditure under the Act..	3,000 00	
ADULTERATION OF FOOD.		
To meet Expenses under the Act 37 Vict., chap. 8. (Will be mainly recouped by fees)..	10,000 00	
PUBLIC WORKS.		
Maintenance and repairs.		
Salaries and Contingencies of Canal Officers...................... 35,170 00		
Collection of Slide and Boom Dues................................ 18,475 00		
Repairs and Working Expenses of above.......................... 438,500 00		
Intercolonial and other Government Railways in Nova Scotia and New Brunswick, and Intercolonial Railway Quebec... 1,600,000 00		
Prince Edward Island Railway...................................... 200,000 00		
Telegraph Lines, British Columbia (including Subsidy) ... 32,200 00		
do between Prince Edward Island and the Mainland.. 1,946 66		
Agent and Contingencies, British Columbia 4,000 00	2,330,291 66	
POST OFFICE.		
For Ontario and Quebec.. 1,229,000 00		
New Brunswick... 155,000 00		
Nova Scotia.. 188,500 00		
Manitoba... 28,000 00		
British Columbia... 80,000 00		
Prince Edward Island..... .... 52,000 00	1,732,500 00	
DOMINION LANDS.		
Surveys of Land, North-West (including Commissions and Staff)...........	60,000 00	
MINOR REVENUES.		
To defray expenses connected with Minor Revenues.......................	10,000 00	5,271,282 66
Total..	....	19,486,616 03

CHAP. 2.

An Act to amend the Act thirty-first Victoria, chapter five, as respects the Public Accounts.

[*Assented to 12th April,* 1876.]

WHEREAS by section twenty-eight of the Act passed in Preamble. the thirty-first year of Her Majesty's reign, intituled "*An Act respecting the collection and management of the re-* 31 V., c. 5, s. *venue, the auditing of public accounts, and the liability of public* 28. *accountants,*" it is provided that "all estimates submitted to Recital. Parliament shall be for the services coming in course of payment during the financial year, and all balances of appropriation which remain unexpended at the end of the financial year shall lapse and be written off"; and whereas in many cases it has been found impossible, especially in the distant Provinces, to obtain the necessary reports upon which to make the payments authorized by law, for some time after the close of the financial year in which the work was done or the service rendered : Therefore Her Majesty, by and with the advice and consent of the Senate and House of Commons of Canada, enacts as follows :—

1. Upon cause being shewn to the satisfaction of the Final time Governor in Council, he may, by Order in Council, extend for closing the time for finally closing the account of any appropriation, counts may for a period of not more than three months from the end of be extended the financial year,—after the expiration of which extended Council. time, and not before, the balance of such appropriation shall lapse and be written off.

CHAP. 3.

An Act to provide for the payment of a temporary grant to the Province of Manitoba.

[*Assented to 12th April,* 1876.]

WHEREAS, from the circumstances stated in the Minute Preamble. of the Governor in Council, bearing date the twenty-sixth day of October, one thousand eight hundred and seventy-five, laid before Parliament during the present session, it appears that it is expedient that Canada should make to the Province of Manitoba a temporary annual grant sufficient to raise the yearly revenue of the Province derivable from Canada to ninety thousand dollars : Therefore Her Majesty, by and with the advice and consent of the Senate and House of Commons of Canada, enacts as follows :—

1

Temporary yearly grant to Manitoba authorized.

1. Manitoba shall receive from Canada, in addition to the subsidy now payable under the Act in that behalf, an annual grant of twenty-six thousand seven hundred and forty-six dollars and ninety-six cents, being the sum required to raise the revenue of the Province derivable from Canada to the amount aforesaid ; the said grant to be payable by half-yearly instalments, and to commence and be reckoned from the first day of July, one thousand eight hundred and seventy-five, and to continue until the end of the year one thousand eight hundred and eighty-one.

Out of Consolidated Revenue Fund.

2. The sums payable under this Act shall be a charge upon and payable out of the Consolidated Revenue Fund of Canada.

CHAP. 4.

An Act to extend the Acts respecting Dominion Notes to the Provinces of Prince Edward Island, British Columbia and Manitoba.

[Assented to 12th April, 1876.]

Preamble.

HER Majesty, by and with the advice and consent of the Senate and House of Commons of Canada, enacts as follows :—

Acts 31 V., c. 46.

33 V., c. 10, 35 V., c. 7 & 38 V., c. 5, extended to the said Provinces.

Provision for redemption of Dominion Notes.

1. The Act passed in the thirty-first year of Her Majesty's Reign, intituled " *An Act to enable Banks in any part of Canada to use Notes of the Dominion instead of issuing Notes of their own,*" as amended by the several Acts, thirty-third Victoria, chapter ten, thirty-fifth Victoria, chapter seven, and thirty-eighth Victoria, chapter five, is hereby extended and shall apply to the Provinces of Prince Edward Island, British Columbia and Manitoba ; and the Provincial and Dominion Notes mentioned in the Act first cited shall be a legal tender in the said Provinces, in like manner as in the other Provinces to which the said Acts now extend : and the Governor may in his discretion establish branch offices of the Receiver General's Department at Charlottetown, Victoria and Winnipeg, respectively, or any of them, for the redemption of Dominion Notes, or may make arrangments with any chartered bank or banks for the redemption thereof, and may allow a fixed sum per annum for such service at all or any of the said places ; and specie or debentures held at any such place for the redemption of Dominion Notes, shall be deemed to be held by the Receiver General.

CHAP.

CHAP. 5.

An Act to amend the Act respecting the Inland Revenue.

[Assented to 12th April, 1876.]

IN amendment of the Act passed in the thirty-first year of Her Majesty's reign, chapter eight, intituled *"An Act respecting the Inland Revenue,"* Her Majesty, by and with the advice and consent of the Senate and House of Commons of Canada, enacts as follows :— *Preamble.*

1. Sub-section four of section sixty-six of the said Act is hereby repealed, and the following sub-section is enacted in its stead, to be read and to have effect, from and after the passing of this Act, as sub-section four of section sixty-six of the said Act, that is to say :— *Sub-section 4 of s. 66 of 31 V. c. 8, repealed, and new sub-section substituted for it.*

" 4. One hundred measures guaged in the cistern, after " saturation is completed, or in the couch-frame, shall be " held to be equal to eighty-seven and a quarter similar " measures by guage of malt, *Gauging barley and malt.*

. " And so in proportion for every greater or less quantity."

2. Sub-section six of section sixty-six of the said Act is hereby repealed, and the following sub-section is enacted in its stead, to be read and to have effect from and after the passing of this Act, as sub-section six of section sixty-six of the said Act, that is to say :— *Sub-section 6 of section 66 of 31 V., c. 8' repealed, and new sub-section enacted in its place.*

" 6. Malt shall be weighed when removed from the kiln " and placed in the warehouse ; but whenever any quantity " of dry malt stated in measures of capacity, as determined " by guage, by computation as provided in this Act or by " actual measurement, is to be stated by an equivalent in " pounds, the computation of the weight thereof shall be " made by determining, by weighing, the weight of a " measure of such malt,—such measure being so taken as to " be, as nearly as may be, a fair average thereof; and the " weight of the measure so ascertained, multiplied by the " number of such measures contained in the quantity of " malt from which it was taken shall be held to be the true " weight of that quantity." *Weight of malt.*

3. This Act may be cited as " *The Inland Revenue Act Amendment Act*, 1876 ; " and shall be read and construed as one with the Act above cited and with sections seventeen, eighteen, nineteen and twenty of the Act passed in the thirty-third year of Her Majesty's reign, chapter nine, amending the said Act above cited. *Short title. One Act with 31 V., c. 8, and with sections 17, 18, 19 and 20 of 33 V., c. 9.*

CHAP.

CHAP. 6.

An Act to amend the Act thirty-eighth .Victoria, chapter twenty-three, respecting the Northern Railway of Canada.

[*Assented to 12th April, 1876.*]

Preamble.
38 V. c. 23.

IN amendment of the Act passed in the thirty-eighth year of Her Majesty's reign, and intituled "*An Act respecting the lien of the Dominion on the Northern Railway of Canada,*" Her Majesty, by and with the advice and consent of the Senate and House of Commons of Canada, enacts as follows :—

Time for payment of £100,000 Stg. extended.

1. The time allowed by the first section of the said Act, for the payment by the Northern Railway Company of Canada of the sum of one hundred thousand pounds sterling, in the manner and with the effect mentioned in the said section, is hereby extended to the first day of November now next, or to such further period as the Governor in Council may deem expedient, not later than six months after the said day : Provided always, that interest at the rate of six per centum per annum for the time of forbearance, after the first of July next, shall be payable on the said sum of one hundred thousand pounds sterling.

Interest from 1st July, 1876.

CHAP. 7.

An Act to provide for the examination of witnesses on oath by Committees of the Senate and House of Commons, in certain cases.

[*Assented to 12th April, 1876.*]

Preamble.

HER MAJESTY, by and with the advice and consent of the Senate and House of Commons of Canada, enacts as follows :—

Examination on oath or affirmation.

1. Whenever any witness or witnesses is or are to be examined by any Committee of the Senate or House of Commons, and the Senate or House of Commons shall have resolved that it is desirable that such witness or witnesses shall be examined upon oath, such witness or witnesses shall be examined upon oath, or affirmation where affirmation is allowed by law.

By whom administered.

2. Such oath or affirmation shall be administered by the chairman or any member of any such Committee as aforesaid.

3

8. Any witness giving false evidence upon any such Perjury. examination shall be subject and liable to all the pains and penalties of perjury, as fixed by the criminal law.

4. The oath or affirmation aforesaid shall be in the follow- Form of oath. ing form : " The evidence you shall give on this examination shall be the truth, the whole truth, and nothing but the truth. So help you God."

CHAP. 8.

An Act to amend the Act thirty-first Victoria, chapter three, respecting the indemnity to Members of both Houses of Parliament.

[*Assented to 12th April,* 1876.]

IN amendment of " *The Members' Indemnity Act,*" Her Preamble. Majesty, by and with the advice and consent of the Senate and House of Commons of Canada, enacts as follows :—

1. The words " seven dollars " are hereby substituted for Section 4 of the words " four dollars," in the fourth section of the said 31 V. c. 3, Act, and the words " or accountant " are hereby added after amended. the word " clerk," in the said section ; and the section as so When to amended shall apply to the present session. apply.

CHAP. 9.

An Act to make more effectual provision for the adminis- tration of the law relating to corrupt practices at elections of members of the House of Commons.

[*Assented to 12th April,* 1876.]

WHEREAS it is expedient to make more effectual pro- Preamble. vision for the administration of the law relating to corrupt practices at elections of members of the House of Commons : Therefore Her Majesty, by and with the advice and consent of the Senate and House of Commons of Canada, enacts as follows:—

1. In case on the trial of an election petition relating to Persons ap- the election of a member of the House of Commons, it is pearing to the determined that any person has been guilty of a corrupt committed practice within the meaning of " *The Dominion Controverted* corrupt prac- *Elections* tices, to be summoned to appear for summary trial. 37 V. c. 9 cited.

Elections Act, 1874," or in case on such trial there is in the opinion of the Judge sufficient evidence available that any person has been guilty of such corrupt practice as aforesaid to warrant his being put on his trial, the Judge shall order that such person shall be summoned to appear at a time and place to be fixed in such summons,—the time not being more than thirty days from the date of the summons, and the place being the nearest convenient court house or other available room,—in order to be summarily tried for the offence, which shall be specified in the summons.

May be bound by recognizance so to appear.

2. The Judge may, by recognizance, bind such person to appear at the said time and place to be tried, and may, by recognizance, bind any person whom he may consider necessary to be examined touching the matter, to attend at the said time and place and give evidence upon the trial; and any such recognizance shall be of the same effect and any forfeiture thereof shall be enforced in the like manner, and any refusal to enter into the same shall entail the same consequences, as if the recognizance had been given or required in any of the Superior Courts of criminal jurisdiction within the Province in which the election was held.

Issue of the summons to be reported by the judge.

3. The Judge shall, forthwith after the issue thereof, report to the Secretary of the Province in which the election was held, for the information of the Lieutenant Governor, and also to the Secretary of State of Canada for the information of the Governor General, the fact of the issuing of the summons in the first section mentioned.

Witnesses to be summoned and by whom.

4. It shall be the duty of the County Attorney, or other officer on whom in case the party had been charged with an indictable offence the like duty would have devolved, to subpœna to attend at the trial the witnesses who at the trial of the election petition deposed to any facts material to the charge, and such other witnesses as he may think requisite to prove the charge.

Counsel for prosecution.

5. It shall be the duty of the Attorney General of Canada to instruct counsel to assist the local authorities in the due prosecution of the accused.

If the accused fails to appear, trial may proceed.

6. In case the accused, being duly served a reasonable time before the time fixed for the trial, or being bound by recognizance to appear to be tried, fails to appear at the time and place fixed for the trial, the trial may proceed in his absence.

Summary trial and judgment, and before whom.

7. The Judge, or, if he be unable to attend, then at his request some other Judge competent under " *The Dominion Controverted Elections Act,* 1874," to try an election petition for any district of the Province within which the electoral district

in

in question is situate, or being one of the judges of a superior court of criminal jurisdiction within such Province,shall, without a jury and in a summary manner, try the accused, and shall, after hearing the counsel for the prosecution and also (if the accused be present), such accused or his counsel, and also such evidence as may be adduced on either side, give such judgment as to law and justice may appertain.

8. The Judge shall be received and attended at the trial in the same manner, as far as circumstances will admit, as if he were holding a sitting of the Provincial court of which he is a member. Reception, &c., of judges.

9. The travelling expenses of the Judge and any expenses necessarily incurred by the sheriff or other officer in connexion with the trial, shall be defrayed out of any moneys which may be provided by Parliament for the purpose. Expenses of trial, &c., how payable.

10. The Judge trying the accused is for all the purposes of such . trial and the proceedings connected therewith, or relating thereto, hereby constituted a court of record, under the name of " *The Court for the summary trial of corrupt practices at Elections,*" and shall, subject to the provisions of this Act, have the same powers, jurisdiction and authority as if he were sitting in any superior court of criminal jurisdiction within the Province; and the record of any such case shall be filed among the records of such superior court, as indictments are and as part of such records. Judge's court to be a court of record. Record of trial to be filed.

11. Witnesses shall be summoned or subpœnaed and sworn in the same manner as nearly as circumstances will admit, and shall be subject to the like penalties for perjury as in cases in a superior court of criminal jurisdiction within the Province. Summoning and swearing witnesses.

12. Any witness, summoned or subpœnaed, whether for or against the accused, to attend and give evidence at the trial, shall be bound to attend, and remain in attendance throughout the whole trial ; and in case he fails, he shall be held guilty of contempt of court and may be proceeded against therefor accordingly. Witnesses bound to attend and give evidence.

13. Upon proof to the satisfaction of the Judge of the service of the subpœna upon any witness who fails to attend, and that the presence of such witness is material to the ends of justice, he may, by his warrant, cause such witness to be apprehended and forthwith brought before him to give evidence and to answer for his disregard of the subpœna ; and such witness may be detained on such warrant before the Judge or in the common gaol with a view to secure his Punishment of witnesses disobeying the order of the court.

presence

presence as a witness, or in the discretion of the Judge he may be released on a recognizance with or without sureties conditioned for his appearance to give evidence and to answer for his default in not attending as for a contempt:

Fine and imprisonment limited. the Judge may, in a summary manner, examine into and dispose of the charge of contempt against such witness, who, if found guilty thereof, may be fined or imprisoned or both, —the fine not exceeding one hundred dollars and the imprisonment being in the common gaol, with or without hard labour, for a term not exceeding ninety days.

Punishment of offender if convicted. **14.** In case of conviction of a corrupt practice the offender shall be sentenced to imprisonment in the common gaol for a term not exceeding three months with or without hard labour and to a fine not exceeding two hundred dollars and to pay the costs of the prosecution—to be taxed by the proper officer under the direction of the Judge; and if the said fine and costs be not paid before the expiration of such term, then to imprisonment for such further time as they shall remain unpaid, not exceeding three months.

Application of fines. **15.** All fines recovered under this Act shall belong to Her Majesty for the public uses of Canada.

Proviso if offender has been already tried. **16.** No summons shall be issued or prosecuted under this Act if it appears to the Judge or court that a criminal prosecution for the same matter against the same person has been tried before the issue of the summons.

Pending prosecution stayed. **17.** Upon the issue of any summons under this Act any criminal prosecution pending in any other court in respect of the same matter shall be stayed.

Offender not to be twice tried. Proviso as to disqualification. **18.** No person tried under the provisions of this Act shall be subject to be otherwise criminally prosecuted in respect of the same matter : Provided that nothing in this section contained shall affect any disqualification imposed on such person under the operation of any Statute.

Report of proceedings of Commissioners under c. 10, of this session that any person has been guilty of corrupt practices. **19.** Where it appears by the report of the Commissioners under the Act of the present session intituled " *An Act to provide for more effectual enquiry into the existence of corrupt practices at Elections of Members of the House of Commons* " that any person named by them has been guilty of a corrupt practice and has not been furnished by them with a certificate of indemnity, such report, with the evidence taken by the Commissioners, shall be laid before the Attorney General of Canada, who shall, if in his opinion there is sufficient evidence available for a prosecution, certify such opinion to the Secretary of State who shall thereupon communicate the report with the evidence to the Lieutenant Governor of the
Province

Próvince in which the election was held ; and it shall be the duty of the Attorney General of Canada to instruct counsel to assist in any prosecution which may be thereon instituted by the local authorities charged with the administration of justice. *Proceedings in consequence.*

CHAP. 10.

An Act to provide for more effectual Inquiry into the existence of Corrupt Practices at Elections of Members of the House of Commons.

[Assented to 12th April, 1876.]

WHEREAS it is expedient to make more effectual provision for inquiring into the existence of corrupt practices at elections of Members of the House of Commons ; Therefore Her Majesty, by and with the advice and consent of the Senate and House of Commons of Canada, enacts as follows :— *Preamble.*

1. In addition to the matters to be reported on by the Judge, under the thirtieth section of " *The Dominion Controverted Elections Act*, 1874," the Judge shall report whether he is of opinion that the inquiry into the circumstances of the election has been rendered incomplete by the action of any of the parties to the petition, and that further inquiry as to whether corrupt practices have extensively prevailed is desirable. *Report under 37 V., c. 10, as to corrupt practices to be made by judge.*

2. When the Judge, in his report on the trial of an election petition under the said Act, states that corrupt practices have, or that there is reason to believe that corrupt practices have extensively prevailed at the election to which the petition relates, or that he is of opinion that the inquiry into the circumstances of the election has been rendered incomplete by the action of any of the parties to the petition, and that further inquiry as to whether corrupt practices have extensively prevailed is desirable, no new writ shall issue for a new election under the thirty-sixth section of the said Act, save by order of the House of Commons. *When the judge reports his opinion that corrupt practices have prevailed, &c., new writ to issue only on order of the House of Commons.*

8. When the House of Commons, by address, represents to the Governor that a Judge in his report on the trial of an election petition under the said Act, states that corrupt practices have, or that there is reason to believe that corrupt practices have extensively prevailed at the election, or that he is of opinion that the inquiry into the circumstances of the election has been rendered *On such report, and that inquiry is desirable, or on Address of House of Commons on petition from electors for the place,*

incomplete

Commission of Inquiry to issue.

incomplete by the action of any of the parties to the petition, and that further inquiry as to whether corrupt practices have extensively prevailed is desirable ; or when the House of Commons by address represents to the Governor that a petition has been, within sixty days after the publication in the *Canada Gazette* of the receipt of the return to a writ of election, by the Clerk of the Crown in Chancery, (if Parliament be sitting at the expiration of the period of sixty days, or, if Parliament be not then sitting, within fourteen days after the then next meeting of Parliament,) presented to the House of Commons, signed by any twenty-five or more electors of the district, stating that no petition charging the existence of corrupt practices has been presented under the Act for the trial of Controverted Elections, and that corrupt practices have, or that there is reason to believe that corrupt practices have, extensively prevailed at the election, and having annexed thereto a solemn declaration under the statute in that behalf, signed by the petitioners, stating that they are such electors, and that the allegations of the petition are true to the best of their knowledge and belief; and when the House of Commons, by such address, prays the Governor to cause inquiry to be made under this Act by one or more Judges of the Supreme Court of Canada, or by one or more judges competent under " *The Dominion Controverted Elections Act,* 1874," to try an election petition for any district of the Province within which the district in question is situate, or by one or more persons named in such address, such persons being County Court Judges, or being Barristers at Law or Advocates of not less than seven years standing, and not holding any office or place of profit under the Crown, it shall be lawful for the Governor to appoint one or more of such judges or such person or persons, as the case may be, to be a Commissioner or Commissioners for the purpose of making inquiry into the existence of such corrupt practices ; and in case any of the Commissioners so appointed die, resign, or become incapable to act, it shall be lawful for the surviving or continuing Commissioners or Commissioner to act in such inquiry as if they or he had been solely appointed to be Commissioners or a Commissioner for the purposes of such inquiry ; and all the provisions of this Act concerning the Commissioners appointed to make any such inquiry shall be taken to apply to such surviving or continuing Commissioners or Commissioner, and in case a sole Commissioner be originally appointed, then to such sole Commissioner.

Who may be appointed commissioners.

In case of decease or inability of any commissioners, surviving or continuing commissioners to act.

Commissioners' oath of office.

4. Every Commissioner shall before taking any other step under this Act, take the following oath, that is to say:—
" I, A.B, do swear that I will truly and faithfully execute
" the powers and trusts vested in me by an Act intituled
" *(here*

" *(here insert the title of this Act)* according to the best of my " knowledge and judgment. So help me God ;" and every such oath shall be taken before a Judge of the Supreme Before whom. Court of Canada or before a judge competent to try an election petition for any district of the Province within which the district in question is situate.

5. It shall be lawful for the Commissioners to appoint, Secretary to and at their pleasure to dismiss, a secretary, and so many commission. clerks, messengers, and officers, as shall be thought necessary by the Minister of Justice for the purpose of conducting the inquiry to be made by them ; and the remuneration of such persons shall be fixed by the Governor in Council.

6. The Commissioners shall, upon their appointment, or Proceedings within a reasonable time afterwards, go to and shall, of commis-from time to time, hold meetings for the purposes of sioners. the inquiry at some convenient place within the district or within ten miles thereof, and shall have power to adjourn such meetings from time to time, and from place to place within the district or within ten miles thereof, as to them may seem expedient ; and they shall give Notice. notice of their appointment and of the time and place of holding their first meeting by publishing the same in two newspapers in general circulation in the district or the neighbourhood thereof : Provided always, that they shall Proviso as to not adjourn the enquiry for any period exceeding adjourn-ments, and as one week, without the approbation of the Minister of to place of Justice : Provided also, that it shall be lawful for them, sitting. with the approbation of the Minister of Justice, to hold meetings for the purposes of deliberation, in the capital city of the Province within which the district is situate, or in the city of Ottawa, and to adjourn the same from time to time, as they may deem fit.

7. The Commissioners shall, by all such lawful means as Duties of to them appear best with a view to the discovery of the commis-sioners. truth, enquire into the manner in which the election, or where the report or petition has referred to two or more elections, the latest of such elections has been conducted, and whether any corrupt practices have been committed at such election, and if so the nature and particulars of such corrupt practices ; and in case they find that corrupt practices In certain have been committed at the election into which they are cases inquiry may extend hereinbefore authorized to inquire, it shall be lawful for them to former to make the like inquiries concerning the latest previous elections. election, and so in like manner from election to election as far back as they think fit ; but where, upon But in such inquiry concerning any election, they do not find that cases only. corrupt practices have been committed thereat, they shall not inquire concerning any previous election ; and they Report to the shall, from time to time, report to the Governor the evidence Governor taken

and particu-
lars to be
contained in
it.

taken by them, and what they find concerning the premises; and especially they shall report with respect to each election the names of all persons whom they find to have been guilty of any corrupt practice thereat, with the particulars thereof, and all other things whereby in their opinion the truth may be better known touching the premises.

Report to be
laid before
Parliament.

8. Every report shall be laid before Parliament within fourteen days after such report is made, if Parliament be sitting at the expiration of the said period of fourteen days, or if Parliament be not then sitting within fourteen days after the then next meeting of Parliament.

Power to
examine and
to command
attendance of
witnesses, and
production of
papers.

9. It shall be lawful for the Commissioners by a summons under their hands and seals, or under the hand and seal of any one of them, to require the attendance before them, at a place and reasonable time to be specified in the summons, of any person whose evidence in their or his judgment may be material to the subject matter of the inquiry, and to require any person to bring before them such books, papers, deeds, and writings as appear necessary for arriving at the truth of the matters to be inquired into ; and all such persons shall attend the Commissioners, and shall answer all questions put to them by the Commissioners touching the matters to be enquired into, and shall produce all books, papers, deeds, and writings required of them and in their custody or under their control according to the tenor of the summons.

To swear
witnesses.

Perjury.

10. The Commissioners, or one of them, shall administer an oath or an affirmation, where an affirmation would be admitted in a court of justice, to every person examined before them ; and any person who, upon such examination, wilfully gives false evidence, shall be liable to the pains and penalties of perjury.

Witnesses not
excused from
answering on
certain
grounds.

Proviso :
witness
giving answer
tending to
criminate
him, may
obtain a certi-
ficate, which
shall stay
prosecution
for offences
acknow-
ledged in his
evidence.

11. No person called as a witness shall be excused from answering any question relating to any corrupt practice at the election forming the subject of inquiry, on the ground that the answer thereto may criminate or tend to criminate himself : Provided always, that where any witness shall answer every question relating to the matters aforesaid which he shall be required to answer, and the answer to which may criminate, or tend to criminate him, he shall be entitled to receive from the Commissioners, under their hands, a certificate stating that he was, upon his examination, required by them to answer one or more questions relating to the matters aforesaid, the answer or answers to which criminated, or tended to criminate him, and had answered every such question ; and if any information, indictment or penal action be at any time thereafter pending in any court against such witness in respect of any corrupt practices committed by him
previously

previously to the time of his giving his evidence, at any election concerning which he may have been so examined, the court shall, on production and proof of such certificate, stay such proceedings, and may, at its discretion, award to him any costs to which he may have been put: Provided that no statement made by any person in answer to any question put by the Commissioners shall, except in case of indictment for perjury, be admissible in evidence in any legal proceeding.

Proviso as to statements made by witnesses.

12. If any person on whom any summons shall have been served by the delivery thereof to him, or by the leaving thereof at his usual place of abode, fail to appear before the Commissioners at the time and place specified therein, then in case the Commissioners be judges of any of the courts hereinbefore referred to, it shall be lawful for any of them and any court of which any of them is a member, to proceed against the person so failing in the same manner as if he had failed to obey any writ of subpœna, or any process lawfully issuing from the court to which such judge belongs, or from such judge; and in case the Commissioners be not such judges, it shall be lawful for them to certify such default under their hands and seals, or under the hand and seal of any one of them, to any court or judge competent to try an election petition under "*The Dominion Controverted Elections Act, 1874*," or any Act amending it, for any district of the Province within which the district in question is situate, whereupon such court or judge shall proceed against such person in manner aforesaid: and if any person so summoned to attend as aforesaid, or having appeared before the Commissioners, shall refuse to be sworn or to make answer to any question put to him by them touching the matters in question, or to produce and show to them any papers, books, deeds, or writings being in his possession or under his control, which they may deem necessary to be produced, or if any person shall be guilty of any contempt of the Commissioners, or their office, the Commissioners shall have the same powers, to be exercised in the same way, as any such judge or court under like circumstances arising in the course of proceedings in an election petition under the said Act may by law exercise in that behalf: and all officers concerned in the administration of justice shall give their aid and assistance in matters within the scope of their duty to the Commissioners in the execution of their office.

Punishment of persons disobeying summons of commissioners.

If the commissioners are not judges.

Or for refusing to answer or produce papers, &c.,

or being guilty of any contempt.

Duty of officers of justice.

13. The Commissioners shall have power, if they deem fit, to award to any witness summoned to appear before them a reasonable sum for travelling expenses and maintenance, according to a scale to be fixed by the Governor in Council, and they shall certify to the Minister of Justice the name of any such witness, and the sum awarded.

Remuneration of witnesses.

3   **14.**

Payment of necessary expenses of commissioners.

14. It shall be lawful for the Governor in Council to order the payment of the necessary expenses of any inquiry under this Act; and every Commissioner not being a Judge shall be paid at the conclusion of the inquiry, besides his travelling and other expenses, such · sum as shall be fixed by the Governor in Council; and every Commissioner shall, after the making of the report hereinbefore directed, lay before the Governor in Council a statement of the number of days he has been actually employed in the inquiry, together with an account of his travelling and

Out of what funds.

other expenses; and any payments by this Act authorized shall be made out of any moneys which may be provided by Parliament for the purposes of Commissions issued hereunder.

Protection of commissioners.

15. The Commissioners shall have such· and the like protection and privileges in case of any action brought against them for any act done or omitted to be done in the execution of their duty, as is given by any Act in force to Justices of the Peace acting in the execution of their office.

CHAP. 11.

An Act to detach a certain portion of the County of Lotbinière and to attach it to the County of Beauce.

[*Assented to 12th April,* 1876.]

Preamble.

WHEREAS the Parish of St. Séverin, in the County and District of Beauce, including therein a portion of the seigniory of Beaurivage, in the County of Lotbinière, has lately been constituted, and whereas the said Parish of St. Séverin forms a separate and distinct municipality, and it is expedient to detach the said portion of the seigniory of Beaurivage from the County or Electoral District of Lotbinière and to attach it to the County or Electoral District of Beauce, for the purposes of representation in the House of Commons : Therefore Her Majesty, by and with the advice and consent of the Senate and House of Commons of Canada, enacts as follows :—

Part of Co. of Lotbinière annexed to Co. of Beauce for electoral purposes.

1. From and after the coming into force of this Act, that portion of the municipality of the Parish of St. Séverin, now forming part of the County of Lotbinière for the purposes hereinafter mentioned, shall be detached from the said County of Lotbinière, and shall be annexed to the County of Beauce for the purposes of representation in the House of Commons.

2

2. The first section of chapter two of the Consolidated How certain Statutes of Canada and the thirtieth and forty-third sub- parts of former sections of section one, of chapter seventy-five of the statutes shall Consolidated Statutes for Lower Canada, in so far as they be construed. apply to representation in the House of Commons of Canada, shall be read and interpreted in conformity with the foregoing provision.

CHAP. 12.

An Act to amend the Acts therein mentioned, respecting the Militia and the Defence of the Dominion of Canada.

[*Assented to 12th April, 1876.*]

IN amendment of the Acts respecting the Militia and Preamble, Defence of Canada: Her Majesty, by and with the advice and consent of the Senate and House of Commons of Canada, enacts as follows:—

1. The first section of the Act passed in the thirty-seventh Sect. 1 of 37 year of Her Majesty's reign, and intituled "*An Act to amend* V., c. 35, *the Acts respecting the Militia and the Defence of the Dominion* repealed. *of Canada, and to extend the same to the Province of Prince Edward Island,*" is hereby repealed.

2. The next enrolment of the Militia under the Act passed When the in the thirty-first year of Her Majesty's reign, intituled enrolment under s. 16 of "*An Act respecting the Militia and Defence of the Dominion* 31 V., c. 40, *of Canada,*" shall be made and completed on or before the shall take twenty-eighth day of February, one thousand eight hundred place. and eighty, and such enrolment shall be made and completed on or before the like day in every fifth year thereafter, in the manner provided by the said Act; and so much of the sixteenth section of the said Act as would require such enrolment to be made at any earlier or other time is hereby repealed: Provided always, that in case of war or Proviso. other emergency, the enrolment mentioned in the said section may be made at any time by order of the Governor in in Council.

3½ -   CHAP.

CHAP. 13.

An Act to make provision for the Collection and Registration of the Criminal Statistics of Canada.

[*Assented to 12th April*, 1876.]

Preamble.

WHEREAS it is expedient to make provision by law for the collection and registration of the criminal statistics of Canada : Therefore Her Majesty, by and with the advice and consent of the Senate and House of Commons of Canada, enacts as follows :—

Schedules of criminal statistics to be filled up and transmitted yearly by certain functionaries to the proper Minister, in forms furnished by him.

1. The clerk, and where there is no clerk, the officer performing like duties, and where there is no such officer, the judge of every court administering criminal justice, and the warden of every penitentiary or reformatory, and the sheriff of every district, shall, before the end of October in each year, fill up and transmit to the Minister of Agriculture, or in case this branch of the subject of statistics and the registration thereof be, by the Governor in Council, assigned to any other Minister, then to such other Minister, such schedules for the year ending the thirtieth day of September preceding, relative, in the case of the clerk, officer or judge to the criminal business transacted in the court, and in the cases of the warden or sheriff to the prisoners committed to his penitentiary, reformatory or gaol, as he shall receive from time to time from the said Minister.

Returns under 32 & 33 Vic., c. 31, s. 81, to be transmitted to the proper Minister yearly.

2. Every officer required by the "*Act respecting the duties of Justices of the Peace out of sessions, in relation to summary convictions and orders*" (being thirty-second and thirty-third Victoria, chapter thirty-one) to transmit to the Minister of Finance true copies of returns made by Justices of the Peace under the said Act, shall, before the end of October in each year, transmit to the Minister of Agriculture, or such other Minister as aforesaid ; true copies of all such returns for the year ending the thirtieth day of September preceding, instead of transmitting the same at the times required by the eighty-first section of the said Act.

Records to be kept for filling up schedules under section 1.

3. It shall be the duty of every person required under the first section hereof to transmit any schedules, to make from day to day and to keep entries and records of the particulars to be comprised in such schedules.

Remuneration of persons filling up and

4. The Minister of Agriculture, or such other Minister as aforesaid, shall cause to be paid out of any moneys which may be provided by Parliament for that purpose, to any clerk,

clerk, officer, warden of a reformatory or sheriff, filling transmitting up and transmitting the schedules required under the first schedules. section of this Act, the sum of one dollar, and the further sum of five cents for each case comprised in such schedules ; and to any officer transmitting the returns required under the second section of this Act the sum of one dollar: Provided that—

(1.) Whenever in any Province 'a system of collecting Proviso as to statistics relative to the prisoners committed to the provin- provincial gaols and cial gaols or reformatories is established, the Governor in reformatories Council may arrange with the Government of such Province for the collection and transmission through such Government of any part of the information to be embraced in the schedules authorized under this Act ; and that—

(2.) In case of such arrangements, the Minister of Agri- Payment in culture, or such other Minister, as aforesaid, may cause to be such case. paid out of any moneys which may be provided by Parliament for that purpose, to the Government of such Province instead of to the sheriffs or wardens, such sum as may be agreed on, not exceeding the amounts which would otherwise be payable for like services, to the sheriffs or wardens.

5. Any person neglecting or refusing to fill up and Penalty on transmit any schedule, or transmit any return required under persons neglecting to the first or second section hereof, or wilfully making a comply with false, partial or incorrect schedule or return under either of the requirements of the said sections, shall forfeit and pay the sum of eighty dol- this Act. lars together with full costs of suit, to be recovered by any person suing for the same by action of debt or information, in any court of record in the Province in which such return ought to have been made or is made, or in the Exchequer Court of Canada,—one moiety whereof shall be paid to the Application party suing, and the other moiety into the hands of Her of penalty. Majesty's Receiver General, to and for the public uses of Canada.

6. The Secretary of State shall, before the end of October Duty of in each year, cause to be filled up and transmitted to the Secretary of State respect- Minister of Agriculture, or such other Minister as aforesaid, ing exercise such schedules for the year ending the thirtieth day of Sep- of prerogative of mercy. tember preceding, relative to the cases in which the prerogative of mercy has been exercised, as he shall, from time to time, receive from the Minister of Agriculture, or such other Minister as aforesaid.

7. All schedules transmitted under this Act shall be Forms to be according to forms from time to time approved by the approved by Governor in Governor in Council, and published in the *Canada Gazette.* Council and published. **8.**

Statistics to
be abstracted
and printed
yearly.

8. The statistics collected by the Minister of Agriculture, or such other Minister as aforesaid, under this Act shall be abstracted and registered, and the results thereof shall be printed and published in an annual report.

Interpreta-
tion.

9. The word "Judge" in the first section of this Act includes any Recorder, District, Stipendiary, or other Magistrate, or other functionary presiding over any court or tribunal administering criminal justice.

CHAP. 14.

An Act to amend " The Railway Statistics Act."

[Assented to 12th April, 1876.]

Preamble.

HER Majesty, by and with the advice and consent of the Senate and House of Commons of Canada, enacts as follows :—

Sect. 2 of 38
V., c. 25,
repealed and
new sect.
substituted.

1. The second section of the Act passed in the thirty-eighth year of Her Majesty's reign intituled : "*An Act to extend and amend the law requiring Railway Companies to furnish returns of their capital, traffic and working expenditure,*" and chaptered twenty-five, is hereby repealed, and the following section shall be taken and read as forming the second section of the said Act :—

Companies to
furnish yearly
returns to
Government,
and in what
form and with
what details.

"**2.** Every company shall annually prepare returns of their capital in accordance with the form contained in Schedule One to this Act, and a copy of such returns signed by the President or other head officer of the company resident in Canada and by the officer of the company responsible for the correctness of each return or any part thereof, shall be forwarded by the company to the Minister of Public Works, not later than three months after the end of the calendar year ; together with a copy of the then last annual return of the traffic and working expenditure which every such company is required to keep, in accordance with the provisions of their respective Acts of incorporation, to be verified in manner and form aforesaid, and furnished in such form as the Minister of Public Works shall approve of or

Penalty for
default.

prescribe. Any company which fails to forward the said returns in accordance with the provisions of this section, shall be liable to a penalty not exceeding ten dollars for every day during which such default continues."

2.

2. All penalties imposed by the said Act hereinbefore cited, as hereby amended, shall be recoverable by the person suing for the same for his own use and benefit in any court having jurisdiction in civil cases to the amount. Recovery of penalties.

3. The foregoing sections shall be read as part of the said Act hereinbefore cited, and the said sections and Act shall be construed accordingly. How this Act shall be construed

---

CHAP. 15.

An Act to make provision for the crossing of Navigable Waters by Railway or other Road Companies incorporated under Provincial Acts.

[Assented to 12th April, 1876.]

WHEREAS it is expedient to make provision for the crossing of navigable waters within any Province by railway or other road companies, incorporated under Acts of the Legislature of such Province : Therefore, Her Majesty, by and with the advice and consent of the Senate and House of Commons of Canada, enacts as follows :— Preamble

1. Whenever any railway company or other road company is lawfully incorporated by an Act of a Provincial Legislature, with power to construct a railway or other road on a line intersected by any navigable water, and it is necessary for such construction that such road should be carried across or along such navigable water, the fifty-fourth, fifty-fifth, fifty-sixth and fifty-eighth sections of " *The Railway Act,* 1868," shall, subject to the provisions of this Act, apply to such company in respect of the carrying such road by such company across or along such navigable water. Certain provisions of 31 V., c. 68 to apply to companies incorporated by Provincial Acts to construct roads crossing navigable waters.

2. Any company proposing to construct any work under this Act shall give public notice for six weeks, in two newspapers published nearest the site of the proposed work, that the plan and proposed site has been submitted to the Railway Committee of the Privy Council under the said fifty-sixth section, and that it is intended to apply to the Governor in Council to authorize the work. Notice to be given by such company.

3. Subject to the provisions of the said fifty-fourth, fifty-fifth, fifty-sixth and fifty-eighth sections, the Governor in Council may, after the expiration of the notice prescribed by the second section of this Act, authorize such company to carry such road across or along such navigable water, pursuant to a plan and on a site to be approved by the Railway Committee How only the road may be carried across or along such waters.

Committee under the said fifty-sixth section, upon such con
ditions as shall appear reasonable : Provided that no unnecessary damage be caused to any lands by reason of the
work, and that compensation be made for any damage
caused to any lands by reason of the work,—the amount of
such compensation in case of disagreement to be settled
under the provisions of " *The Railway Act,* 1868," and any
Act amending the same.

Act 35 V., c.
15, to apply
to the work.

4. In case any company constructs any work under the
provisions of this Act, such company shall, as to the work so
constructed but no further or otherwise, be subject to the
provisions of the Act passed in the thirty-fifth year of Her
Majesty's Reign, intituled : " *An Act respecting Bridges,*"
and the whole of such work shall be deemed to be bridge
within the purview of the said Act and subject to all the
provisions thereof.

Certain
powers re-
served to
Parliament.

5. Parliament may, at any time, annul or vary any Order
of the Governor in Council, made under the third section
of this Act ; and no such legislation shall be deemed an infringement of the rights of the company.

Not to apply
to certain
Rivers.

6. No order shall be made under this Act to authorize the
crossing of the River St. Lawrence or the River St. John.

CHAP. 16.

An Act respecting the Intercolonial Railway.

[Assented to 12th April, 1876.]

Preamble.
38 V., c. 22.

WHEREAS by an Act passed in the thirty-eighth year of
Her Majesty's reign, intituled " *An Act respecting the
Intercolonial Railway,*" it is amongst other things in effect
enacted and declared, that the line of railway from Halifax
to Pictou, in the Province of Nova Scotia, together with
other lines of railway in the said Act mentioned, and all
works and property thereunto appertaining, constitute and
form the Intercolonial Railway, and are vested in Her
Majesty and under the control and management of the
Minister of Public Works : and whereas doubts may arise
whether the railway line and works now under course of
construction from Richmond Station in the City of Halifax,
to North Street in the said City of Halifax, come within the
designation of, and constitute and form part of the Intercolonial Railway under the said Act, and it is desirable to
remove such doubts : Therefore Her Majesty, by and with
the advice and consent of the Senate and House of Commons
of Canada, declares and enacts as follows :—

1.

1. The line of railway from Halifax to Pictou mentioned Line from in the first section of the said Act, comprises the said line Richmond ·from Richmond Station to North Street in the City of North Street, Halifax, forming part of the Intercolonial Railway within Halifax, is the meaning of the said Act, which shall be read and con- said Railway. strued accordingly.

2. Inasmuch as the Intercolonial Railway is a public Minister may work of Canada, the Minister of Public Works has, and he exercise as to may at his option exercise with respect to the same or the con- way, the struction, maintenance or amendment of the same, or any powers given part thereof, or in any respect whatsoever connected there-by 31 V., c. 12. with, any of the rights, powers and authorities granted and conferred in and by the Act passed in the thirty-first year of Her Majesty's reign, intituled: " *An Act respecting the Public Works of Canada.*"

CHAP 17.

An Act respecting the Desjardins' Canal.

[Assented to 12th April, 1876.]

WHEREAS by an Act of the legislature of the late Preamble. Province of Upper Canada, passed in the seventh Recital of year of the reign of His Majesty, King George the Act of U. C. Fourth, chapter eighteen, after reciting that public benefits c. 18. were expected to be derived from connecting Burlington Bay with Lake Ontario, and in order that those bene- fits might be more generally extended to the surround- ing country, it was of manifest importance to form a water communication or canal sufficient for the passage of sloops and other vessels of burden, from the said bay to the village of Cootes Paradise, through the intervening marsh and other lands, and further reciting, that Peter Desjardins and others, had petitioned the Legislature to be by law incor- porated for the purpose of effecting by means of a joint capital or stock, such water communication or canal from the said bay to the said village ;—it is in effect enacted, that certain persons therein named were constituted and declar- ed to be a body corporate and politic, by the name of the "Desjardins' Canal Company ; " and it is further by the said Act enacted that the Company should have full power and authority for the purposes of forming and completing the said canal, to purchase and hold in their corporate capacity such real estate as might be necessary for all the purposes of the said canal and of the said Act ; and it is further in effect enacted, that the said Act now in recital should continue in force for fifty years from the time of the passing

passing thereof, and from thence to the end of the then next
ensuing Session of Parliament, at which time the estate,
rights, titles, tolls and rates of the said canal, with the
waters and navigation thereof, should vest in His Majesty,
His heirs and successors, to and for the use of the said late
Province of Upper Canada in manner aforesaid, unless otherwise provided for by any Act of the Legislature, to be for
that purpose at any time thereafter enacted :

Canal vested
in the Crown
at the end of
the session of
Parliament
next after
fifty years
from passing
the said Act.

And whereas the estate, rights, titles, tolls and rates of the
said canal, with the waters and navigation thereof, will at
the end of the session of Parliament next ensuing the
thirtieth day of January in the year one thousand eight
hundred and seventy-six (being fifty years from the time of
the passing of the said Act hereinbefore in part recited) vest
in Her Majesty, Her Heirs and Successors, to and for the use
of Canada, unless otherwise provided for by any Act for
that purpose to be enacted :

Canal will
then be a
public work
of Canada.

And whereas the said Desjardins' Canal will, from the date
last hereinbefore mentioned, become a public work of
Canada, and as such be and continue vested in Her Majesty
and under the control and management of the Minister of
Public Works ; and it is expedient that the Minister of Public
Works should be authorized to enter into arrangements and
upon the completion of such arrangements to grant, transfer
and convey the said Desjardins' Canal, as is hereinafter authorized : Therefore Her Majesty, by and with the advice
and consent of the Senate and House of Commons of Canada,
enacts as follows :—

Certain sec-
tions of 31
V., c. 12, to
apply to it.

1. The fifty-second, fifty-third, fifty-fourth, fifty-fifth, fifty-
sixth and fifty-seventh sections of the Act passed in the
thirty-first year of Her Majesty's reign, and intituled, *" An
Act respecting the Public Works of Canada"* shall apply
to the Desjardins' canal, which shall, after the expiration of the said charter, be deemed a public work of Canada,
and may be dealt with and treated as if it were in the said
sections of the said Act specially mentioned.

Provision in
case of its
transfer
under the
said sections.

2. In the event of any grant, transfer or conveyance of the
Desjardins' canal, in pursuance of the authority contained
in the said sections of the said Act, the tariff of tolls to be
imposed in respect of the use of the said Desjardins' canal
and its appurtenances, shall be, from time to time, submitted
to the Governor, and no tolls shall be collected unless the rates
be first approved by the Governor in Council.

CHAP.

CHAP. 18.

An Act to amend and consolidate the laws respecting Indians.

[Assented to 12th April, 1876.]

WHEREAS it is expedient to amend and consolidate the Preamble. laws respecting Indians: Therefore Her Majesty, by and with the advice and consent of the Senate and House of Commons of Canada, enacts as follows :—

1. This Act shall be known and may be cited as " *The* Short title Indian Act, 1876 ; " and shall apply to all the Provinces, and and extent of to the North West Territories, including the Territory of Act. Keewatin.

2. The Minister of the Interior shall be Superintendent- Superintend-General of Indian Affairs, and shall be governed in the ent General. supervision of the said affairs, and in the control and management of the reserves, lands, moneys and property of Indians in Canada by the provisions of this Act.

TERMS.

3. The following terms contained in this Act shall be held Meanings as-to have the meaning hereinafter assigned to them, unless such signed to meaning be repugnant to the subject or inconsistent with the Act. terms in this context :—

1. The term "band" means any tribe, band or body of Band. Indians who own or are interested in a reserve or in Indian lands in common, of which the legal title is vested in the Crown, or who share alike in the distribution of any annuities or interest moneys for which the Government of Canada is responsible ; the term "the band" means the band to which the context relates ; and the term "band," when action is being taken by the band as such, means the band in council.

2. The term "irregular band" means any tribe, band or Irregular body of persons of Indian blood who own no interest in any Band. reserve or lands of which the legal title is vested in the Crown, who possess no common fund managed by the Government of Canada, or who have not had any treaty relations with the Crown.

3,. The term "Indian" means   Indians.

First. Any male person of Indian blood reputed to belong to a particular band ;

Secondly.

Secondly. Any child of such person ;

Thirdly. Any woman who is or was lawfully married to such person :

As to illegiti- (a) Provided that any illegitimate child, unless having
mates. shared with the consent of the band in the distribution moneys of such band for a period exceeding two years. may, at any time, be excluded from the membership thereof by the band, if such proceeding be sanctioned by the Superintendent-General :

Absentees. (b). Provided that any Indian having for five years continuously resided in a foreign country shall with the sanction of the Superintendent-General, cease to be a member thereof and shall not be permitted to become again a member thereof. or of any other band, unless the consent of the band with the approval of the Superintendent-General or his agent, be first had and obtained ; but this provision shall not apply to any professional man, mechanic, missionary, teacher or interpreter, while discharging his or her duty as such :

Woman marrying other than an Indian. (c) Provided that any Indian woman marrying any other than an Indian or a non-treaty Indian shall cease to be an Indian in any respect within the meaning of this Act, except that she shall be entitled to share equally with the members of the band to which she formerly belonged, in the annual or semi-annual distribution of their annuities, interest moneys and rents ; but this income may be commuted to her at any time at ten years' purchase with the consent of the band :

Marrying non-treaty Indians. (d) Provided that any Indian woman marrying an Indian of any other band, or a non-treaty Indian shall cease to be a member of the band to which she formerly belonged. and become a member of the band or irregular band of which her husband is a member :

As to half-breeds. (e) Provided also that no half-breed in Manitoba who has shared in the distribution of half-breed lands shall be accounted an Indian ; and that no half-breed head of a family (except the widow of an Indian, or a half-breed who has already been admitted into a treaty), shall, unless under very special circumstances, to be determined by the Superintendent-General or his agent, be accounted an Indian, or entitled to be admitted into any Indian treaty.

Non- treaty Indian. 4 The term " non-treaty Indian " means any person of Indian blood who is reputed to belong to an irregular band. or who follows the Indian mode of life, even though such person be only a temporary resident in Canada.

Enfranchised Indian. 5. The term " enfranchised Indian " means any Indian, his
wife

wife or minor unmarried child, who has received letters patent granting him in fee simple any portion of the reserve which may have been allotted to him, his wife and minor children, by the band to which he belongs, or any unmarried Indian who may have received letters patent for an allotment of the reserve.

6. The term " reserve " means any tract or tracts of land Reserve. set apart by treaty or otherwise for the use or benefit of or granted to a particular band of Indians, of which the legal title is in the Crown, but which is unsurrendered, and includes all the trees, wood, timber, soil, stone, minerals, metals, or other valuables thereon or therein.

7. The term "special reserve" means any tract or tracts Special of land and everything belonging thereto set apart for the Reserve. use or benefit of any band or irregular band of Indians, the title of which is vested in a society, corporation or community legally established, and capable of suing and being sued, or in a person or persons of European descent, but which land is held in trust for, or benevolently allowed to be used by, such band or irregular band of Indians

8. The term " Indian lands " means any reserve or por- Indian lands. tion of a reserve which has been surrendered to the Crown.

9 The term " intoxicants" means and includes all Intoxicants. spirits, strong waters, spirituous liquors, wines, or fermented or compounded liquors or intoxicating drink of any kind whatsoever, and any intoxicating liquor or fluid, as also opium and any preparation thereof, whether liquid or solid, and any other intoxicating drug or substance, and tobacco or tea mixed or compounded or impregnated with opium or with other intoxicating drugs, spirits or substances, and whether the same or any of them be liquid or solid

10. The term "Superintendent-General " means the Superintend- Superintendent-General of Indian Affairs. ent General.

11. The term " agent " means a commissioner, superinten- Agent. dent, agent, or other officer acting under the instructions of the Superintendent-General.

12. The term " person " means an individual other than Person. an Indian, unless the context clearly requires another construction.

RESERVES.

4. All reserves for Indians or for any band of Indians, or Reserves sub- held in trust for their benefit, shall be deemed to be reserved ject to this and held for the same purposes as before the passing of this Act. Act, but subject to its provisions.

5.

Surveys
authorized.

5. The Superintendent-General may authorize surveys, plans and reports to be made of any reserve for Indians, shewing and distinguishing the improved lands, the forests and lands fit for settlement, and such other information as may be required ; and may authorize that the whole or any portion of a reserve be subdivided into lots.

What Indians
only deemed
holders of
lots.

6. In a reserve, or portion of a reserve, subdivided by survey into lots, no Indian shall be deemed to be lawfully in possession of one or more of such lots, or part of a lot, unless he or she has been or shall be located for the same by the band, with the approval of the Superintendent-General :

Indemnity to
Indians dis-
possessed.

Provided that no Indian shall be dispossessed of any lot or part of a lot, on which he or she has improvements, without receiving compensation therefor, (at a valuation to be approved by the Superintendent-General) from the Indian who obtains the lot or part of a lot, or from the funds of the band, as may be determined by the Superintendent-General.

Location
ticket ; in
triplicate :
how dealt
with.

7. On the Superintendent-General approving of any location as aforesaid, he shall issue in triplicate a ticket granting a location title to such Indian, one triplicate of which he shall retain in a book to be kept for the purpose; the other two he shall forward to the local agent, one to be delivered to the Indian in whose favor it was issued, the other to be filed by the agent, who shall permit it to be copied into the register of the band, if such register has been established :

Effect of such
ticket limited.

8. The conferring of any such location title as aforesaid shall not have the effect of rendering the land covered thereby subject to seizure under legal process, or transferable except to an Indian of the same band, and in such case, only with the consent of the council thereof and the approval of the Superintendent-General, when the transfer shall be confirmed by the issue of a ticket in the manner prescribed in the next preceding section.

Property of
deceased In-
dian, how to
descend.

9. Upon the death of any Indian holding under location or other duly recognized title any lot or parcel of land, the right and interest therein of such deceased Indian shall together with his goods and chattels, devolve one-third upon his widow, and the remainder upon his children equally ; and such children shall have a like estate in such land as their father ; but should such Indian die without issue but leaving a widow, such lot or parcel of land and his goods and chattels shall be vested in her, and if he leaves no widow, then in the Indian nearest akin to the deceased, but if he have no heir nearer than a cousin, then the same shall be

Proviso.

vested in the Crown for the benefit of the band : But whatever

ever may be the final disposition of the land, the claimant
or claimants shall not be held to be legally in possession
until they obtain a location ticket from the Superintendent-
General in the manner prescribed in the case of new locations.

10. Any Indian or non-treaty Indian in the Province of
British Columbia, the Province of Manitoba, in the North-
West Territories, or in the Territory of Keewatin, who has,
or shall have, previously to the selection of a reserve,
possession of and made permanent improvements on a
plot of land which has been or shall be included in or
surrounded by a reserve, shall have the same privileges,
neither more nor less, in respect of such plot, as an Indian
enjoys who holds under a location title.

Indians in Manitoba, British Columbia or N. W. Territories, &c., having made improvements.

PROTECTION OF RESERVES.

11. No person, or Indian other than an Indian of the
band, shall settle, reside or hunt upon, occupy or use
any land or marsh, or shall settle, reside upon or occupy
any road, or allowance for roads running through any
reserve belonging to or occupied by such band; and all
mortgages or hypothecs given or consented to by any Indian,
and all leases, contracts and agreements made or purporting to be made by any Indian, whereby persons or Indians
other than Indians of the band are permitted to reside
or hunt upon such reserve, shall be absolutely void.

Who only may settle in thereon.

Certain conveyances, &c., void.

12. If any person or Indian other than an Indian of the
band, without the license of the Superintendent-General
(which license, however, he may at any time revoke), settles,
resides or hunts upon or occupies or uses any such land or
marsh; or settles, resides upon or occupies any such roads or
allowances for roads, on such reserve, or if any Indian is
illegally in possession of any lot or part of a lot in a
subdivided reserve, the Superintendent-General or such
officer or person as he may thereunto depute and authorize,
shall, on complaint made to him, and on proof of the fact to
his satisfaction, issue his warrant signed and sealed, directed
to the sheriff of the proper county or district, or if the said
reserve be not situated within any county or district, then
directed to any literate person willing to act in the premises,
commanding him forthwith to remove from the said land or
marsh, or roads or allowances for roads, or lots or parts of lots,
every such person or Indian and his family so settled, residing
or hunting upon or occupying, or being illegally in possession
of the same, or to notify such person or Indian to cease
using as aforesaid the said lands, marshes, roads or allowances
for roads; and such sheriff or other person shall accordingly
remove or notify such person or Indian, and for that purpose shall have the same powers as in the execution of criminal

Power to re-move persons unlawfully occupying.

Costs of removal. nal process; and the expenses incurred in any such removal or notification shall be borne by the party removed or notified, and may be recovered from him as the costs in any ordinary suit:

Proviso : residence by consent of Superintendent-General. Provided that nothing contained in this Act shall prevent an Indian or non-treaty Indian, if five years a resident in Canada, not a member of the band, with the consent of the band and the approval of the Superintendent-General, from residing upon the reserve, or receiving a location thereon.

Removal and punishment of persons returning after removal. **13.** If any person or Indian, after having been removed or notified as aforesaid, returns to, settles upon, resides or hunts upon or occupies,or uses as aforesaid,any of the said land,marsh or lots, or parts of lots; or settles, resides upon or occupies any of the said roads, allowances for roads, or lots or parts of lots, the Superintendent-General, or any officer or person deputed and authorized as aforesaid, upon view, or upon proof on oath made before him, or to his satisfaction, that the said person or Indian has returned to, settled, resided or hunted upon or occupied or used as aforesaid any of the said lands, marshes, lots or parts of lots,or has returned to, settled or resided upon or occupied any of the said roads or allowances for roads,or lots or parts of lots, shall direct and send his warrant signed and sealed to the sheriff of the proper county or district, or to any literate person therein, and if the said reserve **Warrant to arrest.** be not situated within any county or district, then to any literate person, commanding him forthwith to arrest such person or Indian, and commit him to the common gaol of the said county or district, or if there be no gaol in the said county or district, then to the gaol nearest to the said reserve in the Province or Territory there to remain for the time ordered by such warrant, but which shall not exceed thirty days.

Arrest and imprisonment **14.** Such sheriff or other person shall accordingly arrest the said party, and deliver him to the gaoler or sheriff of the proper county, district, Province or Territory, who shall receive such person or Indian and imprison him in the said gaol for the term aforesaid.

Order to be drawn up and filed. **15.** The Superintendent-General, or such officer or person as aforesaid, shall cause the judgment or order against the offender to be drawn up and filed in his office, and such judgment shall not be removed by *certiorari* or otherwise, or be appealed from, but shall be final.

Punishment of others than Indians trespassing on reserves. **16.** If any person or Indian other than an Indian of the band to which the reserve belongs, without the license in writing of the Superintendent-General or of some officer or person deputed by him for that purpose, trespasses upon

any

any of the said land, roads or allowances for roads in the said reserve, by cutting, carrying away or removing therefrom any of the trees, saplings, shrubs, underwood, timber or hay thereon, or by removing any of the stone, soil, minerals, metals or other valuables off the said land, roads or allowances for roads, the person or Indian so trespassing shall, for every tree he cuts, carries away or removes, forfeit and pay the sum of twenty dollars ; and for cutting, carrying away or removing any of the saplings, shrubs, underwood, timber or hay, if under the value of one dollar, the sum of four dollars, but if over the value of one dollar, then the sum of twenty dollars ; and for removing any of the stone, soil, minerals, metals or other valuables aforesaid, the sum of twenty dollars, such fine to be recovered by the Superintendent-General, or any officer or person by him deputed, by distress and sale of the goods and chattels of the party or parties fined : or the Superintendent-General, or such officer or person, without proceeding by distress and sale as aforesaid, may, upon the non-payment of the said fine, order the party or parties to be imprisoned in the common gaol as aforesaid, for a period not exceeding thirty days, when the fine does not exceed twenty dollars, or for a period not exceeding three months when the fine does exceed twenty dollars : and upon the return of any warrant for distress or sale, if the amount thereof has not been made, or if any part of it remains unpaid, the said Superintendent-General, officer or person, may commit the party in default upon such warrant, to the common gaol as aforesaid for a period not exceeding thirty days if the sum claimed by the Superintendent-General, upon the said warrant does not exceed twenty dollars, or for a time not exceeding three months if the sum claimed does exceed twenty dollars : all such fines shall be paid to the Receiver-General, to be disposed of for the use and benefit of the band of Indians for whose benefit the reserve is held, in such manner as the Governor in Council may direct.

Penalties for offences by trespassers.

Levying penalties or imprisonment of offender for non-payment.

Application of fines.

17. If any Indian, without the license in writing of the Superintendent-General, or of some officer or person deputed by him for that purpose, trespasses upon the land of an Indian who holds a location title, or who is otherwise recognized by the department as the occupant of such land, by cutting, carrying away, or removing therefrom, any of the trees, saplings, shrubs, underwood, timber or hay thereon, or by removing any of the stone, soil, minerals, metals or other valuables off the said land ; or if any Indian, without license as aforesaid, cuts, carries away or removes from any portion of the reserve of his band for sale (and not for the immediate use of himself and his family) any trees, timber or hay thereon, or removes any of the stone, soil, minerals, metals, or other valuables therefrom for sale as aforesaid, he shall be liable to all the fines and penalties provided in the next preceding section in respect to Indians of other bands and other persons.

Punishment of Indians so trespassing.

Or removing timber, &c.

4 **18**

Name of offender need not be mentioned in warrant in certain cases.

18. In all orders, writs, warrants, summonces and proceedings whatsoever made, issued or taken by the Superintendent-General, or any officer or person by him deputed as aforesaid, it shall not be necessary for him or such officer or person to insert or express the name of the person or Indian summoned, arrested, distrained upon, imprisoned, or otherwise proceeded against therein, except when the name of such person or Indian is truly given to or known by the Superintendent-General, or such officer or person, and if the name be not truly given to or known by him, he may name or describe the person or Indian by any part of the name of such person or Indian given to or known by him ; and if no part of the name be given to or known by him he may describe the person or Indian proceeded against in any manner by which he may be identified; and all such proceedings containing or purporting to give the name or description of any such person or Indian as aforesaid shall *primá facie* be sufficient.

Sheriffs, &c., to assist Superintendent.

19. All sheriffs, gaolers or peace officers to whom any such process is directed by the Superintendent-General, or by any officer or person by him deputed as aforesaid, shall obey the same, and all other officers upon reasonable requisition shall assist in the execution thereof.

Superintendent to appoint an arbitrator when property is taken from a band for improvements.

20. If any railway, road, or public work passes through or causes injury to any reserve belonging to or in possession of any band of Indians, or if any act occasioning damage to any reserve be done under the authority of any Act of Parliament, or of the legislature of any province, compensation shall be made to them therefor in the same manner as is provided with respect to the lands or rights of other persons; the Superintendent-General shall in any case in which an arbitration may be had, name the arbitrator on behalf of the Indians, and shall act for them in any matter relating to the settlement· of such compensation; and the amount awarded in any case shall be paid to the Receiver General for the use of the band of Indians for whose benefit the reserve is held, and for the benefit of any Indian having improvements thereon.

SPECIAL RESERVES.

Crown's name may be used in writs respecting special reserves.

21. In all cases of encroachment upon, or of violation of trust respecting any special reserve, it shall be lawful to proceed by information in the name of Her Majesty, in the superior courts of law or equity, notwithstanding the legal title may not be vested in the Crown.

As to trusteeship of reserves lapsing

22. If by the violation of the conditions of any such trust as aforesaid, or by the breaking up of any society, corporation, or ˉcommunity, or if by the death of any person

or

or persons without a legal succession of trusteeship, in whom the title to a special reserve is held in trust, the said title lapses or becomes void in law, then the legal title shall become vested in the Crown in trust, and the property shall be managed for the band or irregular band previously interested therein, as an ordinary reserve.

REPAIR OF ROADS.

23. Indians residing upon any reserve, and engaged in the pursuit of agriculture as their then principal means of support, shall be liable, if so directed by the Superintendent-General, or any officer or person by him thereunto authorized, to perform labor on the public roads laid out or used in or through, or abutting upon such reserve, such labor to be performed under the sole control of the said Superintendent-General, officer or person, who may direct when, where and how and in what manner the said labor shall be applied, and to what extent the same shall be imposed upon Indians who may be resident upon any of the said lands ; and the said Superintendent-General, officer or person shall have the like power to enforce the performance of all such labor by imprisonment or otherwise, as may be done by any power or authority under any law, rule or regulation in force in the province or territory in which such reserve lies, for the non-performance of statute labor ; but the labor to be so required of any such Indian shall not exceed in amount or extent what may be required of other inhabitants of the same province, territory, county, or other local division, under the laws requiring and regulating such labor and the performance thereof. *Indians liable to labor on public roads in reserves, and to what extent.* *Powers of Superintendent.* *Proviso : as to amount of labor.*

24. Every band of Indians shall be bound to cause the roads, bridges, ditches and fences within their reserve to be put and maintained in. proper order, in accordance with the instructions received from time to time from the Superintendent-General, or from the agent of the Superintendent-General ; and whenever in the opinion of the Superintendent-General the same are not so put or maintained in order, he may cause the work to be performed at the cost of such band, or of the particular Indian in default, as the case may be, either out of their or his annual allowances, or otherwise. *Band to cause roads, &c., to be maintained in order.* *Powers of Superintendent.*

SURRENDERS.

25. No reserve or portion of a reserve shall be sold, alienated or leased until it has been released or surrendered to the Crown for the purposes of this Act. *Necessary conditions previous to a sale.*

26. No release or surrender of a reserve, or portion of a reserve, held for the use of the Indians of any band or of any *On what conditions release or sur-*

4½

render to be valid. any individual Indian, shall be valid or binding, except on the following conditions :—

Assent of band.   1. The release or surrender shall be assented to by a majority of the male members of the band of the full age of twenty-one years, at a meeting or council thereof summoned for that purpose according to their rules, and held in the presence of the Superintendent-General, or of an officer duly authorized to attend such council by the **Proviso.** Governor in Council or by the Superintendent-General ; Provided, that no Indian shall be entitled to vote or be present at such council, unless he habitually resides on or near and is interested in the reserve in question ;

Proof of assent.   2. The fact that such release or surrender has been assented to by the band at such council or meeting, shall be certified on oath before some judge of a superior, county, or district court, or stipendiary magistrate, by the Superintendent-General or by the officer authorized by him to attend such council or meeting, and by some one of the chiefs or principal men present thereat and entitled to vote, and when so certified as aforesaid shall be submitted to the Governor in Council for acceptance or refusal ;

Superintendent-General may grant license to cut trees, &c.   3. But nothing herein contained shall be construed to prevent the Superintendent-General from issuing a license to any person or Indian to cut and remove trees, wood, timber and hay, or to quarry and remove stone and gravel on and **Proviso.** from the reserve ; Provided he, or his agent acting by his instructions, first obtain the consent of the band thereto in the ordinary manner as hereinafter provided.

No intoxicant to be permitted at council of Indians.   **27.** It shall not be lawful to introduce at any council or meeting of Indians held for the purpose of discussing or of assenting to a release or surrender of a reserve or portion thereof, or of assenting to the issuing of a timber or other license, any intoxicant ; and any person introducing at such meeting, and any agent or officer employed by the Superintendent-General, or by the Governor in Council, introducing, allowing or countenancing by his presence the use of such intoxicant among such Indians a week before, at, or a week after, any such council or meeting, shall forfeit two hundred dollars, recoverable by action in any of the superior courts of law, one half of which penalty shall go to the informer.

Invalid surrenders not confirmed hereby.   **28.** Nothing in this Act shall confirm any release or surrender which would have been invalid if this Act had not been passed ; and no release or surrender of any reserve to any party other than the Crown, shall be valid.

MANAGEMENT

MANAGEMENT AND SALE OF INDIAN LANDS.

29. All Indian lands, being reserves or portions of reserves surrendered or to be surrendered to the Crown, shall be deemed to be held for the same purposes as before the passing of this Act ; and shall be managed, leased and sold as the Governor in Council may direct, subject to the conditions of surrender, and to the provisions of this Act. *How to be managed.*

30. No agent for the sale of Indian lands shall, within his division, directly or indirectly, unless under an order of the Governor in Council, purchase any land which he is appointed to sell, or become proprietor of or interested in any such land, during the time of his agency ; and any such purchase or interest shall be void ;. and if any such agent offends in the premises, he shall forfeit his office and the sum of four hundred dollars for every such offence, which may be recovered in action of debt by any person who may sue for the same. *Agents not to purchase. Punishment for contravention.*

31. Every certificate of sale or receipt for money received on the sale of Indian lands, heretofore granted or made or to be granted or made by the Superintendent-General or any agent of his, so long as the sale to which such receipt or certificate relates is in force and not rescinded, shall entitle the party to whom the same was or shall be made or granted, or his assignee, by instrument registered under this or any former Act providing for registration in such cases, to take possession of and occupy the land therein comprised, subject to the conditions of such sale, and thereunder, unless the same shall have been revoked or cancelled, to maintain suits in law or equity against any wrongdoer or trespasser, as effectually as he could do under a patent from the Crown ;—and such receipt or certificate shall be *primâ facie* evidence for the purpose of possession by such person, or the assignee under an instrument registered as aforesaid, in any such suit ; but the same shall have no force against a license to cut timber existing at the time of the making or granting thereof. *Effect of former certificates of sale or receipts, unless rescinded. Evidence of possession. Proviso.*

32. The Superintendent-General shall keep a book for registering (at the option of the parties interested) the particulars of any assignment made, as well by the original purchaser or lessee of Indian lands or his heir or legal representative, as by any subsequent assignee of any such lands, or the heir or legal representative of such assignee;— and upon any such assignment being produced to the Superintendent-General, and, except in cases where such assignment is made under a corporate seal, with an affidavit of due execution thereof, and of the time and place of such execution, and the names, residences and occupations of the witnesses, or, as regards lands in the province of Quebec, upon the production *Registers of assignments to be kept. Entries thereof, on what proof made.*

duction

duction of such assignment executed in notarial form, or of a notarial copy thereof, the Superintendent-General shall cause the material parts of every such assignment to be registered in such book of registry, and shall cause to be endorsed on every such assignment a certificate of such registration, to be signed by himself or his deputy, or any other officer of the department by him

Their effect. authorized to sign such certificates;—And every such assignment so registered shall be valid against any one previously

Proviso. executed, but subsequently registered, or unregistered ; but all the conditions of the sale, grant or location must have been complied with, or dispensed with by the Superintendent-General, before such registration is made.

If a subscribing witness be dead, &c. **33.** If any subscribing witness to any such assignment is deceased, or has left the province, the Superintendent-General may register such assignment upon the production of an affidavit proving the death or absence of such witness and his handwriting, or the handwriting of the party making such assignment.

Proof on application for patent. **34.** On any application for a patent by the heir, assignee or devisee of the original purchaser from the Crown, the Superintendent-General may receive proof in such manner as he may direct and require in support of any claim for a patent when the original purchaser is dead, and upon being satisfied that the claim has been equitably and justly established, may allow the same, and cause a patent to issue accordingly ;

Proviso. but nothing in this section shall limit the right of a party claiming a patent to land in the province of Ontario to make application at any time to the commissioner, under the

Con. Stat. U. C., c. 80. " *Act respecting claims to lands in Upper Canada for which no* " *patents have issued.*"

Duty of Superintendent in case of fraud. **35.** If the Superintendent-General is satisfied that any purchaser or lessee of any Indian lands, or any assignee claiming under or through him, has been guilty of any fraud or imposition, or has violated any of the conditions of sale or lease, or if any such sale or lease has been or is made or issued

Cancelling patent. in error or mistake, he may cancel such sale or lease, and resume the land therein mentioned, or dispose of it as if no sale or lease thereof had ever been made; and all such cancellations heretofore made by the Governor in Council or the Superintendent-General shall continue valid until altered.

Obtaining possession after such cancellation, in case of resistance. **36.** When any purchaser, lessee or other person refuses or neglects to deliver up possession of any land after revocation or cancellation of the sale or lease as aforesaid, or when any person is wrongfully in possession of any Indian lands and refuses to vacate or abandon possession of the same, the Superintendent-General may apply to the county judge of the county, or to a judge of the superior court in the circuit,

in

in which the land lies in Ontario or Quebec, or to any judge
of a superior court of law or any county judge of the
county in which the land lies in any other province, or to
any stipendiary magistrate in any territory in which the
land lies, for an order in the nature of a writ of *habere* Order in the
facias possessionem, or writ of possession, and the said nature of writ
judge or magistrate, upon proof to his satisfaction that of possession.
the right or title of the party to hold such land
has been revoked or cancelled as aforesaid, or that such
person is wrongfully in possession of Indian lands,
shall grant an order upon the purchaser, lessee or person
in possession, to deliver up the same to the Superintendent-General, or person by him authorized to receive
the same; and such order shall have the same force as a
writ of *habere facias possessionem,* or writ of possession; and Execution.
the sheriff, or any bailiff or person to whom it may have been
trusted for execution by the Superintendent-General, shall
execute the same in like manner as he would execute such
writ in an action of ejectment or possessory action.

37. Whenever any rent payable to the Crown on any lease Enforcing
of Indian lands is in arrear, the Superintendent-General, or payment
any agent or officer appointed under this Act and authorized of rent.
by the Superintendent-General to act in such cases, may
issue a warrant, directed to any person or persons by him Proceeding
named therein, in the shape of a distress warrant as in ordi- for.
nary cases of landlord and tenant, or as in the case of distress
and warrant of a justice of the peace for non-payment
of a pecuniary penalty; and the same proceedings may
be had thereon for the collection of such arrears as in either
of the said last mentioned cases; or an action of debt as in
ordinary cases of rent in arrear may be brought therefor in
the name of the Superintendent-General; but demand of
rent shall not be necessary in any case.

38. When by law or by any deed, lease or agreement relat- Notice re-
ing to any of the lands herein referred to, any notice is re- quired by
quired to be given, or any act to be done, by or on behalf of law, how to
the Crown, such notice may be given and act done by or by be given.
the authority of the Superintendent-General.

39. Whenever letters patent have been issued to or in the Cancelling
name of the wrong party, through mistake, or contain any patents issued
clerical error or misnomer, or wrong description of any by mistake.
material fact therein, or of the land thereby intended to be
granted, the Superintendent-General (there being no adverse
claim,) may direct the defective letters patent to be cancelled
and a minute of such cancellation to be entered in the New patents.
margin of the registry of the original letters patent, and
correct letters patent to be issued in their stead, which
corrected letters patent shall relate back to the date of those
so cancelled, and have the same effect as if issued at the
date of such cancelled letters patent.

40.

Lands patented twice over.

40. In all cases in which grants or letters patent have issued for the same land inconsistent with each other through error, and in all cases of sales or appropriations of the same land inconsistent with each other, the Superintendent-General may, in cases of sale, cause a repayment of the

Repayment of price in certain cases.

purchase money, with interest, or when the land has passed from the original purchaser or has been improved before a discovery of the error, he may in substitution assign land or grant a certificate entitling the party to purchase Indian lands, of such value and to such extent as to him, the Superintendent General, may seem just and equitable under the

Limitation of time for claim.

circumstances; but no such claim shall be entertained unless it be preferred within five years from the discovery of the error.

Case of deficiency of land provided for.

41. Whenever by reason of false survey or error in the books or plans in the Indian Branch of the Department of the Interior, any grant, sale or appropriation of land is found to be deficient, or any parcel of land contains less than the quantity of land mentioned in the patent therefor, the Superintendent-General may order the purchase money of so much land as is deficient, with the interest thereon from the time

Compensation.

of the application therefor, or, if the land has passed from the original purchaser, then the purchase money which the claimant (provided he was ignorant of a deficiency at the time of his purchase) has paid for so much of the land as is deficient, with interest thereon from the time of the application therefor, to be paid to him in land or in money, as he,

Limitation of time for claim.

the Superintendent-General, may direct;—But no such claim shall be entertained unless application has been made within five years from the date of the patent, nor unless the deficiency is equal to one-tenth of the whole quantity described as being contained in the particular lot or parcel of land granted.

Certain courts may avoid patents issued n error, &c.

42. In all cases wherein patents for Indian lands have issued through fraud or in error or improvidence, the Exchequer Court of Canada, or a superior court of law or equity in any province may, upon action, bill or plaint, respecting such lands situate within their jurisdiction, and upon hearing of the parties interested, or upon default of the said parties after such notice of proceeding as the said courts shall respectively order, decree such patents to be void; and upon a registry of such decree in the office of the Registrar General of Canada,

Practice in such cases.

such patents shall be void to all intents. The practice in court, in such cases, shall be regulated by orders to be from time to time made by the said courts respectively; and any action or proceeding commenced under any former Act may be continued under this section, which, for the purpose of any such action or proceeding shall be construed as merely continuing the provisions of such former Act.

43.

43. If any agent appointed or continued in office under Punishment of agents giving false information as to lands. this Act knowingly and falsely informs, or causes to be informed, any person applying to him to purchase any land within his division and agency, that the same has already been purchased, or refuses to permit the person so applying to purchase the same according to existing regulations, such agent shall be liable therefor to the person so applying Penalty. in the sum of five dollars for each acre of land which the person so applying offered to purchase, to be recovered by Recovery. action of debt in any court, having jurisdiction in civil cases to the amount.

44. If any person, before or at the time of the public Punishment for preventing sale. sale of any Indian lands, by intimidation, combination, or unfair management, hinders or prevents, or attempts to hinder or prevent, any person from bidding upon or purchasing any lands so offered for sale, every such offender, his, her, or their aiders and abettors, shall, for Misdeamenor, fine and imprisonment. every such offence, be guilty of a misdemeanor, and on conviction thereof shall be liable to a fine not exceeding four hundred dollars, or imprisonment for a term not exceeding two years, or both, in the discretion of the court.

MANAGEMENT AND SALE OF TIMBER.

45. The Superintendent-General, or any officer or agent Licenses to cut timber, how granted. authorized by him to that effect, may grant licenses to cut timber on reserves and ungranted Indian lands at such rates, and subject to such conditions, regulations and restrictions, as may from time to time be established by the Governor in Council, such conditions, regulations and restrictions to be adapted to the locality in which such reserves or lands are situated.

46. No license shall be so granted for a longer period than For what time. As to error in description, &c. twelve months from the date thereof; and if in consequence of any incorrectness of survey or other error, or cause whatsoever, a license is found to comprise land included in a license of a prior date, or land not being reserves or ungranted Indian lands, the license granted shall be void in so far as it comprises such land, and the holder or proprietor of the license so rendered void shall have no claim upon the Government for indemnity or compensation by reason of such avoidance.

47. Every license shall describe the lands upon which License must describe the lands : its effect. the timber may be cut, and shall confer for the time being on the nominee, the right to take and keep exclusive possession of the land so described, subject to such regulations and restrictions as may be established ;—And every license shall vest in the holder thereof all rights of property whatsoever in all trees, timber and lumber cut within the limits of the license

license during the term thereof, whether such trees, timber and lumber are cut by authority of the holder of such license

Further rights of holders as to trespassers. or by any other person, with or without his consent ;—And every license shall entitle the holder thereof to seize in revendication or otherwise, such trees, timber or lumber where the same are found in the possession of any unauthorized person, and also to institute any action or suit at law or in equity against any wrongful possessor or trespasser, and to prosecute all trespassers and other offenders to punishment, and to recover damages, if any :—And all proceedings pending at the expiration of any license may be continued to final termination as if the license had not expired.

Return to be made by licensee. **48.** Every person obtaining a license shall, at the expiration thereof, make to the officer or agent granting the same, or to the Superintendent-General a return of the number and kinds of trees cut,and of the quantity and description of sawlogs, or of the number and description of sticks of square timber, manufactured and carried away under such license ; and such statement shall be sworn to by the holder of the

Punishment for evasion. license, or his agent, or by his foreman ; And any person refusing or neglecting to furnish such statement, or evading or attempting to evade any regulation made by Order in Council, shall be held to have cut without authority, and the timber made shall be dealt with accordingly.

Timber to be liable for dues. **49.** All timber cut under license shall be liable for the payment of the dues thereon, so long as and wheresoever the said timber or any part of it may be found, whether in the original logs or manufactured into deals, boards or other stuff,—and all officers or agents entrusted with the collection of such dues may follow all such timber and seize and detain the same wherever it is found, until the dues are paid or secured.

Notes, etc., taken, not to affect lien. **50.** Bonds or promissory notes taken for the dues, either before or after the cutting of the timber, as collateral security or to facilitate collection, shall not in any way affect the lien of the Crown on the timber, but the lien shall subsist until the said dues are actually discharged.

Sale of timber seized after a certain time. **51.** If any timber so seized and detained for non-payment of dues remains more than twelve months in the custody of the agent or person appointed to guard the same, without the dues and expenses being paid,—then the Superintendent-General, with the previous sanction of the Gover-

Balance of proceeds. nor in Council, may order a sale of the said timber to be made after sufficient notice,—and the balance of the proceeds of such sale, after retaining the amount of dues and costs incurred, shall be handed over to the owner or claimant of such timber.

52. If any person without authority cuts or employs or induces any other person to cut, or assists in cutting any timber of any kind on Indian lands, or removes or carries away or employs or induces or assists any other person to remove or carry away any merchantable timber of any kind so cut from Indian lands aforesaid, he shall not acquire any right to the timber so cut, or any claim to any remuneration for cutting, preparing the same for market, or conveying the same to or towards market,—and when the timber or saw-logs made, has or have been removed out of the reach of the officers of the Indian Branch of the Department of the Interior, or it is otherwise found impossible to seize the same, he shall in addition to the loss of his labour and disbursements, forfeit a sum of three dollars for each tree (rafting stuff excepted), which he is proved to have cut or caused to be cut or carried away,—and such sum shall be recoverable with costs, at the suit and in the name of the Superintendent-General or resident agent, in any court having jurisdiction in civil matters to the amount of the penalty;—And in all such cases it shall be incumbent on the party charged to prove his authority to cut; and the averment of the party seizing or prosecuting, that he is duly employed under the authority of this Act, shall be sufficient proof thereof, unless the defendant proves the contrary.

Punishment for unlawfully cutting timber, forfeiture.

Penalty if timber is removed.

How recoverable.

Proof.

53. Whenever satisfactory information, supported by affidavit made before a justice of the peace or before any other competent authority, is received by the Superintendent-General, or any other officer or agent acting under him, that any timber or quantity of timber has been cut without authority on Indian lands, and describing where the said timber can be found, the said Superintendent-General, officer, or agent, or any one of them, may seize or cause to be seized, in Her Majesty's name, the timber so reported to have been cut without authority, wherever it is found, and place the same under proper custody, until a decision can be had in the matter from competent authority ;

Seizure of timber cut without authority.

2. And where the timber so reported to have been cut without authority on Indian lands, has been made up with other timber into a crib, dram or raft, or in any other manner has been so mixed up at the mills or elsewhere, as to render it impossible or very difficult to distinguish the timber so cut on reserves or Indian lands without license, from other timber with which it is mixed up, the whole of the timber so mixed shall be held to have been cut without authority on Indian lands, and shall be liable to seizure and forfeiture accordingly, until satisfactorily separated by the holder.

When it has been indistinguishably mixed with other timber.

All to be deemed cut on Indian lands.

54. Any officer or person seizing timber, in the discharge of

Officer seizing

may command assistance.
Punishment for resistance.
Felony.

of his duty under this Act, may in the name of the Crown call in any assistance necessary for securing and protecting the timber so seized ; and whosoever under any pretence, either by assault, force or violence, or by threat of such assault, force or violence, in any way resists or obstructs any officer or person acting in his aid, in the discharge of his duty under this Act, is guilty of felony, and liable to punishment accordingly.

Conveying away without authority to be stealing.

55. Whosoever, whether pretending to be the owner or not, either secretly or openly, and whether with or without force or violence, takes or carries away, or causes to be taken or carried away, without permission of the officer or person who seized the same, or of some competent authority, any timber seized and detained as subject to forfeiture under this Act, before the same has been declared by competent authority to have been seized without due cause, shall be deemed to have stolen such timber being the property of the Crown, and guilty of felony, and is liable to punishment accordingly ;

Onus of proof that dues have been paid.

2. And whenever any timber is seized for non-payment of Crown dues or for any other cause of forfeiture, or any prosecution is brought for any penalty or forfeiture under this Act, and any question arises whether the said dues have been paid on such timber, or whether the said timber was cut on other than any of the lands aforesaid, the burden of proving payment, or on what land the said timber was cut, shall lie on the owner or claimant of such timber, and not on the officer who seizes the same, or the party bringing such prosecution.

When to be deemed condemned.

56. All timber seized under this Act shall be deemed to be condemned, unless the person from whom it was seized, or the owner thereof, within one month from the day of the seizure, gives notice to the seizing officer, or nearest officer or agent of the Superintendent-General, that he claims or intends to claim the same ; failing such notice, the officer or agent seizing shall report the circumstances to the Superintendent-General, who may order the sale of the said timber by the said officer or agent, after a notice on the spot, of at least thirty days :

Sale.

How seizures may be tried and determined.

2. And any Judge having competent jurisdiction, may, whenever he deems it proper, try and determine such seizures, and may order the delivery of the timber to the alleged owner, on receiving security by bond with two good and sufficient sureties to be first approved by the said agent, to pay double the value in case of condemnation,—and such bond shall be taken in the name of the Superintendent-General, to Her Majesty's use, and shall be delivered up to and kept by the Superintendent-General,—and if such seized timber

Security may be ordered by bond.

If timber be condemned.

timber is condemned, the value thereof shall be paid forthwith to the Superintendent-General, or agent, and the bond cancelled, otherwise the penalty of such bond shall be enforced and recovered.

57. Every person availing himself of any false statement or oath to evade the payment of dues under this Act, shall forfeit the timber on which dues are attempted to be evaded. *Evasion of dues to forfeit timber.*

MONEYS.

58. All moneys or securities of any kind applicable to the support or benefit of Indians, or any band of Indians, and all moneys accrued or hereafter to accrue from the sale of any Indian lands or of any timber on any reserves or Indian lands shall, subject to the provisions of this Act, be applicable to the same purposes, and be dealt with in the same manner as they might have been applied to or dealt with before the passing of this Act. *To be dealt with as heretofore.*

59. The Governor in Council may, subject to the provisions of this Act, direct how, and in what manner, and by whom the moneys arising from sales of Indian lands, and from the property held or to be held in trust for the Indians, or from any timber on Indian lands or reserves, or from any other source for the benefit of Indians (with the exception of any small sum not exceeding ten per cent. of the proceeds of any lands, timber or property, which may be agreed at the time of the surrender to be paid to the members of the band interested therein), shall be invested from time to time, and how the payments or assistance to which the Indians may be entitled shall be made or given, and may provide for the general management of such moneys, and direct what percentage or proportion thereof shall be set apart from time to time, to cover the cost of and attendant upon the management of reserves, lands, property and moneys under the provisions of this Act, and for the construction or repair of roads passing through such reserves or lands, and by way of contribution to schools frequented by such Indians. *Governor in Council may direct investment of Indian funds.* *And the management thereof: expenses how payable.*

60. The proceeds arising from the sale or lease of any Indian lands, or from the timber, hay, stone, minerals or other valuables thereon, or on a reserve, shall be paid to the Receiver General to the credit of the Indian fund. *Proceeds of sales to Receiver General.*

COUNCILS AND CHIEFS.

61. At the election of a chief or chiefs, or the granting of any ordinary consent required of a band of Indians under this Act, those entitled to vote at the council or meeting thereof shall be the male members of the band of the full age *Votes at election of chiefs.*

age of twenty-one years; and the vote of a majority of such members at a council or meeting of the band summoned according to their rules, and held in the presence of the Superintendent-General, or an agent acting under his instructions, shall be sufficient to determine such election, or grant such consent;

In ordinary cases.

Provided that in the case of any band having a council of chiefs or councillors, any ordinary consent required of the band may be granted by a vote of a majority of such chiefs or councillors at a council summoned according to their rules, and held in the presence of the Superintendent-General or his agent.

Periods of election how fixed: and term of office.

62. The Governor in Council may order that the chiefs of any band of Indians shall be elected, as hereinbefore provided, at such time and place, as the Superintendent-General may direct, and they shall in such case be elected for a period of three years, unless deposed by the Governor for dishonesty, intemperance, immorality, or incompetency; and they may be in the proportion of one head chief and two second chiefs or councillors for every two hundred Indians; but any such band composed of thirty Indians may have one chief: Provided always, that all life chiefs now living shall continue as such until death or resignation, or until their removal by the Governor for dishonesty, intemperance, immorality, or incompetency.

Number of chiefs.

Proviso: as to life chiefs.

Chiefs to make regulations for certain purposes.

63. The chief or chiefs of any band in council may frame, subject to confirmation by the Governor in Council, rules and regulations for the following subjects, viz.:

1. The care of the public health;

2. The observance of order and decorum at assemblies of the Indians in general council, or on other occasions;

3. The repression of intemperance and profligacy;

4. The prevention of trespass by cattle;

5. The maintenance of roads, bridges, ditches and fences;

6. The construction and repair of school houses, council houses and other Indian public buildings;

7. The establishment of pounds and the appointment of pound-keepers;

8. The locating of the land in their reserves, and the establishment of a register of such locations.

PRIVILEGES

PRIVILEGES OF INDIANS.

64. No Indian or non-treaty Indian shall be liable to To be taxable be taxed for any real or personal property, unless he in certain holds real estate under lease or in fee simple, or personal cases only. property, outside of the reserve or special reserve, in which case he shall be liable to be taxed for such real or personal property at the same rate as other persons in the locality in which it is situate.

65. All land vested in the Crown, or in any person or Lands held in body corporate, in trust for or for the use of any Indian or trust for In- non-treaty Indian, or any band or irregular band of Indians able. or non-treaty Indians shall be exempt from taxation.

66. No person shall take any security or otherwise obtain No mortgage any lien or charge, whether by mortgage, judgment or to be taken otherwise, upon real or personal property of any Indian or non-treaty Indian within Canada, except on real or personal property subject to taxation under section sixty-four of this Act : Provided always, that any person selling any article to an Indian or non-treaty Indian may, notwithstanding this section, take security on such article for any part of the price thereof which may be unpaid.

67. Indians and non-treaty Indians shall have the right to May sue for sue for debts due to them or in respect of any tort or wrong wrongs. inflicted upon them, or to compel the performance of obligations contracted with them.

68. No pawn taken of any Indian or non-treaty Indian Pawns for for any intoxicant shall be retained by the person to intoxicants whom such pawn is delivered, but the thing so pawned may held. be sued for and recovered, with costs of suit, by the Indian or non-treaty Indian who has deposited the same, before any court of competent jurisdiction.

69. No presents given to Indians or non-treaty Indians, Presents not nor any property purchased, or acquired with or by means for debts. of any annuities granted to Indians or any part thereof or otherwise howsoever, and in the possession of any band of such Indians or of any Indian of any band or irregular band, shall be liable to be taken, seized or distrained for any debt, matter or cause whatsoever. Nor in the province of British Columbia, the province of Nor sold in Manitoba, the North-West Territories or in the territory of provinces,&c. Keewatin, shall the same be sold, bartered, exchanged or given by any band or irregular band of Indians or any Indian of any such band to any person or Indian other than an Indian of such band ; and any such sale, barter, exchange or gift shall Except with be absolutely null and void, unless such sale, barter, assent of exchange or gift be made with the written assent of the ent-General. Superintendent-

Penalty for contravention.

Superintendent-General or his agent ; and whosoever buys or otherwise acquires any presents or property purchased as aforesaid, without the written consent of the Superintendent-General, or his agent as aforesaid, is guilty of a misdemeanor, and is punishable by fine not exceeding two hundred dollars, or by imprisonment not exceeding six months, in any place of confinement other than a penitentiary.

DISABILITIES AND PENALTIES.

Indian may not have homestead in Manitoba and N. W. Territories except as specified.

70. No Indian or non-treaty Indian, resident in the province of Manitoba, the North-West Territories or the territory of Keewatin, shall be held capable of having acquired or acquiring a homestead or pre-emption right to a quarter section, or any portion of land in any surveyed or unsurveyed lands in the said province of Manitoba, the North-West Territories or the territory of Keewatin, or the right to share in the distribution of any lands allotted to halfbreeds, subject to the following exceptions :

(*a*) He shall not be disturbed in the occupation of any plot on which he has or may have permanent improvements prior to his becoming a party to any treaty with the Crown :

(*b*) Nothing in this section shall prevent the Government of Canada, if found desirable, from compensating any Indian for his improvements on such a plot of land without obtaining a formal surrender therefor from the band :

(*c*) Nothing in this section shall apply to any person who withdrew from any Indian treaty prior to the first day of October, in the year one thousand eight hundred and seventy-four.

Indians undergoing punishment by imprisonment, not to receive share of annuity.

71. Any Indian convicted of any crime punishable by imprisonment in any penitentiary or other place of confinement, shall, during such imprisonment, be excluded from participating in the annuities, interest money, or rents payable to the band of which he or she is a member ; and whenever any Indian shall be convicted of any crime punishable by imprisonment in a penitentiary or other place of confinement, the legal costs incurred in procuring such conviction, and in carrying out the various sentences recorded, may be defrayed by the Superintendent-General, and paid out of any annuity or interest coming to such Indian, or to the band, as the case may be.

Payment of annuity may be refused to Indian deserting his family.

72. The Superintendent-General shall have power to stop the payment of the annuity and interest money of any Indian who may be proved, to the satisfaction of the Superintendent General, to have been guilty of deserting his or her family, and the said Superintendent-General may apply the same
towards

towards the support of any family; woman or child so deserted ; also to stop the payment of the annuity and interest money of any woman having no children, who deserts her husband and lives immorally with another man.   And so as to women.

73. The Superintendent-General in cases where sick, or disabled, or aged and destitute persons are not provided for by the band of Indians of which they are members, may furnish sufficient aid from the funds of the band for the relief of such sick, disabled, aged or destitute persons.   Provision for sick, &c., not provided for by the Band.

EVIDENCE OF NON-CHRISTIAN INDIANS.

74. Upon any inquest, or upon any enquiry into any matter involving a criminal charge, or upon the trial of any crime or offence whatsoever or by whomsoever committed, it shall be lawful for any court, judge, stipendiary magistrate, coroner or justice of the peace to receive the evidence of any Indian or non-treaty Indian, who is destitute of the knowledge of God and of any fixed and clear belief in religion or in a future state of rewards and punishments, without administering the usual form of oath to any such Indian, or non-treaty Indian, as aforesaid, upon his solemn affirmation or declaration to tell the truth, the whole truth and nothing but the truth, or in such form as may be approved by such court, judge, stipendiary magistrate, coroner or justice of the peace as most binding on the conscience of such Indian or non-treaty Indian   How Heathen Indians may be sworn.

75. Provided that in the case of any inquest, or upon any inquiry into any matter involving a criminal charge, or upon the trial of any crime or offence whatsoever, the substance of the evidence or information of any such Indian, or non-treaty Indian, as aforesaid, shall be reduced to writing, and signed by the person (by mark if necessary) giving the same, and verified by the signature or mark of the person acting as interpreter (if any) and by the signature of the judge, stipendiary magistrate or coroner, or justice of the peace or person before whom such evidence or information has been given.   Substance of evidence to be reduced to writing and attested

76. The court, judge, stipendiary magistrate, or justice of the peace shall, before taking any such evidence, information or examination, caution every such Indian, or non-treaty Indian, as aforesaid, that he will be liable to incur punishment if he do not so as aforesaid tell the truth..   Indian to be cautioned to tell the truth.

77. The written declaration or examination, made, taken and verified in manner aforesaid, of any such Indian or non-treaty Indian as aforesaid, may be lawfully read and received as evidence upon the trial of any criminal suit or proceedings, when under the like circumstances the writ-   Written declaration, &c., of Indians may be used in like cases as those of other persons.

ten

ten affidavit, examination, deposition or confession of any
other person, might be lawfully read and received as
evidence.

False testimony to be perjury.

78. Every solemn affirmation or declaration in whatever
form made or taken by any Indian or non-treaty Indian as
aforesaid shall be of the same force and effect as if such
Indian or non-treaty Indian had taken an oath in the usual
form, and he or she shall in like manner incur the penalty
of perjury in case of falsehood.

INTOXICANTS.

Punishment of persons furnishing intoxicants to Indians.

79. Whoever sells, exchanges with, barters, supplies or
gives to any Indian, or non-treaty Indian in Canada, any
kind of intoxicant, or causes or procures the same to be
done, or connives or attempts thereat or opens or keeps,
or causes to be opened or kept, on any reserve or special
reserve, a tavern, house or building where any intoxicant
is sold, bartered, exchanged or given, or is found in possession of any intoxicant in the house, tent, wigwam or
place of abode of any Indian or non-treaty Indian, shall,
on conviction thereof before any judge, stipendiary magistrate or two justices of the peace, upon the evidence of
one credible witness other than the informer or prosecutor,
be liable to imprisonment for a period not less than one
month nor exceeding six months, with or without hard

Penalties and application.

labor, and be fined not less than fifty nor more than
three hundred dollars, with costs of prosecution,—one moiety
of the fine to go to the informer or prosecutor, and the
other moiety to Her Majesty, to form part of the fund for the
benefit of that body of Indians or non-treaty Indians, with
respect to one or more members of which the offence was

Of Commanders of vessels furnishing the same.

committed : and the commander or person in charge of any
steamer or other vessel, or boat, from or on board of which
any intoxicant has been sold, bartered, exchanged, supplied
or given to any Indian or non-treaty Indian, shall be
liable, on conviction thereof before any judge, stipendiary
magistrate or two justices of the peace, upon the evidence
of one credible witness other than the informer or prosecutor,

Penalties and application.

to be fined not less than fifty nor exceeding three hundred
dollars for each such offence, with costs of prosecution,—
the moieties of the fine to be applicable as hereinbefore

Imprisonment in default of payment.

mentioned ; and in default of immediate payment of such fine
and costs any person so fined shall be committed to any common gaol, house of correction, lock-up, or other place of confinement by the judge, stipendiary magistrate or two justices
of the peace before whom the conviction has taken place, for a
period of not less than one nor more than six months, with or
without hard labor, or until such fine and costs are paid : and

Punishment of Indian making, selling or having

any Indian or non-treaty Indian who makes or manufactures
any intoxicant, or who has in his possession, or concealed, or
who

who sells, exchanges with, barters, supplies or gives to any in possession other Indian or non-treaty Indian in Canada any kind of any intox-
icant. intoxicant shall, on conviction thereof, before any judge, stipendiary magistrate or two justices of the peace, upon the evidence of one credible witness other than the informer or prosecutor, be liable to imprisonment for a period of not less than one month nor more than six months, with or without hard labor; and in all cases arising under this section, Indians or non-treaty Indians, shall be competent witnesses : but no penalty shall be incurred in Exception. case of sickness where the intoxicant is made use of under the sanction of a medical man or under the directions of a minister of religion.

80. The keg, barrel, case, box, package or receptacle Keg or cask, whence any intoxicant has been sold, exchanged, barter- &c., in which
intoxicants ed, supplied or given, and as well that in which the are carried to original supply was contained as the vessel wherein any be forfeited. portion of such original supply was supplied as aforesaid, and the remainder of the contents thereof, if such barrel, keg, case, box, package, receptacle or vessel aforesaid respectively, can be identified, and any intoxicant imported or manu- Intoxicants factured or brought into and upon any reserve or special and vessels
containing reserve, or into the house, tent, wigwam or place of them may be abode of any Indian or non-treaty Indian, may be seized by seized. any constable wheresoever found on such land or in such place ; and on complaint before any judge, stipendiary And destroy- magistrate or justice of the peace, he may, on the evi- ed by order
of J. P. dence of any credible witness that this Act has been contravened in respect thereof, declare the same for- feited, and cause the same to be forthwith destroyed ; and may condemn the Indian or other person in whose Person in possession they were found to pay a penalty not ex- whose posses-
sion they ceeding one hundred dollars nor less than fifty dollars, and were found the costs of prosecution ; and one-half of such penalty shall subject to belong to the prosecutor and the other half to Her Majesty, penalty from
$50 to $100. for the purposes hereinbefore mentioned ; and in default Imprison- of immediate payment, the offender may be committed to ment in de-
fault of pay- any common gaol, house of correction, lock-up or other place ment. of confinement with or without hard labor, for any time not exceeding six nor less than two months unless such fine and costs are sooner paid.

81. When it is proved before any judge, stipendiary Vessels used magistrate or two justices of the peace that any vessel, boat, in conveying
intoxicants in canoe or conveyance of any description upon the sea or sea contraven- coast, or upon any river, lake or stream in Canada, is tion of this employed in carrying any intoxicant, to be supplied to Act, subject
to seizure and Indians or non-treaty Indians, such vessel, boat, canoe forfeiture. or conveyance so employed may be seized and declared forfeited, as in the next preceding section, and sold, and the proceeds thereof paid to Her Majesty for the purposes hereinbefore mentioned.

Articles exchanged for intoxicants may be seized and forfeited.

82. Every article, chattel, commodity or thing in the purchase, acquisition, exchange, trade or barter of which in contravention of this Act the consideration, either wholly or in part, may be any intoxicant, shall be forfeited to Her Majesty and shall be seized as in the eightieth section in respect to any receptacle of any intoxicant, and may be sold and the proceeds thereof paid to Her Majesty for the purposes hereinbefore mentioned.

Indians intoxicated may be arrested and imprisoned until sober.

And fined.

And further punished if they refuse to say from whom they got the intoxicants.

83. It shall be lawful for any constable, without process of law, to arrest any Indian or non-treaty Indian whom he may find in a state of intoxication, and to convey him to any common gaol, house of correction, lock-up or other place of confinement, there to be kept until he shall have become sober; and such Indian or non-treaty Indian shall, when sober, be brought before any judge, stipendiary magistrate, or justice of the peace, and if convicted of being so found in a state of intoxication shall be liable to imprisonment in any common gaol, house of correction, lock-up or other place of confinement, for any period not exceeding one month. And if any Indian or non-treaty Indian, having been so convicted as aforesaid, refuses upon examination to state or give information of the person, place and time from whom, where and when, he procured such intoxicant, and if from any other Indian or non-treaty Indian, then, if within his knowledge, from whom, where and when such intoxicant was originally procured or received, he shall be liable to imprisonment as aforesaid for a further period not exceeding fourteen days.

To what Judges only an appeal shall lie from conviction under five next preceding sections.

84. No appeal shall lie from any conviction under the five next preceding sections of this Act, except to a Judge of any superior court of law, county, or circuit, or district court, or to the Chairman or Judge of the Court of the Sessions of the Peace, having jurisdiction where the conviction was had, and such appeal shall be heard, tried, and adjudicated upon by such judge without the intervention of a jury; and no such appeal shall be brought after the expiration of thirty days from the conviction.

Want of form not to invalidate conviction.

85. No prosecution, conviction or commitment under this Act shall be invalid on account of want of form, so long as the same is according to the true meaning of this Act.

ENFRANCHISEMENT

Report of Agent when Indian obtains con-

86. Whenever any Indian man, or unmarried woman, of the full age of twenty-one years, obtains the consent of the band of which he or she is a member to become enfranchised.

and

and whenever such Indian has been assigned by the band a ^{sent of Band} suitable allotment of land for that purpose, the local agent ^{to be enfran-chised.} shall report such action of the band, and the name of the applicant to the Superintendent-General; whereupon the said ^{Inquiry there-} Superintendent-General, if satisfied that the proposed allot-^{upon.} ment of land is equitable, shall authorize some competent per-son to report whether the applicant is an Indian who, from the degree of civilization to which he or she has attained, and the character for integrity, morality and sobriety which he or she bears, appears to be qualified to become a proprietor of land in fee simple; and upon the favorable report of such ^{Location} person, the Superintendent-General may grant such Indian a ^{ticket on favourable} location ticket as a probationary Indian, for the land allotted ^{report.} to him or her by the band.

(1.) Any Indian who may be admitted to the degree of ^{Indians ad-} Doctor of Medicine, or to any other degree by any University ^{mitted to degrees in} of Learning, or who may be admitted in any Province of ^{Universities,} the Dominion to practice law either as an Advocate or as a ^{&c.} Barrister or Counsellor or Solicitor or Attorney or to be a Notary Public, or who may enter Holy Orders or who may be licensed by any denomination of Christians as a Minister of the Gospel, shall *ipso facto* become and be enfranchised under this Act.

87. After the expiration of three years (or such longer ^{Patent after} period as the Superintendent-General may deem necessary in ^{certain period of probation.} the event of such Indian's conduct not being satisfactory), the Governor may, on the report of the Superintendent-General, order the issue of letters patent, granting to such Indian in fee simple the land which had, with this object in view, been allotted to him or her by location ticket.

88. Every such Indian shall, before the issue of the ^{Indian to de-} letters patent mentioned in the next preceding section, ^{clare name chosen; and} declare to the Superintendent-General the name and surname ^{to be known} by which he or she wishes to be enfranchised and thereafter ^{by it.} known. and on his or her receiving such letters patent, in such name and surname, he or she shall be held to be also enfranchised, and he or she shall thereafter be known by such name or surname, and if such Indian be a married man his ^{Wife and} wife and minor unmarried children also shall be held to be ^{minor child-ren enfran-} enfranchised; and from the date of such letters patent the pro-^{chised.} visions of this Act and of any Act or law making any distinc-^{Effect of such enfranchise-} tion between the legal rights, privileges, disabilities and ^{ment.} liabilities of Indians and those of Her Majesty's other subjects shall cease to apply to any Indian, or to the wife or minor unmarried children of any Indian as aforesaid, so declared to be enfranchised, who shall no longer be deemed Indians within the meaning of the laws relating to Indians, except in so far as their right to participate in the annuities and interest moneys, and rents and councils of the band of Indians

Proviso as to children attaining majority before their father's probation expires.

Indians to which they belonged is concerned : Provided always, that any children of a probationary Indian, who being minors and unmarried when the probationary ticket was granted to such Indian, arrive at the full age of twenty-one years before the letters patent are issued to such Indian, may, at the discretion of the Governor in Council, receive letters patent in their own names for their respective shares of the land allotted under the said ticket, at the same time that letters patent are granted to their parent :

Proviso as to children found unqualified, or being married.

and provided, that: if any Indian child having arrived at the full age of twenty-one years, during his or her parents' probationary period,. be unqualified for enfranchisement, or if any child of such parent, having been a minor at the commencement of such period, be married during such period, then a quantity of land equal to the share of such child shall be deducted in such manner as may be directed by the Superintendent-General, from the allotment made to such Indian parent on receiving his probationary ticket.

Case of Indian dying before expiration of probation or failing to qualify.

89. If any probationary Indian should fail in qualifying to become enfranchised, or should die before the expiration of the required probation, his or her claim, or the claim of his or her heirs to the land, for which a probationary ticket was granted, or the claim of any unqualified Indian, or of any Indian who may marry during his or her parents' probationary period, to the land deducted under the operation of the next preceding section from his or her parents' probationary allotment, shall in all respects be the same as that conferred by an ordinary location ticket, as provided in the sixth, seventh, eighth and ninth sections of this Act.

As to children of widows probationary or enfranchised.

90. The children of any widow who becomes either a probationary or enfranchised Indian shall be entitled to the same privileges as those of a male head of a family in like circumstances.

Rules for allotting lands to probationary Indians.

91. In allotting land to probationary Indians, the quantity to be located to the head of a family shall be in proportion to the number of such family compared with the total quantity of land in the reserve, and the whole number of the band,

Proviso : as to power of Band in this behalf.

but any band may determine what quantity shall be allotted to each member for enfranchisement purposes, provided each female of any age, and each male member under fourteen years of age receive not less than one-half the quantity allotted to each male member of fourteen years of age and over.

As to Indians not members of the Band, but permitted to reside on their reserve.

92. Any Indian, not a member of the band, or any non-treaty Indian, who, with the consent of the band and the approval of the Superintendent-General, has been permitted to reside upon the reserve, or obtain a location thereon, may, on being assigned a suitable allotment of land by the band

for·

for enfranchisement, become enfranchised on the same terms
and conditions as a member of the band; and such enfranchisement shall confer upon such Indian the same legal
rights and privileges, and make such Indian subject to such
disabilities and liabilities as affect Her Majesty's other
subjects; but such enfranchisement shall not confer upon Proviso.
such Indian any right to participate in the annuities, interest moneys, rents and councils of the band.

93. Whenever any band of Indians, at a council Provision
summoned for the purpose according to their rules, and held when Band
in the presence of the Superintendent-General or of an agent all its mem-
duly authorized by him to attend such council, decides to bers may
allow every member of the band who chooses, and who may enfranchised.
be found qualified, to become enfranchised, and to receive
his or her share of the principal moneys of the band,
and sets apart for such member a suitable allotment
of land for the purpose, any applicant of such band after
such a decision may be dealt with as provided in the seven next
preceding sections until his or her enfranchisement is
attained; and whenever any member of the band, who for Or when In-
the three years immediately succeeding the date on which dian becomes
he or she was granted letters patent, or for any longer period qualified by
that the Superintendent-General may deem necessary, by exemplary
his or her exemplary good conduct and management of pro- conduct.
perty, proves that he or she is qualified to receive his or her
share of such moneys, the Governor may, on the report of the
Superintendent-General to that effect, order that the said Indian be paid his or her share of the capital funds at the credit
of the band, or his or her share of the principal of the annuities of the band, estimated as yielding five per cent. out
of such moneys as may be provided for the purpose by
Parliament; and if such Indian be a married man then he If such In-
shall also be paid his wife and minor unmarried children's dian be a
share of such funds and other principal moneys, and if or widow.
such Indian be a widow, she shall also be paid her
minor unmarried children's share: and the unmarried
children of such married Indians, who become of age during either the probationary period for enfranchisement or for
payment of such moneys, if qualified by the character
for integrity, morality and sobriety which they bear,
shall receive their own share of such moneys when their
parents are paid, and if not so qualified, before they can
become enfranchised or receive payment of such moneys
they must themselves pass through the probationary periods;
and all such Indians and their unmarried minor children And as to un-
who are paid their share of the principal moneys of their married child-
band as aforesaid, shall thenceforward cease in every respect enfranchised
to be Indians of any class within the meaning of this Act, or married In-
Indians within the meaning of any other Act or law. dians.

94. Sections eighty-six to ninety-three, both inclusive, of Provision as
this to Indians in

British Columbia, N.-W. Territories or Keewatin.

this Act, shall not apply to any band of Indians in the Province of British Columbia, the Province of Manitoba, the North-West Territories, or the Territory of Keewatin, save in so far as the said sections may, by proclamation of the Governor-General, be from time to time extended, as they may be, to any band of Indians in any of the said provinces or territories.

MISCELLANEOUS PROVISIONS.

Before whom affidavits to be used under this Act may be made.

95. All affidavits required under this Act, or intended to be used in reference to any claim, business or transaction in the Indian Branch of the Department of the Interior, may be taken before the judge or clerk of any county or circuit court, or any justice of the peace, or any commissioner for taking affidavits in any of the courts, or the Superintendent-General, or any Indian agent, or any surveyor duly licensed and sworn, appointed by the Superintendent-General to enquire into or take evidence or report in any matter submitted or pending before such Superintendent-General, or if made out of Canada, before the mayor or chief magistrate of, or the British consul in, any city, town or other municipality ; and any wilful false swearing in any such affidavit shall be perjury.

Perjury.

Certified copies of official papers to be evidence.

96. Copies of any records, documents, books or papers belonging to or deposited in the Department of the Interior, attested under the signature of the Superintendent-General or of his deputy shall be competent evidence in all cases in which the original records, documents, books or papers, could be evidence.

Governor in Council may exempt Indians from operation of any sections of this Act :— and again remove such exemption.

97. The Governor in Council may, by proclamation from time to time, exempt from the operation of this Act, or from the operation of any one or more of the sections of this Act, Indians or non-treaty Indians, or any of them, or any band or irregular band of them, or the reserves or special reserves, or Indian lands or any portions of them, in any province, in the North-West Territories, or in the territory of Keewatin, or in either of them, and may again, by proclamation from time to time, remove such exemption.

Governor to appoint officers, &c., to be paid out of monies appropriated by Parliament.

98. The Governor may, from time to time, appoint officers and agents to carry out this Act, and any Orders in Council made under it, which officers and agents shall be paid in such manner and at such rates as the Governor in Council may direct out of any fund that may be appropriated by law for that purpose.

Acts and parts of Acts repealed, viz : S. 56 of c. 61,

99. Section fifty-six of chapter sixty-one and section fifty of chapter sixty-eight of the Consolidated Statutes of Canada, section twenty-nine of chapter forty-nine of the Consolidated
Statutes

Statutes for Upper Canada, and so much of chapter eighty-one of the said Consolidated Statutes for Upper Canada as relates to Indians or Indian lands, sections five to thirty-three, inclusive, and sections thirty-seven and thirty-eight of the Act passed in the session held in the thirty-first year of Her Majesty's reign, chaptered forty-two, and the Act passed in the session held in the thirty-second and thirty-third years of Her Majesty's reign, chaptered six, and the Act passed in the thirty-seventh year of Her Majesty's reign, chaptered twenty-one, are hereby repealed, with so much of any Act or law as may be inconsistent with this Act, or as makes any provision in any matter provided for by this Act, except only as to things done, rights acquired, obligations contracted, or penalties incurred before the coming into force of this Act; and this Act shall be construed not as a new law but as a consolidation of those hereby repealed in so far as they make the same provision that is made by this Act in any matter hereby provided for.

and s. 50 of c. 68, Con. Stat. Can. S. 29 of c. 49 of Con. Stat. U. C., part of c. 81 of Con. Stat. U. C. ss. 5 to 33, and ss. 37, 38 of 31 V., c. 42. Acts 32, 33 V., c. 6, and 37 V., c. 21, &c., repealed.

Saving clause as to things done, &c.

100. No Act or enactment repealed by any Act hereby repealed shall revive by reason of such repeal.

Repealed Acts not to revive.

CHAP. 19.

An Act to amend the Dominion Lands Acts.

[*Assented to 12th April*, 1876.]

IN further amendment of "*The Dominion Lands Act*," and of the Act thirty-seventh Victoria, chapter nineteen, intituled: "*An Act to amend the Dominion Lands Act*," hereinafter called and referred to as "the Act of 1874;" Her Majesty, by and with the advice and consent of the Senate and House of Commons of Canada, enacts as follows:—

Preamble. 35 V., c. 23 & 37 V., c. 19.

1. Sub-section two of section two of the Dominion Lands Act passed in the thirty-fifth year of Her Majesty's reign, chapter twenty-three, is hereby amended by inserting after the word "Surveyor-General" where it occurs in the said sub-section, the words "and of plans or documents in any " Dominion Lands or Surveys Office in Manitoba or the North-" West Territories, attested under the signature of the Agent " or Inspector of Surveys, as the case may be, in charge of " such office."

Sub-s. 2 of s. 2 of 35 V., c. 23, amended.

Copies of plans, &c.

2. Sub-section three of the said section two of the said Act is hereby amended by adding thereto the words "or " shall locate military bounty land warrants, or land scrip, or " act as the agent of any other person or persons in such " behalf."

Sub-s. 3 of the same amended.

Agents.

3.

Sub-s. 1 of c. 23, amended.

Military bounty warrants.

3. Sub-section one of section twenty-three of the said Act is hereby amended by adding thereto the following words : " Provided always, that no greater area than twenty per cent " of the land, exclusive of school and Hudson Bay Company " lands, in any township, shall be open for entry by military " bounty warrants, issued after the passing of this Act."

Sec. 33 of same and s. 8 of 1874, amended.

4. The first five lines of section thirty-three of the "*Dominion Lands Act*" as amended by section eight of the Act of 1874, are hereby repealed and the following substituted therefor :—

Entry for homestead right.

" Any person, male or female, who is the sole head of a family, or any male who has attained the age of eighteen years, shall be entitled to be entered for one quarter-section, or a less quantity, of unappropriated Dominion lands, for the purpose of securing a homestead right in respect thereof. (Form A.)"

Sub-s. of 1874 repealed.

New section substituted.

5. The sub-section substituted by the Act of 1874 for sub-section one of the said thirty-third section of the " *Dominion Lands Act*" is hereby repealed, and the following substituted therefor as sub-section one of the said thirty-third section :—

Entry for homestead right ; additional rights attendant on.

Forfeiture.

" 1. The entry of a person as aforesaid for a homestead right shall entitle him to receive at the same time therewith an entry for any adjoining quarter-section then unclaimed, and such entry shall entitle such person to take and hold possession of and cultivate such quarter-section in addition to his homestead, but not to cut wood thereon for sale or barter, and, at the expiration of the period of three years, or upon the sooner obtaining a patent for the homestead under the fifteenth sub-section of this section, shall entitle him to a pre-emption of the said adjoining quarter-section at the Government price of one dollar per acre ; but the right to claim such pre-emption shall cease and be forfeited, together with all improvements on the land, upon any forfeiture of the homestead right under this Act :"

Proviso : as to settlers brought in under Act of 1874.

Provided always, that the right to a pre-emption entry as above given shall not belong to any settler brought in under the provisions of sections fourteen and fifteen of the said Act of 1874.

Sub-s. 5 of s. 33 repealed.

6. Subsection five of the said section thirty-three is hereby repealed, and the following substituted therefor :—

New section as to homestead claims on land then unsurveyed.

" 5. Every person claiming a homestead right on surveyed land must, previously to settlement on such land, be duly entered therefor with the local agent within whose district such land may be situate ; but in case of a claim from actual settlement in then unsurveyed lands, the claimant must file such application within three months after due notice has been

been received at the local office of such land having been
surveyed and the survey thereof confirmed, and proof of
settlement and improvement shall be made to the local agent
at the time of filing such application."

7 Sub-section seven of the said section thirty-three is Sub-s. 7 of s.
hereby repealed, and the following is substituted therefor, 33 repealed.
and shall be read as if numbered sub-section eight; and the New sub-
Form B, which was substituted for that in the Schedule to stituted.
the "*Dominion Lands Act,*" by section thirteen of the Act of
1874, is hereby repealed :—

"8. A person applying for leave to be entered for lands with Affidavit on
a view of securing a homestead right therein, must make entry for
affidavit before the local agent according to the following homestead claim.
form, which is hereby substituted for Form B.

"FORM B.

" *Affidavit in support of claim for Homestead Right.*

"I, A.B., do solemnly swear (*or* affirm, *as the case may be*) Form of
that I am over eighteen years of age; that I have not pre- affidavit.
viously obtained a homestead under the provisions of the
"*Dominion Lands Act;*" that the land in question belongs to
the class open for homestead entry; that there is no person
residing or having improvements thereon; and that my
application is made for my exclusive use and benefit and
with the intention to reside upon and cultivate the said
land. So help me God."

8. Sub-section nine of the said section thirty-three shall Numbering of
be read as being next after sub-section six of the said sub-sections
section and as if numbered seven; and sub-section eight of in s. 33
the said section shall be read as if numbered nine. altered.

9. Sub-section eleven of the said section thirty-three is Sub-s. 11 of
hereby amended by adding thereto the following words : s. 33 amended
"Provided further that, in the case of settlements being as to settle-
formed of immigrants in communities, (such for instance ments by
as those of Mennonites or Icelanders,) the Minister of the communities.
Interior may vary or waive, in his discretion, the foregoing
requirements as to residence and cultivation on each separate quarter-section entered as a homestead."

10. Subsection twelve of the said section thirty-three, is Sub-s. 12 of s.
hereby amended by leaving out all after the word "shall" in 33 amended.
the seventh line to the end of the section, and substituting
the following words: "receive a patent for the land so
purchased."

11. Subsection fourteen of the said section thirty-three is Sub-s. 14
hereby repealed and the following substituted therefor :— repealed.
"14.

New section;
Settler abandoning his claim.

"14. In case it is proved to the satisfaction of the Minister of the Interior that the settler has voluntarily relinquished his claim, or has been absent from the land entered by him for more than six months in any one year without leave of absence from the Minister of the Interior, then the right to such land shall be liable to forfeiture, and may be cancelled by the said Minister, and the settler so relinquishing or abandoning his claim shall not be permitted to make more than a second entry."

Sub-s. 16 *a* of s. 33, amended.
As to cancelled homestead.

12. The subsection inserted under the said Act of 1874, as sixteen *a* of the said section thirty-three, is hereby amended by adding thereto the following words: "and in the case of "a cancelled homestead, with or without improvements "thereon, the same shall not be considered as of right open "for fresh entry, but may be held for sale of the land and of "the improvements, or of the improvements thereon, in "connection with a fresh homestead entry thereof, at the "discretion of the Minister of the Interior."

Additional sub-s. to s. 33.

13. The following additional subsection shall be inserted after subsection seventeen of the said section thirty-three:—

Homestead entry to give certain rights.

"17 *a.* Any person who may have obtained a homestead entry, shall be considered, unless and until such entry be cancelled, as having an exclusive right to the land so entered as against any other person or persons whomsoever, and may bring and maintain actions for trespass committed on the said land or any part thereof."

Sub-s. 18 of s. 33 amended.

14. Subsection eighteen of the said section thirty-three is hereby repealed and the following substituted therefor:—

Certain provisions to apply only to agricultural lands.

"18. The above provisions relating to homesteads shall only apply to agricultural lands ; that is to say, they shall not be held to apply to lands set apart as timber limits, or as hay lands, or to lands valuable for stone or marble quarries, or to those having water power thereon which may be useful for driving machinery."

Section 34 repealed.

15. Section thirty-four of the said "*Dominion Lands Act,*" is hereby repealed, and the following substituted therefor:—

New section as to grazing lands.

"**34.** The Governor in Council may, from time to time, grant leases of unoccupied Dominion Lands for grazing purposes to any person or persons whomsoever, for such term of years and at such rent in each case as may be deemed expedient ; but every such lease shall, among other things, contain a condition by which, if it should thereafter be thought expedient by the Minister of the Interior to offer the land covered thereby for settlement, the said Minister may, on giving the lessee two years notice, cancel the lease at any time during the term."

16.

16. Section thirty-five of the said "*Dominion Lands Act*," is hereby repealed, and the following substituted therefor:—

Section 35 repealed.

"**35**. Leases of unoccupied Dominion lands, not exceeding in any case a legal subdivision of forty acres, may be granted, for the purpose of cutting hay thereon, to any person or persons whomsoever being *bonâ fide* settlers in the vicinity of such hay lands, for such term and at such rent fixed by public auction or otherwise as the Minister of the Interior may deem expedient; but such lease, except as may be otherwise specially agreed upon, shall not operate to prevent, at any time during the term thereof, the sale or settlement of the lands described therein under the provisions of this Act, —the lessee being paid in such case by the purchaser or settler, for fencing or other improvements made on such land, such sum as shall be fixed by the local agent, and allowed to remove any hay he may have made."

New section.
Leases for cutting hay.

Proviso: not to prevent sale or settlement.

17. The subsection substituted by section ten of the Act of 1874 for sub-section five of section forty-six of the "*Dominion Lands Act*," is hereby amended by inserting after the word "behalf" in the last line of the same and between the said word "behalf" and the word "a" the words "but not otherwise."

Sub s. 5 of section 46, amended.

18. Whereas by the provisions of section ten of the Act of 1874, subsection five of section forty-six of the "*Dominion Lands Act*," which provided for the apportionment of woodlots as free grants in connection with and in addition to homestead grants in certain cases, was repealed without reference to rights which might have been acquired under the same; and whereas it is expedient to protect such rights, it is hereby enacted, that any person to whom a wood-lot was apportioned in connection with a homestead under the provisions of the said sub-section five of section forty-six of the Act last mentioned, having duly fulfilled the conditions of such homestead grant required by the said Act, shall receive a patent for such wood-lot as a free grant, as provided in the said sub-section, the Act of 1874 to the contrary notwithstanding.

Protection of rights acquired as to wood lots under repealed subs. of s. 46.

19. Section sixty of the said "*Dominion Lands Act*" is hereby amended by substituting the word "certain" for "all" between the words "in" and "cases" in the sixth line from the bottom; and further, by leaving out all after the word "incurred" in the last line and substituting therefor the following:—"and in default of such fine or penalty and costs being paid forthwith, may sell such timber by public sale after a notice of fifteen days, and may retain the whole proceeds of such sale, or the amount of the penalty and costs only, at the discretion of the Minister of the Interior."

Section 60, amended.

Sale of timber seized.

FOREST

FOREST TREE CULTURE

Entry for tree planting.

20. Any person, male or female, being a subject of Her Majesty by birth or naturalization, and having attained the age of eighteen years shall be entitled to be entered for one quarter-section or less quantity of unappropriated Dominion lands as a claim for forest tree planting.

Form of application; affidavit and fee.

21. Application for such entry shall be made in Form F. in the schedule hereto, and the person so applying shall make an affidavit before the local agent according to Form G. in the schedule hereto, and shall pay at the time of applying an office fee of ten dollars, for which he or she shall receive a receipt and also a certificate of entry, and shall thereupon be entitled to enter into possession of the land.

When only patent may issue.

22. No patent shall issue for the land so entered until the expiration of six years from the date of entering into possession thereof, and any assignment of such land shall be null and void unless permission to make the same shall have been previously obtained from the Minister of the Interior.

Patent after six years on certain conditions.

23. At the expiration of six years the person who obtained the entry, or, if not living, his or her legal representative or assigns shall receive a patent for the land so entered on proof to the satisfaction of the local agent as follows :—

Breaking up for planting.

1. That eight acres of the land entered had been broken and prepared for tree planting within one year after entry, an equal quantity during the second year, and sixteen additional acres within the third year after such date ;

Planting.

2. That eight acres of the land entered had been planted with forest trees during the second year, an equal quantity during the third year, and sixteen additional acres within four years from the date of entry,—the trees so planted being not less than twelve feet apart each way ;

Cultivating the timber.

Proviso.

3. That the above area, that is to say, one-fifth of the land has, for the last two years of the term, been planted with timber, and that the latter has been regularly and well cultivated and protected from the time of planting; provided that in cases where the land entered is less in extent than one quarter-section or one hundred and sixty acres, then the respective areas required to be broken and planted under this and the two next preceding sub-sections shall be proportionately less in extent.

Forfeiture for failure of conditions.

24. If at any time within the period of six years as above, the claimant fails to do the breaking up or planting or either, as required by this Act, or any part thereof, or

fails

fails to cultivate, protect, and keep in good condition such timber, then and upon such event the land entered shall be liable to forfeiture in the discretion of the Minister of the Interior and may be dealt with in the same manner as homesteads which ' may have been cancelled for non-compliance with the law as set forth in sub-section sixteen *a*, inserted in section thirty-three of the "*Dominion Lands Act*," respecting homesteads, by the Act of 1874 :

25. Provided that no person who may have obtained pre-emption entry of a quarter-section of land in addition to his homestead entry under the provisions of sub-section one, of section thirty-three of the said "*Dominion Lands Act*," as amended by the Act of 1874, and by this Act, shall have the right to enter a third quarter-section as a tree planting claim ; but such person, if resident upon his homestead, may have the option of changing the preëmption entry of the quarter-section or of a less quantity of such quarter-section, for one under the foregoing provisions, and on fulfilling the preliminary conditions as to affidavit and fee, may receive a certificate for such quarter-section. or for such quantity thereof as may have been embraced in the application ; and thereupon the land included in such change of entry shall become subject in all respects to the provisions of this Act relating to tree planting. *Proviso: who may not obtain land for planting.* *Option of changing pre-emption entry.*

26. Any person who may have been entered for a tree planting claim under the foregoing provisions, and whose right may not have been forfeited for non-compliance with the conditions thereof, shall have the same rights of possession, and to eject trespassers from the land entered by him, as are given to persons on homesteads under sub-section seventeen *a*, added by this Act to section thirty-three of the "*Dominion Lands Act*," and the title to land entered for a tree planting claim shall remain in the Government until the issue of a patent therefor. and such land shall not be liable to be taken in execution before the issue of the patent. *Rights of persons entered for tree planting.*

SURVEYS AND SURVEYORS.

27. Section seventy-four of the said "*Dominion Lands Act*" is hereby repealed, and the following substituted therefor :— *Section 74, repealed.*

" **74**. There shall be a Board of Examiners for the examination of candidates for such commissions as Dominion Lands Surveyors, or as articled pupils, to consist of the Surveyor General and eight other competent persons to be appointed from time to time by Order in Council, and the meetings of the Board shall commence on the second Monday in the months of May and November in each year, and may be adjourned from time to time ; and the place of meeting shall be at Ottawa, or at some place in Manitoba or the North-West Territories *New section. Board of Examiners and their meetings.*

Territories, as the same shall, from time to time, be fixed, and made public by notice in the *Canada Gazette*."

Examination for articles as pupil.
28. No person shall be admitted as an articled pupil with any Dominion Lands Surveyor unless he has previously passed an examination before the Board of Examiners, or before one of the members thereof, or before some Surveyor deputed by the board for the purpose, as to his ability to write English correctly, and also as to his knowledge of vulgar and decimal fractions, the extraction of the square and cube roots, of the first three books of Euclid, the rules of plane trigonometry, the mensuration of superficies and use of logarithms, and has obtained a certificate of such examination and of his proficiency, from such board.

Notice to Secretary.
29. Applicants for such examination, previous to being articled, shall give notice to the secretary of the board of their desire to present themselves for examination; whereupon such officer shall instruct them accordingly as to the mode in which they must proceed.

Section 75, repealed.
30. Section seventy-five of the said "*Dominion Lands Act,*" is hereby repealed, and the following substituted therefor:—

New section. Examination for admission as surveyor.
"**75.** No person shall receive a commission from the said board authorizing him to practise as a Dominion Lands Surveyor until he has attained the full age of twenty-one years and has passed a satisfactory examination before the said board on the following subjects: that is to say:—Euclid, first four books, and propositions first to twenty-first of the sixth book; plane trigonometry, so far as it includes solution of triangles; the use of logarithms, mensuration of superficies, including the calculation of the area of right-lined figures by latitude and departure, and the dividing or laying off land; a knowledge of the rules for the solution of spherical triangles, and of their use in the application to surveying of the following elementary problems of practical astronomy:—

In practical astronomy.
1. To ascertain the latitude of a place from an observation of a meridian altitude of the sun or of a star;

2. To obtain the local time from an observed altitude of the sun or a star;

3. From an observed azimuth of a circumpolar star, when at its greatest elongation from the meridian, to ascertain the direction of the latter.

Surveying operations in the field, use of instruments, &c.
He must be practically familiar with surveying operations and capable of intelligently reporting thereon, and be conversant with the keeping of field notes, their plotting and representation

representation on plans of survey, the describing of land by metes and bounds for title, and with the adjustments and methods of use of ordinary surveying instruments, and must also be perfectly conversant with the system of survey as embodied in the "*Dominion Lands Acts*," and with the manual of standing instructions and regulations published from time to time for the guidance of Dominion Lands Surveyors.

31. Candidates for examination for commissions as Dominion Lands Surveyors may, at their own request, in addition to the foregoing, be examined as to the knowledge they may possess of the following subjects relating to the higher surveying, qualifying them for the prosecution of extensive governing or topographic surveys or those of geographic exploration, that is to say :— *Voluntary examination in higher branches of study.*

1. Algebra, including quadratic equations, series, and calculation of logarithms ;

2. The analytic deduction of formulas and series, of plane and spherical trigonometry ;

3. The plane co-ordinate geometry of the point, straight line, transformation of co-ordinates, circle and ellipse ;

4. Projections,—the theory of those usually employed in the delineation of spheric surface ;

5. Method of trigonometric surveying, of observing the angles and calculating the sides of large triangles on the earth's surface, and of obtaining the differences of latitude and longitude of points in a series of such triangles, having a regard to the effect of the figure of the earth ;

6. The portion of the theory of practical astronomy relating to the determination of the geographic position of points on the earth's surface, and the directions of lines on the same, that is to say :— *Practical astronomy.*

Methods of determining latitude—

  a. By circum-meridian altitudes, .

  b. By differences of meridional zenith distance (Talcott's method,)

  c. By transits across prime vertical ;

Determination of azimuth—

  a. By extra meridional observations,

6
b

b. By meridian transits ;

Determination of time—

   a. By equal altitudes,

   b. By meridian transits ;

Determination of differences of longitude—

   a. By electric telegraph,

   b. By moon culminations ;

Theory of instruments. 7. The theory of the instruments used in connection with the foregoing, that is to say :—The sextant or reflecting circle, altitude and azimuth instrument, astronomic transit, zenith telescope and the management of chronometers; also of the ordinary meteorological instruments, barometer, mercury and aneroid, thermometers, ordinary and self-**And their use.** registering, anemometer, and rain gauges,—and on their knowledge of the use of the same :

Mineralogy and geology. 8. Elementary mineralogy and geology, so far as respects a knowledge of the more common characters by which the mineral bodies that enter largely into the composition of rocks are distinguished, with their general properties and conditions of occurrence ; the ores of the common metals and the classification of rocks ; and the geology of North America so far as to be able to give an intelligent outline of the leading geological features of the Dominion :

Notice to the Board. Provided that candidates desiring the above extended examination shall inform the board thereof, when giving the notice called for by section eighty-three of the *"Dominion Lands Act."*

Surveyors already admitted may pass such examination. **32.** Gentlemen who may have become qualified to act as Dominion Lands Surveyors previous to the passing of this Act, may, if desirous of so doing, and having given notice in writing to the secretary, at least two months previous to the meeting of the board, of such desire, be examined as to their knowledge of the higher branches of surveying, and other subjects, under the preceding section ; and all candidates for such examination, whether holding commissions previously or otherwise, on passing the same, shall have the fact certified by the board.

Sec. 84, repealed. **33.** Section eighty-four of the *"Dominion Lands Act"* is hereby repealed and the following substituted therefor :—

New tariff of fees. "**84.** The following fees shall be paid under the provisions of this Act,—

1. To the secretary of the board, by each pupil, on giving notice of his desire for examination preliminary to being articled, one dollar ;

2. To the secretary of the board, as the fee due on such examination, ten dollars, and a further sum of two dollars for certificate ;

3. To the secretary of the board, by each pupil, at the time of transmitting to such secretary the indentures or articles of such pupil, two dollars ;

4. To the secretary of the board, by each candidate for final examination, with his notice thereof, two dollars ;

5. To the secretary of the board, by each applicant obtaining a commission, as his fee thereon, two dollars ;

6. To the secretary of the board, as an admission fee by the candidate receiving the commission, twenty dollars, which sum shall also cover any certificate by the board in the case of a candidate passing the higher examination ; but such amount, as also the ten dollars required to be paid under sub-section two of this section, shall be paid to the Receiver General to the credit of Dominion Lands.

84. Section eighty-five of the "*Dominion Lands Act*" is hereby amended by inserting after the word "attendance," at the end of the fourth line, the following words : "and "in the case of the examination of a pupil previous to "being articled, by a member of the board, or by a surveyor "deputed by the board for such purpose, such member or "such surveyor shall be paid five dollars for such exami- "nation. " *Section 85, amended. Special examination of pupil.*

85. Section fifteen of the Act of 1874 is hereby repealed, and the following substituted therefor :— *Section 15, of Act of 1874, repealed.*

"**15.** The expenses, or any part thereof, incurred by any person or persons for the passage money, or subsistence, in bringing out an immigrant, or for aid in erecting buildings on the homestead, or in providing farm implements or seed for such immigrant, may, if so agreed upon by the parties, be made a charge on the homestead of such immigrant ; and, in case of such immigrant attempting to evade such liability by obtaining a homestead entry outside of the land withdrawn under the provisions of the next preceding section, then, and in such case, the expense incurred on behalf of such immigrant, as above, shall become a charge on the homestead so entered, which, with interest thereon, must be satisfied before a patent shall issue for the land ; provided as follows : — *New section. Expenses incurred in bringing out immigrants may be made a charge on their homestead. In case of attempt to evade such charge. Proviso :*

6½   (a).

Amount
limited to
actual cost.

(*a*). That the sum or sums charged for the passage money and subsistence of such immigrant shall not be in excess of the actual cost of the same as proved to the satisfaction of the Minister of the Interior ;

Acknowledg-
ment must
have been
filed.

(*b*). That an acknowledgment by such immigrant of the debt so incurred shall have been filed in the Dominion Lands office ;

Amount
further
limited.

(*c*). That, in no case, shall the charge for principal moneys advanced against such homestead exceed in amount the sum of two hundred dollars ;

Interest
limited.

.(*d*). That no greater rate of interest than six per cent. per annum shall be charged on the debt so incurred by such immigrant.

FORM F.

Application for land for forest tree culture.

I, A.B., do hereby apply to be entered under the provisions respecting forest tree culture of the Act passed in the thirty-ninth year of Her Majesty's reign, intituled : "*An Act to amend the Dominion Lands Acts,*"
in Township number   , in the
                 range
of the
meridian, for the purpose of cultivating forest trees thereon.

FORM G.

Affidavit in support of claim for forest tree culture.

I, A. B., do solemnly swear, (*or* affirm, *as the case may be,*) that I am over eighteen years of age ; that I have not previously obtained an entry of land for forest tree culture. the extent of which, added to that now applied for, will exceed in all one hundred and sixty acres ; that the land now in question is open prairie and without timber, and is unoccupied and unclaimed, and belongs to the class open for entry for tree culture (*or, instead of the above, after the word* "question," *as the case may be, say,* " consists of the "quarter-section heretofore entered by me as a pre-emption right, under the provisions of sub-section one of section thirty-three of the "*Dominion Lands Act*") and that the application is made for my exclusive use and benefit. So help me God.

CHAP.

CHAP. 20.

An Act respecting Roads and Road Allowances in Manitoba.

[Assented to 12th April, 1876.]

WHEREAS in the surveys of townships under the Preamble. "*Dominion Lands Act*," it is provided that Road Allowances, one chain and fifty links in width, shall be laid out between all sections; and whereas it is expedient to place the road allowances, now existing in Manitoba, and those which may hereafter be laid out in the said Province, under the control of the Provincial Legislature : And whereas there existed in the said Province upon, and antecedent to the transfer of the North West Territories to Canada, on the fifteenth day of July, 1870, and before any township surveys were effected, certain thoroughfares or public travelled roads or trails leading from Fort Garry or Winnipeg to the North West Territories, and to the United States, and also others connecting certain settlements within the Province; and whereas application has been made by the Provincial Government to have the said thoroughfares and public travelled roads or trails transferred to the Province, and to have allowances laid out for roads at convenient distances to connect the township road allowances with the public travelled roads through the settlements on the Red and Assiniboine rivers, commonly known as the "Great Highways of the Settlement Belt"; and it is expedient to grant the said application to the extent and on the terms respectively hereinafter set forth : Therefore, Her Majesty, by and with the advice and consent of the Senate and House of Commons of Canada, enacts as follows :—

1. The road allowances in townships surveyed and sub- Certain road divided, and all road allowances set out on block lines allowances to surveyed, in the Province of Manitoba, before the passing of perty of the this Act, shall be the property of the said Province. Province.

2. On the survey and subdivision of any township within And all the Province, after the passing of this Act, and the approval others after of such survey and subdivision of any township, the fact subdivision shall be notified to the Lieutenant-Governor by the are approved. Minister of the Interior, and by virtue of such notification all section road allowances in such township, shall become the property of the said Province.

8. On the Government of Canada receiving notice from And public the Provincial Government of the particular thoroughfares travelled or public travelled roads or trails in the Province which trails, on existed fyling of plan

and descrip-
tion, and
Order in
Council ;
subject to
certain ac-
quired rights

existed as such on the fifteenth day of July, one thousand eight hundred and seventy, and which the said Provincial Government desires to have transferred to the Province, the Governor in Council may pass an Order directing the same to be forthwith surveyed by a Dominion land surveyor and thereafter may transfer each such thoroughfare, public travelled road or trail according to the plan and description thereof to the Province, subject, nevertheless, to any rights acquired under patents for any lands crossed thereby, issued previously to the receipt of such

Proviso as to
width of such
roads.

notice : Provided, that excepting those public thoroughfares in the Province designated by the Provincial Act thirty-four Victoria, chapter thirteen, section one, as "Great Highways " the width of which shall be two chains, no such thoroughfare, public travelled road or trail as abovementioned transferred to the Province, shall be held to have a greater width than one and a half chains or ninety-nine feet.

Roads to be
laid out in
the "outer
two miles."

4. The Minister of the Interior is hereby authorized and required to cause roads to be laid out, in the survey of the " Outer Two Miles " known as the "Hay Privilege " proposed to be granted to the owners of the front lots in the old parishes, as follows :—

In rear of and
between cer-
tain farms.

1. A road one chain and fifty links wide in rear of the farms fronting on the Red and Assiniboine Rivers and between the said farms and the corresponding lots in the " Outer Two Miles " or " Hay Privilege " before-mentioned ;

Between
"outer two
miles" and
sections, &c.,
bounding
thereon.

2. A road one chain and fifty links wide in rear of the lots contained in the " Outer Two Miles " or " Hay Privilege," beforementioned, and between them and the sections, or legal subdivisions thereof, bounding the same, except in cases where the said rear boundary of the said lots may prove to be a regular section line in the township survey ;

Between lots
in "outer two
miles."

3. Roads, each one chain in width, at convenient distances, say every two miles or thereabouts, between lots in the said " Outer Two Miles," and running from the front to the rear thereof :

Where to be
laid out.

Compensa-
tion for land
taken.

4. The roads provided for in the next preceding subsection shall be laid out between such lots as the Minister of the Interior shall indicate with that view, and shall be taken half off each of such lots or the whole width off one of such lots in the discretion of the said Minister; and the persons to whom it is proposed to grant such lots may be compensated by the said Minister for the quantity of land respectively contributed by them to any such road, by the issue of land scrip to them at the rate of one dollar and fifty cents for each acre of land so contributed.

5.

5. On the final completion of the survey and marking off Transfer of such roads to the Province. ·of the lots and roads as above provided in the said " Outer Two Miles," and of the maps thereof, and the approval of the same, the Governor in Council may, on the report of ·the Minister of the Interior, transfer the said several roads provided for by the next preceding section, to the Province.

6. The unpatented land forming part of any road Land how vested, and on what conditions. ·transferred under this Act to the said Province shall be the property thereof,—the legal title thereto remaining in the Crown for the public use of the Province; but no such road ·shall be closed up, or its direction varied, or any part of the land occupied by it sold or otherwise alienated, without the ·consent of the Governor General in Council.

CHAP. 21.

An Act respecting the North-West Territories, and to create a separate Territory out of part thereof.

[Assented to 12th April, 1876.]

WHEREAS it is expedient, pending the settlement of the Preamble. western boundary of Ontario, to create a separate Territory of the Eastern part of the North-West Territories : Therefore Her Majesty, by and with the advice and consent ·of the Senate and House of Commons of Canada, enacts as follows :—

1. All that portion of the North-West Territories, bounded New district formed. ·as follows, that is to say ;—

Beginning at the westerly boundary of the Province of Boundaries thereof. ·Ontario on the International boundary line dividing Canada from the United States of America ; then westerly following upon the said International boundary line to the easterly boundary of the Province of Manitoba ; thence due north along the said easterly boundary of Manitoba to the north- ·east angle of the said Province ; thence due west on the north boundary of the said Province to the intersection by the said boundary of the westerly shore of Lake Manitoba ; thence northerly following the said westerly shore of the said lake to the easterly terminus, thereon of the Portage con- necting the southerly end of Lake Winnepegosis with the said Lake Manitoba known as " the Meadow Portage " ; thence westerly following upon the trail of the said portage to the westerly terminus of the same, being on the easterly ·shore of the said Lake Winnepegosis ; thence northerly following

following the line of the said easterly shore of the said lake to the southerly end of the portage leading from the head of the said lake into "Cedar Lake," known as the "Cedar" or "Mossy Portage;" thence northerly following the trail of the said portage to the north end of the same on the shore of Cedar Lake; thence due north to the northerly limits of Canada; thence easterly following upon the said northerly limits of Canada to the northerly extremity of Hudson's Bay; thence southerly following upon the westerly shore of the said Hudson's Bay to the point where it would be intersected by a line drawn due north from the place of beginning, and thence due south on the said line last mentioned to the said place of beginning —

Name. Shall be and is hereby set apart as a separate district of the said North-West Territories by the name of the District of Keewatin:

Proviso.
Power to re-annex any part to N. w. T. if necessary. Provided always, that the Governor in Council may, by proclamation published in the *Canada Gazette*, at any time when it may appear to the public advantage so to do, detach any portion of the said district from the same, and re-annex it to that part of the North-West Territories not included in the said district; and the portion so detached shall then be subject to the same government and laws as that part of the said Territories to which it is re-annexed.

Repeal of certain Acts hereby consolidated and amended.
34 V., c. 16.
36 V., c. 5.
36 V., c. 34. **2.** The Act passed in the thirty-fourth year of Her Majesty's reign, chaptered sixteen, and intituled "*An Act to make further provision for the Government of the North-West Territories,*" and the Act passed in the thirty-sixth year of Her Majesty's reign, chaptered five, and intituled "*An Act to amend the Act intituled 'An Act to make further provision for the Government of the North-West Territories,'*" and the Act passed in the thirty-sixth year of Her Majesty's reign, chaptered thirty-four, and intituled "*An Act further to amend the Act to make further provision for the Government of the North-West Territories,*"—the provisions whereof are herein amended and consolidated, shall be repealed as respects the said District, on the coming into force of this Act.

Lt.-Governor of District. **3.** The Lieutenant-Governor of the Province of Manitoba, or the person acting as such, shall *ex-officio* be Lieutenant-Governor of the said District of Keewatin.

Council for the district.
Number of Councillors. **4.** The Governor may with the advice of the Queen's Privy Council for Canada, constitute and appoint by warrant, under his sign manual, not exceeding ten nor less than five persons to be members of a Council to aid the Lieutenant-Governor in the administration of the affairs of the said district, with such powers as may be, from time to time, conferred upon them by Order of the Governor in Council.

5.

5. It shall be lawful for the Governor by any Order or Orders to be by him made, with the advice of Her Majesty's Privy Council for Canada, and subject to such restrictions and conditions as to him shall seem meet, to authorize and empower the Lieutenant-Governor of the said district, by and with the advice and consent of the Council appointed to aid him as aforesaid, to make provision for the administration of justice in the said district, and generally to make, ordain and establish all such laws, institutions and ordinances as he may deem necessary for the peace, order and good government of Her Majesty's subjects and others therein, and from time to time to repeal, alter or amend the same in like manner ; and any Order of the Governor in Council giving such authority to the Lieutenant-Governor and his Council, shall be in force unless and until repealed, altered or amended (as it may be) by any subsequent Order of the Governor in Council : Provided always, that all such Orders of the Governor in Council, and all laws and ordinances made by the Lieutenant-Governor, with the advice and consent of his said Council, shall be subject to the provisions hereinafter made.

Governor in Council may empower Lt.-Governor and his council to make laws for the district.

Proviso : laws to be subject to this Act.

6 Subject to the said provisions and those hereinafter made, it shall be lawful for the Governor in Council to make laws for the peace, order and good government of the said district, and of Her Majesty's subjects and others therein, in relation to all matters and subjects in relation to which the Lieutenant-Governor and his Council are not then empowered to make laws, and for that purpose either to make new laws, or to extend and apply and declare applicable to the said district, with such amendments and modifications as he may deem necessary, any Act or Acts of the Parliament of Canada, or any parts thereof, and from time to time to amend or repeal any laws so made and to make others in their stead.

Subject to this Act, Governor in Council may make laws as to matters on which Lt.-Governor and his Council cannot make them.

7. The powers hereby given to the Governor in Council with respect to Acts of the Parliament of Canada, shall belong also to the Lieutenant-Governor and his Council, with respect to the subjects and matters in relation to which they are empowered to make laws, and shall extend to the modification, amendment or repeal (as to the said district) of any Act mentioned in section eleven or in the schedule to this Act, and to the vesting in any judge or judges of any court or courts in Manitoba the power of hearing and determining in that Province either in the first instance or in appeal, but according to the laws in force in the said district, any civil or criminal suit or case arising therein ; and the Lieutenant-Governor shall have power to appoint justices of the peace, and such other officers as may be necessary for administering the laws in force in the said district :

Power to modify certain Acts extended to the district.

J. P's., and other necessary officers.

Provided

Proviso: as to power to make laws: They shall not—

Provided always that no law to be made either by the Governor in Council, or by the Lieutenant-Governor and his Council shall—

1. Be inconsistent with any provision of this Act or of any Act of the Parliament of Canada, expressly referring to the said district, or—

2. Impose any tax or any duty of customs or excise or any penalty exceeding one hundred dollars ; or—

3. Alter or repeal the punishment provided by any Act mentioned in section eleven or the schedule to this Act for any offence ; or—

4. Appropriate any public money, lands or property of the Dominion without the authority of Parliament.

Copies to be transmitted to Governor and laid before Parliament.

A copy of every such law made by the Lieutenant-Governor and his Council shall be mailed for transmission to the Governor in Council within ten days after its passing, and may be disallowed by him at any time within two years after its passing; and a copy of every such law and every law made by the Governor in Council, shall be laid before both Houses of Parliament, as soon as conveniently may be after the making and passing thereof:

Proof of laws. Any copy of any such law made by the Governor in Council, or by the Lieutenant-Governor and his Council, printed in the *Canada Gazette*, or by the Queen's Printer, or the Printer to the Government of Manitoba, at Winnipeg, shall be *primâ facie* evidence of such law and that it is in force.

As to Customs and Excise duties and laws.

8. Unless and until it is otherwise ordered by the Parliament of Canada, the duties of customs and excise shall continue to be the same in the said district as in Manitoba; and except in so far as it may be otherwise provided by any law made under this Act, or made under any former Act and remaining in force in the said district, and subject always to the prohibition of intoxicants hereinafter mentioned, the laws respecting the customs and excise shall be also the same in the said district as in Manitoba.

Laws now in force in the N. W. T. to remain in force in the district until altered.

9. All laws in force in the said district as part of the North-West Territories, at the time of the coming into force of this Act, and not hereby repealed, shall, so far as they are consistent with " *The British North America Act,* 1867," with the terms and conditions of the admission of Rupert's Land and the North-West Territories into the Union, approved of by the Queen, under the one hundred and forty-sixth section thereof, and with any Act of the Parliament of Canada relating to the North-West Territories then in force, and with this

this Act, remain in force in the said district until repealed or altered by the Parliament of Canada, or by the Governor in Council, or the Lieutenant-Governor and his Council, under this Act,—as shall also any order of the Governor in Council made under any Act mentioned in the second section of this Act, until repealed, or altered, as it may be, under this Act.

10. All public officers and functionaries holding office in the North-West Territories at the time of the coming into force of this Act, shall continue to be public officers and functionaries of the said district until it is otherwise ordered under the authority of this Act. *Officers continued.*

11. Unless and until it is otherwise ordered by any law relating to the North-West Territories and in force in the said district, or under this Act, and subject always to the provisions of this Act, the Acts mentioned in. the schedule to this Act as limited in the said schedule, and as amended by any subsequent Acts, shall apply to and be in force in the said district,—as shall also all Acts of the Parliament of Canada relating to the executive government and the several departments thereof, the public works of the Dominion, the postal service, the Canada Pacific Railway, the currency, the Statutes of Canada, the public lands of the Dominion and the survey thereof, commissions of public officers and the oaths of allegiance and of office, and the extradition of certain offenders to the United States of America, and so much of the Act passed in the thirty-eighth year of Her Majesty's reign, and intituled "*An Act to amend and consolidate the Laws respecting the North-West Territories,*" chaptered forty-nine, as is hereinafter mentioned, that is to say;—Sections fourteen to fifty-three of the said Act, respecting—DESCENT OF REAL ESTATE,—OTHER PROVISIONS AS TO REAL ESTATE,—WILLS,—AS TO MARRIED WOMEN, and section seventy-four respecting the PROHIBITION OF INTOXICANTS; and the said sections shall so apply to and be in force in the said district from the coming into force of this Act, whether the said Act shall or shall not have then been brought into force by proclamation in other portions of the North-West Territories : the remaining provisions of the said Act shall not apply to the said district unless expressly extended to it by a law or laws made under the authority of this Act ; and in construing any provision of the said Act as applicable to the said district, the said district shall be held to be intended whenever the North-West Territories are mentioned, unless the context and intention require another construction. *Acts mentioned in this section or in the schedule, to apply to new district.* *Parts of 38 V.. c. 49, to apply.* *Interpretation.*

12. The rule of construction mentioned in the next preceding section shall apply also to sections one to nine, both inclusive, of the Act passed in the thirty-sixth year of Her Majesty's *Certain sections of 36 V., c. 35 to apply to the new district.*

jesty's reign, chaptered thirty-five, and intituled " *An Act respecting the administration of justice and for the establishment of a Police Force in the North-West Territories,*" which sections shall remain in force in and with respect to the said district notwithstanding the coming into force of the Act last cited in the next preceding section, and shall as respects the said district be excepted from the repeal therein

Other sections of the said Act respecting N. W. Police Force, to apply as amended by 37 V., c. 22 and 38 V., c. 50.

proposed. The remaining sections of the said Act of the thirty-sixth year of Her Majesty's reign, chapter thirty-five, relating to the Police Force in the North-West Territories, as amended by the Act passed in the thirty-seventh year of Her Majesty's reign, chaptered twenty-two, and the Act passed in the thirty-eighth year of Her Majesty's reign, chaptered fifty, shall remain in force in the said district, and apply to it, and the Lieutenant Governor of the said district shall (but subject to any order in that behalf from the Governor) have the local disposition of the said force in such numbers and to such extent as the Governor may direct, and may exercise such power in aid of the administration of civil and criminal justice, and for the general peace, order and good government of the said district, and for or in aid of the performance of all duties assigned by the laws in force in the said district, to any constables or officers therein.

Powers of stipendiary magistrates for N. W. T. in the said district.

(1.) And each and every stipendiary magistrate appointed or to be appointed for the North-West Territories, under the said Act passed in the thirty-sixth year of Her Majesty's reign, chapter thirty-five, or under the Act passed in the thirty-eighth year of Her Majesty's reign, chapter forty-nine, shall, notwithstanding the separation of the said District of Keewatin from the remainder of the said Territories for the other purposes of this Act, continue to have, hold and exercise within the said district the same jurisdiction, powers, authority, rights and duties to all intents as if it had still remained part of the said Territories, or this Act had not been passed.

Interpretation clause.

13. The words "the said district" in this Act mean the District of Keewatin hereby constituted ; the words "this Act" include the provisions of former Acts hereby declared applicable to the said district.

Proviso as to 38 V., c. 49.

14. This Act shall not affect the said Act passed in the thirty-eighth year of Her Majesty's reign, chaptered forty-nine, except only as herein expressly provided.

When this Act shall come into force.

15. This Act shall come into force and effect upon, from and after a day to be named in a proclamation to be issued by the Governor in Council for that purpose.

SCHEDULE

SCHEDULE.

Acts of the Parliament of Canada referred to in the eleventh section of this Act

Chapter.	TITLE.
	Acts passed in the First Session, 31st Victoria, 1867, 1868.
14 •	An Act to protect the inhabitants of Canada against lawless aggressions from subjects of foreign countries at peace with Her Majesty.
15	An Act to prevent the unlawful training of persons to the use of arms, and the practice of military evolutions : and to authorize Justices of the Peace to seize and detain arms collected or kept for purposes dangerous to the public peace.
69	An Act for the better security of the Crown and of the Government. *As amended by 32, 33 Vict., chap. 17.*
70	An Act respecting riots and riotous assemblies.
71	An Act respecting forgery, perjury and intimidation in connection with the Provincial Legislatures and their Acts.
72	An Act respecting Accessories to and Abettors of indictable offences.
73	An Act respecting Police of Canada.
74	An Act respecting persons in custody charged with high treason or felony.
	Acts passed in the Second Session, 32, 33 Victoria, 1869.
18	An Act respecting offences relating to the Coin.
19	An Act respecting Forgery.
20	An Act respecting offences against the Person. *As amended by 26 Vict., chap. 50.*
21	An Act respecting Larceny and other similar offences. *As amended by 38 Vict., chap. 40, and other Acts.*
22	An Act respecting Malicious Injuries to Property. *As amended by 35 Vict., chap. 34.*
23	An Act respecting Perjury. *As amended by 33 Vict., chap. 26.*
24	An Act for the better preservation of the peace in the vicinity of Public Works. *As amended by 33 Vict., chap. 23, and 38 Vict., chap. 38.*
29	An Act respecting Procedure in Criminal Cases, and other matters relating to Criminal Law. *Sections 1 to 7, both inclusive, relating to the apprehension of offenders ; sections 81 to 87, both inclusive, relating to the punishment of offences ; and sections 125 to 138, both inclusive, relating to pardons, undergoing sentence, limitation of actions and prosecutions, and general provisions. The whole Act will apply, in Manitoba, to offences committed in the said District of Keewatin, but triable in Manitoba, and the persons committing them.*
30	An Act respecting the duties of Justices of the Peace out of Sessions in relation to persons charged with indictable offences. *So far as respects indictable offences committed in the said District and triable in Manitoba, or committed in some Province in Canada, and the offender apprehended in the said District.*
31	An Act relating to the duties of Justices of the Peace out of Sessions in relation to summary convictions and orders. *Except so much of this Act (or of any Act amending it as gives any appeal from any conviction or order adjudged or made under it.*

SCHEDULE.—*Continued..*

Acts of the Parliament of Canada referred to in the eleventh section of this Act.

Chapter.	TITLE.
32	An Act respecting the prompt and summary administration of criminal justice in certain cases. *In applying this Act to the said District, the expression " competent magistrate" shall be construed as meaning two Justices of the Peace sitting together, as well as any functionary or tribunal having the power of two Justices of the Peace, and the jurisdiction shall be absolute without the consent of the parties charged.*
33	An Act respecting the trial and punishment of juvenile offenders. *In applying this Act to the said District, the expression "any two or more justices" shall be construed as including any magistrate having the powers of any two Justices of the Peace. This Act shall not apply to any offence punishable by imprisonment for two years or upwards, and it shall not be necessary that any recognizance be transmitted to any Clerk of the Peace.*

CHAP. 22.

An Act to amend the Acts therein mentioned, as respects the importation or manufacture of intoxicants in the North-West Territories.

[Assented to 12th April, 1876.]

Preamble.

IN amendment of the Act passed in the thirty-seventh year of Her Majesty's reign, chaptered seven, and of the Act passed in the thirty-eighth year of Her Majesty's reign, chaptered forty-nine, Her Majesty, by and with the advice and consent of the Senate and House of Commons of Canada, enacts as follows : —

Sec. 2 of 37 V., c. 7, and s. 74 of 38 V., c. 49 amended

1. The second section of the Act first above mentioned is hereby amended by inserting after the word "Territories" in the thirteenth line the words "or of the Lieutenant-Gov- "ernor of Manitoba under regulations to be, from time to "time, made by the Governor in Council;" and the seventy-fourth section of the said Act passed in the thirty-eighth year of Her Majesty's reign, chaptered forty-nine, is hereby amended by inserting the same words after the word " Territories," in the seventh line of the said section.

CHAP.

CHAP. 23.

An Act to supply an omission in the Act 37 Vict., chap. 42, extending certain Criminal Laws of Canada to British Columbia.

[*Assented to 12th April,* 1876.]

WHEREAS in the section substituted by the Act passed in the thirty-third year of Her Majesty's reign, chaptered twenty-seven, intituled "*An Act to amend the Act respecting the duties of Justices of the Peace out of Sessions, in relation to summary convictions and orders,*" for the sixty-fifth section of the Act thereby amended, the several courts to which, under the said section, an appeal is given from a conviction had or an order made by a justice or justices of the peace in the several Provinces forming the Dominion of Canada at the time of the passing of the Act first cited are mentioned, but no such provision was or could be made as to the Province of British Columbia, which was not then part of Canada; and, whereas, the Act first cited and the Act thereby amended were, by the Act passed in the thirty-seventh year of Her Majesty's reign, intituled "*An Act to extend to the Province of British Columbia certain of the Criminal Laws now in force in other Provinces of the Dominion,*" extended, with others, to British Columbia, but no provision was made as to the court to which the appeal given by the said substituted section should lie, and it is expedient to remedy such omission: Therefore, Her Majesty, by and with the advice and consent of the Senate and House of Commons of. Canada, enacts as follows:—   •

33 V., c. 27.

32 & 33 V., c. 31, s. 65.

37 V., c. 42.

1. The said substituted sixty-fifth section mentioned in the preamble is hereby amended by inserting therein, immediately before the words "such right of" in the last line but one of the first paragraph of the said section, as printed in the Statutes of the session in which it was passed, the words "and in the Province of British Colum- "bia, to the court of general or quarter sessions of the "peace which shall be held nearest to the place where the "conviction has taken place or the order has been made "from which it is desired to appeal."

Section substituted by 33 V., c. 27, for sec. 65 of 32 & 33 V., c. 31, amended as respects its application to British Columbia.

CHAP. 24.

An Act to provide for the appointment of **Assistant** Inspectors of Penitentiaries in Manitoba and **British** Columbia.

[*Assented to 12th April, 1876.*]

Preamble. WHEREAS, owing to the distance, it is essential to the efficient and economical inspection of Penitentiaries in Manitoba and British Columbia to make provision for the appointment of Assistant Inspectors resident in those Provinces: Therefore Her Majesty, by and with the advice and consent of the Senate and House of Commons of Canada, enacts as follows :—

Assistant Inspectors for Manitoba and British Columbia. **1.** It shall be lawful for the Governor in Council to appoint some fit and proper person to be Assistant Inspector of any Penitentiary established in the Province of Manitoba, and also to appoint some fit and proper person to be Assistant Inspector of any Penitentiary established in the Province of British Columbia.

To represent and report to Inspector. **2.** Such Assistant Inspectors shall act as the representatives of the Inspector, to whom they shall report, and they shall hold office during pleasure.

To be officers of Department of Justice. **3.** They shall be officers of the Department of Justice and shall each receive a salary not exceeding two hundred and fifty dollars per annum, and travelling expenses, to be determined by the Governor in Council.

Their powers to be assigned by Governor in Council. **4.** They shall have, with reference to the Penitentiaries of which they are respectively appointed Assistant Inspectors. such of the powers, and discharge such of the duties imposed by law on the Inspector of Penitentiaries as may be, from time to time, assigned to them respectively by the Governor in Council.

CHAP

CHAP. 25.

An Act to extend the Acts therein mentioned, respecting Weights and Measures, and the Inspection of Gas and Gas Meters to Prince Edward Island.

[*Assented to 12th April, 1876.*]

HER Majesty, by and with the advice and consent of the Senate and House of Commons of Canada, enacts as follows :— *Preamble*

1. The Act passed in the thirty-sixth year of Her Majesty's reign, and intituled : "*An Act respecting Weights and* "*Measures*," as amended by the Act passed in the thirty-eighth year of Her Majesty's reign, and intituled : "*An Act* "*to compel persons delivering certain merchantable liquids in* "*casks, to mark on such casks the capacity thereof*," and the Act passed in the thirty-sixth year of Her Majesty's reign, and intituled : "*An Act to provide for the inspection of Gas* "*and Gas Meters*," shall, from and after the first day of July, in the present year, 1876, extend and apply to the Province of Prince Edward Island, as fully and effectually in all respects as to those Provinces of Canada to which they now extend. *Acts 36 V. c. 47— 38 V., c. 36, and— 36 V., c. 48. extended to P. E. Island.*

2. Upon, from and after the day last above mentioned, the Act of the Legislature of the said Province of Prince Edward Island, passed in the nineteenth year of Her Majesty's reign, and intituled : "*An Act to consolidate the laws relating* "*to Weights and Measures*," and the Act of the said Legislature passed in the thirty-second year of Her Majesty's reign, intituled : "*An Act to add to the Act relating to* *Weights and Measures*," and the Act of the said Legislature, passed in the twenty-fifth year of Her Majesty's reign, intituled : "*An Act for establishing the Standard Weight of Grain and Pulse, and for the appointment of officers for measuring and* *weighing the same*," and so much of the Act of the said Legislature, passed in the session held in the thirty-fifth and thirty-sixth years of Her Majesty's reign, intituled : "*An Act to revive* *and continue certain Acts, therein mentioned*," as revives or continues any of the said Acts or any Act relating to Weights and Measures, shall be repealed, with so much of any Act or law in force in the said Province, as may be inconsistent with the provisions of those hereby extended to the said Province, or with any of them. *Acts of P.E. Island, 19 V., c. 3, 32 V., c. 6, 25 V., c. 14, and— 35-36 V., c.29 repealed, with any other inconsistent laws.*

7

CHAP. 26.

An Act to make further provision in regard to the Supreme Court, and the Exchequer Court, of Canada.

[Assented to 12th April, 1876.]

Preamble.   HER MAJESTY, by and with the advice and consent of the Senate and House of Commons of Canada, enacts as follows:—

EVIDENCE

Proceedings for the examination on interrogatories or by commission, of Persons who cannot for certain reasons, conveniently appear in Court.   **1.** In case any party to any proceeding had or to be had in either the Supreme Court or the Exchequer Court, is desirous of having therein the evidence of any person, whether a party or not. or whether resident within or out of Canada, the court or any judge thereof, if in its or his opinion it is, owing to the absence, age, or infirmity, or the distance of the residence of such person from the place of trial, or the expense of taking his evidence otherwise, or for any other reason, convenient so to do, may, upon the application of such party, order the examination of any such person upon oath by interrogatories or otherwise, before the registrar of the said courts, or any commissioner for taking affidavits in the said courts, or any other person or persons to be named in such order, or may order the issue of a commission under the seal of the court for such examination; and may, by the same or any subsequent order, give all such directions touching the time, place and manner of such examination, the attendance of the witness and the production of papers thereat, and all matters connected therewith, as may appear reasonable.

Such persons hereinafter called "witnesses."   (2.) The person, whether a party or not, to be examined under the provisions of this Act is hereinafter called a "witness."

Duty of persons taking such examination.   **2.** It shall be the duty of every person authorized to take the examination of any witness, in pursuance of any of the provisions of this Act, to take such examination upon the oath of the witness or upon affirmation in any case where **Punishment of witnesses wilfully giving false evidence.** affirmation is allowed by law instead of oath; and any witness who wilfully or corruptly gives any false evidence is guilty of perjury, and may be indicted and prosecuted for such offence in any county or district or other judicial division in Canada where such evidence shall have been given, or if the evidence be given out of Canada, in any judicial division in Canada in which he may be apprehended or be in custody.

2.

3. The court or a judge may, if it be considered for the ends of justice expedient so to do, order the further examination, before either the court or a judge thereof, or other person, of any witness; and if the party on whose behalf the evidence is tendered neglects or refuses to obtain such further examination, the court or judge in its or his discretion may decline to act on the evidence. *Court or Judge may order further examination. Penalty on party refusing to aid in procuring the same.*

4. Such notice of the time and place of examination as shall be prescribed in the order, shall be given to the adverse party. *Notice to adverse party.*

5. When any order shall be made for the examination of a witness and a copy of the order together with a notice of the time and place of attendance signed by the person or one of the persons to take the examination shall have been duly served on the witness, and he shall have been tendered his legal fees for attendance and travel, the refusal or neglect to attend for examination or to answer any proper question which may be put to him on examination, or to produce any paper which he has been notified to produce, shall be deemed a contempt of court and may be punished by the same process as other contempts of court ; but he shall not be compelled to produce any paper which he would not be compelled to produce, or to answer any question which he would not be bound to answer, in court. *Obligation of witness to attend and give evidence on being notified and tendered his legal fees. Proviso : as to production of papers.*

6. If the parties in any case pending in either of the said courts consent in writing that a witness may be examined within or out of Canada by interrogatories or otherwise, such consent and the proceedings had thereunder shall be as valid in all respects as if an order had been made and the proceedings had thereunder. *Consent of parties to examination equivalent to an order.*

7. All examinations taken in Canada, in pursuance of any of the provisions of this Act, shall be returned to the court ; and the depositions certified under the hands of the person or one of the persons taking the same may, without further proof, be used in evidence, saving all just exceptions. *Return of examinations in Canada. Use thereof.*

8. All examinations taken out of Canada, in pursuance of any of the provisions of this Act, shall be proved by affidavit of the due taking of such examinations, sworn before some commissioner or other person authorized under this or any other Act to receive such affidavit at the place where such examination has been taken, and shall be returned to the court, and the depositions so returned, together with such affidavit, and the order or commission, close under the hand and seal of the person or one of the persons authorized to take the examination, may without further proof, be used in evidence, saving all just exceptions. *And if taken out of Canada. Use thereof.*

7½   **9.**

Reading
examination.

9. When any examination has been returned, any party may give notice of such return, and no objection to the examination being read shall have effect, unless taken within the time and in the manner prescribed by general order.

Governor in
Council may
appoint com-
missioners for
receiving
affidavits,&c.,
within or out
of Canada.

10. The Governor in Council may, by one or more commissions, from time to time empower such persons as he may think necessary, within or out of Canada, to administer oaths and take and receive affidavits, declarations and affirmations in or concerning any proceeding had or to be had in the Supreme Court, or in the Exchequer Court; and every oath, affidavit, declaration or affirmation taken or

Effect of such
affidavits.

made as aforesaid shall be as valid, and of the like effect to all intents, as if it had been administered, taken, sworn, made or affirmed before that one of the said courts in which it is intended to be used, or before any judge or competent officer thereof in Canada.

Style of Com-
missioners.

(2.) Any commissioner so empowered shall be styled, " A Commissioner for administering oaths in the Supreme " Court and in the Exchequer Court of Canada."

Further
powers of
commis-
sioners in
Canada.

11. Any commissioner so empowered resident within Canada is authorized to take and receive acknowledgments or recognizances of bail and all other recognizances in the Supreme Court and in the Exchequer Court.

Before whom
affidavits,&c.,
may be made
out of
Canada.
Their effect.

12. Any oath, affidavit, affirmation or declaration, administered, sworn, affirmed or made out of Canada, before any Commissioner authorized to receive affidavits to be used in Her Majesty's High Court of Justice in England, or before any notary public and certified under his hand and official seal, or before the mayor or chief magistrate of any city, borough or town corporate in Great Britain or Ireland, or in any colony or possession of Her Majesty, out of Canada, or in any foreign country, and certified under the common seal of such city, borough or town corporate, or before a judge of any court of supreme jurisdiction in any colony or possession of Her Majesty or dependency of the Crown out of Canada, or before any consul, vice-consul, acting consul, pro-consul or consular agent of Her Majesty exercising his functions in any foreign place, and certified under his official seal, concerning any proceeding had or to be had in the Supreme Court or Exchequer Court, shall be as valid and of like effect to all intents, as if it had been administered, sworn, affirmed or made before a commissioner appointed under the tenth section of this Act.

Documents
purporting to
be under the

13. Any document purporting to have affixed, imprinted or subscribed thereon or thereto, the signature of any
commissioner

·commissioner appointed under this Act, or the signature of ·any such Commissioner authorized to receive affidavits to be used in Her Majesty's High Court of Justice in England, as ·aforesaid, or the signature and official seal of any such notary public as aforesaid, or the signature of any such mayor or ·chief magistrate as aforesaid and the common seal of the corporation, or the signature of any such judge as aforesaid and the seal of the court, or the signature and official seal of any such consul, vice-consul, acting consul, pro-consul or consular agent as aforesaid, in testimony of any oath, affidavit, affirmation or declaration having been administered, sworn, affirmed or made by or before him, shall be admitted in evidence without proof of any such signature or seal being the signature or the signature and seal of the person whose signature or signature and seal the same purport to be, or of the official character of such person. hand or seal of such commissioner or persons to be admitted without proof of that fact.

14. If any person tenders in evidence any such document ·as aforesaid with a false or counterfeit seal or signature thereto, knowing the same to be false or counterfeit, he ·shall be deemed guilty of felony, and shall be subject to the punishment by law provided for felony. Wilfully tendering document with false seal or signature, to be felony.

15. No informality in the heading or other formal requisites to any affidavit, declaration or affirmation made or taken before any person under any provision of this or any other Act, shall be an objection to its reception in evidence in the Supreme Court or the Exchequer Court, if the court or judge before whom it is tendered think proper to receive it; and in case the same be actually sworn to, declared or affirmed by the person making the same before any person duly authorized thereto, and be received in evidence, no such informality shall be set up to defeat an indictment for perjury. Informality not to be an objection to any affidavit, &c., if the Court or Judge thinks proper to receive it. Nor to be set up as defence in case of perjury.

APPEAL IN CONTROVERTED ELECTION CASES.

16. In controverted election appeals under "*The Dominion Controverted Elections Act*, 1874," the Supreme Court may adjudge the whole or any part of the costs in the court below to be paid by either of the parties. Any order directing the payment of such costs shall be certified by the registrar to the court in which the petition was filed, and the same proceedings for the recovery of such costs may thereupon be taken in the last mentioned court as if the ·order for payment of costs had been made by that court or by the judge before whom the petition was tried. Supreme Court may adjudge that costs be paid wholly or in part by either party.

Recovery of such costs.

SPECIAL JURISDICTION.

17. The fifty-sixth section of "*The Supreme and Exchequer Court Act*" is hereby amended by inserting after the word "shall" Sec. 56 of 38 V., c. 11, amended.

"shall "in the third line, the words following : " at the request of the parties, and may without such request if he thinks fit."

EXCHEQUER COURT JURISDICTION.

Sec. 58 of 38 V., c. 11, amended. Words added. Words struck out.

18. The fifty-eighth section of "*The Supreme and Exchequer Court Act*" is hereby amended by adding after the words " Crown alone " in the eighth line, the words following: " And in all cases in which demand shall be made or relief sought in respect of any matter which might in England be the subject of a suit or action in the Court of Exchequer on its plea side against any officer of the Crown ; " and also by striking out the words " or any officer of the Crown " at the end of the said section.

JUDGES.

Sec. 61 of 38 V., c. 11, amended.

19. The sixty-first section of " *The Supreme and Exchequer Court Act*" is hereby amended by striking out the words " on its revenue side " and inserting in lieu thereof " in similar suits."

EXCHEQUER COURT REFERENCES.

Court may refer any matter to Registrar, for certain purposes.

20. The Exchequer Court may for the purposes of taking accounts and making enquiries, refer any cause, matter or petition, over which it has, under any Act, jurisdiction, to the registrar or any other officer of the Court, or to any other referee.

EXCHEQUER COURT JURORS.

Qualification, exemption, &c., of jurors.

21. The qualifications, exemptions and mode of summoning jurors shall be according to the law applicable to the superior courts of the Province where the issues are to be tried.

Number of jurors to be summoned.

22. The number of jurors to be summoned on any panel under a writ of *venire facias* issued pursuant to the fifteenth section of "*The Supreme and Exchequer Court Act*" shall never be less than double nor more than three times the number of jurors required in civil cases to form a jury for the trial of causes in the superior courts of the Province where the issues are to be tried ; but within these limits, the judge who orders the writ of *venire facias* to issue, may exercise his discretion as to the number to be summoned.

Tales in default of jurors.

23. When, from challenges or other causes, a complete jury for the trial of any cause cannot be obtained, the presiding judge may direct the sheriff or other proper officer to summon and return a *tales* according to the law applicable to the superior courts of the Province where the issues are to be tried.

EXCHEQUER

EXCHEQUER COURT EXECUTIONS

24. In addition to any writs of execution which may be prescribed by general rules or orders, the Exchequer Court may issue writs of execution against the person or the goods, lands or other property of any party, of the same tenor and ,effect as those which may be issued by any of the superior courts of the Province in which any judgment or order is to be executed ; and where by the law of the Province a judge's order is required for the issue of any writ of execution, a Judge of the Exchequer Court shall, as regards like executions to issue out of that court, have power to make a similar order. *Writs of execution in addition to those pre-scribed by General Rules or Orders. If Judge's order is necessary.*

25. No person shall be taken in custody under process of execution for debt issued out of the Exchequer Court at the suit of the Crown, unless he could be taken in custody under the laws of the Province in which he happens to be, in a similar case between subject and subject ; and any person taken in custody under such process may be discharged from imprisonment upon the same grounds as would . entitle him to be discharged under the laws in force relating to imprisonment for debt in the Province in which he is in custody. *In what case only a person may be taken in execution.*

26. All writs of execution against real or personal pro-perty as well those which may be prescribed by general rules and orders as those authorized by the twenty-fourth section of this Act shall, unless otherwise provided by general rule or order, be executed as regards the pro-perty liable to execution and the mode of seizure and sale, as nearly as possible in the same manner as similar writs issued out of the superior courts of the Province. in which the property to be seized is situated are by the law of the Province required to be executed ; and such writs shall bind property in the same manner as such similar writs, and the rights of purchasers thereunder shall be the same as those of purchasers under such similar writs. *Writs of and sales under execution to have same effect as like writs from Courts of the Province where the property seized lies.*

27. Any claim made by any person to property seized under a writ of execution issued out of the Exchequer Court or to the proceeds of the sale of such property shall, unless otherwise provided by general rule or order, be heard and disposed of as nearly as may be according to the pro-cedure applicable to like claims to property seized under similar writs of execution issued out of the courts of the Province. *Like provi-sion as to claims to such property or proceeds of sale.*

HABEAS CORPUS.

28. An appeal to the Supreme Court in any *habeas corpus* matter under the said Act shall be heard at an early day whether in or out of the prescribed sessions of the court. *Appeal in habeas corpus case to be heard early,*

29. &c.

Powers of Judges in habeas corpus cases.

29. In any *habeas corpus* matter under the said Act, before a Judge of the Supreme Court, and on any appeal to the Supreme Court in any *habeas corpus* matter under the said Act, the judge or court shall have the same power to bail, discharge or commit the prisoner or person, or to direct him to be detained in custody or otherwise to deal with him as any court, judge or Justice of the Peace having jurisdiction in any such matters in any Province of Canada.

On appeal in habeas corpus cases, prisoner need not be present in Court.

30. On any appeal to the Supreme Court in any *habeas corpus* matter under the said Act, it shall not be necessary, unless the court shall otherwise order, that any prisoner or person, on whose behalf such appeal is made, be present in court ; but the prisoner or person shall remain in the charge or custody, to which he was committed or had been remanded or in which he was at the time of giving the notice of appeal, unless at liberty on bail by order of a judge of the court which refused the application or of a Judge of

Proviso : if Court orders his appearence.

the Supreme Court ; provided that the Supreme Court may, by writ or order, direct that such prisoner or person shall be brought before it.

Jurisdiction in extradition cases taken away.

31. So much of the said Act as confers jurisdiction, whether original or appellate, on the Supreme Court or any judge thereof in *habeas corpus* matters arising out of any claim for extradition made under any treaty, is hereby repealed.

COSTS.

Judges may rule as to costs against the crown.

32. The Judges of the Supreme Court, or any five of them, may, under the seventy-ninth section of the said Act, from time to time, make general rules and orders for awarding and regulating costs in each of the said courts in favour of and against the Crown as well as the subject

How costs to or against the crown shall be paid.

33. Any costs adjudged to Her Majesty in either of the said courts shall be paid to the Receiver General, and the Receiver General shall pay out of any moneys in his hands for the time being legally applicable thereto, or which may be voted by Parliament for the purpose, any costs awarded to any person against Her Majesty.

CERTIORARI.

Writ may issue for certain purposes.

34. A writ of *certiorari* may, by order of the Supreme Court or a judge thereof, issue out of the said court to bring up any papers or other proceedings, had or taken before any court, judge or Justice of the Peace and which may be considered necessary with a view to any inquiry, appeal or other proceeding had or to be had before the Supreme Court.

MISCELLANEOUS.

MISCELLANEOUS.

35. An order in either the Supreme Court or the Exche- Orders for payment of money, how enforced. quer Court for payment of money, whether for costs or otherwise, may be enforced by the same writs of execution as a judgment in the Exchequer Court.

36. No attachment as for contempt shall issue in either No attachment for nonpayment only. the Supreme Court or the Exchequer Court for the nonpayment of money only.

37. The Judges of the Supreme Court shall have the same Judges may make rules and orders for carrying out this Act. power to make rules and orders for carrying out the purposes of this Act as they possess under the seventy-ninth section of " *The Supreme and Exchequer Court Act,*" in reference to the purposes of that Act ; and nothing in this Act contained shall be construed to affect or impair the powers given under the said section.

38. The provisions of "*The Canada Civil Service Act,* 1868," Acts 31 V., c. 34, and 33 V., c. 4, as amended, to apply to officers of the said Courts at Ottawa. and any Acts amending the same, and of the " *Act for better* " *ensuring the efficiency of the Civil Service of Canada, by* ' *providing for the superannuation of persons employed therein,* " *in certain cases,*" and any Acts amending the same shall, so far as applicable, extend and apply to the officers, clerks and servants of the Supreme Court of Canada and of the Exchequer Court of Canada, at the seat of government.

CHAP. 27.

An Act to make further provision for the institution of suits against the Crown by Petition of Right.

[Assented to 12th April, 1876.]

WHEREAS since the passing of the "*Petition of Right* Preamble. 38 V., c. 12. 38 V., c. 11. *Act, Canada* 1875," " *The Supreme and Exchequer Court Act*" has come into force ; and whereas it is expedient to make further and other provision for the institution of suits against the Crown in Canada by petition of right : Therefore Her Majesty, by and with the advice and consent of the Senate and House of Commons of Canada, enacts as follows :

1. " *The Petition of Right Act, Canada,* 1875," is hereby 38 V., c. 12, repealed. repealed.

2. A petition of right may be addressed to Her Majesty Form of petition of right. to the effect of the form No. 1 in the schedule to this Act annexed.

3.

To be left for Governor's fiat, without fee.

3. The petition shall be left with the Secretary of State of Canada, for submission to the Governor General in order that he may consider it, and, if he shall think fit, grant his fiat that right be done ; and nothing shall be payable by the suppliant on leaving or upon receiving back the petition.

Where and how to be filed, &c., after *fiat*.

4. Upon the Governor General's fiat being obtained the petition and fiat shall be filed in the Exchequer Court of Canada, which court shall have exclusive original cognizance of such petitions and thereafter a copy of the petition and fiat shall be left at the office of Her Majesty's Attorney General of Canada, with an endorsement thereon to the effect of the form No. 2 in the schedule to this Act annexed.

No preliminary inquisition. Time for filing defence or demurrer.

5. There shall be no preliminary inquisition finding the truth of the petition, or the right of the suppliant, but the statement in defence, or demurrer or both, shall be filed within four weeks after service, or such further time as shall be allowed by the court, or a judge.

Service on other parties affected by the petition.

6. In case the petition be presented for the recovery of any real or personal property, or any right in or to the same, which shall have been granted away or disposed of by or on behalf of Her Majesty, or Her Predecessors, a copy of the petition and fiat shall be served upon or left at the last or usual or last known place of abode of the person in the possession or occupation of such property or right, endorsed with a notice to the effect of the form No. 3 set forth in the

No *scire facias*

schedule to this Act annexed ; and it shall not be necessary to issue any *scire facias* or other process to such person for the purpose of requiring him to file his statement in defence,

Time for defence or demurrer.

but if he intend to contest the petition he shall, within four weeks after such service or leaving as aforesaid, or such further time as shall be allowed by the court or a judge, file his statement in defence, or demurrer, or both.

What defence may be raised.

7. The statement in defence, or demurrer may raise, besides any legal or equitable defences in fact or in law available under this Act, any legal or equitable defences which would have been available had the proceeding been a suit or action in a competent court between subject and subject ; and any grounds of defence which would be sufficient on behalf of Her Majesty, may be alleged on behalf of any such person, as aforesaid.

Certain issues triable without a jury.

8. Any issue of fact or assessment of damages to be tried or had under this Act, shall be tried or had by a judge without a jury.

Where the trial may be had and evidence taken.

9. The trial of any issue of fact or assessment of damages may, by order of the court or a judge, be had partly at one place and partly at another ; and the evidence of any witness

may,

may, by like order, be taken by commission or on examination or affidavit.

10. In case of failure on behalf of Her Majesty or of such other person as aforesaid, to file a statement in defence or demurrer in due time, the suppliant shall be at liberty to apply to the court or a judge for an order that the petition may be taken as confessed; and it shall be lawful for the court or judge, on being satisfied that there has been such failure, to order that the petition be taken as confessed as against Her Majesty, or such other person, and thereupon the suppliant may have judgment: Provided always, that such judgment may afterwards be set aside by the court or a judge, in their or his discretion, upon such terms as to them or him shall seem fit. *Judgment by default on either side.* *Proviso : may be set aside on terms.*

11. The judgment on every petition of right, shall be that the suppliant is not entitled to any portion, or that he is entitled to the whole or to some specified portion of the relief sought by his petition, or to such other relief, and upon such terms and conditions, if any, as may be just. *Form of judgment.*

12. In all cases in which the judgment commonly called a judgment of *amoveas manus*, was formerly given in England upon a petition of right, a judgment that the suppliant is entitled to relief as herein provided, shall be of the same effect as such judgment of *amoveas manus*. *If for suppliant, to have effect of amoveas manus.*

13. All the provisions of " *The Supreme and Exchequer Court Act*" not inconsistent with this Act shall extend and apply to the jurisdiction by this Act conferred in like manner as if such jurisdiction had been conferred on the Exchequer Court by the fifty-eighth section of the said Act. *Provisions of 38 V., c. 11, to apply.*

14. The Judges of the Supreme Court or any five of them may, from time to time, make general rules and orders for regulating in every particular the pleading, practice, procedure and costs on petitions of right, and for the effectual execution and working of this Act and the attainment of the intention and object thereof, and may, from time to time, alter and amend any rules and orders, and make other rules and orders instead thereof; and such rules and orders may extend as well to matters provided for as to any matter not provided for by this Act, but for which it may be found necessary to provide in order to ensure the proper working of this Act and the better attainment of the objects thereof; and all such rules and orders (being consistent with such express provisions of this Act as are not subject to alteration by rules or orders) shall have the force and effect of law : Provided that copies of all such rules and orders shall be laid before both Houses of Parliament at the next session thereof: Provided also that it shall be lawful for the Governor-General *Judges of Supreme Court to make rules, &c.* *To what such rules may extend.* *Their effect.* *To be laid before Parliament.* *May be suspended by*

Governor in Council or either House of Parliament.
General in Council by proclamation inserted in the *Canada Gazette*, or for either House of Parliament by any resolution passed at any time within thirty days after such rules and orders have been laid before Parliament, to suspend any rule or order made under this Act; and such rule or order shall thereupon cease to have force or effect until the end of the then next session of Parliament.

English rules to apply in default of rules under this Act.
15. In default of other provision either by this Act or by general rules and orders made under the authority of this Act, the rules of pleading, practice and procedure in force with regard to petitions of right in England shall, as to all matters, including the question of costs, so far as applicable, and unless the court or a judge otherwise order, apply and extend to a petition of right filed hereunder.

Payment of costs against Crown.
16. Any costs adjudged to Her Majesty on a petition of right shall be paid to the Receiver General.

Costs may be awarded to suppliant against Crown or other party.
17. Upon any such petition of right, the suppliant shall be entitled to costs against Her Majesty, and also against any other person appearing or pleading or answering to any such petition of right, in like manner and subject to the same rules, regulations and provisions, restrictions and discretion, so far as they are applicable, as are or may be usually adopted or in force, touching the right to recover costs in proceed-

How recoverable.
ings between subject and subject: and for the recovery of any such costs from any such person, other than Her Majesty, appearing or pleading or answering in pursuance hereof to any such petition of right, such and the same remedies and writs of execution as are authorized for enforcing payment of costs upon rules, orders, decrees or judgments in personal actions between subject and subject, shall and may be prosecuted, sued out, and executed on behalf of such suppliant:

Judgment for relief or order for costs to suppliant to be certified to Receiver General.
and whenever on a petition of right judgment is given that the suppliant is entitled to relief and there is no appeal, and whenever upon appeal judgment is affirmed or given that the suppliant is entitled to relief, and whenever any rule or order is made, entitling the suppliant to costs,

Certificate may be left with Minister of Finance.
any judge shall, upon application after the lapse of fourteen days from the making, giving, or affirming of such judgment, rule or order, certify to the Receiver General the tenor and purport of the same, to the effect of the form No. 4 in the schedule to this Act annexed; and such certificate may be sent to, or left at the office of the Minister of Finance.

Payment by Receiver General.
18. The Receiver General shall pay out of any moneys in his hands for the time being legally applicable thereto, or which may be thereafter voted by Parliament for that purpose, the amount of any moneys or costs which shall have been so certified to him to be due to any suppliant.

19.

19. Nothing in this Act contained shall— Act not to affect H. M's.

1. Prejudice or limit otherwise than is herein provided, prerogative rights, or— the rights, privileges or prerogatives of Her Majesty or Her Successors ; or—

2. Prevent any suppliant from proceeding as before the Prevent proceeding as heretofore, or— passing of this Act ; or—

3. Give to the subject any remedy against the Crown Give remedy not allowed in England before 23 & 24 V., c. 34, or— (*a*) in any case in which he would not have been entitled to such remedy in England under similar circumstances by the laws in force there prior to the passing of the Imperial Statute twenty-third and twenty-fourth Victoria, chapter thirty-four, intituled: "*An Act to amend the law relating to Petitions of Right, to simplify the proceedings and to make provisions for the costs thereof,*" or—

(*b*) in any case in which, either before or within two In any case referred to arbitration under Statute. months after the presentation of the petition, the claim is, under the Statutes in that behalf, referred to arbitration by the head of the proper department, who is hereby authorized with the approval of the Governor in Council to make such reference upon any petition of right.

20. All petitions of right which may have been presented As to petitions of right presented under 38 V., c. 12. under the provisions of the Act hereby repealed shall be held and taken to be presented under this Act at the expiration of thirty days from the passing hereof, and shall be, by the Secretary of State, entitled in the Exchequer Court of Canada.

21. The word "relief" comprehends every species of relief Interpretation. "Relief." claimed or prayed for in a petition of right, whether a restitution of any incorporal right, or a return of lands or chattels or a payment of money or damages or otherwise ;

The word "court" means the Exchequer Court of Canada, "Court." "Judge." and the word "judge" means the chief justice or any judge of the same court, unless there be any thing in the context indicating that such words are used in another sense.

22. In citing this Act it shall be sufficient to use the words Short Title. "*The Petition of Right Act*, 1876."

SCHEDULE.

SCHEDULE.

FORMS REFERRED TO IN THE FOREGOING ACT.

No. 1.

PETITION OF RIGHT.

In the Exchequer Court of Canada.
To the Queen's most Excellent Majesty:
County (*or* District) of (*place proposed for trial*) to wit:
The humble petition of A. B. of   , showeth
that (*state with convenient certainty the facts on which petitioner
relies as entitling him to relief*).

Conclusion.

Your suppliant therefore humbly prays that (*state the relief
claimed*).
Dated the   day of   A. D.

      (Signed)   A. B.
          or C. D , Counsel for A. B

No. 2.

The suppliant prays for a statement in defence on behalf
of Her Majesty, within four weeks after the date of service
hereof, or otherwise that the petition may be taken as confessed.

No. 3.

To A. B.
You are hereby required to file a statement in defence to
the within petition in Her Majesty's Exchequer Court of
Canada within four weeks after the date of service hereof.
Take notice, that if you fail to file a statement in defence or
demurrer in due time, the said petition may, as against you,
be ordered to be taken as confessed.
Dated the   day of   A. D.

No. 4.

To the Honorable the Receiver General.
Petition of right of A. B. in Her Majesty's Exchequer Court
of Canada at
I hereby certify that on the   day of
A. D.   it was by the said Court adjudged (*or* ordered)
that the above named suppliant was entitled to, etc.

         (*Judge's signature.*)

           CHAP.

CHAP. 28.

An Act to extend the provisions of the Act thirty first Victoria, chapter thirty-three, respecting the retiring allowance of Judges, to the Chief Justice and Justices of the Court of Error and Appeal for the Province of Ontario.

[*Assented to 12th April, 1876.*]

FOR remedying an omission in the Act hereinafter mentioned; Her Majesty, by and with the advice and consent of the Senate and House of Commons of Canada, enacts as follows:— *Preamble*

1. The third section of the Act passed in the thirty-first year of Her Majesty's reign, intituled: "*An Act respecting the Governor General, the civil list, and the salaries of certain public functionaries,*" shall extend and apply as fully to the Chief Justice and Justices of the Court of Error and Appeal for the Province of Ontario as to the judges and functionaries therein expressly mentioned; and Her Majesty may, under like circumstances and in like manner, grant to any such Chief Justice or Justice an annuity equal to two-thirds of the salary annexed to the office he held at the time of his resignation, to commence immediately after his resignation and continue thenceforth during his natural life, and to be payable *pro rata* for any period less than a year during such continuance, out of any unappropriated moneys forming part of the Consolidated Revenue Fund of Canada. *Sec. 3 of 31 V., c. 33, to apply to the Chief Justice and Justices of the Court of Error and appeal for Ontario.*

CHAP. 29.

An Act to provide for the Salaries of County Court Judges in the Province of Nova Scotia, and for other purposes.

[*Assented to 12th April, 1876.*]

HER MAJESTY, by and with the advice and consent of the Senate and House of Commons of Canada, enacts as follows:— *Preamble.*

1. The salaries of the County Court Judges in the Province of Nova Scotia shall be as follows:— *Salaries of County Court Judges in N.S.*

Six County Court Judges, each............ $2,000 per annum.
The County Court Judge for the County
    of Halifax...................................... 2,400 "   "

To

Travelling expenses.

To each of the County Court Judges there may be paid for actual travelling expenses such sum not exceeding the rate of two hundred dollars per annum, as may be allowed by the Governor in Council.

Increase to $2,400 after three years' service.

The salary of any of the said County Court Judges receiving less than two thousand four hundred dollars per annum shall after a period of three years' service as such County Court Judge, be two thousand four hundred dollars per annum, with travelling expenses as aforesaid.

Payment out of Con. Rev. Fund.

The said salaries and allowances may be paid out of any unappropriated moneys forming part of the Consolidated Revenue Fund of Canada, and *pro rata* for any shorter time than a year, in like manner as the salaries and allowances of other judges.

Sec. 8 of 37 V., c. 4, to apply to County Court Judges in Nova Scotia.

2. The eighth section of the Act passed in the thirty-seventh year of Her Majesty's reign, intituled "*An Act to amend the Act thirty-sixth Victoria, chapter thirty-one, for the readjustment of the Salaries of Judges, and other purposes,*" shall apply to the said County Court Judges in the Province of Nova Scotia, and they shall be entitled to the same retiring allowance or annuity on the same conditions and payable in the same manner as if they were expressly referred to and included in the said section.

CHAP. 30.

An Act to amend " The Insolvent Act of 1875."

[Assented to 12th April, 1876.]

Preamble. 38 V., c. 16.

WHEREAS it is expedient to make certain amendments in "*The Insolvent Act of* 1875" : Therefore Her Majesty, by and with the advice and consent of the Senate and House of Commons of Canada, enacts as follows :—

Sub-s. *b* of s. 2, amended. Publication of Notice.

1. Sub-section *b* of the second section of the said Act is hereby amended by adding after the words " and if no such Gazette is published," the words following : " or if such Gazette is not, in the opinion of the court or judge, published with sufficient frequency to enable the required notice to be conveniently published therein."

Section 4, amended.

2. The fourth section of the said Act is hereby amended by adding after the word " original " in the third line from the end the word " affidavit."

3.

3. The fourteenth section of the said Act is hereby Section 14,
amended. amended by striking out the words "or against whom a writ of attachment has issued as provided by this Act," in the second, third, and fourth lines, and the words "or writ of attachment" in the twelfth line; and by striking out the words "or by section nine" in the fifteenth line; and the words "or who issued the writ of attachment" in the nineteenth and twentieth lines; and the eighteenth section of the said Act is hereby amended by Section 18,
amended. inserting after the word "liquidation" in the ninth line, the following words "or for want of, or for a substantial insufficiency in the affidavits required by section nine."

4. The twentieth section of the said Act is hereby amended Section 20,
amended. by striking out the word "twice" in the third line from the end thereof, and inserting in lieu thereof the word "once," and by inserting after the word "Gazette" in the same line, the words following, "and once in one local or the nearest published newspaper,"

5. The twenty-sixth section of the said Act is hereby Section 26,
amended. amended by inserting after the word "answer" in the fifth line thereof the words "upon oath," and by striking out the word "and" in the eighth line, and inserting in lieu thereof the words "or to be sworn, or"

6. All securities given, or to be given, under the twenty- Right to use
of securities,
under s.s. 28,
and 29. eighth and twenty-ninth sections of the said Act, shall be deposited with the judge, and kept as part of the records of the court, subject to the right of any person entitled to sue upon any such security, to such production and delivery thereof, as may be necessary in order to the exercise of such right.

7. Any creditor of the estate may, in the case of any per- Inspection of
securities by
creditor, and
right to
object and
demand
better. son required, under the said twenty-eighth and twenty-ninth sections, to give security, have inspection of such security, and may, if in his opinion the surety or sureties in such security are insufficient, apply, on notice, to the judge for an order that new or additional sureties be furnished; and the judge may upon such application make such order as shall seem reasonable both as to the furnishing of sureties and as to the costs of the application.

8. The thirty-fifth section of the said Act is hereby Section 35,
amended. amended by striking out the word "as" between the words "Assignee" and "Inspector" in the fourth line from the end, and inserting in lieu thereof the word "or."

9. The thirty-sixth section of the said Act is hereby Section 36,
amended. amended by adding the following words "subject to the proviso as to sale *en bloc* contained in the thirty-eighth section of this Act."

Section 33, amended.

10. The thirty-eighth section of the said Act is hereby amended by adding thereto the following sub-section :—

As to sales *en bloc.*

"(2.) It shall not be necessary to advertise under the provisions of the seventy-fifth section of this Act any proposed sale of the estate *en bloc* under this section, although the estate may comprise real estate."

Section 41, amended. Registers and records of official assignees to be property of H. M.

11. The forty-first section of the said Act is hereby amended by inserting the following at the end thereof :—" And every register of or coming into the possession of an official assignee, and every other record required to be kept by an official assignee in connection with the performance of his duties, shall be held to be the property of Her Majesty ; and upon the death of an official assignee, or his ceasing to hold office, the judge shall be entitled to and shall assume possession and control of such register or other record, which shall thereafter be kept among the records of the court open to inspection as aforesaid."

Section 43, amended.

Remuneration of assignee.

12. The forty-third section of the said Act is hereby amended by inserting after the words " removal of property " in the thirteenth line the following words " the creditors may, in case in their opinion the remuneration of the assignee under the preceding part of this section is inadequate, at any meeting called for the purpose, fix such additional remuneration to be paid out of the estate to the assignee as they shall think reasonable," and by adding, after the word " creditors " in the third line from the end, the following words " and the remuneration of the assignee, whether he be the official or the creditors' assignee, in cases in which the estate is settled by composition."

Section 44, amended.

13. The forty-fourth section of the said Act is hereby amended by adding after the words " five creditors " the following words " if there are five or more, or by all the creditors if there are less than five. "

Section 66, amended.

14. The sixty-sixth section of the said Act is hereby amended by adding at the end thereof the words " or judge."

Section 84, amended.

15. The eighty-fourth section of the said Act is hereby amended by striking out the words " and revalue" in the last line, and by inserting at the end the words " and treat such liability as unsecured."

Section 128, amended.

16. The one hundred and twenty-eighth section of the said Act is hereby amended by striking out the words " either of the superior courts of common law or to the Court of Chancery, or to any one of the judges of the said courts," and substituting in lieu thereof the words " the Court of Error and Appeal, or to any judge of that court."

17.

17. The fourth sub-section of the one hundred and forty- Section 147, seventh section of the said Act is hereby amended by insert- amended. ing after the word " present " in the sixth line thereof the words " in person or represented by proxy."

18. Every assignee shall, before the end of October in each Yearly year, fill up and transmit to the Minister of Agriculture, or returns to be made to the in case this branch of the subject of statistics and the regis- proper tration thereof be, by the Governor in Council, transferred to minister by any other Minister, then to such other Minister, a schedule assignees. showing the particulars contained in the register to be kept by him under the forty-first section of the said Act, and such other schedules for the year ending the thirtieth day of Sep- tember next preceding, relative to the insolvency matters transacted by him, as shall be, from time to time, prescribed by the Governor in Council, according to forms published in the *Canada Gazette;* and it shall be the duty of every Entries to be assignee, to make from day to day and to keep entries and made and kept for this records of the particulars to be comprised in such schedules. purpose.

19. Any assignee neglecting or refusing to fill up and Penalty for transmit any schedule under the eighteenth section of this neglect or for wilfully Act, or wilfully making a false, partial, or incorrect schedule making any thereunder, shall forfeit and pay the sum of forty dollars to- false entry. gether with full costs of suit, to be recovered by any person suing for the same by action of debt or information in any court of record in the Province in which such return ought to have been made, or is made, or in the Exchequer Court of Canada, and one moiety whereof shall be paid to the party suing, and the other moiety into the hands of Her Majesty's Receiver General to and for the public uses of Canada.

20. The statistics collected by the Minister of Agriculture. Statistics collected to or such other Minister as aforesaid, under this Act shall be be published. abstracted and registered, and the results thereof shall be printed and published in an annual report.

21. The word " county " in the said Act includes any Word judicial district in the province of Ontario not organized into " county " explained. a county.

22. No amendment hereby made shall be held to be a Proviso as to declaration of the construction of any provision of the said effect of amendments. Act as applicable to any proceeding heretofore had under the said Act.

CHAP. 31.

An Act to make provision for the winding up of Insolvent Incorporated Banks.

[*Assented to 12th April, 1876.*]

Preamble.

WHEREAS it is expedient to make provision for winding up the estates of insolvent incorporated banks, therefore Her Majesty, by and with the advice and consent of the Senate and House of Commons of Canada, enacts as follows :—

Insolvent Act to apply, subject to certain modifications.

1. Notwithstanding anything contained in " *The Insolvent Act of* 1875," the provisions of the said Act shall apply to incorporated banks, subject to the modifications contained in the one hundred and forty-seventh section of the said Act, and to the following additional modifications which apply to the case of incorporated banks only.

When only writ of attachment may issue or assignment may be made. 34 V., c. 5.

2. No application for a writ of attachment against, and no assignment of the estate shall be made until after the bank has, whether before,or since the passing of this Act, become insolvent by suspension of payment for ninety days, under the provisions of the fifty-seventh section of " *An Act relating to Banks and Banking,*" passed in the thirty-fourth year of Her Majesty's Reign, chaptered five.

Judge may further adjourn proceedings for writ.

3. The judge may adjourn proceedings upon any application for a writ of attachment, for a time not exceeding six months from the time at which the bank suspended payment.

Judge may order preliminary inquiry to be made by persons appointed by him: their powers.

4. The judge may order that the preliminary inquiry authorized by the first sub-section of the said one hundred and forty-seventh section shall be made by a person or persons other than an official assignee, to be by him named on the application of the parties, and the person or persons so named shall have all the rights and discharge all the duties appertaining to the official assignee in connexion with such inquiry; and the judge may extend the time for report upon such inquiry to a period not exceeding thirty days from the date of the order for inquiry.

He may extend time for report.

Bank not to carry on business when insolvent.

5. Nothing herein, or in the said Insolvent Act, contained shall be held to authorize the carrying on or continuing the business after the bank has become insolvent as aforesaid.

Incorporated bank may be Receiver.

6. An incorporated bank may be appointed a receiver or creditors' assignee, and in case a bank is so appointed it may act through one or more of its principal officers to be approved by the judge.

7.

7. The Receiver shall, in addition to the powers vested in Additional him under the said hundred and forty-seventh section, have powers of the powers vested by the fifty-seventh, fifty-eighth and fifty-Receiver. ninth sections of the said Act respecting banks and banking in the " Assignee, or Assignees, or other legal authorities," in the said fifty-seventh section named.

8. After the issue of the writ of attachment the Assignee Additional shall, in addition to the powers vested in him under the powers of Insolvent Act, have like powers to those given to the Assignee after attach-Receiver under the next preceding section of this Act. ment.

9. Publication in the *Canada Gazette*, and in one news- What to be paper issued at or nearest the place where the head office is sufficient situate, of notice of any proceeding of which, under the note-holders. Insolvent Act, creditors should be notified, shall be deemed sufficient notice to holders of notes of the bank intended for circulation.

10. It shall be the duty of the Assignee to ascertain as Reservation nearly as may be the amount of notes of the bank intended of dividends for circulation and actually outstanding, and to reserve until ing notes. the expiration of at least two years after the bank has become insolvent, or until the last dividend, in case that is not made till after the expiration of the said time, dividends ·on such part of the said amount in respect of which claims may not be filed ; and if claims have not been filed and dividends applied for in respect of any part of the said amount before the period herein limited the dividends so reserved shall form the last or part of the last dividend.

11. Nothing shall be done under the fifteenth sub-section As to action of the hundred and forty-seventh section of the said under sub-s. " *Insolvent Act of* 1875," save upon order of the court or 15, of s. 147. judge.

12. The appeal provided for by the hundred and Extent of twenty-eighth section of the said Act, shall extend to all appeal under orders, judgments or decisions of the judge. section 128.

CHAP.

CHAP. 32.

An Act to amend " The Railway Act, 1868."

[Assented to 12th April, 1876.]

Preamble.
31 V., c. 68

WHEREAS it is expedient to amend " *The Railway Act,* 1868 ": Therefore Her Majesty, by and with the advice and consent of the Senate and House of Commons of Canada, enacts as follows:—

Sub-s. 22 of s. 9 amended, respecting arbitrators.

1. The twenty-second sub-section of the ninth section of the said Act is hereby amended by adding after the words " appointed by the parties " in the third line thereof the following words :—" Or the third arbitrator appointed by the two arbitrators," and by adding after the words " so deceased or not acting " in the thirteenth line thereof the words following :—" And in the case of a third arbitrator appointed by the two arbitrators, the provisions of the sixteenth sub-section of this section shall apply."

CHAP. 33.

An Act to amend the Act to make better provision, extending to the whole Dominion of Canada, respecting the inspection of certain Staple Articles of Canadian Produce.

[Assented to 12th April, 1876.]

Preamble.

HER MAJESTY, by and with the advice and consent of the Senate and House of Commons of Canada, enacts as follows:—

Sect. 63 of 37 V., c. 45, amended.

1. Section sixty-three of the Act thirty-seventh Victoria, chapter forty-five, cited in the title of this Act is hereby amended by striking out the words " one inch in width at the large end" and inserting in place thereof the words " five-eighths of an inch at the small end."

Sect. 64 of 37 V., c. 45, amended.

2. Section sixty-four of the Act cited in the title to this Act is hereby repealed, and the following is substituted in place thereof :—

Inspection of certain art'-cles to be compulsory.

" **64.** The inspection of all pickled fish cured for market or exportation, and of all fish oils, codfish tongues, or codfish sounds, cured for such purpose and contained in any such packages as are hereinafter mentioned shall, whenever such pickled

pickled fish, fish oils, or other articles as aforesaid, are removed beyond the limits of the Inspection District in which they are pickled or packed, be compulsory in every Province of the Dominion (except British Columbia and Manitoba) where an Inspector is appointed by law : and if any such pickled fish, fish oil or other article as aforesaid be sold or removed for sale beyond the limits of such district, or shipped or laden in any vehicle for removal, or offered to be removed from any district or place within the Dominion, except Manitoba and British Columbia, without being inspected under this Act, the person so selling or removing the same, or offering the same for sale or removal, shall incur a penalty of not less than one dollar and not more than five dollars for each and every such package." *Exception.*

Penalty for contravention.

3. Sub-section four of section sixty-six of the said Act shall be amended by adding the following words to the first paragraph :— *Sect. 66, sub-s. 4, amended.*

" And every such box of smoked herrings shall contain at " least twenty pounds of fish ; and half boxes shall be " twenty-two inches long, four inches deep and eight inches " wide, and to contain not less than ten pounds of fish." *Weight and size of boxes and half boxes of smoked herrings.*

4. Sub-section eight of the said sixty-sixth section shall be amended by adding the following :— *Sect. 66, sub. s. 8, amended.*

" Every barrel of pickled codfish shall contain two hun- " dred pounds of fish, and every half barrel one hundred " pounds of fish." *Barrels and half barrels of pickled codfish.*

5. Section ninety-seven of the Act cited in the title to this Act is hereby repealed and the following is substituted in place thereof :— *Sect. 97, repealed.*

" **97.** The expression " raw hides " shall mean and include " all green, untanned hides or skins, commonly used in the " manufacture of leather, weighing eight pounds or " upwards." *New provision as to raw hides.*

CHAP

CHAP. 34.

An Act to amend the Act thirty-seventh Victoria, chapter
fifty-one, intituled : " An Act to authorize the incorporation of Boards of Trade in the Dominion."

[Assented to 12th April, 1876.]

Preamble.   **W**HEREAS it is expedient to make further provisions for
the management and incorporation of Boards of Trade
in the Dominion of Canada, and to provide for the incorporation and management of Chambers of Commerce in the
said Dominion : Therefore Her Majesty, by and with the
advice and consent of the Senate and House of Commons of
Canada, enacts as follows:—

Sections 1, 2,
3 of 37 V., c.
51 repealed.   **1.** Sections one, two and three of the said Act cited in the
title of this Act shall, on and from the passing of this Act, be
repealed, and in lieu and place thereof the following sections
are substituted therefor :—

New section
in place of
section 1.
Formation of
Boards of
Trade.   " **1.** Any number of persons not less than thirty, being merchants, traders, brokers, mechanics, manufacturers, managers
of banks or insurance agents, being residents of any village,
town, city, county, or of any district (which word " district "
is hereby defined to be a district established for judicial
purposes by the Legislature of the Province wherein the same
is situate) having a population of not less than two thousand
five hundred, may associate themselves together as a Board
of Trade, and appoint a secretary, with all the privileges
and powers conferred by, and subject to all the restrictions
of this Act."

In place of
section 2.
Certificate of
formation.   " **2.** The persons associating themselves together as a Board
of Trade under this Act shall, under their hands and seals,
make a certificate specifying the name assumed by the association, and by which it shall be known, the name as hereinbefore defined, of the village, town, city, county or district in
which the same is situate and its business transacted, and
the name of the person by them elected secretary to the said
Board of Trade."

In place of
section 3.
Certificate
duly acknow-
ledged to be
sent to Secre-
tary of State.   " **3.** Such certificate shall be acknowledged before a notary
public, commissioner appointed for receiving affidavits, or
justice of the peace, by the secretary of the said Board of
Trade, and shall be forwarded to the Secretary of State, who
shall cause the same to be recorded in a register to be kept
for that purpose ; and a copy thereof duly certified by the
Secretary of State, shall be evidence of the existence of such
association."

2

2. Section five of the said Act cited in the title of this Act is hereby amended by striking out the words " *adding the name of the village, town, or city,* " in the parenthesis in the said section, and substituting therefor the following words " *adding the name, as hereinbefore defined, of the village, town, city, county or district,* " and by striking out the word " secretary " coming between the words " vice-president " and " and " in the tenth line of the said section. Section 5 amended.

3. The said Act cited in the title of this Act is further amended by adding thereto the following section, which shall form section twenty-seven of the said Act :— New section added as section 27.

" **27.** Each, all and every of the provisions of this Act shall apply to the incorporation and management of the commercial institutions styled ' Chambers of Commerce ' now existing or which hereafter may be called into existence in the Dominion of Canada, as fully and effectually as if the words ' Chamber of Commerce ' or ' Chambers of Commerce ' appeared therein in lieu and place of the words ' Board of Trade ' or ' Boards of Trade,' wheresoever the same appear respectively." Act to apply to Chambers of Commerce.

CHAP. 35.

An Act to amend " The Trade Mark and Design Act of 1868. "

[Assented to 12th April, 1876.]

IN amendment of the Act passed in the thirty-first year of Her Majesty's reign, chapter fifty-five, intituled : " *An Act respecting Trade Marks and Industrial Designs ;* " Her Majesty, by and with the advice and consent of the Senate and House of Commons of Canada, enacts as follows :— Preamble. Act 31 V., c 55, cited.

1. The Minister of Agriculture may, at any time before the expiration of the term of five years for which the copyright of any industrial design registered under the said Act either before or after the passing of this Act is valid, on the application of the registered proprietor of such design, grant to such proprietor a renewal of the registration thereof, for such further term, not exceeding five years, as such Minister may, in his discretion, deem to be advisable. Registration of industrial designs may be renewed, and for how long.

2. In case the further term for which the renewal of the registration of any industrial design is so granted has been for less than five years, the Minister may, at any time before the expiration of such further term, on the application of the then Renewals for short terms may be repeated.

then registered proprietor of the design, grant him a further renewal of the registration thereof ; and so on, *toties quoties*;

Limit of the aggregate of such periods.

but so as that no such registration shall be renewed for more than five years in all beyond the term of the validity of the copyright acquired by the registration of the design.

Mode of effecting renewals of registration of industrial designs.

8. Every renewal of a registration under this Act shall be effected as follows :—

The Minister of Agriculture (on receipt of the fee hereinafter prescribed to be paid) shall cause a note to be made in the margin of the proper page of the proper register to the effect that the registration referred to in such note has been renewed for the term mentioned in such note ; and such note shall be placed as near as may be to the entry of the registration to which it refers ; and thereupon such registration shall be renewed for the term mentioned in such note.

Certificates of renewal to be given, and what they shall contain.

4. Whenever the Minister of Agriculture has granted a renewal of the registration of any industrial design, and the same has been renewed, as provided for by this Act, he or his deputy shall make and sign a certificate to that effect, and shall deliver the same, or cause the same to be delivered, to the registered proprietor of such design ; and every such certificate shall contain the date of the registration of the design to which it refers, the number of such design, and the number or letter employed to denote or correspond with the registration, and the day, month and year of the entry of each renewal thereof in the proper register, and the name and address of the registered proprietor thereof at the date of the certificate, and the period of each renewal,—which said certificate, in the absence of proof to the contrary shall be sufficient proof of the design, of the name of the registered proprietor at the date of the certificate, of the registration and of its renewal or renewals, of the commencement and period of registry, of the commencement and period of each renewal, of the person named as proprietor being proprietor, of the originality of the design, and of compliance with the provisions of the said Act and of this Act ; and generally every such certificate, so signed, shall be received in all courts of law or of equity in Canada as evidence of the facts therein stated, without proof of the signature.

Certificates to be proof.

In all courts.

Fees on renewal of registration of industrial designs.

5. A fee of five dollars shall be payable to the Minister of Agriculture for every renewal of registration under the provisions of this Act ; and all fees so received shall be paid over by him to the Receiver General, to form part of the Consolidated Revenue Fund of Canada.

One Act with 31 V., c. 55— and short title of both.

6. This Act shall be read and construed as one Act with the Act cited in its title and preamble and amended by it ;— and the said Act and this Act may be cited collectively as " *The Trade Mark and Design Acts,* 1868 *to* 1876."

CHAP.

CHAP. 36.

An Act respecting the attendance of Witnesses on Criminal Trials.

[Assented to 12th April, 1876.]

WHEREAS it is expedient to make better provision for Preamble. securing the attendance of witnesses on criminal trials: Therefore Her Majesty, by and with the advice and consent of the Senate and House of Commons of Canada, enacts as follows :—

1. Any witness duly subpœnaed to attend and give evi- Witnesses dence at any criminal trial before any court of criminal summoned jurisdiction, shall be bound to attend and remain in atten- must attend. dance throughout the trial.

2. Upon proof to the satisfaction of the judge, of the Judge may service of the subpœna upon any witness who fails to attend cause witness to be arrested or remain in attendance, and that the presence of such wit- to answer for ness is material to the ends of justice, he may, by his warrant, his default. cause such witness to be apprehended and forthwith brought before him to give evidence and to answer for his disregard of the subpœna, and such witness may be detained on such warrant before the judge or in the common gaol with a view to secure his presence as a witness, or, in the discretion of the judge, he may be released on a recognizance, with or without sureties, conditioned for his appearance to give evidence and to answer for his default in not attending or not remaining in attendance ; and the judge may, in a Punishment summary manner, examine into and dispose of the charge of witness found guilty against such witness, who, if found guilty thereof, may, by of such order of the judge, be fined or imprisoned, or both,—the fine default. not exceeding one hundred dollars, and the imprisonment being in the common gaol, with or without hard labor, for a term not exceeding ninety days.

CHAP. 37.

An Act to amend the Criminal Law rela.ing to Violence, Threats and Molestation.

[Assented to 12th April, 1876.]

Preamble.

WHEREAS it is expedient to amend the Criminal Law relating to Violence, Threats and Molestation; Therefore Her Majesty, by and with the advice and consent of the Senate and House of Commons of Canada, enacts as follows :—

38 V., c. 39, repealed.

1. The Act of the thirty-eighth year of Her Majesty's reign, chapter thirty-nine, intituled *"An Act to amend the provisions of 'An Act to amend the Criminal Law relating to Violence, Threats and Molestation'"* is hereby repealed.

Sec. 1 of 35 V., c. 31, repealed and other provisions substituted.

2. The first section of the Act of the thirty-fifth year of Her Majesty's reign, chapter thirty-one, intituled *"An Act to amend the Criminal Law relating to Violence, Threats and Molestation"* shall remain repealed, and the following provisions shall be substituted instead thereof, and shall hereafter be read as forming the first section of the said Act, which shall be construed accordingly :—

Persons wrongfully committing certain acts, viz :

" **1.** Every person who wrongfully and without legal authority, with a view to compel any other person to abstain from doing anything which he has a legal right to do, or to do anything from which he has a legal right to abstain,—

" (1). Uses violence to such other person, or his wife or children, or injures his property ; or—

" (2.) Intimidates such other person, or his wife or children, by threats of using violence to him, her or any of them, or of injuring his property ; or—

" (3.) Persistently follows such other person about from place to place ; or—

" (4.) Hides any tools, clothes or other property owned or used by such other person, or deprives him, or hinders him in the use thereof ; or—

" (5.) Follows such other person with one or more other persons in a disorderly manner in or through any street or road ; or—

" (6.)

" (6.) Besets or watches the house or other place where such other person resides or works or carries on business or happens to be—

" Shall be liable to a fine not exceeding one hundred dollars, or to imprisonment for a term not exceeding three months : *Liable to fine or imprisonment.*

" Attending at or near or approaching to such house or other place as aforesaid, in order merely to obtain or communicate information, shall not be deemed a watching or besetting within the meaning of this section." *Proviso : Interpretation.*

3. Where a person is brought before a functionary or tribunal named in the second section of the said Act of the thirty-fifth year of Her Majesty's reign, chapter thirty-one, in respect to any offence under the provisions of the first section of the said Act as amended by the second section of this Act, the accused may on appearing before such functionary or tribunal declare that he objects to being tried for such offence by such functionary or tribunal, and thereupon such functionary or tribunal shall not proceed with such trial, but may deal with the case in all respects as if the accused were charged with an indictable offence and not with an offence punishable on summary conviction, and the accused may be prosecuted on indictment accordingly : and this section shall be read as part of the said Act. *Persons charged with such offences may object to be tried under sec. 2 of 35 V., c. 31. Proceedings in such case to be by indictment.*

4. A prosecution shall not be maintainable against a person for conspiracy to do any act, or to cause any act to be done for the purposes of a trade combination, unless such act is an offence indictable by Statute or is punishable under the provisions of the Act hereby amended ; nor shall any person, who is convicted upon any such prosecution, be liable to any greater punishment than is provided by such Statute or by the said Act as hereby amended, for the act of which he may have been convicted as aforesaid. *Limitation of prosecution and punishment for conspiracy for purposes of trade combination.*

2. For the purpose of this section, " trade combination " means any combination between masters or workmen or other persons, for regulating or altering the relations between any persons being masters or workmen, or the conduct of any master or workman, in or in respect of his business or employment, or contract of employment or service ; and the word " act " includes a default, breach, or omission. *" Trade combination" and " act " meaning of in this Act.*

CHAP. 38.

An Act to remove doubts under the Acts therein mentioned, respecting the Harbour Commissioners of Montreal, and to amend the same.

[*Assented to 12th April, 1876.*]

Preamble.

36 V., c. 61.

37 V., c. 31.

FOR the removal of doubts under the Act passed in the thirty-sixth year of Her Majesty's reign, intituled "*An Act respecting the Trinity House and Harbour Commissioners of Montreal,*" hereinafter referred to as "The Act of 1873,"---and the Act passed in the thirty-seventh year of Her Majesty's reign intituled "*An Act to amend the Act respecting the Trinity House and Harbour Commissioners of Montreal,*" hereinafter referred to as "The Act of 1874;" Her Majesty, by and with the advice and consent of the Senate and House of Commons of Canada declares and enacts as follows :—

Intent of the said Acts declared. Members and term of office.

1. It was and shall be held to have been the intent of the said Acts ;—that the four members of the corporation of the Harbour Commissioners of Montreal (hereinafter referred to as "the corporation") elected respectively by the Montreal Board of Trade, the Montreal Corn Exchange Association, the Montreal City Council and the Shipping Interest, should respectively, be elected on the first Monday in August, (or if that day were a legal holiday, then on the next following day not being so) as provided by the Act of 1873, subject to the provisions hereinafter made as to the present members ; and that each of them should hold office until the like day in the fourth year from his election, when he should go out of office; but might be re-elected.

Resignation of elective members.

Vacancies how filled.

Error in 37 V., c. 31, s. 7, corrected.

2. Any elective member of the corporation may resign his office by notifying his resignation to the body by which he was elected, in such manner as they may prescribe by by-law ; and the vacancy thereby occasioned or happening in any other manner, shall be filled up in the manner provided by the Act of 1873, the fourteenth, fifteenth, sixteenth, seventeenth and eighteenth sections whereof are hereby declared to have been inadvertently restricted by the seventh section of the Act of 1874, and shall be, and shall be held to have remained in force as to all the elective members, notwithstanding anything in the said seventh section.

Sec. 3 of 37 V., c. 31, repealed.

3. The third section of the Act of 1874 is hereby repealed ; and to establish the order of rotation among the members of the corporation, the present members shall respectively go out of office as follows :—

The

The member representing the Shipping Interest, in August 1876 ;—the member representing the City Council, in August 1877—the member representing the Board of Trade, in August 1878 ;—and the member representing the Corn Exchange in August 1879. Rotation in office.

4. This Act shall be construed as one Act with the said Acts of 1873 and 1874 ; and anything done or any action taken by the Governor, the Minister of Marine and Fisheries, the City Council, the Board of Trade, the Corn Exchange Association, the Shipping Interest " or the corporation," in conformity to the intent of the said Acts as hereby declared, is hereby confirmed and shall be and be held to have been lawful and valid. Construing this Act. Confirmation things done.

CHAP. 39.

An Act to remove doubts under the Acts therein• mentioned respecting the Corporation of the Quebec Harbour Commissioners.

[*Assented to 12th April,* 1876.]

FOR the removal of doubts under the Act passed in the thirty-sixth year of Her Majesty's reign intituled "*An Act further to amend the acts to provide for the management and improvement of the Harbour of Quebec,*" hereinafter referred to as "*The Act of* 1873 " and the Act passed in the thirty-eighth year of Her Majesty's reign and intituled "*An Act respecting the Trinity House and Harbour Commissioners of Quebec,*" hereinafter referred to as "*The Act of* 1875 ; " Her Majesty, by and with the advice and consent of the Senate and House of Commons of Canada, declares and enacts as follows :— Preamble. 36 V., c. 62. 38 V., c. 55.

1. It was and shall be held to have been the intent of the said Acts :— Intent of the said Acts explained.

(1.) That all the members of the Corporation of the Quebec Harbour Commissioners elected by the Council of the Board of Trade of the City of Quebec, and by the Council of the Board of Trade of the Town of Levis, and by the Shipping Interest, except the member elected by the Shipping Interest in August last, under the Act of 1875, should go out of office on the first day of January, 1876 ; Retirement of members.

(2.) That after the day last mentioned the Governor should have power to appoint one member of the said corporation, in addition to the four whom he could appoint under the Act Appointment of additional members by Governor in Council.

Act of 1873, and that the offices of all the other members of
the corporation, except the member elected by the Shipping
Interest in August last, being then vacant, the Council of the
Board of Trade of the City of Quebec, and the Council of the
Board of Trade of the Town of Levis, and the Shipping Interest, had each the power to elect one member of the said
corporation,—the member elected by the Shipping Interest in
August last remaining in office for two years from the time
of his election.

Provision in
case of failure
of election.
(3.)That if any of the said bodies should fail to elect their
member or members within fourteen days after the occurrence of vacancies on the first day of January, 1876, or if such
election should not be forthwith certified to the Minister of
Marine and Fisheries, as required by section seven of the said
Act of 1873, the Governor should have power to appoint the
member or members to fill such vacancy or vacancies, under
section eight of the said Act.

Election and
appointment
up to 1st
Jan., 1876.
(4.) That up to the said first day of January, 1876, the
elections and appointments of members of the said corporation should be made as if the Act of 1875 had not been passed, except that one member should be elected by the Shipping Interest in August 1875 to remain in office two years:
that the other members representing the Shipping Interest
should go out of office at the time appointed for the said
election ; that the said Interest should be represented thereafter (but only until the 1st of January, 1876) by one member
Clerical error
corrected.
instead of three as theretofore, (the word " two " being
inserted instead of " three " in the last line but one of
section eight of the said Act by a clerical error); and that on
and after the 1st of January, 1876, the said Shipping Interest
should be represented by two members.

Vacancies not
to affect
actions of
a quorum.
(5.) That vacancies in the corporation do not prevent or
impair the effect of its action in any matter, provided there
be a quorum of five members present at the meeting at which
such action is taken, and that a majority of them are in favour of such act, as provided by section ten of the Act of
1873.

Number of
members.
(6.) That the said corporation should consist of nine members exclusive of the chairman of the Corporation of Pilots
for and below the Harbour of Quebec, who is *ex officio* a
member of the Corporation of the Quebec Harbour Commissioners, but as respects pilotage matters only.

Omission in
38 V . c. 55,
supplied.
2. And for supplying provisions omitted in the said Act of
1875, it is enacted, that section six of the Act of 1873 be
and the same is hereby repealed, and that the members of
the said corporation elected in January, 1876, and the member elected by the Shipping Interest in August, 1875, and
any

any members appointed by the Governor in place of any
who have not been elected or whose offices have become
vacant, shall respectively hold office as follows, that is to
say :—

The member representing either of the said Boards of Trade Terms of office
until the first Monday in August in the year 1877, and the of elected
members representing the Shipping Interest until the first members.
Wednesday in the same month in the same year, (or if either
of the said days be a legal holiday then until the next following day not being such holiday) ; and others shall then be
elected in their stead by the bodies they respectively represented, and shall hold office until the like day of the week
and month, in the third year from that in which they are
elected, when they shall retire and others shall be elected in
their stead : and to such elections and to the filling of vacancies among elective members, the provisions of the said
Act of 1873 in like matters, not inconsistent with this Act,
shall apply,—members of the said corporation appointed by
the Governor otherwise than for filling vacancies in default
of election or certificate thereof, being appointed and holding office as provided by the said Act of 1873.

3. This Act shall be construed as forming one Act with Act to be
the said Acts of 1873 and 1875, and any thing done or action construed as
taken by the Governor or Minister of Marine and Fisheries one Act with
those of 1873
or by the said corporation, or by either of the said Boards of and 1875, etc.
Trade, or by the said Shipping Interest, in conformity to the
intent of the said Acts as hereby declared, is hereby confirmed and shall be held to be and to have been lawful and valid.

4. The Harbour Commissioners may pay to the Chairman Power to pay
of the Board an annual salary not exceeding two thousand a salary to
dollars out of the revenues of the harbour. their chair-
man.

OTTAWA:

PRINTED BY BROWN CHAMBERLIN,

LAW PRINTER TO THE QUEEN'S MOST EXCELLENT MAJESTY.

1876

TABLE OF CONTENTS.

ACTS OF CANADA.

THIRD SESSION, THIRD PARLIAMENT, 39 VICTORIA, 1876.

PUBLIC GENERAL ACTS.

<table>
<tr><td>CHAP.</td><td></td><td>PAGE.</td></tr>
</table>

INDEX

TO

ACTS OF CANADA,

THIRD SESSION, THIRD PARLIAMENT, 39 VICTORIA, 1876.

PUBLIC GENERAL ACTS.

PAGE

PAGE

ACTS

OF THE

PARLIAMENT

OF THE

DOMINION OF CANADA,

PASSED IN THE

THIRTY-NINTH YEAR OF THE REIGN OF HER MAJESTY

QUEEN VICTORIA,

AND IN THE

THIRD SESSION OF THE THIRD PARLIAMENT,

egun and holden at Ottawa, on the tenth day of February, and closed by Prorogation on the twelfth day of April, 1876.

HIS EXCELLENCY

THE RIGHT HONORABLE, SIR FREDERICK TEMPLE, EARL OF DUFFERIN,
GOVERNOR GENERAL.

VOL. II.
LOCAL AND PRIVATE ACTS.

OTTAWA:
PRINTED BY BROWN CHAMBERLIN,
LAW PRINTER TO THE QUEEN'S MOST EXCELLENT MAJESTY.
ANNO DOMINI, 1876.

39 VICTORIA.

CHAP. 40.

An Act to incorporate "The Chartered Bank of London and North America."

[Assented to 12th April, 1876.]

WHEREAS the persons hereinafter named and others, by Preamble. their petition, have prayed that they may be incorporated for the purpose of establishing a bank in the City of Montreal, and it is expedient to grant the prayer of the said petition : Therefore Her Majesty, by and with the advice and consent of the Senate and House of Commons of Canada, enacts as follows :—

1. James Domville, M.P., of Kingshurst, Province of New Certain persons incorporated. Brunswick, President of the Maritime Bank of the Dominion sons incorporated. of Canada; the Honorable Eugène Chinic, Senator, President of "La Banque Nationale," Quebec; the Honorable John Henry Pope, M.P., Director of the Eastern Townships Bank; the Honorable Henry Adolphus Newman Kaulback, Q.C., Senator, of Lunenburg, Nova Scotia; the Honorable Clement Francis Cornwall, Senator, of Ashcroft, British Columbia; the Honorable Thomas Heath Haviland, Senator, Director of the Bank of Prince Edward Island; Angus Morrison, Esquire, Mayor of Toronto, Ontario, and such others as may become shareholders in the corporation to be by this Act created, and their assigns, shall be, and they are hereby Corporate created, constituted and declared to be a corporation, body name and corporate and politic, by the name of "The Chartered Bank powers. of London and North America."

2. The capital stock of the said Bank shall be one million Capital of pounds sterling divided into twenty thousand shares of stock and shares. fifty pounds sterling each, or five millions of dollars, divided into fifty thousand shares of one hundred dollars each, which said shares shall be, and are hereby vested in the several persons who shall subscribe for the same, their legal representatives and assigns.

3. For the purpose of organizing the said Bank, and of Provisional raising the amount of the said capital stock, the persons Directors and their powers. hereinbefore

d by name shall be provisional direc-
hereinbefore mention- - a majority of them, may cause
tors thereof, and they, o. - giving due notice thereof in
stock books to be opened afte. stock books shall and may
Stock books, and subscription to stock. the *Canada Gazette*; upon whic... riptions of such parties
be received the signatures and subs. holders in the said
or persons as desire to become shar... al and else-
Bank; and such books shall be opened at Montre.
where at the discretion of the provisional directors, and
shall be kept open as long as they shall deem necessary;
When the first meeting of shareholders may be held. and as soon as five hundred thousand pounds sterling or two
million five hundred thousand dollars of the said capital
stock shall have been subscribed upon the stock books, and
fifty thousand pounds sterling or two hundred and fifty
thousand dollars thereof actually paid into some one of
the present chartered banks in Canada, and a certificate
shall have been obtained from the Treasury Board, that
it has been proved to their satisfaction that such amounts
of the capital have been *bond fide* subscribed for and
paid respectively, a public meeting shall be called of
the subscribers thereof by notice, published for at least
two weeks in two newspapers of the said City of Montreal, such meeting to be held in Montreal aforesaid, at
such time and place therein as such notice shall indicate;
Election of directors; their term of office. and at such meeting the subscribers shall proceed to elect
seven directors having the requisite stock qualification, who
shall from thenceforward manage the affairs of the said corporation, shall take charge of the stock-books hereinbefore
referred to, and shall continue in office until the first Wednesday in July, which shall be in the year next after the
year in which they are so elected, and until their successors
Provisional directors superseded. in office shall be duly elected; and immediately upon such
election being had, the functions of the said provisional
directors shall cease.

Number of directors may be increased or diminished. **4.** The number of directors of the said Bank shall be
seven, subject to be diminished or increased from time to time
by by-law, to be passed as provided in the twenty-eighth section of the Act of the Parliament of Canada, passed in the
34 V., c. 5. thirty-fourth year of Her Majesty's reign, intituled: "*An Act relating to Banks and Banking.*"

Chief place of business. **5.** The chief place of business or head office of the said
corporation shall be in the City of Montreal, in Canada;
and the board of directors may establish a place of business
Local directors. Transfers and payment of dividends in United Kingdom. in the City of London, England, and may appoint local
directors; and shares in the capital stock of the said Bank
may be made transferable, and the dividends accruing
thereon may be made payable in the United Kingdom in
like manner as such shares and dividends are respectively
transferable and payable at the chief office of the said Bank
in the City of Montreal; and to that end the directors may
from time to time, make such rules and regulations, and
prescribe

prescribe such forms, and appoint such agent or agents as they may deem necessary.

6. The Act passed in the thirty-fourth year of Her Majesty's reign, chaptered five, and intituled : "*An Act relating to Banks and Banking,*" and all the provisions thereof, shall apply to the Bank hereby incorporated in the same manner as if it were expressly incorporated with this Act, except so far as such provisions relate only to banks already in existence, or to banks *en commandite,* or are not consistent with the provisions of this Act. Act 34 V., c. 5, to apply.

Exception.

7. The said Bank shall obtain from the Treasury Board within two years from and after the passing of this Act, the certificate mentioned and required by section seven of the said "*Act relating to Banks and Banking,*" passed in the thirty-fourth year of Her Majesty's reign, chaptered five ; in default of which this Act shall become and be null and void, and of no effect, and the charter hereby granted, and all and every the rights and privileges hereby conferred, shall be forfeited. Treasury Board certificate to be obtained within two years.

8. This Act shall remain in force until the first day of July, in the year of Our Lord one thousand eight hundred and eighty-one. Duration of Act.

CHAP. 41.

An Act to amend the Act of incorporation of the "Banque Saint Jean-Baptiste."

[Assented to 12th April, 1876.]

WHEREAS the Banque Saint Jean-Baptiste was duly incorporated by the Act of the Parliament of the Dominion of Canada, thirty-eighth Victoria, chapter fifty-nine ; and whereas the provisional directors of the said Bank have by their petition prayed for a prolongation of the delay fixed by the seventh section of the said Act, for obtaining from the Treasury Board the certificate required by the seventh section of the "*Act relating to Banks and Banking ;*" and whereas it is fit that the prayer of the said petition should be granted : Therefore Her Majesty, by and with the advice and consent of the Senate and House of Commons of Canada, enacts as follows :— Preamble.
Act 38 V., c. 59, cited.

34 V., c. 5.

1. The delay of twelve months, fixed by section seven of the said Act, thirty-eighth Victoria, chapter fifty-nine, intituled "*An Act to incorporate the Banque Saint Jean-Baptiste,*" Delay fixed by sec. 7 of 38 V., c. 59, extended to 1st May, 1877.

Baptiste," is by this Act extended and prolonged to the first day of May, one thousand eight hundred and seventy-seven : Provided always, that nothing in this Act contained shall be held to change the existing legal liability of any present subscriber to the capital stock of the said Bank.

Proviso.

CHAP. 42.

An Act respecting " The Mechanics' Bank."

[Assented to 12th April, 1876.]

Preamble.   WHEREAS the Mechanics' Bank, by its petition, has represented that it has sustained heavy losses in the course of its business, whereby the value of its paid up capital stock has been reduced ; and that in order to enable it advantageously to continue business and to realize the largest possible return for its existing shareholders, it is necessary that it should be re-organized upon a different basis, and be authorized to reduce the nominal value of its present shares, and otherwise to adjust and regulate the same, and it is expedient to grant the prayer of the said petition : Therefore Her Majesty, by and with the advice and consent of the Senate and House of Commons of Canada, enacts as follows :—

Nominal value of shares of stock to be reduced to 60 per cent. Directors to make arrangements.   **1.** The shares of the said Bank shall be reduced as to their nominal value to sixty per cent. of their present nominal value ; and new shares shall be issued to the holders of such shares in the said bank in the proportion of six-tenths of a share to the holder of every paid up share therein ; the board of directors are hereby authorized to make such arrangements as to the details of the conversion of the shares in conformity hereto as shall be found most convenient, and in so doing to provide for the conversion or appropriation of balances forming parts of shares in such manner as to do

Proviso : liability of shareholders under 34 V., c. 5 not affected.   justice to the holders thereof : Provided always, that nothing herein contained or done hereunder shall in any way affect or diminish the present liability of the shareholders of the Bank to the creditors thereof, under the " *Act relating to Banks and Banking* " or the present liability of holders of shares unpaid, or not paid in full, to pay up in full the amount of such shares to the present nominal value.

Preferential stock may be issued for five years.   **2.** The said Bank is hereby authorized to issue preferential stock to the extent of three hundred thousand dollars in three thousand shares of one hundred dollars each, the dividends on which stock shall be preferential, as between the holders thereof and the holders of the ordinary stock. at such rate not exceeding eight per cent. in any one year, as shall

shall be fixed by the board, for a period of five years from
the issue of such preferential stock; and during such As to divi-
period dividends shall only be declared or paid on the ordi- dends in such
nary stock, out of the balance of profits which shall cases.
in any year remain after payment of the dividend on
the said preferential stock; but at the end of the said
period of five years such preference shall cease, and the
said preferential stock shall become ordinary stock: Pro- Proviso, in
vided, that the existing shareholders shall under the terms of favor of
issue have a preferential right to subscribe within such time, shareholders.
not less than thirty days, as shall be fixed by the by-law
authorizing the issue, for the new issue, in proportion to the
number of paid up shares held by each.

3. The board are hereby authorized to cancel any ordin- As to shares
ary paid up stock on which the Bank has a lien for debts on which the
due to it by customers to an amount exceeding the present lien.
nominal value of such stock, and to cancel, on such terms as
may be sanctioned by a resolution of the shareholders, any
paid up stock surrendered to the Bank by any of its officers
toward satisfaction of any debt due to it by such officer, and And as to the
it is hereby declared that the new stock into which the new stock.
existing paid up stock of the Bank shall be converted as
hereinbefore provided, shall be held to represent its new
nominal amount only, in the capital of the Bank; and the
difference between the said amount and the total authorized capital of the Bank shall be regarded as unissued, and
shall be capable of being subscribed for upon such terms as
the board shall order, either as preferential stock to the
amount, and upon the conditions hereinbefore provided, or
as new ordinary stock: Provided, that notwithstanding any- Proviso:
thing in this Act contained the total authorized capital of total capital
the Bank embracing both ordinary and preferential stock limited.
shall not exceed one million of dollars.

4. This Act shall not affect any right of action which any Certain rights
individual shareholder may have against any director, or of action not
officer of the Bank; nor shall it have any force or effect Act not to
whatever, until it has been accepted by the shareholders, by have effect
a resolution passed at a special general meeting of such share- by shareholders, called for the purpose, which resolution to have holders.
effect must be concurred in by at least two-thirds of the
holders of paid up stock, present or represented at such
meeting, voting as provided by the "*Act relating to Banks* 34 V., c. 5.
and Banking."

CHAP. 43.

An Act to further amend the Act to incorporate "The London and Canada Bank," and to amend the Act amending the same.

[*Assented to 12th April, 1876.*]

Preamble.
37 Vic., c. 55.
38 Vic., c. 60.

WHEREAS The London and Canada Bank" was duly incorporated by an Act passed in the thirty-seventh year of Her Majesty's reign, chaptered fifty-five ; and whereas the said Act was amended by an Act passed in the thirty-eighth year of Her Majesty's reign, chaptered sixty, and the provisional directors thereof have by their petition prayed that the said Acts may be further amended by again changing the name thereof to that of "The London and Canada Bank," and by extending the time for obtaining from the Treasury Board the certificate required by section seven of "*An Act*

34 V. c. 5. *relating to Banks and Banking,*" and by making other amendments to the said Acts of incorporation, and it is expedient to grant their prayer: Therefore Her Majesty, by and with the advice and consent of the Senate and House of Commons of Canada, enacts as follows :—

37 Vic., c. 55,
.s. 2, repealed.

1. Section two of the Act incorporating the said Bank is hereby repealed, and the following substituted in lieu thereof:

New section.
Capital stock
and shares.

" **2**. The capital stock of the said Bank shall be one million of pounds sterling, divided into twenty thousand shares of fifty pounds sterling each, or five millions of dollars, divided into fifty thousand shares of one hundred dollars each, which said shares shall be and are hereby vested in the several persons who shall subscribe for the same, their legal representatives and assigns."

38 Vic., c. 60,
s. 1, amending
37 V., c. 55,
s. 3, repealed.

2. The section substituted for section three of the Act first above cited, by section one of the Act amending the same, secondly cited, is hereby repealed, and the following substituted therefor :

New section
substituted.
Provisional
directors and
their powers.

" **3**. For the purpose of organizing the said Bank and of raising the amount of the said capital stock, the following persons, that is to say, John M. Grover, John Ham Perry, Joseph Gould, Edward Douglas Armour, shall be provisional directors thereof; and they, or a majority of them, may cause stock-books to be opened after giving due notice thereof, upon which stock-books shall and may be received the signatures and subscriptions of such parties or persons as

Stock books. desire to become shareholders in the said Bank ; and such stock-books shall be opened at the City of London, England,

an

and elsewhere, at the discretion of the provisional directors, and shall be kept open as long as they shall deem necessary; and so soon as the whole amount of the capital stock shall have been subscribed upon the stock-books, and two hundred and fifty thousand pounds sterling, or one million one hundred and twenty-five thousand dollars thereof actually paid into some one of the present chartered banks in Canada, and a certificate shall have been obtained from the Treasury Board that it has been proved to their satisfaction that such amounts of the capital have been *bonâ fide* subscribed for and paid up respectively, a public meeting shall be called of the subscribers thereof by notice published for at least two weeks in some newspaper in the said City of London, such meeting to be held in London, aforesaid, at such time and place as such notice shall indicate; and at such meeting the subscribers shall proceed to elect ten directors having the requisite stock qualifications, who shall, from thenceforward shall manage the affairs of the said corporation and take charge of the stock-books hereinbefore referred to, and shall continue in office until the first Wednesday in July which shall be in the year next after the year in which they are so elected; and immediately upon such election being had the functions of the said provisional directors shall cease, and then, and not before, the bank may commence business." *First meeting of shareholders for election of directors.*

Their term of office.

Provisional directors superseded.

3. The section substituted for section four of the Act first above cited, by section two of the Act amending the same secondly cited, is hereby repealed, and the following substituted therefor: *37 Vic., c. 55, s. 4, repealed.*

"**4.** The chief place or seat of business of the said Bank shall be in the City of Toronto, in Canada, and the board of directors may establish a place of business in the City of London, in England, and may appoint local directors; and shares in the capital stock of the said Bank may be made transferable, and the dividends accruing thereon may be made payable in the United Kingdom, in like manner as such shares and dividends are respectively transferable and payable at the chief office of the said Bank in the City of Toronto; and to that end the directors may, from time to time, make such rules and regulations and prescribe such forms and appoint such agents as they may deem necessary." *New section. Head office.* *Local directors.* *Transfers and payment of dividends in United Kingdom.*

4. The time limited by the third section of the said amending Act, intituled: "*An Act to amend the Act to incorporate 'The London and Canada Bank,' and to change the name thereof to that of 'The Bank of the United Provinces,'*" is hereby extended for the further period of twelve months. *Duration of corporation extended.*

5. Section four of the said amending Act is hereby repealed, and the corporate name of the said Bank is hereby changed from "The Bank of the United Provinces" to "The London, *S. 4 of 38 V., c. 60 repealed. Name changed.*

and

and Canada Bank," but the said corporation shall not therefore be deemed a new corporation, and all real or movable property, shares or stock obligations, debts, rights, claims. privileges and powers heretofore vested in, held or contracted by " The Bank of the United Provinces" are hereby transferred to " The London and Canada Bank," which by its said corporate name is hereby substituted to all intents and purposes for the said " The Bank of the United Provinces."

Rights not affected.

CHAP. 44.

An Act to confirm the amalgamation of the City Bank and the Royal Canadian Bank, and to incorporate the Consolidated Bank of Canada.

[Assented to 12th April, 1876.]

Preamble. Agreement for amalgamation recited.

WHEREAS on the eighteenth day of September, one thousand eight hundred and seventy-five, the City Bank and the Royal Canadian Bank entered into an agreement of amalgamation, thereby agreeing to form one corporation under the name of " The Consolidated Bank of Canada," which agreement was previously authorized by the shareholders of the said two Banks ; And whereas an indenture setting forth the terms thereof was duly executed by the said Banks on the seventeenth and eighteenth days of September last ; And whereas the said Banks have by their joint petition represented that it is for the interest of the shareholders and others interested in the said Banks and of the public. that the said agreement should be confirmed, and the amalgamation of the two Banks authorized upon the terms therein set forth, the said amalgamated Banks consolidated. and the provisions hereinafter contained, enacted, for the better conduct and management of the said Consolidated Bank of Canada, and have prayed that under the said circumstances, an Act of the Parliament of Canada should be passed to contain the provisions hereinafter mentioned ; And whereas it is expedient that the prayer of the said petition be granted : Therefore Her Majesty, by and with the advice and consent of the Senate and House of Commons of Canada, enacts as follows :

Agreement for amalgamation confirmed.

1. The said agreement is hereby confirmed, and the amalgamation of the said City Bank and of the Royal Canadian Bank is hereby authorized upon the terms and conditions in the said agreement of amalgamation as in the schedule to this Act set forth.

The two banks to be

2. And upon, from and after the tenth day of May next
the

the said amalgamated Banks, and the shareholders therein, one from 10th
and their assigns, shall be a corporation, body corporate and May, 1876.
politic by the name of "The Consolidated Bank of Canada," New name.
and shall continue to be such corporation, and shall have
perpetual succession, and a corporate seal, with power to
alter and change the same at pleasure, and may sue and be
sued, implead or be impleaded in all courts of law and equity.

3. The terms and conditions set forth in the said recited Terms and
deed of amalgamation shall constitute the basis of the conditions
union of the two Banks, and it shall be the duty of the recited in the
board of directors of the corporation by this Act created to the basis of
pass and maintain in force such by-laws as may from time union.
to time be necessary to carry out and give effect to the said
terms and conditions.

4. The head office and chief place of business of the said Head office in
amalgamated Bank shall be in the City of Montreal. Montreal.

5. The capital stock of the said Bank shall be four Capital stock
million dollars, divided into forty thousand shares of one and shares.
hundred dollars each.

6. On and from the said tenth day of May next, the pre- Shareholders
sent shareholders of the said Banks shall become and be of both banks
shareholders in the said Consolidated Bank of Canada in the shareholders
amounts, and according to the relative values of the stock of the Con-
of the said amalgamated Banks, as provided for and set forth Bank in
in the said indenture of amalgamation, in lieu of and in which all as-
proportion to the amount of their shares in the said amal- banks shall
gamated Banks, and all the estate and effects, real and per- vest.
sonal, rights, property, credits, *choses in action*, claims and
demands of whatsoever nature or quality, or wherever
situate of the said Banks, shall then become and be vested in
the said Consolidated Bank of Canada, its successors or assigns, as and for its own use absolutely, and it may in its
own name sue for, collect, and get in all and every part of
the said estate, rights and effects ; and the said Consolidated Their notes
Bank shall be bound to redeem and pay all the outstanding redeemed by
bills of both of the said Banks in circulation at the time of it, and may
such amalgamation ; and, so long as it is convenient or expe- as if its own.
dient so to do, but not longer than for one year from the
time when the provisions of this Act shall come into
force, may re-issue such bills from time to time, or
any part thereof, in the same manner and subject to the
same conditions and limitations, and with the same
privileges and remedies against the said Consolidated Bank
of Canada as would exist in respect of bills issued by itself
in its own name. And the said Consolidated Bank of Can- Consolidated
ada shall thereby become and be subject and liable to pay Bank to pay
and discharge all the debts, obligations, bills and promissory amalgamated
notes and other liabilities of each of the said amalgamated banks.
Banks,

Banks, and may be directly sued and proceeded against in respect thereof, as fully and effectually as if the same were originally the debts, obligations, promissory notes or liabilities of the said Consolidated Bank of Canada, and the same

Pending suits by or against either of them may be continued in its own name, or against it, upon a suggestion or *reprise d'instance.*

shall be taken and construed so to be ; and all suits, actions and proceedings pending on the said tenth day of May next in any court of law or equity, or in any court possessing civil jurisdiction in which suits, actions or proceedings the City Bank or the Royal Canadian Bank were plaintiffs or defendants, may be continued to judgment or execution in the name of the Consolidated Bank of Canada, upon a suggestion being entered upon the record by virtue of this Act, at any time before judgment, that the City Bank or the Royal Canadian Bank, as the case may be, became on the tenth day of May, eighteen hundred and seventy-six, the Consolidated Bank of Canada, by virtue of the said agreement of amalgamation and of this Act, or upon a petition *en reprise d'instance* being presented by the Consolidated Bank of Canada, in accordance with the ordinary practice of the courts in the various provinces of the Dominion respectively.

Board of provisional directors ; and annual election of board of directors, on first Wednesday in June.

7. For the management of the affairs of the said corporation there shall be ten directors, who shall be annually elected by the shareholders of the capital stock of the corporation at a general meeting of them, to be held annually on the first Wednesday in June in each year, the first whereof shall be held on the first Wednesday in June next ; and the directors elected by a majority of votes shall be capable of serving as directors for the ensuing twelve months ; and until such election shall be held the said Consolidated Bank of Canada shall be managed and conducted by the whole of the directors of the said two Banks as constituting a board of provisional directors of the said Bank, of whom five shall be a quorum.

One vote per share.

8. And notwithstanding anything contained in any statute of the Parliament of Canada, or in the by-laws of either of the said Banks, every shareholder in either of the said Banks, who shall on the said tenth day of May next be entitled to one or more shares in the said Consolidated Bank of Canada, shall have a vote for each of such shares, but no

First annual meeting may be called, and notice thereof given, by either bank.

vote for any fraction of a share ; And the first annual meeting of the said Consolidated Bank, to be so held on the first Wednesday in June next, may be validly called, and notice thereof may be validly given, by either of the said Banks.

What provisions of Act 34 V., c. 5, shall or shall not apply to this bark

9. The Act of the Parliament of Canada, passed in the thirty-fourth year of Her Majesty's reign, chapter five, intituled, "*An Act relating to Banks and Banking,*" and all the provisions thereof and the amendments thereof, shall apply to the Consolidated Bank of Canada in the same manner as

if

if the same were expressly incorporated in this Act, except in so far as such provisions relate specially to banks in existence before the passing hereof, or to banks *en commandite*, or are inconsistent with this Act.

10. This Act shall remain in force until the first day of July in the year of Our Lord one thousand eight hundred and eighty-one. Duration of Act.

11. This Act shall be a Public Act. Public Act.

SCHEDULE A.

This agreement, made this eighteenth day of September, in the year of Our Lord one thousand eight hundred and seventy-five—Between the City Bank, a corporation duly incorporated under the statutes in that behalf made, and having its chief place of business at Montreal in Canada, of the first part, and the Royal Canadian Bank, a corporation duly incorporated in like manner, having its chief place of business in Toronto, in the said Dominion, of the second part : Agreement.

Whereas, the said Banks have mutually agreed to amalgamate and unite together upon the terms and subject to the provisions hereinafter mentioned : Now, therefore, these presents witness, and it is hereby declared, covenanted and agreed upon by and between the said Banks as follows :—

1. The said Banks shall be amalgamated from and after the tenth day of May next, up to which day both of the said Banks will cause their accounts and books to be made up and posted.

2. The name of the amalgamated Bank shall be " The Consolidated Bank of Canada."

3. The chief place of business of the said amalgamated Bank shall be in the City of Montreal, and the head office for Ontario shall be in the City of Toronto.

4. The capital stock of the amalgamated Bank shall be four millions of dollars, divided into forty thousand shares of one hundred dollars each.

5. The Bank shall be managed by ten directors, and there shall also be a local board at Toronto, to be composed of a chairman, who shall also be a director of the Bank, and of three local directors, who shall be appointed by the board ; and all the members of the local board shall be shareholders of the Bank, duly qualified to be directors, and resident in Ontario. The local board shall be charged with the supervision

Agreement. vision of all agencies situated north and west of Toronto, subject to the instructions and control of the board.

6. In order to equalize the value of the rest account of , the two Banks, parties hereto, the Royal Canadian Bank shall contribute to the amalgamated Bank sixty thousand dollars, or three per cent. upon its capital, and this contribution shall be paid by the shareholders in the Royal Canadian Bank to the amalgamated Bank, on or before the first day of June next. Subject to such payment or deduction, the shares of the Royal Canadian Bank shall be exchanged for shares in the amalgamated Bank at their respective nominal values, and in like manner the shares in the City Bank shall be exchanged for shares in the amalgamated Bank at their nominal , or par value.

7. On or after the first day of June next, in the course of exchanging the stock of the Royal Canadian Bank for the stock of the amalgamated Bank, each shareholder in the Royal Canadian Bank holding a share or part of a share insufficient in all to constitute one share in the amalgamated Bank, or above and beyond the shares convertible into shares of the amalgamated Bank at par, may either pay up in cash the amount required to be added to such share or part of a share to form an amount equal to a share in the amalgamated Bank, or may receive the par value of such share or part of a share in cash from the amalgamated Bank at his option, subject to the deduction of three per cent. for the rest, as herein provided. But the option hereby granted to such shareholder must be exercised within three months after the first day of June next; and after such period of three months such option shall cease, and thereafter each holder of such share or part of a share shall only be entitled to receive the value thereof at par, and upon such payment such share or part of a share shall become vested in the amalgamated Bank, and an amount equal to the total amount of shares or parts of shares so paid for, may be re-issued in shares of the amalgamated Bank as part of its authorized capital of four millions of dollars.

8. The amount of shares required to complete the said capital of four millions of dollars shall be subscribed by the shareholders in the City Bank upon such terms and conditions as the directors of that Bank may deem expedient. But if, in consequence of stringency or derangement of the financial condition of the country, the directors of the City Bank shall not fix the conditions of such subscription and cause books of subscription to be opened so that the said subscription is not obtained on or before the tenth day of May next, the provisional board shall then have power to make such order extending the time for fulfilling this condition as it shall deem expedient, and thereafter the board of the amalgamated

gamated Bank may deal with the question of such addition Agreement. to the capital in any manner that may be considered for the interest of the Bank.

9. The business of the two Banks shall be carried on as heretofore until the tenth day of May next by the directors thereof in the names of the said Banks respectively, but for the benefit and at the risk of the amalgamated Bank, each of the said Banks, however, declaring in favor of its shareholders such dividends as shall be earned by such Bank, subject to the usual margin for rest and bad and doubtful debts; and the dividends to be so declared payable on the first day of June next shall be paid by the amalgamated Bank. But it is understood that the boards of the two Banks shall consult with each other as to any important matter affecting the welfare of the said Banks or either of them, and as to the amount of dividend to be declared.

10. So far as may be compatible with the interests of the amalgamated Bank and with judicious economy, the claims of all officers of both existing Banks shall be considered in a liberal spirit.

11. From and after the said tenth day of May next the said two Banks shall become and shall henceforth be, continue and constitute one united and amalgamated Bank under the said name, title and style of " The Consolidated Bank of Canada," and from and after the said day the said amalgamated Bank shall be vested with all the assets of the said Banks, parties hereto, and shall be responsible for all their obligations and liabilities.

12. The persons who shall be entitled to vote at the first annual general meeting of the shareholders of the said amalgamated Bank shall be those persons in whose names shares of stock in either of the said Banks shall stand in the books of such Bank on the tenth day of May next; and in voting at the said first general meeting the former shareholders in the City Bank shall be entitled to one vote for every share held by them on the said day in the said Bank, and the shareholders in the Royal Canadian Bank shall have one vote for every one hundred dollars of stock held by them on the said day in the Royal Canadian Bank, but shall not have votes in respect of fractional parts of one hundred dollars.

13. Until the said amalgamated Bank shall have completed the preparation for issuing its own notes to the satisfaction of the board, it shall have power to re-issue the notes of either of the two Banks, parties hereto, that may come into its possession.

14. The parties hereto shall give all the aid in their power
respectively

Agreement. respectively towards obtaining legislative sanction for the proposed amalgamation of the said Banks, in conformity with the provisions hereof, and a committee shall be appointed, to be composed of five persons, two of whom shall be selected by the board of each Bank, and the fifth by the four so selected, which committee shall have the power to supervise and arrange for the requisite legislation, and to regulate any minor questions of detail that may arise pending such legislation, or in the passage of such legislation through Parliament.

15. It shall be an instruction to such committee to endeavor to cause it to be enacted by Parliament that the annual meeting of the amalgamated Bank for the election of directors and for the transaction of all business usual at annual meetings, shall be held on the first Wednesday of June in each year, and that the first of such annual meetings shall take place on the first Wednesday in June next, and also that from and after the said tenth day of May next until the election of directors of the said amalgamated Bank the affairs thereof shall be conducted and managed by a provisional board, composed of the then existing directors of the said two Banks, of whom five shall be a quorum.

In witness whereof, the parties hereto have executed these presents, to wit: The City Bank on the seventeenth day of September, in the year of Our Lord one thousand eight hundred and seventy-five, and the Royal Canadian Bank on the eighteenth day of September, in duplicate. The whole under the authority of resolutions duly made and passed by the shareholders of the said Banks respectively, to wit: At a meeting of the shareholders of the said City Bank duly called and held at Montreal on the sixteenth day of the said September, and by the shareholders of the Royal Canadian Bank at a meeting thereof, duly called and held at the City of Toronto, on the fourteenth day of the said September.

Seal of the }   (Signed,)   R. Jas. Reekie,
City Bank. }   *Vice-President.*

                (Signed,)   J. B. Renny,
                                                 Cashier.

Seal of the }   (Signed,)   A. Campbell,
Royal Canadian Bank. }   *President.*

We certify that the foregoing is a true copy of the indenture of union executed by us on behalf of the City Bank and the Royal Canadian Bank respectively, with the approval of the respective shareholders of the said Banks.

                     F. Hincks,
                         President, City Bank.
                   A. Campbell,
                       President, R. C. Bank.

CHAP

CHAP. 45.

An Act to amend the charter of "The St. Lawrence Bank," and to change the name of the said bank to that of "The Standard Bank of Canada."

[*Assented to* 12*th April,* 1876.]

WHEREAS the President and Directors of the St. Law- Preamble. rence Bank have, by their petition, set forth that by the Act of incorporation of the said bank, the nominal value of each of the shares of the said bank is one hundred dollars, and the nominal capital of the said bank is one million dollars, of which eight hundred and thirty-five thousand five hundred dollars have been subscribed, and six hundred and fifty-three thousand one hundred and four dollars and forty cents paid up; but the said capital has been so reduced by losses, that it will be advantageous both to the said bank and the public to have the nominal value coincide and agree with the actual value thereof; and that it will also be advantageous to the said bank and to the public to restore its actual capital to the amount of one million dollars or to such larger amount not exceeding two millions as may be deemed advisable, and to change the name of the said bank to "The Standard Bank of Canada;" and have prayed that in order to carry out and effect such purposes the existing Acts affecting the said bank may be altered, amended and varied as the same are hereinafter altered, amended and varied; and whereas it is expedient to grant the prayer of the said petition : Therefore Her Majesty, by and with the advice and consent of the Senate and House of Commons of Canada, enacts as follows :—

1. The corporate name of the said "The St. Lawrence Corporate Bank" is hereby changed to "The Standard Bank of Canada;" name changed. and the said bank shall be and remain a corporation under the said name of "The Standard Bank of Canada;" and all claims and liabilities either in favor of or against the said "The St. Lawrence Bank" under all or any of the Acts affecting the same, shall enure to or against the said "The Standard Bank New name. of Canada" as fully and effectually to all intents and purposes as they would have enured to or against the said "The St. Lawrence Bank" under all or any of the Acts affecting the same.

2. Until the said "The Standard Bank of Canada" shall Provision as have issued bills or notes in the name of the said corpora- to issue of notes. tion, it may issue the bills or notes of the said "The St. Lawrence Bank" as and for the bills or notes of "The Standard Bank of Canada," and shall redeem such notes in

· 2 **all**

all respects as if the same had been issued in the name of the said " The Standard Bank of Canada."

Nominal value of shares reduced.

34 V., c. 5.

3. For and notwithstanding anything contained in the charter of the said " The St. Lawrence Bank " (being an Act passed in the thirty-fifth year of Her Majesty's reign and chaptered fifty-two), or in the Act passed in the thirty-fourth year of Her Majesty's reign intituled " *An Act relating to Banks and Banking,*" or in any other Act or Acts amending the same, or in any other Act or enactment, each and every now existing share in the capital stock of the said " The St. Lawrence Bank " of one hundred dollars each, shall from and after the passing of this Act represent and be equal to one share of fifty dollars and one half share of twenty-five dollars in the said " The Standard Bank of Canada;"

Capital reduced proportionately.

and the total amount of the said paid-up capital stock of the said " The St. Lawrence Bank " shall be and is hereby reduced in proportion, and shall stand and be the paid-up capital of the said " The Standard Bank of Canada:"

Proviso: as to fractional parts of shares.

Provided, that if by such reduction there shall be any fraction of a share held by any shareholder insufficient to constitute a full share of fifty dollars of the capital stock of the said " The Standard Bank of Canada," such shareholder shall, within two months after the passing of this Act, pay an amount sufficient to make, with such fraction of a share, the sum of fifty dollars, and the said " The Standard Bank of Canada " shall register in his name an additional share of fifty dollars, and no more formal transfer shall be required; but if such amount be not paid as aforesaid, within two months after the passing of this Act, such fraction of a share shall belong to and be vested in the said " The Standard Bank of Canada."

Fractional part forfeited if not made up to one share.

Issue of non-subscribed stock or forfeited stock.

4. The Directors of the said " The Standard Bank of Canada" shall have power, from time to time, to issue stock to the amount of all or any portion of the capital stock of the said " The St. Lawrence Bank," unsubscribed for and which at any time may be forfeited or surrendered to the said " The Standard Bank of Canada " in such manner, to such amount, and payable in such way as they shall think proper.

Power to increase capital stock to $2,000,000.

5. The said Directors may, with the assent of the majority of the shareholders of the said "The Standard Bank of Canada," present at or represented by proxy at any ordinary annual or special general meeting called for that purpose, by by-law or by-laws, increase the capital stock of the said bank, but so that in the whole it shall not exceed two million dollars ; and such additional stock shall be subscribed for in shares of fifty dollars each, and such additional stock shall be issued upon the terms set out by the Act of incorporation of the said " The St. Lawrence Bank," and the Act intituled

Shares.

intituled "*An Act relating to Banks and Banking*" and any amendments thereto: Provided always, that the issuing and subscribing for the additional capital stock authorized b this Act may take place at any time while the charter of the said "The Standard Bank of Canada" remains in force. *Proviso: as to time of issue.*

6. The annual general meeting of the shareholders of the said "The Standard Bank of Canada" shall be held on the second Wednesday in July in each and every year, or on such other day as the said shareholders at any annual or special general meeting called for that purpose may by by-law appoint. *Time for annual general meeting.*

7. This Act shall remain in force until the first day of July, one thousand eight hundred and eighty-one and no longer. *Duration of Act.*

CHAP. 46.

An Act respecting the capital of the Great Western Railway Company, and for the capitalization of certain charges and liabilities.

[*Assented to 12th April, 1876.*]

WHEREAS the net revenue of the Great Western Railway Company has, for some time past, been insufficient to meet the interest on all the bonds and perpetual debenture stock of the Company, and, although their general business and net earnings are now increasing, it may be that the net revenue for the current year ending on the thirty-first day of January, one thousand eight hundred and seventy-seven, will not be sufficient wholly to meet the interest for the same period ; *Preamble. State of the Company's affairs recited*

And whereas the arrears for the past have been temporarily met, but the indebtedness still remains a charge against future revenue ;

And whereas in the general balance sheet of the Company there appear various items assumed to be assets, but which are without value ;

And whereas on the thirty first day of July, one thousand eight hundred and seventy-five there was a sum of five hundred and twenty-one thousand and forty-six pounds, ten shillings and three pence sterling, standing to the credit of the capital account of the Company ;

2¼   **And**

And whereas the Company have by their petition represented that their Directors should be authorized (subject to
the consent in that behalf hereinafter mentioned) to charge
to capital account the said deficiency in net revenue, as well
as the further deficiency (if any) up to and inclusive of the
thirty-first day of January, one thousand eight hundred and
seventy-seven, and such items standing to the credit of the
said general balance sheet as may appear to be without
value, so however that the total amount so charged to capital account shall not exceed three hundred thousand pounds
sterling ;

And whereas the net revenue has also for some time past
been insufficient to provide for the dividends upon the preference stock of the Company, and, notwithstanding the improvement in business, may be insufficient to provide for the
whole of the preference dividends which will be payable up
to and inclusive of the day last aforesaid ; and the Company
have also represented by their petition, that their Directors
should be authorized (subject to the consents in that behalf
hereinafter mentioned) to capitalize the said arrears up to
and inclusive of the said date last aforesaid as hereinafter
mentioned, and that they should be otherwise empowered
as herein provided ;

And it is expedient that the prayer [of the said petition
should be granted :

Therefore Her Majesty, by and with the advice and consent of the Senate and House of Commons of Canada, enacts
as follows :—

Interpreta-
tion.

1. In this Act except where repugnant to or inconsistent
with the context, the word " Company " shall mean the
Great Western Railway Company, and the word " Directors "
shall mean the Directors of the said Company.

Citation of
Acts.

2. The Act passed in the thirty-eighth year of Her Majesty's reign, chaptered sixty-four, and intituled " *An Act to
amend the Acts of incorporation of the Great Western Railway Company,*" may be cited as " *The Great Western Railway
Act*, 1875," and this Act may be cited as " *The Great Western
Railway Act*, 1876."

Directors may
debit capital
account with
deficiency in
net revenue
and depre-
ciated assets.

3. It shall be lawful for the Directors to charge the capital account of the Company with the sums by which the
net revenue of the Company, up to and inclusive of the
thirty-first day of January, one thousand eight hundred and
seventy-six, was insufficient to meet the interest upon the
terminable bonds and perpetual debenture stock of the Company, and with the further sums (if any) by which the net
revenue for the year ending on the thirty-first day of
January,

January, one thousand eight hundred and seventy-seven, may be insufficient to meet the interest on the said bonds and debenture stock for the same period, and with such sums at the credit of the general balance sheet of the Company as shall appear to the Directors to be represented by assets without value, or by an over-valuation of assets: Pro- Not to exceed vided that the total sum so charged to capital, by virtue of £300,000. this section, shall not exceed the sum of three hundred thousand pounds sterling; and provided that nothing herein shall Proviso. be taken to discharge any person or corporation from liability to the Company in respect of any of the sums so charged to the capital account.

4. It shall be lawful for the Directors to capitalize the Directors may whole or any portion of the dividends now in arrear to the capitalize arrears of preference stockholders of the Company, and of such further preference preference dividends (if any) as the net revenue of the Com- dividends. pany may be insufficient to provide for up to and inclusive of the thirty-first day of January, one thousand eight hundred and seventy-seven, by the delivery of certificates for one hundred pounds sterling, or fractional parts of one hundred pounds, as the case may be, of preference stock, to the preference stockholders entitled to such dividends,—which Rank of such additional preference stock shall bear and be entitled to additional the same rate of dividend, stand upon the same footing, have stock. the same priority, and entitle the holder thereof to the same rights as, but no other than the preference stock in respect of which the dividends so capitalized shall have accrued: and in such capitalization the Directors shall have power to Rate of allowance of new create and give at the rate of not less than one hundred stock limited. pounds, nor more than one hundred and forty pounds, of such additional preference stock, for one hundred pounds of such arrears of preference dividends; and such capitalization Dividends shall be in full discharge and satisfaction of the dividends, discharge. or portion of dividends, as the case may be, which the Directors shall have elected to capitalize.

5. And whereas of the borrowing powers of the Company Recital. prior to the passing of this Act as declared by " *The Great Western Railway Act,* 1874, " there are yet unexercised the power to raise under the fourth section of the said Act, by the issue of either terminable bonds or perpetual debenture stock, the sum of thirty-three thousand nine hundred and four pounds sterling, and to raise under the fifth section of the said Act by the creation and issue of perpetual debenture stock the sum of six hundred and eight thousand three hundred and twenty eight pounds sterling, part of the sum therein mentioned ; and whereas it is desirable that the Company should have power to raise the whole of the said two sums, being six hundred and forty-two thousand two hundred and thirty two pounds sterling, by the issue of either class of security, or partly upon one and partly upon the
other,

Power to borrow £642,232 on terminable bonds or perpetual debenture stock.

other, therefore it shall be lawful for the Company to borrow the said six hundred and forty-two thousand two hundred and thirty two pounds sterling by the issue and sale of terminable bonds, or by the creation, issue and sale of perpetual debenture stock, or partly upon one class of security and partly upon the other.

Recital of agreements with W. G. & B. Co. and L. H. & B. Co.

6. And whereas the Company have power to enter into traffic arrangements and agreements with the Wellington, Grey, and Bruce Railway Company, and the London, Huron, and Bruce Railway Company, and to guarantee for the loan of their credit to, and to become guarantors for the railway companies with which they may make such arrangements; and whereas pursuant to such powers the Company have entered into arrangements for the working of, and are now working, the railways of the said companies; and have entered into obligations to acquire the bonds of the said two companies, and have already acquired portions thereof, which they now hold; and whereas the said powers were conferred upon the Company in addition to their express borrowing powers; and inasmuch as the Company can obtain money to replace the capital used, and which may be used from time to time in acquiring such bonds, upon more favorable terms by the issue of their own securities than by the sale of the bonds so acquired; and whereas the total bond issue of the Wellington, Grey, and Bruce Railway Company already acquired and to be acquired, is five hundred and thirty-two thousand pounds sterling, and that of the London, Huron, and Bruce Railway Company is one hundred and eighty-seven thousand five hundred and thirty pounds sterling; therefore it shall be lawful for the Company to raise and borrow money from time to time to replace the money heretofore used, and which may be hereafter used, in acquiring the said bonds of the said two companies, by the issue and sale of perpetual debenture stock, or of terminable bonds, or of both—to be treated as part of the regular perpetual debenture and terminable bond debts of the Company, in addition to those already authorized by the Acts relating to the Company; so, however, that the loan capital raised or created of one class or the other, or of both classes, under the authority of this section, shall not at any time exceed the amount expended in acquiring such bonds, nor in the aggregate exceed the sum of seven hundred and nineteen thousand five hundred and thirty pounds sterling: Provided that whenever the Company shall sell or receive the principal money secured by any bond or bonds of either of the said two Companies which have been or may be so acquired and in respect of which terminable bonds or perpetual debenture stock of the Company shall have been issued under the authority of this section, the Company shall apply the proceeds of such sales, or the amounts so received, in or towards the liquidation and reduction of the loan capital of the Company, which shall be reduced accordingly.

Loan capital of W. G. & B. Co., £532,000.

Of L. H. & B. Co., £187,530.

Company may borrow money to replace capital used in acquiring the said bonds.

Not exceeding £719,530.

Proviso: application of proceeds of sale or receipt of principal of bonds.

7.

7. So that the loan capital raised or created by terminable bonds or perpetual debenture stock shall not in the whole exceed the aggregate amount of the loan capital authorized by Acts relating to the Company, the Directors may, from time to time, pay off or satisfy the terminable bonds of the Company by the issue and sale or exchange of other terminable bonds, or by the creation, issue and sale or exchange of perpetual debenture stock. *Directors may pay off existing bond debts by issue of new bonds or debenture stock.*

8. The terminable bonds and perpetual debenture stock to be hereafter issued may be issued in such proportions, in such manner, at such rates of interest, (not exceeding, as to the perpetual debenture stock, six per centum per annum) and at such price or prices as to premium or otherwise as may be determined from time to time by the Directors. *Manner and terms of issue of bond and debenture stock.*

9. The Company may, by the vote of two-thirds of the shareholders, in terms of the sixth section of "*The Great Western Railway Act,* 1875," at any ordinary or special general meeting of the Company, direct that terminable bonds or perpetual debenture stock shall have an option of conversion into ordinary shares, at such rate and terms of option as the shareholders by such vote may deem advisable when such bonds or debenture stocks are to be issued. *Company by a two-third vote of shareholders may give option of conversion into ordinary stock.*

10. The loan capital of the Company, authorized by Acts relating to the Company, and whether terminable bonds or perpetual debenture stock, shall have co-ordinate lien, and shall be a first mortgage upon the Railways, tolls, and lands, and all and every property of the Company. *The whole loan capital to have co-ordinate lien.*

11. It shall be lawful for the Company from time to time to create and issue in lieu of the whole or any portion of their borrowing powers so many ordinary shares, in addition to their share capital otherwise authorized, as will realize to the Company a sum of money equal to the amount of loan capital in lieu of which such ordinary shares shall be issued; and the borrowing powers of the Company shall be reduced by the amount realized from the ordinary shares so issued; and such ordinary shares may be issued upon such terms as to premium or otherwise as the Company may deem advisable, and either in lieu of unexercised borrowing powers, or for the purpose of paying off or redeeming bonds or debenture stock already issued. *Company in lieu of any portion of borrowing powers may issue ordinary stock to raise an equivalent amount. On what terms.*

12. No powers shall be exercised under the third, fourth, fifth, sixth, or eleventh sections of this Act, unless consent shall be given to the exercise of such powers respectively by the vote of two-thirds of the shareholders in terms of the sixth section of "*The Great Western Railway Act,* 1875," at any ordinary or special general meeting of the Company. *Consent of shareholders required for exercise of certain powers under this Act.*

13.

Consent of preference stockholders to action under s. 4.

13. No powers shall be exercised under the fourth section of this Act, unless with the consent (in addition to the consent required by the twelfth section of this Act) of two-thirds in number and amount of the preference stockholders of the Company present and voting in person or by proxy at a meeting of such preference stockholders to be held on or before the thirty-first day of January, one thousand eight hundred and seventy-seven, in London, England. after such notice in England and Canada as by the Acts relating to the Company would be sufficient for the calling of a special general meeting of the Company,—the object of such meeting being specially set forth in such notice; and at such meeting

Voting at meeting for such purpose.

preference stockholders may be represented by proxies being preference stockholders or ordinary shareholders, appointed in the form and according to the practice now in use res-

Who to preside; certificate of proceedings at such meeting to be filed with Secretary of State.

pecting ordinary shareholders; and the President of the Company, or in his absence the Vice-president, shall preside as chairman at such meeting; and the certificate in writing of the chairman of the giving of such consent as aforesaid thereat shall be taken as *primâ facie* proof of such consent having been duly given,—such certificate to be filed in the office of the Secretary of State of Canada, and certified copies by the said Secretary shall be taken and considered for all purposes as sufficient *primâ facie* evidence of the contents thereof.

CHAP. 47.

An Act further to amend " The St. Lawrence and Ottawa Railway Act."

[Assented to 12th April, 1876.]

Preamble.

WHEREAS the St. Lawrence and Ottawa Railway Company have, by their petition, represented that by an Act passed in the thirty-first year of Her Majesty's reign

31 V. c. 20

known as " *The St. Lawrence and Ottawa Railway Act* " a deed of trust of the eighteenth day of April in the year one thousand eight hundred and sixty-seven, and the certificates thereunder issued were thereby confirmed, and the sum of fifty thousand pounds sterling money of Great Britain thereby secured, and the interest thereon from time to time to become and be payable was thereby declared to be a first security, charge or lien in or upon the said railway, its lands, rights, privileges, franchises and appurtenances, tolls and revenues, rolling stock, plant and machinery, and the lands and premises as particularly in the said deed mentioned; And that by a certain other deed dated the fifteenth day of April in the year one thousand eight hundred and seventy-two a further sum of fifty thousand pounds sterling money
of

of Great Britain was made a mortgage charge or lien upon the said railway as therein mentioned; And that by an Act passed in the thirty-fifth year of Her Majesty's reign known as " *The St. Lawrence and Ottawa Railway Company Amend-* 35 V. c. 67. *ment Act,* 1872 " it was provided that nothing therein contained should in any way vary, lessen or diminish or permit or authorize the Company to vary, lessen or diminish the first security, charge or lien of the deed of trust of the eighteenth day of April in the year one thousand eight hundred and sixty-seven for fifty thousand pounds sterling in and upon the railway, its lands, rights, privileges, franchises and appurtenances, tolls and revenues, rolling stock, plant and machinery (being the security mentioned in the Act hereinbefore recited) or the second security, charge or lien of and under a certain deed or mortgage of the fifteenth day of April in the year one thousand eight hundred and seventy-two for fifty thousand pounds sterling, upon the railway and the tolls, revenues and other properties thereof,—which said two charges or incumbrances of fifty thousand pounds sterling each are, with the priority as between themselves therein mentioned, the first securities, charges or liens, mortgages or pledges on the said railway, and prior to the preference stock, and which are the two charges or incumbrances on the said railway hereinbefore recited; And that since the passing of the last recited Act the Railway Company have expended large sums of money in the construction of the Chaudière Extension in the last recited Act mentioned, and have acquired other property in connection with the same; And that it is necessary and expedient for the Company that they should be enabled to borrow a further sum of money for the purpose of further developing the said railway and for further carrying out the objects contemplated by the said Act passed in the year one thousand eight hundred and seventy-two hereinbefore recited; And that it is expedient that such money should be borrowed or raised either by issue of debenture stock or upon mortgage or mortgage bonds, and that the Company may be empowered from the proceeds thereof to pay off and redeem the first and second securities hereinbefore mentioned,—the assent of the holders of securities under the said two deeds of mortgage to the extent of two thirds of each of the said sums of fifty thousand pounds sterling being first obtained thereto; And whereas the Company have prayed that an Act may be passed for the purposes aforesaid, and it is expedient to grant their prayer, subject to the provisions hereinafter made: Therefore Her Majesty, by and with the advice and consent of the Senate and House of Commons of Canada, enacts as follows:—

1. This Act may be cited for all purposes as " *The St.* Short title *Lawrence and Ottawa Railway Company Amendment Act* 1876."

2.

Interpretation clause.

2. In this Act the term "the Company" means The St. Lawrence and Ottawa Railway Company; the term "undertaking" means the railway, its lands, rights, privileges, franchises and appurtenances, tolls and revenues, rolling stock, plant and machinery, but subject to any incumbrances or equities affecting the same or any parts thereof.

Company may borrow £200,000 sterling, at what rate and with what security and privilege.

3. It shall be lawful for the Company to raise, in their option either by the issue of debenture stock or by mortgage bonds upon the undertaking, a sum not exceeding two hundred thousand pounds sterling money of Great Britain, and bearing interest at a rate not exceeding seven per centum per annum; and the said debenture stock or the said mortgage bonds (as the case may be) and in either case the interest payable thereon, shall be a charge and lien and security upon the undertaking, and shall rank next after the second mortgage or security of the fifteenth day of April in the year one thousand eight hundred and seventy-two, and prior to the preference stock and any other stock of the Company; and the Company may sell and dispose of the debenture stock or mortgage bonds (as the case may be) at such price or prices as they, from time to time, may be enabled to procure for the same.

Mortgage bonds may be issued with coupons.

4. If the Company determine to raise the sum of two hundred thousand pounds sterling by the issue of mortgage bonds, then the Company may, from time to time, raise all or any part of the amount by the issue of mortgage bonds in the form contained in schedule A to this Act annexed, or to the effect of such form, in such sums as they may deem most desirable, with coupons attached for interest not exceeding seven per centum per annum,—which mortgage bonds and coupons may be made payable at such times and at such places and in the currency of Canada, or in sterling money as the Company may think fit; and the same shall without the necessity of any registration bind the undertaking according to the tenor of the same, and of this Act.

A debenture stock may be created.

5. If the Company determine to raise the said sum of two hundred thousand pounds sterling by the creation and issue of debenture stock, then the Company may, from time to time, raise all or any part of the said amount by the creation and issue at such times, in such amounts and manner, on such terms, subject to such conditions, and with such rights and privileges as the Company thinks fit, of stock to be called debenture stock, and may attach to the stock so created such fixed and perpetual preferential interest not exceeding seven per centum per annum payable half yearly or otherwise, commencing at once or at any future time or times when and as the debenture stock is issued or otherwise, as the Company thinks fit.

6.

. The Company shall cause entries of the debenture stock Stock regis-
ter to be kept. from time to time created, to be made in a register to be kept for that purpose, wherein they shall enter the names and addresses of the several persons and corporations from time to time entitled to the debenture stock with the respective amounts of the stock to which they are respectively entitled; and the register shall be accessible for inspection and perusal at all reasonable times to every mortgagee, debenture holder, shareholder and stockholder of the Company, without payment of any fee or charge.

7. The Company shall deliver to every holder of debenture Certificates to
be delivered. stock a certificate stating the amount of debenture stock held by him; and all regulations or provisions for the time being applicable to certificates of shares in the capital of the Company shall apply *mutatis mutandis*, to certificates of debenture stock.

8. Debenture stock shall not entitle the holders thereof Rights of
holders of
debenture
stock. to be present or vote at any meeting of the Company or confer any qualification, but shall in all respects not otherwise hereby provided for, be considered as entitling the holders to the rights and powers of mortgagees of the undertaking, other than the right to require repayment of the principal money paid up in respect of the debenture stock.

9. Debenture stock shall be transmissible and transfer- Transfer of
stock. able in the same manner and according to the same regulations and provisions as other stock or shares of the Company, and shall in all other respects have the incidents of personal estate.

10. Separate and distinct accounts shall be kept by the Separate
accounts to
be kept. Company shewing how much money has been received for or on account of debenture stock, and how much owing on the first and second securities hereinbefore mentioned has been paid off by debenture stock.

11. The interest on any debenture stock, or mortgage Priority of
interest. bonds (as the case may be), issued under this Act shall have priority of payment over all dividends or interest on any preferential shares or stock of the Company, whether ordinary or preference, and shall rank next to the interest payable on the certificates or bonds of the first and second securities hereinbefore mentioned; but the holders of debenture stock or of mortgage bonds (as the case may be) issued under this Act, shall not, as among themselves, be entitled to any preference or priority.

12. If within sixty days after the interest on any such Appointment
of Receiver in
case of non-
payment of
interest. debenture stock or the interest coupon of any such mortgage bonds is payable, the same is not paid, any one or more

more of the holders of the debenture stock, or interest coupons holding individually or collectively the sum of twenty-five thousand pounds sterling of the principal money, may (without prejudice to the right to sue in any court of competent jurisdiction for the interest in arrear) require the appointment by the Court of Chancery of Ontario of a Receiver.

May be appointed by Court of Chancery of Ontario.

Duties and powers of Receiver.

13. On any such application the Court of Chancery of Ontario may, by order, after hearing the parties, appoint some person to receive the whole or a competent part of the tolls or sums liable for the payment of the interest, until all the arrears of interest then due on the debenture stock or mortgage bonds (as the case may be) issued under this Act, with all costs, including the charges of receiving the tolls or sums, are paid ; and upon such appointment being made all such tolls or sums shall be paid to and received by the person so appointed ; and all money so received shall be deemed so much money received by or to the use of the several persons interested in the same, according to their several priorities,—due regard being had in such respect to the respective priorities of the first and second securities now existing, as hereinbefore mentioned. The Receiver shall distribute rateably and without priority, among all the proprietors of debenture stock or mortgage bonds (as the case may be) to whom interest is in arrear, the money which so comes to his hands, after applying a sufficient part thereof in or towards satisfaction of the interest on the first and second securities, now existing as hereinbefore mentioned. As soon as the full amount of interest and costs has been so received, the power of the Receiver shall cease, and he shall be bound to account to the Company for his acts or the sums received by him, and to pay over to the Company any balance that may be in his hands.

Interest in arrear may be recovered.

14. If the interest on the debenture stock or mortgage bonds (as the case may be) under this Act is not paid for sixty days next after any of the respective days whereon the same is payable, the holder for the time being thereof, may, (without prejudice to his power in the next preceding section mentioned) recover the arrears with costs by action or suit in any court of competent jurisdiction.

Application of moneys raised.

15. The money, whether raised by debenture stock or mortgage bonds (as the case may be) under this Act, shall, to the extent of one hundred thousand pounds and of such further sum of money as shall be requisite for interest, be applied exclusively in paying off, in their respective order of priority, the money secured by the first and second securities hereinbefore mentioned ; and the balance or residue of the sum to be raised under this Act, shall be applied to the payment

payment of outstanding debts and obligations and to the general purposes of the Company, as the Company may see fit.

16. On not less than thirty days' notice the Company may call upon and require the last registered holder of any certificate or bond issued under either the first or second securities hereinbefore mentioned, to receive payment of the par value of such certificate or bond, and of all interest which may have accrued or be accruing up to the date of such payment; and the Company may by such payment redeem any and every such certificate or bond in respect of the amount thereby secured, and of all interest accrued thereon, and notwithstanding that any such certificate or bond has not become due or payable; and every such certificate or bond shall, upon such payment and redemption by the Company, be thereby cancelled and utterly void. *Redemption of certain loan certificates.*

17. The notice of any such intended payment and redemption of the certificates or bonds under the first and second securities hereinbefore mentioned, may be given by letter addressed to the last registered holder of each certificate or bond at his last known place of abode or at the bank through which he shall last have received payment of the coupons for interest. *Notice to be given.*

18. If the Company shall have given such notice of their intention to pay off and redeem the certificates or bonds in the preceding section mentioned, then at the expiration of such notice all further interest shall cease to be payable on such certificates or bonds, unless on demand of payment made pursuant to such notice, or unless at any time thereafter the Company fails to pay the principal and interest due at the expiration of such notice of such certificate or bond. *Interest to cease from date of notice*

19. When and as soon as the several certificates or bonds issued under the first or second securities hereinbefore mentioned, and the interest thereon accrued due, are paid off, redeemed and cancelled as hereinbefore mentioned, the deed of trust and mortgage respectively hereinbefore mentioned as the first and second mortgages, liens, charges and securities on the said railway shall be absolutely null and void; and the debenture stock or mortgage bonds (as the case may be) for two hundred thousand pounds sterling authorized by this Act, and all principal money and interest thereby secured, shall be and become and thenceforward continue the first lien, charge and security upon the said undertaking, and prior to the preferential or any other stock. *Upon completion of redemption, stock or bonds under this Act to be first charge on railway.*

20. When and so soon as the two several sums of fifty thousand pounds sterling hereinbefore mentioned, shall have been redeemed and paid off as hereinbefore mentioned the future *Application of earnings of the Company.*

future annual earnings of the Company shall be distributed according to the rank and priority following :—

1. In the payment of working expenses ;

2. In the payment—

(a.) If the sum hereby authorized be raised by mortgage bonds, then of the sum of money secured thereby, as the annual interest thereof, and in the creation and investment of a sinking fund of one per centum per annum on the said sum of two hundred thousand pounds sterling, to meet the principal of the said mortgage bonds at maturity thereof ; or

(b.) If the sum hereby authorized be raised by the issue of debenture stock, then of the annual interest thereon, not exceeding seven per centum per annum ;

3. In payment of a dividend not exceeding eight per centum per annum upon the preference stock and such dividend upon any other stock as the Company may, from time to time, determine ;

4. As the Company may determine.

Sect. 10 of 35 V. c. 67 as to sale of lands amended.   **21.** In amendment of the tenth section of " *The St. Lawrence and Ottawa Railway Company Amendment Act 1872* " it is hereby enacted : That any sale and transfer of any lands therein mentioned shall be good and valid to all intents and purposes, and free and discharged from any mortgage, lien or incumbrance heretofore existing or created by or under authority of the Acts hereinbefore recited, or either of them, or by or under the authority of this Act, or in respect of any sum of money secured thereby. But any money or moneys received in respect of such sale and transfer shall (a) if the sum hereby authorized be raised by means of mortgage bonds, be paid to the credit of the sinking fund hereinbefore mentioned, or (b) if the said sum be raised by means of debenture stock the same shall form part of the capital stock of the Company.

Consent of holders of bonds to be obtained and registered.   **22.** The foregoing sections of this Act shall not take effect until the Company shall have obtained and registered in the office of the Registrar General of Canada, the written consent of three-fourths of the holders of preferential stock and of the holders of certificates or bonds of at least three-fourths in value of the amount of each of the two sums of fifty thousand pounds sterling secured by the first and second securities hereinbefore mentioned, to the provisions contained in the said sections, and to the exercise by the

Certificate thereof.   Company of the powers thereby given them ; and a certificate

ficate signed by the said Registrar General or his deputy, of the registering of the same as aforesaid, shall be evidence thereof.

SCHEDULE A.

FORM OF MORTGAGE BOND.

The St. Lawrence and Ottawa Railway Company

No
£   sterling
The St. Lawrence and Ottawa Railway Company acting by virtue of an Act of the Parliament of Canada known as " *The St. Lawrence and Ottawa Railway Company Amendment Act*, 1876, " are hereby indebted to the bearer hereof in the sum of £   (being part of a loan of £200,000 sterling under the said Act) to bear interest from the date hereof at the rate of   per centum per annum, payable half yearly on the   day of   and on the   day of   . The principal sum thereof shall be payable on the   day of   in the year   and the interest thereon as aforesaid shall be payable on delivery of the coupons therefor according to the terms thereof now forming part hereof.

And for the due payment of the said sum of money and interest, the Company under authority of the said Act of Parliament do hereby bind, as a charge and lien and security thereon, the railway, its lands, rights, privileges, franchises and appurtenances, tolls and revenues, rolling stock, plant and machinery, according to the terms and subject to the provisions of the said Act.

Given under the common seal of the Company at this   day of   in the year of Our Lord

---

CHAP. 48.

An Act to extend the time for the commencement and completion of the Great Western and Lake Ontario Shore Junction Railway ; and for other purposes.

[*Assented to 12th April*, 1876.]

WHEREAS the Great Western and Lake Ontario Shore Junction Railway Company have, by their petition, prayed for an extension of the time for the commencement and completion of their Railway, and that their Act of incorporation may be otherwise amended, and it is expedient to

to grant the prayer of such petition: Therefore Her
Majesty, by and with the advice and consent of the Senate
and House of Commons of Canada, enacts as follows :—

Sect. 19 of 36
V., c. 88,
amended.

1. The nineteenth section of the Act passed in the thirty-
sixth year of Her Majesty's reign, chapter eighty-eight, is
hereby repealed, and the Railway shall be commenced within four years and be completed within six years from the
passing of this Act.

Sections 1
and 5
amended, as
to certain
names.

2. The first and fifth sections of the said Act are hereby
amended by striking the words "Joseph Price, of the City
of Hamilton, Esquire," and "William Kerr Muir, of the
same place, Esquire," out of the said first section, and by
striking the names of "Joseph Price" and "William Kerr
Muir" out of the said fifth section, and by inserting in each
of the said first and fifth sections immediately after the
name "Samuel Barker" therein, the names "Frederick Brough-
ton, Charles Percy, Joseph Hobson and Charles Stiff," and
the said sections as so amended shall henceforth be respectively read as the first and fifth sections of the said Act.

Section 7
amended.

3. The seventh section of the said Act is hereby amended
by striking out the word "nine" from the ninth line thereof
and by inserting the word "seven" in lieu thereof.

Number and
quorum of
Directors
may be varied.

4. It shall be lawful for the shareholders of the Company,
at any annual or special general meeting, from time to time
to reduce or to increase the number of the Directors of the
Company, so, however, that such number be not less than
five, and to determine what number not less than three shall
be a quorum at the meetings of such Directors.

Provision in
case of failure
of election of
Directors.

5 If for any reason, in any year, no election of Directors
shall take place at the annual general meeting, the existing
Directors shall continue to act and retain their powers until
new Directors are elected at any subsequent annual general
meeting or special general meeting called for the purpose.

G. W. R. Co.
may hold
stock in the
Company.

6. The Great Western Railway Company, if so lawfully
empowered, may hold shares in the capital stock of the said
The Great Western and Lake Ontario Shore Junction Railway Company, either in their own name or in the names of
trustees, and such trustees, shall have all the rights, powers
and privileges of ordinary shareholders.

CHAP. 49.

An Act to amend the Act intituled "An Act to incorporate the Clifton Suspension Bridge Company."

[Assented to 12th April, 1876.]

WHEREAS the Clifton Suspension Bridge Company, incorporated by the Act passed in the thirty-first year of Her Majesty's reign and intituled "*An Act to incorporate the Clifton Suspension Bridge Company*," have, by their petition, represented that they are desirous that their said Act of incorporation should be amended as hereinafter set forth, and have prayed for the passing of an Act for that purpose; and it is expedient to grant their prayer: Therefore Her Majesty, by and with the advice and consent of the Senate and House of Commons of Canada, enacts as follows :— *Preamble. 31 V., c. 82.*

1. The fourth section of the Act hereinbefore cited is hereby amended by striking out the words "first Monday of July" in the third line of the said section, and inserting the words "second Tuesday of July" in lieu thereof. *Section 4, amended.*

2. This Act and the Act hereby amended shall be read and construed as one and the same Act. *Act to be one with that amended.*

CHAP. 50.

An Act to continue for a limited time therein mentioned the Canada and Detroit River Bridge Company as a Corporation.

[Assented to 12th April, 1876.]

WHEREAS the Canada and Detroit River Bridge Company have by their petition prayed for an amendment to their Act of incorporation, and whereas it is expedient to grant certain relief to the said Company: Therefore Her Majesty, by and with the advice and consent of the Senate and House of Commons of Canada, enacts as follows :— *Preamble.*

1. The corporate existence of the said Company shall, notwithstanding the non-user of its corporate powers, continue until the end of the next ensuing Session of Parliament: Provided always, that nothing in this Act contained shall authorize the said Company to commence the construction of the bridge by the said Act authorized after the period by the said Act fixed for the said commencement. *Corporation continued. Proviso.*

3   CHAP.

CHAP. 51.

An Act to incorporate the Canada Fire and Marine Insurance Company.

[Assented to 12th April, 1876.]

Preamble. WHEREAS John Winer, George Roach, David Thompson and others, on behalf of themselves and other Directors and shareholders in the Company hereinafter named, and the Canada Fire and Marine Insurance Company incorporated under the Act chapter sixty-seven of the Statutes of the Province of Ontario passed in the thirty-eighth year of Her present Majesty's reign, have, by their petition, represented that they are desirous of becoming incorporated by an Act of the Parliament of Canada under the name of the Canada Fire and Marine Insurance Company, for the purpose of carrying on the business of fire and marine insurance and doing all things appertaining thereto or connected therewith as well in the Province of Ontario where they are now carrying on such insurance business as in other Provinces of the Dominion and in foreign countries ; and it is expedient to grant their prayer : Therefore Her Majesty, by and with the advice and consent of the Senate and House of Commons of Canada, enacts as follows :—

Corporation created and continued. **1.** The shareholders of the Canada Fire and Marine Insurance Company incorporated by an Act of the Legislature of the Province of Ontario passed in the thirty-eighth year of Her present Majesty's reign and chaptered sixty-seven, together with such other persons as may hereafter become shareholders in the Company hereby incorporated, shall be and are hereby constituted a body politic and corporate in law, in fact and in name, by the style and title of the Canada Fire and Marine Insurance Company, for the purpose of carrying on the business of fire and marine insurance and doing all things appertaining thereto or connected therewith, with all

Corporate rights. the powers, privileges and rights hereinafter mentioned ; and shall and may have perpetual succession and shall be capable in law of contracting and being contracted with, and suing and being sued, pleading and being impleaded in any court of law or equity in their corporate name aforesaid ; and they

Proviso : existing rights saved. and their successors shall and may have a common seal, and may change the same at their will and pleasure : Provided always that nothing in this Act contained shall be construed in any manner to affect any contract, matter or thing concerning the said company heretofore incorporated otherwise than is herein expressed, or to affect any action, suit or proceeding commenced on behalf of or against the said company heretofore incorporated, at the time of the passing of this Act, but

but every such action, suit or proceeding may, at the option
of the claimant, be carried on against the Company hereby
incorporated, which is in such case for all the purposes
thereof substituted for the said company heretofore incorporated ; and that all the shareholders in the said company   Shareholders
heretofore incorporated shall be shareholders in the Company   to continue
hereby incorporated, and liable as such shareholders for so   such.
much of their stock subscriptions as are unpaid ; and that all
such subscriptions, and all other property real and personal,
debts, rights, claims and privileges heretofore belonging to or
vested in the said company heretofore incorporated, and all
their interest in the same, shall be held by and are hereby
vested in the said Canada Fire and Marine Insurance Company
hereby incorporated, in the same manner and with all
such benefits and liabilities attaching to the same as existed
at the time of the passing of this Act ; and all the policies   Policies to
and other contracts of insurance and other engagements   remain in
made or entered into by or on behalf of the said company   force.
heretofore incorporated, shall continue to be valid and binding under this Act as against the Company hereby incorporated ; and any person having any claim or demand   And all
against the said company heretofore incorporated, or any   claims on the
shareholder thereof, as such shareholder, shall have the same   company.
claim or demand against the Company hereby incorporated
and against such shareholder thereof.

2. The capital stock of the said Company shall be one   Capital stock
million dollars, divided into ten thousand shares of one   and shares.
hundred dollars each, with the privilege to increase the same   May be
from time to time to any amount not exceeding five millions   increased.
of dollars, by a vote of the shareholders at any annual or
special meeting of shareholders called for that purpose,—
which said shares shall be and are hereby vested in the
several persons who have subscribed or shall subscribe for
the same, their legal representatives and assigns, subject to
the provisions of this Act ; provided that upon every increase   Proviso.
of the capital stock of the Company the sum of at least five
per cent. upon the amount of such increased capital shall be
paid in on subscribing. Aliens as well as British subjects   Aliens may
and whether resident in Canada or elsewhere, may be share-   hold shares
holders in the said Company ; and all such shareholders shall   and vote.
be entitled to vote on their shares equally with British subjects, and shall also be eligible to hold office as Directors or
otherwise in the said Company. But the major part of the   Majority of
Directors of the Company shall, at all times, be persons   Directors to
resident in Canada, and subjects of Her Majesty by birth or   Canada.
naturalization.

3. The shares of capital stock subscribed for shall be paid   Payment of
in and by such instalments and at such times and places as   shares by
the said Directors shall appoint ; no such instalment shall   instalments
exceed ten per cent. of the sum subscribed ; thirty days' notice
of

of each call shall be given, and instalments shall not be made payable more frequently than once in three months:

Proviso. General Acts to apply. Provided that the said Company shall not be authorized to avail themselves of the privileges of this Act, otherwise than in accordance with the provisions of the several Acts of the Parliament of the Dominion relating to fire and marine insurance companies.

Forfeiture and sale of shares for non-payment of calls. 4. If any shareholder shall refuse or neglect to pay the instalments due upon any share or shares held by him, the Directors may declare such share or shares forfeited, together with the amount previously paid thereon, in such manner as may be provided by the by-laws; and such forfeited share or shares may be sold at a public sale by the Directors after such notice as they may direct, and the moneys arising therefrom shall be applied for the purposes of this Act:

Proviso: as to surplus of price. Provided always, that in case the money realized by any sale of shares be more than sufficient to pay all arrears and interest together with the expenses of such sale, the surplus of such money shall be paid on demand to the owner; and no more shares shall be sold than what are deemed necessary to pay such arrears, interest and expenses.

On payment of calls, &c., share to revert to owner. What only need be alleged and proved on the trial in suits for calls. 5. If payment of such arrears of calls, interest and expenses be made before any share so declared forfeited shall have been sold, such share shall revert to the owner as if the same had been duly paid before forfeiture thereof; and in all actions or suits for the recovery of such arrears or calls it shall be sufficient for the Company to allege that the defendant, being the owner of such shares, is indebted to the said Company in such sum of money as the calls in arrear amount to for such and so many shares, whereby an action hath accrued to the Company by virtue of this Act: and on the trial it shall only be necessary to prove that the defendant was owner of the said shares in the Company, that such calls were made, and that notice was given as directed by this Act; and it shall not be necessary to prove the appointment of the Directors who made such calls, or any matter whatsoever other than what is before mentioned: a

Proof of by-laws, &c. copy of any by-law, rule, regulation or minute, or of any entry in any book of the Company, certified to be a true copy or extract under the hand of the President or one of the Vice-Presidents or the Managing Director, or Secretary of the Company, and sealed with the corporate seal, shall be received in all courts and proceedings as *primâ facie* evidence of such by-law, rule, regulation, minute or entry, without proof of the official character or signature of the officer signing the same, or of the corporate seal.

Transfers, how made. 6. No transfer of any share of the stock of the said Company shall be valid until entered in the books of the said Company according to such form as may, from time to time, be be fixed by the by-laws; and until the whole of the capital stock of the said Company is paid up it shall be necessary to obtain the consent of the Directors to such transfer being made: Provided always, that no shareholder indebted to the Company shall be permitted to make a transfer or receive a dividend until such debt is paid or secured to the satisfaction of the Directors; and no transfer of stock shall at any time be made until all calls thereon have been paid in. Proviso: as to debts to Co. and unpaid calls.

7. Each shareholder shall be individually liable to the creditors of the Company to an amount equal to the amount unpaid on the stock held by him, for the debts and liabilities of the Company, but no further. Liability of shareholders limited.

8. The stock, property, affairs and concerns of the said Company shall be managed and conducted by twenty-five Directors, who shall hold office for one year, and shall be elected (at the expiration of the term during which the Directors hereinafter appointed are to hold office) at the annual meeting of shareholders to be held at the City of Hamilton in the month of July next and yearly thereafter on such day as may be appointed by by-law,—not less than ten days' notice of such meeting being given by letter to the shareholders and also by advertisement in some daily newspaper published in said city : and the said election shall be held and made by such of the shareholders present in person or represented by proxy, as shall have paid all calls made by the Directors and then due ; and all such elections shall be by ballot : and the twenty-five persons who shall have the greatest number of votes at any such election shall be Directors, except as hereinafter directed ; and if two or more persons have an equal number of votes, in such a manner that a greater number of persons than twenty-five shall appear to be chosen as Directors, then the Directors who shall have the greater number of votes, or a majority of them, shall determine which of the said persons so having an equal number of votes shall be the Director or Directors, so as to complete the whole number of twenty-five : and the said Directors (as soon as may be after the said election) shall proceed to elect one of their number to be the President, and two to be Vice-Presidents; and if any vacancy should at any time happen amongst the said Directors by death, resignation, disqualification or removal during the current year of office, such vacancy shall be filled for the remainder of the year by the remaining Directors, or the majority of them, electing in such place or places a shareholder or shareholders eligible for such an office: Provided always, that no person shall be eligible to be or continue as Director, unless he shall hold in his name and for his own use stock in the said Company to the amount of twenty shares, whereof at least ten per centum shall have been paid in, and shall have paid all calls made upon his stock, and all liability actually matured and incurred by him

Board of Directors.
Term of office, &c.
Election of Directors.
Ties.
President and Vice-President.
Vacancies, how filled.
Proviso: qualification of Directors.

with

Provisional Directors. with the Company. The first Directors of the Company incorporated under this Act shall be : John Winer, George Roach, David Thompson, Lyman Moore, George Rutherford, John M. Buchan, Thomas Baxter, George Lee, William Harris, C. E. Chadwick, James Reid, F. P. Buckley, H. P. Coburn, H. H. Hurd, Charles Goodhue, John McKinnon, McLeod Stewart, T. H. Marsh, William Elliot, A. Macallum, J. A. Bruce, Dr. E. Vernon, George A. Cox, and A. B. Petrie ;

Term of office. and they shall hold office until the annual meeting of the shareholders of the Company in July next.

Failure of election not to dissolve Company. **9.** In case it should at any time happen that an election of Directors of the said Company shall not be made on any day when, pursuant to this Act, it should have been made, the said Company shall not for that cause be deemed to be dissolved; but it shall be lawful on any other day to hold and make an election at a special general meeting to be called for that purpose by the Directors, who shall continue in office until a new election is made.

When only the company may commence business. **10.** When and so soon as one million dollars of the capital stock of the Company shall have been *bonâ fide* subscribed for, and one hundred thousand dollars thereof shall have been actually paid in, and not before, the Company may commence business under this Act.

One vote for each share. **11.** At all general meetings of the said Company each shareholder shall be entitled to give one vote for every share held by him for not less than fourteen days prior to the time of voting, upon which all calls then due have been paid up; **Proxies.** such votes may be given either in person or by proxy, the **Majority to decide.** holder of any such proxy being himself a shareholder; and all questions proposed for the consideration of the shareholders shall be determined by the majority of votes,—the **Casting vote.** chairman presiding at such meeting having the casting vote in case of an equality of votes.

Proceedings at annual meetings. **12.** At the annual meeting of the shareholders, the election of Directors shall be held and all business transacted without the necessity for specifying such business in the notice of such meeting; and at such meeting a general balance sheet and statement of the affairs of the Company, with a list of all the shareholders thereof, and all such further information as may be required by the by-laws, shall be laid before the **Special meetings.** shareholders: special general meetings of shareholders may be called in such manner as may be provided for by the by-laws; and at all meetings of the shareholders the President or, in his absence, one of the Vice-Presidents, or in the absence of all of them, a Director or shareholder chosen by the shareholders, shall preside, who, in case of an equality of votes, shall give the casting vote in addition to his vote as a shareholder.

13.

13. At all meetings of Directors, five shall be a quorum for the transaction of business; and all questions before them shall be decided by a majority of votes, and in case of an equality of votes the President, Vice-President or presiding Director shall give the casting vote in addition to his vote as a Director. Quorum of Directors and decision of questions. Casting vote.

14. The Directors of the Company, at a meeting held for such specified purpose, may declare such annual or semi-annual dividends upon the capital stock as they shall deem justified by its business, so that no part of the capital thereof be appropriated to such dividends. Dividends.

15. The said Company shall have power and authority to make and effect contracts of insurance with any person or persons, body politic or corporate, against loss or damage by fire or lightning on any house, store or other building whatsoever, and in like manner on any goods, chattels or personal estate whatsoever, for such time or times and for such premiums or considerations and under such modifications and restrictions, and upon such conditions as may be bargained and agreed upon and set forth by and between the Company and the person or persons agreeing with them for such insurance; and the said Company in like manner shall have power and authority to make and effect contracts of insurance with any person or persons, body politic or corporate, against loss or damage by fire, storm or tempest, or other peril of navigation, or from any other cause, of or to ships, boats, vessels or other craft navigating the oceans, lakes, rivers, or high seas, or other navigable waters whatsoever, from any port or ports in Canada to any other port or ports in Canada, or to any foreign port or ports upon the oceans, lakes, rivers or other navigable waters aforesaid, or from one foreign port to another foreign port, or from any foreign port or ports to any port or ports in Canada or elsewhere, upon all or any of the oceans, lakes, rivers and navigable waters aforesaid, and against any loss or damage of or to the cargoes or property conveyed in or upon such ships, vessels, boats or other craft, and the freight due or to grow due in respect thereof, or of or to timber or other property of any description conveyed in any manner upon any of the oceans, seas, lakes, rivers or navigable waters aforesaid, or on any railway, or stored in any warehouse or railway station, and generally to do all matters and things relating to or connected with fire and marine insurances as aforesaid; and to make and to grant all policies therein and thereupon; and to cause themselves to be insured against any loss or risk they may have incurred in the course of their business; and generally to do and perform all other necessary matters and things connected with and proper to promote those objects: and all policies or contracts of insurance issued or entered into by the said Company shall be signed by the President Business of the company. Fire insurance. Marine Insurance. Re-insurance of risks. Execution of policies

President or one of the Vice-Presidents, and countersigned by the Managing Director or Secretary, or otherwise, as may be directed by the by-laws, rules and regulations of the Company, and being so signed and countersigned, shall be deemed valid and binding upon the Company, according to the tenor and meaning thereof.

Power to hold real estate for certain purposes, and in certain cases.

16. The Company shall have power to acquire and hold such real estate as may be necessary for the purpose of its business, and to sell or dispose of the same and acquire other property in its place, as may be deemed expedient ; and to take, hold and acquire all such lands and tenements, real or immovable estate, as shall have been *bonâ fide* mortgaged to it by way of security or conveyed to it in satisfaction of debts previously contracted in the course of its dealings, or purchased at sales upon judgments which shall have been obtained for such debts, or purchased for the purpose of avoiding a loss to the Company in respect thereof or of the owners thereof ; and to retain the same for a period not exceeding ten years : and the Company may invest its funds or any part thereof in the public securities of the Dominion of Canada, or of any of the Provinces thereof, or of any foreign state or states, when required for the carrying on business in such foreign state,—such investment in securities of foreign states not at any time to exceed fifty per cent. of the funds then invested,—or in the stocks of any chartered banks or building societies, or in the bonds or debentures of any incorporated city, town or municipality authorized to issue bonds or debentures, or in mortgages on real estate, in such manner as the Directors may elect ; and may, from time to time, vary or sell the said securities, or mortgage or pledge the same from time to time as occasion may require.

Investment of funds, subject to limitation as to foreign securities.

Directors may make by-laws for certain purposes.

17. The Directors shall have full power and authority from time to time to make, and from time to time to alter such by-laws, rules, regulations and ordinances as shall appear to them proper and needful, touching the well-ordering of the Company, the management and disposition of its stock, property, estate and effects, the calling of special general meetings, the regulation of the meetings of the Board of Directors, the increasing or the decreasing of the number of Directors, the increasing of the capital stock, appointment of a Managing Director, and of local boards to facilitate the details of business, and the definition of the duties and powers of such local boards, the making of calls upon the subscribed capital, the issue and allotment of shares, the appointment and removal of officers and agents of the Company, the regulation of their powers and duties, and the remuneration to be paid to them, the regulation of the transfer of stock and the form thereof, the compensation of Directors, the establishment and regulation of agencies, and the determining of rates, rules and conditions, under which

which the Company's policies shall be issued, transferred or re-purchased : Provided that such by-laws, rules, regulations and ordinances, and all alterations therein, shall be submitted by the Directors to the shareholders at a general meeting thereof, and shall have no force or effect unless and until they are approved by a majority of the voters at such meeting.

Proviso : for confirmation by stockholders.

18. The chief place of business of the Company shall be in the City of Hamilton ; and the said Company shall have full power and authority to comply with the laws of any province, state or country wherein it proposes to carry on business, so far as such laws are not inconsistent with the provisions of this Act or with the laws of Canada, and to appoint therein, under the seal of the Company, local managers, agents, or other officers.

Chief place of business and branches.

19. The Company shall not be bound to see to the execution of any trust, whether expressed, implied or constructive, to which any share or shares of its stock may be subject ; and the receipt of the person in whose name any share stands, shall be a sufficient discharge to the Company for any money paid in respect of such share or shares, notwithstanding any trust to which they or any of them may be held subject, and whether or not the Company shall have had notice of such trust.

Company not bound to see to trusts.

20. If the Directors of the Company declare and pay any dividend when the Company is insolvent, or any dividend the payment of which renders the Company insolvent, or diminishes the capital stock thereof, the Directors declaring such dividend shall be jointly and severally liable as well to the Company as to the individual shareholders and creditors thereof, for the amount of the dividend or dividends so paid ; but if any Director present when such dividend is declared, do forthwith, or if any Director then absent do, within twenty-four-hours after he shall have become aware thereof and able to do so, enter in the minutes of the Board of Directors his protest against the same, and do within eight days thereafter, publish such protest in at least one newspaper, published at or as near as may be possible to the head office of the Company, such Director may thereby and not otherwise, exonerate himself from such liability.

Dividends not to impair capital stock.

Responsibility of Directors.

How a Director may relieve himself.

21. The said Company shall be subject to the provisions of the Act passed by the Parliament of Canada, in the thirty-eighth year of, Her Majesty's reign, and intituled : "*An Act to amend and consolidate the several Acts respecting Insurance in so far as regards Fire and Inland Marine business,*" and to all other general laws in force or that may hereafter be in force respecting fire and marine insurance companies.

General laws to apply

38 V., c. 20

CHAP.

CHAP. 52.

An Act to incorporate the Empire Fire and Marine Assurance Corporation.

[Assented to 12th April, 1876]

Preamble.

WHEREAS D. B. Chisholm, John T. Grange, M.P.P., T. McIlwraith, Robert Duncan, T. C. Livingston, J. T. Middleton, A. Beamer, Geo. A. Clement, Thomas Sutton, S. Frank Wilson, John Stirton, H. Theo. Crawford, George Ennis, A. Neville and others have, by their petition, represented that the establishment of an association for the insurance of fire and marine risks would be greatly beneficial, and have prayed for an Act of incorporation for the purpose of carrying on a business of that nature ; and it is expedient to grant their prayer: Therefore Her Majesty, by and with the advice and consent of the Senate and House of Commons of Canada, enacts as follows :—

Certain persons incorporated.

Corporate name and powers.

1. The persons hereinbefore named and all such persons as shall become shareholders of the said Company shall be and are hereby ordained, constituted and declared to be a body corporate and politic, in law, in fact and in name, by the style and title of the "Empire Fire and Marine Assurance Corporation," for the purpose of carrying on the business of fire and marine insurance, and doing all things appertaining thereto, or connected therewith, in the Dominion of Canada and elsewhere, and shall and may have perpetual succession, and shall be capable in law of contracting. and being contracted with, suing and being sued, pleading and being impleaded in any court of law or equity within the Dominion of Canada or elsewhere in their corporate name aforesaid ; and they and their successors shall and may have a common seal, and may change the same at their will and pleasure.

Provisional Directors.

Stock-books may be opened

2. For the purpose of organizing the said Company, D. B. Chisholm, Thos. McIlwraith, Robert Duncan, Alpheus Beamer and J.T. Middleton, all of the City of Hamilton, Esquires, shall be Provisional Directors thereof; and they or a majority of them may cause stock-books to be opened, after giving due public notice thereof by advertisement for two weeks in one or more of the daily papers published in the city of Hamilton, Ontario,—upon which stock-books shall be recorded the subscriptions of such persons as shall desire to become shareholders of the said Company ; and such books shall be opened in the said City of Hamilton and elsewhere, at the discretion of the said Provisional Directors, and shall remain open as long as they deem it necessary ; and the Provisional Directors are hereby authorized to receive from the shareholders

holders a deposit of five per cent. on the amount of stock Five per cent.
subscribed by them respectively, and to pay all costs and payable on subscribing
expenses incurred in the application for and obtaining the
passing of this Act.

3. When one hundred thousand dollars of the said capital First meeting
stock shall have been subscribed as aforesaid, and at least of shareholders, when to
ten per centum of the amount so subscribed paid into one be held.
or more chartered banks, to be designated by the Provisional
Directors, and not to be withdrawn therefrom except for the
purposes of the Company, the said Provisional Directors
may call a general meeting of shareholders at some place to
be named in the said City of Hamilton,—giving at least ten
days' notice thereof in the *Canada Gazette*, and also in some
daily newspaper published in the said city; at which meeting
the shareholders present in person or represented by proxy,
shall elect a board of Directors, composed of twenty-five Election of
persons, in the manner and qualified as hereinafter pro- Directors.
vided, who shall hold office for one year after their election.

4. The capital stock of the said Company shall be one Capital stock
million of dollars, divided into ten thousand shares of one and shares.
hundred dollars each, with the privilege to increase the same, Provision for
from time to time, to any amount not exceeding two millions increase.
of dollars, by a vote of the shareholders at any annual or
special meeting of shareholders called for that purpose,
which said shares shall be and are hereby vested in the
several persons who shall subscribe for the same, their legal
representatives and assigns, subject to the provisions of this
Act. Aliens as well as British subjects, and whether resi- Aliens may
dent in Canada or elsewhere, may be shareholders in the be shareholders.
said Company; and all such shareholders shall be entitled to
vote on their shares equally with British subjects and shall
also be eligible to hold office as Directors or otherwise in the
said Company; but the major part of the Directors of the Proviso: as to
Company shall, at all times, be persons resident in Canada, Directors.
and subjects of Her Majesty by birth or naturalization; and
provided also, that upon every increase of the capital stock of
the Company the sum of at least five per cent. upon the
amount of such increased capital shall be paid in.

5. The shares of capital stock subscribed for shall be paid Payment of
in and by such instalments and at such times and places as shares.
the said Directors shall appoint; no such instalment shall Calls.
exceed ten per cent. of the sum subscribed; thirty days'
notice of each call shall be given, and instalments shall not
be made payable more frequently than once in three months:
Provided, that the said Company shall not be authorized to Proviso:
avail themselves of the privileges of this Act, otherwise than Company must comply
in accordance with the provisions of the several Acts of the with certain
Parliament of the Dominion relating to fire and marine Acts.
insurance companies.

6.

Forfeiture of shares for non-payment of calls.

6. If any shareholder shall refuse or neglect to pay the instalments due upon any share or shares held by him, the Directors may declare such share or shares forfeited, together with the amount previously paid thereon, in such manner as may be provided by the by-laws; and such forfeited share or shares may be sold at a public sale by the Directors after such notice as they may direct; and the moneys arising therefrom shall be applied for the purposes of this Act:

Proviso: Surplus after sale to belong to owner in default.

Provided always, that in case the money realized by any sale of shares be more than sufficient to pay all arrears and interest together with the expenses of such sale, the surplus of such money shall be paid on demand to the owner; and no more shares shall be sold than what are deemed necessary to pay such arrears, interest and expenses.

Payment of calls, &c., to cause share to revert to owner. What must be alleged and proved in suits for calls.

7. If payment of such arrears of calls, interest and expenses be made before any share so declared forfeited shall have been sold, such share shall revert to the owner as if the same had been duly paid before forfeiture thereof: and in all actions or suits for the recovery of such arrears or calls it shall be sufficient for the Company to allege that the defendant, being the owner of such shares, is indebted to the said Company in such sum of money as the calls in arrear amount to for such and so many shares, whereby an action hath accrued to the Company by virtue of this Act; and on the trial it shall only be necessary to prove that the defendant was owner of the said shares in the Company, that such calls were made, and that notice was given as directed by this Act; and it shall not be necessary to prove the appointment of the Directors who made such calls, or any matter whatsoever other than what is before mentioned: a

Proof of by-laws, &c.

copy of any by-law, rule, regulation or minute, or of any entry in any book of the Company, certified to be a true copy or extract under the hand of the President, or one of the Vice-Presidents, or the Managing Director, or Secretary of the Company, and sealed with the corporate seal, shall be received in all courts and proceedings as *primâ facie* evidence of such by-law, rule, regulation, minute or entry, without proof of the official character or signature of the officer signing the same, or of the corporate seal.

Transfers, how made.

8. No transfer of any share of the stock of the said Company shall be valid until entered in the books of the said Company according to such form as may, from time to time, be fixed by the by-laws; and until the whole of the capital stock of the said Company is paid up it shall be necessary to obtain the consent of the Directors to such transfer being made:

Proviso: Debts to Company and calls must be first paid.

Provided always, that no shareholder indebted to the Company shall be permitted to make a transfer or receive a dividend until such debt is paid or secured to the satisfaction of the Directors; and no transfer of stock shall, at any time, be made until all calls thereon have been paid in.

9.

9. Each shareholder shall be individually liable to the creditors of the Company to an amount equal to the amount unpaid on the stock held by him, for the debts and liabilities of the Company, but no further. Liability of shareholders limited.

10. The transmission of any shares of the stock of the Company, in consequence of the marriage, death or insolvency of a shareholder, or by any other means than an ordinary transfer, shall be made, proved and authenticated in such form, by such proof and generally in such manner as the Directors shall, from time to time, require, or by by-law direct, before any persons claiming such shares shall be entitled to vote thereon or to receive any dividends or money payable in respect thereof. Transmission otherwise than by transfer.

11. The stock, property, affairs and concerns of the said Company shall be managed and conducted by twenty-five Directors, who shall hold office for one year, and shall be elected (at the expiration of the term during which the Directors hereinbefore appointed are to hold office) at the annual meeting of shareholders to be held at the City of Hamilton in the month of July next and yearly thereafter on such day as may be appointed by by-law,—not less than ten days' notice of such meeting being given by letter to the shareholders and also by advertisement in some daily newspaper published in the said city ; and the said election shall be held and made by such of the shareholders present in person or represented by proxy, as shall have paid all calls made by the Directors and then due ; and all such elections shall be by ballot ; and the twenty-five persons who shall have the greatest number of votes at any such election shall be Directors, except as hereinafter directed ; and if two or more persons have an equal number of votes, in such a manner that a greater number of persons than twenty-five shall appear to be chosen as Directors, then the Directors who shall have the greater number of votes, or a majority of them, shall determine which of the said persons so having an equal number of votes shall be the Director or Directors, so as to complete the whole number of twenty-five : and the said Directors (as soon as may be after the said election) shall proceed to elect one of their number to be the President and two to be Vice-Presidents : and if any vacancy should at any time happen amongst the said Directors by death, resignation, disqualification or removal during the current year of office, such vacancy shall be filled for the remainder of the year by the remaining Directors, or the majority of them, electing in such place or places a shareholder or shareholders eligible for such an office : Provided always, that no person shall be eligible to be or continue as Director, unless he shall hold in his name and for his own use stock in the said Company to the amount of twenty shares, whereof at least ten per centum shall have been paid in, and shall have paid all calls made upon his

Board of Directors.
Election of Directors.
Proxies.
Ballot.
Decision in case of equality of votes.
President and two Vice-Presidents.
Vacancies, how filled.
Proviso: Qualification of Directors.

stock

stock and all liability actually matured and incurred by him with the Company.

Provision in case of failure of election.   **12.** In case it should, at any time, happen that an election of Directors of the said Company should not be made on any day when pursuant to this Act it should have been made, the said Company shall not for that cause be deemed to be dissolved; but it shall be lawful on any other day to hold and make an election at a special general meeting to be called for that purpose by the Directors, who shall continue in office until a new election is made

When only the Company may commence business.   **13·** When and so soon as five hundred thousand dollars of the capital stock of the Company shall have been *bona fide* subscribed for, and ten per cent. thereon shall have been actually paid in, and not before, the Company may commence business under this Act.

Votes on shares.   **14.** At all general meetings of the said Company each shareholder shall be entitled to give one vote for every share held by him for not less than fourteen days prior to the time of voting, upon which all calls then due have been paid up; **Proxies.** such votes may be given either in person or by proxy,—the **Majority.** holder of any such proxy being himself a shareholder; and all questions proposed for the consideration of the share- **Chairman.** holders shall be determined by the majority of votes, the chairman presiding at such meeting having the casting vote in case of an equality of votes.

Proceedings at annual meetings.   **15.** At the annual meeting of the shareholders, the election of Directors shall be held and all business transacted without the necessity for specifying such business in the notice of such meeting ; and at such meeting a general balance sheet and statement of the affairs of the Company, with a list of all the shareholders thereof, and all such further information as may be required by the by-laws, shall be laid before the **Special gene- ral meetings.** shareholders : special general meetings of shareholders may be called in such manner as may be provided for by the by-laws ; and at all meetings of the shareholders the President or, in his absence, one of the Vice-Presidents, or in the absence of all of them, a Director or shareholder chosen by the shareholders, shall preside, who, in case of an equality of votes, shall give the casting vote in addition to his vote as a shareholder.

Quorum of Directors and decision of questions.   **16.** At all meetings of Directors, five shall be a quorum for the transaction of business ; and all questions before them shall be decided by a majority of votes, and in case of an equality of votes the President, Vice-President or presiding Director shall give the casting vote in addition to his vote as a Director.

17

17. The Directors of the Company at a meeting held for Dividends·
such specified purpose may declare such annual or semi-
annual dividends upon the capital stock as they shall deem
justified by its business, so that no part of the capital thereof Limitation.
be appropriated to such dividends.

18. The said Company shall have power and authority to Business of
make and effect contracts of insurance with any person or the Company.
persons, body politic or corporate, against loss or damage by
fire or lightning on any house, store or other building what- Fire.
soever, and in like manner on any goods, chattels or personal estate whatsoever, for such time or times and for such
premiums or considerations and under such modifications
and restrictions, and upon such conditions as may be bargained and agreed upon or set forth by and between the
Company and the person or persons agreeing with them for
such insurance ; and the said Company in like manner shall Marine.
have power and authority to make and effect contracts of
insurance with any person or persons, body politic or corporate, against loss or damage by fire, storm or tempest, or
from any other cause, of or to ships, boats, vessels, steamboats or other craft navigating the oceans, lakes, rivers, or
high seas, or other navigable waters whatsoever, from any
port or ports in Canada, to any other port or ports in Canada or to any foreign port or ports upon the oceans, lakes,
rivers, or other navigable waters aforesaid, or from one
foreign port to another foreign port, or from any foreign
port or ports, to any port or ports in Canada or elsewhere,
upon all or any of the oceans, lakes, rivers and navigable
waters aforesaid, and against any loss or damage of or to the
cargoes or property conveyed in or upon such ships, vessels,
boats or other craft, and the freight due or to grow due in
respect thereof, or of or to timber or other property of any
description conveyed in any manner upon any of the oceans,
seas, lakes, rivers or navigable waters aforesaid, or on any
railway, or stored in any warehouse or railway station, and
generally to do all matters and things relating to or connected with fire and marine insurances as aforesaid, and to make
and to grant all policies therein and thereupon ; and to cause Re-insurance.
themselves to be insured against any loss or risk they may
have incurred in the course of their business ; and generally
to do and perform all other necessary matters and things
connected with and proper to promote those objects : and all Policies and
policies or contracts of insurance issued or entered into by contracts.
the said Company shall be signed by the President or one
of the Vice-Presidents, and countersigned by the Managing
Director or Secretary, or otherwise, as may be directed by
the by-laws. rules and regulations of the Company, and
being so signed and countersigned, shall be deemed valid
and binding upon the Company, according to the tenor and
meaning thereof.

19.

Power to hold real estate for certain purposes and subject to certain limitations.

19. The Company shall have power to acquire and hold such real estate as may be necessary for the purpose of its business, and to sell or dispose of the same and acquire other property in its place, as may be deemed expedient ; and to take, hold and acquire all such lands and tenements, real or immovable estate, as shall have been *bonâ fide* mortgaged to it by way of security or conveyed to it in satisfaction of debts previously contracted in the course of its dealings, or purchased at sales upon judgments which shall have been obtained for such debts, or purchased for the purpose of avoiding a loss to the Company in respect thereof, or of the owners thereof; and to retain the same for a period not exceeding five years ; and the Company may invest its funds or any part thereof in the public securities of the Dominion of Canada, or of any of the Provinces thereof, or of any foreign state or states, when required for the carrying on business in such foreign state, or in the stocks of any chartered banks or building societies, or in the bonds or debentures of any incorporated city, town or municipality authorized to issue bonds or debentures, or in mortgages on real estate, or in such other securities of like character, and in such manner and at such rate of interest as may be agreed upon, not exceeding the rate allowed by law in the Province where the investment is made, as the Directors may elect ; and may, from time to time, vary or sell the said securities, or mortgage or pledge the same from time to time as occasion may require ; but not more than fifty per cent. of the whole amount of the investments of the corporation at any time shall consist of the public securities of any foreign state or states.

Investment of funds.

Limitation as to securities of foreign States.

Directors may make by-laws for certain purposes.

20. The Directors shall have full power and authority, from time to time to make and to alter such by-laws, rules, regulations and ordinances as shall appear to them proper and needful, touching the well-ordering of the Company, the management and disposition of its stock, property, estate and effects, the calling of special general meetings, the regulation of the meetings of the Board of Directors, the increasing or the decreasing of the number of Directors, the increasing of the capital stock, the appointment of a Managing Director, and of local boards to facilitate the details of business, and the definition of the duties and powers of such local boards, the making of calls upon the subscribed capital, the issue and allotment of shares, the appointment and removal of officers and agents of the Company, the regulation of their powers and duties, and the remuneration to be paid to them, the regulation of the transfer of stock and the form thereof, the compensation of Directors, the establishment and regulation of agencies, and the determining of rates, rules, and conditions, under which the Company's policies shall be issued, transferred or re-purchased : Provided always, that all such by-laws, rules, regulations and ordinances made

Proviso : not to have effect

made by the Directors as aforesaid, shall only be valid and binding until the next annual general meeting of the shareholders, unless they are then approved by such meeting, and shall thereafter have force and effect as so approved or modified at such meeting ; and provided further, that such bylaws do not contravene the provisions of this Act. until approved by shareholders.

Proviso.

21. The chief place of business of the Company shall be in the City of Hamilton ; and the said Company shall have full power and authority to comply with the laws of any province, state or country wherein it proposes to carry on business, so far as such laws are not inconsistent with the provisions of this Act or with the laws of Canada, and to appoint therein, under the seal of. the Company, local managers, agents, or other officers. Chief place of business and branches.

22. The Company shall not be bound to see to the execution of any trust, whether expressed, implied or constructive, to which any share or shares of its stock may be subject ; and the receipt of the person in whose name any share stands, shall be a sufficient discharge to the Company for any money paid in respect of such share or shares, notwithstanding any trust to which they or any of them may be held subject, and whether or not the Company shall have had notice of such trust. Company not bound to see to trusts.

23. If the Directors of the Company declare and pay any dividend when the Company is insolvent, or any dividend the payment of which renders the Company insolvent, or diminishes the capital stock thereof, the Directors declaring such dividend shall be jointly and severally liable as well to the Company as to the individual shareholders and creditors thereof, for the amount of the dividend or dividends so paid ; but if any Director present when such dividend is declared, do forthwith, or if any Director then absent do, within twenty-four hours after he shall have become aware thereof and able to do so, enter in the minutes of the Board of Directors his protest against the same, and do within eight days thereafter, publish such protest in at least one newspaper, published at or as near as may be possible to the head office of the Company, such Director may thereby and not otherwise, exonerate himself from such liability. Dividends not to impair capital stock.

Responsibility of Directors.

How a Director may avoid it.

24. The said Company shall be subject to the provisions of the Act passed by the Parliament of Canada, in the thirty-eighth year of Her Majesty's reign, and intituled : "*An Act to amend and consolidate the several Acts respecting Insurance in so far as regards Fire and Inland Marine business,*" and to all other general laws in force or that may hereafter be in force respecting fire and marine insurance companies. General laws to apply.

38 V. c. 20.

25 The said corporation shall obtain from the Minister of Finance Company must obtain

4

license under
38 V. c. 20,
within two
years.

Finance within two years from and after the passing of this Act, the license required by Section 5 of the Act passed in the thirty-eighth year of Her Majesty's reign, chapter twenty, in default of which this Act shall become and be null and void, and of no effect, and the charter hereby granted, and all and every the rights and privileges hereby conferred, shall be forfeited.

CHAP. 53.

An Act to incorporate the Atlantic and Pacific Fire and Marine Insurance Company.

[Assented to 12th April, 1876.]

Preamble.

WHEREAS the Honorable John J. C. Abbott, Harrison Stephens, Adolphe Masson, James Crathern, Robert Dalglish, H. A. Nelson and others, have by their petition represented that the establishment of an association for the insurance of fire and marine risks would be greatly beneficial, and have prayed for an Act of incorporation for the purpose of carrying on a business of that nature under the name of the Atlantic and Pacific Fire and Marine Insurance Company ; and it is expedient to grant their prayer : Therefore Her Majesty, by and with the advice and consent of the Senate and House of Commons of Canada, enacts as follows :—

Certain persons incorporated.

Corporate name and purposes.

1. The persons hereinbefore mentioned, and all such persons as now are or hereafter shall become shareholders of the said Company, shall be and are hereby ordained, constituted and declared to be a body corporate and politic in law, in fact and in name, by the style and title of the Atlantic and Pacific Fire and Marine Insurance Company, for effecting insurance against fire and marine risks.

Capital stock and shares.

2. The capital stock of the said Company shall be two million dollars, divided into twenty thousand shares, of one hundred dollars each,—which said shares shall be and are hereby vested in the several persons who shall subscribe for the same, their legal representatives and assigns, subject to the provisions of this Act.

Provisional Directors.

Stock books may be opened.

3. For the purpose of organizing the said Company, the said Honorable John J. C. Abbott, Harrison Stephens, Adolphe Masson, James Crathern, Robert Dalglish, and H. A. Nelson shall be provisional directors thereof ; and they, or a majority of them, may cause stock books to be opened, after giving due public notice thereof, by advertisement, for two

weeks

weeks, in one or more daily papers published in the City of
Montreal, upon which stock books shall be recorded the
subscriptions of such persons as shall desire to become shareholders in the said Company; and such books shall be
opened in the City of Montreal and elsewhere, at the discretion of the said provisional directors, and shall remain open
as long as they deem necessary; and the provisional di- Five per cent.
rectors are hereby authorized to receive from the share- to be paid on
holders a deposit of five per cent. on the amount of the stock each share.
subscribed by them respectively.

4. When and so soon as one million dollars of the First meeting
said capital stock shall have been subscribed as afore- of share-
said, and ten per cent. of the amount so subscribed paid in, only it may
the said provisional directors shall call a general meeting of be held.
shareholders at some place to be named, in the City of Montreal, giving at least ten days' notice thereof in two daily
newspapers published in the said city, at which meeting Election of
the shareholders present in person or represented by proxy Directors.
shall elect not less than nine nor more than thirteen Directors
in the manner and qualified as hereinafter provided, who
shall constitute a Board of Directors, and hold office till
the next annual meeting of the Company, which shall be
held after six months thereafter.

5. The shares of capital stock subscribed for shall be paid Calls on stock.
in by such instalments, and at such times and places, as the
Directors shall appoint; no such instalment shall exceed ten
per cent., and thirty days' notice of each call shall be given;
and executors, administrators and curators paying instalments upon the shares of deceased shareholders shall be,
and they are, respectively indemnified for paying the same:
Provided always, that it shall not be lawful for the said Proviso:
Company to commence their business either of fire or conditions
marine insurance until a sum of not less than two hundred commence-
thousand dollars shall have been actually paid in on account ment of
of the subscribed stock; nor both until at least four business.
hundred thousand dollars have been so paid in.

6. The stock, property, affairs and concerns of the Board of
said Company shall be managed and conducted by Directors.
not less than nine nor more than thirteen Directors,
(one of whom shall be chosen President, and one
Vice-President), who shall hold office until the next
following general election of Directors; and such Direc- Election.
tors shall be shareholders residing in Canada, and be
elected at the annual general meeting of shareholders to be
holden at Montreal on the second Wednesday of January
in each year,—not less than ten days' notice of such meeting Notice.
being given, as hereinbefore provided. Such election shall be
held and made by such of the shareholders present in person, or represented by proxy, as shall have paid all calls Proxies.
4½   made

Ballot.

Ties.

President and V.-P.

Vacancies, how to be filled.

Proviso: qualification of Directors.

made and then due; and all such elections shall be by ballot; and the required number of persons who shall have the greatest number of votes at any such election shall be Directors, except as hereinafter directed; and if two or more persons have an equal number of votes in such a manner that a greater number of persons than are required shall appear to be chosen as Directors, then the Directors who shall have the greater number of votes, or a majority of them, shall determine which of the said persons so having an equal number of votes shall be the Director or Directors, so as to complete the whole number required; and the said Directors (as soon as may be after the said election) shall proceed in like manner to elect by ballot one of their number to be the President, and one to be the Vice-president; but shareholders not residing within the Dominion of Canada shall be ineligible; and if any Director shall move his domicile out of Canada, his office shall be considered as vacant; and if any vacancy should at any time happen amongst the said Directors by death, resignation, disqualification or removal during the current year of office, such vacancy shall be filled for the remainder of the year by the remaining Directors, or the majority of them electing in such place or places a shareholder or shareholders eligible for such office: Provided always, that no person shall be eligible to be or continue as Director, unless he shall hold in his name, and for his own use, stock in the said Company to the amount of forty shares, whereof, after the first election of Directors, at least twenty per cent. shall have been paid in, and shall have paid all calls made upon his stock, and all liabilities actually matured and incurred by him with the Company.

Provision in case of failure of election.

7. In case it should, at any time, happen that an election of Directors of the said Company should not be made on any day when, pursuant to this Act, it should have been made, the said Company shall not for that cause be deemed to be dissolved; but it shall be lawful on any other day to hold and make an election in such manner as may be regulated, directed and appointed by the Directors for the time being; and the Directors in office shall so continue until a new election is made.

Votes on shares.

Proxies.

Proviso.

8. At all general meetings of the said Company each shareholder shall be entitled to give one vote for every share held by him for not less than fourteen days prior to the time of voting, upon which all calls then due have been paid up. Such votes may be given either in person or by proxy,—the holder of any such proxy being himself a shareholder; and all questions proposed for the consideration of the shareholders shall be determined by the majority of votes, the chairman presiding at such meeting having the casting vote in case of an equality of votes: Provided, that no clerk or other

other employee of the said Company shall vote either in person or by proxy at the election of Directors.

9. The said Company shall have power and authority to make and effect contracts of insurance with any person or persons, body politic or corporate, against loss or damage by fire, on any houses, stores or other buildings whatsoever; and, in like manner, on any goods, chattels or personal estate whatsoever, for such time or times, and for such premiums or considerations, and under such modifications and restrictions, and upon such conditions as may be bargained and agreed upon, or set forth by and between the Company and the person or persons agreeing with them for such insurance; and also to make and effect contracts of insurance with any person or persons, body politic or corporate, against loss or damage of or to ships, boats, vessels, steamboats or other craft, navigating the seas or inland navigable waters, or both the one and the other; and against any loss or damage of or to the cargoes or property conveyed in or upon such ships, vessels, boats or other craft, and the freight due or to grow due in respect thereof; or of or to timber or other property of any description conveyed in any manner upon all or any seas or inland navigable waters, or on any railway, or stored in any warehouse or railway station; and, generally, to do all matters and things relating to or connected with marine insurances, and to make and grant policies therein and thereupon; and to cause themselves to be insured against any loss or risks they may have incurred in the course of their business; and, generally, to do and perform all other necessary matters and things connected with and proper to promote those objects; and all policies or contracts of insurance issued or entered into by the said Company shall be under the seal of the said Company, and shall be signed by the President or Vice-president, and countersigned by the Managing Director or Secretary (or otherwise, as may be directed by the by-laws, rules and regulations of the said Company, in case of the absence of any of the said parties), and, being so sealed, signed and countersigned, shall be deemed valid and binding upon them, according to the tenor and meaning thereof: and the chief place of business of the Company shall be in the City of Montreal.

Business and general powers of the Company. Fire Insurance.

Marine.

Re-insurance.

General powers.

Policies, &c., how executed.

Chief place of business.

10. It shall be lawful for the Atlantic and Pacific Fire and Marine Insurance Company to appoint, under the corporate seal of the Company, resident agents at any port or place within the Dominion of Canada, or elsewhere, for the purpose of effecting at such ports or places marine insurance upon ships, freights and cargoes, and insurance against losses by fire on buildings and other property, real and personal, subject to such conditions, restrictions and provisoes as the said Company shall, from time to time, establish and impose; and wherever it shall be found desirable, also to appoint

Agents and sub-boards may be appointed.

point

point and establish local agencies and local Boards of direction or of supervision upon such conditions, with such qualifications and powers, and for such purposes as the Board of Directors shall fix, or as shall be directed by the by-laws of the company.

Forfeiture of shares for non-payment of calls.

11. If any shareholder shall refuse or neglect to pay the instalments due upon any share or shares held by him, the Directors may declare such share or shares forfeited, together with the amount previously paid thereon, in such manner as may be provided by the by-laws; and such forfeited share or shares may be sold at a public sale by the Directors after such notice as they may direct, and the moneys arising therefrom shall be applied for the purposes of this Act: Provided always, that in case the money realized by any sale of shares be more than sufficient to pay all arrears and interest, together with the expenses of such sale, the surplus of such money shall be paid on demand to the owner; and no more shares shall be sold than what shall be deemed necessary to pay such arrears, interest and expenses.

Proviso: surplus to defaulter.

Payment of arrears to annul forfeiture.

12. If payment of such arrears of calls, interest and expenses be made before any share so forfeited shall have been sold, such share shall revert to the owner as if the same had been duly paid before forfeiture thereof; and in all actions or suits for the recovery of such arrears or calls, it shall be sufficient for the Company to allege that the defendant, being the owner of such shares, is indebted to the said Company in such sums of money as the calls in arrear amount to, for such and so many shares, whereby an action hath accrued to the Company by virtue of this Act, and on the trial it shall only be necessary to prove that the defendant was owner of the said shares in the Company, that such calls were made, and that notice was given as directed by this Act, and it shall not be necessary to prove the appointment of the Directors who made such calls, or any other matter whatsoever, other than what is before mentioned: a copy of any by-law, rule, regulation or minute, or of any entry in any book of the Company, certified to be a true copy or extract under the hand of the President or Vice-president, or the Manager or Secretary of the Company, and sealed with the corporate seal, shall be received in all courts and proceedings as *primâ facie* evidence of such by-law, rule, regulation, minute or entry without further proof thereof, and without proof of the official character or signature of the officer signing the same, or of the corporate seal.

Allegations and evidence in suits for calls.

Proof of by-laws, &c.

Quorum and votes at meetings of Directors.

13. At all meetings of Directors five shall be a quorum for the transaction of business; and all questions before them shall be decided by a majority of votes, and in case of an equality of votes, the President, Vice-president or presiding director shall give the casting vote in addition to his vote as a Director.

14.

14. At the annual meeting of the shareholders the elec- Business at annual tion of Directors shall be held, and all business transacted meetings. -without the necessity for specifying such business in the notice of such meeting ; and at such meeting a general bal- -ance sheet and statement of the affairs of the Company, with a list of all the shareholders thereof, and all such further information as may be required by the by-laws, shall be laid before the shareholders. Special general meetings of share- Special holders may be called in such manner as may be provided meetings. for by the by-laws; and at all meetings of the shareholders the President, or, in his absence, the Vice-president, or, in the absence of both of them, a Director chosen by the share- holders shall preside, who, in case of an equality of votes, Casting vote. :shall give the casting vote in addition to his vote as a share- holder.

15. The Directors shall have full power and authority to Directors may make, and, from time to time, to alter such by-laws, rules, make by-laws for certain regulations and ordinances as shall appear to them proper purposes. -and needful, touching the well-ordering of the Company, the management and disposition of its stock, property, estate and effects, the calling of special general meetings, the regu- lation of the meetings of the Board of Directors, the increas- ing the number of Directors, the appointment of a Managing Director and of sub-boards to facilitate the details of business, and the definition of duties and powers of such sub-boards, the making of calls upon subscribed capital, the issue and allotment of shares, the appointment and removal of officers -and agents of the Company, the regulation of their powers and duties and the salaries to be paid to them, the regula- tion of the transfer of stock and the form thereof, the -compensation of Directors, and the establishment and regulations of agencies : Provided always, that all such by- Proviso : by- laws must be • laws, rules, regulations and ordinances made by the Directors confirmed. -as aforesaid, shall only be valid and binding until the next -annual general meeting of the shareholders, unless they are then approved by such meeting, and shall thereafter have force and effect as so approved or modified at such meeting; -and provided further, that such by-laws do not contravene the Proviso. provisions of this Act.

16. The Company shall have power to acquire and hold real Power to hold -estate necessary for the purposes of its business, within the real estate, for what Dominion of Canada, and to sell and dispose of the same and purposes, and acquire other property in its place, as may be deemed expe- how long. -dient, and to take, hold and acquire all such lands and tene- ments, real or immovable estate, as shall have been *bonâ fide* mortgaged to it by way of security, or conveyed to it in sa- tisfaction of debts previously contracted in the course of its -dealings, or purchased at sales upon judgments which shall have been obtained for such debts, or purchased for the pur- pose of avoiding a loss to the Company in respect thereof, or or of the owners thereof, and to retain the same for a period

Investment of funds.

not exceeding ten years ; and the Company may invest its funds, or ,any part thereof, in the public securities of the Dominion of Canada, or of any of the Provinces thereof, or of any foreign state or states (such investments in the securities of foreign states not to exceed fifty per cent. of the investments of the Company for the time being),or in the stocks of any chartered banks or building societies, or in the bonds or debentures of any incorporated city, town or municipality authorized to issue bonds or debentures, or in mortgages on real estate ; and may, from time to time, vary or sell the said securities or mortgages, or pledge the same from time to time as occasion may require.

Transfer of shares, when valid.

17. No transfer of any share of the stock of the said Company shall be valid until entered in the books of the said Company according to such form as may, from time to time, be fixed by the by-laws ; and until the whole capital stock of the said Company is paid up, it shall be necessary to obtain the consent of the Directors to such transfer being made:

Proviso :. debts to Co., must be paid and calls.

Provided always, that no shareholder indebted to the Company shall be permitted to make a transfer or receive a dividend until such debt is paid or secured to the satisfaction of the Directors ; and no transfer of stock shall, at any time, be made until all calls theron have been paid in.

Liability of shareholders limited.

18. Each shareholder shall be individually liable to the creditors of the Company to an amount equal to the amount unpaid on the stock held by him, for the debts and liabilities thereof, but no further.

Suits by and against the company. Witnesses.

19. Suits may be prosecuted or maintained by or against any shareholder by or against the Company ; and no shareholder shall be incompetent as a witness in any proceeding by or against the Company.

Dividends.

20. The Directors of the Company, at a meeting held for such specified purpose, may declare such annual or semi-annual dividends upon the capital stock as they shall deem justified by its business, so that no part of the capital thereof be

Participation of profits by policy holders.

appropriated to such dividends ; and also may, by resolution, order that the holders of policies, or other instruments, shall be paid such portion of the actual realized profits, in such proportions, at such times and in such manner as the said directors may think proper, and may enter into obligations so to do either by endorsement on the policies, or otherwise, in such manner and upon such conditions as shall be

Proviso.

provided by the by-laws of the Company : Provided always, that the holders of policies or other instruments so participating in the profits, shall not be in any wise answerable. or responsible for the debts of the said Company.

21.

21 If the Directors of the Company declare and pay any dividend when the Company is insolvent, or any dividend the payment of which renders the Company insolvent, or diminishes the capital stock thereof, they shall be jointly and severally liable, as well to the Company as to the individual shareholders and creditors thereof, for all the debts of the Company then existing, and for all thereafter contracted during their continuance in office respectively; but if any Director present when such dividend is declared do forthwith, or if any Director then absent do within twenty-four hours after he shall have become aware thereof and able so to do, enter on the minutes of the Board of Directors his protest against the same, and within eight days thereafter publish such protest in at least one newspaper published at, or as near as may be possible to the place in which the office or chief place of business of the Company is situated, such Director may thereby, and not otherwise, exonerate himself from such liability. *Penalty on directors paying dividend out of capital.* *How a director may avoid it.*

22. This Act and the Company hereby incorporated, and the exercise of the powers hereby conferred, shall be subject to the provisions contained in the Act thirty-eighth Victoria, chapter twenty, intituled: "*An Act to amend and consolidate the several Acts respecting Insurance, in so far as regards Fire and Inland Marine Business,*" and to such other legislation on the subject of insurance as may, from time to time, be passed. *General laws to apply.* *38 V., c. 20.*

23. The said Company shall obtain from the Minister of Finance within two years from and after the passing of this Act, the license to carry on business in Canada required by the said Act; in default of which this Act shall become null and void and of no effect, and the charter hereby granted and all and every the rights and privileges hereby conferred shall be forfeited. *Company must obtain license within 2 years.*

CHAP. 54.

An Act to incorporate the Union Life and Accident Assurance Company of Canada.

[Assented to 12th April, 1876.]

WHEREAS H. S. Howland, John Turner, the Honorable T. B. Pardee, M. P. P., H. S. Strathy, W. H. Howland, J. Saurin McMurray, T. Richard Fuller, Thomas Hodgins, M.P.P., John Macnab, J. Maughan, Junior, J. D. Edgar, Thomas McGrosson, George Laidlaw, A. J. Cattanach, R. W. Elliott, W. A. Foster, Robert Bell, M.P.P., and others of the City *Preamble.*

City of Toronto ; R. M. Wanzer, Lyman Moore, the Honorable
Archibald McKellar, William Hendrie, John I. Mackenzie,
D. B. Chisholm, T. C. Livingston, H. Theo. Crawford and
others of the City of Hamilton ; J. H. Fraser, M. P., D. Mac-
millan, M P., of the City of London ; George H. Dartnell,
Whitby ; John T. Grange, M.P.P., Napanee ; C. F. Ferguson,
M. P., Kemptville ; the Honorable R. W. W. Carrall, Senator,
Victoria, B.C., and others have, by their petition, represented
that the establishment of an association for the insurance of
lives would be greatly beneficial, and have prayed for an
Act of incorporation for the purpose of carrying on a business of that nature, and it is expedient to grant their prayer:
Therefore Her Majesty, by and with the advice and consent
of the Senate and House of Commons of Canada, enacts as
follows :—

Certain per-
sons incor-
porated.

1. The persons hereinbefore named and all such persons
as shall become shareholders in the said Company shall
be and are hereby ordained, constituted and declared to be
a body corporate and politic in law, in fact, and in

Corporate
name and
powers.

name, by the style and title of the "Union Life
and Accident Assurance Company of Canada," for the purpose of carrying on the business of life insurance and doing
all things appertaining thereto, or connected therewith, in
the Dominion of Canada and elsewhere, and shall and may
have perpetual succession, and shall be capable in law of
contracting, and being contracted with, and suing and being
sued, pleading and being impleaded in any court of law or
equity within the Dominion of Canada or elsewhere ; and
they and their successors shall and may have a common seal,
and may change the same at their will and pleasure.

Capital stock
and shares.

2. The capital stock of the said Company shall be one
million dollars, divided into ten thousand shares of one hun-

Power to
increase.

dred dollars each ; with the privilege to increase the same
from time to time to any amount not exceeding two millions
of dollars by a vote of the shareholders at any annual or
special meeting of shareholders called for that purpose ;

Proviso :
Five per cent.
to he paid in.

provided, that upon every increase of the capital stock of
the Company the sum of at least five per cent. upon the
amount of such increased capital shall be paid in,—
which said shares shall be and are hereby vested
in the several persons who shall subscribe for the same,
their legal representatives and assigns, subject to the provisions of this Act.

Provisional
Directors.

3. For the purpose of organizing the said Company, the
Honorable Archibald McKellar and H. S. Strathy, Lyman
Moore, J. D. Edgar, D. B. Chisholm, T. C. Livingston, and H.
Theo. Crawford, Esquires, shall be provisional Directors

Stock books
may be
opened.

thereof ; and they or a majority of them may cause stock-
books to be opened, after giving due public notice thereof

yb

by advertisement for two weeks in one or more of the daily papers published in the City of Hamilton, Ontario,--upon which stock-books shall be recorded the subscriptions of such persons as shall desire to become shareholders in the said Company; and such books shall be opened in the said City of Hamilton and elsewhere, at the discretion of the said provisional Directors, and shall remain open as long as they deem it necessary; and the provisional Directors are hereby authorized to receive from the shareholders a deposit of five per cent. on the amount of their stock subscribed by them respectively, and to pay all costs and expenses incurred in the application for and obtaining the passing of this Act.

Five per cent. to be paid in.

4. When one hundred thousand dollars of the said capital stock shall have been subscribed as aforesaid, and at least ten per centum of the amount so subscribed paid into one or more chartered banks, to be designated by the provisional Directors, and not to be withdrawn therefrom except for the purposes of the Company, the said provisional Directors may call a general meeting of shareholders at some place to be named in the said City of Hamilton, giving at least ten days' notice thereof in the *Canada Gazette*, and also in some daily newspaper published in the said city,--at which meeting the shareholders present in person or represented by proxy, shall elect a Board of Directors, composed of not less than five persons, in the manner and qualified as by this Act provided, who shall hold office for one year after their election.

First meeting of shareholders.

Notice.

5. It shall not be lawful for the said Company to issue any policy of insurance, or take any risk, or receive any premium, or transact any business of insurance in Canada until five hundred thousand dollars of the capital stock thereof has been subscribed for and ten per cent. of that amount has been paid in as aforesaid, nor without first obtaining a license from the Minister of Finance of the Dominion, under the Act of the Parliament of Canada passed in the thirty-first year of the reign of Her Majesty, and intituled "*An Act respecting Insurance Companies*," or such other Act as may then be in force respecting life insurance companies.

Business not to be commenced until license is obtained, and $500,000 subscribed and ten per cent. paid in.

31 V. c. 48.

6. The stock, property, affairs and concerns of the said Company shall be managed and conducted by the Board of Directors, who shall hold office until the next annual general meeting of shareholders and election of Directors, to be holden at Hamilton, Ontario, on the anniversary of the first election of Directors or on such other day in each year as may be appointed by by law--not less than ten days' notice of such meeting being given, as provided in section four : the said election shall be held and made by such of the shareholders present in person or represented by proxy, as shall have paid all calls made by the

Board of Directors, term of office.

Election.

Ballot.

'Decision in case of equality of votes.

President and Vice-President.

Vacancies how filled.

Proviso: Qualification of Director.

the Directors and then due; and all such elections shall be by ballot; and the requisite number of persons, as determined under the provisions of section nine, who shall have the greatest number of votes at any such election shall be Directors, except as hereinafter provided; and if two or more persons have an equal number of votes in such a manner that a greater number of persons than the number required (such number to be determined as aforesaid) shall appear to be chosen as Directors, then the Directors who shall have the greater number of votes, or a majority of them, shall determine which of the said persons so having an equal number of votes shall be the Director or Directors, so as to complete the whole number required as aforesaid: and the said Directors (as soon as may be after the said election) shall proceed in like manner to elect by ballot one of their number to be President and one to be Vice-President: and if any vacancy should at any time happen amongst the said Directors by death, resignation, disqualification or removal during the current year of office, such vacancy shall be filled for the remainder of the year by the remaining Directors, or a majority of those of them present at any meeting, electing in such place or places a shareholder or shareholders eligible for such office: Provided always, that no person, except as hereinafter provided, shall be eligible to be or continue as a Director unless he shall hold in his own name and for his own use, stock in the said Company to the amount of forty shares, whereof at least ten per centum shall have been paid in, and shall have paid all calls made and due upon his said stock.

Failure of election not to dissolve Company.

7. In case it should, at any time, happen that an election of Directors of the said Company should not be made on any day when pursuant to this Act it should have been made, the said Company shall not for that cause be deemed to be dissolved; but it shall be lawful on any other day to hold and make an election at a special general meeting to be called for that purpose by the Directors, who shall continue in office until a new election is made.

Quorum and votes at meeting of Directors.

Casting vote.

Who shall preside.

8. At all meetings of Directors five shall be a quorum for the transaction of business; and all questions of business shall be decided by a majority of votes; and in case of an equality of votes, the President, Vice-President, second Vice-President, or presiding Director shall give the casting vote in addition to his vote as a Director. At all such meetings the President or in his absence the Vice-President or in the absence of both the second Vice-President, or in the absence of all of them, a Director, chosen by a majority of the Directors present, shall preside.

Directors may make by-laws for

9. The Directors shall have full power and authority, from time to time, to make and to alter such by-laws, rules, regulations

regulations and ordinances as shall appear to them proper certain and needful, touching the well ordering of the Company, purposes. the management and disposition of its stock, property, estates and effects, the calling of special general meetings, the regulation of the meetings of the Board of Directors, the increasing or the decreasing of the number of Directors, the increasing of the capital stock, the appointment of a second Vice-President, a general Manager and a Secretary, Second Vice-and of local boards to facilitate the details of business, and President and the definition of the duties and powers of such local boards, officers. the making of calls upon the subscribed capital, the issue and allotment of shares, the appointment and removal of officers and agents of the Company, the regulation of their powers and duties, and the remuneration to be paid to them, the regulation of the transfer of stock and the form thereof, the compensation of Directors, and the establishment and regulation of agencies, the adjusting and paying of all claims against the Company, the determining of rates, rules and conditions, under which the Company's policies shall be issued, transferred or repurchased, and generally to do all other necessary matters and things they may deem expedient in conducting and managing the interests, business and affairs of the Company: Provided Proviso :l always, that all such by-laws, rules, regulations and ordi-By-laws not nances made by the Directors as aforesaid, shall only be valid valid until and binding until the next annual general meeting of the shareholders. shareholders, unless they are then approved by such meeting, and shall thereafter have force and effect as so approved or modified at such meeting; and provided further, that such Proviso. by-laws do not contravene the provisions of this Act.

10. The Directors of the Company, at a meeting held for Dividends. such specified purpose, may declare such annual or semi-annual or quarterly dividends upon the capital stock as they shall deem justified by its business: Provided always, that no part of the capital shall be appropriated to such dividend, and also, that a reserve or re-insurance fund sufficient to re-insure the Company's outstanding risks, shall be maintained; and such reserve shall be held for the benefit of policy holders exclusively. The Directors may also, by Participation resolution, order that the holders of policies or other by policy instruments shall be paid such proportion of the actual holders. realized profits, in such portions, at such times and in such manner as the said Directors may think proper, and may enter into obligations so to do, either by endorsement on the policies or otherwise: Provided always, that Proviso. the holders of the policies or other instruments so participating in the profits, shall not be in anywise answerable or responsible for the debts of the said Company. All acts Acts of done by any meeting of the Directors, or by any person act-Directors to be valid not-ing as a Director shall, notwithstanding it may afterwards withstanding be discovered that there was some defect or error in the defects of election, &c. appointment

appointment of any person attending such meeting as a Director, or acting as aforesaid, or that such person was disqualified, be as valid as if any such person had been duly appointed and was qualified to be a Director.

Calls on shares, amount and notice.

11. The shares of capital stock subscribed for shall be paid in and by such instalments and at such times and places as the Directors shall appoint: no such instalment shall exceed ten per cent., of which call thirty days' notice shall be given: and executors, administrators and curators paying instalments upon the shares of deceased shareholders shall be and they are hereby respectively indemnified for paying the same.

Forfeiture and sales of shares for non-payment.

12. If any instalment upon any share be not paid when due the Directors may declare such share forfeited, together with the amount previously paid thereon, in such manner as may be provided by the by-laws; and such forfeited share may be sold at a public sale by the Directors after such notice as they may direct; and the moneys arising therefrom shall be applied for the purposes

Proviso: Surplus to be restored to owner.

of this Act: Provided always, that in case the money realized by any sale of shares be more than sufficient to pay all arrears and interest, together with the expenses of such sale, the surplus of such money shall be paid on demand to the owner; and no more shares shall be sold than are deemed necessary to pay such arrears, interest and expenses.

Share to revert to owner on payment before sale.

13. If payment of such arrears of calls, interest and expenses be made before any share so declared forfeited shall have been sold, such share shall revert to the owner as if the same had been duly paid before forfeiture thereof:

Procedure for recovery of calls by action.

and in all actions or suits for the recovery of such arrears or calls it shall be sufficient for the Company to allege that the defendant, being the owner of such shares, is indebted to the said Company in such sum of money as the calls in arrear amount to for such and so many shares, whereby an action hath accrued to the Company by virtue of this

Proof in such case.

Act; and on the trial it shall be only necessary to prove that the defendant was owner of the said shares in the Company, that such calls were made and that notice was given as directed by this Act; and it shall not be necessary to prove the appointment of the Directors who made such calls, or any matter whatsoever other than what is

Proof of by-laws, &c

before mentioned: a copy of any by-law, rule, regulation or minute, or of any entry in any book of the Company, certified to be a true copy under the hand of the President or one of the Vice-Presidents, or the general Manager or Secretary of the Company, and sealed with the corporate seal, shall be received in all courts and proceedings as *primâ facie* evidence of such by-law, rule, regulation, minute or entry without further proof thereof, and without proof of
the

the official character or signature of the officer signing the same, or of the corporate seal.

14. No transfer of any share of the stock of the said Company shall be valid until entered in the books of the said Company, according to such form as may, from time to time, be fixed by the by-laws; and until the whole of the capital stock of the said Company is paid up it shall be necessary to obtain the consent of the Directors to an absolute transfer being made: Provided always, that no shareholder indebted to the Company shall be permitted to make an absolute transfer of any share or receive a dividend until such debt is paid or secured to the satisfaction of the Directors; and no such transfer of stock shall, at any time, be made until all calls thereon have been paid in.

Transfers not to be valid until registered.

Proviso: Debts to company and calls to be paid before transfer.

15. The transmission of any shares of the stock of the Company, in consequence of the marriage, death or insolvency of a shareholder, or by any other means than an ordinary transfer, shall be made, proved and authenticated in such form, by such proof and generally in such manner as the Directors shall, from time to time, require, or by by-law direct, before any persons claiming such shares shall be entitled to vote thereon or to receive any dividends or money payable in respect thereof.

Transmission otherwise than by transfer.

16. Aliens, as well as British subjects, and whether resident in Canada or elsewhere, may be shareholders in the said Company; and all such shareholders shall be entitled to vote on their shares equally with British subjects, and shall be also eligible to hold office as Directors or otherwise in the said Company; but the major part of the Directors of the Company shall, at all times, be persons resident in Canada and subjects of Her Majesty by birth or naturalization.

All shareholders to have equal rights: aliens may be such.

17. Each shareholder shall be individually liable to the creditors of the Company to an amount equal to the amount unpaid on the stock held by him, for the debts and liabilities thereof, but no further.

Liability of shareholders limited.

18. Every executor, administrator, tutor, curator, guardian or trustee, shall represent the stock in his hands at all meetings of the Company, and may vote accordingly as a shareholder.

Representation of shares in trust.

19. At the annual meeting of the shareholders, the election of Directors shall be held and all business transacted without the necessity for specifying such business in the notice of such meeting; and at such meeting a general balance-sheet and statement of the affairs of the Company, with a list of all the shareholders thereof, and all such further information as may be required by the by-laws,
shall

Business at annual meetings.

Special
general
meetings.
Who to pre-
side.
shall be laid before the shareholders.   Special general meetings of shareholders may be called in such manner as may
be provided for by the by-laws ; and at all meetings of the
shareholders the President, or in his absence, the Vice-
President, or in the absence of both of them, a Director or
shareholder chosen by the shareholders shall preside, who,
in case of an equality of votes, shall give the casting vote in
addition to his vote as a shareholder.

Votes on
shares.
20. At all general meetings of the said Company each
shareholder shall be entitled to give one vote for every
share held by him for not less than fourteen days prior to
the time of voting, upon which all calls then due have been
paid up ; such votes may be given either in person or by
Majority to
decide.
proxy ; and all questions proposed for the consideration of
the shareholders shall be determined by the majority of
votes,—the chairman presiding at such meeting having the
Proxies.
casting vote in case of an equality of votes.   All persons
entitled to vote at any meeting of shareholders may, by
writing under their hands (or if such persons be a corporation, then under their common seal) constitute any person
their proxy to vote at any such meeting.   No person shall
be entitled to vote as a proxy unless he shall be a shareholder
and unless such appointment shall have been produced to
the Secretary and entered in a book to be kept by him for
such purpose

Business of
the Company.
21. The said Company shall have power and authority to
carry on the business of insurance on lives, to grant, make
and effect contracts of insurance with any person or persons.
body politic or corporate upon life or lives. either for a
period of life or lives. or other periods in any way dependent
upon life or lives, and to buy, sell, grant. acquire and
otherwise dispose of the same, or sell annuities either for a
life or lives, or otherwise, and on survivorship, and to buy,
sell, grant and otherwise acquire, and otherwise dispose of
annuities and endowments of every description on the lives
of both adults and children, and to purchase contingent
rights, whether of reversion, remainder, annuities, life
policies or otherwise, and to enter into any transaction de-
pending upon the contingency of life and all other transactions usually entered into by life insurance companies or
May make
certain con-
tracts of
assurance.
associations, including re-insurance.   The Company shall
also have power and authority to make and effect contracts
of insurance with any person or persons, body politic or
corporate, against all accidents or casualties of whatsoever
nature, or from whatsoever cause arising, whereby
the insured may suffer loss or injury, or be disabled ; or in
case of death from any accident, to secure to the representative
of the person assured the payment of a certain sum of money.
upon such terms and conditions as may be agreed upon, and
generally to do and perform all other necessary matters and
                                                          things

things connected with and proper to promote those objects in the Dominion of Canada and elsewhere ; and all contracts or policies of insurance issued or entered into by the said Company shall be signed by the President or one of the Vice-Presidents, and countersigned by the general Manager or Secretary, or otherwise, as may be directed by the by-laws, rules and regulations of the Company, and being so signed and countersigned, shall be deemed valid and binding upon the Company, according to the tenor and meaning thereof.

Policies and contracts how to be executed.

22. The Company shall have power to acquire and hold real estate for the purposes of its business, and to sell or dispose of the same and acquire other property in its place, as may be deemed expedient ; and to take, hold and acquire all such lands and tenements, real or immovable estate, as shall have been *bonâ fide* mortgaged to it by way of security, or conveyed to it in satisfaction of debts previously contracted in the course of its dealings, or purchased at sales upon judgments which shall have been obtained for such debts, or purchased for the purpose of avoiding a loss to the Company in respect thereof, or of the owners thereof ; and to retain the same for a period not exceeding five years : and the Company may invest its funds or any part thereof in the public securities of the Dominion of Canada, or of any of the Provinces thereof, or of any foreign state or states, or in the stocks of any chartered bank or building society, or in the bonds or debentures of any incorporated city, town or municipality authorized to issue bonds or debentures, or in mortgages on real estate, or in such other securities of like character, and in such manner as the Directors may elect ; and may, from time to time, vary or sell the said securities, or mortgage or pledge the same as occasion may require : but not more than fifty per cent. of the whole amount of the investments of the Company, at any time shall consist of the public securities of any foreign State or States.

Company may hold real estate for its own purposes and taken in course of its business.

Proviso.

Investment of funds.

Proviso as to foreign public securities.

23. The Company shall not be bound to see to the execution of any trust, whether expressed, implied or constructive, in respect of any share ; and the receipt of any stockholder, his attorney or agent, in whose name the same may stand in the books of the Company, shall be a valid and binding discharge to the Company for any dividends or money payable in respect of such share. and whether or not notice of such trust has been given to the Company ; and the Company shall not be bound to see to the application of the money paid upon such receipt.

Company not bound to see to trusts on shares.

24. Any certificate or obligation issued by the Company, agreeing to purchase one of its policies for a fixed sum during a stated period when accompanied by the policy duly assigned or transferred, shall be negotiable, and shall convey title to the policy to the party to whom it may be so assigned or transferred.

Conveyance of title to policy.

5

25.

Failure to pay premium to void policy.

25. If any promissory note, cheque, draft or bill of exchange, received by the Company, or any officer or agent thereof, in payment either in whole or in part of any premium or premiums on any policy or policies made or issued by the Company be dishonored, or if the premiums on any policy be not paid when due to the Company, or to one of its duly authorized agents, such policy or policies shall lapse and be null and void, and the Company shall be discharged from all liabilities under the same or in respect

Proviso.

thereof : Provided always, that the Board of Directors in their discretion may subsequently receive such premiums and revive the policies on such terms as they may deem proper.

Proof of claims against the company. Affidavits.

26. Proofs of claims against the Company, under or in respect of any contracts made or policies issued by it, shall be verified by the affidavits, affirmations or declarations of the several persons subscribing thereto. All such affidavits, affirmations or declarations shall be made before the judge of any court of record, or before the mayor of any city or town, or before any notary public ; and all such officers are

Perjury.

hereby authorized to take the same ; and any person who knowingly, wilfully and corruptly makes, in any such affidavits, affirmations or declarations, any false statement of fact, matter or thing in regard to such claims, shall be guilty of wilful and corrupt perjury.

Chief place of business and branches. Compliance with foreign laws.

27. The chief place of business of the Company shall be in the City of Hamilton, Ontario. The said Company shall have full power and authority to comply with the laws of any province, state or country wherein it proposes to carry on business, so far as such laws are not inconsistent with the provisions of this Act, or of the laws of Canada, and establish therein branch offices and agencies, and appoint under the seal of the Company, local boards, managers. medical advisers and other officers.

Company to be subject to any general Act.

28. The said Company shall be subject to the provisions of all general laws now in force or that may be passed in the present or any future session respecting life insurance companies.

License must be obtained from Minister of Finance within two years.

29. The said Company shall obtain from the Minister of Finance within two years, from and after the passing of this Act, the license required by section five of this Act, in default of which this Act shall become and be null and void and of no effect, and the charter hereby granted, and all and every the rights and privileges hereby conferred shall be forfeited.

No Director or officer to be a borrower or surety for one, from Company.

30. No Director or officer of the Company shall become a borrower of any of its funds, nor become surety for any other person who shall become a borrower from the said Company.

.CHAP.

CHAP. 55.

An Act to amend the Acts respecting the " Citizens' Insurance and Investment Company," and to change the name of the said Company to that of the " Citizens' Insurance Company of Canada."

[Assented to 12th April, 1876.]

WHEREAS the Citizens' Insurance and Investment Com- Preamble. pany by their petition have represented, that it would be for the advantage of the said Company that provision should be made for a separate fund, available only to the holders of life policies in the said Company, and that the name of the said Company should be changed ; and whereas it is expedient to grant the prayer of the said petition : Therefore, Her Majesty, by and with the advice and consent of the Senate and House of Commons of Canada, enacts as follows :--

1. The name of the said company is hereby changed to Name of the Citizens' Insurance Company of Canada, by which name Company in future the said Company shall enjoy all the franchises changed. and privileges, and shall hold all the rights and assets, and shall be subject to all the liabilities heretofore held, enjoyed and possessed, or which have heretofore attached to the Citizens' Insurance and Investment Company : and no suit Suits not to now pending shall be abated by reason of the said change abate. of name, but may be continued to final judgment in the name under which it shall have been commenced.

2. From and after the date of the coming in force of this Life insurance Act, the sum of twenty-eight thousand nine hundred and fund to be created, and nineteen dollars and forty-nine cents, being the amount of what to standing at the credit of the business of life insurance consist. heretofore carried on by the said company, on the thirty-first day of December last; and also, the sum of fifty-three thousand dollars deposited in the hands of the Government of Canada, shall constitute and be a separate fund available only to the holders of life policies in the said Company ; and separate books of account shall be kept for all transactions in connection with the business of life insurance. And all moneys received subsequent to the said thirty-first Life pre-day of December last, as premiums upon policies of life miums to be kept separate. insurance or in anywise in respect of such business shall be added to the said sums, and invested and kept distinct and separate from the remaining funds of the Company, and shall be known as the Life Fund of the said Company; and such life fund shall not be available or appli- For what the cable to or liable for any losses or claims whatsoever that fund shall be available.

may happen or be made upon the said Company in respect of fire, accident or guarantee policies; but on the other hand the remaining funds and assets of the Company are not relieved from responsibility for losses on the life busi-

If found insufficient.
ness; and if the life fund should at any time hereafter be found to be insufficient for the payment of losses arising upon life insurance policies, then and in that case, the company shall pay holders of just claims upon life insurance policies issued by the Company out of any or all other funds, stocks or property of the Company from whatever source they may be derived.

CHAP. 56.

An Act respecting loans by " The British American Land Company."

[Assented to 12th April, 1876.]

Preamble.
HER Majesty, by and with the advice and consent of the Senate and House of Commons of Canada, enacts as follows :—

The said company may take eight per cent. per annum on loans.
1. Notwithstanding anything contained in chapter fifty-eight of the Consolidated Statutes of the late province of Canada, intituled: "*An Act respecting Interest,*" or in any other Act, "The British American Land Company," a corporation constituted under and by virtue of letters patent of His Majesty King William the Fourth, bearing date the twentieth day of March, one thousand eight hundred and thirty-four, ratified and confirmed by an Act passed by the Parliament of the United Kingdom of Great Britain and Ireland, in the fourth year of the reign of his said late Majesty King William the Fourth, and recognized by an Act of the legislature of the late province of Canada passed in the session held in the tenth and eleventh years of Her Majesty's reign, intituled:

10, 11 V., c. 107.
" *An Act to facilitate the proof of the charter and Act of* " *incorporation of the British American Land Company.*" and authorized to lend money in certain Provinces in British North America, now forming part of the Dominion of Canada, may hereafter stipulate for, take in advance, exact and recover on any contract or agreement whatsoever for the loan or forbearance of money or money's worth, made in Quebec or Ontario, any rate of interest or discount which may be agreed upon, not exceeding eight per cent. per annum ; but

But shall otherwise remain subject to c. 58, Con. Stat. Can.
subject to the right to take such increased rate of interest or discount, the Acts above cited shall continue to apply to the said Company.

CHAP. 57.

An Act to incorporate " The British Canadian Loan and Investment Company (Limited.) "

[*Assented to 12th April*, 1876.]

WHEREAS the persons hereinafter named have, by their Preamble. petition, prayed that they may be incorporated as a Company under the title of " The British Canadian Loan and Investment Company (Limited), " having for its object the borrowing and lending of money on real estate, and the purchase and dealing in public stocks, bonds, debentures and securities, and in stocks, bonds, debentures and other securities ; and it is expedient to grant their prayer : Therefore Her Majesty, by and with the advice and consent of the Senate and House of Commons of Canada, enacts as follows :—

1. William Thomson, William F. McMaster, the Honor- Certain able John McMurrich, David Galbraith, Donald Mackay, persons incorporated. James Browne, James K. Kerr and Laurence Buchan, and all other and every person and persons, who shall, from time to time, be possessed of any share or shares in the undertaking hereby authorized to be carried on, shall be and are hereby constituted a company and shall be one body politic and corporate by the name of "The British Canadian Loan and Corporate Investment Company (Limited) ;" and by that name shall name and have perpetual succession and a common seal, with power to general powers. break and alter such seal ; and by that name may sue and be sued, plead and be impleaded in all courts of law or equity whatever.

2. The above named persons shall be Provisional Directors Provisional of the Company and shall hold office until Directors of the Directors to hold office Company are elected as hereinafter provided, and during the until election said time the said Provisional Directors shall so hold office of Directors. they shall be vested with the full powers in every respect of ordinary Directors

3. The Company may, from time to time, invest, lend or Company advance the moneys authorized to be received, raised or bor- may lend, rowed by them in and upon the security of real or leasehold advance estate, and may purchase mortgages and stocks and deben- money, and tures of the Dominion or of any of the Provinces of the on what security. . Dominion, or of any city or county in the Dominion, municipal or other corporations, the stocks of incorporated banks, and other securities of like character, or evidences of debt, and the

the same resell as they may deem advisable ; and for that purpose may execute such assignments or other instruments **Company** as may be necessary for carrying the same into effect; the **may recover** Company may stipulate for, take, receive and exact any rate **interest and** **at what rate.** of interest or discount not exceeding eight per centum per annum, that may be lawful in the place where the contract for the same shall be made, and be executory; and they shall have power to do all acts that may be necessary for the advancing of such moneys, for the realizing of such securities and the repayment of the **May receive** moneys lent or advanced thereon with interest ; and for en- **interest on** forcing all agreements made in relation thereto, as to sale, **loans, in** **advance : and** forfeiture or otherwise ; and may stipulate for and demand, **a sinking** and receive in advance half yearly, the interest from time to **fund under** **by-laws.** time accruing on any loans granted by the Company, and may also receive an annual or semi-annual payment on any loan by way of a sinking fund for the gradual extinction of such loan, upon such terms and in such manner as may be **Expenses** regulated by the by-laws of the Company : and it shall be **may be added** lawful for the Company, instead of requiring from the bor- **to principal.** rower the payment of the expenses incidental to any loan at the time the loan is advanced, to give such time for payment of the same as they may be advised, and to add the same to the principal or interest secured by any mortgage or other security securing the loan.

Company   **4.** It shall be lawful for the Company to receive money on **may receive** **money on** deposit, and the Directors may, from time to time, with the **deposit and** consent of the majority of the shareholders present or **borrow** **money on** represented in the general meeting, borrow money upon **their deben-** the debentures of the, Company at such rate of interest **tures.** and upon such terms as they may think proper; which **Form of** **debentures,** debentures and the coupons thereto shall be in the **and amounts.** form or to the effect set forth in the Schedule to this Act annexed; and the Directors may for that purpose make or cause to be made debentures under the common seal of the Company, for sums not less than four hundred dollars or one hundred pounds sterling money, which may be pay- able at any place, and either to the order or bearer, and may have interest coupons attached; and such debentures shall be signed by the President or Vice President and the Manager of the Company, and shall be under the common seal of the Company, and shall be payable at such time and place as **How to be** shall be stated in the said debentures respectively ; and such **signed.** coupons shall be signed by the Manager only, and need not be under seal, and shall be payable at such times and places **Proviso :** as shall be stated in the same respectively : Provided that **purchaser not** no purchaser of a debenture or any debentures of the Com- **bound to** **make certain** pany shall be bound to inquire into the occasion of any such **inquiries.** loan or of the issuing of any such debenture or debentures, or into the validity of any resolution authorizing the same, or **Proviso :** the purpose for which the loan is wanted : Provided also that the

the total amount of the sums to be borrowed as aforesaid, together with the aggregate of the sum or sums then held by the Company on deposit shall never at any time, exceed the amount of the paid up capital of the Company and thirty-three and one third per cent. added thereto. *Total amount limited.*

5. The Company may hold such real estate as may be necessary for the transaction of their business, and such other real property as, being mortgaged or hypothecated to them, may be acquired by them for the protection of their interests; and the Directors shall determine when it is necessary for the purposes of such protection to acquire such real estate; and they may, from time to time, sell, mortgage, hypothecate, lease or otherwise dispose of the same: Provided always, that it shall be incumbent on the Company to sell any real estate so acquired in the prosecution of their business within ten years of the date at which it shall have become the absolute property of the Company. *What real estate the Company may hold.* *Proviso: time of holding it if not held for its own use.*

6. The head office of the Company shall be in Toronto; but the Company may have offices and agencies to transact business at such other places as may be determined upon by the Directors hereinafter referred to. *Head office to be in Toronto with agencies elsewhere.*

7. The capital stock of the Company shall be one million dollars, divided into ten thousand shares of one hundred dollars each, which shall be subscribed for, and ten per centum of the amount subscribed shall be paid in before the Company shall be organized, and twenty per cent. of the amount subscribed shall be paid in before the actual transaction of business is proceeded with; and the remainder shall be called in at such times, and in such portions as the Directors deem advisable: Provided always, that calls on the shareholders shall not be made at periods less than three months apart, and shall, at each call, not exceed ten per cent. of the stock subscribed. *Capital and shares: all to be subscribed and twenty per cent. to be paid before transacting business, and ten per cent. before organizing. Calls. Limitation of calls.*

8. It shall be lawful for the said Company, by a resolution passed at the first or any other general meeting of the shareholders to increase the capital stock from time to time, as may be deemed expedient, to any sum not exceeding the sum of five million dollars; and to raise the amount of the said new stock, either by distribution amongst the original shareholders, or by the issue of new shares, or partly in one way and partly in the other: and the said new stock shall be subject to all such incidents, both with reference to the payment of calls and forfeiture, and as to the powers of lending and borrowing, or otherwise, as the original stock. *Capital may be increased to $5,000,000*

9. No member or shareholder of the Company shall be liable *Limitation of*

liability of
shareholders.

liable for, or charged with the payment of any debt or demand due from the Company, beyond the extent of his shares in the capital of the Company not then paid up.

Liability for
calls.

10. Each shareholder shall be liable to pay the amount of any call made upon him in compliance with the conditions in section nine, to such person and at such time and place as the Directors shall appoint.

Notice before
each call.

11. The Directors shall give at least thirty days' notice before the day appointed for each call, by advertisement in one or more Toronto newspapers and by notice sent by mail to each shareholder.

When a call
shall be con-
sidered as
made.

Interest on
unpaid calls.

12. A call shall be deemed to have been made at the time when the resolution of the Directors authorizing such call was passed ; and if a shareholder shall fail to pay any call due by him, before or on the day appointed for payment thereof, he shall be liable to pay interest for the same at the rate of seven per cent. per annum, from the day appointed for payment to the time of actual payment thereof.

Notice to
shareholders
in default.

That their
shares will be
forfeited if
calls are not
paid.

13. If any shareholder fails to pay any call on the day appointed for the payment thereof, the Directors may, at any time thereafter during such time as the call may remain unpaid, serve a notice on him requiring him to pay such call, together with any interest that may have accrued due thereon by reason of such non-payment ; and such notice shall name a day (not being less than twenty-one days from the date of such notice) and a place on and at which such call and interest, and any expenses that may have been incurred by reason of every such non-payment, are to be paid ; and such notice shall also state that, in the event of non-payment at or before the time and at the place so appointed as aforesaid, the shares in respect of which such call was made will be liable to be forfeited.

In default of
payment
Directors may
declare shares
forfeited.

14. If the requirements of any such notice are not complied with, any share in respect of which such notice has been given, may, at any time thereafter before payment of all calls, interest and expenses due in respect thereof, be declared forfeited by a resolution of the Directors to that effect.

No more
shares to be
sold than will
pay arrears.

15. The Company shall not sell or transfer more of the shares of any such defaulter than will be sufficient, as nearly as can be ascertained at the time of such sale, to pay the arrears then due from such defaulter, on account of any calls, together with interest and the expenses attending such sale and declaration of forfeiture ; and if the money produced by the sale of any such forfeited share or shares be more than sufficient to pay all arrears of calls and interest thereon

due

due at the time of such sale, and the expenses aforesaid, the Surplus how
surplus shall, on demand, be paid to the defaulter, or if not to be dealt
so paid, applied in and towards satisfaction of any calls with.
made thereafter, but prior to such demand being made as
last aforesaid in respect of the remaining unsold shares of
such defaulter.

16. If the payment of such arrears of calls and interest If arrears be
and expenses be made before any share or shares so forfeited paid before
and vested in the Company shall have been sold, such share such sale.
or shares shall revert to the party to whom the same belonged before such forfeiture, in like manner as if such calls
had been duly paid.

17. A declaration in writing by the Secretary or other What shall
thereto duly authorized officer of the Company that a call be sufficient
was made and notice thereof duly served, and that default chaser of
in payment of the call was made in respect of any shares, forfeited
and that the forfeiture of such share was made by a resolution shares.
of the Directors to that effect, shall be sufficient evidence of
the facts therein stated, as against all persons entitled to such
share ; and such declaration and the receipt of the Company
for such price of such share shall constitute a good title to
such share ; and the purchaser shall thereupon be deemed the
holder of such share, discharged from all calls due prior to
such purchase, and shall be entered in the register of shareholders in respect thereof, and shall not be bound to enquire
or see to the application of the purchase money, nor shall
his title to such share be impeached or affected by any irregularity in the proceedings of such sale.

18. The Company may institute and carry on suits or Calls may be
actions against any shareholder for the recovery of arrears recovered by
and calls or for any other debt or engagement; and in such only need be
suits or actions it shall not be necessary to set forth the alleged and
special matter, but it shall be sufficient for the Company to proved.
declare that the defendant is a shareholder and is indebted
to the Company in respect of one call or more, or other money
due, whereby an action hath accrued to the Company by
virtue of this Act ; and on the trial it shall only be necessary
to prove that the defendant was owner of the said shares in
the Company, that such calls were made or such debt due,
that notice was given as directed by this Act ; and in all actions or suits by or against the Company, it shall not be
necessary to prove the appointment of the Directors or any
other matter whatsoever other than what is before mentioned;
and a copy of any by-law, rule, regulation or minute, or of Proof of by-
any entry in any book of the Company, certified to be a true other
copy or extract under the hand of the President, Vice-Presi- documents.
dent, Manager or Secretary of the Company, and sealed with
the corporate seal, shall be received in all courts and proceedings as *primâ facie* evidence thereof, without further proof,
and

and without proof of the official character or signature of the officer signing the same, or of the corporate seal.

When a
general
meeting of
shareholders
may be called.

Notice.

19. When and so soon as the capital stock shall have been subscribed, and ten per cent. of the amount so subscribed paid in, the said Provisional Directors may call a general meeting of shareholders, at some place in the City of Toronto, giving at least four weeks' notice of the time and place for holding such meeting, by publishing the same in the *Canada Gazette,* and also in some daily newspaper published in the said City of Toronto,—at which general meeting the shareholders present or represented by proxy shall elect not fewer than nine nor more than thirteen Directors, who shall constitute a Board of Directors and shall hold office until the first Wednesday in June, in the year following their election.

Directors to
be elected.

Term of office.

Who may be
Directors—
when and
where to be
elected.

Notice of
meeting.

Who may
vote.

Voting to be
by ballot.

If two or more
persons
receive an
equal number
of votes.

Election of
President and
Vice-Presi-
dent.

Vacancies
how filled.

Qualification
of Directors.

20. The said Directors shall be shareholders and they shall be elected, except as above provided, at the annual general meeting of shareholders to be holden in Toronto, on the first Wednesday in June, in each year, or such other day as may be appointed by by-law,—not less than four weeks' notice of such meeting being given as provided in the next preceding section ; and all elections of Directors shall be held and made by such of the shareholders present or represented by proxy as shall have paid the twenty per cent. above prescribed, and all calls made by the Directors and then due ; and all such elections shall be by ballot and the persons who shall have the greatest number of votes at any such election shall be Directors, except as hereinafter directed ; and if there be any doubt or difficulty in such election by reason of two or more persons receiving an equal number of votes, then there shall be a re-ballot, as between such persons, which re-ballot may be repeated as often as deemed advisable by the meeting ; or instead of a re-ballot the Directors as to whose election there is no doubt or difficulty may, if deemed advisable by the meeting, determine by ballot which of the persons having an equal number of votes shall be Director or Directors : and the said Directors as soon as may be after their election, shall proceed in like manner to elect by ballot one of their number to be President, and one to be Vice-President : and if any vacancy shall, at any time, happen amongst the said Directors, by death, resignation, disqualification or removal, or otherwise, during the current year of office, such vacancy shall be filled for the remainder of the year by the remaining Directors or a majority of them electing in such place or places a shareholder or shareholders eligible for such office : Provided, that no person shall be eligible to be or continue as Director unless he shall hold in his own name and for his own use, stock in the said Company to the amount of fifty shares, whereof at least twenty per cent. shall have been paid in and shall have paid all calls made upon

upon his stock and all liability incurred by him to the said Company : Provided further, that notwithstanding anything in this Act contained it shall be competent to the shareholders at any special or general meeting to reduce to not fewer than nine, or to increase to not more than thirteen the number of Directors. And in case it should, at any time, happen that an election of Directors of the said Company should not have been made on the day when pursuant to this Act it should have been made, the said Company shall not for that cause be deemed dissolved ; but it shall be lawful on any other day to hold and have an election in such manner as may be regulated, directed and appointed by the Directors for the time being ; and the Directors in office shall so continue until a new election is made. Number of Directors may be reduced to nine, Or increased to thirteen. Provision if election of Directors be not made on the day appointed.

21. At all meetings of Directors, a majority of the whole board shall be a quorum for the transaction of business ; and all questions before them shall be decided by a majority of votes and in case of an equality of votes, the President, Vice President, or presiding Director shall give the casting vote. Quorum of Directors. Majority to decide.

22. The Directors shall have full power and authority to make and, from time to time, alter such by-laws, rules and regulations and ordinances as shall appear to them proper and needful, touching the well ordering of the Company ; they shall also have full power and authority over the management and disposition of its stock, property, estates and effects ; the regulation of the rates, terms and conditions on which all the business of the Company shall be undertaken and conducted ; the calling of special general meetings ; the regulation of meetings of the Board of Directors ; the making of calls upon the subscribed capital subject to the limitation hereinbefore set forth ; the appointment and removal of all officers and agents of the Company, the regulation of their powers and duties, and the salaries to be paid to them ; the regulation of the transfer of stock and the form thereof ; the compensation of Directors ; the establishment and regulation of agencies ; and generally the Directors may, in addition to the powers expressly conferred upon them, exercise all such powers, execute and give all such covenants, make all such engagements and agreements and do all such acts and things as are and shall be necessary and proper for the due management of the affairs of the Company, and for carrying out the provisions of this Act according to its true meaning and spirit : But every such by-law and every repeal, amendment or re-enactment thereof, unless in the meantime confirmed at a general meeting of the Company duly called for that purpose shall only have force until the next annual meeting of the Company, and in default of confirmation thereof shall, at and from that time only, cease to have force ; and provided further, that such by-laws do not contravene the provisions of this Act. Power of Directors to make by-laws for certain purposes.

By-laws not in force until confirmed at general meeting.

Proviso:

23.

Acts of Directors to be valid notwithstanding defect in their appointment.

23. The acts of the Directors, or of any committee appointed by the Directors, shall, notwithstanding it be afterwards discovered that there was some defect in the appointment of any such Directors or any member of such committee, or that they or any of them were or was disqualified, be as valid as if such person had been duly appointed and was qualified to be a Director.

Before commencing &c, company must obtain certificate of Treasury Board.

24. Notwithstanding anything in this Act to the contrary, the Company shall not be organized nor commence business until they shall have obtained from the Treasury Board a certificate to the effect that it has been proved to the satisfaction of the board that such amounts of capital have been *bona fide* subscribed and paid as are by this Act required to be subscribed and paid respectively before organizing and commencing business or proceeding with the actual transaction of business, under the terms of this Act.

Certificate must be obtained within two years.

25. The Company shall obtain from the Treasury Board, within two years from and after the passing of this Act, the certificate by this Act required to be obtained by the Company before it can commence business; in default of which this Act shall become and be null and void and of no effect, and the charter hereby granted and all and every the rights and privileges hereby conferred shall be forfeited.

Dividends and notice thereof.

26. It shall be the duty of the Directors of the Company to declare and make quarterly or half-yearly dividends of so much of the profits of the Company as to the majority of them may seem advisable, and to give public notice of the payment of such dividends at least ten days previously.

Lien of Company thereon.

27. The Directors may deduct from the dividends payable to any shareholder all such sums of money as may be due from him to the Company on account of calls or otherwise.

Liability of directors paying dividend out of capital or when the Co., is insolvent.

28. If the Directors of the Company declare and pay any dividend when the Company is insolvent, or any dividend the payment of which renders the Company insolvent or diminishes the capital stock thereof, they shall be jointly and severally liable, as well to the Company as to the individual shareholders and creditors thereof, for all the debts of the Company then existing, and for all thereafter contracted during their continuance in office, respectively:

Proviso: how a director may avoid such liability.

Provided, that if any Director present when such dividend is declared do forthwith, or if any Director then absent do within twenty-four hours after he shall have become aware thereof and able so to do, enter on the minutes of the Board of Directors his protest against the same, and within eight days thereafter publish such protest in at least one newspaper published at, or as near as may be possible to the place in which the office or chief place of business of the
                                                        Company

Company is situated, such Director may thereby, and not otherwise, exonerate himself from such liability.

29. The Directors may, from time to time, appoint one or more members of the board to accept and hold any lands or property in trust for the Company, and shall cause all such deeds and things to be made and done as shall be requisite to vest such lands or property in the person or persons so appointed ; and they may, from time to time, remove any such person or persons and appoint another or others instead. *Directors may appoint Trustees.*

30. At all meetings of the Company each shareholder shall be entitled to give one vote for every share held·by him, upon which all calls then due have been paid, for not less than fourteen days prior to the time of voting. Such votes may be given either in person or by proxy, the holder of any such proxy being himself a shareholder and qualified to vote. And all questions proposed for the consideration of the shareholders shall be determined by the majority of votes—the chairman presiding at such meeting having the casting vote in case of an equality of votes : Provided, that no salaried officer, except Directors, and no paid clerk or other employee of said Company shall vote either in person or by proxy at the election of Directors. *Shareholders' votes. Proxies. Majority to decide. Proviso : casting vote.*

31. At every annual meeting of the shareholders the outgoing Directors shall submit a clear and full statement of the affairs of the Company, shewing in detail on the one hand the debts, liabilities and engagements of the Company, and on the other the assets and resources thereof. They shall also exhibit a full statement of the extent and value of the securities held by the Company and such other information as will enable the shareholders to judge of the true position of the Company and its transactions. *Statement of affairs at annual meetings.*

32. The Company shall keep in a book or books a register of the shareholders of the Company, and therein shall be fairly and distinctly entered from time to time the following particulars :—the names and addresses and the occupations, if any, of the shareholders of the Company, and the number of shares held by each shareholder, distinguishing each share by its number, and the amount paid or agreed to be considered as paid on the shares of each shareholder ; and such book or books shall be open to the public at all reasonable times. *Register of shareholders to be kept.*

33. The Company shall transmit annually to the Minister of Finance a statement in duplicate, verified by the oath of the President, and Manager or Secretary, setting out the capital stock of the Company, the proportion thereof paid up, the names of the shareholders, with the places of their abode respectively and the number of shares held by each of them, the *Yearly statement to be sent to the Minister of Finance*

the assets and liabilities of the Company, the amount
of property held by them and such other details as
to the nature and extent of the business of the Company
as may, from time to time, be required by the said
Minister of Finance, or in pursuance of any general Act of

Up to 31st December, then last.

Parliament, passed to regulate trust companies; and such
statement shall be made up to the thirty-first day of December
in each year; and a copy of each such statement shall be

Copies to Parliament.

transmitted by the Company to the Clerk of each House of
Parliament within the first fifteen days of the first session
of Parliament after the day to which it is made up.

Notice of trust on shares not to affect company.

34. Notice of any trust expressed, implied or constructive, shall not be entered on the register, nor shall any such
notice in any way affect the Company as to its shares or any
transfer or any transmission thereof.

Persons to whom shares are allotted to be deemed members.

35. When any person makes application in writing, signed
by him, for an allotment of shares, and any shares or share
are or is allotted to him in pursuance of such application,
he shall be deemed conclusively to have agreed to become a
shareholder of the Company in respect of the shares so allotted, and he shall be entered on the register of shareholders
in respect thereof accordingly.

Shares in the name of two or more persons.

36. If any share stands in the name of two or more persons, the first named in the register of such persons shall, as
regards voting at meetings, receipt of dividends, service of
notices, and all other matters connected with the Company
(except transfer), be deemed the sole holder thereof; no share
in the Company shall be subdivided.

Service on the Company.

37. Any summons, notice, order or other document, required to be served upon the Company, may be served by
leaving the same at the office of the said Company at Toronto.

Authentica- tion of notices by the Company:

38. Any summons, notice, order or proceeding, requiring
authentication by the Company, may be signed by any
Director, Manager, Secretary or other authorized officer of the
Company, and need not be under the common seal of the
Company; and the same may be in writing or in print, or
partly in writing and partly in print.

Service of notice by the Company on members.

39. Notices required to be served by the Company upon
the shareholders may be served either personally or by leaving the same for, or sending them through the post in prepaid letters, addressed to the shareholders at their registered
places of abode.

Notices to members sent by post.

40. A notice or other document served by post by the
Company on a shareholder, shall be taken as served at the
time

time when the letter containing it would be delivered in the ordinary course of post; to prove the fact and time of service it shall be sufficient to prove that such letter was properly addressed, and was put into the post office, and the time when it was put in, and the time requisite for its delivery, in the ordinary course of post.

41. All notices directed to be given to the shareholders shall, with respect to any share to which persons are jointly entitled, be given to whichever of such persons is first named in the register of shareholders ; and notice so given shall be deemed sufficient notice to all the proprietors of such share. *Notice to joint shareholders.*

42. Every person who, by operation of law, transfer or other means whatsoever, shall become entitled to any share shall be bound by any and every notice which previously to his name and address being entered upon the register of shareholders in respect of such share shall have been given to the person from whom he shall derive his title. *Notices binding on transferees.*

43. There shall be a book called the register of transfers provided, and in such book shall be entered the particulars of every transfer of shares in the capital of the Company. *Register for transfers.*

44. The Directors may decline to register any transfer of shares belonging to any shareholder who is indebted to the Company. *As to transfers by debtors to Company.*

45. Every instrument of transfer of any share in the Company shall be executed by the transferrer and transferee, and the transferrer shall be deemed to remain the holder of such share and a shareholder of the Company in respect thereof, until the name of the transferee shall be entered in the register of shareholders in respect thereof. *Transfers how to be executed.*

46. Shares in the Company shall be transferred in the form in the Schedule to this Act annexed, or such other form as the Directors may, from time to time, prescribe. *Form of transfer.*

47. Any person becoming entitled to a share in consequence of the death, bankruptcy or insolvency of any shareholder or in consequence of the marriage of any female shareholder, may be registered as a shareholder upon such evidence being produced as shall, from time to time, be required by the Directors, and on production of a request in writing in that behalf signed by him,—his signature being attested by at least one witness, which shall be conclusive evidence of his having agreed to become a shareholder. *Transfer by bankruptcy, marriage of female members, &c.* *How proved.*

48. Any person who has become entitled to a share in consequence of the death, bankruptcy or insolvency of any shareholder, or in consequence of the marriage of any female shareholder *Nominee of representative of deceased, &c.*

shareholder, may, instead of being registered himself, elect by declaration of transmission to be made and executed as hereinbefore and hereinafter provided to have some person to be named by him registered as a shareholder in respect of such share.

Transfer to nominee.

49. The person so becoming entitled shall testify such election by executing to his nominee an instrument of transfer of such share.

Evidence of transfer.

50. Every such instrument of transfer shall be presented to the Directors accompanied by such evidence as the Directors may require to prove the title of the transferrer, and shall be retained by the Company.

Transfer by personal representative.

51. Any transfer of the share or other interest of a deceased shareholder made by his personal representative shall, notwithstanding such personal representative may not himself be a shareholder, be of the same validity as if he had been a shareholder at the time of his execution of the instrument of transfer.

Interpretation clause.

"Company."
"Directors."
"Secretary."

52. In this Act the following words and expressions have the several meanings hereby assigned to them unless there be something in the subject or context repugnant to such construction, that is to say : the expression "the Company" means the "British Canadian Loan and Investment Company (Limited)" in this Act mentioned and described ; the expressions "the Directors" and "the Secretary" mean the Directors and the Secretary respectively for the time being of the said Company.

Company to be subject to any general Act.

53. The Company hereby incorporated shall be subject to such provisions of any general Acts passed by Parliament, during the present or any future session, as may be declared to apply to loan and investment companies or which Parliament may deem necessary for the public interest.

SCHEDULE.

INSTRUMENT OF TRANSFER OF SHARE.

I, A. B., of   do hereby, for value, transfer to C. D., of   , share (*or* shares) now standing in my name in the books of the   company, to hold to him, his executors, administrators and assigns, subject to the conditions on which I now hold the same, and I, the said C. D., by this writing, accept the said share (*or* shares), subject to the conditions   aforesaid,

aforesaid, and agree to become a shareholder of the said company, as witness our respective hands, this
            day of   , in the year of
Our Lord

.   A. B.
    C. D.

Signed by the above named A. B. }
and C. D., respectively, in the pre- }
sence of   }
            E. F.

DEBENTURE.

Debenture No.   transferable $ (or £   ),
under the authority of an Act of the Parliament of the
Dominion of Canada,   Victoria, chapter   .

" The British Canadian Loan and Investment Company (Limited) " promise to pay to the bearer the sum of
dollars (or   pounds sterling) on the   day of   ,
in the year of Our Lord, one thousand eight hundred and
    , at the head office of the company in Toronto (or at
            in England) with interest at the rate of
per centum per annum, to be paid half yearly on presentation of the proper coupon for the same hereunto annexed,
say on the   days of   and   in each year, at the
head office aforesaid (or at   ).

Dated at Toronto (or   ) the   day of
A. D. 18   .

For the president and directors of " The British Canadian
Loan and Investment Company (Limited)."

            (Seal.)   A. B.,
            President (or Vice President.)
C. D.,
    Manager.

COUPON.

" The British Canadian Loan and Investment Company
(Limited.)"

No.   , $ (or £   ) half yearly dividend due
        day of   , 18   , for $ (or £   )
at   per cent. per annum, payable at the head office, at
Toronto (or at   , England.)

For the president and directors.

            C. D.,
            Manager.

CHAP

CHAP. 58.

An Act to incorporate " The England and Canada Mortgage Security Company."

[*Assented to 12th April, 1876.*]

Preamble.

WHEREAS the persons hereinafter named and others, propose to establish a joint stock company, and have petitioned for an Act of incorporation for the said company, and it is expedient to grant the prayer of the said petition: Therefore Her Majesty, by and with the advice and consent of the Senate and House of Commons of Canada, enacts as follows:—

Certain persons incorporated.

1. William Kersteman, Remy Elmsley, Alexander Robertson, James E. Robertson, Samuel George Wood and all other person and persons, as shall, from time to time, be possessed of any share or shares in the undertaking, shall be united into a Company, and shall be one body politic and corporate by the name of "The England and Canada Mortgage Security Company," and by that name shall have perpetual succession and a common seal, with power to break and alter such seal, and by that name shall sue and be sued, plead and be impleaded in all courts whatsoever.

Capital stock and shares.

Provision for increase.

2. The capital stock of the Company shall be five hundred thousand pounds sterling, divided into fifty thousand shares, of ten pounds each, of which twenty per centum shall be paid in before the actual transaction of business is proceeded with; but it shall be lawful for the said Company, by a resolution passed at the first or any other general meeting of the shareholders, to increase the capital stock, from time to time, as may be deemed expedient to any sum not exceeding the sum of one million of pounds sterling, and to raise the amount of the said new stock either by distribution amongst the original shareholders or by the issue of new shares, or partly in one way and partly in the other, and the said new stock shall be subject to all such incidents, both with reference to the payment of calls and forfeiture, and as to the powers of lending and borrowing or otherwise (as hereinafter provided) as the original stock.

Incidents of new stock.

Business of the Company.

3. The Company, after paying and discharging all costs, charges and expenses incurred in applying for and obtaining the passing of this Act and all other expenses preparatory or relating thereto, may lend and advance money by way of loan or otherwise, for periods of not less than three months, on the security of real estate, and Government stocks and debentures of the Dominion, or of any of the Provinces of the

the Dominion, or of any of the cities or counties therein, and
may buy and sell debts secured by mortgage, or pledge of
freehold and leasehold lands, and may advance or loan
money on such securities.

4. The Directors may, from time, to time, with the consent Borrowing
of the shareholders present or represented in a general meet- powers of the
ing, borrow money on the debentures of the Company, at and rate of
such rates of interest not exceeding eight per centum per interest not
annum as may be lawful or may lawfully be taken, received, cent.
reserved or exacted either by individuals or by bodies
corporate in the place where the contract is made or
is executory and upon such terms as they may
think proper, and the Directors may, for that purpose, make
or cause to be made, debentures under the common seal of
the Company for sums of not less than one hundred pounds
sterling, which may be made payable at any place
either to order or bearer, and may have interest
coupons attached: Provided, that no lender shall be Proviso : in
bound to enquire into the occasion for any such loan favor of
or into the validity of any resolution authorizing the
same or the purpose for which such loan is wanted: Pro- Proviso :
vided also, that the total amount of the sums to be borrowed, total amount
as aforesaid, shall never exceed the amount of the subscribed ed limited.
capital of the Company, which has *bonâ fide* been paid up,
and thirty-three and one-third per cent. added thereto.

5. The Company may hold such real estate, including Power to hold
lands actually required by them for an office in London, real estate
.England, or in the City of Toronto, as may be acquired by purposes, &c.
them for the protection of their investments, and may, from
time to time, sell, mortgage, lease or otherwise dispose of the
same : Provided always, that the Company shall sell any Proviso.
such real estate (the premises occupied by the Company as
aforesaid excepted) within ten years after acquiring it.

6. The head office of the Company shall be in Toronto ; Head office
but the Company may have offices in such other places and agencies,
as the Directors may appoint, and may appoint agents to of debentures,
manage them, and for such other purposes as the Directors &c.
shall determine ; and the debentures, coupons or dividends
of the Company may be made payable at any place in London, England, or in Toronto, or elsewhere.

7. The transmission of the interest in any share of the Transmission
capital stock, in consequence of the marriage, death or of shares
insolvency of a shareholder, or by any other means than than by
an ordinary transfer, shall be authenticated and made in such transfer.
form, by such proof, and generally in such manner as may
be determined by by-law.

8. When any person makes application in writing signed Who shall be
6½   by

deemed members.

by him for any allotment of shares, and any shares or share are or is allotted to him in pursuance of such application, he shall be deemed conclusively to have agreed to become a shareholder of the Company in respect of the shares so allotted, and he shall be entered in the register of share-

Certificate of shares.

holders in respect thereof accordingly, and every shareholder, on the payment of one shilling, may obtain a certificate of membership, and such certificate shall be *primâ facie* evidence of the title of the shareholder therein named to the share or shares therein specified.

Joint holders of shares.

9. If any shares or share stand in the name of two or more persons, the first named shall be deemed the sole holder thereof in all matters connected with the Company.

Transfers, when valid.

10. No share shall be transferred without the consent and approval of the Directors, unless the full amount of such share shall have been paid up, nor shall be held valid until entry thereof has been duly made in the books of the Company.

Enforcement of calls.

What only need be alleged and proved in suits for calls.

11. The Company may enforce payment of all calls and interest thereon by action in any competent court ; and in such action it shall not be necessary to set forth the special matter, but it shall be sufficient to declare that the defendant is the holder of one share or more, stating the number of shares, and is indebted in the sum of money to which the calls in arrear amount, in respect of one call or more upon one share or more, stating the number of calls and the amount of each, whereby an action hath accrued to the Company under this Act ; and a certificate under their seal, and purporting to be signed by the President, Vice-President or general manager of the Company to the effect that the defendant is a shareholder, that such call or calls have been made, and that so much is due by him and unpaid thereon, shall be received in all courts of law and equity as *primâ facie* evidence to that effect.

Interest on calls.

12. Interest shall accrue and fall due at the rate of six per centum per annum upon the amount of any unpaid call from the day appointed for payment of such call.

Forfeiture of shares for non-payment of calls.

13. If after such demand or notice as the by-laws of the Company may prescribe, any calls made upon any share or shares be not paid up within such time as by such by-law may be limited in that behalf, the Directors in their discretion, by vote to that effect, reciting the facts, and the same being duly recorded in their minutes, may summarily declare any shares whereon such payment is not made forfeited, and the same shall thereupon become the property of the Company.

14.

14. The Company shall not sell nor transfer more of the shares of any such defaulter than will be sufficient, as nearly as can be ascertained at the time of such sale, to pay the arrears then due from such defaulter, on account of any calls, together with interest and the expenses attending such sale and declaration of forfeiture, and if the money produced by the sale of any such forfeited share or shares be more than sufficient to pay all arrears of calls and interest thereon due at the time of such sale, and the expenses aforesaid, the surplus shall, on demand, be paid to the defaulter, or if not so paid, applied in and towards satisfaction of any calls made thereafter, but prior to such demand being made as last aforesaid, in respect to the remaining unsold shares of such defaulter.

No more shares to be sold than are required to pay arrears.

15. The Directors shall be elected at the annual general meeting of shareholders to be holden on the first Thursday in May, in each year, or such other day as may be appointed by by-law, not less than one months' notice of such meeting being given; and at such meeting a full and detailed statement of the financial affairs of the Company up to the thirty-first day of December, then last past, shall be submitted to the stockholders and shall appear in the books of the Company and be open for the inspection of the shareholders, and also a similar statement to be prepared at the expiration of every month. Such general meeting may be adjourned by a vote of the majority, and all elections of Directors shall be held and made at such meeting by such of the shareholders present or represented by proxy as shall have paid the ten per cent. above prescribed, and all calls made by the Directors and then due, and all such elections shall be by ballot, and the persons who have the greatest number of votes at any such election shall be Directors except as hereinafter directed; and if there is any doubt or difficulty in such election by reason of two or more persons receiving an equal number of votes, then there shall be a re-ballot as between such persons, or the Directors of whose election there is no such doubt, may determine which of the persons having an equal number of votes shall be Director or Directors, and the said Directors shall then proceed in like manner to elect by ballot one of their number to be President and one to be Vice-President. If any vacancy shall at any time happen amongst the Directors by death, resignation, disqualification, removal or otherwise during the current year of office, such vacancy shall be filled for the remainder of the year by a majority of the remaining Directors : Provided, that no person shall be eligible to be or continue a Director unless he shall hold in his name and for his own use, stock in the said Company to the amount of ten shares, whereof, at least ten per cent. shall have been paid in, and shall have paid all calls made upon his stock and all liability incurred by him to the said Company.

Election of Directors.

Statement of affairs.

Proceedings at and with respect to general meetings. Elections.

Ballot.

Ties.

President and Vice-President. Vacancies, how filled.

Proviso : qualification of Director.

16.

Number of
Directors and
quorum.

16. The number of Directors shall be thirteen, and at all meetings of Directors a majority of the whole board shall be a quorum for the transaction of business, and all questions before them shall be decided by a majority of votes; and in case of an equality of votes, the President, or Vice-President or presiding Director shall give the casting vote.

Term of office
of Provisional
Directors.

17. So soon as the Directors shall have been appointed, the powers and functions of the provisional Directors shall cease and determine.

Provision in
case of failure
of election.

18. If at any time an election of Directors be not made, or do not take effect at the proper time, the Company shall not be held to be thereby dissolved, but such election may take place at any general meeting of the Company duly called for that purpose.

Directors may
make by laws,
and for what
purposes.

19. Directors of the Company shall have full power in all things to administer the affairs of the Company, and to make by-laws regulating the issue and registration of certificates of stock, the transfer of stock, the calling in of amounts due on subscribed stock, the declaration and payment of dividends, the appointment, functions, duties and removal of all agents, officers and servants of the Company; the security to be given by them to the Company, their remuneration and that, if any, of the Directors, the appointment or election of Directors and other officers, and the time and mode of calling and holding ordinary and extraordinary or other meetings of the Company and of the Directors, and where the business of the Company shall be conducted, the requirements as to proxies, and the procedure in all things at such meetings, the imposition and recovery of all penalties and forfeitures admitting of regulation by by-law, and the conduct in all other particulars of the affairs and business of the Company; and may, from time to time, repeal, amend or re-enact the same.

Confirmation
of by-laws by
shareholders
required.

20. Provided always, that all such by-laws, rules, regulations and ordinances made by the Directors as aforesaid, shall only be valid and binding until the next annual general meeting of the shareholders, unless they are then approved by such meeting, and shall thereafter have force and effect as so approved or modified at such meeting.

Copy of by-
law to be
evidence.

21. A copy of any by-law of the Company under their seal, and purporting to be signed by any of the officers aforesaid, shall be received as *primâ facie* evidence of such by-law in all courts of law and equity.

Votes on
shares

22. Every shareholder in the Company shall be entitled to one vote for each share he may hold in the capital stock of the Company at least one month prior to the time of voting: Provided, that no shareholder being in arrears in respect

respect of any call shall be entitled to vote at any meeting of the Company, and the votes of the shareholders may be given in person or by proxy.

23. So soon as the whole of the capital stock shall have been subscribed, and ten per centum thereof paid up and deposited to the credit of the said Company in some chartered bank or agency thereof in Canada, the Directors shall call a general meeting of the shareholders to be held at the head office in Toronto, of which meeting not less than one month's notice shall have been given by public advertisement in the *Canada Gazette*, for the purpose of passing by-laws for the management of the affairs of the Company, the election of Directors, the appointment of officers, and generally for the exercise of the powers conferred on the Company. First meeting of shareholders, when to be held.

24. Annual general meetings and special general meetings of shareholders of the Company shall be called by public notice, advertised for at least one month in the *Canada Gazette*, and in a Toronto newspaper. Annual and special general meetings.

25. The Company shall cause a book or books to be kept by the manager or by some other officer specially charged with that duty, wherein shall be kept recorded: Books to be kept by the manager, &c., and what to contain.

1. A correct copy of the Act incorporating the Company, as also of any and every by-law thereof;

2. The names, alphabetically arranged, of all persons who are or have been shareholders;

3. The address of every such person while such shareholder;

4. The number of shares of stock held by each shareholder;

5. All transfers of stock in the order as presented to the Company for entry thereof;

6. The names, addresses and callings of all persons who are or who have been Directors of the Company with the several dates at which each became or ceased to be a Director.

26. The Company may stipulate for and demand and receive in advance half yearly, the interest from time to time accruing on any loan granted by the Company, and may also receive an annual or semi-annual payment on any loan by way of a sinking fund for the gradual extinction of such loan. Interest may be taken in advance.

Stock and transfer books to be open. **27.** The stock and transfer books shall, during office hours, be kept open for the inspection of shareholders or their representatives, and they may make extracts therefrom; such books shall be *primâ facie* evidence of all facts purporting to be therein stated.

Lands may be held in trust for the Company. **28.** The Directors may, from time to time, appoint one or more members of their board to accept and hold any lands or property in trust for the Company, or remove such person or persons and appoint another or others in their stead.

Responsibility of Directors limited. **29.** Every Director of the Company, his heirs, executors and administrators and estate and effects respectively, shall be charged only with such money as he shall actually receive, and shall not be answerable for his co-Directors or any of them,—but each of them for his own acts, deeds and defaults only,—nor for the acts or deeds of any officer or officers of the Company, nor for the insufficiency of title to any property which may be acquired by order of the Directors, or upon which any moneys of the Company shall be loaned or invested, nor for any loss or misfortune whatever to the Company unless the same shall happen through his own wilful neglect or default.

Division of profits. **30.** The profits of the Company, as far as the same shall extend, shall be divided as follows:—

There shall in the first place be set apart for the purposes of forming a reserve fund to meet contingencies and for equalizing dividends, such sum not less in any year than two and a-half per centum upon the net profits of the business of such year as the Directors shall, from time to time, think fit, and the residue of such profit shall be divided amongst the shareholders in such manner as the Directors, with the sanction of the Company in general meeting assembled shall determine.

Investment of reserve fund. **31.** The Directors may, from time to time, invest the sum set apart as a reserve fund in such good and convertible securities as they, in their discretion, may select.

Dividends not to reduce capital. **32.** The Company shall not declare any dividend whereby the capital stock will be in any way reduced.

Penalty on Directors paying dividends out of capital. **33.** If the Directors of the Company declare and pay any dividend when the Company is insolvent, or any dividend the payment of which renders the Company insolvent, or diminishes the capital stock thereof, they shall be jointly and severally liable, as well to the Company as to the individual shareholders and creditors thereof, for all the debts of the Company then existing, and for all thereafter contracted **How a direc-** during their continuance in office, respectively; but if any
Director

Director present when such dividend is declared do forthwith, or if any Director then absent do within twenty four hours after he shall have become aware thereof and able so to do, enter on the minutes of the Board of Directors his protest against the same, and within eight days thereafter publish such protest in at least one newspaper published at, or as near as may be possible to the place in which the office or chief place of business of the Company is situated, such Director may thereby, and not otherwise, exonerate himself from such liability.

34. The Directors may deduct from the dividends payable to any member, all such sums of money as may be due from him to the Company on account of calls or otherwise.

35. Notice of any dividend that may have been declared, shall be given to each member, and no dividend shall bear interest against the Company.

36. Notices requiring to be served by the Company upon the members, may be served either personally, or by leaving the same for, or sending them through the post office in prepaid letters addressed to the members at their registered places of abode; the proof of such posting will be evidence of service.

37. Any summons, notice, order or proceeding requiring authentication by the Company, may be signed by the Manager or any Director or officer of the Company, and need not be under the common seal of the Company, and the same may be in writing or print, or both.

38. Every person who, by operation of law, transfer or other means whatsoever, shall become entitled to any share or shares, shall be bound by any and every notice which, previously to his name and address being entered upon the register of shareholders in respect of such shares shall have been given to the person from whom he shall derive his title.

39. Every shareholder, until the whole stock has been paid up, shall be individually liable to the creditors of the Company to an amount equal to that not paid thereon.

40. The shareholders of the Company shall not, as such, be held responsible for any act, default or liability whatsoever of the Company, or for any engagement, claim, payment, loss, injury, transaction, matter or thing whatsoever, relating to or connected with the Company beyond the amount of their respective shares in the capital stock thereof not paid up. .

41.

Actions by or against shareholders.　**41.** Any description of action may be prosecuted and maintained between the Company and any shareholder thereof.

Company not to do banking business.　**42.** Nothing in this Act contained shall authorize the said Company to engage in the business of banking, or to issue any note of a character to be circulated as money or as the note of a bank.

Company subject to general Acts.　**43.** The Company hereby incorporated shall be subject to such provisions of any general Acts passed by Parliament, during the present or any future session, as may be declared to apply to loan and investment companies, or which Parliament may deem necessary for the public interest.

Statement to be furnished yearly to the Minister of Finance, and what it must contain.　**44.** The Company shall transmit annually, in the month of January, to the Minister of Finance a statement in duplicate made up to the thirty-first day of December, then last, and verified by the affidavits of the President or Vice-President, and of the General Manager of the Company, setting out the capital stock of the Company, the proportion thereof paid up, the names of the shareholders, with their places of abode and the number of shares held by each of them, the assets and liabilities of the Company, and such other details as to the nature and extent of the business of the Company as may from time to time be required by the Minister of Finance; and a copy of each such statement shall be transmitted by the Company to the Clerk of each House of Parliament within the first fifteen days of the first Session of Parliament after the day to which it has been made up.

Company must obtain certificate from Treasury Board before commencing business.　**45.** Notwithstanding anything in this Act to the contrary, the Company shall not be organized nor commence business until they shall have obtained from the Treasury Board a certificate to the effect that it has been proved to the satisfaction of the Board that such amounts of capital have been *bonâ fide* subscribed and paid up as are by this Act required to be subscribed and paid up respectively before organizing and commencing business under the terms of this Act.

Must obtain the same within two years.　**46.** The Company shall obtain from the Treasury Board within two years from and after the passing of this Act the certificate by this Act required to be obtained by the Company before it can commence business, in default of which this Act shall become and be null and void and of no effect, and the Charter hereby granted and all and every the rights and privileges hereby conferred, shall be forfeited.

CHAP.

CHAP. 59.

An Act to incorporate "The Scottish Canadian Loan Company."

[*Assented to 12th April, 1876.*]

WHEREAS John Turner, David Galbraith, Thomas Mc- Preamble.
Cracken, James David Edgar and others have, by their
petition, represented that they are desirous of organizing a
Company under the name of "The Scottish Canadian Loan
Company," with full powers to lend money and to act as an
agent for the lending of money in the Dominion of Canada,
with the right to raise money by the issue of debentures and
otherwise; and have prayed that they may be incorporated
for that purpose, and it is expedient to grant the prayer of
such petition: Therefore Her Majesty, by and with the advise and consent of the Senate and House of Commons of
Canada, enacts as follows:—

1. The several persons hereinbefore named, and such other Incorpora-
persons as may hereafter become shareholders in the Com- tion.
pany by this Act created, are hereby constituted and declared
to be a corporation under the name and style of "The Corporate
Scottish Canadian Loan Company," and by that name may name, &c.
sue or be sued in all courts.

2. The said above named persons shall be the Provisional Provisional
Directors of the said Company, with power to add to their Directors.
number, and shall hold office as such until Directors of the
Company are elected as hereinafter provided.

3. The said Company are hereby empowered to lay out Application
and invest their capital in the first place in paying and of capital and
discharging all costs, charges and expenses incurred in apply- business of
the Company.
ing for and obtaining the passing of this Act, and all other
preliminary expenses attending the establishment of the
said Company; and the remainder of such capital, or so much
thereof as may, from time to time, be deemed necessary in the
manner and for the purposes hereinafter mentioned, that is
to say: the said Company may, from time to time, lend and Rate of
advance money at such rate of interest, not exceeding eight interest limi-
per cent. per annum, as shall be lawful or may be lawfully ted.
taken, received, reserved or enacted, either by individuals or
by corporate bodies, in the place where the contract for the
same shall be made or be executory, and in advance or
otherwise as may be agreed upon, by way of loan or otherwise, upon the security of real estate in Canada, or Dominion
stock or securities; and may purchase mortgages upon real Buying mort-
estate and Dominion stock or securities, or Provincial gages, &c.
debentures,

debentures, or debentures of cities or counties, and may resell any of such securities, and for that purpose may execute all necessary instruments; and for the foregoing purposes the Company may apply moneys hereinafter authorized to be borrowed by them.

Company may take interest in advance, and payment by instalments.

4. The Company may stipulate for payment of any loan made by them in one sum or in instalments, and may stipulate for and demand and receive in advance, half-yearly, the interest from time to time accruing on any loans granted by the Company, and may add the principal and interest upon any loans together, and make the same payable in instalments, and may also receive an annual, semi-annual or quarterly payment on any loan by way of a sinking fund for the gradual extinction of such loan, and upon such terms and in such manner as may be regulated by the by-laws of the Company; and it shall and may be lawful for the said Company to sell and assign any mortgage or mortgages, or other security made to or held by the said Company.

May add expenses to principal.

5. It shall be lawful for the said Company, instead of requiring from the borrower the payment of expenses incidental to any loan at the time the loan is advanced, to give such time for the payment of the same as may be advised, and to add the same to the principal or interest secured by any mortgage or other security securing the loan.

Company may borrow money; and on what terms and security.

6. The Directors may, from time to time, with the consent of the Company in general meeting assembled, borrow money on behalf of the Company at such rates of interest and upon such terms as they may, from time to time, think proper; and the Directors may for that purpose make and execute any mortgages, bonds or other instruments, under the common seal of the Company, for sums of not less than one hundred dollars each; or assign, transfer or deposit by way of equitable mortgage or otherwise, any of the documents of title, deeds, muniments, securities or property of the Company, and either with or without power of sale, or other special provisions as the Directors may deem expedient:

Proviso: amount limited.

Provided always that the aggregate of the sum or sums so borrowed shall not at any time exceed the amount of the subscribed capital of the Company *bonâ fide* paid up, and thirty-three and one third per cent. added thereto, and no lender shall be bound to enquire into the occasion for any such loan, or into the validity of any resolution authorizing the same, or the purpose for which such loan is wanted:

Proviso: when only the Company may commence business. Must obtain certificates of Treasury Board.

Provided also that the Company shall not commence business unless and until at least twenty per cent. of its subscribed capital has been *bonâ fide* paid up, nor unless the amount thereof so paid up shall be at least two hundred thousand dollars; nor shall such Company organize or transact business until they shall have obtained from the Treasury Board a certificate to the effect that

that it has been proved to the satisfaction of the board that
such amounts of capital have been *bonâ fide* subscribed
and paid up, as are by this Act required to be subscribed
and paid up respectively before organizing and commencing
business under the terms of this Act.

7. The capital stock of the said Company shall be one
million dollars divided into ten thousand shares of one hundred dollars each : Provided that it shall and may be lawful
for the said Company to increase its capital stock to such
sum as shall not in the whole exceed two millions of
dollars, as a majority of the shareholders present or represented at a general meeting expressly convened for that purpose, or at a regular annual meeting, shall agree upon,—in
which case at least six months' notice shall be given of
the intention so to increase the capital stock ; and the
said increased stock may be raised either by distribution
among the original shareholders, or by the issue of new shares,
or partly in one way and partly in the other, but subject
in any case to all the incidents of the original stock. *Capital stock and shares. Provision for increase to $2,000,000. How to be raised.*

8. For the purpose of organizing the said Company the
Provisional Directors or a majority of them may cause stock
books to be opened in which shall be recorded the names
and subscriptions of such persons as desire to become shareholders in the said Company ; and such stock books shall be
opened in such places, and for such length of time as the
said Provisional Directors may deem necessary. *Stock books may be opened.*

9. When and so soon as one million dollars of the said
capital stock shall have been subscribed and at least ten
per cent. of the amount so subscribed paid up, the said
Provisional Directors may call a general meeting of the
shareholders to be held at such place in Canada as they
may determine,—giving at least six weeks' notice of the time
and place of holding such meeting by publishing the same
in some daily newspaper published at the city where such
meeting is to be held, and in the *Canada Gazette* ; at which
meeting the shareholders present or represented by proxy
shall elect not less than nine nor more than thirteen shareholders holding each not less than thirty shares to be
Directors of the said Company, who shall hold office until
they are re-elected or their successors are appointed at the
times and in the manner and with such qualifications as
may be provided by the by-laws of the said Company ; and
the said Directors so soon as may be, after their election
shall choose one of their number to be President and another
to be Vice-President of the said Company. *First meeting of share-holders, when it may be held. Notice. Election of Directors.*

10. The chief place of business of the said Company shall
be at Toronto unless the Board of Directors first elected shall,
by resolution, decide to fix the chief place or seat of business
at *Chief place of business.*

at some other place in Canada, which they shall have full power to do.

11. A register of all securities held by the Company shall be kept, and within fourteen days after the taking of any security an entry or memorial, specifying the nature and amount of such security, and the names of the parties thereto, with their proper additions, shall be made in such register.

12. The Company shall keep, in a book or books, a register of the members of the Company, and therein shall be fairly and distinctly entered, from time to time, the following particulars :—The names and addresses, and the occupations (if any) of the members of the Company, and the number of shares held by such members, and the amount paid, on the shares of each member.

13. Notice of any trust, expressed, implied or constructive, shall not be entered on the register, nor shall any such notice in any way affect the Company as to its shares or any transfer or any transmission thereof.

14. When any person makes application in writing, signed by him or her, for an allotment of shares, and any shares or share are or is allotted to him or her in pursuance of such application, he or she shall be deemed conclusively to have agreed to become a member of the Company in respect of the shares so allotted, and he or she shall be entered on the register of members in respect thereof accordingly.

15. The Directors may reserve the issue of any portion of the shares constituting the present capital of the Company until such further time as they shall think expedient, and may issue any portion of them from time to time as and when they shall think proper.

16. All shares in the capital of the said Company shall be personal estate and transmissible as such.

17. No shareholder shall be liable for or charged with the payment of any debt or demand due from the Company beyond the extent of his shares in the capital of the Company not then paid up.

18. The Directors may, from time to time, make such calls as they shall think fit upon the shareholders in respect of all moneys unpaid upon their respective shares : Provided that no call shall be made without giving notice to the shareholder

shareholder by mailing the same to his last known address, at least thirty days before the day on which such call shall be payable ; but no call shall exceed the amount of ten dol- Limitation· lars per share, and a period of three months at least shall intervene between two successive calls.

19. The said Company may hold such real estate as may Power to hold be necessary for the transaction of their business, or as being real estate. mortgaged to them, may be acquired by them for the pro- tection of their investments, and may, from time to time sell, mortgage, lease or otherwise dispose of the same : Pro- Proviso. vided always, that it shall be incumbent upon the Company to sell any real estate acquired in satisfaction of any debt, or for the protection of any investment, within ten years after it shall have come into their possession.

20. The Directors shall have full power, from time to time, Directors may to make and to alter such by-laws, rules, regulations and make by-laws ordinances, not contrary to law or the provisions of this Act, purposes. as shall appear to them proper and needful for the well ordering of the Company, the management and disposition of its stock, property, estate and effects, the calling of ordinary and extraordinary or other meetings of the said Company, and of the Directors and other officers, and the proceedings at meetings of the Company and of the Directors, the making of calls upon the subscribed capital, the appointment and removal of officers and agents of the Company, the regulation of their powers and duties and the salaries to be paid to them, the compensation of Directors, and for the conduct in all other particulars of the affairs of the Company ; Provided always, that all such by-laws, rules, regulations and Proviso for ordinances made by the Directors as aforesaid, shall only be confirmation. valid and binding until the next annual general meeting of the shareholders, unless they are then approved by such meeting, and shall thereafter have force and effect as so approved or modified at such meeting.

21. If any vacancy should any time occur among the Vacancies said Directors by death, resignation, removal or disqualifica- between tion, such vacancy shall be filled for the remainder of the term of office of the Director dying, resigning or being removed or becoming disqualified, by the remaining Directors or the majority of them, electing in such place or places a shareholder or shareholders eligible for such office.

22. The Company hereby incorporated shall be subject to Company to such provisions of any general Acts passed by Parliament, be subject to during the present or any future session, as may be declared any general to apply to loan and investment companies, or which Parliament may deem necessary for the public interest.

23.

Certificate to be obtained from Treasury Board.

23. The said Company shall obtain from the Treasury Board within two years from and after the passing of this Act the certificate by this Act required to be obtained by the said Company before it can commence business, in default of which this Act shall become and be null and void and of no effect, and the Charter hereby granted and all and every the rights and privileges hereby conferred, shall be forfeited.

CHAP. 60.

An Act to amend the Act thirty-fifth Victoria, chapter one hundred and eight, intituled: "An Act to amend the Act incorporating the London and Canadian Loan and Agency Company (limited)."

[Assented to 12th April, 1876.]

Preamble

35 V., c. 108.

WHEREAS the London and Canadian Loan and Agency Company (limited), have by their petition prayed that the Act amending their Act of incorporation, passed in the thirty-fifth year of Her Majesty's reign, chapter one hundred and eight, may be amended in the manner hereinafter mentioned; and it is expedient to grant the prayer of the said petition : Therefore Her Majesty, by and with the advice and consent of the Senate and House of Commons of Canada, enacts as follows :—

Sect. 8 amended. ;

1. The eighth section of the said Act is hereby amended by adding thereto at the end thereof the words, "for the time being not paid up."

CHAP. 61.

An Act to incorporate " The National Investment Company of Canada, (Limited)."

[Assented to 12th April, 1876.]

WHEREAS the persons hereinafter named and others, Preamble. purpose to establish a joint stock Company, and have petitioned for an Act of incorporation for the said Company ; and whereas it is expedient to grant the prayer of such petition : Therefore Her Majesty, by and with the advice and consent of the Senate and House of Commons of Canada, enacts as follows :—

1. The Honorable M. C. Cameron, Samuel Nordheimer, Incorpora-Edward Gurney, junior, G. W. Torrance, William Alexander, tion. John Stark, William Galbraith, A. V. De Laporte, Benjamin Lyman, Thomas Thomson, Robert Hume, Alfred Hoskin, W. A. Farlane and C. S. Jones, and all or any other person or persons who shall, from time to time, be possessed of any share or shares in the Company, shall be and they are hereby constituted a body corporate and politic under the name and style of " The National Investment Company Corporate of Canada, (Limited)," and shall, by that name, have per-name and petual succession and a common seal, and by the same powers. name be capable of suing and being sued in all courts of justice in Canada.   .

2. The said the Honorable M. C. Cameron, Samuel Nord-Provisional heimer, William Alexander, John Stark, William Galbraith, Directors. A. V. De Laporte, Benjamin Lyman, Thomas Thomson, Robert Hume, Alfred Hoskin, Edward Gurney, junior, G. W. Torrance, W. A. Farlane, and C. S. Jones, shall be Provisional Directors of the said Company.

3. The head office of the said Company shall be in the Head office City of Toronto ; but it shall be lawful for the said Company and branches. to have agencies in various places in the Dominion of Canada, and to appoint persons to manage the same.   `

4. The affairs of the said Company shall be managed by Board of a board of not less than nine, nor more than thirteen Direc-Directors tors ; and the persons named in section one of this Act shall be Directors of the Company until replaced by others duly elected in their stead.

7   **5.**

Capital stock.

Provision for increase.

How to be raised and incidents.

5. The capital stock of the said Company shall be two million dollars divided into twenty thousand shares of one hundred dollars each ; but it shall be lawful for the said Company by resolution, passed at any general meeting of the shareholders, to increase the capital stock from time to time as may be deemed expedient to any sum not exceeding five million dollars, and to raise the amount of the new stock either by distribution amongst the original shareholders, or by the issue of new shares, or partly in one way and partly in the other ; and the said new stock shall be subject to all such incidents, both with reference to the payment of calls and forfeiture, and as to the powers of lending and borrowing or otherwise as the original stock ; and all shares in the capital of the said Company shall be personal estate and transmissible as such.

Stock books may be opened.

Proviso : limitation of shares held by one person.

Ten per cent. to be paid in thirty days.

6. For the purpose of organizing the Company, the Provisional Directors, or a majority of them, may cause stock-books to be opened after giving due public notice thereof in ·some one or more newspapers published in the City of Toronto, in which stock-books shall be recorded the names and subscriptions of such persons as desire to become share-holders in the Company ; and such books shall be opened in the City of Toronto and elsewhere at the discretion of the said Provisional Directors or a majority of them, and shall remain open so long as they may deem necessary : Provided, that no person shall hold more than one thousand shares in the Company ; and provided that each subscriber of stock shall pay ten per centum upon the amount of the stock subscribed by him within thirty days after his subscription ; and in default the said Provisional Directors, in the name of the said Company, or the said Company after its organization, shall be entitled to sue the defaulter for the amount unpaid in respect of such stock.

Meeting for election of Directors, &c., when it may be held.

Notice.

Qualification of Directors.

When only

7. So soon as one million dollars of the capital stock shall have been subscribed, and ten per centum thereof paid up, the said Provisional Directors shall call a general meeting of the shareholders, to be held in the City of Toronto,—of which meeting not less than four weeks' notice shall have been given by public advertisement by four insertions in the *Canada Gazette*, and four weekly insertions in one of the daily newspapers published in the City of Toronto,—for the purpose of passing by-laws for the management of the affairs of the Company, the election of Directors, the appointment of officers, and generally for the exercise of the powers conferred on the shareholders by this Act : Provided always, that no one shall be eligible for the office of Director unless he shall be a shareholder, at all times, whilst holding office, to the amount of thirty shares, and shall have paid up all calls : Provided also, that at least twenty

twenty per cent. of the capital stock subscribed shall be the Company may commence business
paid up before the Company shall commence business, and
that the said general meeting shall not be held nor shall the ness.
Company commence business until the Company shall have
obtained from the Treasury Board a certificate to the effect
that it has been proved, to the satisfaction of the board,
that such amounts of capital have been *bonâ fide* subscribed
and paid up as are, by this Act, required to be subscribed and
paid up, respectively, before organizing or commencing
business under the terms of this Act.

8. So soon as Directors shall have been appointed under Term of office of Provisional Directors.
the next preceding section, the power and functions of the
Provisional Directors shall cease and determine.

9. It shall be lawful for the said Company to lay out and Investment of capital, and business of the Company
invest their capital, moneys borrowed on debentures,
moneys deposited, and the rest or reserve fund, in the first
place in paying or discharging all costs, charges and expenses of and incidental to the obtaining of this Act, and of
the formation and establishment of the said Company, and
the remainder, or so much thereof as may, from time to time,
be necessary, for and towards carrying out the objects of
their undertaking as hereinafter mentioned, that is to say :—
from time to time and at all times to lend and advance
money, by way of loan or otherwise, on real and leasehold
estates in the Dominion of Canada, to be secured by such
real security, by mortgage or otherwise, for such period and
upon such terms, and at such rates of interest as may be Rate of interest to be taken.
agreed upon, and shall be lawful or may lawfully be taken,
received, reserved or exacted either by individuals or by
bodies corporate in the place where the contract is made or
is executory, but not exceeding eight per centum per
annum ; to buy, acquire, hold and dispose of mortgages May buy debentures, &c.
upon real and leasehold estates and the debentures and
other securities of the Dominion of Canada and of the several
Provinces of the Dominion, and to buy and sell evidences of
debt secured by mortgage or pledge of freehold or leasehold
lands ; and the said Company may do all acts that may be General powers.
necessary for advancing such money and for the recovery
and repayment thereof, and for enforcing payment of all
interest accruing therefrom, or any conditions annexed to
such advance or any forfeiture consequent on the non-payment thereof, and give all necessary and proper receipts, acquittances and discharges for the same, and do, authorize and
exercise all acts and powers whatsoever requisite or expedient to be done or exercised in relation to the said
purposes.

10. The Directors may, from time to time, with the con- Power to issue deben-tures
sent of the majority of the shareholders present or repre-
sented

sented in a general meeting, borrow money upon the
debentures of the Company, at such rate of interest and
upon such terms as they may think proper,—which debentures and the coupons thereto shall be in the form or to the
effect set forth in Schedule A to this Act annexed ; and
the Directors may, for that purpose, make or cause to be made
debentures under the common seal of the Company, for
sums not less than four hundred dollars, or one hundred
pounds sterling money, which may be made payable at any
place, and either to order or bearer, and may have interest
coupons attached ; and such debentures shall be signed by
the President or Vice-President and the Manager of the said
Company, and shall be under the common seal of the said
Company, and the coupons shall be signed by the Manager,
and such debentures shall be payable at such time
and place as the said debentures and coupons shall therein
respectively state : Provided, that no purchaser of a debenture or debentures of the said Company shall be bound to
enquire into the occasion of any such loan, or the issuing of
any such debenture or debentures, or into the validity of
any resolution authorizing the same, or the purpose for which
such loan is wanted : Provided also that the total amount
of the sums to be borrowed, as aforesaid, together with the
deposits held by the Company, (if any) shall never· exceed
a sum equal to the amount of the paid up capital and thirty-
three and one-third per cent. added thereto.

Form of debentures; coupons to be attached.

Proviso: no enquiry by purchaser necessary.

Proviso: total amount of debentures limited.

11. The Company may hold such real estate, as may be
necessary for the transaction of their business, or, as being
mortgaged or hypothecated to them may be acquired by
them for the protection of their investments, and may, from
time to time, sell, mortgage, lease or otherwise dispose of the
same : Provided always, that it shall be incumbent upon
the Company to sell such real estate, acquired in satisfaction
of any debt, the premises occupied by the Company aforesaid excepted, within ten years after so acquiring it.

Acquiring lands by the Company.

Proviso: to be sold within a certain time.

12. The Company may stipulate for payment of any loan
made by them in one sum or in instalments, and may
stipulate for and demand and receive in advance, half-
yearly, the interest from time to time accruing on any loans
granted by the Company, and may add the principal and
interest upon any loans together, and make the same payable
in instalments, and may also receive an annual, semi-annual
or quarterly payment on any loans by way of a sinking fund
for the gradual extinction of such loan, upon such terms and
in such manner as may be regulated by the by-laws of the
Company : and it shall and may be lawful for the said Company to sell and assign any mortgage or mortgages, or other
security made to or held by the said Company.

Payments of loans, how they may be made.

13. It shall be lawful for the said Company, instead of
requiring

Expenses in.

requiring from the borrower the payment of the expenses incidental to any loan at the time the loan is advanced, to give such time for the payment of the same as may be advised, and to add the same to the principal or interest secured by any mortgage or other security securing the loan.

cidental to a loan may be added thereto.

14. The general annual meeting of the Company shall be held on the second Wednesday of the month of January in each year, or such other day as may be appointed by the Directors,—of which not less than four weeks' notice shall have been given in the *Canada Gazette*, and one of the daily newspapers published in the city of Toronto; and all elections of Directors shall be held and made by such of the shareholders present, or represented by proxy, as shall have paid the twenty per cent. above prescribed, and all calls made by the Directors and then due; and all such elections shall be by ballot; and the persons who shall have the greatest number of votes at any such election shall be Directors except as hereinafter directed; and if there is any doubt or difficulty in such election, by reason of two or more persons receiving an equal number of votes, then there shall be a re-ballot as between such persons, which re-ballot may be repeated as often as deemed advisable by the meeting; or instead of a re-ballot, the Directors as to whose election there is no such doubt or difficulty, may, if deemed advisable by the meeting, determine which of the persons having an equal number of votes shall be Director or Directors: and the said Directors, so soon as may be after their election, shall proceed to elect one of their number to be President and another Vice-President: and if any vacancy shall at any time happen amongst the said Directors by death, resignation, disqualification, incapacity, or removal, or otherwise, during the current year of office, such vacancy shall be filled for the remainder of the year by the remaining Directors, or a majority of them, electing in such place or places a shareholder or shareholders eligible for such office: Provided always, that the Directors, including the President and Vice-President, shall not exceed seven in number.

Annual meetings.

Election of Directors.

Ties at election.

Election of President, &c.

Vacancies, how filled.

Proviso.

15. At all general meetings of the said Company each shareholder shall be entitled to give one vote for every share held by him for not less than fourteen days prior to the time of voting, upon which share all calls then due have been paid; such votes may be given either in person or by proxy; and all questions proposed for the consideration of the shareholders shall be determined by the majority of votes, in person or by proxy,—the Chairman presiding at such meeting having the casting vote in case of an equality of votes; but no person shall, in right of any debenture, be deemed a shareholder, or be capable of acting or voting as such at any meeting of the Company.

Scale of votes.

Proxies.

Casting vote.

Proviso.

16.

Votes of joint shareholders at meetings.

16. If several persons be jointly entitled to a share or shares, the person whose name stands first on the register of shareholders as one of the holders of such share or shares, shall, for the purposes of voting at any meeting, be deemed the sole proprietor thereof, and on all occasions the vote of such first named shareholder alone, either in person or by proxy, shall be allowed as the vote in respect of such share or shares, and no proof of the concurrence of the other holders thereof shall be required.

Provision in case of failure to elect Directors.

17. If at any time an election of Directors be not made, or do not take effect at the proper time, the Company shall not be held to be thereby dissolved, but such election may take place at any general meeting of the Company duly called for that purpose by the Directors for the time being ; and the Directors in office shall so continue until a new election is made.

Quorum of Directors.

Casting vote.

18. At all meetings of Directors five shall be a quorum for the transaction of business ; and all questions before them shall be decided by a majority of votes ; and in case of an equality of votes, the President, Vice-President or presiding Director shall give the casting vote.

Powers of Directors, as to by-law for certain purposes.

General powers.

Officers, clerks, &c.

19. The Directors shall have full power and authority, from time to time, to make and alter such by-laws, rules, regulations and ordinances as shall appear to them proper and needful touching the well ordering of the said Company ; and such by-laws shall be reduced to writing, and shall have affixed thereto the common seal of the Company; and any copy thereof or extract therefrom certified under the hand of the President, Vice-President or Manager of the said Company shall be evidence in all courts of justice in Canada of such by-laws or extract from them, and that the same were duly made and are in force ; the said Directors shall also have full power and authority over the management of its stock, property, estate and effects, the declaring of dividends and bonuses, and the amount of the same respectively, and the dates and mode of payment thereof; the share of the profits to be set aside as a rest or reserve fund ; and the calling of special general meetings ; the regulation of the meetings of the Board of Directors ; the establishment, appointment and removal of agents and branch offices, and the definition of the duties and powers of such agents and branch offices; the making of calls upon the subscribed capital and the issuing of stock ; the appointment and removal of all agents, officers and clerks of the Company; the regulation of their powers and duties, and the salaries to be paid to them; the compensation of Directors : and generally the Directors may, in addition to the powers expressly conferred upon them, exercise all such powers, give all such covenants, make all such engagements and agreements, and

do

do all such acts and things as are and shall be necessary and proper for the due management of the affairs of the Company, and for carrying out the provisions of this Act accor- ding to its true meaning and spirit: Provided that the Proviso. Directors shall not make any dividend or bonus whereby the capital stock shall be diminished.

20. Provided always, that all by-laws, rules, regulations By-laws may and ordinances may be varied, altered or cancelled at the be amended next annual general meeting, held after the passing of the at a general same, and shall be presumed to have been approved of by meeting. such meeting, except in so far as they shall be varied, altered or cancelled, and shall thereafter have force and effect as if approved: Provided further, that no such variation, altera- Proviso. tion or cancellation shall invalidate anything done in pur- suance or by virtue of such by-laws, rules, regulations and ordinances, or injuriously affect the position or rights of any person: And provided further, that such by-laws do not Proviso. contravene the provisions of this Act.

21. The acts of the Directors, or of any quorum thereof, or Defect of of any committee appointed by the Directors, or by any election not quorum thereof, shall, notwithstanding it be afterwards action of discovered that there was some defect in the appointment Directors or of any such Directors or of any member of any such commit- Committee. tee, or that they or any of them were or was disqualified, be as valid as if such person or persons had been duly ap- pointed, and was qualified to be a Director or Directors.

22. Every Director of the Company, and his heirs, execut- Responsibil- ors and administrators, and estates and effects respectively, ity of Direc- shall be charged and chargeable only with so much money tors limited. as he shall actually receive, and shall not be answerable or accountable for his co-directors or any or either of them, but each of them for his own acts, deeds and defaults only; nor shall the Directors or any of them respectively be answerable or accountable for any person or persons who may be ap- pointed under or by virtue of this Act, or of the by-laws of the Company as aforesaid, or otherwise under and by virtue of the rules and regulations of the Company for the time being in force, to collect or receive any moneys payable to the Company, or in whose hands any money or properties of the Company shall or may be deposited or lodged for safe custody; nor for the insufficiency or deficiency of any title to any property which may, from time to time, be purchased, taken or leased, acquired by order of the Directors, or otherwise, for or on behalf of the Company; nor for the insufficiency or deficiency of any security in or upon which any of the moneys of the Company shall be invested; nor shall any Director be answerable for any loss, damage or misfortune whatsoever which shall happen in the execution of the duties of the office of such Director, or in relation thereto,

thereto, unless the same shall happen through his own wilful neglect or default.

Stock may be reserved. **23.** The Directors may reserve the issue of any portion of the shares constituting the present or any future increased capital of the Company until such further time as they shall think expedient, and may issue any portion of them from time to time as and when they shall think proper.

Issue of such stock. **24.** The shares which may be reserved by the Directors shall be offered to the members in proportion to the existing shares held by them, and such offer shall be made by a notice specifying the number of shares to which the member is entitled, and limiting a time within which such offer, if not accepted, will be deemed to be declined, and after the expiration of such time, or on the receipt of an intimation from the member to whom such notice is given that he declines to accept the shares offered, the Directors may dispose of the same in such manner as they think most beneficial to the Company.

Calls on shares. **25.** The Directors may, from time to time, make calls upon the shareholders of the Company not exceeding ten per centum per annum on each share held by them.

No payment in advance. **26.** No shareholder shall be entitled to pay on the shares held by him more than the calls made thereon by the Directors.

Notice of call. **27.** No call shall be made without giving notice to the shareholder by mailing the same to his last known address at least thirty days before the day on which such call shall be payable ; nor shall such calls be made at intervals of less than thirty days.

Certificate to be delivered on demand. **28.** On demand of the holder of any share, the Company shall cause a certificate of proprietorship of such share to be delivered to such shareholder, and such certificate shall have the common seal of the Company affixed thereto, and shall be signed by the President, Vice-President or Manager : such certificate shall specify the share or number of shares in the undertaking to which such shareholder is entitled and the amount paid thereon ; and such certificate, if lost or destroyed, may be renewed.

Payment of calls. **29.** Each shareholder shall be liable to pay the amount of any call lawfully made upon him to such person and at such time and place as the Directors shall appoint.

Interest on unpaid calls. **30.** A call shall be deemed to have been made at the time when the resolution of the Directors authorizing such call was passed ; and if a shareholder shall fail to pay all calls

calls due from him before or on the day appointed for payment, he shall pay interest for the same at the rate of six per. centum per annum from the day appointed for payment to the time of actual payment, and may be sued for the amount thereof in any court of law or equity having competent jurisdiction; and in any action it shall not be necessary to set forth the special matter, but it shall be sufficient to declare that the defendant is the holder of one share or more, stating the number of shares, and is indebted in the sum of money to which the calls in arrear shall amount in respect of one call or more upon one share or more, stating the number and amount of each of such calls, whereby an action hath accrued to the said Company by virtue of this Act. <small>Suits for calls and allegations therein.</small>

31. On the trial of such action, it shall be sufficient to prove that the defendant, at the time of making such call, was a holder of one share or more in the Company, and that such call was in fact made, and such notice thereof given as is directed by this Act; and it shall not be necessary to prove the appointment of the Directors who made such call, nor any other matter whatsoever; and thereupon the Company shall be entitled to recover what shall be due upon such call, with interest at six per centum per annum, unless it shall be shown that such call or calls was or were not made in conformity with the provisions of this Act. The production of the register book of shareholders of the Company, or a certified extract therefrom, under the signature of the President or Vice-President or Manager of the Company, shall be *primâ facie* evidence of such defendant being a shareholder, and of the number and amount of his shares and of the sums paid in respect thereof. <small>Evidence in actions for calls.</small> <small>Proof of bylaws, &c.</small>

32. If the holder of any share fail to pay a call payable by him in respect thereof, together with the interest which shall have accrued thereon, the Directors, at any time after the expiration of one month from the day appointed for payment of such call, may declare such share forfeited, and that whether the Company have sued for the amount of such call or not. No advantage shall be taken of such forfeiture unless the share shall be declared to be forfeited at a meeting of the Directors to be held after the expiration of three months at least from the day on which notice in writing shall be sent by post to the last known address of the shareholder in default, of the intention to make such declaration of forfeiture; and it shall be lawful for the Directors to confirm such forfeiture at any such meeting, and at any subsequent meeting to direct the share so forfeited to be sold by public auction, private sale or tender, or otherwise be disposed of, and after such confirmation the Directors may sell in manner aforesaid the forfeited shares, and either separately or together in lots, as to them may seem meet. <small>Forfeiture of shares for non-payment of calls.</small> <small>Sale of forfeited shares.</small>

Evidence of forfeiture of share.

33. A declaration in writing by an officer or servant of the Company, or by some credible person (not interested in the matter), made before a notary public under his hand and seal, or before a commissioner for taking affidavits in the Superior Courts of the Province of Ontario, or before a notary public, under his hand and seal, or before a commissioner authorized to take affidavits for use in any of the courts of law or equity in the Province of Quebec, in England, Ireland or Scotland, or before a notary public in the United States of America,—all of whom are hereby authorized to take such declaration,—that the call in respect of a share was made, and notice thereof given, and that default in payment of the call was made, and that the forfeiture of the share was declared and confirmed in manner hereinbefore required, shall be sufficient evidence of the facts therein stated; and such declaration and the receipt of the Manager, or President or Vice-President of the Company, for the price of such share, shall constitute a good title to such share, and thereupon the purchaser shall be deemed the proprietor of such share discharged from all calls made prior to such purchase; and a certificate of proprietorship shall be delivered to such purchaser upon his signing an undertaking to hold the said shares so purchased by him as aforesaid, subject to the provisions of this Act; and he shall not be bound to see to the application of the purchase money, nor shall his title to such share be affected by any irregularity in the proceedings in reference to any such sale.

Certificate to purchaser.

No more shares to be sold than sufficient to meet claim.

34. The Company shall not sell nor transfer more of the shares of any such defaulter than will be sufficient, as nearly as can be ascertained at the time of such sale, to pay the arrears then due from such defaulter, on account of any calls, together with interest and the expenses attending such sale and declaration of forfeiture; and if the money produced by the sale of any such forfeited share or shares be more than sufficient to pay all arrears of calls and interest thereon due at the time of such sale, and the expenses aforesaid, the surplus shall, on demand, be paid to the defaulter, or if not so paid, applied in and towards satisfaction of any calls made thereafter, but prior to such demand being made as last aforesaid in respect of the remaining unsold shares of such defaulter.

Surplus to defaulter.

Redemption of forfeited shares.

35. If the payment of such arrears of calls and interest and expenses be made before any share or shares so forfeited and vested in the Company shall have been sold, such share or shares shall revert to the party to whom the same belonged before such forfeiture, in such manner as if such calls had been duly paid.

Transfer of shares.

36. Subject to the regulations herein contained, any shareholder may sell or transfer his shares or any of them;
but

but no transfer of any share or shares of the stock of the
said Company shall be valid until entered in the books of the
Company according to such form as may, from time to time,
be fixed by by-law : Provided always, that no shareholder Calls must
indebted to the Company shall be permitted to make a have been
transfer or receive a dividend until such debt is paid or sent of
secured to the satisfaction of the Directors, and no transfer Directors.
of stock shall, at any time, be made until all calls thereon
shall have been paid, or without the consent of the Directors
of the Company, unless the entire amount of such share
shall have been paid up.

37. The shareholders of the Company shall not as such Liability of
be held responsible for any debt, act, default or liability limited.
whatsoever of the Company, or for any engagement, claim,
payment, loss, injury, transaction, matter or thing whatsoever
relating to or connected with the Company beyond the extent of their respective shares in the capital stock thereof
not then paid up, and no action shall be brought against any
shareholder therefor until an execution against the Company
has been returned unsatisfied in whole or in part.

38. It shall be the duty of the Directors to declare and Dividends,
make half-yearly dividends of so much of the profits of the when payable
Company, as to them or a quorum of them may seem Notice.
advisable, and to give public notice of the payment of such On what
dividend, at least ten days previously; but no dividend shall conditions
bear interest against the Company : and no dividend shall be
paid in respect of any share or shares, until all calls then
due in respect of that or any other share held by the person
to whom such dividend may be payable shall have been
paid; and the Directors of the said Company shall be at
liberty to apply the dividends, or such portion thereof as
may be necessary, in or towards payment of any overdue
and unpaid calls or call due by the shareholder entitled to
such dividends.

39. Before declaring any dividend, the Directors may, if Reserve fund
they think fit, from time to time, set apart from and out of before declar-
the profits of the said Company such sum as they may think ing dividend.
advisable for the purpose of forming a rest or reserved fund
to meet contingencies, or for enlarging or improving the
estate of the Company, or promoting the objects and purposes for which they are incorporated.

40. At every annual meeting of the shareholders the out- Annual
going Directors shall submit a clear and full statement of the statement of
affairs of the Company for the year preceding, showing in Company.
detail, on the one hand, the debts, liabilities and engagements
of the Company, and on the other the assets and resources
thereof; but such statement shall not disclose the names or
                                                        private

private affairs of any person doing business with the said Company.

Register book of shareholders.   **41.** The Company shall keep a book to be called "The Register Book of Shareholders," and in such book shall be fairly and distinctly entered, from time to time, the names, addresses and additions of the several persons being shareholders of the Company, and the amount of the subscriptions paid on the shares of each member; and such book shall, at all convenient times, be open to the inspection of every shareholder or creditor of the Company, or the agent of such shareholder or creditor, who may demand written extracts therefrom,—which shall be furnished to him on payment of a fee of twenty cents for every one hundred words.

As to shares transmitted in consequence of death, &c., or otherwise than by regular transfer.   **42.** If the interest in any shares shall become transmitted, in consequence of the death, bankruptcy or insolvency of any shareholder, or by any other legal means than by a transfer according to the provisions of this Act, the same shall be authenticated by a declaration in writing as hereinafter mentioned, or in such other manner as the Directors shall require ; and every such declaration shall distinctly state the manner in which and the party to whom such share or shares shall have been so transmitted, and shall be made and signed, and shall be by such party acknowledged before a notary public, under his hand and seal, or a commissioner for taking affidavits in the superior courts of any of the Provinces of the Dominion of Canada, who are hereby authorized to take such acknowledgments, or before a notary

What proof required of declaration.   public, under his hand and seal, or a commissioner duly authorized to take affidavits to be used in any of the superior courts of England, Ireland or Scotland, or the United States of America, if such acknowledgment be taken in Great Britain or Ireland or the United States of America ; and such acknowledgment shall be left with the Manager, and thereupon the Manager shall enter the name of the person entitled under such transmission in the register book of transfers, whereby such person shall be and become a shareholder in the said Company ; and until such transmission shall have been so authenticated, no person or party claiming, by virtue of such transmission, shall be entitled to receive any share of the profits of the Company, nor to vote in respect of any such shares as the holder thereof.

Notices to joint shareholders.   **43.** With respect to any share or shares to which several persons may be jointly entitled, all notices directed to be given to the shareholders shall be given to such of the said persons whose name shall stand first in the register book of shareholders; and notice so given shall be sufficient notice to all the proprietors of such share or shares, unless any of such joint proprietors shall, by writing under his hand, request such notice to be given to him.

44.

44. The Company shall not be bound to see to the execution of any trust, whether express, implied or constructive, to which any of the said shares may be subject; and the receipt of the party in whose name any such share or shares shall stand in the books of the Company shall, from time to time, be a sufficient discharge to the Company for any dividends or other sum of money payable in respect of such share or shares, notwithstanding any trusts to which such share or shares may be subject, and whether or not the Company have had notice of such trusts; and the Company shall not be bound to see to the application of the money paid upon such receipt; and the said Company shall not be affected by any trust, expressed, implied or constructive, whether the same shall or shall not be entered on their books.

Company not bound to see to the execution of trusts.

45. The Directors shall cause notices, minutes or copies, as the case may require, of all appointments made, or contracts entered into by the Directors to be duly entered in books to be, from time to time, provided for the purpose, which shall be kept under the superintendence of the Directors; and every such entry shall be signed by the Chairman of the meeting at which the matter, in respect of which such entry is made, was moved or discussed at or previously to the next meeting of the Company or Directors as the case may be; and a copy of such entry, certified by the President, Vice-President or Manager shall be received as evidence in all courts, and before all judges, justices and others, without proof of such respective meetings having been duly convened, or of the persons making or entering such orders or proceedings being shareholders or Directors respectively, or of the signature of the President, Vice-President or Manager, —all which last mentioned matters will be presumed; and all such books shall, at any reasonable time, be open to the inspection of any of the shareholders.

Minutes of appointments and contracts to be kept.

Effect of certified copies.

46. Any summons, notice, order or other document required to be served upon the Company shall be served by leaving the same at the head office in Toronto with any grown person in the employ of the Company, and who at the time of such service shall be present in the office of the Company, but not otherwise.

Service of process on the Company.

47. Any summons, notice, order or proceeding requiring authentication by the Company may be signed by the President, Vice-President, Secretary or other authorized officer of the Company and need not be under the common seal of the Company; and the same may be in writing or in print, or partly in writing and partly in print.

Authentication of documents of the Company.

48. Notices requiring to be served by the Company upon the members, may be served either personally or by leaving the same for, or sending them through the post in prepaid letters

Service of notices on members by the Company.

letters addressed to the members at their registered places of abode.

Evidence of service by post on members by the Company.

49. A notice or other document served by post by the Company on a member shall be taken as served at the time when a letter containing it would be delivered in the ordinary course of post; to prove the fact and time of service, it shall be sufficient to prove that such letter was properly addressed and was put into the post office, and the time when it was put in, and the time requisite for its delivery in the ordinary course of post.

Effect of notice on members.

50. Every person who, by operation of law, transfer or other means whatsoever, shall become entitled to any share or shares, shall be bound by any and every notice which, previously to his name and address being entered upon the register of members in respect of such share or shares, shall have been given to the person from whom he shall derive his title.

Annual statement to the Government, and its extent.

51. The said Company shall furnish annually, within the first fifteen days of each session to the Parliament, a statement made up to the thirty-first day of December preceding, in duplicate, verified by the affidavit of the President, or Vice-President and the Manager setting out the capital stock of the Company and the proportion thereof paid up, the names of the shareholders, with their places of abode, and the number of shares held by each, the assets and liabilities of the Company, and such other details as to the nature and extent of the business of the Company as may, from time to time, be required by any Act of the Parliament of Canada.

Seal of Company.

52. The said Company shall have a corporate seal, which shall be kept at the head office in the City of Toronto, and the President, Vice-President or Manager shall have full power to execute, sign and deliver and affix the seal of the said Company to all deeds, discharges, releases, leases, transfers, assignments, bonds, indemnities, warrants, agreements, papers, writings and all other instruments and documents which shall or may be necessary or be required to be signed or executed on behalf of or in the conducting of the business of the said Company: Provided always, that the same shall in all cases be signed by the Manager or other

Cheques, bills, &c.

duly authorized officer of the said Company. All cheques, drafts, bills of exchange or letters of credit which shall be made or drawn on behalf of or upon the said Company shall be signed or accepted by the President, Vice-President or a Director of the Company, and countersigned by the Manager or other duly authorized officer of the said Company.

53. In any action or proceeding at law, criminal or civil, Evidence of or in equity, it shall not be necessary to give any evidence seal or signa-to prove the seal of the Company or the signature of the dent. President, Vice-President or Manager or other duly authorized officer ; and all documents sealed with the seal of the Company, or signed with the signature of the President, Vice-President or Manager or other duly authorized officer of the Company, shall be held to have been duly sealed with the seal of the Company, and to have been duly signed by the President, Vice-President or Manager or other duly authorized officer as aforesaid.

54. In this Act the following words and expressions have Interpreta-the several meanings hereby assigned to them, unless there tain words. be something in the subject or context repugnant to.such construction, that is to say :—The word " Company " means " The National Investment Company of Canada, (Limited) ;" words importing the singular number include the plural number, and words importing the plural number include the singular number ; the word "month" means a calendar month ; the word " lands " and the words " real estate " extend to messuages, lands, tenements and hereditaments of any tenure ; the expressions " the Directors " and " the Manager " mean, the Directors and the Manager respectively, for the time being of the said Company.

55. The Company availing themselves of any of the pro-Company to visions of this Act, shall be subject to such provisions of any any general general Acts passed by Parliament during the present or any Act. future session as may be declared to apply to loan and investment companies, or which Parliament may deem necessary for the public interest.

56. The said Company shall obtain from the Treasury Company to Board within two years from and after the passing of this cate of Trea-Act the certificate by this Act required to be obtained by sury Board the said Company before it can transact business ; in default within two of which this Act shall become and be null and void and of no effect, and the Charter hereby granted, and all and every the rights and privileges hereby conferred, shall be forfeited.

SCHEDULE A

Debenture No.   transferable.
   $ (or £)   under the authority of an Act of the Dominion of Canada. Victoria, chapter
   The National Investment Company of Canada, (Limited), promise to pay to the bearer the sum of   dollars (or   pounds sterling) on the   day of   in the year of our Lord one thousand eight hundred and   ,
             at

at the head office of the said Company in the (*state either the head office at Toronto, or their agents in London, England*), with interest at the rate of   per centum per annum, to be paid half-yearly on presentation of the proper coupon for the same as hereunto annexed, say on the days of   in each year, at the office or the agents aforesaid.

Dated at Toronto (*or*   ) the   day of   . A.D. 18

For the President and Directors of the National Investment Company of Canada, (Limited).

                A. B.,

                      President (*or Vice-President.*)

C. D.,
Manager.

COUPON.

THE NATIONAL INVESTMENT COMPANY OF CANADA (LIMITED)

No.   , $ (*or* £   ), half-yearly dividend due   day of   18   on Debenture No. issued by this Company on the   day of   ,   18 for $ (*or* £   ) at   per cent. per annum, payable at the head office at Toronto (*or at their agents in London, England*).

For the President and Directors,

                A. B.,

                      President (*or Vice-President*)

C. D.,
Manager

CHAP

CHAP. 62.

An Act to incorporate the London and Ontario Investment Company, (Limited.).

[Assented to 12th April, 1876.]

WHEREAS the Honorable Frank Smith, of the city of   Preamble.
Toronto, Senator, William Buchanan Hamilton, of
the same place, merchant, David Fisher, of the same place,
banker, James Gooderham Worts, of the same place,
Esquire, George Gooderham, of the same place, distiller,
William Henry Beatty, of the same place, Esquire, John
Gillespie, of the same place, merchant, William Ramsay, of
the same place, merchant, Alexander Fisher, of the same
place, banker, Robert Carrie, of the same place, merchant,
Harvey Prentice Dwight, of the same place, telegraph
superintendent, John Craven Chadwick, of the town of
Guelph, in the County of Wellington, Esquire, and Arthur
Brindley Lee, of the said city of Toronto, merchant, have
petitioned for an Act to incorporate a company for carrying
on the business of investing moneys on mortgages of real
estate and leaseholds, or in Dominion or Provincial securities, municipal debentures or other securities, with power to
borrow moneys and invest the same ; and it is expedient
to grant the prayer of their petition : Therefore Her Majesty,
by and with the advice and consent of the Senate and
House of Commons of Canada, enacts as follows :—

1. The said several persons, and such other persons and   Certain per-
corporations as may become shareholders in the Company   sons incor-
hereby created, are hereby constituted and declared to be a   porated.
corporation and body politic and corporate by the name of
" The London and Ontario Investment Company, (Limited) " ;   Corporate
and by that name shall have perpetual succession and a   name and
common seal, with power to break and alter such seal, and   powers.
by that name may sue and be sued, plead and be impleaded,
in all courts whether of law or equity whatsoever ; and may
acquire, hold and sell such real estate as may be requisite,
from time to time, for the purposes of the Company.

2. The Company shall at all times have an office in   Chief place
Toronto, which shall be their head office ; and they may   of business.
establish such other offices and agencies elsewhere as they
may deem expedient.

3. The capital of the Company shall be two millions   Capital stock
of dollars, in shares of one hundred dollars each,—of which,   and shares.
at least, one million dollars shall be subscribed, and twenty
per cent. on the amount subscribed paid in, (the sum so

Sum to be paid up before commencing business.

Provision for increase of capital to $5,000,000.

How to be raised, &c.

Incidents of new stock.

paid in amounting to at least two hundred thousand dollars) before the actual transaction of business is proceeded with; but the said Company may, by a resolution passed at any general meeting of the shareholders, called for such purpose, increase the capital stock, from time to time, as may be deemed expedient, to any sum not exceeding the sum of five millions of dollars, and may raise the amount of the said new stock either by distribution amongst the original shareholders, or by the issue of new shares, or partly in one way and partly in the other; and the said new stock shall be subject to all such incidents both with reference to the payment of calls and forfeiture, and to the powers of lending and borrowing, or otherwise, as the original stock.

Employment of capital.

4. The Company are hereby empowered to lay out and invest their capital, in the first place, in paying and discharging all costs, charges and expenses incurred in applying for and obtaining the passing of this Act, and all other expenses preparatory or relating thereto, and of the organization of the Company, and prior to the commencement of their business, and the remainder of such capital, or so much thereof as may, from time to time, be deemed necessary, in the manner, and for the purposes hereinafter mentioned, that is to say:—

Business of the Company. Loans.

The Company may, from time to time, lend and advance money by way of loan, or otherwise, on the security of mortgages on real estate, or freehold or leasehold, or on the security of the public securities of the Dominion of Canada or of any of the Provinces thereof, or of the debentures of any city or county in Canada, and may purchase mortgages on real estate, freehold or leasehold, and

Rate of interest limited.

such public securities or debentures, making such loans and purchases upon such terms and conditions and at such rates of interest, not exceeding eight per centum per annum, as shall be lawful, or may be lawfully taken, received, reserved, or exacted, either by individuals or by corporate bodies in the place where the contract for the same shall be made and be executory as to the Company may seem

Powers for collection.

satisfactory or expedient, with power to do all acts that may be necessary for the advancing or laying out such sums of money, and for receiving and obtaining repayment thereof, or selling or getting in invested moneys, and for compelling the payment of all interest, dividends and income accruing from such sums so advanced or invested, and for the observance and fulfilment of any conditions attached to such advances or investments, and to give receipts and acquittances and discharges for the same either absolutely and wholly, or partially; and for all and every and any of the foregoing purposes, and for every and any other purpose in this Act mentioned or referred to, the Company may lay out and apply the capital and property for the time being of the Company, or any part thereof, or any of the

the moneys authorised to be hereafter raised by the Company in addition to their capital for the time being, with General power to authorize and exercise all acts and powers whatso- powers. ever in the opinion of the Directors of the Company requisite or expedient to be done or exercised in relation thereto.

5. The Company may, from time to time, borrow money Company at such rates of interest and upon such terms as they may, may borrow from time to time, think proper; and may, for that purpose, grant make and execute any mortgages, debentures, bonds or other securities. instruments under the common seal of the Company for sums of not less than one hundred dollars each, and may assign, transfer, or deposit by way of equitable mortgage or otherwise, any of the documents of title, deeds, muniments, securities or property of the Company, and either with or without power of sale or other special provisions, as the Directors shall deem expedient; and no lender shall be Proviso : bound to enquire into the occasion for any such loan or into lender not the validity of any resolution authorizing the same, or the application. purpose for which such loan is wanted : Provided that the Proviso : total amount of sums to be borrowed as aforesaid shall amount to be never exceed the amount of the subscribed capital paid up limited. and thirty-three and one-third per cent. added thereto.

6. It shall be lawful for the Company to acquire by pur- May purchase chase, or otherwise, mortgages upon real estate, and to re- mortgages, sell the same at such time and in such manner as to them &c. may seem expedient.

7. In the exercise of any of the powers conferred by this Period of Act, the Company may advance all moneys authorized to loan. be loaned by them for such periods as they may deem expedient,—being not less than six months.

8. The Company may stipulate for, and may demand Payment of and receive in advance half-yearly, the interest from time to interest and sinking fund time accruing on any loans granted by the Company, in advance. and may also receive an annual payment on any loan by way of a sinking fund for the gradual extinction of such loan, and may also impose fines for default in payment of principal or interest, upon such terms and in such manner as may be regulated by the by-laws of the Company and agreed to by the party or parties to be so charged.

9. The Company may hold such real estate as may be Limitation of necessary for the transaction of their business, and also may power to hold real estate. hold for a period not exceeding ten years such real estate as may be acquired by them for the protection of, or for realizing any investment, and may. from time to time, sell, mortgage, lease or otherwise dispose of the same.

10 The business of the Company in Canada shall be Board of
8½   managed Directors ;

qualification
and powers.

managed by not less than nine nor more than thirteen Directors, each of whom shall be the holder of at least one hundred shares of the stock of the Company absolutely in his own right, who, in addition to the powers and authorities given by this Act or by any other Act or law in force in Canada expressly conferred upon them, may exercise all such powers, give all such consents, make all such arrangements and agreements, and generally do all such acts and things as are or shall be by any rule or by-law of the Company directed to be authorized, given, made or done by the Company, and are not thereby expressly directed to be exercised, given, made or done by the Company in general meeting assembled, but subject nevertheless to the provisions of such Act, law, rule or by-law as the case may be.

Provisional Directors; period of office and powers.

11. The said the Honorable Frank Smith, William Buchanan Hamilton, David Fisher, James Gooderham Worts, William Henry Beatty, John Gillespie, William Ramsay, Alexander Fisher and Arthur Brindley Lee, together with such other persons as they may choose to fill vacancies in their number (if any) occurring from time to time, shall be the provisional Directors of the Company and shall hold office as such until other Directors of the Company are elected as hereinafter provided, and shall have power to fill vacancies in their number as afore-

To open stock books.

said, and to open stock-books, and to make a call upon subscribers for stock, and generally so soon as ten per cent.

When the Company may be organized and when they may commence business.

on the amount subscribed for has been paid in, (the sum so paid in amounting to at least one hundred thousand dollars,) to do what may be necessary to organize the said Company and provide for commencing the business thereof; but the said Company shall not be organized nor commence business until they shall have obtained from the Treasury Board a certificate to the effect that it has been proved to the satisfaction of the board that such amounts of capital have been *bonâ fide* subscribed and paid in as are by this Act required to be subscribed and paid in respectively before organizing and commencing business under the terms of this Act

Certain matters to be regulated by by-law.

12. The appointment or election of Directors and officers and the time, place and mode of calling and holding ordinary and special or other meetings of the Company and of the Directors and other officers, and the proceedings at meetings of the Company and of the Directors, shall be subject to and regulated by such rules, regulations and provisions, and meetings of the Company and of the Directors shall have such powers, privileges and authorities, as may be set forth and directed in and by by-laws of the Company passed from time to time at any general meeting of the Company.

13.

13. The said Company may have an agency or agencies Branch offices
in any city or town, cities or towns in England, Scot- and Directors in the United
land or Ireland, and any by-law passed for such purpose Kingdom
shall not be altered or repealed excepting by a vote under by-laws.
of two-thirds of the votes of the members present, or represented by proxy, at any special meeting to be called for such
purpose, nor unless the notice calling such meeting be
published the requisite number of times, namely, once a
week for four weeks in a daily newspaper published in each
city or town in England, Scotland and Ireland, where the
Company shall have an agency.

14. The Directors may regulate by rules and by-laws the Scrip certifi-
issuing of scrip or stock certificates and the transfer of cates and transfer.
shares.

15. At all meetings of the Company every member shall One vote on
be entitled to one vote, either in person or by proxy, for each each share.
share held by him, and no shareholder shall be entitled to Calls must
vote at any meeting unless he shall have paid all the calls be paid.
upon all the shares then held by him.

16. No share shall be subdivided ; and if any share stands Shares held
in the name of two or more persons, the first named in the by more than one person,
register of members shall, as regards voting at meetings, how repre-
payment of dividends, service of notices and all other matters sented and administered.
connected with the Company (except transfer) be deemed
the sole holder thereof,—excepting there be any memorandum
or agreement in writing signed by all the joint holders of
any share, and accepted and agreed to by the Company,
naming one of such persons to be deemed sole holder; and
in such case such person shall be deemed such sole holder
so long as he be living ; and also that excepting as regards
voting at meetings, if the person deemed to be sole holder
of any such share be absent, the person named next or first
(as the case may be) in the register of members shall be permitted to vote.

17. All shares in the capital of the Company shall be Stock to be
personal estate and transferable as such. personal estate.

18. The Directors may, if they think fit, receive from any Payment of
member willing to advance the same, all or any part of the shares in advance.
amounts due on the shares held by such member beyond
the sums then actually called for ; and upon the moneys so
paid in in advance, or so much thereof as shall, from time to
time, exceed the amount of the calls then made upon the
shares in respect of which such advance shall be made, the And allow-
Company may pay interest at such rate, not exceeding six ance of interest.
per cent., as the member paying such sum in advance and
the Directors shall agree upon.

19

Shares may be reserved. **19.** The Directors may reserve the issue of any portion of the shares constituting the present capital of the Company over and above the amount to be subscribed before commencing business until such future time as they shall think expedient, and may issue any portion of them from time to time, as and when they shall think proper.

Issue of such reserved shares.

Proviso.

20. The shares which may be so reserved by the Directors shall (subject to the exception mentioned below) be offered to the members in as fair a proportion as may be practicable to the existing shares held by them; and such offer shall be made by the notice specifying the number of shares to which the member is entitled, and limiting a time within which such offer, if not accepted, will be deemed to be declined; and after the expiration of such time, or on the receipt of an intimation from the member to whom such notice is given, that he declines to accept the shares offered, the Directors may dispose of the same in such manner as they may think most beneficial to the Company; excepting and provided, that no person shall hold more than five hundred shares of the capital stock of the Company.

Register to be kept; its contents. **21.** The Company shall keep, in a book or books, a register of shares and of the members of the Company, in which shall be entered, from time to time, the names and addresses and the occupations (so far as known) of the shareholders of the Company and the number of shares held by each and the amount thereof paid up.

To be evidence. **22.** The register of the members shall be *primâ facie* evidence of any matters by this Act directed or authorized to be inserted therein.

Liabilities of shareholders to be limited. **23.** No member of the Company shall be liable for or charged with the payment of any debt or demand due from the Company beyond the extent of his shares in the capital of the Company not then paid up.

Applicant for shares when accepted to be a shareholder. **24.** When any person makes application in writing. signed by him, for an allotment of shares, and any shares or share are or is allotted to him in pursuance of such application, he shall be deemed conclusively to have become a member of the Company in respect of the shares so allotted, and he shall be entered on the register of members in respect thereof, accordingly.

Representatives of shareholders. **25.** The executors or administrators of any deceased member shall be the only persons recognized by the Company as having any title to his share.

Transmission of shares **26.** Any person becoming entitled to a share in consequence of the death, bankruptcy or insolvency of any member,

member, or otherwise than by ordinary transfer, may be registered as a member upon such evidence being produced as shall, from time to time, be required by the Directors, and on production of a request in writing in that behalf, signed by him (his signature being attested by at least one witness), which shall be conclusive evidence of his having become a member. *otherwise than by transfer.*

27. Every person who, by operation of law, transfer or other means whatsoever, shall become entitled to any share, shall be bound by any and every notice which, previously to his name and address being upon the register of members in respect of such share, shall have been given to the person from whom he shall derive his title. *Notice before transfer to avail as to transferee.*

28. No transfer of share shall be made without the consent and approval of the Directors. *Consent of directors to transfer.*

29. Every instrument of transfer of any share in the Company shall be executed by the transferrer and transferee; and the transferrer shall be deemed to remain the holder of such share, and a member of the Company in respect thereof, until the name of the transferee shall be entered in the register of members in respect thereof. *Execution of transfer.*

30. The Company shall not be bound by or responsible for any trust, expressed, implied or constructive, for or upon which shares shall be held. *Company not liable for trusts.*

31. The Directors may, from time to time, make such calls upon the members in respect of all moneys unpaid upon their respective shares as they shall think fit; but no call, except the first or allotment call, shall exceed the amount of ten per cent. per share, and no calls shall be payable less than two months after the date of the resolution of the Directors making the same; and a period of three months, at the least, shall intervene between the dates fixed for payment of two successive calls. *Calls on stock. Amount and intervals limited.*

32. Each member shall be liable to pay the amount of any calls so made upon him, to such person and at such time and place as the Directors shall appoint. *Payment of calls.*

33. Upon a call being made, at least four weeks' notice thereof shall be given in the *Canada Gazette*, and once a week in a daily paper published in the City of Toronto, and once a week in a daily paper published in any city or town in England, Scotland or Ireland, where the Company shall have an office; and if a shareholder shall fail to pay any call due from him, before or on the day appointed for payment thereof, he shall be liable to pay interest for the same at the rate of ten per cent. per annum, or at such other less rate as the *Notice of calls and interest on arrears.*

the Directors shall determine, from the day appointed for payment to the time of actual payment thereof.

Proof in action for recovery.

34. On the trial of any action for the recovery of money due for a call, it shall be sufficient to prove that the defendant at the time of making such call, was a member of the Company, and that such call was in fact made, and such notice thereof given as is directed by this Act; and it shall not be necessary to prove the appointment of the Directors who made such call, nor any other matter whatever; and thereupon the Company shall be entitled to recover what shall be due upon such call, with interest thereon at the rate aforesaid.

Proceedings in case of non-payment.

Notice to defaulter.

35. If any member fail to pay any call upon the day appointed for the payment thereof, the Directors may, at any time thereafter, during such time as the call may remain unpaid, serve a notice on him requiring him to pay such call, together with any interest that may have accrued due thereon by reason of such non-payment; and such notice shall name a day (not less than sixty days from the date of posting such notice) and a place on, and at which such call and interest, and the expenses of such notice and any other expenses that may have been incurred by reason of such non-payment, are to be paid; and such notice shall also state that in the event of non-payment at or before the time and at the place so appointed as aforesaid, the shares in respect of which such call was made will be liable to be declared forfeited.

Forfeiture of shares.

36. If the requisitions of any such notice are not complied with, any share in respect of which such notice has been given, may, at any time thereafter, before payment of all calls, interest and expenses due in respect thereof, be declared forfeited by a resolution of the Directors to that effect.

Defaulter liable notwithstanding forfeiture.

37. Any member whose share shall have been declared forfeited, shall, notwithstanding such forfeiture, be liable to pay to the Company all calls, interest and expenses owing upon such shares at the time of the forfeiture.

Disposal of forfeited shares.

38. Every share which shall be so forfeited shall be deemed to be the property of the Company, and may be sold, re-allotted, or otherwise disposed of upon such terms, in such manner, and to such person or persons as the Company shall think fit.

Title of purchaser of forfeited shares.

39. A declaration in writing by a Director or the Secretary of the Company, that a call was made and notice thereof duly served, and that default in payment of the call was made in respect of any share, and that the forfeiture of such share was made by a resolution of the Directors to that effect

effect, shall be sufficient evidence of the facts therein stated, as against all persons entitled to such share; and such declaration and the receipt of the Company, for such price of such share, shall constitute a good title to such share, and the purchaser shall thereupon be deemed the holder of such share, discharged from all calls due prior to such purchase, and shall be entered upon the register of members in respect thereof; and he shall not be bound to enquire or see to the application of the purchase money, nor shall his title to such share be impeached or affected by any irregularity in the proceedings of such sale.

40. The Company shall not make any dividend whereby their capital stock shall be in any degree reduced. *Dividend not to reduce capital.*

41. Notice of any dividend that may have been declared, shall be given in such manner as the rules or by-laws of the Company may direct, and shall be payable at such place as the Directors shall name; and no dividend shall bear interest against the Company. *Notice of dividend.*

42. The Directors may deduct from the dividends payable to any member, or retain any such dividends in, or towards payment of all such sums of money as may be due from such member to the Company on account of calls or otherwise howsoever. *Dividends liable for debts.*

43. The acts of the Directors shall, notwithstanding it be afterwards discovered that there was some defect in the appointment of such Directors or any of them, or that they or any of them were or was disqualified, be as valid as if they or he had been qualified and duly appointed. *Defect in election not to invalidate acts of directors.*

44. Notices requiring to be served by the Company upon the members may be served in such manner as shall be, from time to time, provided by the by-laws of the Company. *Notices how served.*

45. The Company shall, if required, transmit annually to the Minister of Finance a statement in duplicate made up to the thirty-first day of December preceding and verified by the oath of the President and Manager or Secretary, setting out the capital stock of the Company and the proportion thereof paid up, the names of the shareholders with their places of abode, and the number of shares held by each, the assets and liabilities of the Company, the amount and nature of the investments made by the Company, both on their own behalf and on behalf of others, and the average rate of interest derived therefrom, distinguishing the classes of securities and the extent and value of the lands held by them, and the said Company shall transmit a copy of each such statement to the Clerk of each House of Parliament within the first fifteen days of the first session *Yearly statement to Minister of Finance, and what it must contain.*

session after the date to which it has been made up : Provided always, that in no case shall the Company be bound to disclose the names or private affairs of any persons who may have dealings with them.

Acts of agents to be valid.   **46.** Notwithstanding any law to the contrary, every deed which any person, lawfully empowered in that behalf by the Company as their attorney, signs on behalf of the Company and seals with his seal, shall be binding on the Company, and have the same effect as if it were under the common seal of the Company.

Company to be subject to general Acts.   **47.** The Company availing themselves of any of the provisions of this Act shall be subject to such provisions of any general Acts passed by Parliament, during the present or any future session, as may be declared to apply to loan and investment companies, or which Parliament may deem necessary for the public interest.

Act to be void unless company commence business within two years. Exception.   **48.** In case the Company incorporated by this Act shall not *bonâ fide* commence business under its provisions within two years from and after the passing of this Act, then this Act shall become and be utterly null and void and of no effect, save and except so much of it as provides or may be construed to provide that the provisional or other Directors may pay or reimburse themselves, or others, all costs and expenses incurred in applying for and obtaining this Act and organizing or proceeding to organize the said Company out of any deposit or shares subscribed for; and the charter hereby granted, and all and every the rights and privileges hereby conferred, shall be forfeited.

CHAP. 63.

An Act to authorize the Shareholders of the "Union Permanent Building and Savings Society" to change the name of the said Society to that of the "Union Loan and Savings Company."

[Assented to 12th April, 1876.]

Preamble.   WHEREAS the Union Permanent Building and Savings Society by their petition have represented that they were incorporated under the authority of the Act passed by the legislature of the late Province of Canada, in the ninth year of Her Majesty's reign and intituled "*An Act to* **Act of Province of Canada, 9 V., c. 90.** *encourage the establishment of certain Societies, commonly called Building Societies, in that part of the Province of Canada formerly constituting Upper Canada,*" and of the Acts amending
                                                                              the

the same; and that by reason of the great extension of their
usiness, the increase in the number of their shareholders,
and the extended character of their financial transactions, it
is necessary that they should seek from Parliament power to
change the name of the said Society; and whereas it would
be for the public advantage as well as for the convenience of
the corporation, that the prayer of the said petition should
be granted: Therefore Her Majesty, by and with the advice
and consent of the Senate and House of Commons of Canada,
enacts as follows:—

1. It shall be lawful for the said Society by by-law to change   Name of
the name of the "Union Permanent Building and Savings   society may
Society" to that of the "Union Loan and Savings Company,"   be changed.
which change shall take effect and shall be held to be effect-   New name.
ual to all intents and purposes from and after a day to be
therein specified: Provided, that the Directors of the said   Proviso:
Society shall advertise the change of name once a week for   Notice to be
one month previous to the change taking effect, in the *Canada*   given.
Gazette and in a newspaper published in the City of Toronto.

2. Upon the said change taking effect, the said Society and   Company
all its then members, their successors and assigns forever,   continued
shall therefrom be, and be thereby held to be constituted,   name.
and shall continue to be a body politic and corporate, under
the name last aforesaid, having its principal place of business in the City of Toronto: and under that name shall be
capable of suing and being sued, pleading and being
impleaded in all courts and places whatsoever.

3. The said Society, under its new name, shall not be   Not to be
deemed to be a new corporation; but it shall have, hold, and   deemed a
continue to exercise all the rights, powers and privileges   tion.
that shall, previously to such change, have been held, exer-   Rights
cised and enjoyed by the said "Union Permanent Building   continued.
and Savings Society" in as full and ample a manner as if
the said Society had continued to exist under its original
name; and all statutory provisions applicable to the said
Society, shall continue applicable to the said "Union Loan
and Savings Company."

4. All real and movable property, shares, or stock obliga-   Property
tions, debts, rights, claims and privileges of the said "Union   vested in the
Permanent Building and Savings Society" shall, from the   company
time such change shall take effect, be held by and vested in   for the
the said Society under its new name; and all the share-   society.
holders in the said Society shall, from such time, continue
shareholders in all respects as before such change of name;
but all legal proceedings heretofore regularly begun by or
against the "Union Permanent Building and Savings
Society" may be continued and be terminated under the name
or style of cause in which they have been instituted.

5.

Officers
continued.

5. The then existing President, Vice-President, Directors and officers of the said "Union Permanent Building and Savings Society," shall continue in office as such in the said Society under its new name, until replaced in conformity with the by-laws of the corporation.

By-laws con-
tinued until
altered.

6. All the then existing by-laws and rules of the said "Union Permanent Building and Savings Society" shall continue to have the full force and effect they now possess, as regards the said Society under its new name, its Directors, officers, shareholders and borrowers, until modified. amended or repealed in accordance with the provisions of this Act.

CHAP. 64.

An Act to authorize the shareholders of "The Security Permanent Building and Savings Society of St. Catharines," to change the name of the said Society to that of the "Security Loan and Savings Company."

[Assented to 12th April, 1876.]

Preamble.

WHEREAS "The Security Permanent Building and Savings Society of St.Catharines," by their petition, have represented that they were incorporated under the authority of the Act passed by the legislature of the late Province of Canada, in the ninth year of Her Majesty's reign, intituled

Act of Pro-
vince of
Canada, 9 V.,
c. 90.

"*An Act to encourage the establishment of certain societies, commonly called Building Societies, in that part of the Province of Canada formerly constituting Upper Canada,*" and of the Acts amending the same; and that by reason of the great extension of their business, the increase in the number of their shareholders and the extended character of their financial transactions, it is necessary that they should seek from Parliament powers to change the name of the said society ; and whereas it would be for the public advantage, as well as for the convenience of the corporation, that the prayer of the said petition should be granted : Therefore Her Majesty, by and with the advice and consent of the Senate and House of Commons of Canada, enacts as follows :—

Corporate
name may be
changed' and
how.
New name.

1. It shall be lawful for the said Society by by-law to change the name of "The Security Permanent Building and Savings Society of St. Catharines" to that of the "Security Loan and Savings Company," which change shall take effect, and shall be held to be effectual to all intents and purposes

purposes from and after a day to be therein specified : Pro- Notice to be
vided, that the Directors of the Society shall advertise the given.
change of name once a week for one month previous to the
change taking effect, in the *Canada Gazette*, and in a newspaper published in the town of St. Catharines.

2. Upon the said change taking effect, the said Society, Effect of such
and all its then members, their successors and assigns for change.
ever, shall therefrom be and be thereby held to be constituted,
and shall continue to be a body politic and corporate under
the name last aforesaid, having its principal place of business in the Town of St. Catharines ; and under that name
shall be capable of suing and being sued, pleading and being
impleaded in all courts and places whatsoever.

3. The said Society, under its new name, shall not be Not to be a
deemed to be a new corporation ; but it shall have, hold and new corpora-
continue to exercise all the rights, powers and privileges Rights, &c.,
that shall, previously to such change, have been held, ex- continued.
ercised and enjoyed by the said "The Security Permanent
Building and Savings Society of St. Catharines " in as full
and ample a manner as if the said Society had continued to
exist under its original name ; and all statutory provisions
applicable to the said Society shall continue applicable to
the said "Security Loan and Savings Company."

4. All real and movable property, shares or stock obliga- Property and
tions, debts, rights, claims and privileges of the said "The liabilities
Security Permanent Building and Savings Society of St. society under
Catharines " shall, from the time such change shall take new name.
effect, be held by and vested in the said Society under its
new name ; and all the shareholders in the said Society
shall, from such time, continue shareholders in all respects as
before such change of name ; but all legal proceedings heretofore regularly begun by or against "The Security Permanent Building and Savings Society of St. Catharines " may
be continued and terminated under the name or style of
cause in which they have been instituted.

5. The then existing President, Vice-President, Directors Officers
and officers of the said "The Security Permanent Building continued.
and Savings Society of St. Catharines " shall continue in
office as such in the said Society under its new name, until
replaced in conformity with the by-laws of the corporation.

6. All the then existing by-laws and rules of the said By-laws con-
"The Security Permanent Building and Savings Society of tinued until
St. Catharines " shall have the same force and effect as prior altered.
to the passing of this Act, and shall be binding in law as
regards the said Society under its new name, its Directors,
officers, shareholders and borrowers, until modified, amended
or repealed in conformity with the provisions of this Act.

                                        CHAP.

CHAP. 65.

An Act to authorize the Shareholders of " The Provincial
Permanent Building and Savings Society " to change
the name of the said Society to that of " The Provincial Loan and Savings Company."

[*Assented to 12th April*, 1876.]

Preamble.

WHEREAS " The Provincial Permanent Building and Savings Society " by their petition have represented that
they were incorporated under the authority of the Act
passed by the legislature of the late Province of Canada, in
Act of Pro- the ninth year of Her Majesty's reign, intituled "*An Act to*
vince of *encourage the establishment of certain Societies commonly*
Canada, 9 V.,
c. 90. *called Building Societies in that part of the Province of*
Canada, formerly constituting Upper Canada," and of the Acts
amending the same, and that by reason of the extension of
their business, the increase in the number of their shareholders and the character of their financial transactions, it
would be for the public advantage as well as for the convenience of the corporation, that the name of the said corporation should be changed; and whereas, it would be for
such advantage and convenience that the prayer of the said
petition should be granted: Therefore Her Majesty, by and
with the advice and consent of the Senate and House of
Commons of Canada, enacts as follows :—

Power to   **1.** It shall be lawful for the said Society by by-law, to
change the change the name of " The Provincial Permanent Building
name of
society.   and Savings Society," to that of " The Provincial Loan and
Savings Company," which change shall take effect, and
shall be held to be effectual to all intents and purposes from
Proviso :   and after a day to be specified in such by-law: Provided,
Directors to that the Directors of the Society shall advertise the change
advertise the
change of   of name once a week for one month previous to the change
name.   taking effect, in the *Canada Gazette*, and in a newspaper
published in the City of Toronto.

Society to   **2.** Upon the said change taking effect the said Society
continue as
a corporation and all its then members, their successors and assigns for
under its new ever, shall therefrom be and be thereby held to be con-
name.   stituted, and shall continue to be a body politic and corporate under the name last aforesaid, having its principal place
of business in the City of Toronto; and under that name
shall be capable of suing and being sued, pleading and being
impleaded in all courts and places whatsoever.

Not to be   **3.** The said Society under its new name shall not be
deemed a new
corporation, deemed to be a new corporation; but it shall have, hold
and

and continue to exercise all the rights, powers and privi- but to con-
leges that shall previously to such change have been held, all its present
exercised and enjoyed by the said Provincial Permanent rights and
Building and Savings Society, in as full and ample a man- powers.
ner as if the said Society had continued to exist under its
original name; and all statutory provisions applicable to the
said Society shall continue applicable to the said Provincial
Loan and Savings Company.

4. All real and movable property, shares or stock obliga- Property,
tions, debts, rights, claims and privileges of the said Pro- shareholders
vincial Permanent Building and Savings Society shall, from proceedings
the time such change shall take effect, be held by and vested not to be
in the said Society under its new name; and all the share- change of
holders in the said Society shall, from such time, continue name.
shareholders in all respects as before such change of name;
but all legal proceedings heretofore regularly begun by or
against the Provincial Permanent Building and Savings
Society may be continued and terminated under the name
or style of cause in which they have been instituted.

5. The then existing President, Vice-President, Directors Officers to
and officers of the said Provincial Permanent Building and continue in
Savings Society shall continue in office as such in the said office.
Society, under its new name, until replaced in conformity
with the by-laws of the corporation.

6. All the then existing by-laws and rules of the said By-laws to
Provincial Permanent Building and Savings Society shall continue in
continue to have the full force and effect they now possess altered.
as regards the said Society under its new name, its Directors,
officers, shareholders and borrowers, until modified, amended
or repealed in conformity with the provisions of this Act.

CHAP. 66.

An Act to incorporate "The Maritime Savings and Loan
Society."

[*Assented to 12th April*, 1876.]

WHEREAS Caleb W. Wetmore, William King Crawford, Preamble.
William Hayward, James H. McAvity, Abijah
Eaton and Alfred A. Stockton, all of the City of Saint
John, in the Province of New Brunswick, propose to estab-
lish a joint stock company, and have petitioned for an Act
of incorporation for the said company; and whereas it is
expedient to grant the prayer of their petition: Therefore
Her

Her Majesty, by and with the advice and consent of the Senate and House of Commons of Canada, enacts as follows:—

Petitioners and others incorporated.

1. Caleb W. Wetmore, William King Crawford, William Hayward, James H. McAvity, Abijah H. Eaton and Alfred A. Stockton, and all and every other person and persons, who shall, from time to time, be possessed of any share or shares in the undertaking hereby authorized to be carried on, shall be united into a Company according to the powers and authorities, rules, orders and regulations hereinafter set forth or referred to, and shall be one body politic and corporate, by the name of "The Maritime Savings and Loan Society," and by that name shall have perpetual succession and a common seal, with power to break and alter such seal, and by that name may sue and be sued, plead and be impleaded in all courts whatsoever, whether at law or in equity.

Corporate name and powers.

Provisional Directors.

2. The said above named persons shall be the provisional Directors of the Company, and shall hold office as such until Directors of the Company are elected as hereinafter provided.

Powers and business of the corporation.

3. The Company are hereby empowered to lay out and invest their capital, in the first place, in paying and discharging all costs, charges and expenses incurred in applying for and obtaining the passing of this Act, and all other expenses preparatory or relating thereto; and the remainder of such capital, or so much thereof as may, from time to time, be deemed necessary, in the manner and for the purposes hereinafter mentioned, that is to say:—The Company may, from time to time, lend and advance money by way of loan or otherwise, for such periods as they may deem expedient, on any real security, or on the public securities of the Dominion of Canada, or of any of the Provinces thereof, or of any city or county therein, or on the public securities of the Province of Newfoundland, and upon such terms and conditions as to the Company shall seem satisfactory or expedient; and may acquire, by purchase or otherwise, in addition to the foregoing securities, mortgages on real estate, and real securities; and may re-sell the same as they may deem advisable: with power to do all acts that may be necessary for advancing such sums of money, and for receiving and obtaining repayment thereof, and for compelling the payment of all interest (if any) accruing from such sums so advanced; and the observance and fulfilment of any conditions annexed to such advance, and the forfeiture of any term or property consequent on the non-fulfilment of such conditions, or for the delay of payment; and to give receipts, acquittances and discharges for the same, either absolutely and wholly, or partially, and to execute such deeds, assignments or other instruments

May lend and advance money out of their capital and on what securities.

Mortgages.

May do all things necessary for the recovery of loans.

instruments as may be necessary for carrying such purchase
or re-sale into effect; and for all and every and any of the
foregoing purposes, and for every and any other purpose in
this Act mentioned or referred to, the Company may lay out
and apply the capital and property for the time being of the
Company, or any part thereof, or any of the moneys authorized
to be hereafter raised or received by the Company in addition
to their capital for the time being; with power to do, authorize
and exercise all acts and powers whatsoever, in the opinion
of the Directors of the Company requisite or expedient to be
done or exercised in relation thereto.

4. The Directors may, from time to time, borrow money **Company may borrow money, and execute mortgages, &c., for that purpose.** on behalf of the Company, at such rates of interest and upon such terms as they may, from time to time, think proper, and the Directors may for that purpose execute any mortgages, bonds, debentures with or without interest coupons attached thereto, or other instruments under the common or corporate seal of the Company for sums of not less than one hundred dollars each: Provided, that the total amount of the **Proviso: Total amount limited.** sums to be borrowed as aforesaid shall never exceed the amount of the subscribed capital of the Company which has been *bonâ fide* paid up: Provided also, that the Com- **Proviso: Conditions preliminary to commencing business.** pany shall not commence business unless and until at least twenty per cent. of its capital has been *bonâ fide* paid up, nor unless the amount thereof so paid up shall be at least two hundred thousand dollars.

5. The Company may stipulate for, take, reserve and exact **Company may exact interest, or discount, and at what rate, or payment as a sinking fund.** any rate of interest or discount not exceeding eight per centum per annum or such lower rate of interest as shall be lawful or may be lawfully taken, received, reserved, or exacted either by individuals or by bodies corporate in the place where the contract shall be made, or be executory, and may also receive an annual payment on any loan by way of a sinking fund for the gradual extinction of such loan, upon such terms and in such manner as may be regulated by the by-laws of the Company.

6. A register of all securities held by the Company shall be **Register of securities.** kept; and within fourteen days after the taking of any security, an entry or memorial specifying the nature and amount of such security, and the names of the parties thereto with their proper additions, shall be made in the register.

7. The capital of the Company shall be one million dollars **Capital and shares. Provision for increase.** in shares of one hundred dollars each, but it shall be lawful for the said Company by a resolution passed at the first or any other general meeting of the shareholders to increase the capital stock, from time to time, as may be deemed expedient, to any sum not exceeding the sum of two million dollars,

and

and to raise the amount of the said new stock, either by distribution amongst the original shareholders, or by the issue of
new shares, or partly in one way and partly in the other ; and
the said new stock shall be subject to all such incidents
both with reference to the payment of calls and forfeitures,
and as to the power of lending and borrowing or otherwise
as the original stock.

Incidents of new stock.

8. No member of the Company as such shall be liable
for or charged with the payment of any debt or obligation
of or demand due from the Company beyond the amount
unpaid on any shares in the capital of the Company held
by him.

Liability of shareholders limited.

9. The Company shall keep in a book or books a stock
register, and therein shall be fairly and distinctly entered,
from time to time, the following particulars ; the names and
addresses and the occupations (if any) of the members of the
Company, and the number of shares held by each member,
and the amount paid or agreed to be considered as paid on
the shares of each member.

Stock register and entries therein.

10. Every person who agrees in writing to become a
member of the Company, and whose name is entered on the
stock register shall be deemed to be a member of the
Company.

Who deemed members.

11. Notice of any trust expressed, implied or constructive, shall not be entered on the register nor shall any such
notice in any way affect the Company as to its shares or any
transfer or any transmission thereof.

Trusts not to affect company.

12. When any person makes application in writing, signed
by him, for an allotment of shares, and any shares or share
are or is allotted to him in pursuance of such application,
he shall be deemed conclusively to have agreed to become a
member of the Company in respect of the shares so allotted,
and he shall be entered on the stock register in respect
thereof accordingly.

Allotment of shares.

13. Every member of the Company shall be entitled to
receive a certificate under the common seal of the Company
specifying the share or shares held by him and the amount
paid up thereon ; and on evidence to the satisfaction of the
Directors being given, that any such certificate is worn out,
destroyed or lost, it may be renewed on such terms as the
Directors may appoint : such certificate shall be *primâ facie*
evidence of the title of the member therein named to the
share or shares therein specified.

Share certifi- cate and renewal thereof.

14. If any share stands in the name of two or more persons, the first named in the register of such persons shall, as
regards

No share to be sub-divided ;

regards voting at meetings, receipt of dividends, service of _{person first} notices and all other matters connected with the Company _{named regarded as} (except transfer), be deemed the sole holder thereof; no share _{sole holder.} in the Company shall be subdivided.

15. The Directors may, from time to time, make such calls _{Calls on stock.} upon the members in respect of all moneys unpaid upon their respective shares as they shall think fit : Provided, _{Proviso :} that thirty days at least before the day appointed for each _{Notice and amount of} call, notice thereof shall be mailed to each shareholder and _{and interval} published for that period in a newspaper published in the _{between calls.} City of Saint John ; but no call shall exceed the amount of ten dollars per share, and a period of three months at least shall intervene between two successive calls.

16. Each member shall be liable to pay the amount of _{Liability for calls.} any call so made upon him to such person or persons and at such times and places as the Directors shall appoint.

17. A call shall be deemed to have been made at the time _{Call deemed} when the resolution of Directors authorizing such call was _{made when authorized.} passed ; and if a shareholder shall fail to pay any call due _{Interest after} from him before or on the day appointed for payment _{day appointed.} thereof, he shall be liable to pay interest for the same at the rate of ten per centum per annum, or at such other less rate as the Directors shall determine, from the day appointed for payment to the time of actual payment thereof.

18. The Directors may, if they think fit, receive from any _{Dividends on shares and on} member willing to advance the same, all or any part of the _{moneys paid} amounts due on the shares held by such member beyond the _{in advance.} sums then actually called for ; and upon the moneys so paid in advance, or so much thereof as shall, from time to time, exceed the amount of the calls then made upon the shares in respect of which such advance shall be made, the Company may pay dividends as upon paid up capital.

19. There shall be a book called the "Register of Transfers" _{Register of transfers.} provided, and in such book shall be entered the particulars of every transfer of shares in the capital of the Company.

20. No transfer of shares shall be made without the con- _{Proviso as to transfer of} sent and approval of the Directors, unless the full amount _{shares.} of such shares shall have been paid up.

21. Every instrument of transfer of any share in the _{Transfers,—} Company shall be executed by the transferrer and transferee, _{how to be executed.} and the transferrer shall be deemed to remain the holder of such share and a member of the Company in respect thereof until the name of the transferee shall be entered in the stock register in respect thereof.

9½   **22**

Form of transfer.   **22.** The Directors of the Company shall have power to prescribe the form of the transfer of shares.

As to transfers by debtors to company.   **23.** The Directors may decline to register any transfer of shares belonging to any member who is indebted to the Company.

Transfer by death, bankruptcy, insolvency of members, &c.   **24.** Any person becoming entitled to a share in consequence of the death, bankruptcy or insolvency of any member, may be registered as a member upon such evidence being produced, as shall, from time to time, be required by the Directors, and on production of a request in writing in that behalf signed by him (his signature being attested by at least one witness) which shall be conclusive evidence of his having agreed to become a member.

Notice to shareholders in default of payment of calls.   **25.** If any member fail to pay any call on the day appointed for the payment thereof, the Directors may, at any time thereafter, during such time as the call may remain unpaid, serve a notice on him requiring him to pay such call, together with any interest that may have accrued due thereon by reason of such non-payment; and such notice shall name a day (not being less than thirty days from the service of such notice) and a place on and at which such call and interest, and any expenses that may have been incurred by **That their shares will be forfeited if calls are not paid.** reason of every such non-payment, are to be paid; and such notice shall also state that in the event of non-payment at or before the time, and at the place so appointed as aforesaid, the shares in respect of which such call was made, will be liable to be forfeited.

In default of payment, Directors may declare shares forfeited.   **26.** If the requisitions of any such notice are not complied with, any share in respect of which such notice has been given, may, at any time thereafter before payment of all calls, interest and expenses due in respect thereof, be declared forfeited by a resolution of the Directors to that effect.

Forfeited shares to be the property of the company. **Proviso: no more shares to be sold than will pay arrears.**   **27.** Every share which shall be so declared forfeited, shall be deemed the property of the Company, and may be sold, re-allotted or otherwise disposed of upon such terms, in such manner and to such person or persons as the Company shall think fit: Provided, that the Company shall not sell nor transfer more of the shares of any such defaulter than will be sufficient, as nearly as can be ascertained at the time of such sale, to pay the arrears then due from such defaulter on account of any calls, together with interest and the expenses attending such sale and declaration of forfeiture: and if the money produced by the sale of any such forfeited share or shares be more than sufficient to pay all arrears of calls and interest thereon due at the time of such sale and the expenses aforesaid, the surplus shall on demand be paid to the defaulter.

defaulter, or if not so paid, applied in and towards satisfaction
of any calls made thereafter, but prior to such demand being
made as last aforesaid, in respect of the remaining unsold
shares of such defaulter.

28. Any member, whose shares shall have been declared
forfeited, shall, notwithstanding such forfeiture, be liable to
pay to the Company the balance due upon all calls, interest
and expenses owing upon such shares at the time of the
forfeiture, after deducting any sum that may have been
realized by the Company from the sale or other disposition
of such forfeited shares. *Dues on forfeited shares to be paid.*

29. The Directors may reserve the issue of any portion of
the shares constituting the present capital of the Company
until such further time as they shall think expedient, and
may issue any portion of them from time to time, as and
when they shall think proper. *Directors may reserve the issue of stock.*

30. The shares which may be so reserved by the Direc
tors shall be offered to the members in proportion to the
existing shares held by them ; and such offer shall be made
by the notice specifying the number of shares to which the
member is entitled, and limiting a time within which such
offer, if not accepted, will be deemed to be declined; and
after the expiration of such time, or on the receipt of an
intimation from the member to whom such notice is given
that he declines to accept the shares offered, the Directors
may dispose of the same in such manner as they think most
beneficial to the Company. *Reserved shares ; how disposed of.*

31. It shall be lawful for the Company to receive money
on deposit for such periods and at such rates of
interest as may be agreed upon : Provided, that the total
amount of money so received on deposit, shall not at any
time exceed the then paid up capital of the Company and
thirty-three and one third per cent. added thereto. *Company may receive deposits of money. Proviso: Total amount limited.*

32. For the purpose of organizing the said Company, the
provisional Directors, or a majority of them, may cause stock
books to be opened after giving public notice thereof by
advertisement in one or more newspapers published in the
said City of Saint John,—in which stock books shall be
recorded the names and subscriptions of such persons as
desire to become shareholders in the Company ; and such
books may be opened in the City of Saint John, in the Province of New Brunswick, and elsewhere, at the discretion of
the said provisional Directors, and shall remain open as long
as they deem necessary. *Provisional Directors may open stock books.*

33. When and so soon as the capital stock shall have been
subscribed, and at least ten per cent. of the amount so
subscribed *When the first general meeting of*

shareholders
may be held.

Notice.

Election of
Directors.

subscribed paid in, the said provisional Directors may call a general meeting of the shareholders, to be held in the said City of Saint John,—giving at least thirty days' notice of the time and place for holding such meeting, by publishing the same at least twice a week in some newspaper published in the said City of Saint John, and also, by serving such notice on each shareholder, either personally or by sending the same through the post as hereinafter provided; at which general meeting the shareholders present or represented by proxy, shall elect seven Directors who shall constitute the Board of Directors, and shall hold office until they are re-elected or their successors are appointed at such time and in such manner as may be provided for by the by-laws of the Company.

Number and
qualification
of Directors.

84. The business of the Company shall be managed by not fewer than nine nor more than thirteen Directors, each of whom shall be the holder of at least forty shares of the stock of the Company.

Number of
Directors may
be increased.

85. The number of Directors by whom the business of the Company shall be managed may, at the first or at any other general meeting of the Company, be increased to any number not exceeding thirteen.

How the
profits of the
company
shall be
disposed of.
Reserve fund.

86. The profits of the Company, so far as the same shall extend, shall be divided and disposed of in manner following, that is to say : There shall, in the first place, be set apart for the purpose of forming a reserve fund to meet contin-gencies or for equalizing dividends, such sum not less in any year than two and one-half per centum upon the net profits of the business of the year, as the Directors shall, from time to time, think fit ; and the residue of such profits shall be divided amongst the members in such manner as the Directors shall determine.

No dividend
to impair
capital.

87. The Company shall not declare any dividend whereby their capital stock will, in any way or degree, be reduced.

Penalty on
directors pay-
ing dividend
out of capital,
&c.

How a direc-
tor may
relieve him-
self from
such penalty.

88. If the Directors of the Company declare and pay any dividend when the Company is insolvent, or any dividend, the payment of which renders the Company insolvent, or diminishes the capital stock thereof, they shall be jointly and severally liable, as well to the Company as to the indivi-dual shareholders and creditors thereof, for all the debts of the Company then existing, and for all thereafter contracted during their continuance in office, respectively ; but if any Director, present when such dividend is declared, do forth-with, or if any Director then absent do, within twenty-four hours after he shall have become aware thereof and able to do so, enter on the minutes of the Board of Directors his pro-test against the same, and within eight days thereafter publish

lish such protest in at least one newspaper published at, or as near as may be possible, to the place in which the office or chief place of business of the Company is situated, such Director may thereby, and not otherwise, exonerate himself from such liability.

39. The Directors may deduct from the dividends payable Lien of company thereon to any member, all such sums of money as may be due from him to the Company on account of calls or otherwise.

40. Notice of any dividends that may have been declared Notice of shall be given to each member either personally or through dividends. the post office, and no dividend shall bear interest against the Dividends not to bear Company.   interest.

41. The chief place of business of the said Company shall Chief place be at the City of Saint John, in the Province of New Brunsof business of the company; wick, which shall be the legal domicile of the Company; branch offices but the said Company shall have power, from time to time, and agencies. and at all times hereafter, to establish such and so many offices and agencies in any part of the Dominion of Canada and elsewhere, and under such regulations for the conduct and management thereof, and to remove and discontinue the same as the Directors of the Company may deem expedient

42. Notices requiring to be served by the Company upon Service of the members may be served personally or by leaving the notice by company on same for, or sending them through the post office in premembers, paid letters addressed to the members at their registered place of abode.

43. All notices directed to be given to the members shall, Notice to with respect to any shares to which persons are jointly joint shareholders. entitled, be given to whichever of such persons is first named in the stock register, and notices so given shall be deemed sufficient notice to all the proprietors of such shares.

44. The appointment or election of Directors and officers, Election of and the times, place and mode of calling and holding ordinary directors, meetings of and extraordinary or other meetings of the Company and of the company, the Directors and other officers, and the proceedings at meet&c.; how ings of the Company and of the Directors shall be subject to regulated. and regulated by such rules, regulations and provisions; and Powers of meetings of the Company, and of the Directors, shall have meetings of shareholders such powers, privileges and authorities as may be set forth or directors. and directed in and by by-laws of the Company passed, from time to time, at any general meeting of the Company.

45. At all meetings of the Company, each shareholder Shareholder's shall be entitled to give one vote for each share then held by votes. him and so held for not less than twenty days prior to the time of voting; such votes may be given in person or by Proxies. proxy,

proxy, the holder of any such proxy being himself a shareholder, but no shareholder shall be entitled, either in person
or by proxy, to vote at any meeting unless he shall have
Majority to   paid all the calls upon all the shares held by him; all
decide.   questions proposed for the consideration of the shareholders
Casting vote.   shall be determined by the majority of votes,—the Chairman
presiding at such meeting having the casting vote in case of
an equality of votes.

Yearly state-   **46**. The Company shall transmit annually to the Minister
ment to be   of Finance, a statement in duplicate made up to the thirty-
sent to the   first day of December then last and verified by the oath of
Minister of   the President and Managing Director or Manager, setting
Finance, and   out the capital stock of the Company, and the proportion
what it must   thereof paid up, the names of the shareholders with their
contain.   places of abode and the number of shares held by each, the
assets and liabilities of the Company, the amount and nature
of the investments made by the Company, and the rates of
interest derived therefrom, distinguishing the classes of
securities, the extent and value of the lands held by them,
and such other details as to the nature and extent of the
business of the Company as may be required by the Minister
of Finance ; and a copy of each such statement shall be
transmitted by the Company to the Clerk of each House of
Parliament within the first fifteen days of the first session
after the day to which it is made up : Provided always, that
in no case shall the Company be bound to disclose the names
or private affairs of any person who may have dealings with
them.

Interpreta-   **47**. In this Act the following words and expressions have
tion clause.   the several meanings hereby assigned to them, unless there
be something in the subject or context repugnant to such
Manager.   construction, that is to say:—The word " manager " includes
Secretary.   the words " cashier " and " secretary ;" the expression " The
Land and   Company " means " The Maritime Savings and Loan Society"
real estate.   in this Act mentioned and described ; the expressions " the
Company.   Directors " and " manager " mean the Directors and the
Directors.   manager respectively, for the time being, of the said Com-
Manager.   pany.

Company to   **48**. The Company hereby incorporated shall be subject to
be subject to   such provisions of any general Acts passed by Parliament
any general   during the present or any future session as may be declared
Acts.   to apply to loan and investment companies, or which
Parliament may deem necessary for the public interest.

Company not   **49**. Notwithstanding anything in this Act to the contrary,
to organize or   the Company shall not be organized nor commence business
commence   until they shall have obtained from the Treasury Board a
without   certificate to the effect that it has been proved to the satis-
certificate of   faction of the Board that such amounts of capital have been
Treasury
Board.

bonâ fide subscribed and paid in as are, by this Act, required to be subscribed and paid in respectively before organizing and commencing business under the terms of this Act.

50. The Company shall obtain from the Treasury Board, within two years from and after the passing of this Act, the certificate by this Act required to be obtained by the Company before it can commence business, in default of which this Act shall become and be null and void and of no effect, and the charter hereby granted and all and every the rights and privileges hereby conferred shall be forfeited. Certificate must be obtained within two years.

CHAP. 67.

An Act to incorporate "The National Exchange Company."

[Assented to 12th April, 1876.]

WHEREAS John Francis Mahon, James Adolphus Mahon, Alexander Johnston, Loftus Cuddy, William Ralph Meredith, John Taylor, Daniel Regan, and Samuel Crawford, propose to establish a joint stock Company, and have, by petition, prayed for the passing of an Act of incorporation for the said Company, and it is expedient to grant the prayer of the said petition : Therefore Her Majesty, by and with the advice and consent of the Senate and House of Commons of Canada, enacts as follows :— Preamble.

1. John Francis Mahon, James Adolphus Mahon, Alexander Johnston, Loftus Cuddy, William Ralph Meredith, John Taylor, Daniel Regan, and Samuel Crawford, and all and every other person and persons, body and bodies politic, who shall, from time to time, be possessed of any share or shares in the undertaking hereby authorized to be carried on, shall be united into a Company, according to the powers and authorities, rules, orders and regulations hereinafter set forth or referred to, and shall be one body politic and corporate by the name of "The National Exchange Company," and by that name shall have perpetual succession and a common seal, with power to break and alter such seal ; and by that name may sue and be sued, plead and be impleaded in all courts of law or equity whatsoever. Certain persons and their associates incorporated. Corporate name and general powers.

2. The said above named persons·shall be the provisional Directors of the Company, and shall hold office as such until Directors of the Company are elected as hereinafter provided. Provisional Directors.

3.

Powers and
business of
the Company.

3. The Company are hereby empowered to lay out and invest their capital in the first place in paying and discharging all costs, charges and expenses incurred in applying for and obtaining the passing of this Act, and all other expenses preparatory or relating thereto ; and the remainder of such capital, or so much thereof as may, from time to time, be deemed necessary, in the manner and for the purposes

May make
loans of
money and on
what secur-
ity, &c., &c.

hereinafter mentioned, that is to say:—The Company may, from time to time, lend and advance money by way of loan or otherwise, for such periods as they may deem expedient, on any real security, or on the public securities of the Dominion, or of any of the Provinces thereof,

Rate of
interest
limited.

and upon such terms and conditions and at such rate of interest, not exceeding eight per cent. per annum, as shall be lawful or may be lawfully taken, received, reserved or exacted either by individuals or by corporate bodies in the place where the contract for the same shall be made or be executory, as to the Company shall seem satisfactory or expedient; and may acquire by purchase or otherwise mortgages on real estate, and real securities and may re-sell the same, as they may deem advisable ;—

Powers for
collecting,
&c.

with power to do all acts that may be necessary for advancing such sums of money and for receiving and obtaining re-payment thereof, and for compelling the payment of all interest (if any) accruing from such sums so advanced, and the observance and fulfilment of any conditions annexed to such advance, and the forfeiture of any term or property consequent on the non-fulfilment of such conditions or for the delay of payment, and to give receipts, acquittances and discharges for the same either absolutely and wholly or partially ; and to execute such deeds, assignments or other instruments as may be necessary for carrying any

Application
of capital for
such pur-
poses.

such purchase or re-sale into effect : and for all and every and any of the foregoing purposes, and for every and any other purpose in this Act mentioned or referred to, the Company may lay out and apply the capital and property, for the time being, of the Company, or any part thereof, or any of the moneys authorized to be hereafter raised or received by the Company in addition to their capital for the

Incidental
and necessary
powers.

time being, with power to do, authorize and exercise all acts and powers whatsoever in the opinion of the Directors of the Company requisite or expedient to be done or exercised in relation thereto.

Borrowing
powers of the
Company.

4. The Directors may, from time to time, with the consent of the Company in general meeting assembled, borrow money on behalf of the Company at such rates of interest and upon

Securities to
be given by
them.

such terms as they may, from time to time, think proper; and the Directors may for that purpose make and execute any mortgages, bonds or other instruments, under the common seal of the Company, for sums of not less than one hundred dollars each ; or assign, transfer or deposit by way of equitable

able mortgage or otherwise, any of the documents of title, deeds, muniments, securities or property of the Company, and either with or without power of sale, or other special provisions as the Directors may deem expedient; and no lender shall be bound to enquire into the *Lenders not* occasion for any such loan, or into the validity *bound to make certain* of any resolution authorizing the same, or the purpose for *inquiries.* which such loan is wanted : and it shall be lawful for the *Money on* Company to receive money on deposit, without giving any *deposit.* such security as aforesaid, for such periods and at such rate of interest as may be agreed upon : Provided that the total *Total amount* amount of money so received on deposit, together with the *borrowed or deposited* aggregate of the sum or sums so borrowed, shall not at any *limited.* time exceed the then paid up capital of the Company, and thirty-three and one third per cent.* added thereto.

5. Provided further that the Company shall not borrow *Proviso:* any money or receive any money on deposit unless and until *Company not to borrow* at least twenty per cent. of its subscribed capital has been *until certain* *bond fide* paid up, nor unless the amount thereof so paid up *requirements are complied* shall be at least two hundred thousand dollars. *with.*

6. The Company may hold such real estate as may be *Power to hold* necessary for the transaction of their business, or as being *land for the transaction of* mortgaged or hypothecated to them, may be acquired by them *their business,* for the protection of their investments, and may, from time to *or taken in satisfaction* time, sell, mortgage, lease or otherwise dispose of the same : *of debt.* Provided always, that it shall be incumbent upon the Com- *Proviso—the* pany to sell any real estate acquired in satisfaction of any *latter to be sold within a* debt within ten years thereafter. *certain time.*

7. The Company may stipulate for, and may demand and *Company* receive in advance, the interest from time to time accruing *may demand and receive* on any loans granted by the Company, and may also receive *interest in* payments on any loans by way of sinking fund, for the *advance with sinking fund.* gradual extinction of such loan upon such terms and in such manner as may be regulated by the by-laws of the Company ; and may require from the borrower the payment of the *Expenses may* expenses incidental to any such loan, either at the time the *be added to principal.* loan is advanced or may give such time for payment of the same as they may be advised, and may add the same to the principal or interest secured by any mortgage or other security securing the loan.

8. The Company may stipulate for, take, reserve and *What interest* exact any rate of interest or discount that may be lawful or *or discount the Company* may be lawfully taken, received, reserved or exacted either *may take.* by individuals or by corporate bodies in the place where the contract for the same shall be made or be executory, but not exceeding eight per centum per annum, and shall not in respect thereof be liable for any loss, penalty or forfeiture on any account whatever ; and may also receive
an

And for a sinking fund. an annual payment on any loan by way of a sinking fund for the gradual extinction of such loan, upon such terms and in such manner as may be regulated by the by-laws of the Company.

Register of securities what to show. **9.** A register of all securities held by the Company shall be kept, and within fourteen days after the taking of any security an entry or memorial, specifying the nature and amount of such security, and the names of the parties thereto, with their proper additions, shall be made in such register.

Capital and number of shares. Power to increase stock to $1,000,000. **10.** The capital of the Company shall be one million dollars, in shares of one hundred dollars each; but it shall be lawful for the said Company, by a resolution passed at any general meeting of the shareholders, to increase the capital stock at any time, or from time to time as may be deemed expedient, to any sum not exceeding one million dollars, and to raise the amount of the said new stock either by distribution amongst the original shareholders or by the issue of new shares, or partly in one way and partly in the Incidents of new stock. other; and the said new stock shall be subject to all such incidents, both with reference to the payment of calls and forfeiture, and as to the powers of lending and borrowing or otherwise as the original stock.

Shares to be personal estate. **11.** All shares in the capital of the Company shall be personal estate, and transmissible as such.

Extent of liability of shareholders. **12.** No member of the Company shall be liable for or charged with the payment of any debt or demand due from the Company beyond the extent of his shares in the capital of the Company not then paid up.

Register of shareholders. **13.** The Company shall keep, in a book or books, a register of the members of the Company, and therein shall be fairly and distinctly entered from time to time the following particulars :—The names and addresses, and the occupations (if any) of the members of the Company, and the number of shares held by such members, and the amount paid or agreed Who to be deemed members. to be considered as paid on the shares of each member; and every person who agrees in writing to become a member of the Company, and whose name is entered on the register of members, shall be deemed to be a member of the Company.

Register to be deemed evidence. **14.** The register of members shall be *primâ facie* evidence of any matters by this Act directed or authorized to be inserted therein.

Company not bound to regard trusts on stock. **15.** Notice of any trust, expressed, implied or constructive shall not be entered on the register, nor shall any such notice in any way affect the Company as to its shares or any transfer or any transmission thereof.

16

16. When any person makes application in writing *Allotment of* signed by him for an allotment of shares, and any shares or *shares and its effect.* share are or is allotted to him in pursuance of such application, he shall be deemed *primâ facie* to have agreed to become a member of the Company in respect of the shares so allotted, and he shall be entered on the register of members in respect thereof accordingly.

17. Every member of the Company shall, on payment of *Certificates.* twenty-five cents, or such less sum as the Directors shall *of shares.* prescribe, be entitled to receive a certificate under the common seal of the Company, specifying the share or shares held by him, and the amount paid up thereon; and on *Renewal of* evidence to the satisfaction of the Directors being given *certificates.* that any such certificate is worn out, destroyed or lost, it may be renewed on payment of the sum of twenty-five cents, or such less sum as the Directors shall prescribe: such certificate shall be *primâ facie* evidence of the title of the member therein named to the share or shares therein specified.

18. If any share stands in the name of two or more per- *Joint share-* sons, the first named in the register of such persons, shall, *holders.* as regards voting at meetings, receipt of dividends, service of notices, and all other matters connected with the Company (except transfer) be deemed the sole holder thereof. No share in the Company shall be subdivided. *No share to be divided.*

19. The Directors may, from time to time, make such calls *Power to* upon the members in respect of all moneys unpaid upon their *make calls.* respective shares as they shall think fit: Provided, that *Notice—calls* twenty-one days at the least before the day appointed for *limited.* each call, notice thereof shall be served on each member liable to pay the same; but no call shall exceed the amount of ten dollars per share and a period of three months shall *Interval* at the least intervene between two successive calls. *between.*

20. Each member shall be liable to pay the amount of *Liability to* any calls so made upon him, to such person, and at such *pay calls.* time and place as the Directors shall appoint.

21. A call shall be deemed to have been made at the time *Interest on* when the resolution of the Directors authorizing such call *calls due and* was passed; and if a shareholder shall fail to pay any call *unpaid.* due from him, before, or on the day appointed for payment thereof, he shall be liable to pay interest upon the same at the rate of ten per cent. per annum, or at such other less rate as the Directors shall determine, from the day appointed for payment to the time of actual payment thereof.

22. The Directors may, if they think fit, receive from any *Payment in* member willing to advance the same, all, or any part of the *advance.* amounts due on shares held by such member, beyond the sums then

Interest may be allowed.

then actually called for ; and upon the moneys so paid in advance, or so much thereof as from time to time shall exceed the amount of the calls then made upon the shares in respect of which such advance shall be made, the Company may pay interest at such rate per annum as the member paying such sum in advance and the Directors shall agree upon.

Transfer Register.

23. There shall be a book called the " Register of Transfers" provided, and in such book shall be entered the particulars of every transfer of shares in the capital of the Company.

Consent of Directors requisite.

24. No share shall be transferred without the consent and approval of the Directors, unless the full amount of such share shall have been paid up.

Execution transfer.

25 Every instrument of transfer of any share in the Company shall be executed by the transferrer and the transferee, and the transferrer shall be deemed to remain the holder of such share, and a member of the Company in respect thereof, until the name of the transferee shall be entered in the register of members in respect thereof.

Arrears must be first paid.

26. The Directors may decline to register any transfer of shares belonging to any member who is indebted to the Company.

Transmission of shares by bankruptcy, marriage of female members, &c.

27. Any person becoming entitled to a share in consequence of the death, bankruptcy or insolvency of any member, or in consequence of the marriage of any female member, may be registered as a member upon such evidence being produced as shall, from time to time, be required by the Directors, and on production of a request in writing in that behalf, signed by him (his signature being attested by at least one witness), which shall be conclusive evidence of his having agreed to become a member.

Liability to forfeiture for non-payment of calls.

Notice of forfeiture.

28. If any member fails to pay any call on the day appointed for the payment thereof, the Directors may, at any time thereafter during such time as the call may remain unpaid, serve a notice on him, requiring payment of such call, together with any interest that may have accrued due thereon by reason of such non-payment; and such notice shall name a day (not less than twenty-one days from the date of such notice) and a place on and at which such call and interest and any expenses that may have been incurred by reason of such non-payment are to be paid ; and such notice shall also state that in the event of non-payment at or before the time and at the place so appointed as aforesaid, the shares in respect of.which such call was made will be liable to forfeiture.

29.

29. If the requisitions of any such notice are not com- Forfeiture of share. plied with, any share, in respect of which such notice has been given, may, at any time thereafter before payment of all calls, interest and expenses due in respect thereof, be declared forfeited by a resolution of the Directors to that effect.

30. Every share which shall be so declared forfeited shall Disposal of forfeited shares. be deemed to be the property of the Company, and may be sold, re-allotted or otherwise disposed of upon such terms, in such manner and to such person or persons as the Company shall think fit.

31. Any member whose shares shall have been declared Liability to payment of arrears. forfeited, shall—notwithstanding such forfeiture—be liable to pay to the Company all calls, interest and expenses owing upon such shares at the time of the forfeiture.

32. There shall be paid in respect of every transfer or Fee on transfers. transmission of shares, such a fee not exceeding fifty cents, as the Directors shall, from time to time, prescribe.

33. The Directors may reserve the issue of any portion of Reservation of shares. the shares constituting the present capital of the Company until such further time as they shall think expedient, and may issue any portion of them from time to time, as and when they shall think proper.

34. The shares so reserved shall be offered to the mem- Offer of reserved shares to members in proportion to their stock. bers in proportion to the existing shares held by them ; and such offer shall be made by a notice specifying the number of shares to which the member is entitled, and limiting a time within which such offer, if not accepted, will be deemed to be declined ; and after the expiration of the time, or on receipt of an intimation from the member to whom such notice is given that he declines to accept the shares offered, the Directors may dispose of the same in such manner as they may think most beneficial to the interests of the Company.

35. So soon as one million dollars of the capital stock shall Amount of capital stock to be subscribed and paid before transaction of business and election of Directors. have been subscribed, and one hundred thousand dollars shall have been paid up, the provisional Directors of the said Company may call a meeting of the shareholders, at some place to be named in the City of London, giving at least ten days' notice by circular, and also in some daily newspaper published in the said city,—at which meeting the shareholders present in person or represented by proxy shall elect seven Directors in the manner and qualified as hereinafter provided, who shall constitute a Board of Directors, and Term of office. shall hold office until they are re-elected or their successors appointed at such time as may be provided for in the by-laws of the Company.

36.

Number of Directors.

36. The business of the Company shall be managed by a Board of not less than nine nor more than thirteen Directors, a majority of whom shall constitute a quorum for the transaction of business.

Directors shall fix salaries of president and employees. Power to make by-laws, &c. Proviso.

37. The Board of Directors shall fix and determine the salaries or compensation for services to be allowed and paid to the President, Cashier, and other employees, and may make and adopt such by-laws, rules or regulations for the internal management of the affairs of the Company, as they may deem expedient and proper : Provided such by-laws shall not be at variance with any of the provisions of this Act, and shall only remain in force until the next general meeting of the shareholders, unless then ratified.

Qualification of Directors.

38. No person shall be eligible for Directorship in the said Company who does not hold in his own name and for his own use at least ten shares of its capital stock.

Annual election of Directors.

39. There shall be an annual election of Directors for the Company, to be held at the City of London, on a day and at a place to be fixed by by-law, and notices of such election shall be mailed to the stockholders or published in one daily and one weekly paper printed at the said City of London, during the ten days preceding the day of election.

President and vice-president, election of and how made.

40. The Directors and their successors at their first meeting, or as soon thereafter as practicable, shall elect by ballot one of their number to the office of President, and another to the office of Vice-President; and the President so elected shall be acknowledged the official head of the Company.

Vacancies how filled.

41. If any vacancy should any time occur amongst the said Directors by death, resignation, removal or disqualification, such vacancy shall be filled for the remainder of the term of office of the Director dying, resigning or being removed or becoming disqualified by the remaining Directors, or the majority of them, electing in such place or places a shareholder or shareholders eligible for such office.

If election not held on day appointed may be held on another day named by Directors.

42. In case it should happen that an election of Directors of the said Company should not be made on any day when pursuant to this Act and in accordance with the provisions of the by-law made in that respect, it should have been made, the said Company shall not for that cause be deemed to be dissolved ; but it shall be lawful on any other day to hold and make an election in such manner as may be regulated, directed and appointed by the Directors for the time being; and the Directors in office shall so continue until a new election is made.

43.

43. At all meetings of the Company each shareholder shall Votes and proxies. be entitled to give one vote for each share then held by him and so held for not less than twenty days prior to the time of voting. Such votes may be given in person or by proxy— the holder of any such proxy being himself a shareholder ; but no shareholder shall be entitled, either in person or by All calls to be paid before voting. proxy, to vote at any meeting unless he shall have paid all the calls then due upon all the shares held by him : all questions Majority to decide. proposed for the consideration of the shareholders shall be determined by a majority of votes, which votes, in all cases, Votes by ballot. shall be cast by ballot,—the chairman presiding at such meeting having the casting vote in case of an equality of votes ; and at all meetings of the Directors the President or Casting vote. Vice-President or presiding Director shall give the casting vote in case of an equality of votes, in addition to his own vote as a Director.

44. The Directors shall appoint a person to the office of Directors to appoint a cashier or manager; duties of. Cashier or Manager, whose duty it shall be to keep the minutes of the Board of Directors, to direct the employees of the Company, to examine accounts and give directions for carrying into effect the general business of the Company, and report to the Directors at their meetings the state and con- dition of the Company.

45. The Cashier and all other employees of the Company Cashier and employees to give bonds. appointed by the Board of Directors shall, before entering upon their several duties, give bonds with sureties satis- .factory to the President for the faithful performance of the various trusts reposed in them : Provided always that no Proviso. Director of the Company shall, at any time, become a surety for any employee of the Company.

46. The Cashier for the time being shall give to sub- Cashier to give receipts for instal- ments scribers to the capital stock of the Company, receipts for instalments paid by them, countersigned by the President for the time being, and no certificate of stock shall be issued to a subscriber until the total amount of his or her subscrip- tions shall have been paid.

47. All certificates of stock in the Company shall be Certificates of stock how signed and counter- signed. signed by the Cashier and President, and countersigned by one of the Directors for the time being, appointed by the Board for that purpose, and such Director shall keep a dupli- cate stock ledger.

48. The profits of the Company, so far as the same shall Division of profits of Company. extend, shall be divided and disposed of in manner follow- ing, that is to say ; there shall, in the first place, be set apart for the purpose of forming a reserve fund, to meet contin- gencies or for equalizing dividends, such sum, not less in any one year than two and a half per centum upon the net

                    profits

profits of the business of such year, as the Directors shall, from time to time, think fit; and the residue of such profits shall be divided amongst the members, in such manner as the Directors with the sanction of the Company in general meeting assembled shall determine.

Dividends not to reduce capital.

49. The Company shall not make any dividend whereby the capital stock shall be reduced. .

Deductions from dividends.

50. The Directors may deduct from dividends payable to any member, all such sums of money as may be due from him to the Company on account of calls or otherwise.

Notices of dividends.

51. Notice of any dividend that may have been declared shall be given to each member—and no dividend shall bear interest against the Company.

Chief office in London.

52. The Company shall have its chief office in the City of London, and may establish such other offices or agencies elsewhere in the Dominion of Canada as they may deem expedient.

Service of notices by the Company.

53. Notices required to be served by the Company upon the members, may be served either personally, or by leaving the same for, or sending them through the post office in prepaid letters addressed to the members at their registered places of abode.

Notices to members sent by post.

54. A notice or other document served by post by the Company on a member, shall be taken as served at the time when the letter containing it would be delivered 'in the ordinary course of post; to prove the fact and time of service it shall be sufficient to prove that such letter was properly addressed and was put into the post office, and the time when it was put in, and the time requisite for its delivery in the ordinary course of post.

Notices to joint shareholders.

55. All notices directed to be given to the members shall, with respect to any share to which persons are jointly entitled, be given to whichsoever of such persons is first named in the register of members, and notice so given shall be deemed sufficient notice to all the proprietors of such shares.

Notice binding on transferees.

56. Every person who, by operation of law, transfer or other means whatsoever, shall become entitled to any shares, shall be bound by any and every notice which, previously to his name and address being entered upon the register of members in respect of such share, shall have been given to the person from whom he shall derive his title.

Certified copies of by-laws, &c., to

57. A copy of any by-law, rule, regulation or minute, or of any entry in any book of the Company, certified to be

a true copy or extract under the hand of the President or be received as
Vice-President, or the Cashier or Secretary of the Company, *primâ facie*
and sealed with the corporate seal, shall be received in all evidence
courts and proceedings as *primâ facie* evidence of such by- ther proof.
law, rule, regulation, minute or entry without further proof
thereof, and without proof of the official character or signature of the officer signing the same, or of the corporate seal.

58. The appointment or election of Directors and officers, Certain mat-
and the times, place, and mode of calling and holding ters may be
ordinary and extraordinary or other meetings of the Com- by-law.
pany, and of the Directors and other officers, and the proceedings at meetings of the Company and of the Directors
shall be subject to and regulated by such by-laws, rules,
regulations and provisions ; and meetings of the Company Meetings.
and of the Directors shall have such powers, privileges and
authorities, as may be set forth and directed in and by by-
laws of the Company passed from time to time at any general meeting of the Company.

59. The Company shall transmit annually to the Minister Annual state-
of Finance a statement in duplicate, made up to the thirty- ment to
first day of December and verified by oath of the President ister and
and Cashier, setting out the capital stock of the Company and what it must
the proportion thereof paid up, the names of all the share- show.
holders with their places of abode and the number of shares
held by each, the assets and liabilities of the Company, the
amount and nature of the investments made by the Company,
both on their own behalf and on behalf of others, and the
average rate of interest derived therefrom,—distinguishing the
classes of securities, the extent and value of the lands held
by them, and such other details as to the nature and extent
of the business of the Company as may be required by the
Minister of Finance ; and the Company shall transmit a copy
of each such statement to the Clerk of each House of Parliament within the first fifteen days of the first session after
the date to which it has been made up : Provided always, Proviso.
that in no case shall the Company be bound to disclose the
name or private affairs of any person who may have dealings with them.

60. In this Act the following words and expressions have Interpreta-
the several meanings hereby assigned to them, unless there tion.
be something in the subject or context repugnant to such
construction, that is to say :— the word " Cashier " includes
the words Manager, Secretary and clerk ; the expression
" The Company," means the National Exchange Company ;
" The Directors and the Cashier " mean the Directors and
Cashier respectively for the time being of the said Company.

61. The Company hereby incorporated shall be subject to Company to
such provisions of any general Acts passed by Parliament be subject to
10½   during Act.

during the present or any future session as may be declared to apply to loan and investment companies, or which Parliament may deem necessary for the public interest.

To obtain certificate from Treasury Board before organizing or commencing. **62.** Notwithstanding anything in this Act to the contrary, the Company shall not be organized nor commence business until they shall have obtained from the Treasury Board a certificate to the effect that it has been proved to the satisfaction of the Board that such amounts of capital have been *bonâ fide* subscribed and paid up as are by this Act required to be subscribed and paid up respectively before organizing and commencing business under the terms of this Act.

Certificate must be obtained within two years. **63.** The Company shall obtain from the Treasury Board, within two years from and after the passing of this Act, the certificate by this Act required to be obtained by the Company before it can commence business, in default of which this Act shall become and be null and void and of no effect, and the Charter hereby granted and all and every the rights and privileges hereby conferred, shall be forfeited.

CHAP' 68.

An Act to amend the Act to incorporate "The Commercial Travellers' Association of Canada."

[Assented to 12th April, 1876.]

Preamble. WHEREAS by the Act to incorporate "The Commercial Travellers' Association of Canada" it was declared that the said Association had for its objects the moral, intellectual and financial improvement, advancement and welfare of its members ; and whereas one purpose of the said Association was to insure its members against accidents, and doubts have been expressed whether such purpose falls by legal construction within the objects so defined : Therefore Her Majesty, by and with the advice and consent of the Senate and House of Commons of Canada, declares and enacts as follows :—

Association may make contracts for Accident Insurance. **1.** The said Association shall have and has power and authority, with and out of the funds thereof, to make contracts of insurance with any Accident Insurance Company, against accidents or casualties arising to the members of the said Association whereby they may suffer loss or injury, or be disabled or die, and also to apply its funds from time to time in benefits or bonuses to members thereof during sickness or disability from accident, casualty, or otherwise, or at death to the families or personal representatives of such

members,

members, and to make and from time to time to alter such by-laws, rules and regulations as may be necessary for any such purpose.

2. And it is hereby declared, that the Association has power and authority to grant any sum of money to the family or representatives of any of the members of the Association, who have died by reason of any accident since the incorporation of the said Association, or to grant any sum of money to any of the members of the said Association who are living, but have suffered loss or injury or have been disabled since the incorporation of the said Association. *And may grant relief to certain of its members.*

3. At any annual meeting of the Association members may vote by proxy in the election of officers in such manner as shall be provided by by-law. *Votes by proxy.*

CHAP. 69.

An Act to amend the Act to incorporate " The Canada Shipping Company."

[*Assented to 12th April*, 1876.]

WHEREAS " The Canada Shipping Company " have petitioned for amendments to their Act of Incorporation, and it is expedient to grant the prayer of their petition : Therefore Her Majesty, by and with the advice and consent of the Senate and House of Commons of Canada, enacts as follows :— *Preamble.*

1. The said Company are hereby authorized, from time to time, as occasion may require, and by such amounts as may, from time to time, be deemed advisable, to increase their capital stock to an extent not exceeding in all five millions of dollars currency, either by the allotment of new shares to the persons who may be holders of the stock of the Company at the time of the increase, or by the admission of new subscribers, or by any other equitable means the said Company, acting by its shareholders or Directors, may decide upon. *Capital stock, may be increased to $5,000,000, and by what means.*

2. All the provisions of the Statute of Canada, thirty-first Victoria, chapter eighty-eight, in regard to the making and the recovery of calls, as well as in regard to by-laws, and generally all the powers granted by the said cited Statute in so far as they are applicable, shall apply to the increase of stock authorized by the present Act, save and except as hereinafter provided. *Act of incorporation 31 V., c. 88, to apply.*

3.

Shares to be
$100 each.

3. The capital stock of the said Company, old and new, shall be divided into shares of one hundred dollars, currency, each, and the present shares being each for one thousand dollars, shall be divided each into ten shares of one hundred dollars; and the Directors may, by resolutions, rules, orders or by-laws, require the surrender of such scrip certificates or vouchers for shares as may exist or may have been granted in respect of the present existing shares, and grant such new certificates in accordance with the amendments herein contained as they may judge advisable.

New certificates for
existing
shares.

Company
may purchase
cargo, to be
carried exclusively by
their vessels.

4. The Company are hereby empowered, by themselves or their agents, when they find it necessary or advisable so to do, to purchase, and afterwards sell, cargoes or parts thereof to be carried exclusively by the vessels of the said Company.

Company
may purchase
vessels, &c.

5. The Company are hereby empowered to purchase, acquire and sell all kinds of ships, steamers, steamships, boats, vessels and craft generally, as well as appurtenances, ships' stores and furnishings, either from individuals or companies, and may pay for the same in money or other value, or in shares in the capital stock of the said Canada Shipping Company, provided the number of shares issued for all purposes shall not exceed the number authorized by the present Act.

Proviso.

Name of
Company
changed.

6. The Company, for and notwithstanding anything in the said recited Act contained, shall hereafter be known and designated as "The Canada Shipping Company (Limited)."

CHAP. 70

An Act to amend the Act thirty-eighth Victoria, chapter ninety-three, intituled, "An Act to incorporate the Canadian Gas Lighting Company."

[*Assented to 12th April,* 1876.]

Preamble.
33 V., c. 93.

WHEREAS the "Canadian Gas Lighting Company" has petitioned for certain amendments to its Act of Incorporation; and whereas it is expedient to grant the prayer of the said petition: Therefore Her Majesty, by and with the advice and consent of the Senate and House of Commons of Canada, enacts as follows:—

Sect. 1
amended.

1. Section one of the said Act of incorporation is amended to read as follows:

"1.

" 1. The said petitioners and all such other persons as Certain per-
sons incor-
porated. shall be shareholders in the corporation hereby created, shall be, and they are hereby made, a body corporate and politic, by the name of the " Canadian Gas Lighting Company," and Corporate
name and
powers. shall have the power to work the said inventions and processes, and also the Patent known as Rigby's Excelsior Patent for the manufacture and sale of illuminating gas, and the apparatus to produce the same, in any part of the Dominion of Canada, and may hold, use, or dispose of the same for the benefit of the business of the said Company. Moreover, the May hold
real estate
for their own
use. said Company may acquire and hold by purchase or otherwise immovable property, for the efficient and convenient carrying on and development of the business of the said Company, and may sell or otherwise dispose of the same, and in place thereof acquire other immovable property for the same purpose."

CHAP. 71.

An Act to amend the Act incorporating " The Ottawa Gas Company," to confirm a resolution of their Shareholders placing preferential and ordinary ·stock on the same footing, and to confirm, amend and extend their corporate powers.

[Assented to 12th April, 1876.]

WHEREAS under the provisions of a certain Act of the Preamble. Parliament of the late Province of Canada passed in Act of Pro-
vince of
Canada, 29 the twenty-ninth year of the reign of Her Majesty Queen Victoria, intituled : " *An Act to change the name of the Bytown* V., c. 88,
recited in
part. " *Consumers' Gas Company and to confirm, amend and extend* " *their corporate powers under the name of The Ottawa Gas* " *Company,*" the capital stock of the said the Ottawa Gas Company was increased from ten thousand pounds to fifty thousand pounds, and the said Company were empowered at a general meeting of the holders of the then present subscribed stock by a resolution to be ratified by the President and Directors under the seal of the Company, to declare and make any number of the shares of such stock preferential stock, upon such terms and conditions and with such advantages to the subscribers and holders of such preferential stock, over the residue of such stock as they should see fit : And whereas at a general meeting of the said holders of the then present subscribed stock duly held on the twenty-third day of August in the year of Our Lord one thousand eight hundred and sixty-nine they, by resolution ratified by the President and Directors under the seal of the Company, declared
clared

clared and made thirteen hundred and twenty-two of the
shares of such capital stock, preferential stock, upon the
terms and conditions and with certain advantages in the
said resolution set forth; And whereas at another general
meeting of the said stockholders duly held on the twenty-
first day of April in the year of Our Lord one thousand eight
hundred and seventy-three they, by resolution ratified by
the President and Directors under the seal of the Company,
declared and made thirteen hundred and twenty-two of the
shares of the unsubscribed capital stock of the Company
" preferential stock second issue" upon the terms and conditions and with certain advantages therein set forth; And
whereas at another general meeting of the said shareholders
and of the first and second preferential stockholders duly
held on the first day of June in the year of Our Lord one
thousand eight hundred and seventy-five they, by resolution
ratified by the President and Directors under the seal of the
Company, and with the unanimous consent of all the preferential stockholders, allotted three thousand nine hundred
and sixty-six shares of the said unsubscribed capital stock
of the Company amongst the then holders of preferential
stock, in the proportion of two shares for each share of preferential stock, first issue, held, and of one share for each
share of preferential stock, second issue, held, in consideration that from thenceforth the said preferential stockholders, both of first and second issue, should cease to be
preferential stockholders, and that all shares should be held
on the same footing, with the same rights and powers as if
the said preferential stock had never been created; And
whereas to meet the requirements of the rapidly increasing
population of the City of Ottawa, the City of Hull, and the
villages of New Edinburgh and Rochesterville, it is necessary that the capital stock of the said Company should be
increased; And whereas the said the Ottawa Gas Company
have by their petition prayed that the said resolution of the
first day of June in the year of Our Lord one thousand eight
hundred and seventy-five, may be confirmed by Act of Parliament, their capital increased, and their corporate powers
confirmed, amended, and extended, and it is expedient to
grant the prayer of the said petition: Therefore Her Majesty, by and with the advice and consent of the Senate and
House of Commons of Canada, enacts as follows :—

A certain
resolution of
the Company
declared
legal.

1. The said resolution of the stockholders of the said
Company passed at a general meeting held on the first day
of June one thousand eight hundred and seventy-five, allotting certain unsubscribed capital stock to the holders of preferential stock, both first and second issue, and with the
consent of all such preferential stockholders, declaring that
thenceforth all preferential stock should cease to be preferential, and that all shares of the capital stock of the said
Company should be non-preferential and on the same
footing

footing as if no preferential stock had ever been created, is
hereby declared to have been legally passed, and to be
legally operative and binding, and all shares of the capital
stock of the said Company now held by subscribers are and
shall be non-preferential.

2. It shall and may be lawful to and for the said Com- Increase of
pany to add to their present capital stock any sum not exceed- capital stock
ing three hundred thousand dollars, divided into shares of provided for.
twenty dollars each ; provided that such increase of the Proviso.
capital stock shall be agreed upon by a majority of the votes
of the shareholders present at any annual general meeting or
meetings, or at any special meeting or meetings called from
time to time for that purpose.

3. Any new stock of the said Company to be issued on Issue of new
any such increase of the capital stock shall be allotted to the stock.
then shareholders of the said Company *pro rata* at par : Pro- Proviso, as to
vided always, that any of such increased stock which shall allotment.
not be taken up and subscribed for by any shareholder
within one month from the time when notice of the allotment thereof shall have been mailed, prepaid, in the post
office at the City of Ottawa, to his address, may be opened for
subscription to the public in such manner and on such
terms as the Directors of the said Company may determine.

4. The shares of such stock subscribed for shall be paid in Calls on
by such instalments, and at such times and places and under shares.
such regulations as the Directors of the said Company may,
from time to time, appoint ; and executors, administrators, Payment by
trustees or curators paying instalments on the shares of executors, &c.
deceased shareholders, shall be and they are hereby respectively indemnified for paying the same.

5. It shall not be obligatory upon the said Company to Stock may be-
open books of subscription, or to sell or allot the whole issued from
amount of stock authorized by this Act ; but the said Com- time to time.
pany may, from time to time, limit the number of shares for
which books of subscription shall be opened, or which shall
be allotted, offered for sale, or otherwise disposed of, to such
amount as may be, from time to time, agreed and decided
upon by a majority of the votes of shareholders present at
any general or special meeting of the shareholders as aforesaid, called for that purpose.

6. The notice of any special meeting or meetings of the Notice of
stockholders of the said Company called by the Directors or special
stockholders thereof, in pursuance of the Act of incorporation meetings.
thereof or of this Act, shall be given by inserting a notice
specifying the time, place, and object of such meeting in at
least

least two daily newspapers published in the city of Ottawa in each issue thereof, during the two weeks next preceding the day fixed for such meeting.

Existing en-
actments to
apply.
7. All the provisions of the Act incorporating the said Company, and the Acts amendatory thereof, which were or now are applicable to the present stock of the said Company, not inconsistent with the provisions of this Act, shall apply to the new stock subscribed or allotted under this Act.

CHAP. 72.

'An Act to extend the provisions of " An Act relating to the Upper Ottawa Improvement Company."

[Assented to 12th April, 1876.]

Preamble.
WHEREAS the' Upper Ottawa Improvement Company have petitioned to have their charter extended and certain additional powers conferred on them, and it is expedient to grant the prayer of their petition : Therefore Her Majesty, by and with the advice and consent of the Senate and House of Commons of Canada, enacts as follows :—

Certain
works au-
thorized, and
confirmed.

38 V., c. 77.
1. Those works which have been recently constructed on the Upper Ottawa, known as " Melons Chenail Boom " and " Allumette Boom," are hereby authorized and confirmed. subject always to compulsory removal after notice as is provided in section two of the Act passed in the thirty-eighth year of Her Majesty's reign, intituled, "*An Act relating to the Upper Ottawa Improvement Company.*"

Land selec-
tion privilege
extended.
2. The privilege of selecting and acquiring ten separate and distinct parcels of land as provided in the said second section is hereby extended to the first day of May, one thousand eight hundred and eighty-one, and the same shall not be taken to have been reduced or impaired by the construction of the said works in the first section of this Act mentioned.

Dues for
boom work-
ing expenses.
3. The said Company shall have a further power to levy and collect tolls, dues and charges for boom working expenses, the same having been first approved by the Governor in Council and published in the *Canada Gazette* pursuant to the provisions of section nine of the said cited Act, which section shall apply thereto ; and the Order in Council to 'be adopted thereunder shall be deemed the only authority required for the tolls, dues and charges, and also for the works of the Company.

4.

4. The Company may become parties to bills of exchange Company and promissory notes either as makers, endorsers, drawers, may be parties to acceptors or holders, and may sue and be sued thereon, pro- promissory vided the same are made, drawn, endorsed, accepted or taken notes, &c. in accordance with a by-law or by-laws to be passed by the shareholders.

5 The by-laws of the Company shall not require publica- No publica- tion¹ in any newspaper, but the same shall be printed and laws re- posted in the office of the Company and be open to inspec- quired. tion at all reasonable hours : Provided always, that copies Proviso. of all such by-laws shall be appended to the Company's annual report made to the Minister of Public Works.

CHAP. 73.

An Act to amend the Act thirty-fifth Victoria, Chapter one hundred and eleven, intituled : " An Act to incor- porate The Mail Printing and Publishing Company (Limited.)"

[Assented to 12th April, 1876.]

WHEREAS The Mail Printing and Publishing Company Preamble. (Limited), duly incorporated as such by Act of Parliament, thirty-fifth Victoria, chapter one hundred and eleven, have by their petition prayed to be permitted to increase their capital stock by the issue of five hundred preferential shares, representing fifty thousand dollars, current money of Canada, and it is expedient to grant their prayer : Therefore Her Majesty, by and with the advice and consent of the Senate and House of Commons of Canada, enacts as follows :—

1. Immediately after the coming into force of this Act, Preferential the said Company shall have power to increase their capital shares may be stock by the issue of five hundred preferential shares, of one hundred dollars currency each, for which purpose a stock- book shall be opened in the office of the said Company.

2. Of the opening of such stock-book, notice shall be Notice to be given to each shareholder by the Secretary of the said given. Company, by circular bearing the ordinary last known address of such shareholder, or, in case of his absence, of his duly authorized agent, deposited and registered in the post office in the City of Toronto, and by advertisement, during fourteen consecutive days in The Mail newspaper.

3.

Shareholders to have preference, during one month.

3. During a period of one month from the opening of the said stock-book, each shareholder of the said Company shall be entitled to subscribe for such preferential shares to the extent of one preferential share for every two shares held by him in the original capital stock of the said Company; at the expiration of that month any preference stock not then taken up may be divided *pro rata* among the shareholders who have already subscribed to the preference stock. one month being allowed them for decision.

Disposal of remainder of shares.

4. After the expiration of such second month, it shall be competent for anybody approved of by the Directors of the Company to subscribe for any portion of the said preferential shares which may not then have been taken up under the provisions of the next preceding section by the shareholders of the said Company.

To bear interest from payment. Calls.

5. The said preferential shares shall be called preference stock, and shall bear interest on all such portions thereof as shall be actually paid up, from the date of payment; and calls on such preference stock may be made by the Directors of the said Company from time to time, in their discretion.

Transfer of preference shares.

6. Shares of preference stock shall be transferable only in the manner and on the conditions provided by the by-laws of the said Company, with respect to the transfer of shares of the original stock of the Company, and they shall confer voting power in the same ratio.

To be first charge on net earnings for interest at 10 per cent.

7. The net earnings of the said Company, after the payment of all their outstanding liabilities, shall be applied towards the payment of interest at the rate of ten per centum per annum on the preferential stock, and any surplus remaining shall be applied as a dividend on the original capital stock of the Company.

Rights of preference shareholders.

8. In case it should become necessary, or be determined by a vote of the shareholders to wind up the affairs of the said Company, the shareholders of the preferential stock shall be paid in preference to the shareholders of the original capital stock.

Act not to affect right of action; and to be accepted by shareholders before taking effect.

9. This Act shall not affect any right of action which any individual shareholder may have against any Director, or officer of the Company, nor shall it have any force or effect whatever, until it has been accepted by the shareholders, by a resolution passed at a special general meeting of such shareholders, called for the purpose, which resolution to have effect must be concurred in by at least two-thirds of the votes of holders of paid up stock present, or represented by proxy, at such meeting, voting as provided by the original Act of incorporation.

CHAP.

CHAP. 74.

An Act to enable The Welland Vale Manufacturing Company to obtain an extension of a Patent known as "Rodden's Improved Capped Ferrule or Socket."

[Assented to 12th April, 1876.]

WHEREAS the Welland Vale Manufacturing Company, having their chief place of business at St. Catharines, in the County of Lincoln and Province of Ontario, and being a Company incorporated by letters patent under the Great Seal of the Province of Ontario, dated the twenty-third day of October, in the year of Our Lord one thousand eight hundred and seventy-three, have by their petition represented that on and prior to the twenty-second day of September, in the year of Our Lord one thousand eight hundred and seventy-five, they were the holders of letters patent under the Great Seal of the Dominion of Canada, dated the twenty-second day of September, one thousand eight hundred and seventy, for improvements in sockets for forks, hoes, chisels, and other articles, known as "Rodden's Improved Capped Ferrule or Socket;" the said letters patent having on the day last aforesaid been granted to one William H. Rodden, who in or about the month of March, in the year of Our Lord one thousand eight hundred and seventy-three, being insolvent, made an assignment under the Insolvency laws of Canada of all his estate and effects—amongst which were the letters patent referred to—to one William T. Mason, an Official Assignee duly appointed ; That on or about the ninth day of September, in the year of Our Lord one thousand eight hundred and seventy-three, the said William T. Mason assigned and transferred the said letters patent to one Edward C. Jones, and one William Chaplin, who are now respectively the President and Secretary of the said Company and hold the said Patent in their names ; That on or before the expiration of the said letters patent, which were granted for the term of five years, the Company, or the said Edward C. Jones and William Chaplin were entitled, on application therefor, to a renewal of the same, as provided for in section seventeen of the Statute passed in the thirty-fifth year of Her Majesty's reign and chaptered twenty-six ; but inadvertently the Company, or the said Edward C. Jones and William Chaplin omitted to make such application on or before the expiration of the said Patent, but did make such application some five weeks after, at which time the said application could not be entertained, it not being then competent for the Commissioner of Patents to grant a renewal of the same ; And whereas the said Company have petitioned for an Act authorizing the Commissioner of Patents to receive such application and grant a renewal of the said Patent, as provided

Preamble.

Case recited.

vided

vided for in the said Patent Act, in as ample a manner as if
application had been duly made before the expiration of the
said Patent : Therefore Her Majesty, by and with the advice
and consent of the Senate and House of Commons of Canada,
enacts as follows :—

Extension of   **1.** Notwithstanding anything to the contrary contained in
patent may
be granted   the "*Act respecting Patents of Invention*," being chapter
under S. 17 of twenty-six of the Statutes of Canada, passed in the thirty-fifth
35 V., c. 26. year of Her Majesty's Reign, it shall be lawful for the Commissioner of Patents to receive the application of the said
Welland Vale Manufacturing Company for a renewal of the
said Patent, and to grant such renewal of the said Patent or
such extension of the said Patent to the said Edward C. Jones
and William Chaplin, with the consent of the said Company,
as provided for in the seventeenth section of the said Patent
Act above referred to, in as full and ample a manner as if the
application for such renewal had been duly made within the
time provided for in that behalf.

Certain   **2.** Any person who by use or otherwise shall, within the
rights saved
of persons   period between the twenty-second day of September, in the
having used   year of Our Lord one thousand eight hundred and seventy-
the invention. five, and the extension of the said Patent under this Act,
have acquired any right in respect of such improvements or
invention, shall continue to enjoy the same to all intents and
purposes, as if this Act had not been passed.

CHAP. 75.

An Act to enable Ozro Morrill to obtain a patent for
certain inventions and improvements in Sewing
Machine Shuttles.

[Assented to 12th April, 1876.]

Preamble.   WHEREAS Ozro Morrill has, by his petition, represented,—
Case recited.   that he is a British subject resident in Canada, and
is sole assignee of the inventions and improvements in sewing machine shuttles made by John Reece, also a British
subject and resident in Canada; that on the eighteenth day
of November, one thousand eight hundred and seventy-
one, letters patent of the Dominion of Canada were
issued to the said John Reece for such of his said
inventions as were made prior to the date of the said letters
patent ; that subsequently letters patent were procured in
the United States of America, Great Britain, France and
Russia for all the inventions and improvements made by
the

the said John Reece, prior to the respective dates of the said
letters patent including certain valuable improvements made
by him subsequent to the date of the said Canadian patent ;
that the said Ozro Morrill having been advised, and believ-
ing that the said Canadian patent was broad enough in its
terms to protect all the improvements made by the said
Reece expended large sums of money in buildings, tools and
machinery in the Province of Quebec, for the purpose of
manufacturing sewing machines containing the said inventions and improvements; that it is a matter of doubt
whether the said Canadian patent validly covers and pro-
tects all the said improvements, and whether the said Ozro
Morrill, by reason of having commenced the manufacture
and sale of sewing machines of the description supposed to
be protected by the said Canadian patent can now obtain a
valid patent in Canada to protect such of the said improvements as might be held not to be included in and protected
by the said Canadian letters patent, and that he the said
Ozro Morrill is liable to sustain great loss and damage
unless relief be granted in accordance with the prayer of
his petition ; and whereas it is expedient to grant the prayer
of the said petition: Therefore Her Majesty, by and with
the advice and consent of the Senate and House of Commons of Canada, enacts as follows :—

1. Notwithstanding anything to the contrary contained
in " *The Patent Act of* 1872," it shall be lawful for the
Governor General if he shall see fit, and upon being satisfied of the truth of the statements so made by the said
petitioner, to grant letters patent to the said Ozro Morrill,
for such of the inventions and improvements of the said
John Reece in sewing machine shuttles as have been made
by him since the date of the said Canadian letters patent
and not included therein, in as full and ample a manner, with
the same privileges and to the same effect, as if patents had
been issued at the time when the said several inventions
and improvements were respectively made,—the said letters
patent so to be issued in virtue of this Act, to continue and
have force for the term of five years from the date thereof:
and the same may be extended at the expiration of five
years, and at the expiration of ten years, from the date of
issue, upon compliance with the ordinary conditions prescribed in the said " *Patent Act of* 1872," respecting exten-
sions of patents. *Letters patent may be issued for certain in-ventions under 35 V., c. 26.* *Extension may be grant-ed under the said Act.*

2. If any person has commenced to manufacture in Canada,
sewing machine shuttles containing the inventions and
improvements of the said John Reece, which may be included in the letters patent so to be issued in virtue of this
Act, the right of such person to manufacture and sell such
inventions and improvements in Canada shall not be pre-
judiced by this Act. *Existing rights saved.*

OTTAWA:

PRINTED BY BROWN CHAMBERLIN,

LAW PRINTER TO THE QUEEN'S MOST EXCELLENT MAJESTY.

1876.

TABLE OF CONTENTS

TO

ACTS OF CANADA.

THIRD SESSION, THIRD PARLIAMENT, 39 VICTORIA, 1876.

LOCAL AND PRIVATE ACTS.

INDEX

LOCAL AND PRIVATE ACTS OF CANADA.

THIRD SESSION, THIRD PARLIAMENT, 39 VICTORIA, 1876.